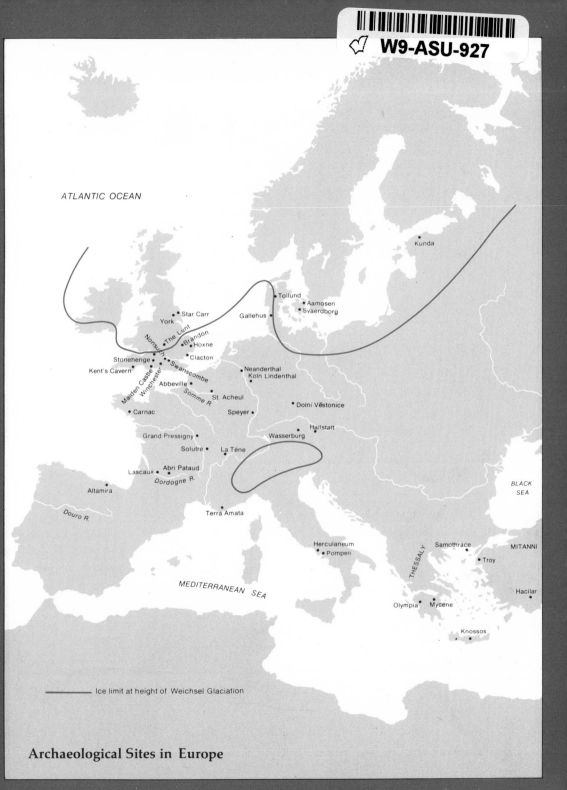

ATLANTIC OCEAN

• Kunda

• Tollund
Gallehus • Aamosen
• Svaerdborg
York • Star Carr
• The Lunt
Nonsuch • Brandon
• Hoxne
Stonehenge • Clacton
Kent's Cavern • Swanscombe
• Neanderthal
Koln Lindenthal
Maiden Castle
Winchester Abbeville
Somme R. • St. Acheul
• Carnac
• Dolní Věstonice
Speyer •
Grand Pressigny • Hallstatt
Solutré • La Tène Wasserburg
Lascaux • Abri Pataud
Altamira Dordogne R.

Douro R.
Terra Amata

MEDITERRANEAN SEA

BLACK
SEA

MITANNI

Herculaneum
• Pompeii Samothrace
THESSALY • Troy

Hacilar

Olympia • Mycene

Knossos

——— Ice limit at height of Weichsel Glaciation

Archaeological Sites in Europe

IN THE BEGINNING

Decked out for the hunt, King Assurbanipal of Assyria pursues his quarry, as depicted in a bas-relief from the seventh century B.C.

BRIAN M. FAGAN
University of California, Santa Barbara

IN THE BEGINNING

AN INTRODUCTION TO ARCHAEOLOGY

Fourth Edition

LITTLE, BROWN AND COMPANY
Boston   Toronto

Library of Congress Catalog Card No. 80-81388

ISBN 0-316-259926

9   8   7   6   5   4   3   2   1

HAL

Published simultaneously in Canada
by Little, Brown & Company (Canada) Limited

Printed in the United States of America

Cover photo is from the Pech-Merle cave, France.

Credits for Illustrations

The author wishes to thank the publishers, authors, photographers, and illustrators for granting permission to use their material. The sources for the text figures appear below, except for those given with the illustration. The figures without specified credits have been drawn specially for this book.

Frontispiece: Reproduced by Courtesy of the Trustees of the British Museum.

Chapter 1
1.2   The Bettmann Archive, Inc.
1.3   Reproduced by Courtesy of the Trustees of the British Museum.
1.4   Hester A. Davis, "Is There a Future for the Past?" *Archaeology*, Vol. 24, No. 4, Copyright 1971, Archaeological Institute of America.
1.5   The Metropolitan Museum of Art, Bequest of Joseph H. Durkee, Gift of Darius Ogden Mills, and Gift of C. Ruxton Love, by Exchange, 1972.

1.6   The Bettmann Archive, Inc.
1.7   George Holton/Photo Researchers, Inc.
1.8   Colonial Williamsburg Photograph
1.9   Courtesy of Dr. Braidwood and the Oriental Institute, University of Chicago

Chapter 2
2.1   Alinari/Editorial Photocolor Archives
2.2   Rapho/Photo Researchers, Inc.
2.4   Royal Anthropological Institute of Great Britain and Ireland, redrawn from "The Swanscombe Skull: A Survey of Research on a Pleistocene Site" (occasional paper no. 20, Fig. 26.3).
2.5   The Bettmann Archive, Inc.
2.6   Robert Lackenbach/Black Star
2.7   From the Collection of the Museé de L'Homme, photo by J. Oster

Chapter 4
4.1   Irven DeVore/Anthro Photo File

(Illustration credits continued on page 536.)

For Judy
With fondest love

TO THE READER ⤇

Many people think of archaeology as a romantic subject, a glamorous pastime associated with pyramids, mysterious inscriptions, and buried treasure. This stereotype originated in the last century, when both archaeologists and the ancient civilizations they uncovered became legendary. Today, over 150 years of archaeological investigations have turned archaeology into a meticulous scientific discipline. But the excitement is still there, in the many, diverse, and highly detailed reconstructions of life in the past from finds that sometimes seem trivial. Archaeologists have established the direction of the wind during a bison hunt on the Great Plains about 8000 years ago, learned what plants made up the wreaths created for Tutankhamun's funeral, and even examined the garbage produced in modern urban America. This book describes how archaeologists make and study such finds to illuminate the human past.

In the Beginning introduces the history and methods of archaeology and its significance today. It discusses archaeological concepts and procedures, and shows how archaeologists describe cultures in time and space to interpret the prehistoric past. One objective of this book is to provide a comprehensive summary of the field for people who have little or no experience in it. A second objective is to alert you to a major crises facing archaeology in the 1980s. All archaeological sites are finite records of the past, and once destroyed they can never be replaced. But the treasure hunting of individuals and the explosive increase in construction of buildings, roads, dams, and the like have destroyed thousands of archaeological sites all over the world. Without access to intact sites, we cannot possibly complete a picture of the human past, so the crisis of site destruction is, in its way, as important as the ecological crisis we face. *In the Beginning* aims to alert you to the need of living responsibly with your cultural heritage.

Archaeology, struck by a knowledge explosion, must rely more and more on sophisticated systems models and applications of quantitative methods. But the relatively small size of this book and the necessity of providing an overall view of the subject prevent me from considering too many technical nuances of contemporary archaeology. I hope you will pursue the topics that interest you in more advanced and specialized archaeology courses or in the many excellent books and articles listed in the Bibliography and Suggested Readings at the end of the book or in the Guide to Further Reading at the end of each chapter.

The chapters of the book begin with previews that highlight the major themes and concepts. Whenever practicable, drawings and photographs illustrate what the text describes in words. I use specialized terms as little as possible and define every new term when it first appears. In addition, a glossary at the end of the book provides definitions of the terms used in the book as well as of some words you may encounter in other reading.

I have written this book from predominantly English-language sources, for two main reasons. First, my reading in the vast archaeological literature has been necessarily selective and mostly in English. And, second, for most of you English is your native tongue. Although linguistic abilities and time have thus biased this volume toward the achievements and writings of English-speaking archaeologists, archaeology is indeed a global activity, conducted with great energy and intelligence by every nation and in every corner of the world.

B. M. F.

TO THE INSTRUCTOR ❧

Like its predecessors, the fourth edition of this introductory archaeology text results from the experience of many people. Literally hundreds of instructors have assigned previous editions, and thousands of students have used them. This edition has benefited from the comments of many of these teachers and students (including at least one student who is now a teacher). Of course, the fourth edition also reflects my own perceptions of contemporary archaeology and of the fantastic theoretical and methodological changes it has undergone in the last decade. Archaeology's many traits, interacting variables, and different forms of feedback make it almost as much of a cultural system, evolving in a multilinear way, as the many cultures it studies.

I have changed about 60 percent of *In the Beginning* for this fourth edition. Part I now concentrates on the significance of archaeology, the basic goals of the discipline, its current crisis, and the wide diversity of archaeologists. Part II traces the early origins of archaeology and how it developed into the science it is today. Part III has been completely rewritten to cover the critical problems of culture, data, and context in time and space, before describing how archaeologists acquire and describe their data in the field and laboratory. Recovering data is the subject of Part IV, which has been reorganized and expanded to cover not only basic survey and excavation methods but also the actual processes by which archaeologists survey and dig sites. I also pay more attention to how the archaeological record has been transformed by natural and human phenomena since it was deposited, an aspect of archaeology that is receiving increasing attention. The chapter on technology and artifacts in Part V gives more attention to metals, ceramics, and the analysis of different artifact forms.

The second half of *In the Beginning* covers the reconstruction of past lifeways and the interpretation of culture change. Part VI covers not only prehistoric subsistence, social organization, and religious beliefs but also emphasizes analogy, experimental archaeology, and ethnoarchaeology. If there is one major trend in contemporary archaeology, it is an increasing concern with how archaeologists interpret the surviving traces of prehistoric cultures; and ethnoarchaeology, particularly, offers a unique opportunity to develop the theoretical models for such interpretation. In Part VI also, the coverage of settlement archaeology concentrates on settlement studies in Mesoamerica, where enormous amounts of data are available for sophisticated quantitative analysis.

Part VII, on the interpretation of culture change, is now divided into two chapters dealing with the traditional descriptive methods of culture history and the methods of processual archaeology that have amplified the traditional methods in recent years.

In the Beginning ends with chapters on cultural resource management and on opportunities and responsibilities in archaeology. At the suggestion of reviewers, I have placed the chapter on cultural resource management near the end of the book because it draws on the whole spectrum of archaeological approaches described in the text.

For the benefit of students, I have added chapter previews that focus on main themes and have expanded the glossary of key terms and concepts. For clarity, I have deleted many superfluous examples. At the request of many of the book's users, I have also replaced footnotes with a parenthetical system of reference and corresponding bibliography.

I espouse no particular theory of archaeology here, but rather survey modern prehistoric archaeology in its broad scope, giving each instructor a basis for amplifying the text with his or her own viewpoint and theoretical persuasion. Evaluations of the book indicate its usefulness to air many archaeological viewpoints; as one reviewer said, "This is the fun with the book." Long may it continue to be so.

Modern archaeology is so wide ranging and complex that one could easily write a 1000-page text on the subject. Thus I have had to skate over some topics, such as population carrying capacity, in almost indecent haste. These topics are important, to be sure, but the limitations of space require concentration on basics rather than on the more experimental methodologies. I leave it to each of you to fill in details on topics you think are given inadequate treatment. However, I urge you to give full coverage to one vital topic: the growing crisis of site destruction. This entire subject demands full factual and moral coverage in introductory courses, where many students arrive with the notion of finding buried treasure or collecting beautiful artifacts. Many of us have firsthand experience with treasure hunters and with tragically bulldozed sites. Every course in archaeology must place responsibility for preserving the past emphatically on the public. It is for this reason that this book ends with a stark statement of basic archaeological ethics for everyone.

Many people have assisted in the preparation of this new edition. I am indebted to the wise advice of Professors Paul V. Aiello, Ventura College; Brad Bartel, San Diego State University; Paul R. Fish, Arizona State Museum; James F. O'Connell, University of Utah; Stephen M. Perlman, Virginia Commonwealth University; David Sanger, University of Maine, Orono; and William A. Turnbaugh, University of Rhode Island.

My friendships within the College Division of Little, Brown extend back over a decade. Jane Aaron supported me throughout the long revision process, making a laborious and sometimes frustrating task much easier; she joins Milton Johnson, Woody Chittick, and Frank Graham as one of the major contributors to the success of this text. And without the loyal assistance and cheerful efficiency of many other people in Boston—particularly, this time around, Lee Ripley, Cynthia Chapin, and Tina Schwinder—this book would never have appeared. The association with Little, Brown has enriched not only this book, but also my life.

B. M. F.

BRIEF CONTENTS ❧

CONTENTS ❧

PART I 🙌

BACKGROUND TO ARCHAEOLOGY

Like earnest mastodons petrified in the forests of their own apparatus the archaeologists come and go, each with his pocket Odyssey and his lack of modern Greek. Diligently working upon the refuse-heaps of some township for a number of years they erect on the basis of a few sherds or a piece of dramatic drainage, a sickly and enfeebled portrait of a way of life. How true it is we cannot say; but if an Eskimo were asked to describe our way of life, deducing all his evidence from a search in a contemporary refuse dump, his picture might lack certain formidable essentials.

LAWRENCE DURRELL
Prospero's Cell

Why study archaeology? What is the importance of this popular and apparently romantic subject? We begin to answer these questions by looking at the place of archaeology in the twentieth-century world, at its important role in our cultural enrichment and in the writing of world history. Unfortunately, the discipline faces a crisis brought about by the rapid destruction of important sites by industrial development and treasure hunting. Furthermore, the credibility of archaeologists is undermined by all sorts of pseudo-archaeologies that purport to tell the truth about lost worlds, ancient astronauts, and sunken continents.

The reality of archaeology is much less romantic but just as fascinating. We define archaeology by placing it within its broader context as part of anthropology and history.

CHAPTER 1 ✣

ARCHAEOLOGY INTRODUCED

Preview

- Modern archaeology is the scientific study of past cultures and technologies—whether ancient or modern—by scientific methods and theoretical concepts that have been devised for that purpose.
- Archaeology covers the human past, from the earliest peoples up to modern times.
- Archaeology had its origins in treasure hunting, Renaissance classicism, and grave robbing, but it has evolved into a highly precise discipline. It has become an integral part of twentieth-century life as a component of popular culture and modern intellectual curiosity.
- Archaeology provides the only viable means of writing the history of many of the world's societies, whose documented past began in recent times. As such, it is a vital support for nationalist feeling and the fostering of cultural identity.
- Archaeologists have important contributions to make to the resolution of modern land disputes and to modern resource management.
- The destruction of sites, fostered by greedy collectors and industrial development, is the most serious crisis that archaeology is faced with today. Archaeological sites are a finite resource that can never be replaced. If the present rate of destruction continues, there is real danger that few undisturbed archaeological sites will remain by the end of this century.

- Archaeologists also face a challenge from people who promote "pseudo-archaeologies" that purport to explain the past, such as the extravagant theories of Erich von Däniken.
- Archaeology is part of the science of Anthropology, which is the study of humankind in the widest possible sense. Archaeologists use a battery of special methods and techniques to examine human societies in the past.
- There are many types of archaeologists. Prehistoric archaeologists study prehistory, that is, human history before written records; historical archaeologists use archaeology to supplement documentary history; while Classical archaeologists study ancient Greece and Rome.
- Modern archaeology has three basic goals: the study of culture history, the reconstruction of past lifeways, and the study of cultural process.
- In contrast to American archaeologists, Old World scholars think of archaeology as an extension of documentary history into the remote past.

Archaeology has always been thought of as a romantic subject. In actual fact, however, modern archaeology is a rigorous and demanding scientific discipline. We use the word discipline because archaeology consists of a broad range of scientific methods and techniques for studying the past, methods and techniques that are used carefully and in a disciplined way. In this chapter we explore archaeology's role in the twentieth-century world and the crisis of destruction that archaeology faces; define archaeology in relation to anthropology and history; and look at the different types of archaeologists.

WHY STUDY ARCHAEOLOGY?

Most people associate archaeologists with buried treasure, the Great Pyramids, and grinning skeletons. The archaeologist is often depicted as an elderly, eccentric scholar in a sun helmet digging up inscribed tablets in the shadow of Egyptian temples. They are thought to be typical absentminded professors, who are deeply absorbed in the details of ancient life and care little for the pressures and frustrations of modern life. Archaeology is believed to open doors to a world of romance and excitement, to discoveries like the spectacular tomb of the Egyptian pharaoh Tutankhamun, opened by English archaeologists Howard Carter and Lord Carnarvon in 1922. Even today, many people believe that archaeologists spend their lives solving great mysteries and finding lost civilizations. Any course or lecture on archaeology is filled with people who are indulging their fascination with the past. Hopefully, you are reading this book for the same reason.

Few archaeologists are fortunate enough to discover a royal burial or a forgotten civilization, however. Most of them excavate for a lifetime without finding anything more spectacular than some fine pottery or delicately made stone tools. But archaeology is still a fascinating subject, one that captures the imagination of scholar and lay person alike. It was the British archaeologist Stuart Piggott who once called archaeology "the science of rubbish." And there is much truth in that statement. Archaeologists spend their lives investigating the surviving and abandoned remains of ancient societies. However, it is not gold or fine objects that interest them but the information that comes from digging up finds and properly recording them. The modern archaeologist is as much interested in why people live the way they do as in the objects they made and the buildings they erected.

On the face of it, the study of archaeology, however fascinating, seems to be a luxury we can ill afford in a world confronted by economic recessions and widespread poverty and famine. But to regard archaeology in such a way would be to treat the entire cultural heritage of humankind as irrelevant and unnecessary to the quality of our lives; whereas, in reality, it is integral (White, 1974).

Early Archaeologists.   The first people to study archaeology did so because they enjoyed digging into the past (Daniel, 1967), both out of curiosity and for fun. A century and a quarter ago, archaeology was no more than a lighthearted pastime. People would gather from far and wide to witness the opening of an Egyptian mummy or the excavation of an ancient burial mound. "Eight barrows were examined," wrote Englishman Thomas Wright (1852) of an archaeological picnic in 1844. "Most of them contained skeletons, more or less entire, with the remains of weapons in iron, bosses of shields, urns, beads, brooches, armlets, bones of more amulets, and occasionally more vessels." The day's festivities ended with a "sumptuous repast" and a tour through the landowner's "interesting collection of antiquities" (Daniel, 1975) (Figure 1.1).

Figure 1.1   A nineteenth-century barrow excavation as depicted in *Gentlemen's Magazine*, 1840.

The first archaeologists to dig in Egypt, as well as those who discovered the Maya and the Assyrians, were no more than amateurs (Fagan, 1975; 1979). Normally ardent travelers, they learned how to dig as they went along, their objective being to discover and remove as many spectacular finds as they could in the time they had available. Englishman Austen Henry Layard was in his twenties during the mid-1840s, when he dug into the ancient mounds of the Biblical sites of Calah and Nineveh in Iraq. He discovered the lost civilization of the Assyrians and gave up archaeology by the time he was thirty-five. Layard achieved worldwide fame as a result of his bestselling book *Nineveh and Its Remains* (Layard, 1849). The Mayan civilization of Mexico and Guatemala was first described by American travel writer John Lloyd Stephens, who traveled in the forests of the Yucatan with artist Frederick Catherwood in 1839 (Figure 1.2). His *Incidents of Travel* (Stephens, 1841) became an instant bestseller. Both Layard's and Stephens's works were as much volumes of travel and adventure as they were archaeological reports. One has the impression that they had great fun on their travels. "The reader is perhaps curious to know how old cities sell in Central America. Like other articles of trade they are regulated by the quality in the market and the demand," wrote Stephens. "I paid fifty dollars for Copán . . . for which Don José Maria thought me only a fool; if I had offered more, he would probably have considered me something worse." Stephens wanted to transport the Copán sculptures to New York, as others had removed antiquities from Egypt and Mesopotamia to the museums of Europe. Fortunately for science, he failed (Fagan, 1977), and today's traveler can still enjoy the same sculptures in their natural setting.

Figure 1.2 A lithograph by Frederick Catherwood of the Mayan site, Chichén Itzá.

The foundations of modern archaeology lie not only in the adventuresome spirit, but also in the intellectual curiosity of the early travelers and archaeologists. None was more single-minded than Heinrich Schliemann, a German businessman who made several fortunes before retiring and devoting the remainder of his life to searching for the cities that were described in Homer's poems (Ceram, 1953). His career reads like a dream. He was born into a poor German family and started work as a grocer's assistant at age 15. During a period as a merchant's clerk in Amsterdam, Schliemann devoted himself to learning Russian and other languages with fanatical intensity. Within a few years he was a wealthy merchant in St. Petersburg, Russia. In his early forties he gave up business, married a young Greek wife, and set out to find Homer's legendary city of Troy. His feverish search ended at the mound of Hissarlik in northwestern Turkey. Schliemann always worked on a large scale. He recruited 150 men and moved no less than 325,000 cubic yards of soil in his early seasons. His excavation techniques were modeled on those used to dig the Suez Canal in Egypt some years earlier. By 1873, Schliemann had found no less than seven cities and a great gold treasure, which he proudly displayed on his wife's neck (Ceram, 1953; Schliemann, 1881; Stone, 1975). But his archaeological methods were brutal—he destroyed almost as much as he discovered.

Until the last decades of the nineteenth century, archaeological excavations still resembled treasure hunts—and they often were. "It is sickening to see the rate at which everything is being destroyed, and the little regard paid to preservation," wrote Egyptologist Flinders Petrie in 1883. One can hardly blame him for his remarks. Early excavators in Egypt, such as the notorious Giovanni Belzoni, a strongman turned tomb robber, literally mined the ancient Egyptians for gold. Belzoni would push his way into mummy caves and even sit down on a corpse to rest. "When my weight bore on the body of an Egyptian, it crushed like a band-box," he recalled (Fagan, 1975). Belzoni often found himself smothered in dust and decayed bones, and he was not above using corpses and coffins for firewood. The losses to science from such activities were incalculable. How often do we read that such and such a find "crumbled to dust," or that exposure to the open air resulted in the object "dissolving before our very eyes"?

Most early archaeologists were interested in carrying away precious objects for display in foreign museums and were concerned only minimally with preserving the great sites they dug for future generations. But their depredations did lead to the popular fascination that archaeology holds for many today.

Archaeology as Entertainment.   Despite its roots in nineteenth–century excavations, scientific archaeology as a serious and popular field of investigation is a cultural phenomenon of the twentieth century. Sixty years ago professional archaeologists were few and far between; today hundreds of museums, archaeological surveys, and universities are staffed with trained graduates in archaeology. A sharp increase in popular interest in the past has developed in recent decades, an interest sparked in part by an explosion of popular literature on archaeology. Colorful, imaginative reconstructions of early humans camping on the African savannah appear in Time-Life books and on the pages of the *National Geographic.* Spectacular archaeological discoveries merit prominent headlines in many newspapers. Archaeology is as much part of popular culture as football or the automobile. Thousands of people read archaeology books for entertainment, join archaeological societies, and flock to popular lectures on the past.

The advent of the jetliner and the package tour has helped make archaeology a medium of popular entertainment as well. Fifty years ago only the wealthy and privileged could take a tour up the Nile, visit the Greek temples, and explore Mayan civilization. Now package tours can take you to Egypt, to the Parthenon, and to Teotihuacán. The jumbo jet and the air-conditioned bus can take you to such remote sites as Petra in Jordan or the Inca cities in Peru. The famous sites of antiquity give the modern traveler a sense of time that dwarfs the day-to-day concerns of the twentieth century. The immensity of the pyramids of Gizeh in Egypt, and the prodigious labor that built them; the white columns of the Temple of Poseidon at Sounion, touched with pink from the setting sun; the ruins at Tikal bathed in the light of the full moon—as sights alone, these overwhelm the senses. Tutankhamun's golden mask or a giant Olmec head with its snarling grin (Figure 1.3) lifts us to a realm where achievement endures and perceptions seem of a higher level. It is this sense of physical reality from the past that holds our human secrets, if we could only read its meaning, that draws people to archaeology—a casual interest for some; but for others an all-consuming passion.

Archaeology and Cultural Heritage.   Every society on earth has some form of the origin myth—folklore that is the official, sanctioned account of how it came into being. Our own society is no exception. "And God said, 'Let us make man in our image, after our likeness: and let them have dominion over the fish of the sea, and over the fowl of the air, and over the cattle, and over all the earth, and over every creeping thing

Figure 1.3 A ceremonial Olmec axe head, depicting a god who combines the features of a man and a jaguar. His face is stylized, with flamelike eyes and drooping mouth. (One-half actual size.)

that creepeth on the earth.' "—thus reads the first chapter of Genesis, a majestic account of the Creation that was accepted as the authorized version of human origin for centuries.

Origin myths, such as that of Genesis, developed in response to humanity's deep seated curiosity about its origins. For more than two thousand years, Westerners have speculated about their ancestry and tried to develop theoretical models to explain their origins. Some of these models are purely philosophical, while others are based on scientifically collected data. Much of this data comes from archaeological surveys and excavations. Archaeology is fascinating because it enables us to test theoretical models of evolving societies: why some people have flourished, while others have vanished without trace, and still others have sunk into complete obscurity.

Our curiosity about the past stems not only from a preoccupation with our ultimate origins, but from strong feelings of nostalgia as well.

We live in a world of rapid change and diminishing natural resources, in a crowded, over-populated urban environment. As population increase and ecological problems deepen, we find ourselves nostalgic for simpler, earlier times. The life of prehistoric peoples, determined by the seasons of vegetable foods and the movements of game, is perceived as a time of natural simplicity. Archaeology gives insight into those less complicated societies of the past.

Archaeology also contributes valuable information to our collective cultural heritage. Most American Indian groups only came into contact with literate Western civilization during the past three centuries. Before European contact, Indian history was not written; it consisted, for the most part, of oral traditions handed down from generation to generation. Archaeology and archaeological sites are the only other possible sources for American Indian history. Only as archaeologists probe into their ancestry will the first chapter of American history be written.

One of the most remarkable examples of archaeology's ability to reveal the history of the Indian comes from Ozette, Washington, where Richard Daugherty has excavated the remains of a Makah Indian village that was buried by a series of mud slides about 500 years ago (Kirk, 1974). Preservation conditions at the site were so exceptional that archaeologists were able to recover complete details of the village's plank houses and their contents, down to stored food and whale bone harpoons. By working closely with the Tribal Council, Daugherty was able not only to interpret the objects found on the site, but also to help the Council raise a large sum of money for a local museum in which to display the finds. In this way, he brought the hitherto forgotten history of the Makah into the consciousness not only of the Indians themselves, but of the public as well (Fagan, 1978a).

The Ozette example is by no means unique, for more and more archaeologists are working closely with American Indians and other ethnic groups. E. Charles Adams has excavated at the Hopi village of Walpi in the Southwest, and has worked in close cooperation with the local people. Pre-civil war lifeways among black slave communities in the Southeast are the subject of long-term excavations there, and archaeologists working in Alexandria, Virginia, have studied the history of black neighborhoods using archaeology, historical records, and oral traditions (Cressey, 1980).

Political Uses of Archaeology.   Many newly independent nations, anxious to foster nationalism, are encouraging archaeological research as the only way to uncover the early roots of the peoples who lived there before colonial times. The Tanzanian and Zambian governments in

Africa have sponsored excavations for years, whose results soon appear in the pages of university textbooks and schoolbooks. The primary goal of archaeology there, as in many parts of the world, is to write unwritten history, not from archives and dusty documents, but from long abandoned villages and rubbish heaps. That this type of archaeology is essential is clear from the remarks of President Kenneth Kaunda of Zambia, when presented with a book on Zambian history written by a group of archaeologists and historians. With intense pride he said, "This is our history. Now we can look people from other countries in the face and tell them that we have a history and a national identity to be proud of." It is difficult to convey the intense pride that came through in his remarks.

In a far less admirable way, a number of governments have used archaeology for political ends. The Nazis used it to produce "evidence" for the evolution of a master race in Europe. During the late 1960s, the government of Rhodesia in southern Africa claimed that the Zimbabwe ruins, a famous complex of stone buildings, were the work of Phoenician colonists who had settled south of the Zambezi river over 2000 years ago. They chose to ignore over half a century of archaeological research that showed Zimbabwe had been built by indigenous African peoples between A.D. 1000 and 1500. The reason for the claims were easily discerned: A Phoenician date for Zimbabwe would be evidence for white settlement in southern Africa long before the arrival of the local people (Garlake, 1973). Fortunately, most attempts to make this type of political use of archaeological evidence are doomed to failure, simply because people are not that naive.

Archaeology as a Social Science.   Archaeologists bring a unique perspective to the social sciences of which they are a part: a way of understanding how people have dealt with the world around them from the earliest times. This contributes to a much better understanding of not only our own history, but also that of the environment, the world climate, and the formation of our landscape. The long abandoned settlements that archaeologists study are repositories of precisely dated geological, biological, and environmental data that can add a vital time depth to studies of the contemporary world. For instance, preservation conditions are so good in the dry pueblos of Arizona that wood, fossil pollen grains, and other environmental evidence are found in abundance. It is proving to be possible, because of this, to study the gradual evolution of southwestern agriculture through many centuries and determine how the local people responded to changes in rainfall and other environmental conditions. The results of such researches are invaluable to students of modern agriculture who are trying to expand crop production in the desert. Archaeological sites are an important storehouse of information for a host of natural and physical sciences.

Chemists and physicists have made important contributions to the study of the past as well, through development of such approaches as the radiocarbon dating method and sophisticated ways of studying prehistoric trade through spectographic analysis.

Archaeolgists have many practical tasks to perform in today's world that further amplify their role as social scientists. One such task is the settling of territorial claims by excavation. In the eighteenth century an archaeological investigation figured in the settling of a border dispute between the British and the Americans over the site of Samuel de Champlain's settlement at Dochet island on the St. Croix River, between Maine and Canada. An antiquarian dug to find the site of the fort. Excavations have occasionally featured in Indian lands disputes, and we can expect that archaeologists will provide expert testimony in many future cases.

Recent federal legislation requires archaeological impact studies to be made on all government-funded development projects to ensure that minimum damage is done to archaeological resources in the course of construction work. This legislation has led to a massive expansion of archaeological work through North America (see Chapter 20). It is designed to protect the finite data base of archaeological sites that are studied not only by archaeologists, but also by scientists from many other disciplines.

Archaeology has also played a direct role in contemporary American society, especially in the area of resource and waste management. University of Arizona archaeologist William Rathje, for example, has studied the garbage dumps in Tucson for a long time (Rathje, 1974). He examines patterns in garbage disposal from Tucson households, analyzes the evidence from the dump using the latest archaeological research designs and techniques, and joins to it data gleaned from interviews with householders and other sources. His study has revealed startling information on wasteful habits in Arizona households of many economic and social backgrounds, which could be used to help suggest better strategies for consumer buying and resource management.

Rathje argues that studies of modern garbage, such as this, offer a unique source of knowledge about ourselves, as well as about the past. The objects we use shape our lives in many ways, and understanding how they do this is important to learning about the past and anticipating the future (Rathje, 1979).

The archaeologist, then, has an important role to play in the twentieth-century world, a world where an understanding of other cultures is vital to our survival. To say that archaeology is a luxury is to deny the cultural achievements of our predecessors and to deny to many millions of people the opportunity of learning about their roots and ancestry.

As more and more non-Western societies abandon their traditional lifeways in the face of modern technological civilization, archaeologists are becoming the guardians of the world's dying cultures. As people leave their traditional village sites and move into cities or modern housing, their old settlements crumble to the ground. Only the archaeologist's spade, combined with oral tradition and the work of early anthropologists, can hope to recover the full details of the dying culture. The remarkable anthropological studies of San hunter-gatherers in the Kalahari desert of Southern Africa by Richard Lee and others included studies not only of the living people but of their recently abandoned campsites as well (Yellen, 1977). In this and other field studies, the archaeologist joins with the anthropologist in trying to study and describe a society that is slowly becoming extinct in the face of pressure from the outside world.

In short, archaeology satisfies our intellectual curiosity about the nature of humanity. With its broad perspective of time and circumstance, contemporary archaeology is as much part of our lives as are history, anthropology, physics, and an army of more exotic specialties. For some, it is the only source of their cultural history.

THE CRISIS IN ARCHAEOLOGY

Unfortunately, archaeologists are an endangered species. The sites that they investigate are being destroyed so rapidly that a sizable portion of the world's archaeological heritage has already vanished forever. Unlike trees or animals, archaeological sites are a finite resource. Once destroyed by a bulldozer or a treasure hunter, an archaeological site is gone forever. The archaeologist's archives are buried in the soil, and the only way to preserve them is to leave them alone and intact until they can be investigated with rigorous and scientific care. Both human nature and the need for the world's growing populations to satisfy their needs have wrought terrible destruction on the discipline.

Collectors and the Morality of Collecting. Our materialistic society places much emphasis on wealth and the possession of valuable things.

Many people have an urge to possess the past, to keep a piece of antiquity on their mantel. Projectile points, Acheulian hand axes, Benin bronzes, or Maya pots all add an exotic touch to the prosaic American living room. Many archaeological artifacts, such as those Benin bronzes, have a high antique and commercial value. They are "Buried Treasure," valued as museum pieces and by the major collectors of the world, commanding enormous prices at auction and in salesrooms. Glorious finds of antiquity are displayed without context, often because their archaeological associations are unknown. High commercial values and the human urge to own have resulted in unscrupulous treasure hunting and a flourishing illegal trade in antiquities, which rapes sites for gold and other precious ornaments, as well as pottery, sculpture, and all the other artifacts that today's covetous collectors seek to own and trade.

The destruction of archaeological sites for commercial ends is reaching alarming proportions, but it is nothing new. The dilettantes of eighteenth-century Italy, Giovanni Belzoni in Egypt, and Lord Elgin in Greece were merely the best known of those who satisfied the educated European's lust for antiquities. The thirst for pre-Columbian antiquities goes back at least a century. The only difference is that today the traffic in tomb robbing and illegal antiquities is better organized, more lucrative, and fueled by inflation, insatiable greed, and the aggressive acquisition policies of public and private museums.

This pressure to acquire objects of interest and value has escalated in the twentieth century as more museums compete for fewer and fewer valuable and authentic pieces. In some countries, like Italy and Costa Rica, tomb robbing is a full-time, if technically illegal, profession. The Italian *tombaroli* concentrate on Etruscan tombs (Hamblin, 1970). Their finds command high prices from foreign dealers, and the government does little to control either the looting or the export trade. Entire Inca cemeteries have been dug up in search of gold ornaments. Thousands of Egyptian tombs have been rifled for papyri and statues. And the problem is not confined to ancient civilizations. North America literally bristles with pot hunters, who think nothing of ravaging sites for their projectile heads and potsherds. The looting of even a single projectile head destroys a small part of our nation's finite archaeological resource. The cumulative effects of treasure hunting, pot hunting, and mine detectors is catastrophic.

Why do people collect antiquities? In 1921 Henri Codet, a French doctor, wrote a pioneering dissertation on collecting. He concluded that it has four underlying motives: "the need to possess, the need for spontaneous activity, the impulse to self-advancement, and the tendency to classify things" (Meyer, 1977). Another Frenchman once said of collecting: "It is not a pastime, but a passion and often so violent that it is inferior to love or ambition only in the pettiness of its aims." People collect everything from beer cans to phallic symbols, and anything collectible is considered by collectors to be portable and private—and it is their duty to preserve it. It follows that everything has a market value and can be purchased, the market value depending on the demand for the category of artifact or its rarity or aesthetic beauty. The archaeological context of the artifact is unimportant, and information about the people who made it is usually irrelevant: all that matters is the object itself (Figure 1.4).

Protecting antiquities is complex and incredibly difficult, for in the final analysis, it involves an appeal to people's moral values and requires almost unenforceable legislation that ultimately would take away a potential source of livelihood, however illegal, from thousands of poverty-stricken peasants and more prosperous middlemen who have some political influence. Many countries are now feeling more nationalistic about their past and their own archaeological sites. When collecting began, there were no museums in such countries as Egypt or Turkey to house the finds of early archaeologists. Now most countries have museums, many have antiquities services and stringent archaeology laws that control the export of archaeological finds—at least in theory. The trouble is that the laws cost a fortune to administer and enforce, and even such comparatively wealthy countries as Mexico are unable to police even the most famous of sites. But public opinion in Egypt and other countries shows some pride in the national heritage. It is galling to see the prized sculptures and antiquities of one's past adorning museums in London, Copenhagen, and New York. Yet the tide of public opinion cannot stem the collectors' mania or the ruthless policies of major museums. Perhaps the most notorious example of questionable acquisition by a large museum was perpetrated by the Metropolitan Museum of Art in New York when it purchased a Greek painted vase priced at no less than a million dollars in 1972 (Hess, 1974). The Euphronios vase dates to the sixth century B.C. and is one of the finest examples of its type ever found (Figure 1.5). The Met claimed that the vase came from a private collection that had been intact for almost half a century. But others suspected that the vase was dug up in an illegal excavation of an Etruscan tomb north of Rome and sold by tomb robbers. The controversy still continues. Fortunately some universities and museums have adopted more stringent acquisitions policies, although it is too early to say whether they have had any effect. Changing public attitudes, more cautious policies, and a shortage of fine antiquities may slow the traffic, but the damage has already been done.

Figure 1.4 The wrong and the right way to dig. Archaeology is a hobby for both these groups, but the top group is destroying evidence of the past by their digging techniques while the bottom group is preserving it. The latter, alas, happens all too rarely.

Figure 1.5   The Euphronios Vase, sixth century B.C., showing dead Sarpedon being carried by Thanatos and Hyponos. (Height, 18 inches; diameter, 21-11/16 inches.)

The Destruction of Archaeological Sites.   Pot hunters and treasure hunters have left thousands of archaeological sites looking like rabbit burrows and have so damaged them that archaeological inquiry in such areas is impossible. The ravages of industrial activity, strip mining, and agriculture have all taken their catastrophic toll on many archaeological sites as well.

In some areas of the United States, the damage to sites has reached epidemic proportions. Virtually no undisturbed sites remain. It has been estimated, for example, that less than 5 percent of the sites in Los Angeles county remain undisturbed by pot hunters or development activity. As Charles McGimsey has pointed out in his landmark book, *Public Archaeology* (1972): "This nation's past is contained in the soil. That soil is being disturbed and redistributed at an ever increasing rate. Those of us alive today will be the last ever to see any significant portion of it in an undisturbed state."

How can we stem this wanton destruction? Don Graybill (1978) has recently estimated that we are rapidly losing the opportunity to study many ancient societies on a regional basis because the sites to study them have been destroyed. The only way to minimize future damage is to spend vast sums of money to enforce much stricter antiquities laws, and to carry out large-scale surveys to inventory the finite resource base of sites before it is too late. At the same time, a massive shift in public attitudes about archaeology is needed—one that makes people respect the past as a valued possession. There is a need to educate people to a responsible attitude toward the past—an attitude that considers destruction of vital sites an invalid exchange for prestige and wealth. Archaeologists have not done much to educate the general public about the crisis facing the irreplaceable archives of the prehistoric and historic past. McGimsey (1972) puts the situation in a nutshell: "No one may act in such a manner such that the public right to knowledge of the past is unduly endangered or destroyed."

PSEUDOARCHAEOLOGIES

Modern archaeology is highly technical and, let us be honest, sometimes rather dull. In contrast, the flood of "pseudo-archaeologies" that has appeared in recent years positively drip with romance and excitement, with "unexplained" secrets, lost civilizations, and great temples buried in dense rainforests. The Lost Continent of Atlantis, the Ten Lost Tribes of Israel, expeditions in search of Noah's Ark—all provide superb raw material for the armchair adventurer.

Pseudoarchaeologies are nothing new, and they have always been lucrative businesses. In the mid-nineteenth century, thousands of Americans bought books that described great mound-building civilizations that flourished and did battle in the Midwest. Their descendants supposedly have moved from earth into space. Perhaps the most notorious pseudoarchaeology of recent times is that perpetuated by Erich von Däniken and his Ancient Astronauts. The 1960s saw America fascinated with space, with the possibility of living creatures on other planets. Had the human experience been duplicated on other planets? Had people from other worlds landed on earth long before our civilization emerged? Yes, argues Erich von Däniken in a series of books and films that have made him millions of dollars. According to von Däniken, "foreign astronauts visited the earth thousands of years ago. The crew of the spaceship soon realized that the earth could support intelligent life" (von Däniken, 1970; 1971). They found some primitive humans on earth and fertilized some of the females. Millennia later the spacemen returned and found *Homo sapiens* scattered over the earth. So they repeated their breeding experiments and eventually produced a "creature intelligent enough to have the rules of society imparted to it" (von Däniken, 1970). These new beings started art and agriculture, eventually their own civilizations, regarding their progenitors as "benevolent gods who were interested in their welfare." But soon warfare began and people began to destroy many of the sacred places. And then centuries later people started to excavate these ancient temples. The impact of the astronauts on prehistoric people, argued von Däniken, was about equivalent to that of Captain Cook and his mariners on the Tahitians—devastating.

The world at large adored von Däniken's incredible hypotheses, but archaeologists were puzzled. They found it impossible to follow his reasoning, for his archaeological evidence is laced with Biblical allusions, in one of which he claims that Sodom and Gomorrah were destroyed by an atomic bomb! The Ark of the Covenant was an electrified transmitter that enabled Moses to communicate with the astronauts. After this theological *tour-de-force* we are led through a mishmash of archaeological evidence from all over the world cited as grounds for proving that astronauts did land on earth thousands of years ago. Von Däniken claims, for example, that an astronaut complete with helmet was carved at Copán in Guatemala and that the Sun God statue at Tiahuanaco, Bolivia (Figure 1.6), is a depiction of a golden spaceship that came from the stars.

Von Däniken's brand of pseudoarchaeology is unusual only because he has moved into space for his heroes. Like his predecessors, and like many people fascinated by escapism and space fiction, he is intoxicated by the mystery and lure of vanished tribes and lost cities engulfed in swirling mists (Story, 1976; Wauchope, 1972). Of course, not all of the pseudoarchaeologists turn to space for their explanations. In order to answer the intense controversy that surrounds the question of the early settlement of the Americas, Barry Fell and other authors have alleged that North America was settled by foreigners long before the Vikings and Christopher Columbus arrived. They use as their evidence isolated artifacts and alleged inscriptions that are sometimes little more than crude forgeries and are invariably without well-documented archaeological contexts. Many of their theories bear no resemblance whatsoever to archaeological reality (Fell, 1977).

While flamboyant nonarchaeology of the type expounded by von Däniken and Fell will always appeal to those who believe that "there is a faint possibility that . . .", it does not excuse discounting archaeologists as "elitists" or "scientific fuddy-duddies" because they reject such wild theories that are unsupported by scientifically gathered evidence. This is, however, exactly what has been happening in recent years. One reason is that archaeologists have made little effort to popularize their own subject. They have been too busy digging up the past all over the world and communicating the results of their research to their colleagues. With the pressures of constant site destruction and the need to

Figure 1.6 The Gate of the Sun God at Tiahuanaco, Bolivia. According to von Däniken, the gate represents "a flying god flanked by forty-eight mysterious figures. Legend tells of a golden spaceship which comes from the stars."

remove as much as possible from the ground before it is too late, one can hardly blame them.

The credibility of modern archaeology, then, depends on the ability of archaeologists to communicate the results of their scientific research to wider audiences in intelligible and enjoyable terms. They have a formidable task, for as we have seen, popular attitudes toward archaeology tend toward the romantic and the exotic. Today's archaeology is far from exotic, and although it is highly technical, it is still extremely fascinating. Hopefully, this book will give you an understanding of how scientific archaeologists go about their work.

ARCHAEOLOGY, ANTHROPOLOGY, AND HISTORY

Anthropology and Archaeology.   Anthropology is the scientific study of humankind in the widest possible sense. Anthropologists study human beings as biological organisms and as people with a distinctive and unique characteristic—culture. They carry out research on contemporary human societies and on the development of humankind from the very earliest times. This enormous field is subdivided into a series of subdisciplines.

Physical anthropology involves the study of human biological evolution and the variations between different living populations. Physical anthropologists also study the behavior of living nonhuman primates, such as the chimpanzee and the gorilla, research that can throw light on the behavior of the earliest humans.

Cultural anthropology is concerned with the analysis of human social life, both past and present. The primary concern is the study of human culture and of the ways in which it has adapted to the environment. There are a number of different specialists within the field of cultural anthropology:

Ethnographers spend most of their time describing the culture, technology, and economic life of living and extinct societies.

Ethnologists engage in comparative studies of different societies, a process that involves attempts to reconstruct general principles of human behavior.

Social anthropologists analyze social organization, the ways in which people organize themselves.

The objectives of archaeologists are the same as those of cultural anthropologists, except that archaeologists study ancient societies. Thus, one can safely describe an archaeologist as a special type of anthropologist, one who studies the past. Both anthropologists and archaeologists study humankind; the only difference between them is the types of evidence they use to do so.

Archaeology.   Archaeology is the application of scientific techniques and theoretical concepts to the study of the material remains of cultures (Clark, 1939; Deetz, 1967; Fagan, 1978). It covers all of human history, from the time of the earliest humans right up to the present.

To understand what archaeology involves requires some knowledge of the material evidence it examines. As we shall see in Chapter 8, some raw materials preserve much more readily than others. Stone and clay vessels are virtually indestructible, while wood, skin, metals, and bone are much more friable. Thus, in most archaeological sites, only the most durable remains of human material culture are preserved for the archaeologist to study. Any picture of the prehistoric past obtained from archaeological investigations is likely to give a very one-sided picture of that life. As a result, the unfortunate archaeologist is like a detective fitting together a complicated series of clues to give a generalized impression and explanation of prehistoric culture and society. Much effort has gone into developing sophisticated methods for studying the prehistoric past. Often, it is somewhat like taking a handful of miscellaneous objects—say two spark plugs, a fragment of a china cup, a needle, a grindstone, and a candle holder—and trying to reconstruct the culture of the makers of these diverse objects on the basis of the collection alone.

Some people think that archaeology is a set of techniques, such as accurate recording, precise excavation, and detailed laboratory analysis. Such a narrow definition, however, deals only with "doing archaeology," the actual process of recovering data from the soil. Modern archaeology is far more than a set of techniques, for it involves not only recovering, ordering, and describing the past, but also interpreting the evidence from the earth.

Theory in Archaeology.   A broad definition of archaeology includes not only the subject matter but also the techniques used to describe and explain it. Over a century and a half of serious work all over the world has resulted in the development of a whole battery of methods and techniques for describing and explaining the past. But these methods and techniques in themselves are not enough. They are related to a body of theoretical concepts that provide both a framework and a means for archaeologists to look beyond the facts and material objects for explanations of events that took place during our long history.

Much archaeological research and theory is strongly influenced by contributions made by other academic disciplines, such as specialists in other fields of anthropology and in biology, chemistry, geography, history, physics, and computer technology, to mention only a few. Multidisciplinary research is essential to modern archaeology.

Archaeology and Prehistory.   The term *archaeology* originally embraced the study of ancient history as a whole, but the word was gradually narrowed in meaning to its present definition—the study of material remains and human cultures using archaeological theory and techniques (Daniel, 1975).

In 1833, a French scholar named F. Tournal coined the word *prehistory* to refer to that portion of human history that extends back before the time of written documents and archives. Prehistory, which is studied by prehistoric archaeologists, encompasses the enormous time span of human cultural evolution that extends back at least three million years.

Archaeology and History.   The earliest written records were compiled on the banks of the Tigris and Euphrates rivers in what is now Iraq about 5000 years ago. It is at that point that *history*, the study of human experience through written documents, begins.

Archaeology is our primary source of information for 99 percent of human history on this planet. Written history describes less than one-tenth of one percent of that enormous time span. Although in the Near East, written records extend back 5,000 years, the earlier portions of that period are illuminated very little by the documents. In other parts of the world, prehistory ended much later. Continuous written history in Britain began with the Roman conquest some 2000 years ago; while decipherable records in the New World commenced with Christopher Columbus, even though the Maya had a record-keeping system and a form of calendar. Some parts of the world did not come into contact with literate peoples until much more recently. The pastoral Khoi-Khoi of the Cape of Good Hope emerged from prehistory in 1652 and were first known to the outside world when Bartholomew Diaz met them in the late fifteenth century. The tribes of the Central African interior had their first contact with David Livingstone in 1855. Continuous government records of this area did not begin until the late nineteenth century, while parts of New Guinea and the Amazon basin are still emerging from their prehistoric past.

There is a sharp contrast between documentary history and the view of our past as it is reconstructed from the archaeological record. In the first place, historians work with accurate chronologies (Dymond, 1974). They can date an event with certainty to within a year, and possibly even as closely as a minute or second. Secondly, their history is that of individuals, groups, governments, and even several nations interacting with each other, reacting to events, and struggling for power. They are able to glimpse the subtle interplay of human intellects, for their principal players have often recorded their impressions or deeds on paper. But there still tend to be gaps in the historian's record. Details of political events are likely to be far more complete than those of day-to-day existence or the trivia of village life, which were often of little consequence to contemporary observers, no doubt because they experienced such commonplace things in the same way as we drive our cars. Such minor details of past human behavior do absorb students of ancient society, especially archaeologists interested in broad patterns of human change and early cultures, and it is here that the archaeologist may be useful to the historian (Finley, 1971).

THE DIVERSITY OF ARCHAEOLOGISTS

Since no single archaeologist could possibly be expert in the entire time span of archaeology, most archaeologists specialize. Archaeologists can pursue one of the following specialties:

Prehistoric archaeologists (prehistorians) study prehistoric times, from that of the earliest humans right up to the frontiers of documentary history. There are dozens of different specialties among prehistorians. For example, paleoanthropologists are experts in the living floors and artifacts of the earliest humans. This specialty involves close cooperation with physical anthropologists interested in human biological evolution and with geologists concerned with the complex strata in which the earliest human dwellings are found. Others are experts in stone technology, studying the early peopling of the world and the subsistence strategies of prehistoric hunter-gatherers. Those who specialize in the origins of agriculture and literate civilization have a pressing concern with ceramics, domesticated grains and animal bones, and a wide range of site types and economic lifeways. Since modern prehistoric archaeology is global in its coverage, there are both New and Old World archaeologists, each focusing on specific regions such as the North American Southwest, Mesoamerica, or Peru. Even these large areas are too big for specialist researchers to work alone, so they tackle a specific region, site, or detailed problem within a larger site, region, or area. Our knowledge of world prehistory today is made up of the efforts of hundreds of archaeologists working in all parts of the world, on small problems or larger ones, on a regional survey or on a ten-year excavation at a single settlement. And, of course, some prehistorians are experts on soil analysis, ancient animal bones, the use of computers and statistical methods in archaeology, or simply on excavation itself.

Classical archaeologists study the remains of the great Classical civilizations of Greece and Rome (Figure 1.7). Many of them work in close collaboration with historians, amplifying documentary records and filling in details of architectural and art history. Traditionally, Classical archaeologists have been much concerned with art objects and buildings, but some of them are now beginning to study the types of economic and social problems discussed by prehistoric archaeologists in this book (Wheeler, 1954).

Egyptologists and *Assyriologists* are among the many specialist archaeologists who work on specific civilizations or time periods. These specialties require unusual skills. Egyptologists, for instance, have to acquire a fluent knowledge of hieroglyphs to help them study the ancient Egyptians, while Assyriologists, experts on the Assyrians of ancient Iraq, have to be conversant with cuneiform script.

Figure 1.7   The Parthenon in Athens. Most Classical archaeologists are much concerned with art history and architecture.

Historical archaeologists study archaeological sites with the aid of written records. They examine medieval cities, such as Winchester and York in England; they excavate Colonial American settlements (Figure 1.8), Spanish Missions, and nineteenth-century forts in the west; and they even study a whole range of interesting historical artifacts, from bottles to uniform buttons (Fontana, 1968; Noël Hume, 1969; South, 1977).

Both historical and archaeological data are such that there are always gaps in the reconstruction of the past. Even on sites where historical records are exceptionally complete, archaeology can provide invaluable information to amplify them (Schuyler, 1978). Medieval Winchester, for example, is known to us from a rich archive of official records, which include title deeds for houses. In the Brooks area of the city, Martin Biddle and his colleagues were able to connect houses found in excavations with their long-dead owners. They excavated the quarter of humble artisans' houses, then carried out a lengthy title search in the city archives that enabled them to identify the ownership of individual houses whose foundations were exposed in their trenches (Selkirk, 1970). Perhaps one of the most vivid discoveries of historical archaeology comes from the fortress of Masada in Israel. The first century historian Josephus Flavius describes how the Romans besieged a group of Jewish patriots in the fortress in A.D. 73. The defenders chose to commit mass suicide rather than surrender. Excavations in the mid-1960s revealed minute details of the daily lives of the besieged and of their heroic deaths. Thus, a combination of archaeology and history has painted a vivid and surprisingly complete picture of the siege.

Historical archaeology comes into its own in studies of the last 5,000 years, for which abundant documentary records are available. But historical records can also be important in throwing light on societies that had limited written records. A case in point is the Classic Mayan civilization, which flourished in Mesoamerica between about A.D. 200 and 900. The Maya developed a complex writing system that enabled them to record religious, political, and astronomical events with elaborate glyphs sculpted on stone and wood, as well as set down in large books. Although only partially deciphered to date, these records are beginning to provide an invaluable new perspective on a civilization that was hitherto known almost entirely from archaeological investigations (Thompson, 1972).

Underwater archaeologists study sites and ancient shipwrecks on the sea floor and lake bottoms, and even under rapids in Canadian lakes. A whole array of specialist techniques have been developed by scuba-diving archaeologists for recording these underwater sites (Bass, 1966).

Figure 1.8   Foundations of the Public Hospital for the Insane at Colonial Williamsburg in Virginia, which were revealed by archaeological excavation in 1972.

This field of archaeology is so specialized that we lack the space to cover it here.

Industrial archaeologists study buildings and other structures dating to the Industrial Revolution or later, such as Victorian railway stations, old cotton plantations, windmills, and even slum housing in England (Buchanon, 1972; Hudson, 1976). Anyone entering this field needs at least some training as an architectural historian.

These are but a few of the many specialties within archaeology. Modern archaeology is so complex that there are experts in dozens of different aspects of the subject, ranging from mice bones to soil profiles to the techniques of ancient metallurgy. The unifying aspect of all the specialties is their common interest in studying humanity in the past.

THE GOALS OF ARCHAEOLOGY

Whether they are concerned with the most ancient of human societies or with those of more recent centuries, most archaeologists agree that their research has three broad goals in mind:

The study of sites and their contents in a context of time and space, from which one derives descriptions of long sequences of human culture. This descriptive activity is the reconstruction of culture history.

The reconstruction of past lifeways.

The study of cultural process (Trigger, 1978).

By no means would every scholar, however, agree that all three of these objectives are equally valid, or indeed that they should coexist. In practice, however, each tends to complement the others, especially when an archaeologist designs his or her research to answer specific questions, rather than merely digging as a preliminary to describing rows of excavated objects.

Culture History.   The term *culture history* means, quite simply, the description of human cultures as they extend backward thousands of years into the past. An archaeologist working on the culture history of an area is concerned purely with describing the prehistoric cultures of that region. Culture history is derived from the study of sites and the artifacts and structures in them in a context of time and space. By investigating groups of prehistoric sites and the many artifacts in them, it is possible to erect local and regional sequences of human cultures that extend over centuries, even millennia (see Chapters 12 and 18). Most of the activity involved is descriptive, the accumulation of minute chronological and spatial frameworks of archaeological data as a basis for observing how particular cultures evolved and changed through prehistoric times. Culture history is reconstructed by building up local sequences of archaeological sites into regional and even larger-scale frameworks of changing human cultures. It is an essential preliminary to any work on lifeways or cultural process (see Chapter 19).

Many archaeologists concerned with culture history feel inhibited, by poor preservation of artifacts and sites, from making inferences about the more intangible aspects of human prehistory, such as religion and social organization, arguing that archaeologists can legitimately concern themselves only with the material remains of ancient human behavior. Unfortunately, this rather narrow view of culture history sent many people off in unprofitable directions, into a long and painstaking preoccupation with artifact types and local chronologies that turned much of archaeology into a form of glorified stamp collecting.

Past Lifeways.   The study of past lifeways—the ways in which people have made their livings in the past—has developed into a major concern since the 1930s. This new goal of archaeology developed as people realized that the prehistory of humankind was played out against a complicated background of environmental change. Every human culture was, they realized, a complex and constantly changing adaptation to specific environmental conditions.

The study of prehistoric lifeways in their environmental contexts began with Grahame Clark's research at Star Carr and other sites in Europe (Chapter 4), and with Julian Steward and others in the United States (Clark, 1954; Steward, 1955; Steward and Setzler, 1977). These scholars realized that artifacts and structures alone give a very one-sided view of humanity and its environmental adaptations. So they began to concentrate on reconstructing ancient subsistence patterns from animal bones, carbonized seeds, and other food residues recovered from meticulous excavations. They called in the assistance of pollen analysts and soil scientists, as well as botanists, so that they could look at archaeological sites in a much wider, multidisciplinary context. The context of such studies was still descriptive archaeology, with its preoccupations with space and time, but there was a different emphasis: the contexts of space and time relative to the interplay of changing human settlement patterns, subsistence strategies, and ancient environments.

Robert Braidwood took a team of scientists from other disciplines with him when he started work on the early history of agriculture in the Zagros Mountains of the Near East (Figure 1.9). He recovered evidences of animal domestication as early as 6000 B.C. and developed a new theory for the origins of food production based on more precise environmental data than ever before (Braidwood and Howe, 1962). Richard MacNeish worked closely with botanists as he traced the early history of maize in the Tehuacán Valley of Mexico (MacNeish, 1970). Conditions there were so dry that he was able to show how the settlements of the Tehuacán people had slowly changed as they relied more heavily on maize cultivation after 5000 B.C. As long ago as 1948, Gordon Willey carried out a detailed survey of the coastal Virú Valley in Peru, where he plotted the distributions of hundreds of prehistoric sites from different chronological periods against a changing valley environment (Willey, 1953). This was a pioneer attempt at reconstructing prehistoric settlement patterns, obviously a key part of any attempts to reconstruct prehistoric lifeways.

Such factors as population density and carrying capacity of agricultural land are clearly central to any understanding of ancient lifeways.

Figure 1.9   Robert Braidwood's excavation at the village of Jarmo in the Zagros Mountains of the Near East was among the first team investigations to study early agriculture.

The thrust of this goal of archaeology is still, however, descriptive, within a theoretical framework that saw human cultures as complicated, ever-changing systems. These systems not only interacted with other cultural systems but with the natural environment as well.

Cultural Process.   A third goal of archaeology has developed in the past twenty years that is concerned not only with descriptions of the past but also with explanations of culture change in prehistory. Archaeologists concerned with this goal attempt to explain the nature of cultural change, process, and evolution in prehistory, topics that we explore more fully in Chapter 19. The ultimate goal of these prehistoric archaeologists is to explain why human cultures in all parts of the world reached their various stages of cultural evolution. Human tools are seen as part of a system of interrelated phenomena that include both culture and the natural environment. Prehistoric archaeology, they argue, is a science, one in which much more rigorous research methods must be used than hitherto. Archaeologists should design their research work within a framework of testable propositions that may be supported, modified, or rejected on the basis of excavated and analyzed archaeological data.

This approach to archaeology, sometimes called the "new archaeology," is concerned primarily with finding out the "ways in which human populations (in their own way) do the things other systems do" (Binford and Binford, 1968). The many archaeologists of this persuasion believe that the past is inherently knowable, provided that rigorous research methods and designs are used and that field methods are impeccable. They feel strongly that archaeology is more than a descriptive science and that archaeologists can explain cultural change in the past.

As we shall see in Chapter 4, it is debatable just how "new" the new archaeology is. For this reason the rather ghastly term "processual archaeology" is more frequently used to describe this approach to prehistory, a label that emphasizes its concern for cultural process and explantion of the past.

Differing Goals: New and Old World Archaeologists.   Not only are there disagreements about goals among archaeologists as a whole, but American scholars have a different viewpoint from many Old World prehistorians as well. In the United States archaeologists have long believed that anthropology is the study of humankind in the widest sense. Thus American scholars have regarded archaeologists as anthropologists who excavate the material remains of humans of the past, giving anthropology a time dimension. European archaeologists, on the other hand, lean toward a definition of anthropology as part of history. In the Old World, the arts of excavation have been developed to a high pitch by a historical tradition that began with A. H. L. Fox Pitt Rivers and continued with Sir Mortimer Wheeler and many postwar archaeologists. Both British and Continental prehistorians have placed great emphasis on the recovery of data from the ground, on the tracing of settlement patterns and structures, on economic reconstruction, and on the detailed analysis of artifact types and complicated typologies. Many European archaeologists have acquired international reputations on the basis of their skill as excavators or museum people. The archaeologist is seen as a craftsperson with diverse skills, not the least of which is the effective reconstruction of the past, both to amplify the written record and also to create a historical story, albeit incomplete, for periods when no archives exist to throw light on the deeds of chiefs or the attitudes of individuals.

But, for all the differing approaches and perceived goals of archaeology, every archaeologist, of whatever viewpoint, would agree that we cannot hope to carry out archaeological research without a body of sound theory, good descriptive archaeology, and detailed information on prehistoric lifeways to form the basis for testing our newly generated hypotheses.

Guide to Further Reading

Ceram, C. W. *Gods, Graves, and Scholars.* New York: Alfred A. Knopf, 1953.
A classic account of early archaeologists, which provides a wonderful introduction to the heroic days of archaeology.

Deetz, James. *Invitation to Archaeology.* Garden City, N.Y.: Natural History Press, 1967.
An admirable brief introduction to prehistoric archaeology that gives the reader a brief overview of the subject.

Fagan, Brian M. *Archaeology: A Brief Introduction.* Boston: Little, Brown, 1978.
A short version of In the Beginning *that covers more ground than Deetz in about the same length.*

McGimsey, Charles. *Public Archaeology.* New York: Seminar Press, 1972.
A pungent statement about the crisis in archaeology that should be read by everyone interested in the preservation of the past.

PART II 🦢

A SHORT HISTORY OF ARCHAEOLOGY:

SIXTH CENTURY B.C. TO 1980

The Four Stages of Public Opinion

  I (Just after publication)
  The Novelty is absurd and subversive of Religion & Morality. The pro-
  pounder both fool & knave.
 II (Twenty years later)
  The Novelty is absolute Truth and will yield a full & satisfactory explanation of things in general—The propounder man of sublime genius & perfect virtue.
III (Forty years later)
  The Novelty won't explain things in general after all and therefore is a
  wretched failure. The propounder a very ordinary person advertised by a
  clique.
 IV (A century later)
  The Novelty a mixture of truth & error. Explains as much as could reasonably be expected. The propounder worthy of all honour in spite of his
  share of human frailties, as one who has added to the permanent possessions of science.

THOMAS HUXLEY
Notes, 1873

No one can fully understand modern, scientific archaeology without having some notion of its roots. The first archaeologists were little more than philosophers and antiquarians who were searching for curiosities, buried treasure, and intellectual enlightenment. These treasure hunters were the predecessors of the early professionals, scholars who concentrated on site description and believed that human society evolved through a series of simple stages, the final stage being modern civilizations. Since World War II archaeology has undergone a major transformation from a basically descriptive discipline into a many-sided activity that is greatly concerned with trying to understand the processes by which human cultures changed and evolved in the past. If there is one major lesson to be learned from the history of archaeology, it is that no development in the field took place in isolation. All innovations in archaeology are the result of steady advances in the quality of scientific research.

CHAPTER 2 ❧

THE ORIGINS OF ARCHAEOLOGY:
SIXTH CENTURY B.C. TO 1870

Preview

- Archaeology has its origins in the intellectual curiosity about the past felt by a number of Classical writers, such as Hesiod, who engaged in much speculation about the stages of early human history.
- With the Renaissance this curiosity about the past, which manifested itself in excavations at Pompeii and elsewhere, was renewed. But speculations about early prehistory were shackled by the dogma of the Christian church.
- With a greater knowledge of human biological and cultural diversity in the later eighteenth century, people began to speculate about the relationships between different groups and about the notion of human progress from simple to complex societies.
- The fact that humanity had been in existence for more than 6,000 years was proven by the discovery in the Somme Valley, France, and elsewhere, of the bones of extinct animals in direct association with tools made by humans. However, these discoveries could not be placed in a scientific context without the development of both uniformitarian geology—the new science of paleontology—and the theory of evolution by natural selection.
- The notion of human social evolution followed in the train of biological evolution. Many archaeologists thought of prehistoric cultures as being arranged in geological-like layers of progress from the simple to the complex. A simple form of unilinear evolution was

espoused by such pioneer anthropologists as Sir Edward Tylor and Lewis Morgan, who portrayed humanity as having progressed from simple savagery to complex, literate civilization.

In this chapter we examine the early history of archaeology as it developed out of the philosophical speculations of Classical and Renaissance scholars. Much early nineteenth-century archaeology was concerned with the origins of humankind and with proving that people lived on earth long before 4004 B.C., the date for the Creation determined by Archbishop James Ussher in the seventeenth century. Developments in evolutionary biology, geology, and paleontology had a strong influence on nineteenth-century archaeology. Anthropology, the study of humankind, developed out of the social sciences in the 1870s, and immediately formed a close relationship with archaeology. This was manifested in the common scholarly belief that all human societies evolved from a state of simple hunting and gathering to civilization in a series of stages, but that not all societies reached the highest pinnacle of achievement—modern civilization. The material in Chapter 2 covers everything up to the time when scholars were beginning to challenge this evolutionary approach.

THE FIRST ARCHAEOLOGISTS

Philosophical Speculations.   Although King Nabonidus of Babylon did excavate an ancient palace at Ur-of-the-Chaldees in the sixth century B.C., he could hardly be called an archaeologist. Archaeology has developed as a scientific discipline only in the last two hundred years, and it is a young and vigorous discipline whose basic principles are still much debated. But a philosophical interest in the prehistoric past goes back far earlier than the eighteenth century. The Greeks and Romans reflected about human origins and about the diversity of humankind. Homer had written about a glorious, heroic past of kings and warriors, of a time when gods mingled freely with humans. But how had humanity fared before the time of Homer's *Iliad?* In the eighth century B.C. the philosopher Hesiod wrote that humanity had passed through five great ages of human history—the earliest, one of Gold, when people "dwelt in ease"; the last, an Age of War, when people worked terribly hard and experienced great sorrow (Daniel, 1975; Plumb, 1969). Speculations of this type, which reflected the idle curiosity of the day, are widespread in Classical and even early Chinese writings.

The Renaissance.   The Renaissance saw a quickening of intellectual curiosity, not only about the nature of humanity but about the Classical world as well. People of leisure and wealth began to follow in the footsteps of the Renaissance scholars, traveling widely in Greece and Italy, studying antiquities, and collecting examples of Classical art. The same travelers were not above a little illicit excavation to recover fine statuary from ancient temples and Roman villas. Soon the cabinets of wealthy collectors bulged with fine art objects, and the study of Classical art became a major scholarly preoccupation. When the King of the Two Sicilies commissioned the Cavaliere Alcubierre to excavate the famous Roman city of Herculaneum in 1738, a new era in Classical archaeology began, one that made Classical archaeology a discipline predominantly concerned with art and architecture, with temples and other large, spectacular monuments (Ceram, 1953) (Figure 2.1). And the Herculaneum excavations revealed incredibly full details of a Roman town destroyed by an eruption of Vesuvius in A.D. 79. The many fine objects dug up by Alcubierre and his successors took Classical archaeology into artistic realms that were spectacular and that offered exciting prospects for wealthy collectors and those scholars who considered themselves expert antiquarians.

Antiquarians and Excavators.   Many of the early collectors and scholars came from Britain, France, and Germany. Their less wealthy colleagues stayed at home and spent their time speculating about ancient British and European history instead. Who were the ancient Britons? Were they the sophisticated warriors that Julius Caesar had described when he visited Britain in 55 B.C.? Or were they to be compared to the American Indians? When the famous English artist John White returned from North America with his vivid drawings of the simple Indian tribes of the new colony, intellectual curiosity about the ancient Britons reached a fever pitch. The pioneer antiquarian John Aubrey (1626–1697) described them as "two or three degrees less savage than the Americans. The Romans subdued and civilized them" (Daniel, 1975).

There was little enough for people to go on. The prehistoric Europeans left behind them few tangible signs of their existence, except for thousands of earthen mounds, some extensive earth fortification works, and a few very conspicuous monuments, the most famous of

Figure 2.1   Herculaneum, destroyed by an eruption of Vesuvius in August A.D. 79 and excavated in 1738.

which was Stonehenge in southern England (Figure 2.2). This remarkable series of stone circles was hailed as a famous temple. It was here that the ancient Druids, a flamboyant priesthood described by Julius Caesar, had performed their pagan rites, just as Aubrey believed (Piggott, 1968). Everyone realized that Europe had been populated by primitive tribes long before the Roman conquest. But how long had they lived there, and what was the nature of their history? If the American Indians and South Sea islanders, first revealed to an astonished world in the eighteenth century, were any guide, then the ancient Europeans had enjoyed many different life styles and elaborate customs. There were only two ways to tackle the problem—by excavating ancient burial mounds and settlements and by philosophical speculation about human conditions and origins.

The tools and burials of the ancient Europeans had been turning up for centuries, revealed by the plowshare and house-building operations. Stone and bronze axes, strange clay pots, even gold ornaments and skeletons found buried with elaborate ornaments formed a confusing jumble of information about prehistoric times. When local landowners began to excavate burial mounds and other monuments on their properties, the confusion increased even more. Some burials contained bronze and gold ornaments, others only stone implements; still others were mere cremations deposited in large urns. Which burial mounds were the earliest? Who had deposited the skeletons, and how long ago? No one had yet developed a way of putting in order the hundreds of years of prehistory that preceded the Greeks, Romans, and ancient Egyptians of Biblical fame.

SCRIPTURES AND FOSSILS

The Biblical Legend. One reason that antiquarians of the seventeenth and eighteenth centuries were confused was that they had no idea of how long people had been living on earth. They had no means of dating the past or of classifying the jumble of finds that cluttered their

Figure 2.2 Stonehenge, the Bronze Age ceremonial center in southern England that became an early focus of antiquarian interest. This picture was taken before the restoration of the stones in 1958.

cabinets. Above all, they did not know how all these finds fitted into the story of the Creation in the Bible.

The dogma of the Christian church rested firmly on the first chapter of Genesis, which stated that God created the world and its inhabitants in six days. The story of Adam and Eve provided an entirely consistent explanation for the creation of humankind and the world's population. The Bible's early chapters are full of complicated genealogical tables for the early families that populated the earth. Scholars used the tables for calculating the date of the Flood and the date of the Creation. In the seventeenth century, Archbishop James Ussher, using the genealogies in the Old Testament, calculated that the world was created in 4004 B.C. This dating was refined by Dr. John Lightfoot of Cambridge, who published a monograph in 1642 in which he declared that humanity was created at 9:00 A.M. on October 23, 4004 B.C. (Daniel, 1962). These calculations and propositions received almost universal acceptance. They became a dogmatic canon defended with almost fanatic frenzy in the nineteenth century. It was a comfortable proposition, allowing approximately 6,000 years for all of human history. All kinds of romantic legends were concocted to fill these 4,000 years in order to produce some explanation for the chaotic jumble of antiquities found by the antiquarians.

What Is Humanity?   While antiquarians were puzzling over the marriage of prehistoric times with the story of the Creation, political and social philosophers were speculating intensely about the state of human society. The great scientist Sir Isaac Newton, for example, argued that the universe ran more like a clock than by the hand of God (Slotkin, 1965). This concept of a clock led writers of the Enlightenment, such as John Locke and Jean Jacques Rousseau, to philosophize about the rules and laws that could perpetuate a sophisticated civilization. "What is humanity?" they asked. "Does it need a despotic government—or a minimum of social control?"

Many scholars began to feel that such humans as the South Sea islanders, the American Indians, and the Australian aborigines—people who lived in a "state of nature," with minimal social controls—were inferior, for they were deprived of the benefits of modern civilization. Others, like Rousseau, depicted contemporary savages such as the Tahitians as living in Eden-like innocence in pastoral groves (Moorehead, 1966). People were better off, he said, without civilization's institutions, rules, and repressions.

The philosophers began to rebel openly against the church and its way of interpreting the world and its history, and they had sound grounds for doing so. Captain Cook, who traveled in the South Seas, and others who traveled in the Americas and Africa had brought home new information about all manner of primitive societies flourishing at various levels of cultural development; none of them, however, were as advanced as that of eighteenth-century Europe (Figure 2.3). Daringly, in a world where accusations of heresy were a serious matter, they began to formulate a theory of human progress, one that helped not only to explain how Europeans had achieved a life style so far removed from that of the South Sea islands, but also to put human prehistory into a new perspective. People like the Marquis de Cordorcet theorized that humanity had progressed through successively higher stages of development up to modern times. But the question of questions remained unanswered. How long had this progress been going on? Could

Figure 2.3   An Australian aborigine with his lightweight toolkit. (A nineteenth-century engraving.)

it really have happened within the short 6000-year time span allowed by the official Biblical chronology?

Axes and Extinct Animals.   As antiquarians dug into burial mounds and philosophers argued about human progress, discoveries were beginning to come to light that threw serious doubt on Ussher's dating. For centuries, farmers had happened upon the bones of extinct animals in clays and river gravels on the banks of such rivers as the Somme in France and the Douro in Portugal. They had found hundreds of strangely shaped stones as well, stones whose shapes so differed from those of natural stones that it was difficult to explain them away as anything but human-made axes. Scientists generally scoffed at the idea that these "thunderbolts" or "meteorites" were of human manufacture. But a few people had quietly disagreed, among them the sixteenth-century scholar Michele Mercati, who called the alleged thunderbolts "weapons used by people ignorant of the use of metals" (Mercati, 1717). A century later, the works of an author who said that Mercati's "weapons" were made by people who lived before Adam were burned in public.

Then the bones of large animals extinct in the region, such as the elephant and hippopotamus, began to be found in European river gravels. These bones were jumbled with Mercati's axes in such a way that the animals and human tools appeared to be contemporary. In 1715, for example, a stone axe and elephant bones were unearthed in river gravels in the very center of the city of London. Many people believed that the elephant was of Roman vintage; but others felt that the axe had been made by an ancient Briton who did not know how to use metals.

Nearly a century later, an English country squire named John Frere collected carefully chipped stone axes from a gravel pit near the small village of Hoxne, Suffolk (Figure 2.4). The axes came from a depth of 3.7 meters (12 feet) below the surface of the ground, at the same level as bones of extinct animals. Frere took the trouble to publish his remarkable finds, describing the axes as weapons of war used by people ignorant of metals. "The situation," he wrote, "in which these weapons were found may tempt us to refer them to a very remote period indeed, even beyond that of the present world." In other words, the tools were made earlier than 4004 B.C.—and the Creation (Daniel, 1967).

John Frere's remarkable discovery caused little excitement at the time. In the early nineteenth century, most people, even the most eminent scientists, still fervently believed that God created the world in 4004 B.C. Humankind had inhabited the world for 6000 glorious

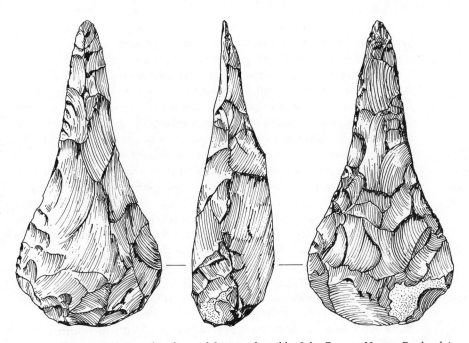

Figure 2.4   A stone hand axe of the type found by John Frere at Hoxne, England, in 1797.

years, living in a beautiful world that "teemed with delighted existence" created by the Lord. Although scholars were now familiar enough with stone implements, they were not ready to accept the idea that they came from a world that was much older than the Garden of Eden. That humankind had been in existence for longer than 6,000 years, and that the earth and living organisms had developed on a far larger time scale than the Ussherian estimate—these were still viewed as wild ideas. And until proofs of these notions could be established, no one would be able to explain the discoveries of extinct animals and stone tools at all satisfactorily.

Catastrophism and Uniformitarianism.   The eighteenth century was a period of awakening interest not only in archaeology but also in geology and the natural sciences. It was then that the science of paleontology was born, a science devoted to the study of fossil animals. A remarkable Frenchman, Georges Cuvier (1769–1832) spent his lifetime studying fossil mammals, distinguishing hundreds of different species and developing paleontology into a complex science. He laid out a geological history of the world by using dozens of fossil animals as type indicators for different geological layers and epochs. He discovered, for example, a period when great dinosaurs had been the dominant creatures on earth. But, since no early human fossils were found, Cuvier could continue to argue that all humanity had been created by God in the Garden of Eden 6000 years earlier. The dinosaurs and other early creatures had been wiped out by series of great catastrophes. As one fauna was destroyed, God created a new one to replace it. The Biblical flood, indeed, was the last catastrophic event in a long series of cataclysms. Cuvier's *catastrophism* was a popular theory that appealed greatly to theologians, confirming as it did "the power, wisdom and greatness of God as manifested in Creation" (Daniel, 1962). Under the Cuvier rubric, the layers of rocks seen in cliffs and other exposed strata resulted from a periodic major upheaval that literally destroyed the earth before a new rebirth—not once, but on many occasions.

But many field geologists were puzzled. The Industrial Revolution had sparked an orgy of canal building involving vast earthmoving projects that exposed more geological strata than ever before. One of those who studied these new exposures was William Smith (1769–1839), a geologist so engrossed by geological stratigraphy that his friends nicknamed him "Strata" Smith. This remarkable geologist recognized that the geological processes of erosion, accumulation, weathering, and earthquake movement, which were still occurring, were far more likely agents of geological change than were successive catastrophes. Smith produced a complicated geological table identifying geological strata and fossil animal types that appeared and disappeared at the same time everywhere on earth. He emphasized that the rocks of the earth had formed as a result of continuous natural geological processes. The catastrophes proposed by Cuvier and others were not needed to explain geological change. Every gale that battered the coast, every flash flood or sandstorm, and every earthquake movement were among the natural phenomena that had gradually shaped the earth into its modern form. None of the strata examined by Smith or his colleagues showed any signs of successive cataclysms on a regional, let alone a global, scale.

In 1785, James Hutton (1726–1797) published his celebrated *Theory of the Earth* in which he proposed that the earth was formed by quite natural and gradual processes. Hutton's thesis soon became known as the doctrine of *uniformitarianism* (Daniel, 1975). It caused immediate controversy, dividing geologists into two camps: those who believed in the new doctrine and those who said that denial of catastrophism meant denial of the Biblical story of the Creation. To accept uniformitarianism meant that one was quite prepared to accept a date for human origins far older than the mere 6000 years of Biblical dogma.

The issue came to a head when Sir Charles Lyell (1797–1875) published his three-volume *Principles of Geology* (1830–1833). Locality by locality, stratum by stratum, Lyell summarized the meticulous findings of the new geology in a form that was intelligible not only to geologists but to the wider public as well. *Principles of Geology* became a popular bestseller, attracted dozens of newcomers to geology, and placed the doctrine of uniformitarianism on a new footing, bolstered by solid evidence from the field gathered at hundreds of sites all over Europe. Most important of all, *Principles of Geology* was read by scientists in other fields, among them an obscure biologist named Charles Darwin.

EVOLUTION AND NATURAL SELECTION

In his book, Charles Lyell had used a generalized philosophy of gradual change when he described the different types of fossils found in successive strata of the earth. The *Principles of Geology* appeared just as Charles Darwin was leaving England on his five-year voyage (1831–1836) on the *H.M.S. Beagle* (Moorehead, 1961). As Darwin began the classic series of observations in South America and elsewhere that led him toward his theories of evolution and natural selection, he sat down to read Lyell. From that moment on, he looked at the earth with different eyes—as a continually changing world formed and modified by quite natural geological processes.

Upon his return to England, Darwin started the first of a series of notebooks on what he called "the species question"—ways in which species changed through time. In 1838 he read Thomas Henry Malthus's great *Essay on the Principle of Population*, first published in 1798. Darwin immediately realized at this point that he was on the track of an idea of great importance. Malthus had argued that human reproductive capacity far exceeds the available food supply. In other words, people must compete with one another for the necessities of life. Competition causes famine, war, and all sorts of misery. Similar competition occurs among all living organisms. Darwin wondered if new forms had in part been formed by this "struggle for existence," in which the well-adapted individuals survive and the ill-adapted are eliminated.

The doctrine of evolution was nothing new at that time. Many scientists before Darwin, including Lamarck, Buffon, the sociologist Herbert Spencer, and even Darwin's own grandfather, had recognized that animals and plants had not remained unaltered through the ages but were continuously changing. They had hinted that all organisms, including human beings, were modified descendants of previously existing forms of life. With the aid of Lyell's book, Malthus's ideas, and his own field observations of fossil and living organisms, Darwin removed evolution from the realm of speculation by showing *how* change could occur.

As Darwin delved more deeply into the "species question," he realized that his new theory would imply that accumulated favorable variations over long periods must result in the emergence of new species and the extinction of old ones. A timid man, Darwin procrastinated over the publication of his results. To publish them would bring the

Figure 2.5 A period cartoon by Thomas Nast lampooning Darwin's connection of apes with humans.

Mr. Bergh to the Rescue
The Defrauded Gorilla. "That *Man* wants to claim my Pedigree. He says he is one of my descendants."
Mr. Bergh. "Now, Mr. Darwin, how could you insult him so?"

powerful wrath of the church down on his head. Evolution flew right in the teeth of the sacrosanct account of the Creation in Genesis. So, for twenty years, he sat on his revolutionary ideas, only agreeing to their publication in 1858, when he found out that a colleague working in Asia had reached the same general conclusions. A year later Charles Darwin achieved immortality with the publication of *On the Origin of Species,* a preliminary sketch, he said, of the theory of evolution by natural selection.

On the Origin of Species described the basic mechanisms of evolution. "As many more individuals of each species are born than can possibly survive, and as consequently there is a frequently recurring struggle for existence, it follows that any being, if it vary however slightly in any manner profitable to itself . . . will have a better chance of surviving, and thus be naturally selected. . . . This . . . I have called natural selection, or the survival of the fittest" (Darwin, 1859).

Darwin's book was greeted with both acclaim and vicious criticism, as scientists and theologians took sides in a controversy that lasted for generations. Those who believed in the Creation were profoundly disturbed, for evolution not only implied that human beings had developed over a far longer period of time than 6,000 years, but also that they were descended from apes. No other tenet of evolution caused as much furor as the suggestion that humanity began as apes. Cartoonists lampooned the idea; clerics were horrified; parents worried about the effects of such revelations on their children (Figure 2.5) (Howell, 1965). Darwin himself was well aware of the implications of evolution for the antiquity of humankind. He cautiously made but one mention of the subject. "Light," he remarked in *On the Origin of Species,* "will be thrown on the origin of man and his history" (Darwin, 1859).

Evolution by natural selection gave a theoretical explanation for the diversity of both fossil and living forms—no more relying on supernatural intervention, hypothetical catastrophes, or other improbable and undemonstrable occurrences. Evolution by means of natural selection does not, of course, entirely explain biological phenomena. But natural selection did provide one single, direct way of accounting for biological change as time passsed. It made a mockery of the 6,000 years of the Creationists, and like uniformitarianism, provided a valid intellectual framework for seeking the origin of humankind in much earlier times. Many of the scientists who read *On the Origin of Species* were closely connected with several new archaeological discoveries that seemed to date from much earlier than 6,000 years before. What was needed was clear archaeological proof of an earlier date for humanity.

THE ANTIQUITY OF HUMANKIND

The first in a whole series of discoveries that were to revolutionize archaeology was made by Father J. MacEnery, an English Catholic priest. In digging into the lower layers of Kent's Cavern near Torquay in Devon between 1824 and 1829 (Daniel, 1975), he found the remains of extinct animals associated with stone implements. The layer in which they were found happened to be sealed by a zone of stalagmite, a cave deposit having the consistency of cement, which takes a long time to form. MacEnery discussed his finds with some well-known Creationists. They refused to accept the contemporaneity of the bones and stones and insisted that ancient Britons had made ovens in the stalagmite, thereby introducing their implements into the older, lower levels.

While MacEnery did not publish his results for fear of ridicule, a Frenchman named Jacques Boucher de Perthes was not afraid to make known his own findings. In 1837, de Perthes, who was a customs officer at Abbeville in northwestern France, began collecting stone implements and fossils from the gravels of the Somme River. Immediately, he began to find hand axes and the bones of extinct animals in the same sealed gravel beds in such numbers that he was convinced that he had found pre-Flood people. He insisted that human beings had lived before the last catastrophic cataclysm, before the start of Ussherian time. Unfortunately, de Perthes was rather pompous, and his findings were ridiculed when he published them in 1841 (de Perthes, 1841). But he persisted in his investigations and spent his spare time visiting quarries, acquiring a huge collection of fossil bones and stone axes, and arguing that humans had lived before the Flood.

In 1856, a strange skull was found in a cave near Neanderthal, Germany, one that greatly puzzled scientists. It had great, beetling brow ridges (Figure 2.6) and a squat skullcap that were quite unlike the smooth, rounded cranium of modern *Homo sapiens* (Huxley, 1863). The scientists were divided into two camps. Some regarded the Neanderthal skull as that of a pathological idiot, or even of one of Napoleon's soldiers. But a minority of them believed that the new find was that of a primitive human, perhaps that of the maker of all the crude stone tools that had been found from one end of Europe to the other. By this time, news of Boucher de Perthes's discoveries had drifted across the channel. They came to the ears of two eminent English scientists, antiquarian John Evans and the geologist Joseph Prestwich. The two men visited de Perthes at Abbeville in 1859 and examined his museum and the quarry sites. At one place John Evans actually found an axe in

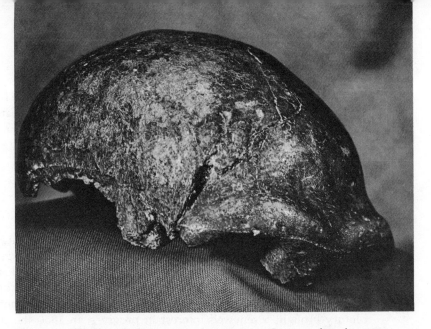

Figure 2.6   The Neanderthal cranium from western Germany found in 1856.

the same level as the bones of a hippopotamus. The sheer quantity of finds was such that Evans and Prestwich realized that here, at last, was the proof of a great antiquity for humankind, something that the new theories of uniformitarianism and evolution had made intellectually possible. Extinct animals and humans in existence thousands of years before the Garden of Eden were, indeed, contemporaneous.

In June 1859, John Evans spoke to the Society of Antiquaries in London; his paper contained this statement: "This much appears established beyond doubt, that in a period of antiquity remote beyond any of which we have hitherto found traces, this portion of the globe was peopled by man" (Evans, 1860).

There followed a rapid and fairly general acceptance of the idea, as a scientific fact, that humans had been living on this earth longer than 6,000 years. The great biologist Thomas Huxley (1825–1895), perhaps the most vigorous champion of Darwin's new ideas, stated that evolution "will extend by long epochs the most liberal estimate that has yet been made of the Antiquity of Man." He also posed the "question of questions for mankind": "the problem which underlies all others, and is more deeply interesting than any other— . . . the ascertainment of the place which man occupies in nature and of his relations to the universe of things" (Huxley, 1863). At last, people were realizing that the past before the advent of written records was knowable and that it was possible to measure enormous time scales back to when people lived at the same time as animals that are now extinct. And, the "question of questions" posed by Thomas Huxley is still at the heart of all archaeological research.

HUMAN PROGRESS: EVOLUTIONISM

As we have seen, the notion of human progress was nothing new. Popular in the eighteenth century, it suffered a decline in popularity during the Napoleonic wars, when civilization seemed, philosophically, to have come apart. But the spectacular social and economic changes brought about by the Industrial Revolution in the nineteenth century brought a renewed interest in progress. In 1850 the prolific sociologist Herbert Spencer (1820–1903) was already declaring that "progress is not an accident, but a necessity. It is a fact of nature" (Spencer, 1855). Darwin's theories of evolution seemed to many a logical extension of the doctrines of social progress. The new theories opened up enormous tracts of prehistoric time for Victorian archaeologists to fill. The oldest finds were Boucher de Perthes's crude axes from the Somme Valley. Later in prehistory, apparently, other people started to live in the great caves of southwest France, at a time when reindeer, not hippopotami, were living in western Europe. And the famous "lake dwellings," abandoned prehistoric villages found below the water's edge in the Swiss lakes during the dry years of 1853–1854, were obviously even more recent than the cave sites of France (Daniel, 1975). What was the best theoretical framework for all these finds? Could notions of human progress agree with the actual archaeological discoveries? Did prehistoric peoples' technology, material culture, and society develop and progress uniformly from the crude tools of the Somme Valley to the sophisticated iron technology of the La Tène culture of Europe? Had cultures evolved naturally along with the biological evolution that brought humanity through all the stages from savagery to civilization?

Many archaeologists began to treat prehistoric peoples as geological artifacts. Intoxicated by thousands of stone tools and archaeological sites of unbelievable richness, they gaily cataloged their finds into a long series of epochs, like geological eras, stages through which every human society would ultimately pass. It was a logical step, they thought. The universal progress of humankind enjoyed the status of what one French archaeologist called a "Great Law" (de Mortillet,

1867). But, as archaeological research extended beyond Europe and into the New World, the incredible diversity of early human experience became visible in the archaeological record. The great civilizations of the Near East were recovered by Henry Layard and others, and the great Mesoamerican religious complexes were described anew (Layard, 1849, Stephens, 1841). Upper Paleolithic art was accepted as authentic some years after the Altamira paintings were discovered in northern Spain in 1879 (Figure 2.7) (Cartailhac, 1901). Yet many parts of North America and Africa showed no signs of higher civilizations. Furthermore, the New World civilizations and European cave art seemed to imply that humanity sometimes regressed. The great religious centers of Mesoamerica had been abandoned, for instance, and art equal to that from the French caves did not reappear for many thousands of years. Scientists became less and less certain that people had a common, consistently progressing universal prehistory. Obviously, humankind had progressed considerably overall since the remote millennia of its simple origins, and life had improved for humanity—for the Victorians, at any rate. But was that progress uniform in the same way that geological progress was seen to be?

Edward Tylor (1832–1917).   Archaeologists were not the only people to be thinking about human progress (Harris, 1968; Hatch, 1973). The early anthropologists, pioneers of a discipline that developed out of a strong Victorian interest in human institutions, were evolutionists, too.

Figure 2.7   Bison in a polychrome cave painting in Altamira, Spain. The Altamira art style represents the ultimate artistic achievement of the Upper Paleolithic hunter-gatherers of western Europe, about 12,000 B.C. Finally accepted as genuine in 1904, the Altamira paintings are now, alas, closed to the public.

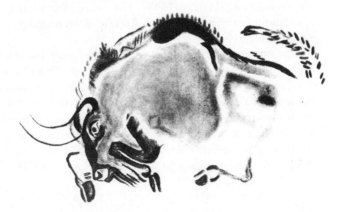

E. B. Tylor, one of the fathers of anthropology in the English-speaking world, was an avid believer in reasoned human progress (Tylor, 1871). He surveyed human development in all its forms, from crude stone axes of the Somme Valley in France to Maya temples to Victorian civilization. The origins of civilized institutions, he argued, might be found in the simpler institutions of ruder peoples. If the stone axes made by the Australian natives were like the stone axes obtained from ancient European river terraces, then perhaps the marriage customs of the native Australians were similar to those of the Paleolithic inhabitants of Europe. Most of his data came from two sources: accounts of contemporary primitive peoples and archaeological findings from the past. He arranged these to reflect a tripartite sequence of human development—from simple hunting *savagery*, as he called it; through a stage of simple farming, which he called *barbarism*; to *civilization*, the most complex of all human conditions.

Lewis Morgan (1818–1881).   The American anthropologist Lewis Morgan went even further than Tylor. He distinguished no fewer than seven ethnic periods of human progress, which were outlined in his famous book *Ancient Society* (1877). Like Tylor, however, Morgan's stages began with simple savagery and had human society reaching the height of its achievements in a "state of civilization" (Willey and Sabloff, 1980). His seven stages, he said, had developed quite rationally and independently in different parts of the world.

The theories of Lewis Morgan exercised a strong influence on the ideas of Karl Marx and Friedrich Engels, the Communist social philosophers. They drew on his ideas of primitive communism—the notion that people shared available resources—and proceeded to say that this type of sharing was gradually eroded by the emerging forces of industrial civilization (Harris, 1968). His work was also to influence the development of modern North American archaeology, with its strong evolutionary bias.

Such notions of human progress were easy to defend in a world whose frontiers were still under exploration. There was no such thing as a "world prehistory" in the 1870s, merely thousands of scattered archaeological finds, most of them from Europe, the Mediterranean, or North America. Nearly all of these were from thoroughly unscientific excavations that would make a modern archaeologist shudder. It was hardly surprising that even expert scientists turned to the comfortable framework of biological and social evolution to explain the astonishing diversity of humankind.

Guide to Further Reading

Daniel, Glyn. *One Hundred and Fifty Years of Archaeology*. London: Duckworth, 1975.
The classic account of the history of archaeology, with strong emphasis on the Old World.

_____. *The Idea of Prehistory*. London: Watts, 1962.
A popular account of the events that led to the acceptance of the antiquity of humankind.

Daniel, Glyn, ed. *The Origins and Growth of Archaeology*. Baltimore: Pelican Books, 1967.
A series of extracts from the writings of early archaeologists that can serve to amplify the other readings in this guide.

Willey, Gordon, and Sabloff, Jerry. *A History of American Archaeology*. San Francisco: W. H. Freeman, 1980. 2nd ed.
A detailed account of the development of New World archaeology from the Spanish occupation until recent times.

CHAPTER 3 🦢

ARCHAEOLOGY COMES OF AGE:
1870 to 1950

Preview

- Unilinear evolution was recognized by early twentieth-century archaeologists as being far too simple a scheme to provide a satisfactory explanation of prehistory. Some scholars began to turn to diffusionist schemes, which presumed that many cultural innovations had emanated from ancient Egypt and other similar centers of higher civilization.

- These diffusionist explanations proved just as unsatisfactory. Under the influence of Franz Boas (1858–1942) and Vere Gordon Childe (1892–1957), archaeologists began to pay much more attention to the precise description of artifacts and sites and became preoccupied with culture history and chronologies.

- American archaeologists made extensive use of the Direct Historical Approach to prehistory, working back in time from known historical cultures to prehistoric societies. This approach was first developed in the southwest, most notably by A. V. Kidder. In addition, standard taxonomic systems, one of which is the Midwestern Taxonomic System, developed in the 1930s and came into use over wide areas.

- The advent of radiocarbon dating in the late 1940s coincided with a greater concern with the natural environment and the study of human ecology. The anthropologist Leslie White developed a theory of multilinear evolution to explain the past, while his colleague Julian Steward formulated the principles of cultural ecology, the study of

the relationships between human cultures and their natural environments.
- W. W. Taylor's *A Study of Archaeology*, published in 1948, was a
  landmark critique of American archaeology that chided archaeologists for their preoccupation with description and chronology rather
  than with cultural change. This pioneer work and the researches of
  Julian Steward and Leslie White established, once and for all, the
  close relationship between archaeology and anthropology.

This chapter takes us from the beginnings of professional archaeology
in the last decades of the nineteenth century through the 1950s, a
period during which tremendous strides in archaeological research
were made. The first professional archaeologists rejected simple evolutionary schemes as well as the diffusionist views of prehistory that
represented every significant innovation as originating in one location
and then spreading all over the world. Influenced strongly by such
scholars as Franz Boas and V. Gordon Childe, they concentrated on
describing sites and objects and on trying to date their finds. They used
a number of well-tried approaches, including the Direct Historical
Approach and the Midwest Taxonomic System. The advent of radiocarbon dating in the late 1940s solved one of their most pressing
problems, that of developing accurate chronologies for prehistoric cultures.

Most of the archaeologists mentioned in this chapter were content to
describe the past, rather than explain how and why cultures changed.
But the years after World War II saw the development of new approaches that took into account environmental change and the relationships between human cultures and ecological processes. These
innovations took archaeology in new directions, leading it away from
simple description and toward the development of multilinear evolutionary frameworks for prehistoric times.

UNILINEAR EVOLUTION AND DIFFUSIONISM

The spectacular discoveries of the late nineteenth century took place at
a time when anthropology was coming of age as one of the social
sciences. The British social anthropologist Sir James Frazer laid out the
long-term objectives of anthropology in 1890. Anthropologists, he

said, were assigned the task of discovering the general laws that regulated human history in the past and that would continue to control human development in the future. They were to study "the origin, or rather the rudimentary phases, infancy, and childhood of human society" (Frazer, 1890). His remarks reflected a growing professionalism among students of humankind, a professionalism that coincided with a gradual refinement of excavation methods and ways of classifying the past.

Unilinear Evolution.   Anthropology developed from a mingling of several diverse intellectual philosophies (Harris, 1968). These included biological evolution, the notion of social progress, and the idea of cultural evolution. One of the most important influences was the constant contacts between Western civilization and other human societies with completely different social institutions. It was easy for anthropologists, corresponding as they did with missionaries and pioneer settlers from all over the world, to argue that Victorian civilization was the pinnacle of human achievement. The huge volume of anthropological and archaeological data they collected was used to build a universal scheme of *unilinear cultural evolution.* In other words, all human societies had the potential to evolve from a simple hunter-gatherer lifeway to a state of literate civilization, but many of them had never made it.

Today, unilinear evolution seems far too simple an explanation for the evolution of human society. But, one must remember that the first archaeologists looked at the world through ethnocentric eyes; that is, they assumed that their own civilization was the contemporary highpoint of human achievement. However, as more and more basic data accumulated from anthropological researches and archaeological excavations all over the world it became clear that a universal scheme of unilinear evolution was a totally unrealistic way of interpreting world history.

Diffusion and Diffusionists.   As archaeological knowledge blossomed in the late nineteenth century—and in America, particularly in the early twentieth—the great human cultural diversity that existed during prehistoric times was slowly recognized. But scholars still faced many hard questions. What were the origins of human culture? When and where was metallurgy introduced? Who were the first farmers? If people did not develop according to universal evolutionary rules, how then *did* culture change and cultural diversity come about? Archaeologists began to expect that population movements, migrations, and invasions would explain prehistory.

The *diffusion* of ideas from one people to another was recognized early as a valid explanation for cultural change in prehistory. Diffusion was an especially popular notion with late nineteenth-century archaeologists, who both reacted against the idea that cultures changed uniformly and realized that culture change could be explained by outside influences. The newly discovered Near Eastern civilizations raised problems that lent themselves to diffusion as the answer: What were, for instance, the origins of such peoples as the Mycenaeans (found by Heinrich Schliemann in the 1870s) (Ceram, 1953)? Many archaeologists began to go along with diffusionist theories when they tried to explain why Near Eastern civilizations were so rich as compared with the apparently poor European cultures of the same period. Furthermore, they argued, how could the brilliant New World civilizations in Mexico and Peru have arisen if not by long-distance migration from the civilized centers in the Near East?

In its more extreme forms, diffusionism is the assumption that many major human inventions originated in one place and then diffused to other parts of the world by trade, migrating populations, cultural contact, or bold explorers. Simple diffusionist ideas were very popular in the early years of this century. They had the advantage of being easy to formulate and understand, and there was something romantic in the idea of vast migrations of adventurous people from one end of the world to the other. Early in this century, for example, the British anatomist Grafton Elliot Smith became obsessed with the techniques of Egyptian mummification, sun worship, and monumental stone architecture. The achievements of ancient Egyptian civilization were so unique, he argued in *The Ancient Egyptians,* published in 1911, that all of world civilization and much of modern Western culture diffused from the Nile Valley (Smith, 1911). It was the People of the Sun who had achieved all this, people who were not afraid of voyaging all over the globe in search of gold, shells, and precious stones. Everywhere they went, they took their archaic civilization with them. Thus, sun worship, irrigation, agriculture, and metallurgy, as well as stone architecture—to mention only a few traits—spread all over the world, across the Atlantic and the Pacific, too. Although relatively few archaeologists ever took Elliot Smith particularly seriously, the public did. His several books enjoyed great popularity among those who were fascinated with the ancient Egyptians and who liked their prehistory simple, romantic, and exciting.

Smith's diffusionist views of human history were far too simplistic, and just as inadequate as unilinear cultural evolution, if not more so. Slowly, the first professional archaeologists of the twentieth century realized they were dealing with very complex problems. Fortunately, they set aside attempts to write universal histories and concentrated on the collection of basic data from archaeological sites.

Diffusionist theories have remained popular, albeit in a modified form. In their most extreme manifestations they still reach incredible levels of absurdity, as people have sought to prove that Black Africans colonized America before Columbus or that the Vikings settled Minnesota thousands of years ago.

DESCRIPTIVE ARCHAEOLOGY

The first professional archaeologists and anthropologists lived at a time when the traditional cultures of non-Western societies were withering away under the onslaught of modern technological civilization. They felt their overwhelming priority to be the collection of basic information about vanishing cultures. This collection of this data was an essential preliminary to the elaborate theoretical approaches used in archaeology today.

Franz Boas (1858—1942).   The American anthropologist Franz Boas was among those who insisted on far more detailed field research (Hatch, 1973). He and his students helped establish anthropology—and by implication, archaeology along with it—as a form of science, by applying more precise methods to collecting and classifying data. They collected an incredible amount of data on pot designs, basketry, and thousands of other cultural details. Artifacts and customs were meticulously studied and used as the basis for explanations of the past.

The enormous inventories of cultural traits, such as types of moccasins and designs of bows and arrows collected by American ethnographers in the 1920s, led to some quite false interpretations of American Indian culture, interpretations that were later disproved by archaeological research. For example, ethnologists of this period saw the arrival of Europeans, and especially of domestic horses, as an event unparalleled in importance; they saw the Great Plains quickly filling with nomadic buffalo hunters and raiders of the type made familiar to us by Hollywood films. The plains were described as being sparsely populated before the horse arrived, because water was scarce and ploughs were not available to till the soil. Yet the subsequent work of such archaeologists as W. D. Strong, who dug at Signal Butte, Nebraska, revealed that the Great Plains has been inhabited by hunter-gatherers and horticulturalists for many hundreds of years before the advent of Europeans and horses turned the plains into a macabre carnival of nomads (Strong, 1935). Archaeology, then, became a source of information against which one checked the historical reconstructions produced by ethnologists.

Vere Gordon Childe (1892–1957).   Perhaps the most brilliant of these archaeologists was an Oxford-trained Australian, Vere Gordon Childe. Childe was a brilliant linguist who acquired an encyclopedic knowledge of the thousands of prehistoric finds in museums from Edinburgh to Cairo. Once he had mastered the data, a task made easier by his language skills, Childe (1925) set out to describe European prehistory in outline. Childe's aim was to distill from archaeological remains "a preliterate substitute for the conventional politico-military history with cultures, instead of statesmen, as actors and migrations instead of battles" (Childe, 1958).

Gordon Childe classified cultures by their surviving characteristic culture traits—pots, implements, house forms, ornaments—constantly found together. Such cultures were the material expression of "peoples." Not supplying a chronological record for themselves, the cultures might have widespread or limited distribution in time and space. Cultural successions were reconstructed within limited geographic areas and compared with those from neighboring regions; the culture traits—presumed to have spread from one area to another—were carefully checked. This type of methodology became widespread in the 1930s and 1940s, a time when archaeology was still largely a descriptive discipline. But Childe went further, for he was one of the few archaeologists who realized that the cataloging of artifacts was useless unless conducted with some frame of reference. So he used the data from hundreds of sites and dozens of cultures to formulate a comprehensive viewpoint of Old World prehistory that became a classic one. The origins of agriculture and domestication and of urban life were, he felt, two great, revolutionary turning points in world history. He thought in terms of two great stages, those of the "Neolithic and Urban Revolutions." Each so-called revolution saw the development of new and vital inventions that could be identified in the archaeological record by characteristic artifacts. The Neolithic and Urban Revolutions were really a technological and evolutionary model, combined with an economic one, so that the way people got their living was the criterion for the comparison of different stages of world history. Childe dominated archaeological thinking in Europe until the late 1960s. But his ideas had less impact in the New World, largely because Childe himself never studied or wrote about American archaeology.

CULTURE HISTORY

Boas, Childe, and their disciples made data collection a primary objective of both New and Old World archaeology. But archaeology itself developed somewhat differently on each side of the Atlantic. The Europeans were studying their own prehistoric origins and tended to concentrate on constructing descriptive, historical schemes that traced the development of European society from its hunter-gatherer origins up to the threshold of recorded history. As Gordon Childe showed, the prehistoric peoples of the Near East and temperate Europe were the logical ancestors of the Greeks, Romans, and other civilizations. It was no coincidence that Arnold Toynbee and other world historians adopted Childe's universal schemes when they made prehistoric times the first chapter of their great historical syntheses.

The New World: Direct Historical Approach.   New World archaeologists were in a very different position. Their most logical way to work was from the known, historical Indian cultures backward into prehistoric times (Fagan, 1977; Willey and Sabloff, 1980). This approach was pioneered in the 1880s by Cyrus Thomas of the Bureau of American Ethnology. He and fellow archaeologists from other institutions excavated dozens of earthworks in the Ohio valley. They used pottery and other small finds to demonstrate the continuity between prehistoric and modern Indian culture. The early Southwestern archaeologists adopted a similar approach in the 1890s, carrying out research that traced modern Indian pottery styles centuries back into the past. This work culminated in the excavations at Pecos Pueblo carried out by Harvard archaeologist A. V. Kidder between 1915 and 1929 (Kidder, 1924). These excavations established a cultural sequence that is still used in a modified form today. Later researchers, such as W. D. Strong, applied similar methods to Plains archaeology with great success (Strong, 1935).

This *direct historical approach*—working from the known, historic sites to the unknown, prehistoric settlements, preferably those of known peoples—has serious limitations, however. It works quite satisfactorily as long as one is dealing with the same basic cluster of finds, such as pottery forms and the like. Once one excavates sites occupied by people with totally different cultures, however, continuity is lost and the direct historical approach can no longer be used.

The Midwestern Taxonomic System.   The influence of Franz Boas was strongly felt among archaeologists of the 1920s to the 1950s, who concentrated on collecting and classifying enormous numbers of prehistoric finds from hundreds of sites all over the Americas. They began to arrange these in increasingly elaborate regional sequences of prehistoric cultures, but they ran into trouble because no two archaeologists could agree on how to classify the pottery and other objects. Thus, no one could compare one area to another using common terms. Fortunately, a group of scholars headed by W. C. McKern got together and developed a set of definitions that soon became known as the "Midwestern taxonomic system" (McKern, 1939). This system was an attempt to tie together sequences of prehistoric cultures all over the Midwest by using the similarities between different collections of prehistoric artifacts.

The Midwest taxonomic system came into widespread use over much of the central and eastern United States. By the 1940s James Ford, James Griffin, and Gordon Willey began to look further afield than local regions. They had at their disposal a mass of unpublished archaeological data from hundreds of sites excavated during the Depression (Ford and Willey, 1941; Griffin, 1946). Their studies in the eastern United States revealed a steady development in prehistoric material culture over many thousands of years. They distinguished periods within which broad similarities in prehistoric culture could be found and designated those periods as developmental stages. This work was extended by Willey and Phillips in 1958, in an important monograph, which applied essentially the same techniques to the whole of the New World, and devised developmental stages for the entire continent (Willey and Phillips, 1958). The stages Willey and Phillips proposed were defined by technology, economic data, settlement patterns, art traditions, and social factors rather than by chronology, which to their way of thinking was a less important consideration.

Chronology and Time Scales.   No question worried the archaeologists of the 1920s to the 1950s more than that of establishing the age of their sites and finds. Once one reached the limits of direct historical ties, there was no means of dating early American cultures. The first breakthrough came in the early years of this century, when University of Arizona astronomer A. E. Douglass started his famous studies of annual growth rings in southwestern trees (see Chapter 6). By 1929, Douglass had developed an accurate chronology for southwestern sites that was eventually extended back from modern times into the first century B.C. Unfortunately, however, tree-ring dating could only be used in the dry areas of the Southwest, where trees had a well-defined annual growth season. It is not suitable to climates with even distribution of rainfall.

In other areas, archaeological chronology was largely a matter of intelligent guesswork until 1949, when University of Chicago scientists J. E. Arnold and W. F. Libby (1949) described the radiocarbon method for dating organic materials from archaeological sites (Libby, 1955). Within a few years, radiocarbon dates were processed from hundreds of sites all over the world. For the first time, there was a widely accepted chronological framework for New World prehistory that superseded the guesswork of earlier years. Archaeologists finally could compare sites and cultures from widely separated areas, using an unbiased time scale. As a result, they were able to deemphasize chronology and classification and concentrate, instead, on the reasons *why* American Indian cultures had changed in the past.

CULTURAL ECOLOGY

With the advent of the radiocarbon dating method, the new emphasis in archaeology was on interpretation, based on carefully studied regional sequences. One conclusion was obvious: Human material culture and social organization had developed from the simple to the infinitely complex. From then on, many accounts of world prehistory or broad syntheses of large culture areas allowed for the general notion of progress in prehistory. Childe with his revolutions, Robert J. Braidwood in the Near East, and Gordon Willey in North America—all attempted to look at culture history with the knowledge that human culture is in constant and dynamic relationship with its environment and with other factors that interact with it (Braidwood and Howe, 1962; Childe, 1942; Willey, 1966, 1971).

Julian Steward: Multilinear Evolution. At about this time, the anthropologist Julian Steward started thinking about ways of identifying common cultural features in dozens of societies distributed over many cultural areas (Steward, 1955). Were there ways in which one could identify such common features? In contrast to the ardent evolutionists, who insisted that all societies passed through similar stages of cultural development, Julian Steward assumed that certain basic types of culture would develop in similar ways under similar conditions. However, very few actual concrete features of culture would appear among many human societies in a similar, regular order that was repeated again and again. In other words, cultural evolution was multilinear; that is, it had proceeded on many courses, not just on a single universal track, as Tylor and others had believed.

Before Steward, such people as Alfred Kroeber, Lewis Morgan, and Leslie White had long thought of culture as a form of "layered cake," with technology as the bottom layer, social organization the middle, and ideology the top (White, 1949). Steward not only added the environment to the cake, but also looked for causes of cultural change. To do so, he developed a method for recognizing the ways in which such change is caused by adaptation to the environment.

Steward called his study of environment and culture change *cultural ecology*. He began by making several important points:

> Similar adaptations may be found in different cultures in similar environments.

> No culture has ever achieved an adaptation to its environment which has remained unchanged over any length of time.

> Differences and changes during periods of cultural development in any area can either add to societal complexity, or result in completely new cultural patterns (Steward, 1955).

Steward used these principles as a basis for studying cultures and culture change in widely separated areas. To study different cultures, he would isolate and define certain distinguishing characteristics in each culture, a nucleus of traits he called the "cultural core." For instance, he observed that African San, Australian aborigines, and Fuegian Indians were all organized in patrilineal (descent through the father) bands. They formed a cultural type. Why? Because their ecological adaptation and level of social organization were similar. Although the environments of these groups differed greatly, ranging from desert to cold and rainy plains, the practical requirements of the hunting and gathering lifeway grouped all these people into small bands, each with its own territory. The social structure and general organization of the bands in each area were very similar, and their adaptation to their environment fundamentally the same, despite many detailed differences. Steward used his "cultural core" device to isolate and define distinguishing characteristics of the hunter-gatherer and of other specific culture types from all the miscellaneous data on hand.

Steward spent a great deal of time studying the relationships between environment and culture that form the context and reasons for certain critical culture features. While a culture trait, be it a new house type or a particular form of social organization, might be found at one location because it diffused there, that did not explain why the people accepted the trait in the first place. Steward used cultural ecology to attack such questions and also such problems as why the adjustment of human societies to different environments results in certain types of behavior. To diffusion and evolution, he added a new concept—changing adaptations to the natural environment. In other words, the study of culture change involved not only the study of human cultures but of changing environmental conditions as well.

A STUDY OF ARCHAEOLOGY

Steward's work appeared at a time when American archaeology was completely preoccupied with chronology and artifacts. Every issue of each archaeological journal was crowded with arid reports of pottery chronologies that seldom referred to their content or meaning as human implements. It was as if archaeologists were classifying insects or collecting postage stamps. Then, in 1948, archaeologist W. W. Taylor published his famous *A Study of Archaeology,* a devastating critique of American archaeology's preoccupation with chronology (Taylor, 1948).

Taylor called for a "conjunctive approach" to archaeology, a shift in emphasis from chronological sequences and distributions to detailed, multileveled studies of individual sites and their features, such as cultural layers, floors, or hearths. The conjunctive approach brought together all possible sources of evidence on a site—technology, style, ecological evidence, architecture, and information on social life—to focus on the people who lived at the site and on the changes in their culture.

Studying the people meant seeing their artifacts in context, as products of total cultural systems and trying to reconstruct these systems as completely as possible, including even the less tangible parts, such as their social organization and religious institutions. This view contrasted with that of Childe and his contemporaries on the other side of the Atlantic, who preferred to limit their study of artifacts. Taylor tried to introduce into archaeology a view of culture that envisaged the discipline as an integral part of anthropology. He felt both disciplines should work together to arrive at general truths about human culture (Kluckhohn, 1943).

All of this was a far cry from the simple evolutionary and diffusionist schemes of earlier decades. Julian Steward's and W. W. Taylor's research brought twentieth-century archaeology to the threshold of great theoretical change. They established, once and for all, the close relationship between archaeology and anthropology. *A Study of Archaeology* showed, with incisive clarity, that one of archaeology's primary goals must be to develop adequate explanations for human prehistory, a far more sophisticated aim than mere excavation, collection, and description.

Guide to Further Reading

The references for Chapter 3 will suffice, with the addition of the following:

Taylor, W. W. *A Study of Archaeology.* Menasha, Wisconsin: American Anthropological Association, 1948.
The controversial, pioneer statement on archaeology that was one of the major stepping-stones for the development of processual archaeology in the 1960s.

White, Leslie. *The Evolution of Culture.* New York: McGraw Hill, 1949.
White's classic work on cultural evolution is one of the foundations of modern archaeology and anthropology.

CHAPTER 4 ❦

TOWARD PROCESSUAL ARCHAEOLOGY:
1950 TO 1980

Preview

- In the 1950s, statistical methods which had long been used in the natural and physical sciences, began to be used in archaeology. The new approaches that this engendered gave archaeologists the ability to form far more meticulous and detailed descriptions and to manipulate larger quantities of data.
- Lewis Binford, strongly influenced by Leslie White, Julian Steward, and Albert Spaulding, formulated a new archaeological method and theory that used explicitly scientific methods. He proposed that archaeological data be tested against formal hypotheses and that careful research designs be used for planning all inquiries.
- Beyond the use of the formal scientific method, there were other trends toward the development of a more scientific archaeology, including a new interest in living archaeology, or ethnoarchaeology. This is the study of surviving hunter-gatherers as a means of gaining insights into prehistoric societies. Many people realized that before long archaeology would be the only means of explaining cultural variations among nonindustrial societies.
- With the development of a more scientific archaeology there was increasing attention paid to the works of philosophers of science, such as Thomas Kuhn, and to the principles of General Systems

theory. As archaeologists began to move away from simple explanations of the past, they used systems approaches to aid in their depiction of a given human culture as a complicated system of interacting elements that in turn interacted with the ecological system of which it was a part.

- Systems approaches developed hand-in-hand with cultural ecology, that is, with studies of the changing relationship between prehistoric societies and the environments in which they flourished. Settlement archaeology depended heavily on statistical methods and the use of computers to order large quantities of field data.

- The new emphasis on scientific approaches has generated a major debate as to whether archaeology is humanities or science. The fully scientific archaeology of the future will have to incorporate the scientific evidence with valid empirical generalizations of history.

Archaeology, like all the social sciences, has changed almost beyond recognition in the past thirty years. The development of the digital computer, the widespread use of statistical methods, and the influence of the philosophy of science have all played their part in transforming archaeology from a largely descriptive discipline into something much more comprehensive. Chapter 4 starts with a discussion of these developments and shows how much more sophisticated ecological and evolutionary approaches and a greater concern with deductive scientific methods and theory building took archaeology in new directions. Scholars, such as Lewis Binford, Kent Flannery, Albert Spaulding, and Julian Steward, realized the significance of the major trends in social science and began the difficult task of applying them to archaeology. The chapter ends with a brief glance at the major approaches to processual archaeology, which is described in more detail in Part VII.

SCIENCE AND ARCHAEOLOGY

Statistical Methods.   It was in the 1950s that statistical methods first began to have an impact on archaeology and anthropology. Although archaeologists had been counting tools and other finds for years, only a few instances of the use of chi-square (X^2) techniques and other statistical devices were mentioned by Albert Spaulding (1960), the pioneer in this field, in an early paper on the subject. This approach to archaeological evidence resulted from both the changing interests of research workers and the digital computer's application as an aid for ordering and handling enormous numbers of tools. Statistical methods came into fashion rapidly, as archaeologists realized that the new methods gave them opportunities for far more meticulous and detailed descriptions of archaeological finds than had ever been carried out before. Albert Spaulding has forecast that the future of archaeology is bound up with the success or failure of efforts to properly apply quantitative methods to archaeological data.

Lewis Binford and the Scientific Method.   While a graduate student at the University of Michigan, a young archaeologist named Lewis Binford came into contact with a group of eminent scholars who had done much to develop the archaeology of the 1940s and 1950s. Among them were James Griffin, who taught him descriptive archaeology; Albert Spaulding, who introduced him to statistical techniques for handling specific problems; and Leslie White, who exposed him to logic and urged him to steep himself in the philosophy of science. Binford learned that theory was a meaningful word, and he realized that there were close links between archaeology and ethnography. He arrived at the idea that the ultimate objective of archaeology was a search for universal laws that govern cultural change.

In the 1960s, Binford wrote a series of closely reasoned and classic papers that caused a ferment in archaeological circles. He advocated more rigorous scientific testing in archaeology, arguing that statements about the significance of the archaeological record had been evaluated previously according to how far back our knowledge of contemporary peoples could be projected onto prehistoric contexts and onto our judgment of the professional competence and honesty of the archaeologists interpreting the past (Binford, 1962; 1972). Simple induction had been drawn on for inferences about the archaeological record, with guidance from ethnographic data and experimental archaeology. Binford argued that, although induction and inferences are perfectly sound methods for understanding the past, independent methods of testing propositions about the past must be developed and must be far more rigorous than the time-honored value judgments arrived at by assessing professional competence.

With a scientific approach involving interaction between previous data, new ideas, and new data, a research problem can be approached from a collection of observed data that enables one to pose research hypotheses. The general problems may have to do with change, like: How and why did the hunter-gatherers of the Near East turn to agriculture and domestic animals for their livelihood? Or the problems may instead touch on cultural relationships: Is a new pottery type that suddenly appears in a Midwest cultural sequence the result of trade, population movement, or independent invention?

Working hypotheses were nothing new in archaeology. What was new about Binford's approach was that he advocated that these hypotheses be tested explicitly against archaeological data collected in the field and against other alternatives that have been rejected. Once a hypothesis is confirmed, it can join the body of reliable knowledge upon which further hypotheses can be erected. And these may, in their turn, require additional data or even the development of entirely new approaches to the excavation and collection of archaeological information. What Binford was suggesting, then, was that the explicit scientific method commonly used in science should now be applied to archaeological research.

Binford's papers, lectures, and many seminars provoked widespread interest among American archaeologists, many of whom joined him in reevaluating the scientific methods of archaeology. He and his disciples challenged the assumption that the archaeological record's incompleteness precludes reliable interpretation of the nonmaterial and perishable components of prehistoric society and culture. All artifacts found in an archaeological site have functioned at one time within a particular culture and society. They occur in meaningful patterns that have a systematic relationship to the economies, kinship systems, and other contexts within which they were used. Moreover, all of these artifacts were at the mercy of such transient factors as fashion or decorative style, each of which has, in itself, a history of acceptance, use, or rejection within the society. Thus, artifacts are far more than mere material items; rather, they are reflections of many of the often intangible variables that went into determining the actual form of the objects preserved. Binford argued that "data relevant to most, if not all, the components of past sociocultural systems *are* preserved in the archaeological record (Binford and Binford, 1968). The archaeologist's task is to devise methods for extracting this information that deal with *all* determinants operating within the society or culture being studied.

Lewis Binford was not alone in his thinking. In the early 1960s British archaeologist David Clarke wrote a monumental critique of prehistoric archaeology, in which he argued for more explicit scientific methods, greater rigor, and the development of a body of theory to replace what he rather picturesquely called "the murky exhalation that represents theory in archaeology" (Clarke, 1968). Unfortunately, David Clarke died before he fulfilled his potential as a leader in archaeological thinking.

LIVING ARCHAEOLOGY (ETHNOARCHAEOLOGY)

One of the spin-offs of this new concern with greater scientific rigor was a renewed interest among archaeologists in living peoples. Lewis Binford was not, of course, the first archaeologist to look at ethnography, for many scholars were worrying about the extinction of preindustrial societies all over the world (Binford, 1968; Sollas, 1911; Thompson, 1956). As early as 1865, Lord Avebury had urged his archaeological colleagues to compare Stone Age cultures with modern hunter-gatherer peoples. The Direct Historical Approach evolved from American archaeologists' recognition that modern Indian cultures had long roots in prehistory.

Binford (1977; 1978) urged, however, that once different comparisons are chosen, researchers should explicitly state the implications and then test each in turn against archaeological data. The best conditions for making such tests were in the field, observing cultural adaptations among living hunter-gatherers and subsistence agriculturalists. Before long, he argued, archaeology would be the only source of explanations of cultural variations among nonindustrial societies.

Some anthropologists, among them Richard Lee, who studied the !Kung San of the Kalahari desert, realized the archaeologists' difficulties and arranged to take a prehistorian with them to study the remains of long-abandoned campsites and compare them to modern settlements (Lee and DeVore, 1976; Yellen, 1977) (Figure 4.1). Richard Gould, an anthropologist who worked among the Australian aborigines, deliberately went out of his way to gather information on abandoned campsites that could be of use to archaeologists (Gould, 1977). Lewis Binford himself has worked among the Nunamiut Eskimo and the Navajo on variability in adaptation systems, seeking viable analogies between living cultures and archaeological materials and trying to develop workable models of culture as rigorous yardsticks for studying variability (Binford, 1978).

Figure 4.1 An anthropologist making a plane table survey of a San camp in the Kalahari. The data from such surveys are of great value in interpreting the archaeological record.

SYSTEMS THEORY AND ECOLOGY

Systems Theory. Another element in the development of a more scientific archaeology was the influence of both philosophers of science, such as Thomas Kuhn (1970), and of general systems theory (Watson, Redman, and LeBlanc, 1971; Redman, 1973). As archaeologists moved away from simple explanations and unilinear evolution toward much more elaborate theories, they began to examine the delicate and complex relationships between human societies and their ever-changing environments. Systems approaches involved thinking of human cultures as complicated systems of interacting elements, such as technology and social organization, which interacted, in turn, with the ecological systems of which they were a party (see Chapter 19). The systems approach has strongly influenced archaeology because of the intense concern with the relationships between prehistoric peoples and their environments.

Ecology and Archaeology. Ecological thinking about archaeology has a long history. Much of it is based on the assumption that human cultures could affect their environments, and vice versa (Trigger, 1971). One school of thought, the environmental determinists, believed that forms in nature, which are active, determined human culture, which is passive. Franz Boas and other anthropologists went so far as to argue that the environment was passive and that human culture developed because some environmental possibilities were selected and others ignored.

The advent of modern ecology, with its distinctions among various ecosystems, caused these simple notions to be rejected in favor of more holistic views of culture and environment. These new approaches assume that cultural ecology studies the total picture of the way in which human populations adapt to, and transform, their environments. Human cultures are thought of as open systems, because it is acknowledged that their institutions may be connected with those of other cultures and with the environment. Open-system ecology is very realistic. It assumes a great deal of variation between individual modern and archaeological cultures. Any explanation of culture has to be able to handle the real patterns of variation found in living cultures, not just the artificial ones erected by classifiers of archaeological cultures. So many factors influence cultural systems that order can be sought only by understanding what Canadian archaeologist Bruce Trigger has called "those processes by which cultural similarities and differences are generated" (Trigger, 1971). Many complex factors are external to the culture and cannot be controlled by the archaeologist; one cannot reconstruct the whole cultural system from only one part of it (in archaeological cultures, the surviving artifacts and food residues). Every facet of the cultural system has to be reconstructed separately, using the evidence specifically relevant to that facet, until in time a picture of the whole cultural system, as comprehensive as possible, is available. The issue is a society's total adaptation to both its natural and cultural environments. As Trigger points out: "Developments affecting any one aspect of the culture can ultimately produce further adjustments throughout the system and affect the system's relationship with the natural environment" (Trigger, 1971).

Studying prehistoric societies within the context of their natural environments involves examining the relationships between prehistoric settlements and their surrounding landscape. A series of important studies done in Mexico have assumed that the patterns of human settlement throughout time provide a reliable way of studying the changing adaptations of human cultures to an environment over a long period of time (Flannery, 1976; Sanders, Parsons, and Santley, 1979) (see Chapter 16). Such studies can be conducted only with detailed background knowledge of the specific environment in which the culture flourished, changed, and eventually died. One of the brightest prospects for archaeology lies in studying human cultural systems within the changing economic, demographic, and social variables interacting within an environmental setting over long periods of time.

Some of the most sophisticated research in archaeology is being done in open-system ecology formats, as archaeologists wrestle to develop a meeting ground between a broad view of cultural change and the need to look at each changing culture and its microadaptation to a dynamic environment; both clearly are needed (Flannery, 1976).

A HUMANITY OR A SCIENCE?

The new emphasis on systems theory, scientific method, and new approaches to ecology has changed the tactics of archaeological research in the 1980s. The result has been a state of ferment, a fascinating intellectual climate in which practically every familiar theory in archaeology has been challenged. The ferment between archaeologists has led to two general viewpoints on the goals of the discipline (Flannery, 1973; Spaulding, 1973).

1. The first sees archaeology as examining the activities of past human beings. This activity would categorize it as history, a discipline with its own limitations, resources, and explanatory methods.
2. The second viewpoint argues that we cannot go far in understanding past societies through archaeology without assuming that human behavior has always been subject to certain general laws and principles that operate at all levels of cultural development. The only way these laws can be studied is by using the scientific method. Hence, archaeology is a science.

Many archaeologists favor neither viewpoint, but rather, see history and science as distinctive approaches, each with their own uses and merits. Everyone agrees, however, that mathematical models, statistical approaches, and rigorous scientific methods will play an increasingly vital role in the archaeology of the remainder of the twentieth century.

Albert Spaulding (1973) makes the point well, as he contemplates two centuries of gradually evolving archaeological endeavor:

"We simply do not know what the fully scientific archaeology of the future might be. But we do know we will never approach an answer if we do not try to develop a scientific archaeology, and we do know that a scientific archaeology must incorporate the evidence and valid empirical generalizations of history."

In other words, archaeology is rapidly adopting the methods of science, but in so doing, we should not reject the careful research of earlier generations of less scientifically oriented archaeologists. Like all academic disciplines, archaeology has evolved along many lines, with each generation building on the achievements—and mistakes—of its predecessors.

Guide to Further Reading

The references for Chapters 2 and 3 are useful here as well.

Binford, Lewis R. *An Archaeological Perspective.* New York: Seminar Press, 1972.
   A highly personal account of the development of processual archaeology by its leading proponent. The volume includes Binford's major early papers.

Redman, Charles L., ed. *Research and Theory in Current Archaeology.* New York: John Wiley Interscience, 1973.
   A volume of essays that provides a critique of the way in which processual archaeology is evolving. The essays by Kent Flannery and Albert Spaulding are especially important.

Watson, Patti Jo; LeBlanc, Steven; and Redman, Charles L. *Explanation in Archaeology.* New York: Columbia University Press, 1971.
   A fundamental source on the development of processual archaeology.

PART III

DATA AND CONTEXT

"Time which antiquates antiquities, and hath an art to make dust of all things."

SIR THOMAS BROWNE,
Hydriotaphia (1658)

Part III describes the most basic concepts behind archaeological research, those of culture and context. Every archaeological site and every find has a context, not only within some long-extinct culture but also in time and space. In this section of the text, we examine the concept of culture in archaeology, the nature of archaeological data, and the ways in which people have established archaeological contexts. Fundamental to context are methods of defining human activities in space, and especially those of measuring prehistoric time. We describe the various methods that have been devised for dating prehistoric cultures from the very earliest times.

CHAPTER 5 ❦

CULTURE, DATA, AND CONTEXT

Preview

- Culture is regarded by archaeologists as humankind's primary means of adapting to the natural environment. Human culture is made up of our behavior and its results, both of which consist of a complex and constantly interacting set of variables. Our culture is always adjusting to both internal and external change.
- Archaeologists work with the tangible remains of human activity that still survive in the ground. Archaeological finds are not culture in themselves but products of it, and they are linked to culture in a systematic way.
- Archaeologists think of human cultures as complex systems of interacting variables. This viewpoint is based loosely on principles of General Systems theory, a way of searching for general relationships in the empircal world.
- Culture and the environment in which it is found represent a number of articulated systems in which change occurs through a series of minor, linked variations in one or more of these systems. A major objective of archaeology is to understand these linkages. According to this viewpoint, a cultural system is a human culture that is changing in constant response to external and internal stimuli.
- Cultural process is the identification of the factors responsible for the direction and nature of change within cultural systems. Processual archaeology is the analysis of the causes of cultural change, and

77

analysis that involves looking at relationships between those variables that could lead to cultural change.

- The archaeological record consists of the surviving traces of human behavior found in archaeological sites, be they in the form of food remains, tools, or entire cities.
- Data are material recognized as significant as evidence by archaeologists and collected and recorded as part of the research process.
- Artifacts, features, structures, and ecofacts constitute four broad classes of archaeological data. The context of these finds in time and space is an integral part of archaeological data as well.
- The matrix is the physical substance that surrounds an archaeological find.
- Provenience is the precise, three-dimensional position of an archaeological find within the matrix.
- The Law of Association states that objects found in the same archaeological layer, in circumstances which make it clear that they were deposited there at the same time, are of similar age.
- The Law of Superposition, which is derived from geology, states that archaeological finds discovered in stratified layers were deposited in a relative order. Those found in the lowest levels were deposited before those found in the higher levels. There are, of course, occasional exceptions to this law.
- Archaeological context is derived from recording of the matrix, provenience, and association. Context is a position in time and space, but it also involves assessing why a find is in a particular context.
- Context is affected by the way in which the find was made or used by its original owners, the way in which it was deposited in the ground, and its subsequent history in the ground.
- The primary context of a find is its original context; the secondary, that which resulted from some later disturbance.
- There are four levels of spatial context, each of which coincides with an actual level of human behavior: artifacts, structures, sites, and regions. This behavior is reflected by the patterning of finds in the ground.
- Artifacts are objects that exhibit any physical attributes that can be assumed to be the result of human activity. Assemblages are patternings of finds that represent the behavior of entire communities; subassemblages are patterns of artifacts that represent the behavior of single individuals.
- Archaeological sites are places where traces of ancient human activity are to be found. They can range in size from a small scatter of stone tools to an entire city. Sites are classified according to archaeo-

logical context, artifact content, geographical location, or function.
• Archaeologists seeking to understand the prehistory of areas larger than a single site work with well-defined geographical regions and with archaeological cultures, that is, consistent patternings of artifact assemblages. A culture area is a large geographical area through which artifacts characteristic of a culture can be identified.
• A settlement pattern is the distribution of human settlement across the natural landscape.

The concepts of culture, space, and time in archaeology are inseparable. The accurate measuring of age in calendar years and of spatial context lie at the very core of all archaeological research. Indeed, as Albert Spaulding has pointed out, a very minimal definition of archaeology is that it is the study of the interrelations between the form of artifacts found in a site and their date and spatial location relative to the problem being studied (Spaulding, 1960).

This chapter introduces you to some basic concepts of archaeological research, to culture, to data in the form of artifacts, and to the matrix, provenience, and context of the data. The provenience and context of all archaeological data are based on the two fundamental laws of superposition and association. From basic concepts, we move on to discuss spatial context, not the limitless frontiers of the heavens, but a precisely defined location for every find made during an archaeological survey or excavation.

THE CONCEPT OF CULTURE

In Chapter 1, we stated that "Anthropologists study human beings as biological organisms and as people with a distinctive and unique characteristic—culture. . . . Archaeologists are a special type of anthropologist, whose concern is past human culture." There are few concepts in anthropology that have generated as much controversy and academic debate as those that are expressed in that statement (Kroeber and Kluckholn, 1952). Perhaps the best general definition of archaeology was written by British anthropologist Sir Edward Tylor more than a century ago. He stated that culture is "That complex whole which includes knowledge, belief, art, morals, law, custom, and any other capabilities and habits acquired by man as a member of society" (Tylor, 1871). To that definition, modern archaeologists would add the statement that archaeology is our primary means of adapting to our environment.

Culture is a distinctively human attribute, for we are the only animals to use our culture as our *primary* means of adapting to our environment (Keesing, 1974). It is our adaptive system. While biological evolution has protected the polar bear from Arctic cold with dense fur and has given the duck webbed feet for swimming, only humans make thick clothes and igloos in the Arctic and live under light, thatched shelters with minimal clothing in the tropics. We use our culture as a buffer between ourselves and the environment, one that has become more and more elaborate through the long millennia of prehistory. We are now so divorced from our environment that removal of our cultural buffer would render us almost helpless and probably lead to rapid extinction of the human race within a very short time. Thus, human cultures are made up of human behavior and its results; they obviously consist of a complex and constantly interesting set of variables. Human culture, never static, is always adjusting to both internal and external change, whether environmental, technological, or societal (Deetz, 1967; Dunnell, 1971).

The Nature of Culture.   Culture can be subdivided in all sorts of different ways—into language, economics, technology, religion, political or social organizations, and art. But human culture as a whole is a complex, structured organization in which all our various categories shape one another. All cultures are made up of myriad tangible and intangible traits, the contents of which result from a complex adaptation to a wide range of ecological, societal, and cultural factors. Much of human culture is transmitted from generation to generation by sophisticated communication systems that permit complex and ongoing adaptations to aid survival and help rapid cultural change take place— as, for example, when less-advanced societies come into contact with higher civilizations.

Everyone lives within a culture of some kind; and every culture is qualified by a label, such as "middle-class American," "Eskimo," or "Masai." The qualification conjures up certain characteristic attributes or behavior patterns typical of those associated with the cultural label. for example, one attribute of a middle-class American might be the hamburger; of the Eskimo, the kayak; of the Masai, a long-handled, fine-bladed spear. Our mental images of cultures are associated with popular stereotypes, too. To many Americans, Chinese culture conjures up images of paper lanterns and willow-pattern plates; French culture, good eating and fine wines. We are all familiar with the distinctive "flavor" of a culture that we encounter when dining in a foreign restaurant or arriving in a strange country. Every culture has its own individuality and recognizable style, which shapes its political and judicial institutions and morals (Frankfort, 1951; Renfrew, 1972).

Culture and Material Remains.   Culture consists of many interacting elements, many of them highly perishable. No one has been able to dig up a religious philosophy or a language; so, as was stated earlier archaeologists have to work with the tangible remains of human activity that still survive in the ground. But the intangible aspects of human culture can radically affect the artifacts and other results of human behavior that the archaeologist recovers. Every object found in an excavation is a reflection not only of the technology that made it but also of the values and uses a society placed on such objects, and in the final analysis, of the many and complex societal and religious limitations that they placed on the use of such artifacts. In other words, the tangible remains of the past found by archaeologists are a patterned reflection of the culture that produced them. Artifacts are not culture in themselves, but they are products of it and are linked to culture in a systematic way (Figure 5.1).

Figure 5.1   Temple of the Inscriptions at Palenque, Yucatan, Mexico. This is one of the many Mayan sites shaped by the distinctive religious beliefs that were shared by all Mayan peoples.

CULTURAL SYSTEMS

As archaeologists have developed more rigorously scientific means for studying human cultures, they have begun to think of cultures as complex systems of interacting variables. Thus, rather than referring to cultures, they have begun to use the term *cultural systems.* Stuart Struever (1971) has provided us with one of the best definitions of a cultural system. It is: "Culture and its environments represent a number of articulated [interlinked] systems in which change occurs through a series of minor, linked variations in one or more of these systems."

One of the major objectives of archaeology is to understand the linkages between parts in both the cultural and environmental systems, as reflected in archaeological data.

The systems approach to culture is derived from general systems theory, a body of theoretical concepts developed as a means of searching for "general relationships in the empirical world" (Watson, LeBlanc, and Redman, 1971). A system is defined as "a whole which functions by virtue of the interdependence of its parts." In other words, the relationship between the parts is the critical element that has to be described and explained. Systems theory is widely used in chemistry and physics, where relationships can be defined with great precision. It has come into use in archaeology as a concept to aid in the understanding of the ever-changing relationship between human cultures and their environment. The systems approach to human culture argues that geographical distance between settlements, differences in activities conducted at various sites, and a host of other spatial differences, both large and small, have affected human culture as deeply as has time. Because of this, many archaeologists use a definition of culture that emphasizes cultural systems that are constantly changing in response to external and internal stimuli (Doran, 1970).

CULTURAL PROCESS

Systems theory deals with relationships and variations in relationships; in other words, it deals with precisely the phenomena involved in explaining the processes by which cultures change. Modern scientific archaeology is deeply concerned with analyzing the causes of cultural change, that is, the cultural process.

The word *process* implies a patterned sequence of events that leads

Figure 5.2 A San hunter-gatherer in the Kalahari Desert searches the bole of a tree for water. "... human culture is, from the ecologist's viewpoint, merely one element in the ecosystem...."

one from one state of affairs to another. This patterned sequence is determined by a process of decision making that sets the order of events. For example, a forty-foot sailing yacht starts as a pile of materials—wood, aluminum, copper, bronze—and then a patterned sequence of manufacturing events turns the material into a new and gleaming ship. Archaeology is a processs, too. It involves designing the research project, formulating the hypothesis, collecting and interpreting the data, testing the data, and then, finally, publishing the results.

Causes are events that force people to make decisions about how to deal with new situations. As such, they are distinct from the actual process of decision making—the mechanisms that lead to any kind of change. For instance, a change in the natural environment from year-round rainfall to a seasonal pattern is a cause.

The term *cultural process* is used in archaeology to refer to the "identification of the factors responsible for the direction and nature of change within cultural systems" (Sharer and Ashmore, 1979). *Processual archaeology* is the analysis of the causes of culture change, an analysis that involves looking at relationships between variables that could lead to cultural change. These possible causes are then tested against actual archaeological data, often within a systems theory context.

As more and more archaeological data have become available, the older, overly simplistic explanations of cultural process in prehistory, such as universal evolutionism and diffusionism, hardly reflect accurately the actual situations as we now see them. Clearly, no one element in any cultural system is the primary cause of change; instead, a complex range of factors—rainfall, vegetation, technology, social restrictions, and population density—interact with one another and react to changes in any element in the system. It follows, then, that human culture is, from the ecologist's viewpoint, merely one element in the ecosystem, a mechanism of behavior whereby people adapt to an environment (Figure 5.2).

ARCHAEOLOGICAL DATA

The cultures studied by archaeologists are reconstructed using archaeological data. Archaeological data is any material remains of human activity, whether a scatter of broken bones, a ruined house, a gold mask, or a vast temple plaza. Archaeologists use a number of terms to define these remains for research purposes.

The archaeological record is the general term that denotes any and all of the surviving traces of human behavior found in archaeological sites, whether in the form of food remains, tools, or entire cities. The archaeological record is the equivalent of the historian's archives.

Data is the material recognized by the archaeologist as significant evidence, all of which is collected and recorded as part of the research. Archaeological data is sometimes referred to as *evidence.* Data can be broken down into four broad classes:

1. *Artifacts*—humanly manufactured or modified objects (Figure 5.3).
2. *Features*—artifacts that cannot be removed from the ground, such as post holes and ditches.
3. *Structures*—houses, granaries, temples, and other buildings that can be identified from patterns of post holes and other features in the ground.
4. *Ecofacts*—a term sometimes used to refer to food remains, such as bones, seeds, and other finds, which throw light on human activities.

Figure 5.3   A magnificent example of an Iron Age helmet from the River Thames in London (20.5 cm. diameter at base). Objects like this are useful for cross dating archaeological sites all over Europe.

Archaeological data does not consist of artifacts, features, structures, and ecofacts alone however; it consists also of their context in space and time. Lewis Binford made the point when he said that "data relevant to most, if not all, the components of past sociocultural systems are preserved in the archaeological record. . . . Our task, then, is to devise means for extracting this information" (Binford, 1972).

MATRIX AND PROVENIENCE

All scientifically collected or excavated archaeological finds, be they a complete site or a single object, occur within a matrix and have a specific provenience.

The *matrix* is the physical substance that surrounds the find. It can be gravel, sand, mud, or even water. Most archaeological matrices are of natural origin—the result of the passage of time and the work of external phenomena, such as wind and rainfall. The early camp sites at Olduvai Gorge in Tanzania were situated on the edge of a shallow and ever-fluctuating lake 1.75 million years ago. The scatter of tools and bones left by the departing inhabitants was soon covered by a layer of thin lake sand carried by advancing shallow water. This matrix preserved the tools in their original position for thousands of millennia (Leakey, 1971). An archaeological matrix can also be humanly made. One example of this is the huge earthen platforms of Hopewell burial mounds in the Midwest (Willey, 1966).

Provenience is the precise three-dimensional position of the find within the matrix as recorded by the archaeologist. Provenience is derived from accurate record keeping during excavations and site surveys, from evidence that is inevitably destroyed once a site is dug or artifacts collected from a surface site.

Every human artifact has a provenience in time and space. The provenience in time can range from a radiocarbon date of 1400 ± 60 years before the present for a Mayan temple to a precise reading of A.D. 1980 for a dime released by the United States Mint; or frequently, it can simply consist of an exact position in an archaeological site whose general age is known. Provenience in space is based, in the final analysis, on associations between tools and other items that were results of human behavior in a given culture. Provenience is determined by the use of two fundamental archaeological laws: the Law of Association and the Law of Superposition.

The Law of Association.   The Law of Association (Figure 5.4) was first stated by Danish archaeologist J. J. A. Worsaae in 1843. Worsaae, who was working with prehistoric burials, stated the principle very clearly:

> The objects accompanying a human burial are in most cases things that were in use at the same time. When certain artifact types are found together in grave association after grave association, and when more evolved forms of the same tools are found in association with other burials, then the associations provide some basis for dividing the burials into different chronological groups on the basis of association and artifact styles.

Worsaae eventually proved the chronological validity of the law of association by stratigraphic excavations in dozens of burial sites.

Instances of archaeological associations are legion. The first evidence of a high antiquity for humankind came from the discovery of associations of stone axes and the bones of extinct animals in the same geological layers. Many early Mesoamerican farmers' houses are associated with storage pits for maize and other crops. In this and many other cases, it is the horizontal association between artifacts and houses, or dwellings and storage pits, or artifacts and food residues that provide the archaeological association. Unassociated artifacts, examined devoid of an association with other finds, yield relatively little information of value. Much of the most valuable archaeological data is derived from precise studies of associations between different finds in the ground.

Figure 5.4 Some instances of archaeological associations. (a) The burial pit, dug from the uppermost layer, contains not only a skeleton but also a dagger that lies close to its foot. The dagger is associated with the skeleton, and both finds are associated with the burial pit and the layer from which the grave pit was cut into the subsoil. (b) In contrast, a pot and a stone axe are found in two different layers, separated by a sterile zone, a zone with no finds. The two objects are not in association. (c) Two different household clusters with associated pits and scatters of artifacts. These are in association with each other. (d) An association of two contemporary communities.

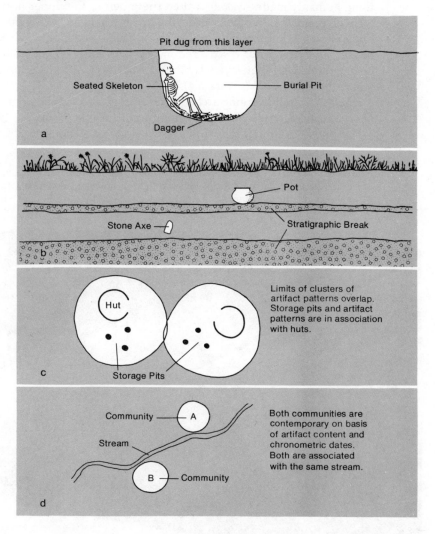

The Law of Superposition.   The time dimension of archaeology is based on basic principles of stratigraphic geology set down by the uniformitarians of the early nineteenth century. "Strata" Smith's classic studies of British geology were based on the Law of Superposition (Daniel, 1975). It was easy for archaeologists to adopt this law, for many of their most important finds were made within geological layers or contexts.

The Law of Superposition states that the geological layers of the earth are stratified one upon another, like the layers of a cake. Cliffs by the seashore and quarries are easily accessible examples. Obviously, any object found in the lowermost levels—whether a stone or something humanly made—was deposited there before the upper horizons were accumulated. In other words, the lower levels are *earlier* than the upper strata. The same law applies to archaeological sites: The tools, houses, and other finds discovered in the different layers of a site can be dated relative to the layers by their association with the stratum in which they are found (Figure 5.4).

The basis of all scientific archaeological excavation is the accurately observed and carefully recorded stratigraphic profile (Wheeler, 1954).

We return to stratigraphy and superposition in Chapter 6.

Figure 5.5   An iron arrowhead embedded in the backbone of a skeleton from a battle cemetery at Maiden Castle, England. The artifact comes from a Roman cultural context; the skeleton, from native British. Nevertheless, they are still associated in the archaeological record.

ARCHAEOLOGICAL CONTEXT

Archaeological context is derived from a careful recording of the matrix, provenience, and association of the finds. Context is far more than just a find spot, a position in time and space. It involves assessing how the find got to its position and what has happened since its original owners abandoned it. Anyone wanting to reconstruct human behavior or ancient cultural systems must pay careful attention to the context of every find.

Context is affected by a number of factors:

1. The manufacture and use of the object, house, or other find by its original owners. For example, the orientation of a house may be determined by the position of the sun on summer afternoons. Since the archaeologist's objective is to reconstruct ancient behavior, this aspect of context is of vital importance.
2. The way in which the find was deposited in the ground. Some discoveries, like royal burials or caches of artifacts, were deliberately buried under the ground by ancient people; others vanished as a result of natural phenomena. Dilapidated houses that have been abandoned slowly become covered by blowing sand or rotting vegetation. The Roman city of Herculaneum in Italy, however, was buried quickly by a catastrophic eruption of Vesuvius in August A.D. 79.
3. The subsequent history of the find in the ground. For example, was the burial disturbed by later graves, or was the site eroded away by water?

Primary and Secondary Context. The context of any archaeological find can be affected by two processes: the original behavior of the people who used or made it and later events.

Primary context is the original context of the find, undisturbed by any factor, whether human or natural, since it was deposited by those who were involved with it. For example, the Iron Age warrior depicted in Figure 5.5, who was buried at Maiden Castle in A.D. 43, died from his wounds in a battle against a Roman legion. His kinfolk buried him swiftly in a shallow grave. The skeleton survived intact in its primary context until Sir Mortimer Wheeler excavated the undisturbed burial in the late 1930s (Wheeler, 1943).

Secondary context refers to the context of a find whose primary context has been disturbed by later activity. Very frequently, the excavators of a burial ground will find incomplete skeletons whose graves have been disturbed by the deposition of later burials. In other instances, such as

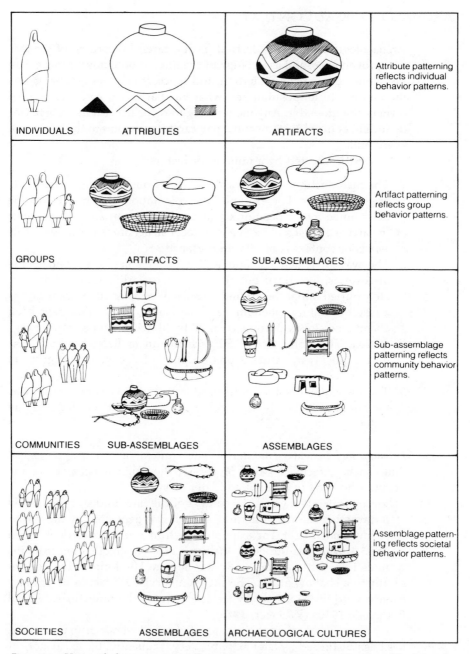

Figure 5.6 Human behavior as it is reflected in archaeological classifications. The hierachy begins with attributes and artifacts and ends with entire archaeological cultures.

in the case of the tomb of Pharaoh Tutankhamun, tomb robbers may disturb the original grave furnishings in a frantic search for gold or precious oils. In still other instances, finds can be shifted by the natural forces of wind and weather. Many of the Stone Age tools found in European river gravels have been transported for considerable distances by floodwaters to a location far from their original place of use. In all of these cases, the disturbed finds are in a secondary context.

Spatial Context. Spatial context is important to archaeologists, because it enables them to determine the distance between different objects or features, between entire settlements, or between settlements and key vegetational zones and landmarks. Important distances can be a few inches of level ground between a dagger and the associated skeleton of its dead owner, a mile separating two seasonal camps, or a complicated series of interrelated distance measurements separating dozens of villages that are part of an elaborate trading system carrying luxury goods through several geographic regions hundreds of miles apart.

One can identify four levels of spatial context, each of them coinciding with an actual level of human behavior (Figure 5.6).

1. *Artifacts:* individual human activity.
2. *Structure:* household or group activities (structures can, of course, include public buildings, such as temples, which are used by more than one household).
3. *Site:* community activity, groups of contemporary houses, stores, temples, and other structures.
4. *Region:* the activities of groups of people reflected by sites distributed on the landscape. These are sometimes referred to as a settlement pattern.

These four levels of spatial context are closely tied to actual cultural behavior. An artifact itself can provide valuable information on technology and actual use. But in order to infer cultural behavior the artifact's association must be known, both with other artifacts and with the matrix in which it was found. For example, the patterning of artifacts in space around an abandoned iron smelting furnace or near the bones of a slaughtered bison kill is tangible evidence for specific human behavior. An unassociated projectile head will never give you anything more specific than the inference that it was used as a weapon. But a patterning of projectile heads, scraping tools, and large boulders associated with a bison skeleton has a context in time and space that allows much more detailed inferences.

The basic assumption behind all studies of artifacts in space is that they were used for rational purposes and that characteristic groups of them were used for specific activities, such as ironworking, butchery, and hunting. It follows that similarly patterned groups of artifact types found on other sites resulted from basically similar activities, even if there are differences in detail. For instance, during the earlier millennia of the Stone Age, people enjoyed much the same basic level of hunting and gathering culture throughout Africa, Europe, and India. This is reflected in thousands of similar-looking stone axes found in sites as widely separated as the Thames valley and the Cape of Good Hope in South Africa.

ARTIFACTS, SUBASSEMBLAGES, AND ASSEMBLAGES

Artifacts.   Artifacts are commonly defined as "anything which exhibits any physical attributes that can be assumed to be the result of human activity" (Dunnell, 1971). This definition implies that the term *artifact* covers every form of archaeological find, from stone axes, bronze daggers, and clay pots to butchered animal bones, carbonized seeds, huts, and all other manifestations of human behavior that can be found in archaeological sites. Some archaeologists define artifacts by breaking them down into three categories: features, structures, and ecofacts (forms of archaeological evidence that will be covered in more detail later in this book).

Whichever definition of artifact is preferred, it is assumed by all that any object or any event of manufacture or consumption is a product of human activity if its location or any other of its features cannot be accounted for by natural processes. In other words, artifacts are compared to natural objects and distinguished from them, not by individual features but by a whole patterning of different, humanly caused features. It is this patterning that is important. For example, a simple flake removed from an elaborate ceremonial obsidian knife blade may not necessarily show evidence of human modification. But the patterned, consistently repeated occurrence of several dozen or hundreds of small flakes—flakes that together formed a knife—is highly diagnostic of human activity. Normally there is no difficulty at all in telling humanly made or caused artifacts from those caused by water action, fire, hyena kills, or all the other natural phenomena that one can run across.

Figure 5.7 Mesopotamian *tell,* a site that was occupied over thousands of years.

Subassemblages. A single artifact, such as an arrowhead or a basket, is made up of a combination of attributes (see Chapter 12), which make up a constant pattern of behavior reflected in the finished artifact. When such artifacts are found in patterned associations that reflect the shared cultural behavior of minimal groups, then they are classified in what are commonly called *subassemblages* (Deetz, 1967). A hunter, for example, uses a bow, arrows, and a quiver. A blacksmith uses hammers, tongs, and bellows to make hoes or spears, and so on. Subassemblages represent the behavior of individuals.

Assemblages. When a number of different subassemblages of artifacts, let us say a collection of hunting weapons, baskets, pounders, and digging sticks, traces of windbreaks, and stone vessels, are found in a contemporary association, they reflect in their patterning the shared activities of a total community and are known as *assemblages.* With assemblages, one is looking at the shared behavior of a community as a whole, shared behavior that is frequently reflected in the remains of houses, the features associated with them, and the community settlement patterns.

ARCHAEOLOGICAL SITES

Archaeological sites are places where traces of past human activity are to be found. Sites are normally identified through the presence of artifacts. Sites can range in size from a large city, such as Teotihuacán, in the Valley of Mexico, to a tiny scatter of hunter-gatherer artifacts in Death Valley, California. There are millions of archaeological sites in the world, many of them still undiscovered. Some were occupied for a few short hours, days, or weeks; some were occupied for a generation or two and then abandoned forever. Other localities, such as Mesopotamian occupation mounds, or *tells,* were reoccupied again and again for hundreds, even thousands, of years and contain many stratified layers (Figure 5.7). In contrast, the single occupation site may contain little more than a surface scatter of potsherds or stone tools or a single occupation layer buried under a few inches of topsoil. Archaeological sites can consist of a simple association (an isolated burial and a single pot), many associations making up an assemblage of artifacts representing a single community, or a whole series of assemblages stratified one above another.

Classification of Sites. Archaeological sites can be classified in a number of ways:

By archaeological context. The context of the artifacts in the site can be used to distinguish between sites such as surface locations, singlelevel occupations, and stratified settlements.

By artifact content. The site is labeled according to its specific artifact content: pottery, stone tools, milling stones, and so on. The associations, assemblages, and subassemblages of artifacts in the site are used to label it as Stone Age, Mayan, and so on.

By geographical location. Most human settlements have been concentrated in certain well-defined types of geographical locations, and these sites can be referred to as cave sites, valley-bottom sites, foothill sites, and the like.

By artifact content related to site function. Since subassemblages are reflections of individual human behavior, sites can be classified by using the characteristic patternings of the artifacts found in them.

Common Site Function. The following are some common site functions.

Living, or habitation sites are the most common, for they are the places where people have lived and carried out a multitude of activities. The artifacts in living sites reflect domestic activities, such as food preparation, as well as toolmaking. Dwellings are normally present. The temporary camps of early humans at Olduvai Gorge are living sites, as are Stone Age rockshelters, southwestern pueblos and Mesopotamian *tells.* Habitation sites of any complexity are associated with other sites that reflect specialized needs, such as agricultural systems, cemeteries, temporary camps, and so on.

Kill sites are places where prehistoric people killed game and camped around the carcasses while butchering the meat. Kill sites are relatively common on the Great Plains. The Olsen-Chubbock site is a good example of this. Projectile points and butchery tools are associated with kill sites.

Ceremonial sites may or may not be an integral part of a living site. The Mesopotamian *ziggurat* dominated its mother city, while Mayan ceremonial sites, such as Tikal, were surrounded by habitation areas. Other famous ceremonial sites, such as Stonehenge in England or the Great Serpent Mound in Ohio, are isolated monuments. Ceremonial artifacts, such as sting ray spines which were used in mutilation rituals, and statuary, may be associated with sacred sites.

Burial sites include both cemeteries and isolated tombs. People have been burying their dead since at least 70,000 years ago and have often taken enormous pains to prepare them for the afterlife. Perhaps the most famous burial sites of all are the Pyramids of Gizeh. Burials, such as that of the Egyptian pharaoh Tutankhamun absorbed the energies of hundreds of people in their preparation. Many burials are associated with special grave furniture, jewelry, and ornaments of rank.

Trading, quarry, and art sites represent a special category of site in that some kind of specialist activity was carried out. The special tools needed for the mining of copper, obsidian, and other metals identify quarry sites. Trading sites are identified by large quantities of exotic trade objects and by their strategic position near major cities. The Assyrian *karum* that flourished outside the Hittite city of Kanesh in 1900 B.C. is one example of this. Art sites, which abound in southwest France, southern Africa, California, and other areas, are identified by painted frescoes on the walls of caves and rockshelters.

Shipwrecks are another class of site, and they are found in many parts of the world, even at the foot of rapids in midwestern rivers (Bass, 1966). These are sealed associations of artifacts, which often provide vital information on prehistoric trading and require specialized recovery techniques, which are not described in this book.

CULTURES, REGIONS, AND SETTLEMENT PATTERNS

The spatial units we have referred to thus far are all confined to the boundaries of a single community. They reflect the activities of the maximum number of people who occupied a single settlement at some time during a cycle of settlement. Although a great deal of archaeological research is carried out on single sites, archaeologists often seek to understand the prehistory of a much wider area. Several communities or a scattered population living in a well-defined region may be linked together in the same subsistence or settlement system. Such commonly held systems, and the human activities that derive from them, make up an entire culture. Culture behavior is identified through the patterning of an entire assemblage. The study of an entire culture involves working with much larger bodies of archaeological information, as well as with background geographical and environmental data.

Archaeological Cultures and Other Units.   A number of spatial units are in common use:

Archaeological cultures are consistent patternings of assemblages, the archaeological equivalents of human societies. Archaeological cultures consist of the material remains of human culture preserved at a specific space and time at several sites.

Culture Areas are large geographical areas in which artifacts characteristic of an archaeological culture exist in a precise context of time and space. For example, one can refer to both a Mayan cultural system and a Mayan culture area.

Archaeological Regions are generally described as well-defined geographical areas bounded by conspicuous geographical features, such as ocean, lakes, or mountains. Once having defined a region geographically, the researcher will try to identify its ecological and cultural boundaries throughout prehistoric times.

Most regional approaches involve far more than comparing the artifacts from a few scattered settlements. They are based on a research strategy that is aimed at sampling the entire region, and on objectives that seek to reconstruct many more aspects of prehistoric life than those uncovered at a single site. These include both social organization and economic strategies (see Chapter 16).

Settlement Patterns.   A settlement pattern is the distribution of sites and human settlement across the natural landscape. Settlement patterns are determined by many factors: by the environment, by economic practices, and by technological skills. Settlement archaeology is part of the analysis of the interactions between people and their environment.

In spatial terms, the archaeologist's studies of the behavior of a human society as a whole are based on models and hypotheses that are tested by data from many disciplines. This data bears on the ways in which communities and their associated contemporary assemblages are grouped into larger units on the landscape. By the same token, it also bears on the ways in which prehistoric societies interacted with the ever-changing natural environment.

Spatial context is vital to scientific archaeology, for it provides one of the critical dimensions of archaeological data. The other critical dimension is time, which we will consider in the next chapter.

Guide to Further Reading

The literature on basic archaeological concepts is sketchy at best, but the following are some key references.

Childe, V. Gordon. *Piecing Together the Past.* London: Routledge and Kegan Paul, 1956.
An outdated but still outstanding source on basic archaeological concepts, with a strong European orientation.

Deetz, James. *Invitation to Archaeology.* Garden City, N.Y.: Natural History Press, 1967.
An entertaining and succinct introduction to culture in archaeology.

Hole, Frank, and Heizer, Robert F. *An Introduction to Prehistoric Archaeology.* 3d ed. New York: Holt, Rinehart, and Winston, 1973.
An advanced archaeological textbook, with superb bibliographies that give considerable coverage to the basics.

Watson, Patti Jo; LeBlanc, Steven; and Redman, Charles. *Explanation in Archaeology.* New York: Columbia University Press, 1971.
A fundamental source that describes processual archaeology in rather technical terms.

Wheeler, R. E. M. *Archaeology from the Earth.* Oxford: Clarendon Press, 1954.
An elegant guide to excavation that contains much of value about fundamental concepts.

Willey, Gordon R., and Phillips, Philip. *Method and Theory in American Archaeology.* Chicago: University of Chicago Press, 1958.
A classic essay on basic culture history in North American archaeology.

CHAPTER 6 ❦

TIME: RELATIVE CHRONOLOGY

Preview

- Chronological ordering of prehistoric times was a major problem for early archaeologists. In an attempt to deal with this, C. J. Thomsen developed the Three-Age system, a technological framework that was widely used in the Old World. New World archaeologists used the direct historical approach to determine the framework for the Americas.
- Chronometric (absolute) dates are dates expressed in years. In contrast, relative dates represent relationships in time that are used to correlate prehistoric sites or cultures with one another. These are based on the law of superposition.
- Most relative dating in archaeology is based on stratigraphic observations in archaeological sites. Not only the layers in a site but also the ways in which they were formed and the finds in them are carefully observed and recorded.
- Cultural disturbances, which result from human behavior, can affect stratigraphy. Natural disturbances such as erosion or flooding, can change stratigraphic contexts through natural means.
- Early archaeologists studied the evolution of artifact styles throughout time. This approach has developed into formal ordering, or what is called the technique of seriation. This technique is based on the assumption that artifacts come into fashion, enjoy a period of maximum popularity, and then slowly go out of style. Tested against the

evidence of New England tombstones and other modern artifacts, seriation has been developed into an effective way of ordering sites in a chronological sequence.

- Cross dating, which is widely used in Europe and Mesoamerica, uses artifacts of a known age, such as coins and artifacts that were widely traded, to provide relative dates for sites in areas where no historical chronology exists.

- Obsidian hydration, a technique based on the measurement of hydration layers in this volcanic glass, is sometimes used to provide relative dates for sites in California and Mexico.

- The Pleistocene, or Great Ice Age, has been relative dated by such geological events as the major glaciations and interglacials as well as by fluctuations in sea level. Bones from such extinct species as Pleistocene elephants have been used to provide an approximate relative chronology for the Pleistocene, a technique known as geochronology.

- Pollen analysis, or palynology, uses the fossil pollens of grasses and forest trees to study prehistoric vegetational cover with great accuracy. Pollen samples provide not only ecological information about glaciations and interglacials, but also insights into the environments surrounding archaeological sites. Palynology has even been used to date individual rooms within southwestern pueblos.

The measurement of time and the ordering of prehistoric cultures in chronological sequence has been one of the major preoccupations of archaeologists since the very beginnings of scientific research. In this chapter we examine the ways in which archaeologists establish chronological relationships between different artifacts, sites, and other features. This type of relative chronology is based on stratigraphic principles that were first developed by geologists.

Early antiquarians and theologians wrestled with the enigma of the Biblical legend of the Creation and the finds of fossil animals and human artifacts. Since the establishment of a high antiquity for humankind in 1859, however, accurate measurement of time has become one of the principal preoccupations of those who study the prehistoric past. How does one classify the past and measure the age of the great events of prehistory? The time dimension of archaeology is a vital element in our description and interpretation of prehistory. Yet, our own perspectives of time and philosophies of life have taken very little account of these vast new chronological horizons (Leone, 1978).

Consider for a moment how you view time. What is the earliest date you can remember? Mine is my third birthday—I have a vague memory of balloons and lots of people. My continuous memory of people as individuals and of day-to-day events begins at age 8. Most adults have a somewhat similar span of recollection and a chronological perspective on their lives extending back into early childhood. Our sense of personal involvement in human history, too, extends only over the period of our lifetimes. We have but an indirect involvement with the lives of our parents, relatives, or other friends, some of whom may have been alive 50 to 70 years before we were born. Perhaps our profoundest involvement with time occurs toward the end of our lives, with a period covering the lives of our immediate family. But we do have, also, a marginal sense of longer chronologies and a perspective on events within them—our family ancestry, the history of our community, of our nation—and in these days of ardent internationalism, with the world as well, though few people have a sense of perspective for the whole span of human experience.

THE THREE-AGE SYSTEM

In Chapter 3, we saw how the classification of the past was a major problem for early excavators. Confronted with a jumble of artifacts from burial mounds or settlements, they had no means of subdividing or measuring the past. Until the nineteenth century, the world had been comfortably secure. People had speculated freely about their origins but only within the narrow horizons of the Biblical account of the Creation. What happened before the Creation was a blank. Christians had contemplated eternity, but it was the shadowless, changeless eternity of God. Ussher's 6000 years sufficed for all prehistory, even if subdividing these six millennia presented a problem.

Scandinavian archaeologists were the first to develop a framework into which the bewildering mixture of artifacts from their excavations could be fitted. At the end of the eighteenth century, they were writing about ages of stone, copper, and iron, which flourished in prehistoric times. But as late as 1806, Professor Rasmus Nyerup of the University of Copenhagen complained that "everything which has come down to us from heathendom is wrapped in a thick fog; it belongs to a space of time which we cannot measure" (Daniel, 1976). Nyerup and others were responsible for the setting up of a Danish National Museum that housed a confusing collection of artifacts from bogs, burial chambers, and shell middens. The first curator of the Museum, Christian Jurgensen Thomsen (1788–1865), was appointed in 1816. Thomsen put the Museum collections in order by classifying them into three groups, representing ages of Stone, Bronze, and Iron, using sealed finds in graves as a basis for his classification. He claimed that his Three Ages were chronologically ranked (Thomsen, 1836).

Thomsen's bold classification was taken up by another Dane, J. J. A. Worsaae, who proved the basic stratigraphic validity of the system. By studying archaeological finds from all over Europe, Worsaae demonstrated the widespread validity of what became known as the Three-Age System (Worsaae, 1843). This system was a technological subdivision of the prehistoric past. It gave archaeologists a broad context within which their own finds could be placed. Thus, Thomsen's Three Ages, which were a first attempt at a chronology of relationship for the prehistoric past, were widely adopted as a basis for classifying prehistoric sites in the Old World. This framework for Old World prehistory, in a modified form, survives today (Table 6.1).

Table 6.1   Some nomenclature of Old World archaeology.

Approximate age	Geological epoch	Three-Age terminology	Important events
3000 B.C. – 7800 B.C. –	HOLOCENE	Iron Age Bronze Age Neolithic Mesolithic	Writing in the Near East Origins of food production
8000 B.C. – 35,000 B.P. –	END OF PLEISTOCENE	Upper Paleolithic	Origins of blade technology
70,000 B.P. – 400,000 B.P. – 1.75 million B.P. – 5 million B.P. –	PLEISTOCENE	Middle Paleolithic Lower Paleolithic	Hand axes in widespread use
13 million B.P. –	PLIOCENE		Origins of toolmaking
25 million B.P. –	MIOCENE		No humans
34 million B.P. –	OLIGOCENE		

Note: This table is for general reference throughout the text.

NEW WORLD CHRONOLOGY

The Three-Age System of the Scandinavians was not adopted in North America. Systematic archaeological research flourished in the New World after 1859, but early attempts to find Paleolithic sites there were unsuccessful. The complicated cultural strata of the European rivers, with their rich storehouses of hand axes, did not exist, but what did exist—the relationships between the Indian population and the finds of the archaeologist—was soon established. Stratigraphic observations and local cultural sequences did not preoccupy American archaeologists, unlike the Europeans. Few researchers bothered to apply meticulous excavation techniques to later New World archaeological sites, in which, in any case, almost no metals were found.

Not until 1914 did chronology and detailed stratigraphic observations of the past become important in American archaeology, when N. C. Nelson (Nelson, 1914), and later A. V. Kidder began to use potsherds in southwestern sites as stratigraphic indicators. Kidder's classic excavations at the Pecos Pueblo (Kidder, 1924) brought about a conference there in 1927, which delineated eight sequential stages of Pueblo culture. With that event the foundations of accurate stratigraphic and chronological studies in American archaeology were soundly laid in the classic archaeological laboratory of the Southwest.

As we saw in Chapter 4, the direct historical approach and the development of tree-ring dating in the southwestern United States provided at least one area of the Americas with an accurate chronological framework. Most other regions were without accurate chronologies in calendar years until the advent of radiocarbon dating in the 1950s.

CHRONOMETRIC (ABSOLUTE) AND RELATIVE DATING

Prehistoric chronologies cover enormously long periods of time—millennia and centuries—as opposed to days or minutes. Some idea of the scale of prehistoric time can be gained by piling up a hundred quarters. If the whole pile represents the time that humans have been on earth, the length of time covered by historical records would equal considerably less than the thickness of one quarter.

Archaeologists commonly refer to dates expressed in years as chronometric or absolute dates. Julius Caesar landed in Britain in 55 B.C.; Washington, D.C., was founded in A.D. 1800. The current chronometric dates for the earliest humans begin around four million years ago. Though not nearly as precise as the date for Caesar, they are, nevertheless, expressed in years. Dating experts draw widely on techniques invented by chemists and physicists and used by geologists for chronometric dating (see Chapter 7).

Relative dates correlate prehistoric sites of cultures with one another by their relative age. They are based on the law of superposition.

Relative dates are simpler to establish than are chronometric dates. If I place a book on the table and then pile another one on top of it, clearly the upper one of the two was placed on the table after, at a later moment in time, than the original volume. The second book became part of the pile after the first—though how long afterward we have no means of telling.

Stratigraphy and Superposition.   Most relative chronology in archaeology has its basis in large- or small-scale stratigraphic observations in archaeological sites of all ages. As the eminent British archaeologist Sir Mortimer Wheeler has cogently argued, the basis of scientific archaeological excavation is the accurately observed and carefully recorded stratigraphic profile (Wheeler, 1954).

Superposition is fundamental to studying archaeological sites, for many settlements, such as Near Eastern mounds or Indian villages in the Ohio Valley or cave sites, contain multilevel occupations whose decipherment is the key to their relative chronology. Sir Mortimer Wheeler has ably described the processes of human occupation as applied to stratigraphy:

> The human occupation of a site normally results in the accumulation of material of one kind or another on and about the area occupied. Objects are lost or discarded and become imbedded in the earth. Floors are renewed and old ones buried. Buildings crumble and new ones are built on the ruins. A flood may destroy a building or a town and deposit a layer of alluvium on its debris and later, when the flood has subsided, the level site may be reoccupied. Sometimes, the process is in the reverse direction. Evidences of occupation may be removed as in the deepening of an unsurfaced street by traffic, or the digging of a pit for the disposal of rubbish or for burial. . . . In one way or another the surface of an ancient town or village is constantly altering in response to human effort or neglect; and it is by interpreting rightly these evidences of alteration that we may hope to reconstruct something of the vicissitudes of the site and its occupants (Wheeler, 1954).

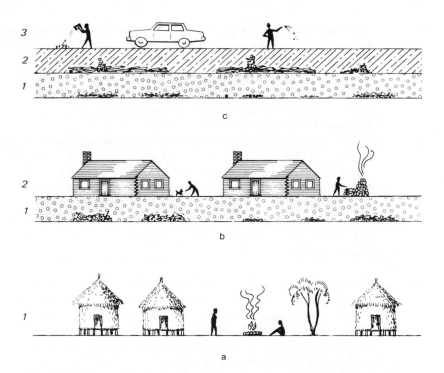

Figure 6.1 Superposition and stratigraphy: a). A farming village built on virgin subsoil. After a time, the village is abandoned, and the huts fall into disrepair. Their ruins are covered by accumulating soil and vegetation. b). After an interval, a second village is built on the same site, with different architectural styles. This in turn is abandoned; the houses collapse into piles of rubble and are covered by accumulating soil. c). Twentieth-century people park their cars on top of both village sites and drop litter and coins which, when uncovered, reveal to the archaeologist that the top layer is modern. An archaeologist digging this site would find that the modern layer is underlaid by two prehistoric occupation levels; that square houses were in use in the upper of the two, which is the later (law of superposition); and that round huts are stratigraphically earlier than square ones here. Therefore, village 1 is earlier than village 2, but when either was occupied or how many years separate village 1 from 2 cannot be known without further data.

Stratigraphy, as applied to archaeological sites, is on a much smaller scale than that of geology, but often, it is correspondingly more complicated (Harris, 1979). Most archaeological relative chronology employs careful observations of sequences of occupation levels as well as the correlation of these with cultural sequences at other sites in the same area. Successive occupation levels may be found at the same spot, such as in a cave, fort, or mound site, where many generations of settlers lived within a circumscribed or restricted area. In other cases,

however, the chronological sequence can be horizontal. Such a situation arises when economic or political conditions dictate a regular
movement of villages when fields are exhausted or residence rules
modified. In this case, a cultural sequence may be scattered throughout
a series of single-level occupation sites over a large area and can be put
together only by judicious survey work and careful analysis of the
artifacts found in the different sites.

The artifacts, food bones, or other finds recovered from the layers of
a site are as critical as the stratigraphy itself. Each level in a settlement,
however massive or small, has its associated artifacts, the objects that
the archaeologist uses as indicators of cultural and economic change.
Indeed, the finds in each layer—and their associations—often provide
the basic material for relative chronology. Furthermore, the relative
dating of many sites is complicated by other questions. Has the site
been occupied continuously? Do stratigraphic profiles reflect a continuous occupation over a long period of time or a sequence that has been
interrupted several times by warfare or simple abandonment of the
site? Such problems can be resolved by careful examination or excavated profiles (Figures 6.1, 6.2, and 6.3).

Another factor that may affect the interpretation of stratigraphy is
the breaks, or disruptions, in the layering caused by human activity
and by natural phenomena. These disruptions in a site form a vital part
of the context of archaeological data.

Figure 6.2   An idealized section through an Upper and Middle Paleolithic cave in
France. The four archaeological culture layers are separated by sterile layers, the
Mousterian being earlier than the Aurignacian, and so on. Most stratigraphic
sequences are, of course, much more complicated than this hypothetical example.
(After Oakley.)

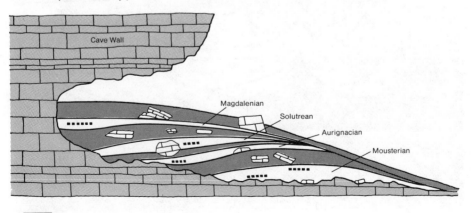

Cultural transformations are those resulting from human behavior. For example, later occupants of a village may dig rubbish pits or graves into earlier strata. Cattle may be kept on the site, their hooves removing the soil and disturbing the upper levels of the underlying horizons; this process also may be caused by later people cultivating the rich soils of an abandoned village site. Building activities may cause foundation trenches, and even stone walls, to be sunk into earlier levels. The local inhabitants' technological level has a direct bearing on their ability to destroy evidence of earlier occupation. Obviously, the inhabitants of a Near Eastern city are more likely to have destroyed evidence of earlier occupation with constant rebuilding than are a group of farmers without metal tools, who merely reoccupy earlier village sites with minimal disturbance of the underlying levels. Modern construction activity, road building, or deep plowing can also disturb a site and its contents, as can the depredations of pot and treasure hunters, who have no concern of scientifically collected data.

Figure 6.3   A stratigraphic section through a town site in Cambridge, England, showing profiles of prehistoric and Roman enclosures and huts with a post hole (P.H.), gullies, and ditches. The complex stratigraphy is interpreted by correlating the various features with their horizontal layers, a difficult task in this case because of the jumbling of layers. For example, the lowest ditch was cut into bedrock (E) and was truncated by a later ditch. (One thirty-second actual size).

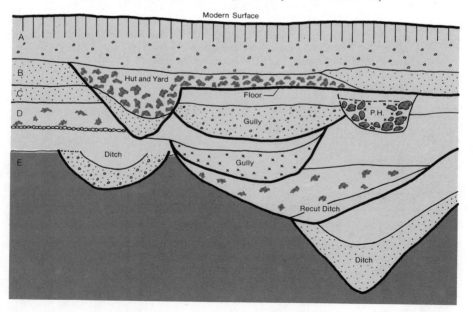

Natural transformations are those caused by natural phenomena. A sudden flood can cover an abandoned village in a thick layer of mud. Volcanic ash buried Roman Herculaneum in A.D. 79. Burrowing animals, too, enjoy archaeological sites, working their way through the soft, organic soils of caves and village sites and disrupting stratigraphy over large areas of the settlement. Natural transformations are of vital importance, for they determine the state of preservation of data. Preservation conditions differ widely from site to site and must be assessed carefully for each location. An understanding of both cultural and natural transformation conditions is essential to precise interpretation of archaeological data.

ARTIFACTS AND RELATIVE CHRONOLOGY

Manufactured artifacts are the fundamental data archaeologists use to study human behavior in the past. These artifacts are reflections of ancient human behavior and how it has changed throughout time. One only has to look at the simple stone-chopper of the earliest humans and compare it to the latest and most sophisticated digital computer to get the point. Most artifact changes in prehistory, however, are extremely gradual. They are cumulative, minor changes in such elements as, say, shape, decoration, or lip angle of clay pots that lead ultimately to a quite different vessel form, one that is hardly recognizable as related.

Early Artifact Studies.   Early archaeologists were very concerned with the evolution of objects throughout time and studied minute details of these changes. If animals evolved, they argued, why not artifacts as well? As early as 1849, John Evans described the stater of Philip II of Macedon (Figure 6.4) and its progressive alteration in the hands of British coiners who had little interest in the Greek prototype (Evans, 1849–50). Evans noted the degeneration in the design and used it to devise a chronological sequence for the coins. But he and others soon found that in tool design many variables affected changes, among them improved efficiency, stylistic degeneration, or simply, popularity. British General Pitt Rivers was the first to apply the term *typology*—a method used in natural science to work out relationships in the form and structure of organisms within an evolutionary sequence—to analysis of human-made objects (Pitt Rivers, 1887). Pitt Rivers's typologies were based on another important principle: certain technological trends are irreversible. To take an obvious example, an aeronautical

Figure 6.4 The derivation of the British stater from the stater of Philip II of Macedon, as studied by Sir John Evans. The faces of the original Macedonian coins are at the left.

enthusiast, given the photographs of a series of aircraft types dating from the beginnings of aviation up to the present, could place them in approximate order, even if he had no idea of the dates of the photographs. It would simply be impossible to envision a typological sequence in which the earliest aircraft was a supersonic jet and the latest a Bleriot monoplane of 1912: the modifications needed would be both illogical and incredible.

Another scholar, the Egyptologist Sir Flinders Petrie, also contributed much to the early study of artifact chronology. In 1902 he wanted to arrange a large number of pre-Dynastic tombs from the Nile Valley in chronological order. He eventually placed them in sequence by studying groups of pots found with the skeletons, arranging the vessels in such a way that their stylistic differences reflected gradual change (Petrie, 1889). The handles on the jars were particularly informative, for they changed from functional appendages into more decorative handles and, finally, degenerated into a series of painted lines. Flinders Petrie built up a series of pottery stages at Diospolis Parva to which he assigned "sequence dates," the fifty stages running from SD 30 to SD 80. SD 30 was the oldest in the group. Petrie correctly assumed that the earliest of his wares was not, in fact, the most ancient Egyptian pottery. His sequence dates were subsequently applied over wide areas of the Nile Valley, providing an admirable relative chronology for early Egyptian pottery that remained in use for many years. When one found a pot of a known type in the sequence date series, the pot itself and all the objects associated with it could be dated to that stage in the sequence.

Seriation.   The last fifty years have seen a rapid development in tech-niques of *seriation,* or chronological ordering, of artifacts. Recent stud-ies of seriation are based on the assumption that the popularity of any artifact or culture trait is a transient thing. The mini skirt becomes the midi or maxi, dancing styles change from month to month, records hit the top forty but are forgotten within a short time, and each year's automobile model, hailed as "brand new," is soon relegated to the sec-ondhand lot. Other traits may have a far longer life. The chopper tools of the earliest humans were a major element in early tool kits for hundreds of thousands of years. Candles were used for centuries be-fore kerosene and gas lamps came into fashion. But each had its period of maximum relative frequency, or popularity. Figure 6.5 shows how such popularity distributions are made up by the use of bar graphs

Figure 6.5   At the left, nine excavated sites (A to I) contain different percentages of three distinct pottery types. At the right, the nine sites have been seriated by rearranging the bars of type percentages into battleship curve order. At the far right, later excavations are eventually fitted into the sequence.

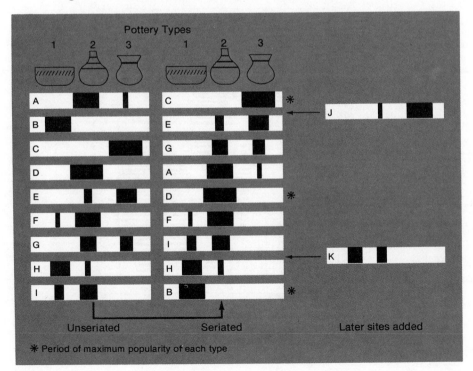

plotted against strata or other archaeological associations. Each distribution of artifacts or culture traits plotted has a profile that has been described as resembling a large battleship's hull viewed from the air (Figure 6.6).

The technique of seriation is based on the assumption that the popularity of pottery types, stone artifact forms, or other culture traits peaks in a "battleship curve," the widest part of the graph representing the period of maximum popularity. Thus, it is argued that sites within a restricted and uniform geographic area showing similar plots of pottery or other artifact types are of broadly the same relative date. A series of sites or surface collections can be linked in a relative chronol-

Figure 6.6   A seriation graph in the making. Each strip of paper represents a statigraphic unit; the ten columns of black bars are different pottery types. Each strip has the pottery counts for the level plotted on it in bar graph form. The strips, placed in position with paper clips onto graph paper pinned to a backboard, produce the most viable seriated sequence. (The diagram is almost complete.)

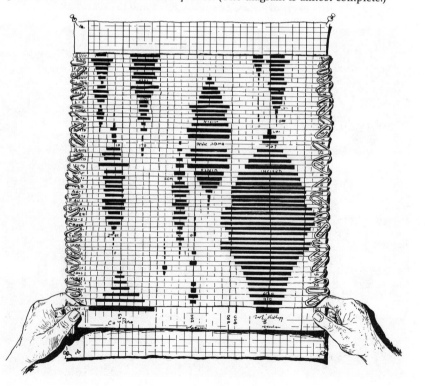

ogy, even though, without chronometric dates, one cannot tell when they were occupied, provided that the samples of artifacts used are statistically reliable. Edwin Dethlefsen and James Deetz tested the battleship curve assumption against some historical data, using a series of Colonial gravestones from a New England cemetery (Deetz, 1967; Dethlefsen and Deetz, 1966) (Figure 6.7). The gravestones dated by the inscriptions on them, show three decorative styles—death's head, cherub, and urn and willow—that yield an almost perfect series of battleship curves following one upon the other. Seriation is also applied to stylistic change within a single series of artifacts that may in themselves form a battleship curve. The same principle, which was used by Petrie with his pre-Dynastic jars, applies and a battleship curve results. Once the sequence of artifact types has been established, it is possible to insert new sites or single components from multilevel settlements into the carefully correlated sequence of seriated artifact types. This is done simply by comparing the percentages of types found in the new site with those in the correlated sequence as a whole. The new site is inserted into the sequence with considerable precision, on the assumption that closely similar artifacts were made at approximately the same time and that the lifetime of these particular tools coincides, albeit approximately, at all sites in a restricted culture area. If the collections are radiocarbon dated, then the seriation can be given an accurate date in years,too (Durrell, 1970).

The so-called battleship curve seriation method has been widely used in American archaeology, especially by the late James Ford, who used battleship-curve seriations extensively in the southeastern United States (Ford, 1962). Figure 6.8 illustrates a fine example of a seriated pottery sequence, that from the Tehuacán Valley in Mexico, famous for its evidence for early cultivation of maize in Mesoamerica (Mac-Neish, 1970). It shows how three distinctive phases of Tehuacán culture were ordered in a relative chronology with the seriated counts of many different pottery types.

You will notice that Figure 6.8 contains no absolute dates; the illustrated seriation is based on changing pottery forms and nothing else. In fact, of course, the chronological validity of the Tehuacán sequence has been confirmed by radiocarbon dating. Today's seriators use sophisticated statistical techniques to produce the seriation and to test the viability of their conclusions (Hole and Shaw, 1967; Johnson, 1968; LeBlanc, 1975; Marquardt,1978). Sound sampling procedures are obviously essential if seriation is to be used extensively, so it is necessary to establish that the samples collected were selected randomly (see Chapter 9).

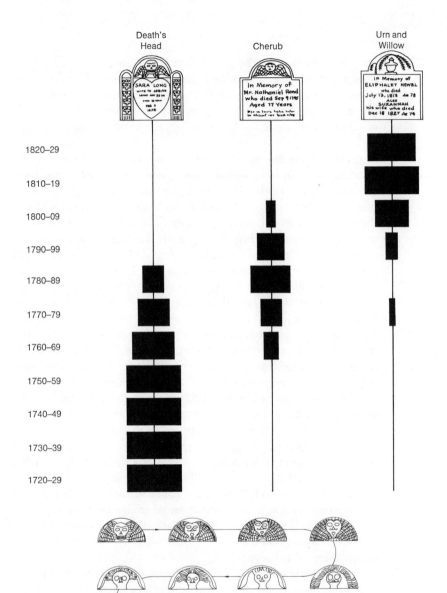

Figure 6.7 Above, Deetz's seriation of stylistic sequences of gravestones from Stoneham, Massachusetts. These dated battleship curves prove that all objects have a period of maximum popularity. Below, seriation of a stylistic change within a single New England gravestone motif. This type of seriation deals with the minute changes in a motif and shows how culture traits change very gradually throughout time.

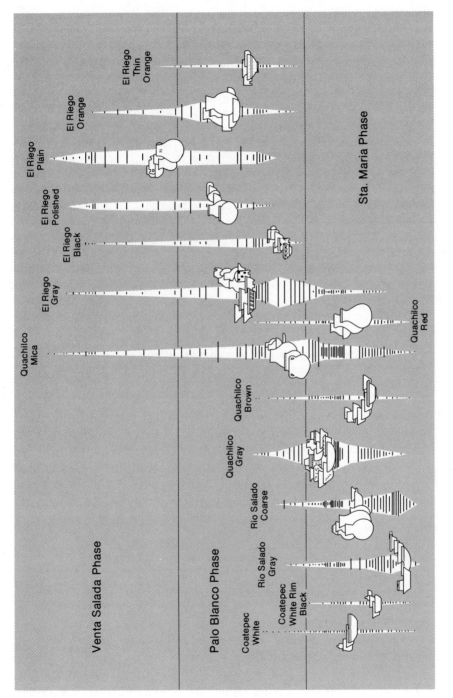

Figure 6.8   The battleship curve principle was used to develop this seriated ceramic sequence from the Tehuacán Valley in Mexico.

Although seriation can work well with undated artifact sequences, it works even better when radiocarbon dates or other accurate dating methods are available. When artifact types change rather predictably throughout a period of time, and these changes are well documented and dated in such a way that the direction of change is established, then it is possible to assign undated sites with similar artifacts to an approximate relative position on the crude time scale. This is the approach pioneered by John Evans, one that, of course, works well only when the artifacts being studied are of a type that changed in a distinctive and readily identifiable way.

Cross Dating.   Cross dating is one of the classic relative dating techniques of archaeological research. It has been applied to many sites in the New and Old worlds. In its classic application, cross dating is based on the use of dated objects, such as coins or pottery types, whose precise ages are known in their localities of ultimate origin (Childe, 1956).

When a dated artifact, such as a coin, turns up in an otherwise undated prehistoric occupation level far from its place of origin, it is safe to conclude that the horizon was laid down no earlier than the date of the article of known age. An Indian village site in Virginia that yielded an Elizabethan coin bearing a date of A.D. 1588 obviously dates to 1588 or later.

Such items as Chinese porcelain, Roman glass vessels, faience or glass beads, cotton and flax fabrics, bronze daggers, and Greek wine amphorae were luxuries that were diffused widely throughout the Old World, often to the barbarian tribes on the fringe of the unknown. The dates of styles of Chinese porcelain or Greek vases, changing according to the fashion's dictates, are firmly established in historical records. Such objects are found hundreds and even thousands of miles from the source of manufacture in undated prehistoric camps or trading centers. Since the date of the import is known at its source, the settlement in which it is found can be relatively dated to a period contemporary with, or younger than, the exotic object of known age (Garlake, 1973; Piggott, 1965).

Cross dating has been widely applied to sites where objects of known age are absent, too. In these instances, a well-studied sequence of different artifacts, whose development throughout time has been established by excavation, seriation, and stratigraphy, can be used to fit sites in neighboring areas into the master sequence simply by taking the artifacts in them and matching them with the dated collections from the central area. Perhaps the largest study of this type in recent years was conducted in the Tehuacán Valley in Mexico, where the excellent artifacts and seriations from Richard MacNeish's many excavations were combined with radiocarbon dates to fix the chronological time spans of each cultural phase in the valley (MacNeish, 1970). Armed with the precise chronological sequence, MacNeish's team was able to fit new sites and their artifactual contents into the sequence by both radiocarbon dating and cross dating of the seriated artifacts in the site. In some instances, the relative chronology established by cross-dated artifacts was more accurate than a radiocarbon date that was out of line with the master chronology established on the massive Tehuacán sequence. The Tehuacán sequence was used as a cross dating yardstick to correlate sites and cultural sequences all over Mexico. Obviously, individual trade artifacts with a short life at Tehuacán are best for such cross datings, for their short life gives the cross dating considerable precision. Artifacts, such as ceramics or stone tools, give less accurate results, for entire pottery styles may be only partially copied by others or may take time to spread from one area to another. But approximations are better than no relative chronology at all.

Readers interested in the working details of both seriation and cross dating are referred to the specialist literature (Marquardt, 1978).

Obsidian Hydration. Obsidian is a natural glass substance often formed by volcanic activity. It has long been prized by humankind for its sharp edges and excellent qualities for stone toolmaking. Projectile heads, hand axes, blades, even mirrors, were made from this much prized and widely traded material in both the New World and Old World. When a piece of obsidian is fractured, the freshly exposed surface absorbs water from its surroundings, forming a measurable hydration layer (Friedman, Clark, and Smith, 1969; Taylor and Meighan, 1978). As the surface becomes saturated with a layer of water molecules, they slowly diffuse into the main body of the obsidian, forming a zone with much higher water content than the interior of the obsidian piece.

Hydration is measured by making thin sections of obsidian artifact edges and examining them microscopically to obtain mean measurements of the hydration layer. Experiments have shown that the temperature, climate, and obsidian composition can affect the rate at which the water diffuses. By carefully controlling these variables, it is possible to compare hydration values from different sites within particular geographical areas. A number of experiments have been conducted in northern California and the Valley of Mexico, correlating radiocarbon-dated sites and layers with readings from obsidian artifacts. Since obsidian hydration tests are cheap to perform, it is possible for a researcher to obtain large numbers of dated samples. These can be arranged in chronological order, so that the investigator can examine small stylistic changes in artifacts through time.

The potential implications of this method are exciting. Unfortunately, however, many factors can contaminate the hydration: surface exposure or burning of artifacts, the reuse of tools, and climatic change. It seems unlikely that the method will ever be a highly accurate dating technique.

PLEISTOCENE GEOCHRONOLOGY

Most people have heard of the Great Ice Age, known to geologists as the Pleistocene, a period of recent geological time when much of Europe and North America experienced a bitter, arctic climate (Butzer, 1974). It was during this period that most of human prehistory was played out—against a background of complex and often dramatic climatic change that radically affected the pattern of human settlement. A relative chronology for human evolution that links archaeological sites with major Pleistocene climatic events can be obtained from the study of Pleistocene geochronology (Greek: *geos* = earth; *chronos* = time).

The Ice Age began over two million years ago and ended, by conventional definition, 8000 years before Christ, only shortly after the last great glacial period. During this two-million-year period, the world's climate underwent major fluctuations, changes that saw now-temperate Europe, for example, exhibit both subtropical and arctic climates within a 100,000-year period. The Arctic and Antarctic ice sheets expanded and contracted as the fluctuations of Pleistocene climate ranged from cold to warm and back again. The expanded ice sheets locked up enormous bodies of water, causing world sea levels to fall by several hundred feet. This opened up vast areas of the continental shelf to human settlement. A land bridge joined Siberia and Alaska, a huge flat plain that was traversed by the first hunter-gatherers more than 25,000 years ago (Figure 6.9). The low-lying coastal zones of Southeast Asia were far more extensive 15,000 years ago than they are now, and they supported a thriving population of hunter-gatherers. The fluctuations and distributions of vegetation zones also affected the pattern of human settlement and the course of human history.

From the point of view of archaeology, the major climatic events of the last two million years provide an admirable framework for a rela-

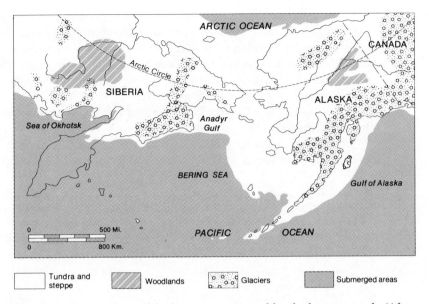

Figure 6.9   The Bering Land Bridge as reconstructed by the latest research. (After Jason Smith.)

tive chronology of human culture. Although almost no human beings lived on, or very close to, the great ice sheets that covered so much of the Northern Hemisphere during glacial periods, they did live in regions affected by geological phenomena associated with the ice sheets; they inhabited coastal areas, long dried-up lakes, and river floodplains. When human artifacts are found in direct association with Pleistocene geological features of this nature, it is sometimes possible to tie in archaeological sites with the relative chronology of Pleistocene events derived from geological strata.

Geochronology: Glaciations, Interglacials, and Sea Levels.   The glaciers and ice sheets that make up the framework for geochronological studies were formed in mountainous, high-latitude areas, and on continental plains during the Pleistocene. Prolonged periods of arctic climate and abundant snowfall caused glaciers to form over enormous areas of northern Europe, North America, and the Alpine areas of France, Italy, and Switzerland. At least four times during this period, arctic conditions prevailed over the Northern Hemisphere. These alternated with prolonged *interglacial* phases, when world climate was considerably warmer than it is today.

Every ice sheet had a *periglacial zone,* an area affected by climatic influences from the glaciers. Twenty-five thousand years ago, the persistent glacial anticyclone that was centered over the northern ice sheet caused dry, frosty winds to blow over the periglacial regions. The dry winds blew fine particles of dust, known as *loess,* onto the huge, rolling plains of central and eastern Europe and northern America.

The loess plains of central and eastern Europe were inhabited by hunter-gatherers who preyed on mammoth and big game (Klein, 1969). They lived in long houses built of bones and skins that, when excavated, were found at least partially sunk in the loess soil (Figure

Figure 6.10   Big-game hunters' long houses in western Russia, *ca.* 25,000 years ago. At the top is the plan of a long house from Kostenki IV, and at the bottom is a reconstruction based on finds at Push Kari. The latter was nearly 12 meters long and 3.7 meters wide and stood in a shallow depression.

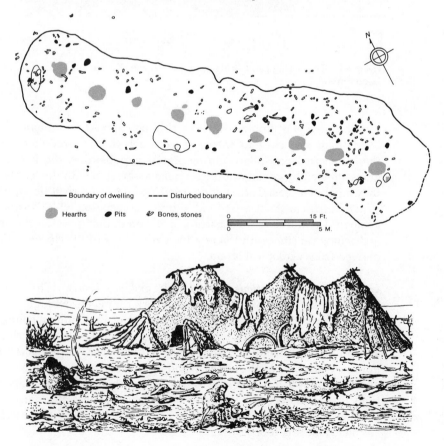

6.10). The relative dates of these settlements have been established by correlating the occupation levels with the different periods of loess accumulation that took place during the Pleistocene. Much later, Danubian peoples, the first farmers of temperate Europe, settled almost exclusively on these same light loess soils, for they were eminently suitable for the type of simple slash-and-burn agriculture practiced by these pioneer farmers (Piggott, 1965).

In addition to the formation of loess plains, the growth of an ice sheet on land had other effects (Buber, 1974). The water that falls as snow to form the ice sheets and glaciers comes ultimately from the oceans. When large areas in the northern latitudes were covered in ice, enormous quantities of water—sufficient to reduce the general level of the oceans by many meters—were immobilized on land. This *eustatic* effect was accompanied by an *isostatic* effect as well. The sheer dead weight of the massive ice sheets caused the loaded continental blocks of the land masses to sink to some degree into the viscous underlying layers of the earth, some ten kilometers (six miles) below the surface. While the isostatic effect was obviously confined to ice-covered areas, the eustatic effect was felt all over the world. At their maximum, the sea levels of the world may have been lowered as much as 200 meters (660 feet). Major geographical changes resulted from this. For instance, until roughly 4500 B.C., Britain was joined to the continent by a strip of marsh, which covered what is now the North Sea and part of the English Channel (Figure 6.11).

Many prehistoric settlements occupied during periods of low sea level are, of course, buried deep beneath the modern oceans. Numerous sites on ancient beaches have been found dating to periods of higher sea level. American archaeologist Richard Klein has excavated a coastal cave at Nelson Bay in the Cape Province of South Africa, which at present overlooks the Indian Ocean (Klein, 1977). Large quantities of shellfish and other marine animals are to be found in the uppermost levels of the cave. But, in the lower levels, occupied roughly 11,000 to 12,000 years ago, fish bones and other marine resources are very rare. Klein suspects that the seashore was many miles away at this time, for world sea levels were much lower during a prolonged period of arctic climate in northern latitudes. Today the cave is only 45 meters (50 yards) from the sea.

Animal Bones and Human Evolution.   Stone Age hunters killed a wide range of large and small mammals for food, whose broken bones are often preserved in river gravels, living floors, and other sites. The animals hunted most often were species that are now extinct, such as

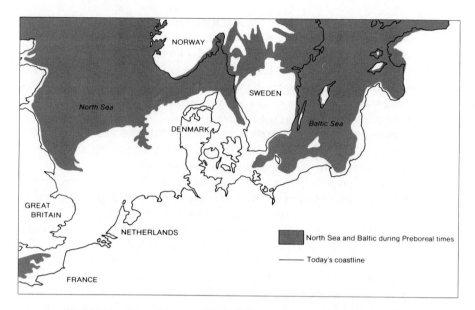

Figure 6.11   Great Britain and Scandinavia at the end of the Pleistocene, showing sea levels *ca.* 7000 B.C.

the giant pigs and buffalo found at Olduvai Gorge in Tanzania. Paleontologists have classified Pleistocene faunas from many localities, often using the remains of these animals, and they have tried to build up a very simple relative chronology of mammal types throughout the Pleistocene.

It has been found that the evolution of large mammals proceeded rapidly during the last five million years. Elephants, for example, changed radically during each European interglacial (Oakley, 1969). The evolving species can be distinguished by the distinctive cusp patterns of their teeth (Figure 6.12).

Unfortunately, however, the use of vertebrate fauna is severely limited by the difficulty of identifying different mammal species. Certain animals are more sensitive to climatic change than others. Some are tolerant of both cold and warm climates, while others prefer warm weather but can stand perversely low temperatures with remarkable resilience. Furthermore, so many environmental factors affect the distribution of mammals and the extinction of one species at the expense of another that it is very difficult to be sure that one is dealing with a chronological, as opposed to an environmental, difference. But, with early Pleistocene sites, the uses of animal bones as chronological indicators are magnified simply because enormous time scales are involved and minor details are obscured.

Pollen Analysis.   Vegetation is one of the best indicators of ecological change, for it depends on climate and soil for survival and is a sensitive barometer of climatic alteration. Pollen analysis, or *palynology,* is a comprehensive way of studying ancient vegetation; it was developed in

Figure 6.12   Grinding surfaces of the third upper molars of four types of Pleistocene elephant, illustrating the differences in enamel patterns from earlier (bottom) to later (top) types. (After Oakley; one-fifth actual size.)

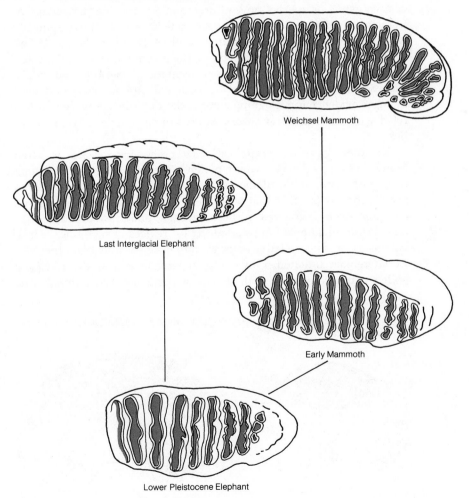

1916 by a Swede, Lennart van Post, who used forest trees. Subsequently, this analysis extended to all pollen-liberating vegetation. The principle of pollen analysis is simple (Faegri and Iverson, 1966). Large numbers of pollen grains are dispersed in the atmosphere and have remarkable preservative properties if deposited in an unaerated geological horizon. The pollen grains can be identified microscopically (Figure 6.13) with great accuracy and used to reconstruct the vegetation that grew near the spot where they are found.

Pollens are normally only identifiable under a very powerful microscope. Samples are taken through stratigraphic sections at close intervals and subjected to identification and statistical treatment. The grains of each genus or species present are counted, and the percentage of frequencies calculated. The counts are then correlated stratigraphically with one another to provide a sequence of vegetational change. When sufficient sections have been analyzed, the palynologist is able to *zonate* the vegetation according to distinct vegetational periods and to use such zones, and the characteristic pollen diagrams associated with them, as evidence for assigning a particular deposit to a place within a relative chronological framework worked out at a series of type localities.

Palynology has obvious applications to prehistory, for sites are often found in swampy deposits where pollen is preserved, especially fishing or fowling camps and settlements near water. Isolated artifacts, or even human corpses (such as that of Tollund man found in a Danish bog), have also been discovered in these deposits; pollen is sometimes obtained from small peat lumps adhering to crevices in such finds. Thus, botanists can assign relative dates even to isolated finds that otherwise would remain undated. Obviously, an archaeological site having a pollen graph coinciding with that of a particular vegetational zone

Figure 6.13 Pollen grains: left, spruce; right, silver fir. (After Oakley; both 340 times actual size.)

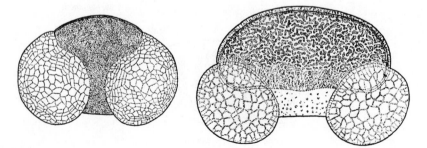

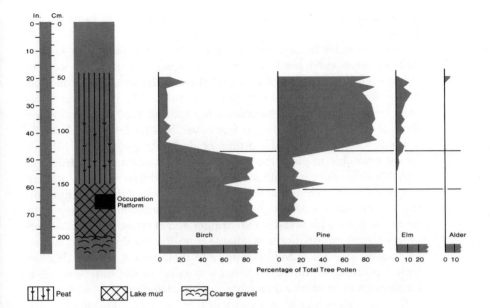

Figure 6.14   A simplified pollen diagram from a hunter-gatherer campsite at Star Carr, England, showing the changes in vegetational cover around the site from about 9000 B.C. up to *ca.* 6500 B.C. At the left is a vertical scale in inches and centimeters. Beside it is a column indicating the geological layers found at that spot on the site. The occupation level, which has been radiocarbon dated to about 7800 B.C., is shown at a depth of 160–170 cms. At the right are separate graphs, showing the proportions of four major tree types through the years. During the occupation of the site, birch trees were the dominant species near the lake, where the people lived. Pine trees were fairly common, too, but elm and alder, both trees associated with warmer weather, were almost nonexistent. In about 7000 B.C. the proportion of birch trees fell sharply, there was a rapid increase in the pine cover, and elms became much more common. At the end of the sequence pine trees were being supplanted by elms and a few alders, and the birch trees were much more rare. It can be seen that the climate had warmed up considerably since the Star Carr people camped among the birch trees. Interestingly, the inhabitants seem to have had no effect on the tree cover. In addition, grass pollens, indicative of open country, are rare in this diagram.

belongs within that particular period. An example appears in Figure 6.14.

Pollen analysis has important applications for later prehistory as well. Improved recovery and excavation methods have opened up all sorts of new possibilities. Southwestern archaeologists now have a regional pollen sequence at their disposal, one that provides not only climatic information but also invaluable information on the functions of different pueblo rooms and different foods that were eaten by the Indians.

Pollen samples from pueblo rooms at Broken K pueblo in eastern Arizona were even used to place individual rooms in the correct chronological order. James Hill and Richard Hevly (1968) collected pollen samples from about fifty rooms in the pueblo, which was occupied, tree rings told them, between A.D. 1100 and 1300—a period when the area was gradually losing its tree cover. By correlating the individual pollen samples with the profile of declining tree cover, Hill and Hevly were able to place the various rooms in order of construction.

At the Lehner site in southern Arizona, three different pollen profiles were combined to show that the groundcover around this early hunting site was probably a desert grassland. The climate seems to have been much the same as it is today (Mehringer and Haynes, 1965). So much palynological information is available from the Southwest that it may be possible to place individual sites into their correct relative chronological position in the vegetational sequence on the basis of pollen frequencies in samples taken from the undated site.

Relative chronology is an invaluable tool for archaeological research. Unfortunately, however, it does not provide accurate dates in years, the ultimate objective of all chronological research. Chapter 7 outlines the major methods used to date archaeological sites in calendar years.

Guide to Further Reading

Brothwell, D. R., and Higgs, Eric, eds. *Science in Archaeology.* 2 ed. New York: Praeger, 1969.
A series of essays on dating and other scientific approaches to archaeology. There are some articles that cover relative chronology.

Butzer, Karl. *Environment and Archaeology.* 2 ed. Aldine: Chicago, 1974.
The fundamental synthesis of Pleistocene geochronology. This is recommended for more advanced readers.

Deetz, James. *Invitation to Archaeology.* Garden City, N.Y.: Natural History Press, 1967.
The best account of seriation for the lay person yet written, penned by someone closely involved with basic research in this field.

Taylor, R. E., and Meighan, C., eds. *Chronologies in New World Archaeology.* New York: Academic Press, 1978.
A series of articles on chronology in American archaeology. Up to date and informative.

CHAPTER 7 ❧

TIME: CHRONOMETRIC DATING

Preview

- Although historical records provide a fairly accurate chronology for much of the past 5,000 years, archaeologists rely heavily on chemical and physical chronometric dating methods.
- Potassium argon methods are used for dating the earliest humans. These can be used to determine dates from the origins of the earth up to about 400,000 years ago. This radioactive counting method is based on the measurements of accumulations of argon 40 in volcanic rocks. It has been used to date Olduvai Gorge and other early sites to between one and three million years.
- Radiocarbon dating is the most widely used method. It can be used at sites between 75,000 and 400 years ago. Based on the decay rate of carbon 14 to nitrogen in organic objects, it can be used to date a wide range of such materials as charcoal and bone to even skin and leather. The accuracy of radiocarbon dating is subject to statistical errors, owing to past variations in the C-14 content of the atmosphere, and thus it has to be calibrated against tree-ring chronologies.
- Fission track dating is based on measurement of the uranium content of many minerals and volcanic glasses and examination of the fission tracks in the material caused by the fragmentation of massive concentrations of energy-charged particles. It has applications in sites between a million and 100,000 years old, where volcanic rocks are found in humanly occupied levels.

- The annual sedimentary layers, or varves, of melting and retreating glaciers in the Americas and Scandinavia have provided a means of dating geological events at the end of the Ice Age.
- Thermoluminescence may prove to be a method of dating potsherds, whose baked clay traps electrons, which are released for measurement by sudden and intense heating under controlled conditions. The visible light rays emitted during heating are known as thermoluminescence. This method is still highly experimental.
- Amino acid racemization can be applied to small fragments of fossil bone dating from about 100,000 to 5,000 years ago. Amino acids, which form collagen, a fibrous protein that forms 90–95 percent of all organic material in bones, slowly racemize. This chemical reaction can be measured, and dates obtained, provided temperature and other variables are controlled. This controversial method has been applied to human remains from California and East Africa.
- Dendrochronology (tree-ring dating) has its principal application in the American Southwest. It provides an accurate chronology for about 2,000 years of Southwestern prehistory, and it has many uses on more recent sites in Europe and elsewhere. Dendrochronologists count the annual growth rings on trees, such as the bristlecone pine, and correlate them into long sequences of growth years that are joined to a master chronology. Wooden beams and other archaeological wood fragments are correlated with this master chronology to provide accurate dates for pueblos and other sites.
- Archaeomagnetic dating can be used to date clay samples from furnaces and other features, by measuring the thermoremnant magnetism of the clay and correlating it with records of changes in the earth's magnetic field. It is mainly used to date pottery kilns and similar structures dating to the last 500 years, when records of the magnetic field have been recorded.
- Historical records and calendars developed by such people as the Ancient Egyptians and the Maya are of immense value for dating their literate civilizations. A great deal of valuable chronological information can also be obtained from objects of known age, such as clay pipes or coins. But, again, these objects are confined to the most recent periods of human history.

More effort has been devoted to invent methods of chronometric dating in archaeology than to almost any other aspect of the subject. It is hardly surprising, for fundamental questions about the past are involved. How old is this tool? How long ago was that site occupied? Are these villages contemporary? These are probably the first questions asked by anyone curious about an artifact or a prehistoric village, as well as by the archaeologists. They remain some of the most difficult questions to answer.

An impressive array of chronological techniques has been developed to date the past. Some have become well-established, reliable methods of dating. Others, after a brief vogue, have been ejected into academic oblivion upon the discovery of some fatal flaw. In practice, the huge span of human cultural history is dated by a number of scientific methods; the chronological span is shown in Table 7.1. Potassium argon dating provides a somewhat generalized chronology for the first two-thirds of human history, its recent limits reaching up to some 400,000 years ago. The other major radioactive technique, radiocarbon dating, covers a period from approximately 75,000 years ago up to as recently as A.D. 1500, when the standard errors become too large when compared with the small time spans involved. No one has yet developed a dating method to cover the 350,000 years or so between the outer limits of radiocarbon dating and the beginnings of potassium argon chronology.

As for recent periods, historical documents provide a fairly accurate chronology for kings and political events going back over 5,000 years in the Near East and shorter periods elsewhere in the world. In the New World, prehistory ends with European settlement of the Americas in the fifteenth century. These more recent periods, frequently times when archaeology can be used in conjunction with historical documents or oral records, are covered by many other dating methods, including the use of imported objects of known historical date and dendrochronology. Dates in years not only tell how old a site is, but also illuminate the relationships between different communities, cultures, or larger geographic or social units.

CHEMICAL AND PHYSICAL DATING METHODS

Let us now look at the principal methods of chronometric dating used to develop absolute chronologies for world prehistory. Our discussion starts with the chemical and physical dating methods used to date the earlier millennia of prehistory and ends in modern times with the use of objects of known age.

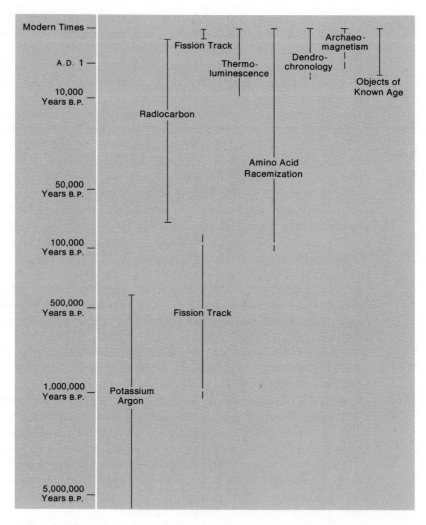

Table 7.1 Chronological spans of major chronometric methods in archaeology.

POTASSIUM ARGON DATING

Principles. The only viable means of chronometrically dating the earliest archaeological sites is through the potassium argon method (Dalrymple and Lamphere, 1970). Geologists use this radioactive counting technique to date rocks as old as 2 billion and as recent as

400,000 years ago. Potassium (K) is one of the most abundant elements in the earth's crust and is present in nearly every mineral. In its natural form, potassium contains a small proportion of radioactive ^{40}K atoms. For every 100 ^{40}K atoms that decay, 11 percent become Argon 40, an inactive gas that can easily escape from its material by diffusion when lava and other igneous rocks are formed. As volcanic rock forms by crystallization, the concentration of Argon 40 drops to almost nothing. But the process of regular and reasonable decay over time of ^{40}K will continue, with a half-life of 1.3 billion years. So, it is possible to measure the concentration of Argon 40 that has accumulated since the rock formed, using a spectrometer. Since many archaeological sites were occupied during a period when extensive volcanic activity occurred, especially in East Africa, it is possible to date them through associations of lava with human settlements.

Datable Materials and Procedures.   Potassium argon dates have been obtained from a wide range of igneous minerals, of which the most resistant to later argon diffusion are biotite, muscovite, and sanidine. Microscopic examination of the rock is essential to eliminate the possibility of contamination by recrystallization and other processes. The samples are processed by crushing the rock, concentrating it, and treating it with hydrofluoric acid to remove possible atmospheric argon from the sample. The various gases are then removed from the sample and the argon gas isolated and subjected to mass spectrographic analysis. The age of the sample is then calculated using the Argon 40 and ^{40}K contents and a standard formula. The resulting date is quoted with a large standard deviation—in the case of early Pleistocene sites, in the order of a quarter of a million years.

Archaeological Applications.   Fortunately, many early human settlements in the Old World are found in volcanic areas, where such deposits as lava flows and tuffs are found in profusion.

The first, and one of the most dramatic, archaeological date to be obtained from this method came from Olduvai Gorge, Tanzania, where Louis and Mary Leakey found a long sequence of human culture extending over much of the Lower and Middle Pleistocene, associated with human fossils. Olduvai, a jagged slash in the Serengeti Plains, was formed by earth movement and erosion that exposed the beds of a long-forgotten Pleistocene lake overlying a layer of volcanic tuff. Early humans camped around the shores of the lake; their living floors are preserved in the sides of the gorge, and their implements and broken animal bones lie on them where they were dropped by their owners, to be preserved under layers of fine lake silt. The remains of early humans have been found on the living floors, associated with the tools and bones, together with lumps of lava deposited naturally by the lake. Some layers overlying and underlying the floors have been dated by the potassium argon technique. Samples from a living floor where the first cranium of *Australopithecus boisei* was discovered were dated to about 1.75 million years (Figure 7.1) (Leakey, 1971). At the time, these and other nearly contemporary dates were a sensation, for most people had imagined that the Pleistocene began about a million years ago. With a single discovery, humankind had almost doubled its antiquity. Even earlier dates have come from the Omo Valley in southern Ethiopia, where American, French, and Kenyan expeditions have investigated extensive Lower Pleistocene deposits long known for their rich fossil beds. Fragmentary Australopithecines were found at several localities, but there were no traces of tools; potassium argon dates gave readings between 2 and 4 million for deposits yielding hominid fossils. Tools were found in levels between two dates of 2 and 2.5 million years. Chopper tools of undoubted human manufacture have come

Figure 7.1 Skull of *Australopithecus boisei,* with reconstructed jaw, from Bed I at Olduvai Gorge, Tanzania, potassium argon dated to about 1.75 million years ago.

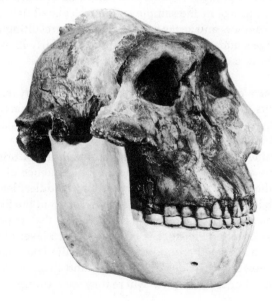

from Koobi Fora in northern Kenya, dated to about 1.85 million years, at the present time one of the earliest dates for human artifacts (Curtis, 1975).

Limitations.   Potassium argon dates can be taken only from volcanic rocks, and preferably from actual volcanic flows. The laboratory technique is so specialized that only a trained geologist should take the samples in the field. Archaeologically, it is obviously vital that the relationship between the lava being dated and the human settlement it purports to date be worked out carefully. The standard deviations for potassium argon dates are so large that a higher degree of accuracy is almost impossible to achieve.

Chronological Limits (Table 7.1)   Potassium argon dating is accurate from the origins of the earth up to about 400,000 years before present.

RADIOCARBON DATING

Principles.   Radiocarbon dating is perhaps the best known and most widely used of all chronometric dating methods. It was in 1949 that J. R. Arnold and W. F. Libby published a paper in *Science* describing the dating of organic samples from objects of known age by their radiocarbon content (Arnold and Libby, 1949). The paper caused an archaeological furor, but once checked out, it was soon applied to organic materials from prehistoric sites hitherto undated by any reliable chronometric method. Over thirty years have elapsed since the radiocarbon dating method became a regular part of the archaeologist's tool kit. For the first time a world chronology for prehistory has begun to emerge, based almost entirely on dates obtained from Libby's technique.

The radiocarbon dating method is based on the fact that cosmic radiation produces neutrons that enter the earth's atmosphere and react with nitrogen. They produce the carbon isotope carbon 14, an isotope that contains fourteen rather than the usual twelve neutrons in the nucleus. With these additional neutrons, the nucleus is unstable and is subject to gradual radioactive decay. Willard Libby calculated that it took 5,568 years for half of the C-14 in any sample to decay, the so-called half-life of carbon 14. He found that the neurons emitted radioactive particles when they left the nucleus and developed a method for counting the number of emissions in a gram of carbon.

Carbon 14 is believed to behave exactly like ordinary carbon from a chemical standpoint, and together with ordinary carbon it enters into the carbon dioxide of the atmosphere, in which a constant amount of carbon 14 is to be found. The tempo of the process corresponds to the rates of supply and disintegration. Since living vegetation builds up its own organic matter by photosynthesis and by using atmospheric carbon dioxide, the proportion of radiocarbon present in it is equal to that in the atmosphere. The very short lifetime of individual plants is negligible compared with the half-life of radiocarbon. As soon as an organism dies, no further radiocarbon is incorporated into it. The radiocarbon present in the dead organism will continue to disintegrate slowly, so that after 5,568 years only half the original amount will be left; after about 11,100 years, only a quarter; and so on. Thus, if you measure the rate of disintegration of carbon 14 to carbon 12, you can obtain an idea of the age of the specimen being measured. The initial amount of radiocarbon in a particular sample is low, so the limit of detectability is soon reached. Samples earlier than 75,000 years contain only miniscule quantities of carbon 14 (Grootes, 1978).

Datable Materials and Procedures. Radiocarbon dates can be taken from samples of a wide range of organic material. About a handful of charcoal, burnt bone, shell, hair, skin, wood, or other organic substance is needed. The samples themselves are collected with meticulous care during excavation from impeccable stratigraphical contexts, so that an exact location, specific structure, or even hearth is dated. Several dates

Figure 7.2 A radiocarbon laboratory at the University Museum, University of Pennsylvania. Left: The equipment used to purify the sample and convert it to gas. Right: The equipment used for measuring radioactivity.

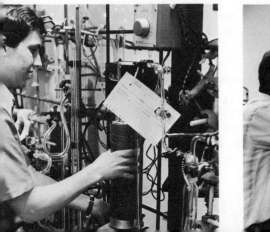

should be taken from each level, as one sample may have been contaminated by a variety of factors. Modern rootlets, disturbances in the stratigraphy, and even packing with cotton wool or in newspapers can introduce younger carbon into an ancient sample, although some more obvious contaminations are eliminated by careful laboratory treatment.

The first stage in the dating procedure is a physical examination of the sample. The material is then converted into gas, purified to remove radioactive impurities, and then piped into a proportional counter (Figure 7.2). The proportional counter itself is sheltered by massive iron shields to protect it against background radiation. The sample is counted at least twice at intervals of about a week. The results of the count are then compared to a modern count sample, and the age of the sample is then computed by a formula to produce the radiocarbon date and its statistical limit of error.

When a date is received from a radiocarbon dating laboratory it reads as follows:

$$3621 \pm 180 \text{ radiocarbon years before present (b.p.)}$$

The figure 3621 is the age of the sample in radiocarbon years before the present. With all radiocarbon dates, A.D. 1950, the date Libby announced the method, is taken as the present by international agreement. Note that the sample reads in *radiocarbon years*, not calendar years. Corrections must be applied to make this an absolute date.

The radiocarbon age has the reading ± 180 attached to it. This is the standard deviation, an estimate of the amount of probable error. The figure of 180 years is an estimate of the range within which the date falls. Statistical theory provides that there is a 2 out of 3 chance that the correct date is between the span of one standard deviation (3441 and 3801). If we double the deviation, chances are 19 out of 20 that the span (3261 to 3981) is correct. Most dates in this book are derived from C-14 dated samples and should be recognized for what they are—statistical approximations.

The conventional radiocarbon method relies on the measurement of a beta-ray decay rate to date the sample. A number of laboratories are now experimenting with an ultrasensitive mass spectrometer to count the individual C-14 atoms in a sample instead. This exciting new approach has numerous advantages which promise to overcome many of the disadvantages of the traditional method. One can date much smaller samples—samples as small as a fragment of straw in a potsherd—and the results will be more accurate than conventional readings. It takes only a few minutes to measure samples that hitherto took hours to study. The outer chronological limits of radiocarbon dating can be extended to 75,000 years and perhaps beyond. Furthermore, this technique is so precise that it distinguishes carbon 14 from all other particles, making cosmic ray bombardment no longer a problem. The mass spectrometry approach to radiocarbon dating will make it possible to obtain more accurate dates from a far wider range of materials. It should result in many refinements to existing radiocarbon chronologies (Pavlish and Banning, 1980).

Archaeological Applications.   Radiocarbon dates have been obtained from African hunter-gatherers' settlements dating to as long as 50,000 years before the present, from Paleo-Indian bison kills in the American Plains, from early farming villages in the Near East and the Americas, and from early cities and spectacular temples associated with the world's early civilizations. The method can be applied to sites of almost any type where organic materials are found, provided they date to between about 75,000 years ago and A.D. 1500.

Limitations.   Radiocarbon dates can be obtained only from organic materials, which means that relatively few artifacts can be dated. But associated hearths with abundant charcoal, broken animal bones, and burnt wooden structures can be dated. Artifacts contemporary with such phenomena are obviously the same age as the dated samples. The context of any dated sample has to be established beyond all doubt, and having a block of samples from the same division is preferable, so that they can be treated statistically and tested for probable degree of accuracy. It should also be noted that it is the moment of death of an organism that is dated. All radiocarbon dates are, of course, statistical computations, and if uncalibrated, merely the statistically most likely radiocarbon age.

Calibration of Radiocarbon Dates.   Just when archaeologists thought that they had at last found an accurate and reliable means of dating the past, radiocarbon dates for tree rings of the California bristlecone pine were published. The readings were consistently younger with trees before 1200 B.C., because Libby had made a false assumption when he originally formulated the radiocarbon method. He had argued that the concentration of radiocarbon in living things remained constant as time passed, so that prehistoric samples, when alive, would contain the same amount of radiocarbon as living things today.

In fact, changes in the strength of the earth's magnetic field and

C14 / corrected date	Radiocarbon date (Half-life of 5,568 years)	Calibrated date: Corrected date in years[a]
Earlier Later	A.D. 1800	A.D. 1685
	A.D. 1500	A.D. 1440
	A.D. 1000	A.D. 1030
	A.D. 500	A.D. 535
	250 B.C.	320 B.C.
	500 B.C.	550 B.C.
	1000 B.C.	1250 B.C.
	1500 B.C.	1835 B.C.
	2000 B.C.	2520 B.C.
	2500 B.C.	3245 B.C.
	3000 B.C.	3785 B.C.
	3500 B.C.	4375 B.C.
	4000 B.C.	4845 B.C.
	4500 B.C.	5350 B.C.
Corrected C14 date date		

[a] The corrections are tabulated at 500-year intervals and are based on a table published by R. M. Clark in 1975, a statistical treatment of the various laboratory calculations so far available. It is anyone's guess how much earlier or later radiocarbon ages earlier than 4500 B.C. would be if calibrated.

Table 7.2   Approximate variations between radiocarbon ages and calibrated radiocarbon dates between 4500 B.C. and modern times.

alterations in solar activity have considerably varied the concentration of radiocarbon in the atmosphere and in living things. Thus, samples of 6,000 years ago were exposed to a much higher concentration than living things today. It is possible, fortunately, to correct radiocarbon dates by using accurate dates from tree rings. Since 1966, dendrochronology experts have been systematically radiocarbon dating tree-ring samples of known age and have developed calibration curves, which are used for converting radiocarbon dates into actual dates in years. One provisional calibration curve is illustrated here (Table 7.2). Archaeologists have been understandably cautious about using the calibration curves until they know how accurate they are (Renfrew, 1973; Suess, 1965). British archaeologist Colin Renfrew has calibrated the radiocarbon dates for European prehistory, and he claims that many long-accepted chronological relationships are now reversed as a result. According to him, the famous megalithic, stone-built tombs of western

Europe are older than the pyramids of Egypt, their supposed predecessors. The final layout of Stonehenge constructed in 1600 B.C., (the
complex of prehistoric stone circles in southern Britain), was originally
thought to have been inspired by Mycenaean designs. When the calibrated dates were released, it was found that Stonehenge dated to
before 1800 B.C., much older than the Mycenaean civilization in question. The new, calibrated radiocarbon chronology for Europe, argues
Renfrew, allows us to think of distinctive European societies that developed their own institutions without the Oriental influence favored
by so many archaeologists. Few prehistorians have jumped so whole-
heartedly into the new chronologies as Renfrew, but widespread calibration of radiocarbon dates is certain to be a reality within a few years.
In the meantime, most people think of radiocarbon dates as nothing
more than *radiocarbon ages*—not dates in actual years. Earlier dates will
remain radiocarbon ages of unknown accuracy, because there is as yet
no means of extending dendrochronology further back into the past.

Chronological Limits (Table 7.1).   Carbon 14 dating is accurate from *ca.*
75,000 years B.P. to A.D.

FISSION TRACK DATING

Principles.   Fission track dating is a new chronometric method that
promises to have important archaeological applications in the future.
The principle of the method is that many minerals and natural glasses,
such as obsidian, contain very small quantities of uranium that under-
goes slow, spontaneous decay. Most uranium atoms decay by emitting
alpha particles, but spontaneous fission causes the decay of about one
atom in every two million. The fission decay rate and its extent are
constant, and the date of any mineral containing uranium can be obtained by measuring the amount of uranium in the sample by counting
the *fission tracks* in the material. These fission tracks are narrow trails of
damage in the material caused by fragmentation of massive, energy-
charged particles. The older the sample, the more tracks. It is possible
to examine fission tracks under high magnification and to calculate the
sample's age by establishing the ratio between the density of the tracks
and the uranium content of the sample.

Datable Materials and Procedures.   Two counts of fission tracks are
needed for each sample. The materials used, which must have a high

uranium content, can be either volcanic rocks, such as lava flows that originated more recently than the beginnings of prehistory, or manufactured materials, such as certain types of artificial glass. In the case of rocks, the time of origin of the rocks is being dated, not the time of their utilization. An optical microscope is used to examine the tracks in the sample, which have first been etched with hydrofluoric acid. This procedure serves to enlarge the tracks and to make them more visible. The first count establishes the density of the tracks, the second makes a count of the uranium content in the sample. This is done by inducing fission of uranium 235 through neutron irradiation. The age of the sample is the ratio between the number of observed tracks resulting from natural fission to those resulting from induced fission.

Archaeological Applications.   The fission track dating technique is still new to archaeology, but it promises to become a fairly precise means of dating samples between 100,000 and 1,000,000 years old. The method can be used to date a wide range of mineralogical materials, but in archaeology, it is applicable only to sites that were subjected to volcanic activity just before, during, or shortly after occupation. Sites overlain or underlain by lava can be given upper or lower age limits by dating the lava. Because many early sites are found in volcanic areas, such as the Great Rift Valley of East Africa, the method has obvious applications.

Few results from the fission track method have been published, but volcanic pumice from Bed I at Olduvai Gorge, where the early hominid fossils were found, was dated to 2.03 ± 0.28 million by the fission track method. This reading was in reasonably close agreement with Leakey's original date of about 1.8 million years, obtained from potassium argon readings for the same stratum. In another case, modern manufactured glass with a high uranium content, used to make a nineteenth-century candlestick, was dated accurately to the last century. (Brill, 1964; Fleischer, 1975).

Limitations.   The limitations of fission track dating are much the same as those of potassium argon dating. Only volcanic rocks contemporary with a human settlement and formed at the time the site was occupied can be used.

Chronological Limits (see Table 7.1).   Fission track dating is accurate from one million to 100,000 years before the present. There is some limited application to historic artifacts as well.

VARVES

Until the development of such chronometric dating methods as the potassium argon, fission track, and radiocarbon techniques, the chronology of the major events of the Pleistocene epoch was mostly uncertain, despite many efforts to develop viable time scales.

An accurate chronology for parts of the Pleistocene has been developed by counting varves, annually deposited layers of silt laid down in glacial lakes by runoff from melting ice sheets (Zeuner, 1958). As long ago as 1878, Swedish geologist Baron Gerard DeGeer recorded this phenomenon and began a chronology for retreating ice sheets at the end of the Pleistocene, a timescale that in places now extends back as far as 17,000 years. Varve dating is applicable only in areas where ice sheets were present during the Pleistocene and where it is possible to develop a continuous varve chronology from modern times to link up with Pleistocene varves. Although experiments with varve chronology have been attempted in North America, Africa, and South America, the method's main application is in Scandinavia, for dating the closing stages of the Pleistocene. Archaeological sites are rarely dated by varve readings, for Pleistocene settlements near glacial lakes are very uncommon. But it is sometimes possible to correlate varve sequences with other Pleistocene features associated with human occupation.

THERMOLUMINESCENCE

Principles, Datable Materials, and Procedures.   Thermoluminescence, a pottery dating method with a formidable sounding name, is still in the developmental stage (Aitken, 1977; Fleming, 1979). It holds considerable promise and may one day provide absolute dating of even isolated potsherds. The principle is simple. The materials from which pottery, dating method with a formidable sounding name, is still in electrons as atomic defects or impurity sites. This stored energy can be released by heating the pottery, at which time visible light rays are emitted, known as thermoluminescence. All pottery and ceramics contain some radioactive impurities to a concentration of several parts per million. These materials emit alpha particles at a known rate, depending on how densely concentrated they are in the sample. When an alpha particle is absorbed by the pottery minerals around the radioactive impurities, it causes mineral atoms to ionize. Electrons are then released from their binding to the nuclei and later settle at a metastable stage of higher energy. This energy is stored, unless the parent material is heated—for example, during the firing of the pot—when the trapped electrons are released and thermoluminescence occurs. After the pot is fired, alpha particles are again absorbed by the material, and the thermoluminescence increases with time until the pot is heated again. Thus, to date a clay vessel involves measuring the thermoluminescence of the sample, as well as its alpha-radioactivity and its potential susceptibility to the production of thermoluminescence. In the laboratory, the trapped electrons are released from a powdered pottery fragment by sudden and violent heating under controlled conditions.

Archaeological Applications and Limitations.   The method is still being developed, and there are numerous factors that affect its accuracy. As with other dating methods, results have been obtained initially from vessels of known age; because of these results, several investigators claim accuracies of ±10 percent for prehistoric dates. Other proponents of the method are more cautious, however. The potential of thermoluminescence will not fully be assessed for some time; but its future use could be unlimited for later prehistory, for pottery is one of the most common archaeological finds. Theoretically, thermoluminescence works with all previously heated objects. Experiments with accidentally and intentionally heated stones have produced results that may presage a new dating technique that could be applied directly to stone artifacts. This would bridge the gap between radiocarbon dating and potassium argon dating. But it is too early to say whether the method is workable, because it is still highly experimental.

AMINO ACID RACEMIZATION

Principles, Datable Materials, and Procedures.   This new method for dating fossil bones provides a potentially valuable tool for studying the origins of modern humans. It can be applied to small fragments of fossil bone dating from about 100,000 years ago to *ca.* 5000 years before the present (Bada and Hoffman, 1975).

Racemization dating is based on the fact that amino acids, which make collagen, a fibrous protein that forms 90 or 95 percent of all organic material in bones, consist only of L-isomers (molecules that rotate polarized light to the left). Over long periods of geological time, however, these L-amino acids slowly racemize (a process of change in the rotation direction of polarized light) and produce corresponding D-isomers (molecules that rotate polarized light to the right). Both L- and D-amino acids are found in fossil bones. The D:L amino acid ratio increases with the age of the bone. Racemization is a chemical reaction that is sensitive to temperature change. The average temperature to which the bone has been exposed has to be estimated, from pollen diagrams or other data, to allow for temperature change errors. Alternatively, a calibrated amino acid reading can be obtained by taking a D:L amino acid ratio from a radiocarbon-dated bone. The corrections taken from the comparison of both readings can then be applied to D:L readings from other sites in the same region. The most common amino acid used in fossil bone dating is Aspartic acid, which has one of the fastest racemization rates of all the stable amino acids. Aspartic acid's half-life is about 15,000 years at a temperature of 20° C, which means that the technique can be used to date bones much earlier than the 75,000-year limit of C-14. Since only a few grams of fossil bone are needed, amino acid racemization can be used to date samples too small to be dated by radiocarbon.

Archaeological Applications.   Amino acid racemization has been applied with interesting results to Paleo-Indian skeletons from California. Two skeletons found north of San Diego have been dated to *ca.* 50,000 years, a date that could reopen the controversy about the date of the earliest Americans. Additional dates in excess of 40,000 years have been calculated from samples taken from prehistoric skeletons found near Del Mar, Scripps Institute of Oceanography, and La Jolla, in southern California (Figure 7.3). Amino acid racemization readings taken from relatively recent sites in Olduvai Gorge, Klasies River Mouth Cave in South Africa, and other locations for the most part agree with radiocarbon dates or chronological evidence from other sources.

Amino acid racemization methods are still in their infancy, but they appear to have great promise.

Limitations.   Since the method dates bones, the problem of associating the bones with artifacts is vital. The important southern California dates mentioned above come from skeletons whose archaeological contexts are still uncertain. Clearly, a dated skeleton that is out of cultural and archaeological context is almost useless. Environmental factors play an important part in establishing the reliability of dates, too. In the case of samples more than 10,000 years old, one has to allow for fairly radical fluctuations in air temperatures as a result of the last

Figure 7.3   Laguna cranium from California, one of the early specimens dated by amino acid racemization and radiocarbon to 17,150 ± 1470 years ago.

glaciation. Although temperature estimates can be generated by evaluation and calculation, humidity may affect racemization rates as well. Those experimenting with this important dating method no doubt will produce techniques for overcoming these problems.

Chronological Range (see Table 7.1).   Amino acid racemization is accurate from one hundred thousand years or more to the present.

DENDROCHRONOLOGY

Principles.   Dendrochronology, or tree-ring dating, was developed in Arizona by Dr. A. E. Douglass in about 1913 (Bannister, 1969). However, the idea of using tree rings as a method of dating archaeological sites is much older. As early as 1788, the Reverend Manasseh Cutler was counting the rings on trees growing on archaeological sites near Marietta, Ohio, and suggested that the site he was studying was about a thousand years old. But the prehistoric time scale established from tree rings goes back considerably further into the past, especially in the Southwest, where it has been applied successfully to wooden beams in ancient pueblos preserved by dry, desert conditions. Both the slow-growing sequoia and the California bristlecone pine *(Pinus aristata)* provide long tree-ring sequences, the latter providing a continuous tree-ring chronology of 8,200 years. One pine tree 4,900 years old has been reported.

Everyone is familiar with tree rings, concentric series of circles, each circle representing annual growth, visible on the cross section of a felled trunk. These rings are formed on all trees but especially in areas where there is a marked seasonal weather change, either a wet and dry season, or a marked alternation of summer and winter temperatures. As a rule, trees produce one growth ring a year, which is formed by the cambium lying between the wood and the bark. When the growing season starts, sets of large cells are added to the wood. These cells become thicker walled and smaller as the growing season progresses; by the end of the growth season, cell production has ceased altogether. This process occurs every growing year; and a distinct line is formed between the wood of the previous season, with its small cells, and the wood of the next, with its new, large cells. The thickness of each ring may vary according to the tree's age and annual climatic variations, thick rings being characteristic of good growth years.

Weather variations within a cricumscribed area tend to run in cycles. A decade of wet years may be followed by five dry decades. One season may bring a forty-year rainfall record. These cycles of climate are reflected in patterns of thicker or thinner rings, which are repeated from tree to tree within a limited area. Dendrochronologists have developed sophisticated methods of correlating sets of rings from different trees so that they build up long sequences of rings from a number of trunks that may extend over many centuries (Figure 7.4). By using modern trees, whose date of felling is known, they are able to reconstruct accurate dating as far back as 8,200 years ago. Actual applications to archaeological wood are much harder, but archaeological chronology for the American Southwest now goes back to 59 B.C.

Datable Materials and Procedures.   The most common dated tree is the Douglas fir. It has consistent rings that are easy to read and was much used in prehistoric buildings. Piñon and sagebrush are usable, too. Since the latter was commonly used as firewood, its charred remains are of special archaeological interest. The location of the sample tree is important. Trees growing on well-drained, gently sloping soils are best, for their rings display sufficient annual variation to make them more easily datable. The rings of trees in places with permanent abundant water supplies are too regular to be usable.

Samples are normally collected by cutting a full cross section from an old beam no longer in place, by using a special core borer to obtain

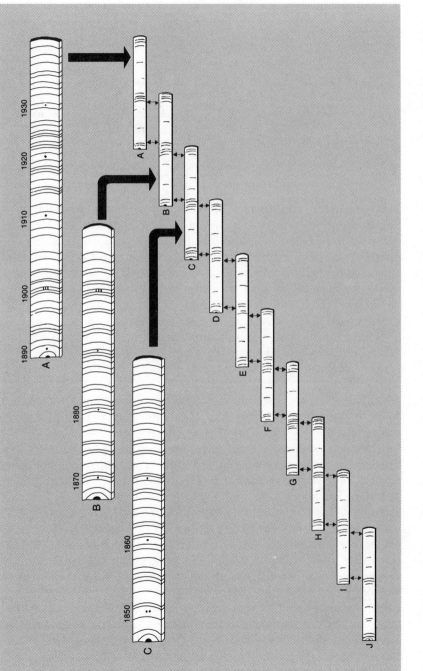

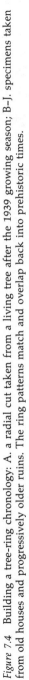

Figure 7.4   Building a tree-ring chronology: A. a radial cut taken from a living tree after the 1939 growing season; B–J. specimens taken from old houses and progressively older ruins. The ring patterns match and overlap back into prehistoric times.

samples from beams still in place, or by V-cutting exceptionally large logs. Delicate or brittle samples are impregnated with paraffin or coated with shellac before examination.

Once in the laboratory, the surface of the sample is leveled to a precise plane. The analysis of tree rings consists of recording individual ring series and then comparing them against other series. Comparisons can be made by eye or by plotting all of the rings on a uniform scale, so that one series can be compared with another. The series so plotted can then be matched with the master tree-ring chronology for the region. Measuring the tree rings accurately, too, can add precision to the plottings.

Archaeological Applications.   The extremely accurate chronology for Southwestern sites has been achieved by correlating a master tree-ring sequence from felled trees and dated structures with beams from Indian pueblos. The beams in many such structures have been used again and again, and thus some are very much older than the houses they were most recently used to support. The earliest tree rings obtained from such settlements date to the first century B.C. but most timbers were in use between A.D. 1000 and historic times.

One of the most remarkable applications of tree-ring dating was carried out by Jeffrey Dean, who collected numerous samples from wooden beams at Batatakin, a cliff dwelling in northeastern Arizona dating to A.D. 1270. Dean ended up with no less than 292 samples, which he used to reconstruct a history of the cliff dwelling on literally a room by room basis (Dean, 1970). He found that three room clusters were built in 1267, and a fourth was added a year later. In 1269 the inhabitants trimmed and stockpiled a supply of beams for later use. These beams were not actually used until 1275, when ten more room clusters were added to Batatakin. Dean also found that the site was abandoned between 1286 and 1300. Such intrasite datings are only possible with a large number of samples to hand.

Dendrochronology has been used widely in Alaska, the Mississippi Valley, northern Mexico, Canada, Scandinavia, England, and Germany (Bannister and Robinson, 1975). But progress in several areas was slowed by a lack of old trees and of readily cross-datable samples as well as by evidence of irregular climatic fluctuations. In Ireland, living oaks have been dated back to A.D. 1649, and this chronology has been extended back, using beams from churches, forts, and farmhouses, to A.D. 1380. Medieval farmhouses and a Hanseatic ship buried in Bremen have taken tree-ring chronologies in Germany back to A.D. 1266. Celtic and Roman beams have been strung together in a floating chronology that has been cross dated with archaeological data for the period *ca.* 717 B.C. to *ca.* A.D. 339. Modern oak chronologies based on Trier and Speyer cathedrals in Germany go back to A.D. 383. These two chronologies have been joined to form a tree-ring sequence going back some 2,700 years. Dutch tree-ring experts have even used the oak panels utilized by painting masters to date and authenticate their paintings!

Arizona tree-ring laboratories are trying to analyze data on annual variability in rainfall from the many trees encompassed by their chronologies. A network of archaeological and modern chronologies provides a basis for reconstruction of changing climatic conditions over the past two thousand years. These varying conditions will be compared with the complex events of southwestern prehistory over the same period (Fritts, 1976). And, as mentioned earlier, radiocarbon dates are calibrated with the aid of dendrochronology.

Limitations. Dendrochronology has traditionally been limited to areas with well-defined seasonal rainfall. In locales where the climate is generally humid or cold, or in an area where trees enjoy a constant water supply, the difference in annual growth rings is either blurred or insignificant. Again, the context in which the archaeological tree-ring sample is found affects the usefulness of the sample. Many house beams, for example, are trimmed or reused several times, in order to remove the outside surface of the log. The felling date cannot be established accurately without carefully observing the context and archaeological association of the beam. For this reason, several dates must be obtained from each site. Artifacts found in a structure whose beams are dated do not necessarily belong to the same period, for the house may have been used over a period of several generations. Like any other chronometric dating method, dendrochronology requires meticulous on-site observations and very careful sample collection.

Chronological Range (Table 7.1)   Dendrochronology is accurate from approximately 2000 years ago to the present, with possibility of wider application. However, non-archaeological tree ring dates extend back 8200 years.

ARCHAEOMAGNETIC DATING

Principles.   We know that the direction and intensity of the earth's magnetic field varied throughout prehistoric time. Many clays and clay soils contain magnetic minerals, which when heated to a dull red heat, will assume the direction and intensity of the earth's magnetic field at the moment of heating. Thus, if the changes in the earth's magnetic field have been recorded over centuries, or even millennia, it is possible to date any suitable sample of clay material that is known to have been heated by correlating the thermoremanent magnetism of the heated clay with records of the earth's magnetic field (Figure 7.5) (Traling, 1971; 1975). Archaeologists frequently discover structures with well-baked clay floors, ovens, kilns, and iron-smelting furnaces, to name only a few, whose burnt clay can be used for archaeomagnetic dating. Of course, reheated clays (clays used again after their original heating) will change their magnetic readings and are thus useless for archaeomagnetic dating.

Thermoremanent magnetism results from the ferromagnetism of

Figure 7.5 The meandering of the geomagnetic North Pole, worked out over a period of 8000 years.

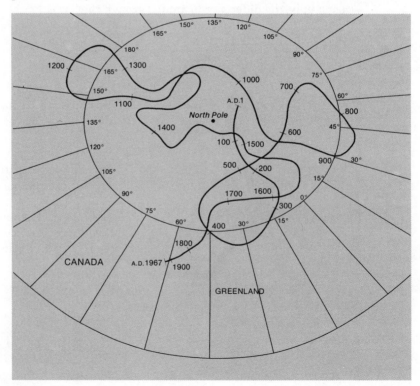

magnetite and hematite, minerals that are found in significant quantities in most soils. When the soil containing these minerals is heated,
the magnetic particles in magnetite and hematite change from a random alignment to one that conforms with that of the earth's magnetic
field. In effect, the heated lump of clay becomes a very weak magnet
that can be measured by a device called a parastatic magnetometer. A
record of the magnetic declination and dip similar to that of the actual
earth's magnetic field at the time of heating is preserved in the clay
lump. The alignment of the magnetic particles fixed by heating is called
thermoremanent magnetism.

Datable Materials and Procedures.   The selection of a kiln or other
baked structure for magnetic dating is far from straightforward. Substantial floors of well-baked clay are best for the purpose. Tiny pillars
of burnt clay, of such a size that they will fit into a brass-framed
extraction jig, are extracted from the floor. The jig is oriented to present-day north-south and fitted over the pillars, which are then encap-
sulated in melted dental plaster. The jig and pillar are carefully removed from the floor, and then the other side of the jig is covered with
dental plaster as well. The clay sample is placed under suspended
magnets and rotated. The scale will record the declination and dip of
the remnant magnetism in the clay.
    An absolute date for the sample can then be obtained if the long-
term, or *secular,* variation of the earth's field for the region is known.

Archaeological Applications and Limitations.   From the archaeological
point of view, archaeomagnetism has but limited applications, because
systematic records of the secular variation in the earth's magnetic field
have been recorded from only a few areas. Declination and dip have
been recorded in London for 400 years, and a very accurate record of
variations covers the period from A.D. 1600. France, Germany, Japan,
and the southwestern United States have received some attention.
From the latter, clay samples associated directly with dendrochron-
ological or radiocarbon samples have been tested, with one set of
readings from sixteen pre-Columbian villages extending back almost
2000 years. At the moment the method is limited, but as local variation
curves are recorded from more areas, archaeomagnetism is likely to be
far more useful for the more recent periods of prehistory, when kilns
and other burned clay features were in use.

Chronological Range (Table 7.1).   Archaeomagnetic dating is potentially useful from 2000 years ago to the present.

CALENDARS AND OBJECTS OF KNOWN AGE

Calendars.   Certainly, a calendar developed by an ancient civilization itself provides an excellent way of dating archaeological sites, provided that the calendar can be linked to our own chronology. The Mesopotamians and ancient Egyptians developed sophisticated calendars, and the Maya of the Yucatan had a calendric system that is justly famous (Coe, 1976). Calendars were used to regulate the agricultural and religious year in Egypt and Mesopotamia and played a vital role in organizing secular and religious life in the Yucatan.

The Maya enjoyed both a secular 365-day calendar and a 260-day religious calendar for timing religious ceremonies (Figure 7.6). They also developed a system of dating their own civilization in years, starting from a mythical date long before their own society was in being. Their dating system, known as the Long Count, is recorded on many stelae, along with inscriptions that signal important events or transfer

Figure 7.6   Mayan stelae are carved stone monuments that often record important dates in the lives of their rulers. (This stela records a date equivalent to A.D. 771.)

Figure 7.7 Part of an evolutionary series of bowl changes that occurred with English smoking pipes dating to between 1730 and 1830.

of priestly power. Attempts that have been made to link the Long Count and the Christian calendar place the span of the Mayan calendar from about 3113 B.C. to A.D. 889. Much of this time span is, of course, long before the Maya themselves emerged as a fully fledged state. But the Long Count stelae are a useful check on the dates of such well-known Mayan sites as Tikal and Palenque.

The most reliable chronometric dates are, of course, those obtained from historical documentation of archaeological sites. We know that King Henry VIII began to build his palace at Nonsuch, England, in A.D. 1538, as well as the chronology of Plimoth Plantation in Massachusetts, from contemporary records, and our primary interest lies in discovering details of settlement layout or day-to-day life. Many later sites yield easily dated artifacts, such as coins dropped by the inhabitants on the floors of buildings or elsewhere in the settlement's strata. Such objects can provide accurate dates for the earliest age of the archaeological sites being investigated.

Objects of Known Age.   Objects of known age found in African, North American, and European prehistoric sites include a bewildering array of artifacts, ranging from dated coins and glass bottles to Chinese porcelain and all manner of imported ceramics. The latter include American domestic tableware, English imported china, and Spanish *majolica* vessels in historic sites in North America. Ivor Noël Hume has compiled an invaluable compendium of artifacts from Colonial America that is a useful source book for anyone interested in such objects (Hume, 1969). Some of these types of finds can act as invaluable artifacts for cross dating prehistoric sites.

One of the most useful Colonial American artifacts is the imported English kaolin pipe (Figure 7.7). Not only were pipes manufactured, imported, smoked, and thrown away within a very short time, but the shape of the pipe body changed in an easily recognizable evolutionary chain. Clay pipes were so cheap that everyone, however poor, used and discarded them almost like cigarettes. Not only the pipe bowls but the length of the stem and the diameter of the holes changed between A.D. 1620 and 1800, and these characteristics have been used to date these artifacts and the sites associated with them with considerable precision (Oswald, 1975).

Stanley South and others have used statistical techniques to study the relationships between eighteenth-century English imported pottery and historic sites in North Carolina. They argued that once enough percentage relationships had been worked out, they would be able to date sites of unknown age by using the frequencies of imported pottery types (South, 1972). A surprisingly good correspondence was found to exist between the calculated median dates and the known historical date of the pottery forms.

Roger Grange (1972) has taken this method a step further and applied the ceramic dating formula to the Pawnee and Loup Loup ceramic tradition of the Great Plains. This tradition was estimated, from historical data and archaeological cross dating, to date from the period A.D. 1825 to 1846, when Pawnee potmaking died out, back to about A.D. 1500. Grange calculated median dates by using archaeological data derived from seriation, which gave the range of different types. He found that there was a fair degree of correspondence between the median dates and those obtained from the more conventional analyses. This was especially true when the greatest peaks of popularity for different pottery types were used as the basis of the formula calculations. Formula dating of this type may have considerable potential in areas where tree-ring chronologies or calibrated radiocarbon dates provide a basis for accurate median age calculations. And the advantages for cross dating of newly discovered sites are obvious.

The potential range of historic objects that can be dated to within surprisingly narrow chronological limits is enormous. Many people collect beer cans and openers, barbed wire, firearms, uniform buttons, even horseshoes. All of these artifacts, to say nothing of such prosaic objects as forks, electrical switch plates, and scissors, can be dated to within a few years by use of mail order catalogs, U.S. patent records, and a great deal of patient detective work. As Bernard Fontana has eloquently pointed out, bottles, buckets, and horseshoes may be the unrespectable artifacts of archaeology but, unlike many of their prehistoric relatives, they can be dated with great accuracy (Fontana, 1968). What better way to learn about archaeology than to study and date our own material culture!

Guide to Further Reading

The literature on chronometric dating is enormous, but the following volumes can be of great use to the student.

Brothwell, D. R., and Higgs, Eric S. *Science in Archaeology.* 2d ed. New York: Praeger, 1969.
A series of articles on major dating methods that provide admirable introductions to the subject.

Michael, H. N., and Ralph, E. K., eds. *Dating Techniques for the Archaeologist.* Cambridge: MIT Press, 1971.
Another series of articles on basic dating methods, but the content here is highly technical.

Michel, J. W. *Dating Methods in Archaeology.* New York: Seminar Press, 1973.
Probably the most widely read book on dating presently available. A good follow-up to this chapter.

Taylor, R. E., and Meighan, C. W. *Chronologies in New World Archaeology.* New York: Academic Press, 1978.
Essays on New World chronological problems.

CHAPTER 8 ⚜

THE PRESERVATION OF ARCHAEOLOGICAL DATA

Preview

- Traditionally, archaeologists have argued that the archaeological record is incomplete, since many items of material culture have been lost to decay and destruction.
- Lewis Binford and others have refused to accept the assumption that archaeology yields information only on material culture. They argue that data relevant to all components of past sociocultural systems are preserved in the archaeological record and that much depends on the recovery methods used to obtain archaeological data.
- Preservation conditions depend largely on the soil and general climatic regimen in the area of a site. Inorganic objects, such as stone and baked clay, can often survive almost indefinitely. But organic materials, such as bone, wood, leather, and so on, only survive under exceptional conditions, such as dry climate, in permafrost areas, and when waterlogged. The surviving picture of the past obtained from excavations is often confined to inorganic materials.
- Waterlogged and peat bog conditions are especially favorable to the preservation of wood and vegetal remains. This chapter discusses the Danish bog corpses and the Ozette site in Washington State as examples of these types of sites.
- Dry conditions can preserve almost the full range of human artifacts, the best examples being the remarkably complete preservation of ancient Egyptian culture and the comprehensive finds made in desert caves, such as Hogup cave in Utah, in the American West.

- The burials of horsemen at Pazyryk in Siberia provide an instance of how refrigerated conditions in the soil can preserve such organic materials as human skin, horse trappings, and even woven rugs. Arctic sites in Alaska have yielded priceless information on ancient ivory carving and Eskimo material culture.
- Later human activity can radically affect archaeological preservation. People can discard only certain types of artifacts, and many variables can affect the layout of settlements and other considerations. The example of Fulani compounds in West Africa is an instance of the difficulties of interpretation involved.
- Some people, such as the Southwestern Indians, recycled wooden beams and other materials, distorting the archaeological record. Sites are reused, lower strata are often disturbed, and sometimes succeeding generations will preserve an important building, such as a temple, for centuries. Modern warfare, industrial activity, even deep agriculture and cattle grazing can affect the preservation of archaeological remains.

Modern archaeologists have developed a battery of methods to recover fragile objects from the soil, for preservation is a major factor both in the discovery of archaeological sites and in our reconstruction and explanation of the past. This short chapter reviews archaeologists' approaches to site preservation and gives examples of unusually complete recoveries of the past. It examines, also, ways in which ancient human behavior can affect the preservation of archaeological data.

THE INCOMPLETE ARCHAEOLOGICAL RECORD

Traditionally, archaeologists have argued that the archaeological record is incomplete, since many items of material culture have been lost to decay and destruction. Wooden implements, baskets, and feather headdresses are in this category. Our interpretations of the archaeological record thus depend on how representative the surviving stone implements, pottery, or other objects are of the total material culture. It follows that the reliability of our statements about this culture also depends on how strongly we can believe that the nonmaterial elements of society and culture are reflected in the incomplete collection of finds that has come down to us.

These traditional cautionary arguments have been challenged by American archaeologist Lewis Binford and other prehistorians, who refuse to accept the assumption that archaeology yields information only on material culture. The distinction between "material culture" (artifacts, houses, and the products of human culture) and "nonmaterial" culture (kinship, social organization) is regarded as totally artificial, for every aspect of a human sociocultural system interacts with many other complex variables. According to Binford, "data relevant to most, if not all, the components of past sociocultural systems *are* preserved in the archaeological record" (Binford, 1968). The archaeologist's task, then, as Binford sees it, is to develop means for extracting such information from the data recovered from excavations and archaeological surveys.

This school of thought refuses to attribute the limitations on our knowledge of the past to the quality of the archaeological record and the state of its preservation in the soil. The limitations, according to them, lie in our methodological naiveté, in unsophisticated methodologies that many archaeologists are seeking to improve by means described at intervals in this book. The discussion of "preservation" that follows deals with the actual finds and conditions of preservation found in archaeological sites all over the world, for obviously everyone needs as much information to work with as can be obtained from their sites.

Organic and Inorganic Materials.   Preservation conditions depend largely on the soil and the general climatic regimen in the area of a site. Under highly favorable conditions, a wide range of artifactual materials is preserved, including such perishable items as leather containers, basketry, wooden arrowheads, or furniture. But under normal circumstances, usually only the most durable artifacts survive. Generally, the objects found in archaeological sites can be divided into two broad categories: inorganic and organic materials.

Inorganic objects are such materials as stone, metals, and clay. Prehistoric stone implements, such as the choppers of the earliest humans, made over two million years ago, have survived in perfect conditions for archaeologists to find. Their cutting edges are just as sharp as they were when abandoned by their makers. Clay pots are among the most durable human artifacts, especially if they are well fired. It is no coincidence that much of prehistory is reconstructed from chronological sequences of changing pottery styles. Fragments (potsherds) of well-fired clay vessels are practically indestructible and have lasted as long as 10,000 years in some Japanese sites.

Organic objects are made of living substances, such as wood, leather, bone, or cotton. They rarely survive in the archaeological record. When they do, they give a much more complete picture of prehistoric life than do inorganic finds. Organic materials formed a vital part of most societies' toolkits. For example, hunter-gatherers of southwestern France made extensive use of antler and bone for hunting tools and weapons (Grasiozi, 1960). Some of their finest artistic achievements were executed on fragments of these organic materials with the use of fine flint engravers. The preservation of organic materials depends heavily on local preservation conditions. Let us examine some of the more favorable preservation conditions that archaeologists encounter.

PRESERVATION OF ORGANIC MATERIALS

The best way to describe different preservation conditions is through descriptions of specific sites.

Waterlogged Environs.   Waterlogged or peat-bog conditions are particularly favorable for preserving wood or vegetal remains, whether the climate is subtropical or temperate. While tropical rain forests, such as those of the Amazon basin or the Congo, are far from kind to wooden artifacts, many archaeological sites are found near springs or in marshes where the water table is high and where perennial waterlogging of occupation layers has occurred since they were abandoned.

Tollund man.   Danish bogs have yielded a rich harvest of wooden hafted weapons, clothing, ornaments, traps, and even complete corpses, such as that of Tollund man (Glob, 1969). This unfortunate individual's body was found by two peat cutters in 1950, lying on its side in a brown peat bed in a crouched position, a serene expression on the face and eyes tightly closed (Figure 8.1). Tollund man wore a pointed skin cap and a hide belt—nothing else. We knew that he had been hanged, because a cord was found knotted tightly around his neck. The Tollund corpse has been shown to be about 2000 years old and to belong to the Danish Iron Age. So perfect were preservation conditions in the acidic bog soil that much of his skin survives, and his peaceful portrait has been included in many archaeological volumes.

A formidable team of medical experts examined his cadaver, among them a paleobotanist who established that Tollund man's last meal consisted of a gruel made from barley, linseed, and several wild grasses and weeds, eaten some twelve to twenty-four hours before his death. He is thought to have been a sacrificial victim of a fertility cult, hanged to ensure the success of crops and the continuation of life.

Figure 8.1   Tollund man.

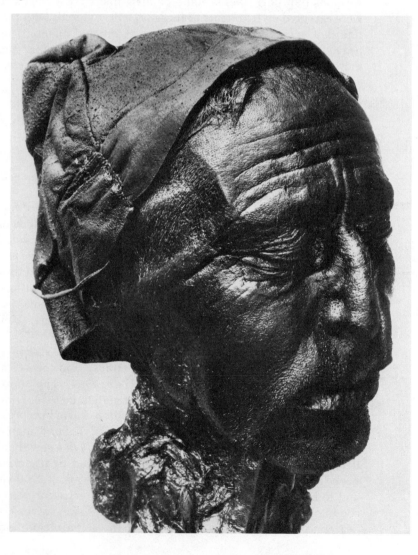

Figure 8.2 Ozette, Washington. Excavation of the walls, sleeping benches, and planks of a prehistoric house uncovered by a mudslide. The waterlogged conditions have preserved wood and fiber perfectly.

Ozette. Richard Daugherty of Washington State University has worked at the Ozette site on the Olympia Peninsula in the Pacific Northwest for many years (Kirk, 1974). The site first came to his attention in 1947, as part of a survey of coastal settlements. Ozette had been occupied by Makah Indians until some twenty or thirty years before, and traces of their collapsed houses could be seen on top of a large midden. It was not until 1966–1967 that Daugherty was able to start excavations at the site, which was being threatened with obliteration by wave action and mud slides. A trial trench revealed large deposits of whale bones and yielded radiocarbon samples that dated back 2500 years. Most important of all, the muddy deposits had preserved traces of wooden houses and the organic remains in them. Then, in 1970, a call from the Makah Tribal Council alerted Daugherty to a new discovery. High waves had cut into the midden and caused the wet soil to slump, revealing traces of wooden fish-hooks, boxes, and even a canoe paddle. Even a cursory glance showed that the Ozette site contained the remains of collapsed wooden houses buried under an ancient landslide.

Daugherty and his colleagues have worked at Ozette ever since, uncovering the remains of four cedarwood long houses and their contents (Figure 8.2). The excavations were fraught with difficulty and involved using high-pressure hoses and sprays to clear the mud away from the delicate woodwork. All the finds were then preserved with chemicals before final analysis. The wet muck that mantled the houses had engulfed them suddenly in a dense, damp blanket that preserved literally everything except flesh, feathers, and skins. The houses were perfectly preserved, one uncovered in 1972 measuring 21 meters long and 14 wide. There were separate hearths and cooking platforms and hanging mats and low walls as partitions. Over forty thousand artifacts have so far come from the excavations, including conical rain hats made of spruce roots, baskets, wooden bowls still impregnated with seal oil (Figure 8.3), mats, fish hooks, harpoons, combs, bows and arrows, even fragments of looms, and ferns and cedar leaves. A fine artistic tradition in wood excited the excavators: it included a whale fin carved of red cedar and inlaid with 700 sea-otter teeth. No one had ever seen one of these objects before, although Captain Cook had illustrated one in his report of a voyage to the Northwest coast in 1778.

The Ozette site is a classic example of how much can be recovered from an archaeological site when waterlogged conditions exist. But Ozette is important in other ways, too, for the Makah Indians who lived there are enthusiastically involved in the excavations. For the first time, they have a tangible history, one that extends back at least two thousand years before the advent of the whites. Existing oral traditions and written records for the Makah do not go back further than A.D. 1800. The Makah abandoned Ozette only in modern times, to move nearer a school in the 1920s. The archaeological excavations have traced the continuity of this village of whale catchers and fisherfolk back far into prehistory, thus giving a new sense of identity to the Makah of today.

Figure 8.3   A bowl for oil, from the Ozette site, carved in the form of a man and complete, even to a braid of human hair.

Dry Conditions.   Very arid environments such as those of the American Southwest or the Nile Valley, are even better in terms of preservation than waterlogged localities.

The tomb of Tutankhamun.   Undoubtedly one of the most famous of all archaeological discoveries is the amazing tomb of Tutankhamun (*ca.* 1345 B.C.), unearthed by Lord Carnarvon and Howard Carter in 1922 (Carter and others, 1923–33). The undisturbed burial chamber was opened, revealing the grave furniture in the exact same state in which it had been laid out by the king's mourners. Gilded wood chests, cloth, ivory caskets, models of chariots and boats, and the mummy were all perfectly preserved, together with a bewildering array of jewelry and paintings shining as brightly as the day they were painted, even showing the somewhat hasty execution accorded them by the artist. Tutankhamun's sepulchre provides as vivid a glimpse of the past as we are ever likely to obtain. Papyrus texts have been preserved by the dry Egyptian conditions in many Nile Valley cemeteries, too, giving an unrivaled picture of the ancient Egyptian world (Johnson, 1978).

Hogup.   C. Melville Aikens has spent many years excavating the Hogup cave in Utah, where deep, dry deposits contain a record of human occupation that began at least 9000 B.P. and lasted into historic times (Aikens, 1970). Preservation conditions are so good that Aikens and his colleagues were able to recover stone artifacts, basketry, netting fragments, bone artifacts, and the remains of large and small animals. The early deposits of the cave were literally strewn with the chaff of pickleweed seeds, seeds that were also found in human feces (dung) from the site. During the earlier periods of occupation, there was open water and marshland not too far from the cave, which is evidenced by the discovery of plentiful waterfowl and marsh plants in the deposits. After 3000 B.P. the waterfowl disappeared and the pickleweed declined sharply, demonstrating that the marshes were flooded by lake waters. The drier environment that evolved in modern times resulted in an increased exploitation of vegetable foods and small mammals. Few sites contain a wider range of evidence for hunting and food gathering as does Hogup. And it is precisely these basically dry conditions, which have persisted over the West since the end of the Pleistocene, that have enabled this evidence to be preserved so well.

Arctic Conditions.   Arctic sites, too, are excellent for the preservation of the human past. The circumpolar regions of Siberia and the New World have acted like a giant freezer, in which the processes of decay have been held in check for thousands of years. Close to the Arctic Sea, the carcasses of mammoths have survived thousands of winters in a state of perennial refrigeration. The Beresovka mammoth from Siberia was studied in 1901 by a Soviet expedition whose dogs ate the flesh of the Pleistocene beast as it was being dismembered (Digby, 1926). The hair was perfectly preserved, and the remains of its last meal were found on its tongue and in its stomach.

Pazyryk.   Russian archaeologist Sergei Rudenko was responsible for some remarkable excavations at the 2300-year-old Pazyryk burial mounds in Siberia, not far from the Chinese and Mongolian borders (Rudenko, 1970). Although the mounds are south of the permafrost zones of Siberia, the sites themselves are permanently frozen because a special microclimate has been formed inside them by the heat-conducting properties of the stone cairn forming each mound's core.

The mounds covered burial shafts filled with logs and rocks. Log chambers containing the burials lay under this filling. The bodies were deposited in log coffins, were usually partly clothed and accompanied by wooden pillows and tables with dishes of food. Cheese and food residues were still found inside them. Horses were buried with their masters, having been dispatched with a pole axe and placed in the burial shafts. Bridles, saddles, and head decorations accompanied the horses. Solid-wheeled wooden trolleys were found in each barrow; one a four-wheeled carriage with a draft pole. The horse carcasses were so well preserved in the frozen conditions that their hides could be studied: none had their winter coats. The horses were rather emaciated, as if they had survived a hard winter and had been slaughtered in early summer.

The refrigerated conditions of the mounds preserved not only an array of wooden artifacts, horse harnesses, carpets, and even felt wall-coverings and canopies with elaborate naturalistic motifs, but also the clothes and flesh of the individuals buried there. Linen shirts adorned with braid, caftans decorated with leather and gold discs, and head-dresses of felt and leather came from the coffins, as did women's bootees, aprons, and stockings. Much of the clothing was elaborately decorated, whereas the individual's hair was shaved. In addition to small ornaments, several bodies bore remarkable and elaborate tattooing. One chief's body showed a lively picture of a monster like a lion-griffin or some other imaginary creature. Deer, birds, and carnivores also adorned his body, with tattooing over the heart and arms and also on the legs. Presumably, the figures had some magical significance as well as a decorative intent.

The remarkable discoveries at Pazyryk have a local importance, because they show the long cultural ancestry of the modern pastoral tribes of southern Siberia. To archaeology as a whole, they reveal the potential richness of archaeological sites under the preservation conditions sometimes found in the Arctic.

Ipiutak. Eskimo archaeology has benefited enormously from the arctic cold, where permafrost, especially in Greenland and the more northern parts of the Arctic territory, has refrigerated wooden objects, bone and ivory artifacts, and the remains of animals hunted by the artifact makers. A remarkable site is the Ipiutak settlement near Point Hope on the Chukchi Sea, dated to the first few centuries A.D. (Collins, 1937). Over 60 semisubterranean dwellings were excavated out of an estimated 600–700 on the site. The floor level of the Ipiutak houses was about 50 centimeters (19 inches) below the ground, with the squarish floor between 3 and 7 meters (10 and 23 feet) in diameter. A central fireplace lay on the floor of packed gravel or logs, while sleeping benches of gravel and earth lined three walls. Vertical logs or poles, caulked with finer timbers, formed the walls; the whole structure, including the wooden roof, was covered with arctic moss. In a nearby cemetery, wooden coffins containing a single burial were built in small pits, most of them at least a half-meter (19 inches) deep. Few grave goods were associated with these burials—in contrast to another series of skeletons deposited only a few centimeters below the surface. These bodies, when discovered, were found partially disarticulated, lying in a deposit of wood fragments, which included some flamboyant ivory carvings and midden soil. The excavators inferred that the dead had been deposited on the ground, enclosed in a wooden frame or a pile of logs. Elaborate ivory carvings were invariably associated with the surface burials at Ipiutak, preserved by the cold conditions that have persisted at the site since its abandonment. Ipiutak art is dominated by small sculptures of bears, walruses, and other animals, while composite masks and delicate spiral ornaments were probably fastened to the grave coverings. It is sobering to realize that under temperate conditions only stone artifacts and the outlines of the Ipiutak houses and bed platforms would have survived the 2,000 years since the settlement was occupied (Dumond, 1977).

Special Conditions.   Geological deposits, such as oil-bearing layers in Poland or tar beds in the New World, have supplied many fossil remains of large mammals trapped in the treacherous deposits thousands of years ago. A dog corpse from a Basketmaker site in the Southwest survived so well in dry soil that the flies that fed on the putrefying corpse were found with the skeleton. Viking ships are preserved in the acid soils of temperate climates by the stones, clay, and peat packed around them by their owners. Even the wine of Roman times has come down to us. In 1867 a bottle of wine dating from the third century A.D. was found in a Roman sarcophagus at Speyer; the bottle was still full, and the liquid was analyzed to be wine mixed with honey. A thick layer of olive oil covered the wine, poured into the bottle by the original bottler to preserve the contents; this had become resinated, which prevented the wine from evaporating (De Laet, 1956).

In spite of these exceptional instances, most soils tend to be destructive. Acid soils destroy organic objects rapidly, but the dark discolorations of post holes and hut foundations often remain and challenge the archaeologist to reconstruct structures whose actual substance has vanished. The granitic soils of subtropical regions tend to be highly destructive, while the chalk deposits of Europe preserve animal bones, burials, and metals moderately well. The great loess belts of central Europe have mantled many Upper Paleolithic settlements, preserving the floor plans of the mammoth-hunters' camps, some of the earliest human structures ever recovered (Klein, 1969).

PRESERVATION AND HUMAN ACTIVITY

The preservation of archaeological remains can, of course, be influenced by the ancient peoples themselves.

Discards.   The patterns of artifact discard can be very subtle and understanding them often requires knowledge that is still beyond our grasp.

Cozumel.   At the Mayan trading center on Cozumel, Yucatán, for example, the people invested very little material wealth in temples, tombs, or other permanent monuments (Sabloff, 1975). Their capital was kept fluid and on hand, a different investment in resources than that found at other Mayan ceremonial centers, which invested heavily in religious monuments and tangible displays of wealth. The different investment in resources reflected the activities and significance of each type of locality. The interpretations of such patterns of discard, of the remains that are left for interpretation after the long centuries and millennia of natural destruction have taken place, present enormous difficulties for archaeologists.

Fulani.   In a fascinating discussion of thirty-six modern, inhabited Fulani compounds in North Cameroon, West Africa, Nicholas David attempted to show the "fit" between the houses in the compounds and their Fulani inhabitants (David, 1971). He found that so many variables affected the layout of the compounds that only the most general observations were possible. The huts in the compound could, sometimes, be used to estimate the numbers of adult women or male family heads. But what about bachelors or children? Fish-drying ovens of puddled mud and large hearths were signs of economic specialization and of evening classes for study of the Koran in the modern settlements. But had an archaeologist dug up the compound centuries after its abandonment, only the ovens would have survived. The house of the chief musician gave no clue to his profession, nor did those of many part-time specialists. The granaries used to store grain supplies were not built on stone foundations that were likely to survive: the only sign of the basic subsistence economy in the archaeological record might be the special grinding huts in the compound. Furthermore, while in prehistoric times the compounds might have reflected the status of different families—wealthy people, poor, free Fulani, and slaves, today there is no slavery and a far more homogeneous society. Above all, in earlier times wealth was not necessarily reflected in house size. All houses were about the same size, a dimension dictated, so David found, by white ant infestation. When insecticides became available in the late 1960s, houses started to get larger. The absolute limits of archaeological inference were soon met when David attempted to fit the material culture and houses to social structure. David found, for example, that in modern country villages people built houses to suit their precise needs. Land is abundant and free. But in modern towns, where the Fulani have to buy land and modify their property for their needs within a much tighter framework, people either have to move to new quarters or adapt their lifestyle to fit their limited space. The constraints are far more severe.

Any archaeologist working anywhere has to face the peculiar problems that David demonstrated with his Fulani compounds. What are the distorting effects of human discard patterns on the archaeological record, on surface site survey, and on the limits to which we can take the interpretation of sites and finds? These are questions that few archaeologists have yet tackled head on, but they form a critical facet of the preservation question.

Recycling.   Not only do people discard artifacts, but they recycle them as well. A stone axe can be resharpened again and again, until the original, large artifact is just a small stub that has been recycled literally into extinction. It takes a great deal of effort to build a mud brick house from scratch. Very often, an old house is renovated again and again, its precious wooden beams recycled and used again in the same structure or in another building. Such recycling can distort the archaeological record, for what appears to be a single structure can in fact be one that has been used again and again. Tree-ring dating of pueblos in the Southwest is complicated by the constant reuse of wooden beams. In some cases, too, the Indians would cut a stock of beams and stockpile them for later use.

Not only individual artifacts, but also entire archaeological sites can be recycled. For example, a settlement flourishes on a low ridge in the Near East. After a generation or two the site is abandoned, and the inhabitants move elsewhere. Later, people return to the site, level the abandoned houses, and build their own dwellings right on top of them. This type of recycling can result in the sealing and preservation of later levels, but by the same token, it can also result in the reuse of building materials from earlier houses.

Heirlooms.   Sometimes, successive generations find a particular structure or artifact so valuable that they consciously preserve it for the benefit of their descendants.

Eridu.   The great temple, or *ziggurat,* of the city of Eridu in Mesopotamia was first erected around 5000 B.C. This important shrine was visible for miles around and was rebuilt on the same site time and time again for over two thousand years. Tracing the complex history of this structure has consumed many hours of excavation time. Reconstructing the sequence of mud-brick construction through generations of recycling of successive structures involves understanding the processes by which mud brick architecture came into being and how it decays (Lloyd, 1963).

Ceremonial artifacts.   Many prehistoric societies valued ritual objects, such as masks, ceremonial axes, and other symbolic artifacts that were associated with ancestor worship. Sometimes, these ceremonial artifacts were buried with a dead priest or leader, as was the case with Tutankhamun and some of the Mayan leaders. In such cases, it is easy enough to tell their age and association with a grave dug at a particular period. In other instances, ceremonial artifacts can be treasured for generations, being displayed only on special occasions or kept in a special relic hut. An interesting example of such heirlooms is that of the sacred relics of the Bemba tribe of Central Africa, which included ceremonial iron gongs and bow stands that were at least two hundred years old (Richards, 1937). Tragically, these were destroyed by political protestors in the early 1960s, which caused great trauma among the older Bemba. By treasuring such objects, however, the owners can unwittingly distort the archaeological record. Fortunately, in most cases it is possible to identify instances of curation by the style of the artifacts. In the case of Tutankhamun's tomb, for example, Carter found objects that had belonged to earlier pharaohs in the grave furniture. Presumably, they had been placed in the tomb to fill in gaps in the royal inventory caused by the pharaoh's unexpected death.

There are many other potential causes of human distortion of the archaeological record. These can include deliberate destruction of cemeteries, the erasure of inscriptions from temples at royal command, or the ravages of warfare, both ancient and modern. The trench warfare of World War I did terrible damage to archaeological sites. Even more destructive are the depredations of treasure hunters and antiquities dealers supplying the greedy needs of museums and private collectors (Meyer, 1977).

An archaeologist must always evaluate the preservation conditions at every site investigated to determine the preservation factors—both human and natural—that affected the integrity of the archaeological record.

Guide to Further Reading

Good surveys of preservation in archaeology are few and far between. The following will provide some useful references.

Clark, J. G. D. *Archaeology and Society.* New York: Barnes and Noble, 1939.
This is a classic archaeological text that still contains much information of value, especially on the preservation of archaeological remains.

————. *Star Carr.* Cambridge: Cambridge University Press, 1954.
A definitive monograph about a waterlogged site, which is a classic of its type.

Glob, P. V. *The Bog People.* London: Faber and Faber, 1969.
A popular account of bog corpses found in Denmark. Includes a description of the Tollund find.

Kirk, Ruth. *Hunters of the Whale.* New York: William Morrow, 1974.
A popular narration about the Ozette site in Washington State. Gives a summary of preservation and excavation problems.

Rudenko, Sergei. *Frozen Tombs of Siberia: The Pazyryk Burials of Iron Age Horsemen.* Translated by M. W. Thompson. Berkeley: University of California Press, 1970.

PART IV

RECOVERING ARCHAEOLOGICAL DATA

A mere hole in the ground, which of all sights is perhaps the least vivid and dramatic, is enough to grip their attention for hours at a time.

P. G. WODEHOUSE
A Damsel in Distress

Part IV deals with the ways in which archaeologists acquire data in the field. As we stressed earlier, the acquisition of such data depends on a sound research design and the formulation of specific hypotheses before reconnaissance, site survey, or excavation can be begun. Our knowledge of the past is limited, not only by preservation in the ground but also by our own data recovery methods. Chapters 9 through 11 describe some of the fundamental principles and processes of archaeological fieldwork, as well as some of the many special problems encountered by archaeologists in the field. And, rather than draw on a single case study, we have chosen to give many examples, relying on your instructors to use case studies derived from their own experience.

CHAPTER 9 ✦

THE PROCESS OF ARCHAEOLOGICAL RESEARCH

Preview

- Modern archaeology makes use of scientific methods developed not only by archaeologists but also by scientists in many other disciplines.
- A well-qualified archaeologist commands a wide variety of skills, both in archaeological method and theory and in practical methodology. This expertise includes an ability to select and work with specialists in other academic disciplines. Practical fieldwork experience and considerable administrative and managerial skill is also required on even the smallest research project. All archaeologists have to develop precise analytical and writing skills that enable them to communicate their results and record them for posterity.
- Archaeologists use science as a means of acquiring knowledge and understanding about those parts of the natural world that can be observed. They do this by working with two forms of reasoning: inductive reasoning, which takes a set of specific observations and then makes a generalization from them, and deductive reasoning, which starts with a generalization and proceeds to specific implications.
- The process of archaeological research begins with the formulation of highly specific research designs that are flexible enough to allow changes in the overall project as field research proceeds.

- The research project is formulated in terms of the problem to be investigated and the geographical area involved. The process of formulation means carrying out background research and then developing a series of hypotheses to be tested against data acquired in the field.
- Once the field team is assembled, the acquisition of data through reconnaissance, site survey, and excavation begins. This acquisition process requires the recording of provenience, archaeological context, and a great deal of basic information about the site, its natural environment, and its archaeological finds.
- The processing of archaeological data requires the analysis and interpretation of the archaeological finds, which involves sorting, classifying, and ordering the finds, and then testing the hypotheses developed as part of the research design.
- The final stage in the archaeological research process is the publication of the results for posterity.
- The modern archaeological research process is heavily dependent on statistical manipulation of data, for there are rarely sufficient resources for total excavation of sites or for a comprehensive survey of even small areas. Thus, archaeologists rely heavily on sampling methods to ensure unbiased samples of data.
- All sampling is based on a data universe, an arbitrarily chosen research area, be it a geographic region, a site, or an assemblage of artifacts. This universe is subdivided into arbitrarily or nonarbitrarily chosen sample units, which form a population.
- Nonprobabilistic sampling involves selection using such criteria as vegetational cover or intuition as a basis for sampling. Probabilistic sampling is designed to provide unbiased data for use in probability testing.
- Probabilistic samples are selected on a simple random, systematic, or stratified basis, depending on the complexity of the problem being studied.
- Sampling methods are widely applicable in archaeology, especially when quantitative approaches are being used on archaeological data.

"The excavator without an intelligent policy may be described as an archaeological food-gatherer, master of a skill, perhaps, but not creative in the wider terms of constructive science," wrote Sir Mortimer Wheeler in his classic description of archaeological research (Wheeler, 1954). This chapter shows just how true his remarks were. Modern archaeology makes use of scientific methods developed not only by archaeologists themselves but also by scientists in many other disciplines. It is a complex process that involves research design, field surveys, and actual excavation, as well as lengthy laboratory analysis of many different types of finds. Above all, modern archaeological research is a multidisciplinary effort, one that ideally involves a closely knit group of researchers with many and diverse skills.

After discussing the qualifications of a good archaeologist, we look at the relationship between science and archaeology, at inductive and deductive reasoning, and then examine the process of archaeological research itself. This short chapter is an important preliminary to the discussions of archaeological data acquisition that follow.

THE ARCHAEOLOGIST'S SKILLS

Early archaeologists needed few qualifications beyond a liking for the past, some experience at excavation, and an ability to classify artifacts. Sir Leonard Woolley, the famous excavator of Ur-of-the-Chaldees in Mesopotamia in the 1920s, was completely self-trained and learned excavation in a few seasons in the Sudan. He became an archaeologist as a result of an interview with an Oxford college president, who told him: "*I have decided that you shall become an archaeologist!*" Fortunately for science, Woolley obeyed him (Fagan, 1979).

The archaeologists of the 1980s, however, require specialist training in a wide variety of administrative, technical, and academic skills. Modern archaeology has become so complex that few individuals can possibly master all the skills needed to excavate a large city or even a medium-sized settlement where preservation conditions are exceptionally complete. In the 1920s Leonard Woolley excavated Ur with a handful of Europeans, three expert Syrian foremen, and several hundred workers. An expedition to an equivalent site today would consist of a carefully organized team of experts whose skills reflect the precise hypotheses about the site that were to be tested in the field.

Let us examine, then, some of the basic skills an archaeologist needs.

Theoretical Skills.   The archaeologist must have the ability to define research problems in the context of existing knowledge about them. This existing knowledge includes not only the current status of the research on a specific problem, such as the origins of humankind or the earliest human settlement of Ohio, but also the latest theoretical and methodological advances in archaeology that could affect the definition and solution of the problem.

The research problem will be defined in terms of specific objectives, or goals, to be achieved. The archaeologist must have the expertise to formulate the precise hypotheses to be tested in the research. As the research proceeds, he or she will have to be able to evaluate and put together the results of the work in the context of the original objectives.

Methodological Expertise.   Every archaeologist must have the ability to plan the methods to be used in the research to achieve the theoretical goals laid out at the outset. Methodological skills include the ability to select between different methods of data collection, to decide which analytical methods are most effective for the data being handled. Excavation of sites requires a whole range of methodological skills, from deciding which sampling and trenching systems to use, to devising recording methods, to dealing with special preservation conditions where fragile objects have to be removed intact from their matrix.

One important aspect of methodological expertise involves the ability to select and work with specialists from other disciplines. This involves not only an understanding of multidisciplinary research but also a knowledge of the uses and limitations of the work of, say, geologists or zoologists, for the specific problems one is investigating.

Technical Skills.   Methodological and technical skills overlap, especially in the field. The scientific excavation of any site or a large-scale field survey requires not only the ability to select a method or a recording system but also to execute it under working conditions. Archaeological excavations require great precision in measurement and excavation, the deployment of skilled and unskilled labor, and implementation of find recovery systems that keep artifacts in order from the moment they are found until they are shipped to the laboratory for analysis. At issue here is the provenience of the artifacts and features and of the associated ecofacts. The field archaeologist has to assume the roles of supervisor, photographer, surveyor, digger, recorder, writer, and soil scientist, as well as be able to deal with any unexpected jobs, such as uncovering the delicate bones of a skeleton or setting up details of a computer program. On large sites, expertly trained students or fellow archaeologists may assume such specialist tasks as photography; on small sites, the archaeologist often must perform this and all other tasks alone.

Administrative and Management Skills.   Modern archaeology requires—or actually, demands—a high level of administrative and management skills from its practitioners. Today's archaeologist has to be able to coordinate the activities of specialists from other disciplines, organize and deploy teams of volunteer students and paid labor, and raise and administer research funds that have been obtained from outside sources. He or she must always be aware of all aspects of a research project as it develops, from arranging for permits and supplies of stationery and digging tools to doing the accounts.

Above all, anyone working on an archaeological project has to be an expert in human relations, in keeping people happy at demanding work, which is often carried out under difficult and uncomfortable conditions. The diplomatic side of archaeological excavations is often neglected. But the folklore of archaeology abounds with stories of disastrous excavations run by archaeologists with no sensitivity to their fellow workers. A truly happy excavation is a joy to work on, a dig where people smile, argue ferociously over the interpretation of stratigraphic profiles, and enjoy the companionship of a campfire in the evenings.

Writing and Analytical Skills.   If there is one basic lesson to be learned at the beginning of any archaeological endeavor, it is that all excavation is destruction, destruction of finite archives in the ground that can never be restored to their original configuration. Every archaeologist has the responsibility to not only analyze his or her finds in the laboratory, but also to prepare a detailed report on the particular fieldwork that has been done, which forms an important part of the permanent record of archaeological research. Regrettably, the shelves of museums all over the world are filled with finds from sites that have been excavated but never written up.

At first glance, the list of qualifications for a professional archaeologist can be extremely formidable. But, in practice, a sound classroom training combined with a great deal of fieldwork experience can give one the necessary background.

ARCHAEOLOGY, SCIENCE AND THE SCIENTIFIC METHOD

At various places in the text we have referred to scientific archaeology, scientific method, and testing of hypotheses against data collected in the field (Thomas, 1974). It is now time to ask the question: Is archaeology a science? The answer to this question is a qualified yes. In the sense that archaeologists study human societies in the past by scientifically recovering and analyzing data that consist of the material remains of these societies, it is a science. But in the sense that archaeology, as a part of anthropology, studies the intangible philosophic and religious beliefs of a society, it is not a science.

What exactly do we mean by the word "scientific"? Science is a way of acquiring knowledge and understanding about those parts of the natural world that can be measured. It is a disciplined and carefully ordered search for knowledge, carried out in a systematic manner. This is a far cry from the ways in which we acquire our personal experience of religious philosophies, social customs, or political trends. Science involves using methods of acquiring knowledge that are not only cumulative but also subject to continuous testing and retesting. Over the years, scientists have developed a set of general procedures for acquiring data, known as the scientific method, which has come into widespread use. While the scientific method may be applied in somewhat different ways in botany than it is in zoology or anthropology, the basic principles are the same: the notion that knowledge of the real world is both cumulative and subject to constant rechecking. The scientific method has many applications to archaeological data, and its use classifies much of archaeology as a science.

The Scientific Method.   Science establishes facts about the natural world by observing objects, events, and phenomena. In making these observations, the scientist proceeds by using either inductive or deductive reasoning.

Inductive reasoning takes a set of specific observations and then makes a generalization from them. For example, I once found nearly 10,000 wild vegetable remains in a 4000-year-old hunter-gatherer camp in central Zambia. Over 42 percent of them were from the *bauhinia,* a shrub prized for its fruit and roots, which flowers from October to February. The *bauhinia* is still eaten by San hunter-gatherers in the Kalahari today. From this knowledge I induced that *bauhinia* has been a preferred seasonal food for hunter-gatherers in this general area for thousands of years (Fagan and Van Noten, 1971).

Deductive reasoning works the other way around. That is, the observer starts with a generalization and proceeds to form specific implications. In this case, I would have formulated a hypothesis (or series of hypotheses) about San and prehistoric hunter-gatherer *bauhinia* eating, and then tested it with ethnographic fieldwork and archaeological investigations. My hypothesis would then be confirmed, rejected, or refined.

A classic and often cited example of the application of both inductive and deductive approaches comes from field studies done in the Great Basin in the western United States by anthropologist Julian Steward, who spent much of the 1920s and 1930s working on Shoshonean ethnography. The mass of field data that he collected led him to make a series of inductive generalizations about the ways in which the Shoshoneans moved their settlements throughout the year (Steward,1938).

In the late 1960s this pioneer work was greatly refined by David Hurst Thomas, who approached the Shoshoneans' settlement patterns deductively. First, he took Steward's theory about the settlement patterns and devised a set of hypotheses about the densities and distributions of artifacts in the various ecological zones of the Great Basin. "If the late prehistoric Shoshoneans behaved in the fashion suggested by Steward, how would the artifacts have fallen on the ground?" he asked (Thomas, 1969; 1973; 1979). He developed a total of over 100 hypotheses relating to Steward's original theory. Next, he devised a set of tests to verify or invalidate his hypotheses. He expected to find specific forms of artifacts associated with particular types of activity, such as hunting, in seasonal archaeological sites where hunting was said to be important. Given local preservation conditions, he placed major emphasis on the distribution and frequency of artifact forms. Then, he collected the necessary archaeological data in the field to perform his tests. Finally, Thomas tested each of his hypotheses against the field data and rejected about 25 percent of his original hypotheses. The remainder were supported by the data and provided a major refinement of Steward's original generalization. Later fieldwork gave him abundant opportunities to refine his original hypotheses and to collect more field data to further confirm them.

Thomas's Great Basin research is a good example of the cumulative benefits of deductive reasoning and scientific method in archaeological research.

Most early archaeological research was, and much contemporary work still is, inductive. At present, there is a tendency to dismiss all inductive research as being scientifically unsound, for it involves a certain amount of insight or intuition rather than a precise application of scientific method. Such a dismissal is totally unrealistic, however, for it means rejecting all of the early archaeological knowledge acquired by those scholars who did not use scientific method.

The importance of scientific method, on the other hand, cannot be underestimated. This has been put very well by Sharer and Ashmore: "Science advances by disproof, proposing the most adequate explanations for the moment, knowing that new and better explanations will later be found. This continuous self-correcting feature is the key to the scientific method" (Sharer and Ashmore, 1979).

THE PROCESS OF ARCHAEOLOGICAL RESEARCH

The archaeology of today is becoming more and more explicitly scientific and sophisticated. Essential to it is the formulation of much more specific research designs. In this section we describe the process of archaeological research, from the formulation of the research design to the publication of the final report.

Research Designs.   Lewis Binford was among the first archaeologists to see the necessity for highly specific research designs (Binford, 1964). To this end, he called for more regional studies, for investigations in which the archaeologist would aim at solving specific problems, and for the testing of hypotheses with representative samples of data drawn from a well-defined region. Such research is so complex that it requires highly specific research designs to execute. Under this approach, the research problem itself often determines the sites to be investigated.

A research design is a formal process whose purpose is to direct the carrying out of an archaeological investigation (Daniels, 1972). It has two objectives: to ensure the scientific validity of the results, and to carry out the research as efficiently and economically as possible. The process of archaeological research, then, is controlled by the research design, which takes the project through a series of stages. These stages, described below, are by no means common to all research projects; for although the term "research design" sounds very rigid and inflexible, in practice the design for any project has to be flexible enough to allow changes in the overall project as field research proceeds.

Formulation.   Any archaeological research begins with a series of fundamental decisions about the problem or area to be studied. A research problem can be as grandiose as a determination of the origins of agriculture in the Southwest—a truly enormous project—or as specific as a determination of the date of the second phase of Stonehenge's construction. The initial decisions will identify both the problem and the geographical region in which it will be investigated. This latter can be a single site or an entire geographical region. These decisions immediately limit the scope of the research design.

Once the problem and the area are identified, the researcher must do a great deal of background research, which will involve both library work and field investigations. He or she must read up on previous archaeological research on the problem and study the geology, climate, ecology, anthropology, and general background of the area. Several field visits to the area are essential, both to examine fieldwork conditions and to get a feel for the region. Water supplies, camp sites, and labor sources have to be identified. Landowners' permissions to dig and survey are essential, and government permits may be needed. At least some preliminary fieldwork is needed to aid in the formulation of the research design, especially in areas where no archaeology has been carried out before.

The objective of all this preliminary work is to refine the problems under investigation to the point where one can begin to define the specific research goals. These goals will almost invariably include the testing of a series of specific hypotheses. These hypotheses can be related to earlier research carried out by previous investigators, or they may be entirely new ones that have emerged during the preliminary formulation of the research problem. Yet others will be added as the research work proceeds. The generation of hypotheses at this stage is vital, for they determine the types of data that will be sought in the field. It is necessary to define these types of data, at least in general terms, before one goes into the field.

Let us take an example of two hypotheses, which were designed as part of a research project into early food production in Egypt:

> The earliest cereal agriculture near Kom Ombo developed among hunter-gatherers who had been exploiting wild vegetable foods very intensively. The emergence of agriculture came about as a result of the intensification of gathering and rapid population growth causing shortages of wild cereals. So people began to grow wild cereals for themselves.

What sorts of data would be needed to test these hypotheses at Kom Ombo? The archaeologist formulating the project of which this hypothesis forms a part would be looking for the following:

1. sites in areas where wild cereals could have grown, where preservation conditions would allow for the survival of vegetal remains
2. food residues in the form of carbonized and discarded vegetable foods and the bones of domesticated animals
3. implements used for harvesting and processing both wild and domesticated grains, grindstones, sickles, and so on

4. evidence for such features as storage pits or baskets, which indicate the deliberate conservation of food supplies
5. sites that were occupied for longer than the relatively short periods of time favored by most hunter-gatherers: farmers have to watch over their crops.

Armed with both hypotheses and lists of the types of evidence likely to be encountered in the field, the archaeologist can plan for the necessary equipment, facilities, and people needed to carry out the job. Even more important, the project can be formulated in terms of experts, whose specialist knowledge will be needed either in the field or in the laboratory. The necessary contacts with experts are best made before the fieldwork begins and funds are obtained. A surprising number of specialists are needed for even quite simple investigations. For example, the Kom Ombo hypothesis could ideally require the long- or short-term services of the following specialists:

1. a geologist to assist in the geological dating of sites in the Nile valley
2. a soil scientist to study occupation levels and organic soils
3. a radiocarbon dating laboratory to date carbon samples
4. a botanist to supervise the recovery of vegetal remains and to identify them
5. a pollen analysis expert to work on any such samples recovered in the excavations
6. a zoologist to study the animal bones

The larger-scale project may take an integrated team of experts from several disciplines into the field—an expensive enterprise but one that often yields important results. The study of early agriculture in the Near East was revolutionized by Robert Braidwood of the University of Chicago in the 1950s, when he took such a team of experts with him to the Zagros mountains. The research team was able to trace the development of agriculture and animal domestication from its beginnings among nomadic hunter-gatherers on the highlands over 9000 years ago (Braidwood and Howe, 1962).

The final stage in the formulation of the research project is the acquisition of the necessary funding. This can be a frustrating and time-consuming process, for sources of monies for archaeological fieldwork are always in short supply. Most excavations organized in the Americas are funded either by the National Science Foundation, or if within the United States, by some other government agency, such as the National Park Service. Some private organizations, such as the National Geographic Society or the Wenner Gren Foundation for Anthropological Research, support excavations. Some foundations limit their support to the study of specific topics. For instance, the L. S. B. Leakey Foundation of Pasadena only supports research into primate behavior and the origins of humankind and certain types of urgent anthropological fieldwork. Few archaeologists are expert fund raisers, for it requires a great deal of time. But some excavations, such as the Koster project in Illinois (Brown and Struever, 1973), rely heavily on private donations. The organizers expend a great deal of time on fund raising to support each field season and the laboratory work that follows it.

Data Collection.   Once the field team is assembled and the funds are in hand, the actual implementation of the project begins. The first stage is to acquire equipment, set up camp, and organize the research team in the field. Once that process is complete, the actual collection of archaeological data can begin.

This collection of data involves two basic processes: the location and survey of sites and the scientific excavation of carefully selected sites.

The location of archaeological sites is obviously the first stage in the collection of data. As we will see in Chapter 10, reconnaissance can be carried out on foot, in vehicles, or even on the back of a mule. A variety of techniques are used to ensure that a representative sample of sites is located and investigated before excavation. Then the surfaces of the sites are carefully investigated and samples of artifacts lying at ground level are collected, to record as much as possible about the location without the expense of excavation. This recording process can include photographs, some surveying and measurement, and even some probing of the site with borers or remote sensing devices. Obviously, the amount of information collected from surface surveys is much more limited than that from excavations.

Archaeological excavations are ultimately a process of recording subsurface features and the provenience, or precise relationships, of the artifacts within the site. A wide variety of techniques are used to collect and record archaeological data from beneath the ground, as described in Chapter 11. As is obvious, the scope of archaeological excavation can range from a small test pit to a large-scale investigation at a site such as Meadowcroft rockshelter in the Ohio valley, where excavation has extended over many seasons (Adovasio, and others, 1975).

Data Processing, Analysis, and Interpretation.   The end-products of even a month's excavation on a moderately productive site are a daunting accumulation. Box upon box of potsherds, stone tools, bones, and other finds are stacked in the field laboratory and must be cleaned, labeled, and sorted. Hundreds of slides and photographs must be processed and cataloged. Rolls of drawings, which contain important information on the provenience of the finds from the trenches must also be cataloged. Then there are radiocarbon and pollen samples, burials, and other special finds that need examination by specialists. The first stage in processing the data, then, occurs at the site, where the finds are washed, sorted, and given preservation treatment sufficient to transport them to the archaeological laboratory for more thorough examination.

The detailed analysis of the data is carried out over many months in a laboratory where the necessary facilities for such research work are available. These analyses include not only the classification of artifacts and the identification of the materials from which they were made, but also studies of food remains, pollen samples, and other key information sources. All these analyses are designed to provide information for the interpretation of the archaeological record. Some tests, such as radiocarbon dating or pollen analysis, are carried out in special laboratories with the necessary technical equipment for the work. We describe various approaches to archaeological analysis in chapters 12 through 17.

The interpretation of the resulting classified and thoroughly analyzed data involves not only making a synthesis of all the information from the investigation, but the final testing of the basic hypotheses formulated at the beginning of the project. From these tests emerge models for the reconstruction and explanation of the prehistory of the site or region under investigation. We look at some of these models and interpretations in Part VII.

Publication.   The archaeologist's final responsibility is to publish the results of the research project. The process of archaeological excavation destroys all or part of a site forever; and unless the investigator publishes the results of the excavation, vital scientific information will be lost forever. The ideal scientific report publishes not only the research design and hypotheses formulated, but also the data used to test them and to interpret the site or region, so that the same tests can be replicated by others (Grinsell, Rahtz, and Williams, 1970).

All archaeological research is cumulative, in the sense that everyone's investigations are eventually superseded by later work, which uses more refined recovery methods and new analytical approaches. But unless every archaeologist publishes the results of his or her completed work, the chain of research is incomplete, and a fragment of human history will vanish into complete oblivion. It is sad that the pace of publication has lagged far behind that of excavation. The reason is not hard to discern: excavation is far more fun than writing reports!

DATA ACQUISITION AND SAMPLING

The acquisition and analysis of archaeological data are activities that are limited by the availability of time and money. To begin with, location of every site in a survey area is an impossible goal; additionally, no one has the time and money to dig even a few sites in their entirety. The fieldworker has two goals:

1. To make as careful a survey as possible and then carry out selective excavations on sites that look promising. This approach is the ideal, but often is not carried out. Sites located or chosen for excavation are found or selected on a far from random basis. For instance, an archaeologist might choose to dig a site near a well or close to a road or airstrip, simply for logistical convenience. One site might be the largest or have more surface finds than the others. These might be chosen because they "looked good." A multitude of conscious and unconscious factors can influence our selection of a site for excavation, factors that can introduce serious biases into our field data.
2. To carry out archaeological reconnaissance and excavation using rigorous sampling methods. The ideal would be to recover information on the full range of variation in the archaeologial record relevant to one's research project. The only approach to this end is to use sampling techniques that reduce to a minimum the risk of one-sided data or limited information being collected.

Archaeologists have long recognized that they are working with limited information. But a model that provides a framework for assessing whether the data samples collected are truly a random sample of the actual information in the ground provides a basis for calculating statistical probabilities.

Sampling Defined.   Sampling has been defined as the "science of controlling and measuring the reliability of information through the theory of probability." Systematic and carefully controlled sampling of archaeological data is essential if we are to rely heavily, as we do, on statistical approaches in the reconstruction of past lifeways and cultural process. For example, if we are interested in past adaptations to environmental conditions, we must systematically sample many different types of sites in each environmental zone; not merely those that look important or likely to yield spectacular finds. Sampling techniques enable us to ensure a statistically reliable basis of archaeological data from which we can make generalizations about our research data. As these generalizations are often estimates of probability, they must be based on unbiased data.

Sampling Terminology.   Sampling design is an integral part of the formulation of a research project and research design, and must be fitted specifically to the particular problem posed by the researcher. For the data to be most useful, it is necessary to define clearly, and in highly specific terms, what the sample will actually represent. Because relatively little can be known about the populations with which one is dealing, probability sampling of archaeological data can be very misleading in a strictly statistical sense. Sampling approaches are useful in reducing bias, and as aids to decision making about data collection, but their value as precise statements of probability is much more limited.

The first stage in any sampling design is to define the boundaries of the area being investigated, the data universe.

The data universe is the area that is chosen for investigation. It can be a single site; portions of a settlement; a well-defined geographical region, such as a river valley; or a chronological period, as, for example, between 1000 B.C. and A.D. 350 in Ohio.

Sample units are the units chosen for the investigation of the data universe. *Nonarbitrary units* are sample units that might coincide with obvious, quite natural units, such as rooms in a pueblo, graves within a cemetery, or highly distinctive local environments. *Arbitrary units* are just that—spatial units chosen to subdivide an area into convenient sections for investigation. These can be of any shape or size. Some of the most common are grid squares, sometimes called quadrats; long, rectangular units, which are almost like pathways across an area, often known as transects; and simple site locations, or points. Sample units are purely a research tool, and as such, they contain archaeological data. The only assumption made, whether arbitrary or nonarbitrary units are used, is that the data in each are similar enough, or sufficiently complementary, to allow comparison of one unit to the other.

Populations are the total of all sampling units. They are not the same as data universes, which are a definition of a research area. Sample units may be devised to survey only the southern part of a river valley, for example. These units, perhaps transects across a densely forested plain, form a population. But the population of sample units is only a small part of the data universe. In many cases, however, the population may end up yielding data that is applicable to the universe as a whole.

The data pool is the *potential* information available to the researcher within the data universe. Sampling methods are designed to acquire as much of the data pool as possible, the data acquired coming from sample units within the populations of the data universe. Even without using formal sampling methods, the amount of information that can be obtained from a data pool is limited. Sampling methods are designed to maximize data acquisition and to do so on a statistically sound basis.

Sampling the Data. A data universe is easy enough to define on paper and in theory. But the reality of access in the field may be very different. Funds and people may be limited; and access to the area may be restricted by landowners, rugged landscape, the vegetational cover, or even political events. And, in the case of a site chosen for excavation, one should always leave a portion undisturbed so that later generations of archaeologists can check the work, using more sophisticated methods. The sampling of the data universe depends, in the final analysis, on both the amount of the universe accessible and what method is used to sample the population of the sample units set up.

Nonprobabilistic sampling selects the sample units to be investigated on the basis of intuitive or pragmatic criteria chosen by the investigator. These can include such realistic considerations as access to only a few sites being possible in a dense rain forest, the precedent of generations of earlier research that lead one to concentrate on certain types of conspicuous sites, or simply the archaeologist's long experience. This type of sampling is fine for many specific tasks, *provided* that the sample units, the data universe, and the population being investigated are clearly defined ahead of time. Without such precise terms of reference, it is difficult to assess whether the sample data collected is truly representative of the data universe as a whole. Nonprobabilistic sampling often tends to concentrate on the more conspicuous sites. Is one justified, for instance, in arguing that the burial practices in one Hopewell burial mound were similar to those at a site three miles away, and at another twenty miles away? The answer to this is no, unless one's terms of reference for making generalizations are carefully defined ahead of time.

Probabilistic sampling is much more effective and appropriate in situations where one is seeking to generalize about a large data universe from a small sample population. The discipline of statistics and statistical theory makes considerable use of probability theory, a means of relating small samples of data in mathematical ways to much larger populations. The classic example of this is the political opinion poll, which is based on a tiny sample (perhaps 1500 people) used to draw much more general conclusions about national feelings on an issue. In archaeological terms, probabilistic sampling improves the chance that the conclusions reached on the basis of the samples are relatively reliable. This outcome depends, however, on very carefully drawn research designs and precisely defined sample units.

Probabilistic sampling in archaeology is still in its infancy, for the peculiar nature of archaeological data, as opposed to that in, say, physics, makes the development of sampling strategies difficult (Mueller, 1975). Once the sampling units are carefully defined and chosen, the archaeologist can elect to take a sample of individual units or of statistical clusters of them. This is often a decision of convenience. One example of clusters of sample units is a series of transects that lie close to one another, yet are assumed to include the range of data variability found in the entire population. It is obviously cheaper to survey such a cluster than to travel between several individual sample units scattered over an entire data universe of thousands of square miles.

Sampling frames are the lists of chosen units that form the sample of the total population to be tested. The sample frame is compiled as a means to proceed to the selection of units for investigation. The units are listed in order and form the *sample size*. There has been much debate about the desirable size of archaeological data samples (Asch, 1975). Obviously, the ideal sample is a total population, but in practice the dictates of time and funds make samples much smaller. Obviously, too, the larger the sample, the smaller the chance there is of missing an important variation in the population.

Probabilistic Sampling Schemes.   Archaeologists rely on three basic probability sampling schemes:

1. *Simple random sampling* takes the sample frame, determines the sample size, and then randomly selects the number of units required from the frame. The actual selection of numbered units can be done with reference to a table of random numbers, until the requisite number of units has been selected. Any method, like drawing cards from a hat, will do, provided the selection is absolutely random. This method is used when it is not necessary to take into account such variables as landscape or site topography, or sometimes when an absolutely virgin area is being worked. This approach treats all samples as absolutely equal, without reference to any external variables that may affect an individual sample.

2. *Systematic sampling* is a refinement of simple random sampling. A single unit is chosen, and then others are selected at equal intervals from the first one. One might, for example, excavate every fifth square on a grid of equal-sized squares laid out across a shell midden. This approach is useful for studying artifact patterning; but it is less effective when studying such situations as, say, the rooms of a pueblo, where a regular pattern of human behavior may cause one to accidentally sample only a portion of the activities at a site.

3. *Stratified sampling* is used when sample units are not uniform. The population is subdivided into separate groups, or strata, which reflect the observed range of variation within the population. Strata can be different ecological zones, different occupation layers or artifact classes, or groups of trenches. Such units enable intensive sampling of some units and less detailed work on others.

Charles L. Redman applied stratified sampling methods to a thirteenth century A.D. pueblo in the El Morro valley of west central New Mexico (Redman, 1975). He only had time to clear about one-quarter of the 500 rooms in the pueblo, so he stratified the site into four corners and four sides—each side was divided into four sampling blocks. Redman randomly selected one corner and one block from each area for clearance. He was able to select large blocks from areas that were well separated from one another but still use random sampling methods. Fourteen rooms in pairs selected from each side of the pueblo and from the corners, were excavated. Thus, the population was stratified to ensure the testing of at least one room from each row and of compartments of different sizes, as identified during preliminary investigation. It proved possible to sample this large site systematically, with a minimal expenditure of time and funds.

Using Sampling and Statistical Methods in Archaeological Research.   The use of formal sampling techniques in archaeology is still in an initial stage, and anyone using them must have a sound background in statistics or have access to a qualified statistician. The effective use of formal sampling methods depends, however, on a thorough knowledge of the archaeological problems to be investigated, a knowledge that must be acquired before starting one's research design and consulting a statistician. The sampling methods used must be appropriate to the data being acquired and to the range and size of the research project. Much more sophisticated sampling methods are needed for studying, for example, a settlement pattern through a millennium of human occupation in a Peruvian river valley, than are required for a straightforward analysis of a stone tool assemblage of 600 artifacts.

Sampling methods are applied to archaeological reconnaissance and site survey, to excavations, and to artifact analyses. Any quantitative treatment of archaeological data must be based on formal sampling methods. A detailed description of these methods is beyond the scope of these pages. The reader is referred to the specialist literature on the subject (Mueller, 1975).

Modern archaeology relies heavily on statistical methods as well as sampling techniques. Statistical procedures have two objectives in archaeology. The first of these, *descriptive statistics,* is a battery of standard procedures through which large bodies of data are reduced to manageable proportions. These include frequency distributions of different artifact attributes and types, various forms of graphs, and measures (central tendency and dispersion, that is, means, modes, and medians). These enable one to establish clustering or dispersion of different variables and measurement of degrees of variability.

The second objective, *inferential statistics,* provides systematic procedures for generating sensible conclusions about the whole when only a part is known. Archaeologists most often work with only samples of data, and therefore face a fundamental problem: How far can one generalize from sample findings? Common sense inferences have been used for generations, but the enormous bodies of data now available make such approaches much less effective than before. A body of statistical tools has been developed that forms a process of reasoning from a sample statistic to a population as a whole. At issue here is the need to determine the chances of error when making inferences about a population as a whole. In other words, what are the probabilities that statistical decisions based on small samples of data are reliable. Probability statistics involves a battery of well-defined statistical tests that are used to assess the significance of distributions obtained from descriptive procedures, such as binomial distributions, normal curves, and chi-square tests. (For a more technical description of these, see Thomas, 1976.) It is important to realize that statistical methods enable archaeologists not only to organize their data in an intelligible way, but also to attempt predictions as to the probability that their inferences from small samples are valid for larger populations.

Guide to Further Reading

Binford, Lewis R. "A Consideration of Archaeological Research Design." *American Antiquity* 29:425–441.
    Binford summarizes the key points about sound archaeological research design.

Hester, Thomas R.; Heizer, Robert F.; and Graham, John A. *Field Methods in Archaeology*. Menlo Park: Mayfield, 1975.
A basic field manual on survey and excavation for the beginner.

Mueller, James W., ed. *Sampling in Archaeology*. Tucson: University of Arizona Press, 1975.
A set of essays on sampling problems, which were a fundamental source for this chapter.

Thomas, David Hurst. *Predicting the Past: An Introduction to Anthropological Archaeology*. New York: Holt, Rinehart and Winston, 1976.
A short account of the basic methods of anthropological archaeology, which provides invaluable background for this chapter.

CHAPTER 10 ✒

FINDING ARCHAEOLOGICAL SITES

Preview

- Two processes are involved in the location of archaeological sites: reconnaissance and site survey.
- Many archaeological sites are discovered by accident, through industrial activity, modern agriculture, or as the result of natural happenings, such as floods and earthquakes.
- Many famous archaeological sites—like the Pyramids—have never been lost to human knowledge. But other, less conspicuous locations are found only by planned ground reconnaissance. Archaeological sites manifest themselves in many ways: in the form of mounds, middens, caves, and rockshelters. Many more are much less conspicuous and are located only by soil discolorations or surface finds.
- There are several levels of intensity of ground reconnaissance, ranging from general surveys leading to the location of only the largest sites down to precise foot surveys that aim to cover an entire area in detail. Even these are not totally effective, and all reconnaissance is, at best, a major sampling of the research area.
- In most cases, total survey is impracticable, so archaeologists rely on probabilistic and nonprobabilistic sampling methods to obtain unbiased samples of the research area.
- Key indicators of archaeological sites include conspicuous above-ground features, vegetational coverage, soil colors, and surface finds.

- A whole battery of new reconnaissance techniques involve aerial photography and remote sensing. Photographs taken from the air can be used to locate sites that are spread over huge areas. Pioneer efforts have been made with side scan aerial radar and scanner imagery.
- Subsurface features are often detected with the aid of resistivity surveys, which measure the differences in electrical resistivity of the soil between disturbed and undisturbed areas. Proton magnetometers are used to locate iron objects, fired clay furnaces, and other features.
- Site survey is designed to obtain information on subsurface features at previously located sites, as well as to collect and record artifacts and other surface finds. These categories of data are used to test hypotheses about the age, significance, and function of the site.
- Site survey depends on accurate mapping. The Teotihuacán project from Mexico illustrates the results that can be obtained with a site survey.
- Surface collections may be made by gathering every artifact on the surface of the site, by selecting for diagnostic artifacts, or by using random sampling. Surface collections are used to establish the activities that took place on the site, for locating major structures, and for gathering information about the most densely occupied areas of the site.
- Surface survey is much cheaper than excavation and is highly effective, provided the methods used are based on explicit research designs and the results are checked by precise excavations.

Numerous writers have spoken lyrically about the ravages of time on the monuments of antiquity, some with pathos, some with humor. W. S. Gilbert, in the second act of the *Mikado*, in 1885, said:

> There's a fascination frantic
> In a ruin that's romantic
> Do you think you are sufficiently decayed?

There was a sense of romance in the antique and the decayed, a sense experienced by every visitor to the Parthenon in Athens or to the Pyramids. Time has transformed the abandoned sites of our ancestors in many different ways. Some sites, such as Stonehenge and the Pyramids of Gizeh in Egypt, have never passed into oblivion. People have always realized that they were the work of earlier human beings. Others, like the thousands of sites in the Great Basin and in Australia, have vanished almost without a trace. It takes a trained archaeological eye to identify them.

Until fairly recently, archaeologists paid relatively little attention to the techniques for locating archaeological sites and interpreting them without actual excavation. A new emphasis on regional archaeological studies, innovative remote sensing techniques, and above all, the urgent need to save and record sites before they are destroyed by twentieth-century development activity has changed all this. The pages that follow review some of the techniques that archaeologists use to locate and study archaeological sites without digging them.

There are two basic processes involved in the location of archaeological sites:

Archaeological reconnaissance, which is the systematic attempt to locate, identify, and record the distribution of archaeological sites on the ground and against the natural geographical and environmental background.
Site survey, which is the collection of surface data and the evaluation of the archaeological significance of each site.

CHANCE DISCOVERIES

The ingenious people who calculate such things estimate that something like a quarter of all archaeological sites have been discovered as a result of natural or human activity. Whole chapters of the past have emerged through accidental discoveries of sites, spectacular artifacts, or skeletons. Ploughing, peat cutting, road-making, and other day-to-day activities have been a fruitful source of archaeological discoveries. Industrial activity, highway construction, airport expansion, and other destructive pastimes of twentieth-century humankind have unearthed countless archaeological sites, many of which have to be investigated hurriedly before the bulldozers remove all traces. Deep ploughing, freeway construction, and urban renewal are bitter enemies of the past. Yet dramatic discoveries have resulted from our despoiling of the environment. Some states require highway contractors to allocate a proportion of their contract budgets for the investigation of any archaeological sites found in the path of their freeways—this at least permits some investigation of accidentally discovered settlements. But many construction programs pay little heed to the pleas of the archaeologist and bulldoze away the past with minimal concern (see Chapter 20).

The excavation for Mexico City's *Metro* (subway) provided a unique opportunity for accidental discoveries of archaeological sites. The shallow tunneling, which extended for more than twenty-six miles under the city, yielded a wealth of archaeological material. Mexico City is built on the site of Tenochtitlán, the capital city of the Aztecs. Tenochtitlán, destroyed by the Spanish under Hernando Cortes in 1521, was a wonderful city whose markets rivaled those of most of the major Spanish cities in size. Little remains of Tenochtitlán on the surface today, but the contractors for the *Metro* found more than 40 tons of pottery, 380 burials, and even a small temple dedicated to the Aztec God of the Wind, Ehecatl-Quetzalcoatl (Figure 10.1). The temple is now preserved on its original site in the Pino Suárez station of the *Metro* system, part of an exhibit commemorating Mexico City's ancestor. The tunneling operations, happily, were under the constant supervision of a large group of archaeologists under the direction of Jorge Gussinyer of the world famous National Museum of Anthropology. The archaeologists were empowered to halt digging whenever an archaeological find of importance was made. As a result, many new sculptures and artifacts were saved from destruction for the national collections.

Hydroelectric schemes and flood control programs in North America and elsewhere have destroyed thousands upon thousands of archaeological sites without a trace—and have accelerated the discovery of others. Some of these projects have stimulated much intensive survey. The Aswan Dam scheme in Nubia provided a rare opportunity for intensive investigation of Pleistocene geology and Stone Age sites in the area to be flooded by Lake Nasser (Wendorf and others, 1968).

Figure 10.1   The temple of Ehecahl-Quetzalcoatl, found during the digging of the Mexico City *Metro*.

Nearer home, the flood-control schemes initiated by the Tennessee River Valley Authority and by the Army Corps of Engineers elsewhere in the agriculturally rich South have led to many river basin surveys (Phillips, Ford, and Griffin, 1951).

Nature itself sometimes uncovers sites for us, which may then be located by a sharp-eyed archaeologist looking for natural exposures of likely geological strata. Erosion, flooding, tidal waves, low lake levels, earthquakes, and wind action can all lead to the exposure of archaeological sites. One of the most famous sites to be exposed in this manner is Olduvai Gorge in Tanzania, a great gash in the Serengeti Plains, where nature, through earth movement, has sliced through hundreds of meters of Pleistocene lake bed to expose numerous living floors of early humans (Leakey, 1951). Fossil animal bones were found in the Gorge's exposed strata by Professor Wilhelm Kattwinkel as early as 1911, which led to a fossil-hunting expedition under Professor Hans Reck, and ultimately, to Louis and Mary Leakey's long and patient investigations in the Gorge. The results of their excavations are spectacular—a series of living floors stratified one above another, upon which hominid fossils, broken animal bones, stone implements, and even traces of possible structures have been found and dated to ages ranging from 400,000 for *Homo erectus* to 1,750,000 years before the present for living floors in the earliest bed of the gorge.

In late 1957, another remarkable discovery was made, this time in the semiarid country in southeastern Colorado (Wheat, 1972). Wind erosion exposed what appeared to be five separate piles of bison bones in an arroyo near Kit Carson. Some projectile points were also found with the bones. The bone bed, known as the Olsen-Chubbuck site, lay in a filled buffalo trail, of a type which crisscrossed the plains in early frontier days (Figure 10.2). The bones were carefully excavated and shown to come from *Bison occidentalis,* an extinct species. Separate piles made up of different bone types, such as limb bones, pelvic girdles, and so on, gave a clue to the hunters' butchery techniques. They had cut up the carcasses systematically, piling the detached members in the arroyo in separate heaps, dismembering several bison at a time. The remains of nearly 200 bison came from the arroyo, but only a proportion was fully dismembered. Clearly, the arroyo was a trap into which the beasts had been stampeded. (They have a keen sense of smell but poor vision; a lumbering herd of these gregàrious beasts can be readily stampeded into an abrupt declivity, and the leaders have no option but to plunge into the gully and be immobilized or disabled by the weight of those behind them.) So vivid a reconstruction of the Paleo-Indians' hunt could be made that the excavators were even able to guess at the

Figure 10.2 A layer of excavated bison bones from the Olsen-Chubbuck site in Colorado, a kill site found by a cowboy.

direction of the wind on the day of the stampede. The vivid traces of this hunt of 6500 B.C. were buried in the arroyo by nature and exposed again eight thousand years later, to be discovered by the vigilant eye of an amateur archaeologist.

ARCHAEOLOGICAL RECONNAISSANCE

Many famous archaeological sites have never been lost. The Parthenon, on the Acropolis at Athens, was remembered even when Athens itself had become an obscure Medieval village. The temples of Ancient Egyptian Thebes were famous as long ago as Roman times and have never vanished from historical consciousness (Fagan, 1975). Others, such as Homeric Troy, were remembered in Classical literature, but their precise locations were only rediscovered as a result of prolonged archaeological investigations.

Heinrich Schliemann devoted his entire career to locating the site of

Homeric Troy. Born in conditions of extreme poverty, he started life as
a grocer's assistant. By the time he was 30, Schliemann was a wealthy
merchant in Russia, having made a fortune in the textile trade. In the
late 1860s he retired from business to devote the rest of his life to a
search for Homer's Troy. In 1870 he started excavations at the large
mound known as Hissarlik in northwest Turkey. Within a few seasons,
he located the remains of several prehistoric towns, one of which, he
claimed, was Priam's Troy (Ceram, 1953; Schliemann, 1881; Stone,
1975).

Of course, most of the world's archaeological sites are far less conspicuous than the Pyramids, and unlike Troy they have no historical
records to testify to their existence. The early antiquarians discovered
sites primarily by locating burial mounds, stone structures, hillforts,
and other conspicuous traces of prehistoric human impact on the European landscape. The *tells* of the Near East, occupied by generation
after generation of city dwellers, were easily recognized by early travelers, and the temples and monuments of ancient Egypt have attracted
antiquarian and plunderer alike for many centuries. New World archaeological sites were described by some of the first conquistadores.
Later, in 1576, Copán, the ruined Mayan city, was studied by García de
Palacio. Mayan sites were vividly cataloged by John Lloyd Stephens
and Frederick Catherwood in the mid-nineteenth century, and the
wonders of Mesoamerican civilization laboriously recovered from the
rain forest that engulfed them (Figure 10.3).

Archaeological reconnaissance did not become a serious part of archaeology until field archaeologists began to realize that people had
enacted their lives against the background of a contemporary landscape and that all that remained for archaeology to find would be what

Figure 10.3 Copán in Honduras, a conspicuous archaeological site found by a
Spanish priest in 1576 and made famous by Stephens and Catherwood in the
nineteenth century.

Francis Bacon defined as "some remnants of history which have casually escaped the shipwreck of time." In the Southwest during the late nineteenth century, the immortal Adolph F. Bandelier, historian, archaeologist, ethnographer, and novelist, walked thousands of miles in search of archaeological sites. The early twentieth century gave rise to a great deal of this more systematic type of field archaeology in Europe. J. P. Williams Freeman and O. G. S. Crawford, among others, traced Roman roads and ancient field systems, walking and bicycling over the countryside in search of known and unknown sites. In Bolivia and Peru, Max Uhle, a German, was among those who pioneered systematic field survey in the New World. The techniques developed by these scholars form the basis for much archaeological fieldwork today (Crawford, 1953).

Ground Reconnaissance.   Most archaeological sites are discovered as a result of careful field survey and thorough examination of the countryside for both conspicuous and inconspicuous traces of the past (Willey, 1953). A survey can vary from the search of a single city lot for historic structures or of a tiny side valley with a few rockshelters in its rocky walls, to a large-scale survey of an entire river basin or water catchment area—a project that would take several years to complete. In all cases, the theoretical ideal is the same: to recover all traces of ancient settlement in the survey area. Terms like *complete survey* or *comprehensive reconnaissance* are often used to describe surveys that claim to have recovered all, or nearly all, the sites in a particular region.

Archaeological sites manifest themselves in many different ways: in the form of tells, mounds of occupation debris; middens, mounds of food remains and occupation debris; or conspicuous caves or temples. But many others are far less easily located, existing, perhaps, merely as a small scatter of stone tools or a patch of discolored soil. Still other sites leave no traces at all of their presence above the ground and may come to light only when the subsoil is disturbed, as was the case with the temple of Ehecatl-Quetzalcoatl, found during excavation of Mexico City's *Metro* line. Thus, it can be seen that no surface survey, however thorough, and however sophisticated its remote sensing devices, will ever achieve complete coverage. The key to effective archaeological survey lies in proper research designs and in the use of rigorous sampling techniques to provide a reliable basis of probability to extend the findings of the survey from a sample zone to a wider region.

The comprehensiveness of any survey is affected by other factors, too. Many surveys are carried out in intensively populated areas or on private farmland. Some landowners may refuse access to their lands.

To their credit, most farmers or landlords do not. Indeed, an owner may recall past discoveries on his land, hitherto unsuspected by archaeologists. Inaccessibility can be further complicated by such factors as dense vegetation, crops, and floodwaters. In many areas of Mexico and California, for example, the obvious months for site survey are at the end of the dry season, when the vegetation is dry or even burnt off. But in lush, lowland floodplains, such as those of the American South, large tracts of the survey area may be totally inaccessible all year. Only the most conspicuous sites, like mounds, show up under such conditions. And, of course, thousands of sites are buried under housing developments and parking lots, concrete, or huge earthmoving operations that have radically altered the landscape in many places.

A great deal depends, too, on the intensity of the survey in the field. The survey area can be traversed by automobile, horseback, mule, camel, bicycle, or—most effectively—on foot. Most famous field archaeologists of this century have been avid walkers. In fact, one well-known archaeologist used to boast that he had walked off the feet of all of his students and colleagues in pursuit of the past! Footwork is important, for it enables the archaeologist to develop an eye for topography and the relationships of human settlement to the landscape.

Michael Schiffer of the University of Arizona has identified four basic types of intensive ground reconnaissance (Schiffer and House, 1976):

1. Conspicuous and accessible sites are located by superficial survey, such as that by Catherwood and Stephens with Mayan sites in the Yucatan in the 1840s. The investigator visits only very conspicuous and accessible sites of great size and considerable fame. These operations, however, hardly scratch the archaeological surface.
2. In the next level of survey, assisted by local informants such as landowners, the relatively conspicuous sites at accessible locations are discovered. This type of survey was used frequently in the 1930s for the classic river basin surveys in the lower Mississippi Valley. It can be very effective, but it tends to give a rather narrow view of the archaeological sites in an area.
3. Limited area reconnaissance involves door-to-door inquiries on a very comprehensive level, supported by actual substantiation of claims that a site exists by checking the report on the ground. This type of survey, with its built-in system of verification, tends to yield more comprehensive information on sites. But it still does not give the most critical information of all—data on the ratios of one site type to another—nor does it provide an assessment of the percentage of accessible sites that have been found. When archaeologists

are concerned with the total inventory of archaeological sites in an area, such information is vital.

4. In the last type, foot survey, a party of archaeologists covers an entire area by walking over it, perhaps with a set interval between members of the party. This is about the most rigorous reconnaissance method that exists, but it does work, as evidenced by the Cache River project in Arkansas. There, selected zones of the basin were surveyed by people walking sixty meters apart (Schiffer and House, 1976). When Paul Martin and Fred Plog surveyed 5.2 square miles of the Hay Hollow Valley in east-central Arizona in 1967, for example, they supervised a team of eight people who walked back and forth over small portions of the area (Martin and Plog, 1973). Each worker was nine meters from the next, their pathways carefully laid out by compasses and stakes. Two hundred and fifty sites were recorded by this survey, at the cost of thirty person days per square mile. One would think that every site would have been recorded. Yet two entirely new sites were discovered in the same area in 1969 and 1971, a series of prehistoric irrigation canals were spotted by an expert on some aerial photographs, and some sandstone quarry sites were found.

Total and Sample Reconnaissance.   As we have said, the chances of any archaeological survey recording every site in even a small area are remote. Obviously, total survey of an area is desirable, and sometimes, near total coverage can be achieved by the use of a combination of aerial survey and ground reconnaissance. In the vast majority of cases, however, it is impracticable to cover an entire area, either because of the expense involved, or because the groundcover or terrain is too dense to allow for searching every corner of the region. Some survey areas are simply too large for a small research team to cover in the course of even several seasons. In all these cases, archaeologists must rely on sampling the survey area, using either nonprobabilistic sampling or probabilistic sampling, depending on the type of conditions in the area being surveyed.

Nonprobabilistic sampling, as we mentioned in Chapter 9, is used in situations where dense vegetational cover or difficult ground conditions make it practically impossible to select a portion of a survey area on a random, statistical basis. The classic examples of surveys using nonprobabilistic sampling are those done in the rainforests of Mesoamerica and the Amazon basin, where the vegetation is so thick that even modern roads are in constant danger of being overgrown. Most archaeological sites found in rainforest areas are located near well-trodden roads and tracks. The early archaeologists located sites by following narrow paths through the forest cut by *chicleros*, local people who collected resin from forest trees and guided them to the sites. Even today, archaeologists can pass right through the middle of a large site in the forest, or within a few feet of a huge pyramid, and see nothing (Chartkoff, 1978). Some large Mayan ceremonial centers such as Mirador in the northern Peten, have been located by air survey, but they are so difficult to get to that they have never been investigated thoroughly (Sharer and Ashmore, 1979).

Most archaeological reconnaissance has been nonprobabilistic, and site distributions often reflect the distribution of roads and the presence of archaeologists rather than actual prehistoric settlement patterns (Clark, 1967).

Probabilistic sampling, as stated in Chapter 9, involves the use of probability theory. It maximizes the probability that the site distribution in a chosen sample area is similar to that for the area as a whole. This type of approach has the advantage of allowing people not only to project the total number of sites in a research area, but also to calculate the proportion of larger sites to smaller ones, and so on, information of vital importance in the study of evolving human settlement patterns (see Chapter 16).

Archaeological reconnaissance based on probability survey is still in its infancy, for few attempts have yet been made to assess the efficiency of the different sampling programs that have been designed (Mueller, 1975). The best way of testing the efficacy of a particular sampling approach is to take a totally surveyed area and cover it again, using a variety of sampling approaches that are tested against one another. Experiments of this type have been conducted in the Southwest (Mueller, 1974) and in the Valley of Oaxaca in Mexico (Plog, 1976).

Most sampling surveys begin with the division of the survey area into arbitrary units. The size of sample units is determined by careful estimation of possible site densities and such data as topography, accessibility, and so on. Highly specific questions are posed at this stage. How large should the sample units be? What proportion of the area should be sampled to ensure a total site estimate within, say, ten percent of the actual total? What field techniques should be used to traverse the chosen sample areas? Will transect or square units be more effective for sampling the area?

Unfortunately, one key element is missing in the planning of survey research, that of ancient population densities. Having this information would allow one to zero in, with highly precise sampling strategies, on the most densely populated areas. In practice, many surveys combine both unit squares and transects to provide not only generalized information on site densities but also intensive surveys of carefully sampled units of the research area. The burden is on the archaeologist to prove that certain areas were, or were not, occupied, and how intensively. And this, in the many situations where the problem is to inventory the archaeological resource base in a specific area, can be achieved only by careful research design and the use of probability sampling methods. Examples of archaeological surveys that used sampling techniques will be found in Chapters 16 and 20, which deal with cultural resource management and settlement archaeology, respectively.

In cases where total reconnaissance is impracticable, probabilistic sampling approaches are by no means invariably the best solution to effective coverage of an area. In many regions, such as the well-forested, deep-river valleys of the eastern United States, probabilistic sampling is impracticable due to local conditions. In these and other obvious circumstances, the fieldworker has to fall back on nonprobabilistic approaches, where intuition and experience play important roles.

IDENTIFYING SITES

The competent fieldworker can identify archaeological sites with an ease born of experience that can astound the lay onlooker. I remember being astonished when, on a survey in the Zambezi valley in Central Africa in 1959, my senior and very experienced colleague stopped suddenly and picked up half a stone flake from a gravel covered with Stone Age artifacts. "This is the other half of a flake I found here in 1938," he told me. I flatly disbelieved him. But he was right. We located the original in the local museum collections, and the two halves were reunited. My colleague's archaeological memory was astounding, but it was also a result of long experience with local conditions.

The following are some key indicators of archaeological sites.

1. Conspicuous earthworks, stone ruins, or other surface features are among the most obvious indicators. Good examples are the Adena and Hopewell burial mounds of the Ohio valley, the pueblos of the American Southwest, and the fortified *pa's,* or defensive earthworks, built by the Maori in New Zealand (Bellwood, 1979).
2. Vegetational cover is a useful indicator, for grass may grow more

lushly on areas where the subsoil has been disturbed or the nitrogen content of the soil is greater. On the other hand, many California shell middens are covered with stunted vegetation caused by the artifact-filled, acidic soil that contrasts sharply with the surrounding green grass at the end of the rainy season. They can be spotted literally miles away. Sometimes specific types of tree or brush are associated with archaeological sites. One good example is the breadnut, or *ramon*, tree, which was once cultivated by the Maya. These trees are still common near ancient sites and have been used as guides to the location of many archaeological locations.

3. Soil discolorations are a sure sign of archaeological sites. In many cases the dark, organic soils of long-abandoned villages show up in plowed land as dark zones, often associated with potsherds and other artifacts. Burrowing animals living in such areas leave telltale traces in the form of organic earth and artifacts, which their activities have brought up to the surface.

4. Surface finds of artifacts, and broken bones, and other materials may show up in dry areas as dense concentrations of debris that stand out from the surrounding ground. In some cases, millennia of wind erosion may remove the soil mantling the artifacts and leave them exposed on the surface.

AERIAL RECONNAISSANCE AND REMOTE SENSING

Today's growing inventories of archaeological sites would never have been possible without the assistance of new reconnaissance techniques that rely heavily on twentieth-century technology. Some of these enable one to discover archaeological sites without even going into the field (Lyon and Avery, 1977).

Aerial Photography. The potential of aerial photography for archaeological reconnaissance was first recognized during World War I by O. G. S. Crawford in the West and by German archaeologists serving in the Sinai. The latter photographed ancient fields, streets, buildings, and other features that showed up with astonishing clarity (Crawford and Keiller, 1928). The famous aviation pioneer Charles Lindbergh flew Alfred Kidder over areas of Arizona and New Mexico in search of ancient village sites. These pioneer flights were followed by hundreds of later sorties. Archaeological photography has also benefited from

Figure 10.4   An aerial photograph of Chan Chan, in coastal Peru, shows the general layout of this remarkable settlement, occupied *ca.* A.D. 1200.

technological advances made during World War II and by space exploration. Today, thousands of hitherto unknown sites have been plotted on maps for the first time, whole field systems and roadways have been incorporated into panoramas of prehistoric or Roman landscapes in Italy and North Africa, and well-known sites such as Stonehenge and the many Mesoamerican and South American temples, have been photographed in the context of their landscapes (Figure 10.4).

Aerial photography gives an unrivaled overhead view of the past. Sites can be photographed from oblique or vertical angles, at different seasons or times of day, and from many directions. Numerous sites that have left almost no surface traces on the ground have come to light through the all-embracing eye of the air photograph (Deuel, 1969; Vogt, 1974).

Shadow sites.   Many earthworks or other complex structures have been leveled by plough or erosion, but their reduced topography clearly shows up from the air. The rising or setting sun can set off long shadows, which emphasize the relief of almost-vanished banks or ditches, so that the features of the site stand out in the oblique light. Such phenomena are sometimes called "shadow sites."

Crop and soil marks.   These are found in areas where the subsoil is suitable for revealing differences in soil color and in the richness of

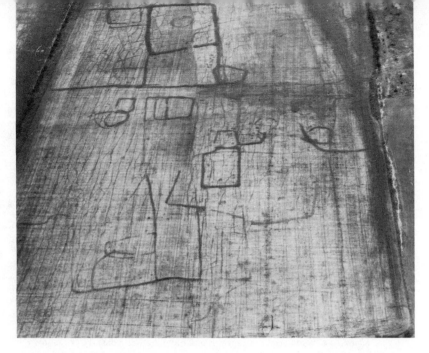

Figure 10.5 A crop mark site, from Thorpe, Achurch, Huntingdonshire, England. Under favorable circumstances, such marks can be clearly seen from the air.

crop growth on a particular soil (Figure 10.5). Such marks cannot be detected easily on the surface, but under favorable circumstances they can be seen clearly from the air. The principle upon which the crop mark is based is the fact that the growth and color of a crop are largely determined by the amount of moisture the plant can derive from the soil and subsoil. If the soil depth has increased by digging features, such as pits and ditches, and then filling them in, or by heaping up additional earth to form artificial banks or mounds, the crops growing over such abandoned structures are high and well nourished. The converse is also true in areas where soil has been removed and the infertile subsoil is near the surface, or where there are impenetrable surfaces, such as paved streets, below ground level and crops are stunted. Thus a dark crop mark can be taken for a ditch or pit, while a lighter line will define a more substantial structure. Soil marks result from ploughing soil from such features as banks, which show up as a lighter color, in contrast to the darker, deeper soil around them. Soil marks are useful in chalk country, where subsoil is a brilliant white.

Examples of aerial photography. A classic example of air photography was provided by Gordon Willey, who used a standard Peruvian Air Force mosaic of the cultivated valley bottoms and margins of the Virú Valley in northern coastal Peru to survey changing settlement patterns there (Willey, 1953).Willey employed these photographs as the basis for a master site map of the valley and was able to plot many different archaeological features. Three hundred and fifteen sites in the Virú Valley were located, many of them stone buildings, walls, or terraces that showed up quite well on the mosaics. Some much less conspicuous sites were also spotted, among them midden heaps without stone walls, refuse mounds that appeared as low hillocks on the photographs, and small, pyramidal mounds of insignificant proportions. Adobe houses did not show up as clearly as stone structures. An enormous amount of time was saved, time that otherwise would have been spent walking over rough countryside. The aerial photographs enabled Willey and his team to pinpoint many sites before going out in the field. The finds were later investigated on the spot. The result was the fascinating story of shifting settlement patterns in Virú over many thousands of years, which has become a classic study of its kind.

Most aerial photographs are taken with black-and-white film, which gives superior definition and is much cheaper to use and reproduce than color. The wide range of filters that can be used with black-and-white give the photographer much greater versatility in the field.

Some valuable experiments have been made with color photography, which is useful in detecting natural rather than cultural features. But it suffers from the disadvantage of being more expensive and less tolerant of errors by the photographer.

Infrared film, which has three layers, sensitized to green, red, and infrared, detects reflected solar radiation at the near end of the electromagnetic spectrum, some of which is invisible to the human eye. The different reflections from various cultural and natural features are translated by the film into distinctive "false" colors. Bedrock comes up blue on infrared film, but vigorous grass growth on alluvial plains shows up bright red. Experiments at the famous Snaketown site in the American Southwest did not show up new cultural features, but tonal contrasts within a color indicated various cultural components at the site. Vigorous plant growth showing up red on infrared photographs has been used as a means of tracking shallow subsurface water sources where there were formerly springs used by prehistoric peoples. The infrared data could lead the archaeologist to likely areas for hunting camps and villages where few surface indications now remain (Gumerman and Lyons, 1971; Harp, 1978).

It is important to note that no archaeological aerial photography is fully effective without checking the results on the ground. Even an expert can make many errors in interpreting surface features from air photographs.

Nonphotographic methods. Archaeological sites can be detected from the air using nonphotographic techniques, as well, but they are always very expensive.

Side-scan aerial radar (SLAR). This technique is used by the military to look at the ground from an oblique angle, and is effective even through dense cloud cover. Radar can sometimes penetrate through dense vegetation as well, and can be used to show up areas where many changes in topography have taken place or disturbance of the subsoil of large sites. It has also been applied to underwater sites to locate wrecks on the sea floor.

Scanner imagery. This can be used to record infrared radiation beyond the practical spectral response of photographic film. A scanning system collects the emitted energy with an oscillating mirror that scans the ground surface. The radiation thus recorded is converted to an electrical signal with a cryogenic detector. A radiation map, which can be inspected on a television screen or on film is the product of this system. Infrared imagery has been used most dramatically in north-central Arizona, where prehistoric garden plots, barely visible on the ground, have shown up in sharp focus on scanning plots. The borders of the plots are enhanced on the image, because the thicker volcanic ash at the edges of the gardens has a lower thermal inertia than the soil in the middle of the plots. The buried and obscure features of the field system have absorbed and radiated solar energy in differing amounts from the surrounding soil.

LANDSAT 1 and 2. These are the Earth Resources Technology Satellites that scan the earth. They are equipped with readers that record the intensity of reflected light and infrared radiation from the earth's surface. The data from the scanning operations is converted electronically into photographic images, and from then, into mosaic maps. Normally, however, these maps are taken at a scale of about 1:1,000,000, far too imprecise for anything but the most general of archaeological surveys. The pyramids and plazas of Teotihuacán in the Valley of Mexico might appear on such a map, but certainly not the types of minute archaeological distribution information that the average survey seeks. One can imagine applications of satellite sensing on really large-scale distribution problems, such as Roman roads in North Africa, but the basic imprecisions of the method still leave it in the experimental stage as far as most archaeology is concerned.

Figure 10.6   A periscope being used to investigate an Etruscan tomb.

SUBSURFACE DETECTION

Once sites have been located it is often possible to learn much more about them by using a variety of geophysical methods, most of which involve mechanical devices, for subsurface detection of buried features. Many of these relatively new techniques were developed for use in oil or geological prospecting. Most are expensive; some are very time consuming. But their application can sometimes save many weeks of expensive excavation, and on occasion, aid in the formulation of an accurate research design before a dig begins.

Nonmechanical detection.   In this method, the surface of the site is thumped with a suitable heavy pounder. The earth resonates in different ways, so much so that a practiced ear can detect the distinctive sound of a buried ditch or a subsurface stone wall. Bowsing, more an art than a geophysical method, really works—with practice. The author has used it on several occasions to detect the presence of walls.

The auger, or core borer.   This is a tool used to bore through subsurface deposits to find out what depths of archaeological deposit, and of
what consistency, lie beneath the ground. This technique has its value
during an excavation, but it has the obvious disadvantage that valuable
artifacts may be destroyed by the probe. Augers were used quite successfully at the Ozette site in Washington to establish the depth of
midden deposits (Kirk, 1974). Some specialized augers are used to lift
pollen samples. Augers with a camera attached to a periscope head are
also used to investigate the interiors of Etruscan tombs (Figure 10.6).
The periscope is inserted through a small hole in the roof of the tomb
and the interior inspected. If the contents are undisturbed, then excavation proceeds. But if tomb robbers have emptied the chamber, many
hours of labor have been saved.

Mechanical Detection.   There are several types of mechanical detection: (1) resistivity survey, (2) magnetic survey, and (3) pulse radar.

Resistivity survey.   The electrical resistivity of the soil provides some
clues to subsurface features on archaeological sites (Coles, 1972).
Rocks and minerals conduct electricity, mainly because moisture containing mineral salts in solution is present in the deposits. A resistivity
survey meter can be used to measure the variations in the resistance of
the ground to an electric current. Stone walls or hard pavements obviously retain less dampness than a deep pit filled with soft earth or a
large ditch that has silted up. These differences can be measured accurately, so that disturbed ground, stone walls, and other subsurface
features can be detected by systematic survey. To survey a site, all that
is needed is the meter, which is attached to four or five probes. A grid
of strings is laid over the site and the readings taken from the probes
plotted as contour lines of equal resistance. These show the areas of
equal resistance and the presence of features, such as ditches and walls
(Figure 10.7). This method works best on well-drained soils, and it has
been used more widely in Europe than elsewhere.

Magnetic survey.   Magnetic location of buried features is used to find
iron objects, fired clay furnaces, pottery kilns, hearths, and pits filled
with rubbish or softer soil. The principle behind the method is simple.
Any mass of clay heated to about 700° C and then cooled acquires a
weak magnetism. Rocks, boulders, and soil will also acquire magnetism if iron oxides are present when they are heated. When the remnant magnetism of fired clay or of other materials in a pit or similar
feature is measured, it will give a reading different from that of the

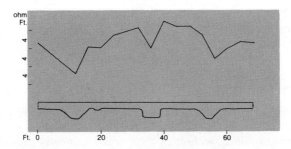

Figure 10.7 An electrical resistance survey across a Bronze Age burial site at Dorchester, Oxford, England. The upper curve represents the traverse made across the site with the instrument, with the probes set 1.2 meters (4 feet) apart. The lower line is a schematic section across the site; the dips indicate the two outer ditches and the burial pit, the positions of which were subsequently confirmed by excavation.

intensity of the earth's magnetic field normally obtained from undisturbed soils. The proton magnetometer is the instrument most commonly used to detect archaeological features by magnetic detection. A site is surveyed by laying out 15-meter (50-feet) square units, each of them divided into 1.5-meter (5-feet) grid squares. The measurement is taken with a staff to which are attached two small bottles filled with water or alcohol enclosed in electric coils. The magnetic intensity is measured by recording the behavior of the protons in the hydrogen atoms in the bottle contents. The magnetometer itself amplifies the weak signals from the electrical coils. Features are traced by taking closely spaced measurements over areas where anomalies in the magnetic readings are found. Magnetic detection has been used very successfully to record pits, walls, and other features in the middle of large forts or fortified towns, where total excavation of a site is clearly uneconomical. This method has been used widely in Europe and on earthen pyramids at La Venta, Mexico, but it is subject to some error, due to such modern features as barbed wire fences, electric trains, and electric cables (Steponaitis and Brain, 1976).

Pulse radar. The pulse induction meter applies pulses of magnetic field to the soil from a transmitter coil. This instrument is very sensitive to metals and can be used to find pottery and metal objects and graves containing such objects. A soil conductivity meter can be used to detect subsoil features by measuring changes in the conductivity of the soil. Anomalies spotted by the instrument can be plotted with good accuracy, and pits as small as 30 centimeters (11.8 inches) in diameter and 10 centimeters (3.9 inches) deep have been located. Individual metal objects can also be detected by this method, which adds great promise for the future.

RECORDING SITES

Archaeological reconnaissance is useless unless one records the exact geographical location of the sites. The newly discovered sites have to be plotted on aerial photographs or survey maps, so that they can be placed in their exact relationship to the local topography and environment. Good maps are an essential preliminary to the recording process.

It is not enough, however, just to plot a site on a good map and record its precise latitude, longitude, and if possible, map grid reference. Most expeditions develop a site record form as well, such as the one illustrated in Figure 10.8. This requires the person who discovers the site to note down information not only about location but also about surface features, the landowner, and threats to the site. On this form data about surface finds are recorded and this information is also related to inventory numbers. Some states, such as Arkansas, are programming all of their site records to a computer, so that a huge body of archaeological information can be recalled at short notice.

In addition to the above, every archaeological site in the United States is given a name and a number. For example, sites in Santa Barbara county, California, are given the prefix CA-SBa- and are numbered sequentially.

Readers interested in learning more about site recording should consult the specialist literature on this complicated subject (Hester, Heizer, and Graham, 1975).

SITE SURVEY

Archaeological reconnaissance has as its objective the discovery and pinpointing of site locations. Once this process is completed, each site is surveyed carefully, with the following objectives in mind:

1. To collect and record information on subsurface features, such as walls, buildings, and fortifications, traces of which may be detected on the surface. Such features may include ancient roads, agricultural systems, and earthworks, which are first detected from the air and then investigated on the ground (Bradford, 1957).

2. To collect and record information on artifacts and other finds lying on the surface of the site.

3. To use both the above general categories of data to test hypotheses about the age, significance, and function of the site.

By combining information from several sites or settlements from an entire archaeological region, it is possible to gain a general impression of a study area before any excavation commences, or to use this data as an adjunct to subsurface investigations at several locations.

Reconnaissance and surface survey have received increasing attention from archaeologists in recent years, especially in the American Southwest and in Mesoamerica. In almost every case, archaeological reconnaissance and survey precedes excavation of sample sites from the region or of selective excavations on a major site that has been subjected to intensive surface survey. With the increased emphasis on studying ancient settlement patterns in their ecological context, precise survey methods have become of great importance.

Teotihuacán. Perhaps the largest archaeological survey project ever undertaken was the Teotihuacán Mapping Project directed by George Cowgill and René Millon. Teotihuacán lies northeast of Mexico City and is one of the great tourist attractions of the Americas. This great pre-Columbian city flourished from about A.D. 1 until 700. Up to 150,000 people lived in Teotihuacán at the peak of its prosperity. Huge pyramids and temples, giant plazas, and enormous market formed the core of the well-organized and well-planned city. The houses of the priests and nobles lay along the main avenues, while the artisans and common people lived in crowded compounds of apartments and courtyards (Millon, 1973).

The sheer size of Teotihuacán is mind boggling, and a detailed survey of its hundreds of structures and alleyways was a monumental undertaking. Cowgill and Millon realized that the only effective way to study the city was to make a comprehensive and all-embracing map of all the precincts, for without it they would never have been able to study the processes by which Teotihuacán grew to such an enormous size. Fortunately, Teotihuacán's streets and buildings lay close to the surface, unlike the vast city mounds of the Near East, where only excavation yields settlement information.

The mapping project began with a detailed ground reconnaissance, conducted with the aid of aerial photographs and large-scale survey maps. The field data was collected on 147 map data sheets of 500-meter squares at a scale of 1:2000.

Intensive mapping and surface survey, including surface collections

Figure 10.8 Two pages of the site file form used by the state of Florida, showing the standard of data now required from field surveys. This approach assumes that all sites are valuable archaeological resources, each of them a part of the total inventory of sites forming an archaeological data base that can be consulted for many purposes.

STATE OF FLORIDA
DEPARTMENT OF STATE
Division of Archives, History and Records Management
DS-HSP-3A Rev. 4-77

FLORIDA MASTER SITE FILE

FDAHRM 802==

Site No. ______ 1009==

Site Name ______ 830==

Other Name(s) for Site ______ 930==

Other Nos. for Site ______ 906==

NR Classification Category: ______ 916==

County ______ 808==

Instructions for locating site (or address) ______

______ 813==

Location: ______ / ______ / ______ 868==
subdivision name / block no. / lot no.

Owner of Site: Name ______ ;

Address ______ 902==

Occupant, Tenant, or Manager:
Name ______ ;

Address ______ 904==

Reporter (or local contact):
Name ______ ;

Address ______ 816==

Recorder:
Name & Title ______ ;

Address ______ 818==

Survey Date ______ 820== Type Ownership ______ 848==

Inventory Status ______ 914==

Previous Survey(s), Excavation(s) or Collection(s): (*enter activity/title of project or survey/ name/date/respository*)

______ 839==

Recording Station ______ 804==
Specimens (Inventory Numbers) ______ 870==
Specimens (Present Repository of Materials) ______
______ 880==

Date of Visit to Site ______ 828== Recording Date ______ 832==

Photographic Record Numbers ______
______ 860==

Location of Site (Specific):

Map Reference (incl. scale & date)_____   809==

Township	Range	Section	¼ Sec.	¼ ¼ Sec.	¼ ¼ ¼ Sec.
					812==

LATITUDE AND LONGITUDE COORDINATES DEFINING A POLYGON LOCATING THE PROPERTY

Point	LATITUDE				LONGITUDE		
	Degrees °	Minutes '	Seconds "		Degrees °	Minutes '	Seconds "
	°	'	"		°	'	"
	°	'	"		°	'	"
	°	'	"		°	'	"
	°	'	"		°	'	"

=========== OR ===========

LATITUDE AND LONGITUDE COORDINATES DEFINING THE CENTER POINT OF A PROPERTY OF LESS THAN TEN ACRES

°   '   "   °   '   "   800==

UTM Coordinates: _____   890==

Zone   Easting   Northing

Description of Site:

Original Use(s) of Site_____   838==

Site Size (approx. acreage of property) _____ /   833==

Condition of Site:

Check one

☐	Excellent	863==	☐	Deteriorated	863==
☐	Good	863==	☐	Ruins	863==
☐	Fair	863==	☐	Unexposed	863==
			☐	Redeposited	863==

Integrity of Site:

Check one or more

☐	Altered	858==	☐ Restored ()(Date:	)()	858==
☐	Unaltered	858==	☐ Moved ()(Date:	)()	858==
☐	Destroyed	858==	☐ Original Site		858==

Condition of Site (Remarks): ( )(_____

_____)( ) 863==

Threats to Site:

Check one or more

☐ Zoning ( )(	)( ) 878==	☐ Transportation ( )(	)( ) 878==
☐ Development ( )(	)( ) 878==	☐ Fill ( )(	)( ) 878==
☐ Deterioration ( )(	)( ) 878==	☐ Dredge ( )(	)( ) 878==
☐ Borrowing ( )(	)( ) 878==		
☐ Other (See Remarks below):	878==		

Threats to Site (Remarks): _____

_____

_____   879==

of artifacts, were then conducted systematically within the 20-square kilometer limits of the ancient city defined by the preliminary reconnaissance. Ultimately, the architectural interpretations of the surface features within each 500-meter square were overprinted on the base map of the site. These architectural interpretations were based not only on graphic data but also on a mass of surface data collected on special forms and through artifact collections, photographs, and drawings. Extensive use of sophisticated sampling techniques and quantitative methods was essential for the successful completion of the map.

By the end of the project more than 5000 structures and activity areas had been recorded within the city limits. The Teotihuacán maps do not, of course, convey to us the incredible majesty of this remarkable city; but they do provide, for the first time, a comprehensive overview of a teeming, multifaceted community that contained vast public buildings, plazas, and avenues, and thousands of small apartments and courtyards, which formed individual households and pottery, figurine, and obsidian workshops, to mention only a few of the diverse structures in the city. The survey also revealed that the city had been expanded over the centuries according to a comprehensive master plan. (For more on Teotihuacán, see Chapter 16.)

Mapping.   Archaeological survey on any scale depends, as was the case with the Teotihuacán survey, on precise mapping. Maps are a convenient way of storing large quantities of archaeological information. Mapping specialists, called cartographers, have developed many effective and dramatic ways of communicating information graphically, devices that are very useful inclusions in archaeological reports (Figure 10.9).

Figure 10.9   Examples of archaeological maps. Left: A topographic map that shows the relationship between sites and the landscape. Right: A planimetric map that shows the different features of a site.

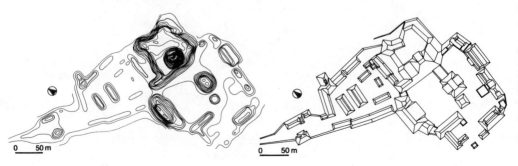

0   50 m   0   50 m

Topographic maps.   The distributions of archaeological sites are plotted on large-scale topographic maps that relate the ancient settlements to the basic features of the natural landscape (Figure 10.9, left). This master base map can be overlain with plots that show vegetational cover—either prehistoric or modern—soil types, and even prehistoric trade routes.

Planimetric maps.   These are commonly used to record details of archaeological sites. They are used to relate different archaeological features to each other and contain no topographic information (Figure 10.9, right).

Site plans.   These are specially prepared maps made by archaeologists to record the horizontal provenience of artifacts, food residues, and features. Site plans are keyed to topographic and other surveys from a carefully selected point (datum point), such as a survey beacon or a landmark that appears on a large-scale map. This datum point provides a location from which a grid of squares can be laid out over the area of the site, a grid that is normally open-ended, so that it can be extended to cover more ground if necessary. The grid provides a system of coordinates for recording provenience. The arms of the grid are normally oriented, using true north. A site grid is of critical importance during excavation for use in three-dimensional recording. It also plays a vital role in the recoding of surface finds during the initial survey process.

Readers interested in survey and mapping techniques as they relate to archaeology are referred to the specialist literature (Hester, Heizer, and Graham, 1975; Barker, 1977).

Surface Collection.   The artifacts and other archaeological finds discovered on the surface of a site are a potentially vital source of information about the people who once lived there. Surface collection has the following objectives:

1. the gathering of representative samples of artifacts from the surface of the site for the purposes of establishing the age of the area and the various periods of occupation
2. the establishment of the types of activity that took place on the site
3. the gathering of information on the areas of the site that were most densely occupied and that might be most productive for either total or sample excavation
4. the location of major structures that lie, for the most part, below the surface.

Limitations.   There are many limitations to surface collecting. A site is often occupied more than once by different peoples. The surface of a site has been exposed to the ravages of weathering, erosion, rainfall, and human activity for centuries, which may result in the *comminution* (pulverizing) of potsherds, stone tools, and bone fragments, so that almost nothing may remain on the surface. Pot hunters and previous investigators may have removed hundreds of artifacts, leaving behind nothing but insignificant fragments. The surface indications on a cave site, mound, or prehistoric village may be misleading or may tell one little about the people who abandoned it. In many cases, however, surface survey has been shown to provide good information on subsurface activities; and it is much cheaper than excavation.

Methods.   There are various ways to collect artifacts from the surface of a site. Some archaeologists collect everything from the surface, take their finds home to the laboratory, and then analyze them at leisure. This approach is commonly used in areas where little archaeological research has been carried out before.

When dealing with a well-known area or with sites containing distinctive artifacts, it is possible to collect only diagnostic artifacts, such items as potsherds, stone artifacts, or other characteristic finds that are easily classified and identified. These key finds may enable one to assess what periods of occupation are represented at the site.

Another way is by random sampling. Since total collecting is impossible on sites of any size where surface finds are abundant, some type of sampling technique is used to obtain a valid random sample of the surface artifacts. A common random sampling approach involves laying out a grid of squares on the surface of the site and then collecting everything found in randomly selected units. Once such a "controlled collection" has been made, the rest of the site is then covered for highly diagnostic artifacts.

How large should a surface sample be? There is general agreement among American archaeologists that a surface collection of at least 100 sherds should contain representatives of most pottery types at a site. As Frank Hole and Robert Heizer point out, however, there is no apparent evidence for this agreement (Hole and Heizer, 1973). It is also agreed that rigorous sampling techniques are essential to obtain even this minimal sample at the individual site level (Barker, 1977). Surface collection and sampling is often combined with small test-pit excavations to get preliminary data on stratigraphic information (see also South and Widmer, 1977)

Evidence of the activities of the inhabitants of a region can be obtained from surface collections but only in circumstances where the relationship between remains found on the surface and below the ground is clearly understood. In some cases, the surface finds may be an accurate reflection of site content; while in others, they may not. This problem is compounded not only by natural erosion and other factors but also by the depth of the occupation deposits on the site. Obviously, almost no finds from the lowest levels of a thirty-foot deep village mound will lie on the surface today, unless erosion, human activity, or animal burrows bring deeply buried artifacts to the surface.

With shallow sites, such as Teotihuacán and many prehistoric settlements in the American West, it is a reasonable assumption that the artifacts on the surface are an accurate reflection of those slightly below the surface (Millon, 1973; Yellen, 1977). This assumption provides a basis for studying activities from surface finds. However, any conclusions derived from surface collections have to be verified by subsequent excavation.

Figure 10.10   Paleo-Indian fluted projectile heads from the Plains. Judge and Dawson used such surface collections to trace changing site distributions through time.

The Rio Grande Valley.   Working in this major drainage area near Albuquerque, New Mexico, James Judge and Jerry Dawson were able to study hunting and living patterns among Paleo-Indian cultures of about 8000 years ago (Judge and Dawson, 1972). They used stone tools to define different site types, distinguishing between general localities, where no diagnostic artifacts were found, and specific sites, where Paleo-Indian projectile heads of diagnostic type were found (Figure 10.10). In this area were found base camps and processing sites, where food was prepared, as well as armament sites, where hunting tools were predominant. By distinguishing these site types on the basis of artifact collections, Judge and Dawson showed how the older Paleo-Indian sites were much farther away from large bodies of water than the later settlements and campsites, which were closer to the greatly reduced streams and rivers of later, more arid, times.

Site survey has the great advantage that it is much cheaper than excavation, provided that the methods used are based on explicit research design and that the conclusions are checked by precise and carefully designed test excavations. Many of the most exciting studies of cultural process and changing settlement patterns of recent years have depended heavily on archaeological reconnaissance and site survey. We describe some of these in Chapter 16, when we examine settlement studies in archaeology.

Guide to Further Reading

Crawford, O. G. S. *Archaeology in the Field.* New York: Praeger, 1953.
Field archaeology of the classic type, involving close observation of the ground on foot. The work has a British orientation, but it is a sound, old-fashioned essay.

Deuel, Leo. *Flights into Yesterday.* London: Macdonald, 1969.
A competent introduction to aerial photography.

Millon, René. *The Teotihuacán Map. Urbanization at Teotihuacán, Mexico, volume I.* Austin: University of Texas, 1973.
A complicated survey and mapping project that serves as a prime example of a survey project.

Mueller, James A. "The Use of Sampling in Archaeological Survey." *Society for American Archaeology,* Memoir 28.
A useful study of field survey sampling problems for the advanced reader.

Vogt, E. Z., ed. *Aerial Photography in Anthropological Field Research.* Cambridge: Harvard University Press, 1974.
A survey of aerial photographic applications in anthropology. A useful source book.

CHAPTER 11 ❧

ARCHAEOLOGICAL EXCAVATION

Preview

- Excavation is one way in which archaeologists acquire subsurface data about the past. The methods used today were refined by Mortimer Wheeler and others from the principles of stratigraphic observation and recording developed by Pitt-Rivers and others a century ago.
- Modern excavations are often conducted by multidisciplinary research teams made up of specialists from several disciplines, who work together on a carefully formulated research design.
- All archaeological excavation is destruction of a finite resource. Accurate planning, recording, and observation methods are essential.
- The Koster site in Illinois, where the excavators developed a sophisticated data flow system to keep their research design updated, illustrates the essential nature of the research design.
- Sites can be excavated totally, or as is more commonly the case, selectively. Vertical excavation is used to test stratigraphy and to make deep probes of arachaeological deposits. The digging of test pits, often combined with various sampling methods, is done to give an overall impression of an unexcavated site before major digging begins. Horizontal, or area, excavation is used to uncover far wider areas and, especially, to excavate site layouts and buildings.
- The process of archaeological excavation begins with a precise site

survey and the establishment of a site recording grid. A research design is formulated and hypotheses developed for testing. The placement of trenches is determined by the location of likely areas or by sampling methods. The process of excavation involves not only digging but also recording of stratigraphy and find proveniences, as well as observations of the processes that led to the formation of the site.

- Careful stratigraphic observation in three dimensions is the basis of all good excavation and is used to demonstrate relationships between different layers and between layers and artifacts.
- Three-dimensional recording methods are used to establish the provenience of artifacts and features.
- Excavation is followed by analysis and interpretation and, lastly, publication of the finds to provide a permanent record of the work carried out.
- Among the special excavation problems discussed are the recovery of fragile objects and human skeletons and the digging of postholes and structures.
- The chapter ends with a summary, using photographic and textual examples, of some of the best known archaeological excavations throughout the world and the various problems encountered in them.

Excavation! The very word conjures up romantic images of lost civilizations and royal burials, of long days in the sun digging up inscriptions and gold coins. Yet, though the image may remain, the techniques of modern excavation are far less romantic than they are rigorous and demanding, requiring long training in practical field techniques. Excavation is the major way in which archaeologists acquire data about the past. Unlike reconnaissance and surface survey, excavations recover data from beneath the surface of the ground—where preservation conditions are best—and accurate information on provenience, context, and association can be recovered intact. This chapter discusses some of the basic principles of archaeological excavation—the organization, planning, and execution of a scientific dig.

A SHORT HISTORY OF EXCAVATION

The earliest archaeologists were little more than treasure hunters, who thought nothing of excavating several burial mounds in the course of a single day (Daniel, 1975). At the same time, the great civilizations of the Near East and Egypt were being unearthed from millennia of oblivion by such men as Henry Layard and Heinrich Schliemann, who were hastily uncovering and removing literally tons of antiquities from their proper archaeological contexts. "Nothing was done with any uniform plan," complained Sir Flinders Petrie, an eminent Egyptologist of eighty years ago. "It is sickening to see the rate at which everything is being destroyed, and the little regard paid to preservation" (Daniel, 1967).

However, the foundations of scientific excavation had already been laid at the time when Petrie was complaining about the work of his colleagues. A century before, Thomas Jefferson, the third President of the United States and author of the Declaration of Independence, had spent time investigating Indian burial mounds in Virginia, which were rumored to be huge sepulchres. He decided to excavate one "to satisfy myself whether any and which of these opinions was just," he wrote. Here, for the first time, was a deliberate archaeological excavation undertaken to verify one of several hypotheses about Indian mounds. Jefferson cut a perpendicular trench through the mound "so that I might examine its internal structure." The trench was dug down to the natural soil and was wide enough to allow Jefferson to record the different layers of the mound. He was able to recognize at least three layers of human bones, horizons where the Indians had gathered together dozens of bones before piling stones on top of them. His *Notes on the State of Virginia*, published in 1784, contains a description of his excavations and conclusions. It is one of the first recorded instances of stratigraphical observation in archaeology (Fagan, 1977; Willey and Sabloff, 1980).

It was not until nearly a century later that scientific excavation developed anywhere. The first truly scientific digs were carried out by Austrian and German archaeologists working in Greece in the 1870s. One of these was the Austrian Alexander Conze, who began excavating at the Sanctuary of the Great Gods on the island of Samothrace in 1873, with a team of scientists that included a photographer and two architects. The dig lasted two years, and the resulting monograph was beautifully illustrated and full of accurate plans. Another, the German Ernst Curtius, began excavations in 1875 at Olympia, which lasted for

six seasons. His excavations were conducted with Teutonic thorough-
ness; he made careful plans of the architecture and detailed studies of
the stratigraphy, and he developed new methods of digging and recording that eventually came into widespread use in excavations all
over the Near East.

The sense of purpose and discipline the Austrians and Germans
introduced into the digging process was also practiced by a military
gentleman in England. This man was General Lane Fox, who retired
from active duty in 1880, inherited the Rivers estate in southern England, and changed his name to Pitt-Rivers. He devoted the last twenty
years of his life to a detailed exploration of the archaeological sites on
or near his estate. Pitt-Rivers's methods were elaborate and painstaking; he recorded every object found in his trenches in such a manner
that its exact find spot could be identified in the future, with reference
to sections and plans of the dig. Three-dimensional recording was a
cornerstone of his excavations, as were accurate stratigraphic profiles
with the finds recorded on them, a large and competent staff, and
prompt and meticulous publication of his results. The General is a
colossus in the history of archaeological excavation; the labor involved
in producing the elegant blue and gold monographs describing his
excavations must have been enormous (Pitt-Rivers, 1887; Thompson,
1977).

American archaeologists became involved in scientific investigation
of pre-Columbian sites at about the same time. Beginning with Cyrus
Thomas in the Ohio valley and Adolph Bandelier in the Southwest,
archaeologists started to develop the direct historical method, working
back from the known to the unknown (Fagan, 1977; Willey and Sabloff, 1980). Scientific archaeology developed most rapidly in the
Southwest. Much early research consisted of cleaning up many of the
major pueblos after the depredations of the massive treasure hunting
operations of the late-nineteenth century. A small team of archaeologists, including N. C. Nelson and A. V. Kidder, spent season after
season developing precise chronological and stratigraphical frameworks for the area.

N. C. Nelson, a robust and earthy Scandinavian, was the first person
to use potsherds for establishing Southwestern chronology. He took a
cluster of sites in the Galisteo Basin of New Mexico and dug small
stratigraphic trenches through their deposits. The resulting chronological sequence of pottery forms began with the Basket-Maker period
dating to the first millennium A.D. and ended with Spanish and historic
artifacts dating to about A.D. 1680. The Harvard-trained archaeologist
A. V. Kidder carried Nelson's work to its logical conclusion with the

large-scale excavations at Pecos pueblo from 1915 to 1926. His studies of potsherds and stratigraphical profiles led him to delineate a long sequence of Southwestern prehistory that "owes to outside sources little more than the germs of its culture" (Kidder, 1924). Kidder's cultural sequence has withstood the test of time, even if detailed modifications of his scheme have been made.

It took a long time for the lessons of Pitt-Rivers, Nelson, and others to be learned by the wider archaeological community. European archaeologists were generally quicker to apply the rigorous principles enumerated by the General than were Americans. A great exponent of the art of scientific excavation was the Englishman Sir Mortimer Wheeler, whose short monograph, *Archaeology from the Earth* (1954), is an elegant and lively part of any archaeologist's library. He and his contemporaries refined and applied Pitt-Rivers's methods with consistent energy. With them, the central emphasis in excavation shifted from the finding of objects to the developing of a strategy for an excavation campaign, one that would be oriented toward the solution of archaeological problems rather than toward discovery for its own sake. Precise digging and recording methods developed in England and Scandinavia were soon being applied as far afield as India and South Africa (Daniel, 1975).

Modern scientific excavation owes a great deal to such people as Wheeler, who realized that good fieldwork depended on careful organization, multidisciplinary teamwork, and very accurate recording and excavation methods. The popular stereotype of archaeology as a frenzied treasure hunt, then, has no grounding in reality, as the following pages will show.

THE ORGANIZATION OF ARCHAEOLOGICAL EXCAVATIONS

In the last century there has been a total transformation of archaeology, from treasure hunting and curiosity to scientific investigation and problem-oriented excavation. As a result, the organization of excavations has become increasingly complex.

In the early days, someone like Heinrich Schliemann or Austen Henry Layard would supervise huge teams of several hundred workers. Even as late as the 1920s, Leonard Woolley excavated the ancient Mesopotamian city of Ur-of-the-Chaldees with only a handful of qualified scholars and up to three hundred unskilled laborers. Today's excavation is limited in scope by ever-rising costs and by the sheer complexity of the data that now can be recovered from a site. Some of the more elaborate sites are dug by teams of specialists with very little unskilled help. Others are staffed by volunteer laborers, interested amateurs, and students, who gain practical experience of all aspects of excavation, from the use of a shovel to the recording of a complicated stratigraphic profile.

The director of a modern archaeological field expedition needs skills other than just those of a competent archaeologist. He or she also has to be able to fill the roles of accountant, politician, doctor, mechanic, personnel manager, and even cook. In addition, on a large dig, though manual labor may not be the director's responsibility, logistic problems are compounded, and he or she will head a large excavation team made up of site supervisors, artists, photographers, and numerous minor functionaries (Atkinson, 1953; Hester, Heizer, and Graham, 1975). Above all, the field director has to be the leader of a multidisciplinary team of specialist fieldworkers.

Multidisciplinary Research Teams.   The complexities of modern archaeology are such that all excavation projects now require multidisciplinary teams made up of archaeologists, botanists, geologists, zoologists, and other specialists who work together on closely integrated research problems, such as the origins of food production. The team approach is particularly important in the cases where environmental problems are most pressing, where the excavations and research seek the relationships between human cultures and the rest of the ecosystem.

A good inter- or multidisciplinary study is one that is based on an integrated research design that brings a closely supervised team of specialists together to test a series of carefully formulated hypotheses against data collected by all of them. Note that we say "data collected by all of them." Many archaeologists pay lip service to the need for multidisciplinary research teams but then recruit a few experts to act as highly paid technicians on the excavation, that is, merely to do such jobs as identifying animal remains and plant fragments or recording and interpreting geological layers. There have been cases of natural scientists actually excavating archaeological sites that were rich in, say, vegetable remains, and then retaining an archaeologist to interpret the artifacts in the site! An effective multidisciplinary archaeological team must be just that—a team, whose combined findings are used to test specific hypotheses.

Multidisciplinary research teams have been employed with great success at early hominid campsites in East Turkana, Kenya, where geologists provided the background environmental data; zoologists, the identifications and interpretations of the fossil animals found in the sites; and archaeologists, the data on surviving cultural remains; while physical anthropologists studied the human remains found in the three- to three-million-year-old sites. This approach is logical, but it is rarely carried to its logical extreme, where the experts would design their research together, share an integrated field mission, and communicate on a day-to-day basis about their findings and research problems. Much of the East Turkana research has been carried out by carefully selected teams of specialist experts, whose research experience is not in, say, Pleistocene geology as a whole, but in the specific types of geological deposits and stratigraphic and ecological problems found in East Turkana (Isaac and McKown, 1977).

The criteria, then, for selecting the members of multidisciplinary research teams include not only academic skills, but also an ability to communicate with people in other disciplines, highly specific specialist qualifications and, above all, a willingness to work closely with a group of scholars who are all committed to solving common problems. Such people are hard to find, and thus truly effective interdisciplinary research teams are few and far between. More loosely knit team approaches in which each member of a group pursues his or her own research but contributes to more general overall goals are far more common. The well-known Southwest Archaeological Group, whose members meet annually before the field season to reach consensus on approaches and research methods is an excellent example of this (Brown and Struever, 1973).

Excavation Staff.   Large, elaborate excavations that take several seasons to complete are staffed not only by a director and other specialist experts, but by several other technicians as well. Among the technicians are:

Site supervisors. Skilled excavators, often graduate students, are responsible for the excavation of trenches and recording of specific locations. The large-scale digs of medieval York in northern England are divided into different localities, each with a skilled excavator who supervises the volunteers doing the actual digging.

Recording experts. Some very large excavations will have a full-time surveyor, who does nothing but draw and record the stratigraphic profiles and structures found in the dig. Expert archaeological photographers are in great demand and will expose thousands of slides and black-and-white prints during even a short season. Their task is to create a complete record of the excavation from beginning to end (Harp, 1975).

Artifact and small finds staff. Even a small excavation can yield a flood of artifacts and flora and fauna remains that can literally overwhelm the staff of a dig. A skeletal laboratory staff to bag the finds and wash, rough sort, and mark them for eventual transport to the laboratory is essential on any but the smallest excavation. Some knowledge of preservation techniques is essential as well. Large excavations, such as the Koster site in Illinois, may actually employ computer records to handle the analysis of the finds (Struever and Holton, 1979).

Foremen. Paid foremen can become skilled archaeological excavators in their own right, but their primary responsibility is the management of paid laborers, especially on overseas excavations. Some of them devote their entire working lives to archaeology. Perhaps the most famous archaeological foremen are found in Egypt and Iraq, where successive generations of the same family have served on excavations for decades. Sir Leonard Woolley worked with the same foreman, Sheikh Hamoudi, from 1912 to 1941. Hamoudi, who became almost a part of Woolley's family, was famous for his invective and for his sensitivity to the moods of the workmen (Fagan, 1979).

In these days of rising costs and financial stringencies, most excavations are conducted on a comparatively small scale. There will usually be a team of students or paid laborers under the overall supervision of the director and perhaps one or two assistants; the assistants may be graduate students with some technical training in archaeological fieldwork and can take some of the routine tasks from the director's shoulders, allowing him or her to concentrate on general supervision and interpretative problems. But, in many cases, the director will not only be in charge of the research and the arrangements for the excavation but will also personally supervise all trenches excavated on the site. On that one person, therefore, devolve the tasks of recording, photography, drawing, measurement, and labor supervision. The director may also take a turn at the recovery of fragile burials and other delicate objects that cannot be entrusted to students or workmen; he or she is also responsible for maintaining the excavation diaries and find notebooks, the storage and marking of artifacts, and the logistics of packing finds and shipping them to the laboratory.

So varied are the skills of the excavator that much of a professional archaeologist's training in the field is obtained as a graduate student working at routine tasks and gaining experience in the methods of excavation and site-survey under experienced supervision. For the director, such students provide not only useful supervisory labor but also an admirable hone upon which to try out favorite theories and discuss in ruthless detail the interpretation of the site. Many an elaborate and much-cherished theoretical model has been demolished over a disputed profile or an evening campfire! Opportunities to gain excavation experience are always open, and notices of digs can be found on many college and university bulletin boards. The camaraderie and happiness of a well-run, student-oriented excavation is one of the more worthwhile experiences of archaeology.

PLANNING AN EXCAVATION

Excavation is the culminating process in the investigation of an archaeological site. It recovers from the earth data obtainable in no other way (Barker, 1977). Like historical archives, the soil of an archaeological site is like a document whose pages have to be deciphered, translated, and interpreted before they can be used to write an accurate account of prehistory. If there is one general remark about the history of archaeological excavation that is applicable to all areas of the world, it is that data recovery methods have been far too crude. Today's archaeologists are presented with the reality that their excavation methods are becoming more and more precise and slow moving just as the destruction of archaeological sites is proceeding at a record pace.

The first lesson that any budding excavators learn is that their work is potentially destructive. Excavation is destruction—the archaeological deposits so carefully dissected during any dig are destroyed forever and their contents removed. Here, again, there is a radical difference between archaeology and the sciences and history. A scientist can readily recreate the conditions for a basic experiment; the historian can return to his archives for a reevaluation of the complex events in a politician's life. But all that remains after an excavation is the finds from the trenches, the untouched portions of the site, and the photographs, notes, and drawings that record the excavator's observations for posterity. Thus, accurate recording and observation play an overwhelmingly vital role in the day-to-day work of archaeologists, not only for the sake of the accuracy of their own research, but because they are creating an archive of archaeological information that may be consulted by others (Alexander, 1970). Archaeological sites are nonrenewable resources, and much of the present concern in archaeology is directed at the need to conserve most rigorously those undisturbed sites that still survive.

Austen Henry Layard, Heinrich Schliemann, and the other pioneers were looking for archaeological treasure; Thomas Jefferson, on the other hand, spent many summer days excavating for information about the inhabitants of Virginian burial mounds. Today, we follow in Jefferson's footsteps and search for the past in the widest sense, excavation being but one method at our disposal, even if it is a vital one. Thousands of observations can be made, even on a small-scale excavation. Unfocused excavation is useless, for the manageable and significant observations are buried in a mass of irrelevant trivia. A problem focus is essential for every excavation to hold the observations to a reasonable and controllable limit. Any excavation must be conducted from a sound research design that seeks to solve specific and well-defined problems.

Research Plans.   "Problem-oriented" research has become a platitudinous catchword used by almost every archaeologist, even if his or her research designs are far from explicit. As archaeology becomes more explicitly scientific and more sophisticated, much more specific research designs are essential (Figure 11.1). Lewis Binford, who wrote about the need for sound research design in archaeological research, has argued that archaeologists have no defined criteria for selecting "important" sites. Excavations are traditionally conducted on larger sites, on sites that look more productive, or on sites that are nearest to roads. These criteria bear no resemblance to what is actually required, which is representative and unbiased data to answer a particular problem—a problem whose limits are ultimately defined by available money and time. Unbiased data, which do not reflect the investigator's

Figure 11.1   An organized horizontal grid excavation.

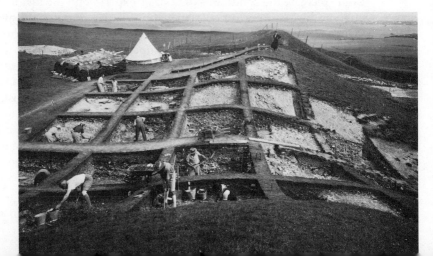

idiosyncrasies, can properly yield probabilistic estimates of the culture from which the samples were drawn. This kind of information requires explicit sampling procedures, not only to select a few sites from an area to excavate, but also to control the reliability of the information by using probability and statistics.

Excavation costs are such that problem-oriented digging is now the rule rather than the exception, with the laboratory work forming part of the ongoing evaluation of the research problem. The large piles of finds and records accumulated at the end of even a small field season contain a bewildering array of interdigitating facts that the researcher has to evaluate and reevaluate as inquiry proceeds, by constantly arranging propositions and hypotheses, correlating observations, and reevaluating interpretations of the archaeological evidence. Finds and plans are the basis of the researcher's strategy and affect fieldwork plans for the future. The days when a site was excavated because it "looked good," or because sheer lack of imagination precluded the development of a research strategy, are slowly being replaced by a constant reevaluation of research objectives.

The need for sound planning and design is even more acute in ecological research in archaeology, where archaeologists try to understand changes in human culture in relation to human environmental systems. Let us take the example of the Koster excavation in Illinois, one of the largest and most complex digs ever undertaken in North America, to illustrate this point.

The Koster Site.   The Koster site lies in the lower Illinois valley. It is a deep accumulation of twenty-six prehistoric occupation layers extending from about 10,000 years ago to *ca.* A.D. 1100 to 1200 (Struever and Holton, 1979). The wealth of material at Koster first came to light in 1968 and has been the subject of extremely large-scale excavation ever since. The dig has involved the collaboration of three archaeologists and six specialists from such other disciplines as zoology and botany, as well as the use of a computer laboratory.

Even a superficial examination of the site showed that a very careful research design was needed, both to maximize available funds and to ensure adequate data control. In developing the Koster research design, James Brown and Stuart Struever (1973) were well aware of the numerous, complex variables that had to be controlled and the need to carefully define their sampling procedure and the size of the collecting units.

They were faced with a number of formidable difficulties. Thirteen of the Koster cultural horizons are isolated from their neighbors by a zone of sterile slopewash soil, which makes it possible to treat each as a separate excavation and analysis problem—as if it were an individual site—although, in fact, the twelve are stratified one above another. Because the total site is more than 7.1 meters (30 feet) deep, the logistical problems are formidable, as in all large-scale excavations. One possible strategy would have been to sink test pits, obtain samples from each level, and list diagnostic artifacts and cultural items. But this approach, though cheaper and commonly used, is quite inadequate to the systems model that the excavators developed to study the origins of cultivation in the area and cultural change in the lower Illinois valley. Large-scale excavations were needed to uncover each living surface, so that the excavators could not only understand what the living zones within each occupation were like but also, after studying in detail the sequence of differences in activities, make statements about the processes of cultural change.

Due to the large scale of the excavations, Brown and Struever saw the need for immediate feedback from the data flow from the site during the actual excavation. Changes in the excavation method would, no doubt, be needed during the season's fieldwork to ensure that maximum information was obtained. To accomplish this, both excavation and data-gathering activities were combined into a data flow system (Figure 11.2) to ensure feedback to the excavators that would be as close to instantaneous as possible. The categories of data—animal bones, artifacts, vegetable remains—were processed in the field, and

Figure 11.2   The Koster site data flow system.

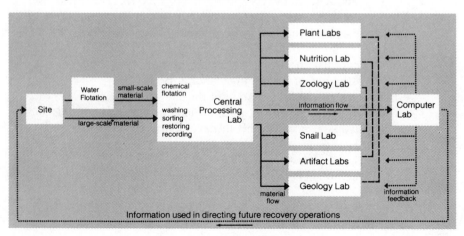

the information from the analyses was then fed by remote access terminal to a computer in Evanston, Illinois, many miles away. Pollen and soil samples were sent directly to specialist laboratories for analysis. The effects of the data flow system are highly beneficial. The tiresome analysis of artifacts and food residues is completed on the site, and the data are available to the excavators in the field in a few days, instead of months later, as is usually the case. The research design can be modified in the field at short notice, with ready consultation between the team members in the field. A combination of instant data retrieval, comprehensive and meticulous collecting methods involving, among other things, flotation methods (see Chapter 14), and a systems approach to both excavation strategy and research planning have made the Koster project an interesting example of effectively used research design in archaeology.

In many projects, excavation is only part of the overall research design. As a method, it should be used sparingly, for the end result is always the destruction of a site (Barker, 1977). Under these circumstances, no one can challenge the necessity for highly specific, problem-oriented excavation at all times.

TYPES OF EXCAVATION

Archaeological excavation is designed to acquire as much raw data as possible, given available financial and other resources. Its ultimate objective is to produce a three-dimensional record of an archaeological site, in which the various artifacts, structures, and other finds are placed in their correct provenience and context in time and space. The process of excavation, described below, involves the archaeologist in constant choices about the methods to be used, the types of trenches to be laid out, and the tools to be used, to mention only a few of the decisions to be made.

Total and Selective Excavation. As we saw in Chapter 9, not only the size and character of a site but also sampling techniques can play an important part in deciding which excavation methods are used. In the early days of archaeology, many sites were excavated completely. Total excavation of a site has the advantage of being comprehensive, but it is expensive and it leaves none of the site intact for excavation at a later date with, perhaps, more advanced techniques. *Selective excavation* is much more commonplace. Many prehistoric sites are simply too large for total excavation and can only be tested selectively, using sampling methods or carefully placed trenches. Selective excavation is used to obtain stratigraphic and chronological data as well as samples of pottery, stone tools, and animal bones. From this evidence, the archaeologist can decide whether or not to undertake further excavation. Some of the world's most important archaeological sites have been excavated selectively.

Vertical and Horizontal Excavation.   Invariably, vertical excavation is selective digging, the uncovering of a limited area of a site for the purposes of recovering specific information. Most vertical excavations are probes of deep archaeological deposits, their real objective being to reveal the chronological sequence at a site. Horizontal excavation is used to expose contemporaneous settlement over a larger area.

Vertical Excavation.   *Test pits,* sometimes called by the French name *sondages,* are a frequently used form of vertical excavation. They consist of small trenches large enough to accommodate one or two diggers and are designed to penetrate to the lower strata of a site to establish the extent of archaeological deposits (Figure 11.3). The digging of test pits is done to obtain samples of artifacts from lower layers, and this method may be supplemented by the use of augurs or borers.

Figure 11.3   A line of test pits on a Mesoamerican site, laid out at 15 meter intervals and aligned with the site grid.

Figure 11.4 A classic example of vertical excavation from Sir Mortimer Wheeler's excavations at Maiden Castle, Dorset, England. Note the recording posts on either side of the cutting and the workmen, which give an idea of the scale of the dig.

By their very nature, test pits are a preliminary to larger-scale excavation, for the information they reveal is limited, at best. Some archaeologists will only use them outside the main area of a site, on the grounds that they will destroy critical strata. But carefully placed test pits can provide invaluable insights into the stratigraphy and artifact content of a site before larger-scale excavation begins.

Test pits are also used to obtain samples from different areas of sites, such as shell middens, where dense concentrations of artifacts are found throughout the deposits. In cases like this, test pits are excavated on a grid pattern, the positioning of the pits being determined by probabilistic sampling or by a regular pattern such as alternate squares.

Vertical trenches are much larger, deeper cuttings and are used to establish such phenomena as sequences of building operations, the histories of complex earthworks, and long cultural sequences in deep caves (Figure 11.4). Vertical trenches have been widely used to excavate Near Eastern mounds, such as the Tepe Yahya site in Iran (Lamberg-Karlovsky, 1970). They may be used, also, to obtain a cross section across a site threatened by destruction or to examine outlying structures near a village or cemetery that has been dug on a large scale. Vertical excavations of this kind are almost always dug in the expectation that the most important information to come from them will be the record of layers in the walls of the trench and the finds from them. But, clearly, the amount of information to be obtained from such cuttings is of limited value compared to that from a larger excavation.

Tunneling is a form of vertical excavation done in a horizontal plane. Austen Henry Layard made use of tunneling to penetrate into the deep horizons of the Kuyunjik mound at the ancient city of Nineveh on the Tigris. Today, tunneling operations are confined to specialized excavations that investigate the center of huge earthworks and other deep structures.

Horizontal, or Area, Excavation.   Horizontal, or area, excavation is done on a much larger scale than vertical excavation, and is as close to total excavation as archaeology can get. An area dig implies covering wide areas to recover building plans or the layout of entire settlements (Figure 11.5). The only sites that are almost invariably totally excavated are very small hunting camps, isolated huts, and burial mounds. The Tudor palace at Nonsuch in southeastern England is a famous example of this type of dig. The ground plan of the entire palace had been lost and was recovered by horizontal excavation, adding a new portrait to the already glittering history of Henry VIII's reign (Dent, 1962).

The problems with horizontal digs are exactly the same as those with any excavation—stratigraphic control and accurate measurement. Area excavations imply the exposure of large, open areas of ground to a depth of several meters. A complex network of walls or post holes may lie within the area to be investigated. Each feature relates to other structures, a relationship that must be carefully recorded to enable the site to be interpreted correctly, especially if several periods of occupation are involved. If the entire area is uncovered, it is obviously difficult to measure the position of the structures in the middle of the trench, far from the walls at the excavation's edge. To achieve better control of

Figure 11.5   The horizontal excavation of an open area: an Iroquois long house, Howlett Hill site, Onondaga, New York. The small stakes mark the house's wall posts; hearths and roof supports are found inside the house.

measurement and recording, it is better to use a system that gives a network of vertical stratigraphic sections across the area to be excavated. This is often done by laying out a grid of square or rectangular excavation units, with walls several meters thick between each square (see Figure 11.6). Such areas may average 3.7 meters (12 feet) square in size, or larger. As the figure shows, this system allows stratigraphic control of considerable areas. Large-scale excavation with grids is extremely expensive and time-consuming and is difficult to use in areas where the ground is irregular, but it has been employed with great success at many excavations, being used to uncover structures, town plans, and fortifications. Many area digs are "open excavations," where large tracts of a site are exposed layer by layer without the use of a grid.

Stripping off overlying areas with no archaeological significance to expose buried subsurface features is another type of large-scale excavation. Stripping is especially useful when a site is buried only a short distance below the surface, and the structures are preserved in the form of post holes and other discolorations in the soil.

Horizontal excavation depends, of course, on precise stratigraphical control. It is normally combined with vertical trenches, which provide

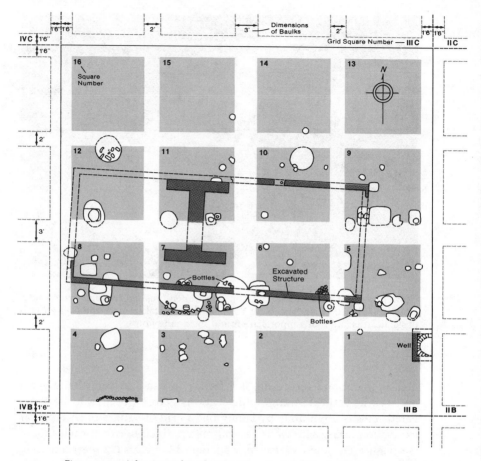

Figure 11.6   A horizontal grid excavation showing the layout of squares relative to an excavated structure at Colonial Williamsburg.

the information necessary for the accurate peeling off of successive horizontal layers. Many excavations involve the use of both vertical and horizontal excavations, with horizontal digging being the result of initial vertical trenches that reveal structures to be uncovered.

TOOLS OF THE TRADE

Every archaeological site poses different technical problems, not least of which is the decision about what types of tools will be used to excavate them (Atkinson, 1953). The choice of digging tools radically affects the excavation as a whole. The following are some of the options.

Earth-moving equipment is sometimes used to remove the sterile overburden covering large areas of a site, or when speed of excavation is vital. Backhoes are sometimes used to cut crude test pits, when sites are threatened by immediate destruction. The use of mechanical equipment is always limited, however, for such devices are highly destructive of fragile archaeological remains.

Spades, shovels, mattocks, picks, and forks, are used for loosening and moving large amounts of soil. The traditional archaeological symbol is the spade, which has a flat back and straight edge, and is used for cleaning walls. Shovels, with their scoop-like shape, are used for piling up earth in a trench preparatory to its being examined; they have innumerable applications in cleaning straight edges and tidying trenches, and they are the principal working tool of the archaeologist under conditions where much ground has to be uncovered.

Tools for loosening soil are the mattock, the pick, and the fork. The mattock and the pick may be considered together, because they are variants on the same type of tool; when used with care, they are a delicate gauge of soil texture, an indication used often in larger sites. The traditional Near Eastern excavation used teams of pickmen, shovelers, and basket carriers to remove the soil and dump it off the site.

The most common archaeological tool is the diamond-shaped trowel, its straight edges and tip having innumerable uses: soil can be eased from a delicate specimen; the edges can scrape a feature in sandy soil into higher relief; and as a weapon of stratigraphic recording, it can trace a scarcely visible stratum line or barely discernible feature. In addition, it is used for clearing post holes and for other minor work, so much so it is rarely out of a digger's hand on smaller sites.

Brushes are among the most useful tools, especially for dry sites. The most commonly used is the household brush with fairly coarse bristles that can be held by the handle or the bristles. Wielded with short strokes, it effectively cleans objects found in dry and preferably hard soil. The excavator uses various paintbrushes for more delicate jobs. The one-inch or one-half-inch domestic paintbrush has wide application in the cleaning of animal bones and more coarse specimens. Fine, camel's-hair artists' brushes are best for most delicate bones, beads, and fragile ironwork.

Small tools, some improvised on the site, aid in clearance of delicate finds. Six-inch nails may be filed to a point and used for delicate cleaning jobs on bones and other fragile artifacts. The needle is another tool used to clear soil from such delicate parts of skeletons as the eye sockets and cheekbones. One of the most useful digging tools is the dental pick, available in a bewildering variety of shapes. Often, dental picks can be obtained without charge through dentists, who discard them as soon as they show signs of wear. Continental European archaeologists have used a small, hooked digging tool, called a *crochet*, for many years; this is widely used for those excavations where a trowel is too big but where smaller tools are too slow and inefficient.

Screens are important tools because many finds, such as coins, glass beads, shells, small tacks, nails, and other artifacts, are minuscule. Most deposits from sites where small artifacts are likely to occur are laboriously sifted through fine screens of one-half to one-eighth-inch size. Flotation techniques are also widely used (see Chapter 14).

Surveying tools normally include lines or metal tapes, plumb bobs, string, spirit levels, drawing boards, drawing instruments, a plane table, and a surveyor's level and compass—all essential for accurate recording of site plans and sections and for setting up the archaeological archive.

Storage containers are vital on any excavation to pack and transport the finds to the laboratory, as well as to store them permanently. Paper and plastic bags are essential for pottery, animal bones, and other small finds; while vegetal remains and other special items may require much more delicate packaging. Cardboard cartons, supermarket bags, even large oil drums, can be used for storage of finds. One of the tragedies of archaeology is the gradual disappearance of the metal tobacco can, which served generations of archaeologists faithfully.

This by no means exhausts the list of equipment at the archaeologist's disposal, for much depends on conditions in the field and the types of finds encountered.

THE PROCESS OF ARCHAEOLOGICAL EXCAVATION

There is only one way to learn how to excavate and fully understand the process of archaeological excavation, and that is to go to a field school or on a dig and learn by doing it. *In the Beginning* is not a how-to manual, and can give you only an outline summary of the process of excavation, couched in the most general terms. The interested reader is also urged to consult the specialist literature (Alexander, 1970; Atkinson, 1953; Barker, 1977; Hester, Heizer, and Graham, 1975).

The description of the process of excavation that follows can be applied, in general terms, to any archaeological site. One must realize, however, that only a very few digs are conducted under ideal conditions, with unlimited time, adequate funds, and superb facilities. As Philip Barker puts it: "Just as 'all art constantly aspires toward the condition of music,' all excavation should aspire to the condition of total excavation." In other words, the ideal should always be kept in mind (Barker, 1977).

The excavator's aim should be to explain the origin of every layer and feature encountered in the site, whether naturally or humanly made. It is not enough to just excavate and describe the site; one must explain, also, how the site was formed. This process is achieved by removing the superimposed layers of the site one by one. In so doing, the archaeologist records the full details of each layer and its contents as they are excavated. The process of archaeological excavation involves deciding where to dig, the actual digging, the recording of the evidence contained in the excavation, and the interpretation of the site and the processes by which it was formed.

Deciding Where to Dig.   All archaeological excavation begins with a precise surface survey and the making of an accurate contour map of the site. A grid is then laid out over the site (see Chapter 10). The surface survey and the collections of artifacts made as part of it determine the working hypotheses that the archaeologist uses as a basis for deciding where to dig.

The first decision to be made is whether a total or a selective excavation is to be carried out. This decision depends on the size of the site, the hypotheses to be tested, and the available time and money. Most excavations are selective. Anyone contemplating a selective dig is faced with choosing the areas of the site to be dug. The choice can be clearcut and nonprobabilistic, or it can be based on complex sampling approaches. For example, a selective excavation to determine the age of one of the stone uprights at Stonehenge obviously will be located at the foot of the stones. But the excavation of a shell midden with no surface features may be determined by probabilistic sampling and the selection of random grid squares that are excavated to obtain artifact samples.

In many cases, an excavation can involve both probabilistic and nonprobabilistic choices. In the case of the Maya ceremonial center at Tikal in Guatemala, the archaeologists were anxious to learn something about the hundreds of mounds that lay in the hinterland around the main ceremonial precincts (Coe, 1967). They extended at least 10 km. from the center of the site and were identified along four strips of carefully surveyed ground, extending out from Tikal. Since, obviously, the excavation of every mound and structure identified on the surface was impossible, a test pit program was designed to collect random samples of datable pottery so that the chronological span of the occupation could be established. By using a proportional, stratified random sampling scheme, the investigators were able to select about 100 mound structures for testing and obtain the data they sought.

The choice of where to dig can be determined, also, by logistical considerations, such as access to the trench, something that can present problems in small caves; by the time and funds available; or, regrettably very often, by the imminent destruction of part of a site that is close to industrial activity or road construction. But, ideally, the archaeologist will dig where the results will be maximized and the best chance of acquiring data to test working hypotheses exists.

In some cases, the location of excavations may be established by test digging. For example, when Richard MacNeish (1978) surveyed the Tehuacán valley in Mexico, he tested 39 sites with vertical trenches and selected eleven of them for more extensive excavation (see figure 11.16). The sites chosen were those from which MacNeish felt he could obtain maximal information on different chronological periods. This strategy was brilliantly successful. The excavations enabled him to trace the early history of domesticated maize (see Chapter 20).

Stratigraphy and Sections.   The actual mechanics of archaeological excavation are best learned in the field. There is an art in skillful use of the trowel, brush, and other implements to clear archaeological deposits (Atkinson, 1953; Barker, 1977). Stripping off layers exposed in a trench requires a sensitive eye for changing soil colors and textures, especially when excavating postholes and other features, and a few hours of practical experience are worth thousands of words of instructional text. Photographs at the end of this chapter will give some idea of the practical problems involved.

We touched briefly on archaeological stratigraphy in Chapter 6, where we made the point that the basis of all excavation is the properly recorded and interpreted stratigraphic profile (Wheeler, 1954). A section through a site gives one a picture of the accumulated soils and occupation levels that constitute the ancient and modern history of the locality. Obviously, anyone recording stratigraphy is concerned as much with the history of the natural processes that the site has undergone since abandonment as with the actual formation of the ancient site itself. The soils that cover the archaeological finds have undergone processes of transformation that radically affect the ways in which artifacts are preserved or moved around in the soil. Burrowing animals, later human activity, erosion, wind action, grazing cattle—all of these can modify a series of superimposed layers in drastic ways. Charles Darwin pointed out that even the common earthworm's activities affect the world's soils (Atkinson, 1957; Darwin, 1881).

Archaeological stratigraphy tends to be much more complicated than geological layering, for the phenomena observed are much more localized, and the effects of human behavior tend to be intensive and often involve constant reuse of the same location (Adams, 1975; Drucker, 1972). Subsequent activity can radically alter the context of artifacts, structures, and other finds. For example, a village site can be leveled and then reoccupied by a new community that digs the foundations of its structures into the lower levels, and sometimes even reuses the building materials of earlier generations. Post holes and storage pits, as well as burials, are sunk deep into older strata; their presence can only be detected by changing soil colors or the artifact content.

Anyone attempting to interpret archaeological stratigraphy has to take the following into account:

1. Human activities at the various times in prehistory when the site was occupied and the effects, if any, on earlier occupations.
2. Human activities, such as plowing, industrial activity, and so on, *subsequent* to the final abandonment of the site (Wood and Johnson, 1978).
3. Natural processes of deposition and erosion at the time of prehistoric occupation. Cave sites, for example, were often abandoned at times when the walls were shattered by frost and fragments of the rock face were showering down on the interior. Such phenomena appear as dense layers of rock fragments that can separate different prehistoric occupations (McBurney, 1959).
4. Natural phenomena that have modified the stratigraphy *after* the abandonment of the site.

The interpretation of archaeological stratigraphy involves reconstructing the depositional history of the site and then interpreting the significance of the various natural and occupation levels that are observed. This means distinguishing between different types of human activity; between deposits that result from rubbish accumulation, architectural remains, and storage pits; and between activity areas and other artifact patternings.

Vertical trenches and sections are by no means the only way of recording archaeological stratigraphy. In many cases—Koster is a good example—safety considerations make it impossible to maintain vertical sections to any great depths, and the sides of the trenches are stepped. The only essential is that the section be absolutely clean when the time comes to record it with camera and pencil.

Philip Barker, an English archaeologist and expert excavator, advocates a combination of horizontal and vertical excavation for recording archaeological stratigraphy. He points out (1977) that a vertical profile gives a view of stratigraphy in the vertical plane only. Many important features appear in the section as a fine line and are only susceptible in the horizontal plane. The principal purpose of a stratigraphic profile is to record the information for posterity, so that later observers have an accurate impression of how it was formed. Since stratigraphy demonstrates relationships—between different sites and structures, artifacts, and natural layers—he advocates cumulative recording of stratigraphy, for this would enable the archaeologist to record layers in section and in plan at the same time. Such recording requires extremely skillful excavation. Various modifications of this technique are used in both Europe and North America. The Scandinavians have developed fine-tuned stratigraphic observations in which each layer is removed entirely and its surface surveyed with great accuracy. As a result, theoretically, one can reconstruct the stratigraphy at any point on the site (Biddle and Kjølbye-Biddle, 1969; Hatt, 1957).

All archaeological stratigraphy is three-dimensional, that is to say, it involves observations both in the vertical and horizontal planes. The ultimate objective of archaeological excavation is to record the three-dimensional relationships throughout a site, for these relationships are what provide the provenience.

Archaeological Recording.   *Notebooks* are an important part of record keeping. An archaeologist maintains a number of different notebooks throughout the excavation, including the site diary or daybook. This large notebook records all events at the site—the amount of work done, the daily schedule, the number of people on the digging team, and any labor problems that may arise. Dimensions of all sites and trenches are recorded. Any interpretations or ideas on the interpretations, even those considered and then discarded, are meticulously recorded in this book. Important finds and significant stratigraphic details are also noted carefully, as is much apparently insignificant information, which may, however, prove to be vital in the laboratory. The site diary purports to be a complete record of the procedures and proceedings of the excavation. It is more than just an aid to the fallible memory of the excavator; it is a permanent record of the dig for future generations of scientists who may return to the same site to amplify the original findings. Site diaries can be a most important tool in the hands of later researchers. For instance, the Knossos site diaries kept by Sir Arthur Evans as he uncovered Minoan Civilization for the first time have been used again and again by later investigators in Crete (Boardman and Palmer, 1963).

A small-finds register is also important in the records on any dig. In many cases, while some artifacts, such as pottery or stone implements, may be very common, others, such as iron tools or beads, will turn out to be extremely rare and have special significance. A small-finds notebook will help in assessing their significance.

Site plans may vary from a simple contour plan for a burial mound or occupation midden to a complex plan of an entire prehistoric town or of a complicated series of structures (Hester, Heizer, and Graham, 1975). Accurate plans are important, for they provide a record of not only the features of the site but also the measurement recording grid set up prior to excavation to provide a framework for the trenching.

Stratigraphic records can be drawn in a vertical plane, or they can be drawn axonometrically (Figure 11.7). Any form of stratigraphic record is a complex process and requires not only drawing skills but also considerable interpretative ability. The difficulty of recording varies with the site's complexity and with its stratigraphic conditions. In many cases, the different occupation levels, or geological events, are clearly delineated in the stratigraphic sections. On other sites, the layers may be much more complex and less visible, especially in drier climates, where the soil's aridity has tended to leach out colors.

Sections can be recorded with a horizontal datum string set up on the wall, whose ends are related to the site grid. All features on the profile are then carefully recorded with reference to the datum line. Some archaeologists have also used scaled photographs or surveying instruments to record sections, the latter being essential with large sections, like those through city ramparts.

Three-dimensional recording is the process of recording artifacts and structures in time and space. The provenience of archaeological finds is recorded with reference to the site grid (see Figure 11.8). Three-dimensional recording is carried out with a surveyor's level, or with tapes and plumb bobs. It assumes particular importance on sites where artifacts are recorded in their original positions, or on those where different periods in the construction of a building are being sorted out.

Grids, units, forms, and labels are the backbone of all recording efforts. Site grids are normally laid out with painted pegs and strings that are stretched over the trenches when recording is necessary. Small-scale recording of complex features may involve the use of an even smaller grid that covers a single square of the entire site grid.

In an interesting variant on the grid, Hallam Movius erected a permanent site grid *over* the deep deposits in the Abri Pataud rockshelter, Les Eyzies, France (Figure 11.9) (Movius, 1977). Using plumb bobs, a grid of 2-meter squares of metal pipe provided a framework for vertical and horizontal measurements on the surface of the deposits. Similar grids are sometimes erected over underwater wrecks in the Mediterranean (Bass, 1966).

The various squares in the grid and the levels of the site are designated by grid numbers (Figure 11.9, bottom), which provide the means for identifying the location of finds, as well as a basis for recording them. The labels attached to each bag or marked on the find bear the grid square numbers, which are then recorded in the site notebook. A great deal of time is saved if standardized forms are used to record site

Figure 11.7   A magnificent example of cumulative recording, recorded axonometrically. A portion of London's pre-fifteenth-century waterfront recovered by excavation in waterlogged deposits.

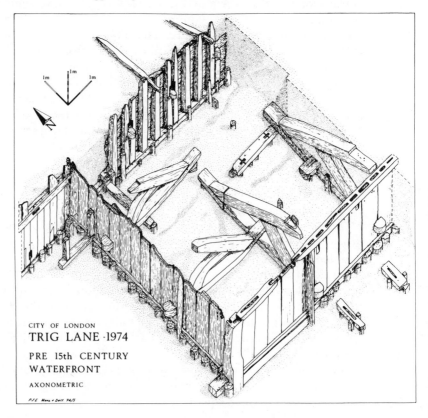

CITY OF LONDON
TRIG LANE ·1974

PRE 15th CENTURY
WATERFRONT

AXONOMETRIC

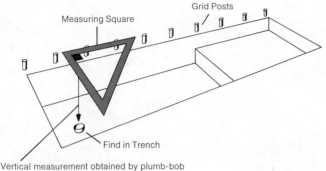

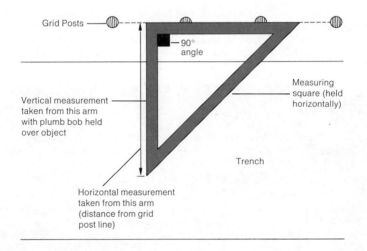

Figure 11.8   Three-dimensional recording. Top: The use of a measuring square. Bottom: A close view of the square from above. The horizontal measurement is taken along the edge, perpendicular to the grid post line; the vertical measurement, from that arm with a plumb bob.

data. The forms relating to, say, radiocarbon samples can then be assembled in order in a looseleaf notebook for later reference in the laboratory and museum.

Analysis, Interpretation, and Publication.   The process of archaeological excavation itself ends with the filling in of the trenches, and the transportation of the finds and site records to the laboratory. The archaeologist retires from the field with a complete record of the excavations

Figure 11.9 The site grid at Abri Pataud. Top: The 2-meter grid recording system at Abri Pataud, France. This permanent grid was used over many seasons of excavation. Bottom: Measuring the horizontal coordinates of a recently excavated find at Abri Pataud. Note the small board recording the grid square number and level.

and with all the data needed to test the hypotheses that were formulated before going into the field. But with this, the job is far from finished; in fact, the work has hardly begun. The next stage in the research process is the analysis of the finds, a topic covered in Chapters 12–17. Once the analysis is completed, interpretation of the site can begin (see Chapters 18–19).

In these days of high printing costs, it is impossible to publish the finds from any but the smallest sites in complete detail. Fortunately, there are many data retrieval systems that enable us to store data on computer tape and microfilm, so that they will be available to the specialists who need it.

Beyond publication, the archaeologist has one final obligation—to place the finds and site records in a convenient repository where they will be safe and readily accessible to later generations.

SPECIAL EXCAVATION PROBLEMS

Not all excavation consists of sifting through shell mounds or uncovering huge palaces. A great deal of archaeological fieldwork is dull and monotonous; but, occasionally, archaeologists are confronted with unexpected and exciting challenges that require special excavation techniques. Imagine being confronted with a royal grave, such as that of Tutankhamun, which took Howard Carter nearly ten years to excavate, or with the mass of waterlogged artifacts that came from the trenches at Ozette, Washington. In both cases, the excavators had to develop special techniques for dealing with these fragile discoveries.

Let us examine some of the most common excavation problems.

Fragile Objects.   Narratives of nineteenth-century excavation abound with accounts of spectacular and delicate discoveries that crumbled to dust on exposure to the air. Regrettably, similar discoveries are still made today; but in many cases, spectacular recoveries of fragile artifacts have been made. In almost every case, the archaeologist responsible has had to use great ingenuity, often with limited preservation materials on hand.

Leonard Woolley faced a number of very difficult recovery problems when he excavated the Royal Cemetery at Ur-of-the-Chaldees in the 1920s (Woolley, 1954). In one case, he recovered an offering stand of wood, gold, and silver, portraying a he-goat with his front legs on the branches of a thicket, by pouring paraffin wax over the scattered remains. Later, he rebuilt the stand in the laboratory and restored it to a close approximation of the original.

Arthur Evans, who discovered the Palace of Minos in Crete, realized that the walls of the palace were covered with fine frescoes, of which only tiny fragments still remained. Painstakingly, he recovered the small fragments and then pieced together the original frescoes. Unfortunately, there was little evidence of the original, and some of his reconstructions are regarded as somewhat fanciful.

The conservation of archaeological finds has become a highly specialized field of endeavor (Dowman, 1970; Organ, 1968; Plenderleith and Werner, 1973), which covers every form of find, from textiles to leather, human skin, and basketry. Many conservation efforts, like those used to preserve the Danish bog corpses, can take months to complete (Glob, 1969).

One of the largest-scale conservation efforts was mounted at Ozette, Washington, where the sheer volume of waterlogged, wooden artifacts threatened to overwhelm the excavators. The finds that needed treatment ranged from tiny fishhooks to entire planks. A large conservation laboratory was set up nearby, in Neah Bay, where the finds were processed after transportation from the site. Many objects were left to soak in polyethylene glycol to replace the water that had penetrated into the wood cells, a treatment that takes years for large objects. (A similar technique, incidentally, was used with the Swedish warship *Vasa*, which was raised from the bottom of Stockholm harbor.) The results of this major conservation effort can be seen in the Neah Bay Museum, where many of the artifacts are preserved (Kirk, 1974).

Burials. Human burials have been encountered either as isolated finds or in the midst of a settlement site. Some projects are devoted to the excavation of an entire cemetery. In all cases where graves are excavated, the burial and its associated grave, funerary furniture, and ornamentation are considered as a single excavation unit or grave lot.

The unearthing and recording of human burials is considered by the layperson to be one of the most romantic aspects of the archaeologist's job. No doubt this is true when the skeletons are adorned with an array of rich grave goods. But, in fact, the excavation of burials is a difficult and routine task that must be performed with care, because of the delicacy and often bad state of the bones. The record of the bones' position and the placement of the grave goods and body ornaments is as important as the association of the burial, for the archaeological objective is reconstructing burial customs as much as establishing chronology (Anderson, 1969).

Although the pharaohs of Egypt were sometimes buried under great pyramids, and at Palenque, Mexico, a great burial chamber was covered by the Temple of the Inscriptions, most burials are normally located by means of a simple surface feature, such as a gravestone or a pile of stones, or by an accidental discovery during excavation. Once the grave outline has been found, the skeleton is carefully exposed from above. The first part of the skeleton to be identified will probably be the skull or one of the limb bones. The main outline of the burial is then traced before the delicate backbone, feet, and finger bones are uncovered. The greatest care is taken not to displace the bones or any of the ornaments or grave goods that surround them. In many cases the burial is in a delicate state, and the bones may be soft; therefore, they are exposed gradually, giving them time to dry before they are coated with a suitable chemical, such as polyvinyl acetate or Bedacryl. The hardened bones can then be removed to the safety of the laboratory (Bass, 1971; Brothwell, 1965). Normally, the undersurfaces of the bones are left in the soil, so that the skeleton may be recorded photographically before removal (Fig. 11.10). The photography of skeletons requires careful use of the camera to avoid parallax errors. A scale must be included in the photograph so that the relative size of the subject may be apparent to the viewer. The burial is either removed bone by bone; or it is surrounded with a cocoon of plaster of paris and metal strips, the inside of which is packed with earth, and the whole structure is then transported to the laboratory, where it is cleaned at leisure. This technique is expensive and is generally used only used when a skeleton is of outstanding scientific importance or when it is to be displayed in a museum. Usually, however, the bones are carefully removed, one by one, hardened with chemicals, and then packed in cardboard cartons or wooden boxes with cotton, wool, and straw for transport to the laboratory.

Some burials are deposited in extremely elaborate funerary chambers, so much so that the contents of the tomb may reveal information on not only the funeral rites, but also, as in the case of the Ur-of-the-Chaldees royal burials, on the social order of the royal court.

The great royal tombs of the Shang civilization of northern China are an example of complex tombs, where careful excavation made possible the recording of many chariot features that would otherwise have been lost (Shang, 1977). The shaft, axle, and lower parts of the chariot wheels are visible as discolored areas in the ground. The area was dug to recover the dimensions and character of the chariots, which were found at the entrance ramps of the great Shang tombs. The charioteers were buried to accompany their masters.

Structures and Pits.   The excavation of houses and household clusters involves not only careful uncovering of the structures themselves but also of the artifacts associated with them. Humankind has constructed every type of dwelling, from simple brush shelters to elaborate palaces. The recovery of the floor plans of such dwellings requires extremely sensitive excavation methods.

Open excavations are normally used to uncover structures of considerable size (Barker, 1977). Grids allow stratigraphic control over the building site, and especially, over the study of successive occupation stages. In many cases, the structures may have been built of such

Figure 11.10   A classic Maya collective tomb at Guattan in the Motagua Valley, Guatemala, excavated by Norman Hammond. Note the clean excavation, the carefully cleaned up skeletons, and the stone lining of tomb.

Figure 11.11 The Bronze Age palace of Nestor from Mycenaean Greece.

perishable materials as wood or matting. Wooden houses are normally recognized by the post holes of the wall timbers and, sometimes, foundation trenches. Clay walls collapse into a pile when a hut is burnt or falls down; thus, the wall clay may bear impressions of matting, sticks, or thatch. Stone structures are often better preserved, especially if mortar was used, although sometimes the stone has been removed by later builders, and only foundation trenches remain (Figure 11.11). Stratigraphic cross sections across walls give an insight into the structure's history. The dating of most stone structures is complicated, especially when successive rebuilding or occupation of the building is involved (Figure 11.12).

Some of the most spectacular buildings in the archaeological record are those that leave few traces on the surface. Figure 11.5 shows an Iroquois long house that was identified purely from subsurface markings in the soil. Numerous long houses have been identified from early farming sites in Europe in the same way (Piggott, 1965).

The pueblos of the American Southwest offer another type of excavation problem. The many rooms of the pueblos contain complicated deposits that are full of occupation debris and many artifacts (Figure 11.13). Efforts have been made to record the artifact patternings in these rooms, in order to establish both the activities carried out in them and the possible residential patterns (Hill, 1970).

Storage and rubbish pits are commonly found on archaeological sites and may reach several meters in depth (Figure 11.14). Their contents furnish important information on dietary habits gleaned from

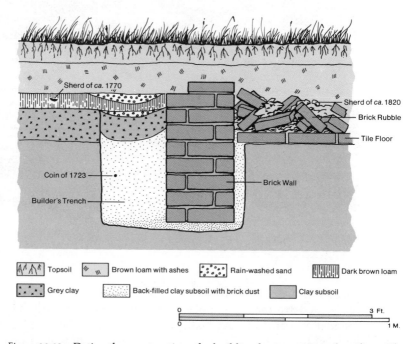

Topsoil | Brown loam with ashes | Rain-washed sand | Dark brown loam

Grey clay | Back-filled clay subsoil with brick dust | Clay subsoil

Figure 11.12 Dating the construction of a building by its associated artifacts. The brick wall was built in a foundation trench that was filled with brick dust and clay. Someone dropped a coin dated 1723 into the clay as the trench was being filled. Obviously, then, the building of which the wall forms a part dates to no earlier than 1723.

Figure 11.13 Mesa Verde, a southwestern pueblo in Colorado.

food residues or caches of seeds. Trash pits are even more informative. Garbage pits and privies at Colonial Williamsburg have yielded a host of esoteric finds, including wax seals from documents that were used as toilet tissue (Noël Hume, 1969). Some historic pits can be dated from military buttons and other finds.

Storage and trash pits are normally identified by circular discolorations in the soil. The contents are then cross-sectioned, and the associated finds analyzed as an associated unit (Figure 11.14). Large pits, which contain literally thousands of seeds and other informative materials, are excavated with particular care.

Figure 11.14   A double storage pit at Maiden Castle, Dorset, which was cut into the chalk subsoil.

Postholes are normally associated with houses and other such structures. The posts they once contained were buried in holes that were dug larger than the base of the post itself. Once the structure was abandoned, the post might be left to rot, be removed, or cut off. The traces each of these outcomes leave in the ground differ sharply and can be identified with careful excavation. Sometimes it is possible to find fragments of the post or of the charcoal from its burning, which enable one to identify the type of wood used. Some interesting experiments in Britain have shown that most small posts will last about 15 years in damp ground (Morgan, 1975), but much depends on soil conditions.

These are but a few of the many unusual excavation problems that may confront the archaeologist in the field. Each archaeological site offers special challenges to the investigator, challenges of preservation, recording, or interpretation. But, whatever the nature of the site, we always return again and again to stratigraphy and settlement patterns, to chronologies and cultural sequences, and to research designs, sampling, and careful surveys—principles of excavation that originated with the nineteenth-century archaeologists and have been refined progressively over the years. Though individual methods may vary from site to site and from area to area, no one denies the fundamental objective of archaeological excavation: the recovery and recording of data from below the ground in as systematic and scientific a way as possible.

SOME WELL-KNOWN ARCHAEOLOGICAL EXCAVATIONS

This section provides a summary, using photographs and text, of some of the different types of excavation problems encountered throughout the world and the methods used to deal with them.

Hunter-Gatherer Camp Sites.   The earliest humans lived in small camp sites that are sometimes represented in the archaeologial record by little more than a scatter of broken animal bones, crude stone artifacts, and other occupation debris. Figure 11.15 shows a portion of a slaughtered elephant uncovered in Bed I at Olduvai Gorge, Tanzania. The original position of the bones was recorded before their removal. Such living sites are normally excavated in their entirety, using horizontal trenching.

Figure 11.15   Portion of a slaughtered elephant from Olduvai Gorge, Tanzania.

Caves and Rockshelters.   Figure 11.16 shows the excavations at Cox-catlán rockshelter in the Tehuacán valley in Mexico, where important evidence for early maize cultivation was recovered. Cave excavation like this tends to be selective and is carried out both horizontally and vertically. The Coxcatlán site was excavated in alternate squares, each of which was treated as a separate unit.

Perhaps the most meticulous rockshelter excavation ever carried out was at Abri Pataud in the Dordogne (Figure 11.9), where Hallam Movius dug on a coordinated, master plan basis. He removed over 6 meters (20 feet) of occupation levels over a 12-square meter (60-square feet) area, using a horizontal technique that enabled the excavators to record the exact provenience of every find and major feature.

Figure 11.16   Coxcatlán, Tehuacán Valley, Mexico.

Middens.   A midden is a dump of food remains and occupation debris. The constituents of shell middens include sea shells, fish bones, ash, stone, and several other forms of food remains (Gifford, 1916). These sites are commonplace on the world's coasts. The excavation problems are twofold: identifying stratigraphic features in the monotonous deposits, and working out adequate sampling procedures to obtain statistically reliable samples of the occupation and food residues in the site. Many modern shell midden excavations are conducted with the aid of random sampling methods that facilitate the collection of unbiased samples of midden contents for later analysis. Horizontal excavation techniques are often used, as at the Galatea Bay midden illustrated in Figure 11.17 (Shawcross, 1967; Terrell, 1967).

Mound Excavations.   The great *tells*, or occupation mounds, of the Near East result from centuries, even millennia, of human occupation. Such large settlements require huge labor forces to excavate, even on a modest scale. Figures 11.18 and 11.19 contain, respectively, a stratigraphic profile through the ramparts of the ancient city of Harappa in the Indus valley, Pakistan, and a photograph of the actual excavation, a deep probe into the depths of the city's citadel. In this case, vertical excavation provided the history of the defenses (Wheeler, 1967).

Figure 11.17   Galatea Bay midden, North Island, New Zealand.

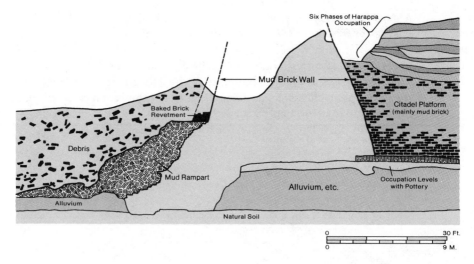

Figure 11.18   A section through the defenses of the citadel at Harappa, Pakistan.

Clearly, with sites of these great dimensions, only a sampling of the deposits can be made. In the final analysis, the most important primary objective is to obtain details of the stratigraphy of the settlement (Figure 11.20). Mound stratigraphy is rarely simple, for both humans and animals complicate it: burrowing animals saunter through the soft soil of the occupation levels, disturbing burials, huts, and hearths; rubbish, burial, and storage pits are dug into lower levels; drains, new street levels, and house foundations disturb natural accumulations. As Braidwood and Howe remarked about early farming village mounds in the Near East: "The . . . strata of the archaeological sites may pitch and toss in ways their surface contours seldom suggest. . . ." (Braidwood and Howe, 1962).

Small burial mounds may be excavated in their entirety, using a quadrat method of excavation that removes the mound to its foundations while leaving unexcavated control sections across the site (Figure 11.21)

Village and Town Sites.   Larger habitation sites, such as farming villages, complete prehistoric towns, or even Medieval cities, are best investigated by area excavation, if sufficient resources are available and their deposits are shallow enough.

Figure 11.19   Wheeler's excavation through the mud-brick rampart at Harappa. The lower figure stands on the original ground surface.

A remarkable example of this type of archaeology came from Winchester, where the history of a row of cottages, eleven houses, and two churches was recreated from documents and archaeological research (Selkirk and Selkirk, 1970). The Brooks area of Winchester was formerly a cloth-working area, where dyeing and fulling was done (Figure 11.22). The Brooks houses had workrooms and shops facing the street, with the water channels for the dying process penetrating the front walls; working and living quarters were behind or on top of the shop. A title deed to one house shows that by 1366 it was owned by Richard Bosynton, a leading fuller of his day, who became City Cofferer (treasurer) in 1380–1381. Bosynton appears as a strong character, who was fined sixpence in 1390 for polluting the stream that ran by the Brooks houses with dyer's waste. He sold part of his house in 1407 when he retired, and the surviving deed describes the house in detail at the time. Another house was owned by William Bolt, a vigorous businessman, who evicted a feckless tenant named John Shovelar in 1402 as a result of a complex law case. Shovelar had been in trouble with the courts for, among other offenses, erecting a public urinal on his property—urine was a vital ingredient in the fulling process, acting as a type of soap. In

Figure 11.20 Two approaches to mound trenching: (a) A stepped trench from the summit exposes a small amount of the original occupation, if this is the mound's center. All earth must be lifted out. (b) A stepped cutting at the mound's edge may miss the core, but soil is easily disposed of. In both approaches, stepping the walls prevents collapse.

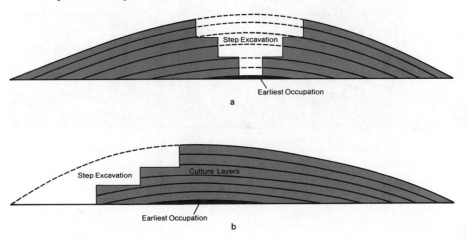

this and other instances at Winchester, documents and excavations were linked to provide a remarkably graphic picture of life in a medieval town.

These are but a few examples of archaeological excavations. Your instructors, undoubtedly, will share others from their own digging experience with you.

Figure 11.21   A quadrat excavation on a round barrow from Wiltshire, England, photographed from above.

Figure 11.22 A view of the Brooks site, Winchester, England. The outlines of the thirteenth-century cottage walls and of small rooms are clear, as is the narrow lane in front of the dwellings.

Guide to Further Reading

The best excavation manuals are from Britain, which is hardly surprising, in view of the long tradition of fieldwork and excavation there. The British are lucky in having a wide range of very challenging excavation problems to confront, and the literature reflects this. The following are the major publications on excavation.

Alexander, John. *The Directing of Archaeological Excavations.* London: John Baker, 1970.
Provides a very wide coverage of different site problems.

Atkinson, R. J. C. *Field Archaeology.* London: Methuen, 1953.
An older manual, but superb in its clear exposition of basic approaches.

Barker, Philip. *The Techniques of Archaeological Excavation.* London: Batsford, 1977.
An expert guide to excavation that can be used in conjunction with Alexander and Atkinson. Strong European orientation.

Hester, Thomas N.; Heizer, R. F.; and Graham, John. *Field Methods in Archaeology.* 6th ed. Palo Alto: Mayfield, 1975.
The American manual used widely in field schools.

Wheeler, R. E. M. *Archaeology from the Earth.* Oxford: Clarendon Press, 1954.
An archaeological classic that describes excavation on a grand scale with verve and elegance. A must for every archaeologist's bookshelf, if only for its common-sense information.

PART V ❧

ANALYSIS OF THE PAST

ARTIFACTS AND TECHNOLOGY

"Intelligence . . . is the faculty of making artificial objects, especially tools to make tools."

HENRI BERGSON,
L'Evolution Créatrice (1907)

Part V begins our exploration of the ultimate objectives of archaeology: the construction of culture history, the reconstruction of past lifeways, and the study of cultural process. Upon returning from the field, we begin by sorting the data that came from the excavation into various categories. From there, we concentrate on artifacts and prehistoric technology. We outline the basic principles of archaeological classification and examine the ways in which ancient peoples used organic and inorganic raw materials. A proper understanding of technology and its uses and limitations is an essential preliminary to any discussion of prehistoric lifeways and culture change in the past.

CHAPTER 12 ❧

DATA IDENTIFICATION AND CLASSIFICATION

Preview

- The first stage in laboratory analysis is the processing of field data into a form that will enable one to analyze and interpret it. The basic processing of data takes place as excavation proceeds: finds are washed, conserved, labeled, and sorted into basic categories, such as bone (animal and human), stone, shell, wood, and so on. The finds are also inventoried during this stage.
- The classification of artifacts in archaeology is somewhat different from our day-to-day classifications of the objects around us.
- Two systems of classification are taxonomy and systematics. Taxonomy is a classification system of concepts and terms used by many sciences, among them archaeology. Systematics is a way of creating units that can be used to categorize things as a basis for explaining archaeological, or other, phenomena. It is a means of creating units of classification within a scientific discipline.
- The objectives of archaeological classification are to organize data into manageable units, to describe types, and to identify relationships between different types.
- Archaeological classification begins with the identification of artifact attributes, the characteristics that serve to distinguish one artifact from another. Form attributes are such features as the shape of an artifact, while technological attributes include the materials used to

make an artifact and the way in which it was manufactured. Attributes can be selected either by close examination of a collection of artifacts, or they can be derived statistically.

- Modes are attributes that define types; that is, they are clusters of attributes that have been placed in a cultural context.
- Archaeological types are groupings of artifacts created for purposes of comparison with other groups. This grouping may or may not coincide with the actual tool types designed by the manufacturers. Types are based on modes, or clusters of attributes.
- Natural types are those that are identified with reference to our own cultural background. They are based on the assumption that all artifacts are the results of human behavior, the products of society and culture that placed a series of complex limitations and technological boundaries around the artifacts. These are functional types, designed to coincide closely with actual categories established by the original owners. It is difficult to achieve this goal in archaeology, except where there is cultural continuity between prehistoric and recent societies in areas such as the American Southwest.
- Analytical types are purely arbitrary categories set up by archaeologists for their own specific research purposes. One commonly used system is the convenience type, by which artifacts are divided according to their obvious characteristics. This approach relies heavily on the archaeologist's experience. Another is classification according to norms; that is, two or three obvious attributes that are found across a wide range of artifacts. Norms are assumed to represent the normal range of variation based on visual inspection, as well as on measurements and statistical calculations, and are often designed to identify the "average" artifact. Convenience type and norms are both intuitive approaches.
- Statistical types are based on probability techniques, which rely on computer analysis of individual attributes to determine clusters of attributes. The cluster patterns are then tested for random and nonrandom significance. A statistical type may be defined as a group of artifacts displaying a consistent assemblage of attributes whose combined properties give a characteristic pattern.

Once the excavations and surveys are completed, the archaeologist is confronted with the enormous task of organizing, analyzing, and interpreting the data. This chapter describes the first stage in the long process of identification and classification of artifacts.

PROCESSING ARCHAEOLOGICAL DATA

The first stage in any laboratory analysis is one that starts in the field—the processing and organizing of the data so that it can be analyzed and interpreted. The basic processing of archaeological data goes on simultaneously with excavation, for the excavator needs to know where the data are weak and where they are strong. The objective of data collection is to test working hypotheses, and the data acquired for these purposes are normally highly specific. It would be nothing less than stupid to discover in the laboratory that you failed to collect data needed to verify part of your hypothesis simply because you did not monitor it. The wise excavator keeps an eye on the data flowing from the trenches and plans further excavation to obtain larger samples, if they are required.

Preliminary Processing. An essential part of preliminary data processing is the packing, conservation, and marking of the artifacts and other finds. As we stressed in Chapter 5, the provenience of archaeological finds is a major key to understanding their significance. It is no coincidence, then, that most archaeologists develop a careful sequence of stages for processing artifacts and other small finds.

The field laboratory. The first stages in processing newly excavated archaeological data are entirely routine and are common to all finds (Figure 12.1). Most excavations maintain some form of field laboratory where the finds are taken for preliminary examination. It is here that the major site records are kept and developed, stratigraphic profile drawings kept up to date, and radiocarbon samples and other special finds packed for specialist examination. The field laboratory is staffed by a small group of people whose job is to ensure that all data is processed promptly, packed carefully, and labeled and recorded precisely. The successful laboratory is one that is organized to cope with a steady flow of finds, all of which are handled promptly, thus enabling the director of the excavation to evaluate the available data on a daily—even hourly—basis.

Cleaning. The laboratory staff's first task is to clean the newly excavated finds. In the case of stone implements or potsherds, fresh water is used for cleaning. More delicate artifacts may have to wait for special laboratory treatment, or they may simply be brushed clean with a fine brush. Cleaning the artifacts is an essential process, for it enables at least a superficial examination of the find a short time after its discovery, which is part of the process of evaluating the data.

Figure 12.1   Preliminary data processing: archaeologists sorting pottery finds at a site.

Labeling.   "Never let the sun set on an unmarked artifact," one of my professors used to say. He was right, for an artifact without provenience is almost useless. The finds should arrive in the laboratory in a bag or container with a label attached, and they should never be separated from this label throughout the cleaning and conservation process. Sometimes special drying trays are used, with individual compartments for each batch of finds. With these, the label is pinned to the side of the compartment while the finds dry out. Large or especially important artifacts are normally marked with black ink and the mark covered with clear lacquer. A large number of potsherds or stone waste flakes are placed in labeled bags, with labels inside and outside the bag.

Conservation.   Fragile artifacts, animal or human bones, or very small finds, may need special conservation work, which begins as soon as the find reaches the laboratory; sometimes even in the trench itself. Entire burials can be lifted out of a trench in their original matrix by being encased in plaster of paris. But most conservation work is carried out in the laboratory. Some sites, such as Ozette, Washington, require a special laboratory for treating thousands of waterlogged wooden finds, often for months on end. Much of the wood was lifted in a waterlogged state and slowly dried out in the laboratory.

Conservation can involve many activities: reassembling of fragmented pots, a time-consuming and delicate process; hardening of bones, using such chemicals as polyvinyl acetate; or treatment of iron objects. In most cases, field conservation measures are designed to transport the find to the laboratory safely, where it will be examined and preserved at leisure.

Sorting and inventorying.   These procedures begin with a rough sorting of the finds, which is based, normally, on the raw material involved.

Finds are counted and recorded within broad categories—bone, stone tools, and so on—to give a general impression of the data and to record the numbers in each category and within each level. This count data is carefully related to provenience and context. Subsequently, the artifact counts may be refined by cataloging each individual specimen. Some excavations maintain loose-leaf catalogue books. Others, such as the Koster dig in Illinois, record their artifact data on a computer terminal hooked up to data banks hundreds of miles away (Struever and Holton, 1979). Cataloging is a very time-consuming process, and therefore, normally, it is reserved for highly significant artifacts and for special lots, such as the contents of storage pits or inventories from house floors. Data of this type is vital for studies of household and other activities.

Packing and storage.   These make up the final stage of preliminary data processing. Potsherds, animal bones, and stone tools are placed in bags and taken to the laboratory in cartons. Radiocarbon samples, soil specimens, vegetable remains, and other such materials are packed separately, ready for shipment to specialists. Such delicate finds as burials are packed with great care, using tissue paper and special packing materials to prevent breakage in transit. Packing, like all preliminary processing, requires great skill and patience, far more than that accorded your china by a moving company! A complex site can devour huge quantities of packing materials. Howard Carter used several miles of wadding to pack the wooden finds from Tutankhamun's tomb (Carter and others, 1923–33).

The preliminary data processing ends with the storage of the finds in the permanent laboratory. Days, months, and sometimes even years later the long tasks of classification and analysis begin. The remainder of this chapter will discuss objectives and methods of classification and ordering of artifacts.

CLASSIFICATION OF ARTIFACTS

Ordering in Daily Life.   Our attitude toward life and our surroundings is one that involves constant classification and sorting of enormous quantities of data. We classify different types of eating utensils: knives, forks, and spoons—each type has a different use and is kept in a separate compartment in the drawer. We group roads according to their surface, finish, and size. A station wagon is classified separately from a truck. In addition to classifying artifacts, life-styles, and cultures, we also make choices among them. If we are eating soup, we choose to use a spoon. Some people eat rice with a fork, some use chopsticks, and others have decided that a spoon is more suitable. In this case, there is a variety of available choices, the final decision often being dictated by cultural usage rather than functional pragmatism.

Everyone "classifies," because doing so is a requirement for abstract thought and language. But, everyday classes are not often best for archaeological purposes. In our daily life we habitually use classification as a tool for and a part of our life-style. Like the computer, however, it should be a servant rather than a master. Sometimes our classifications of good and bad—for example, those based on color of skin or on our definitions of what is moral or immoral, pornographic or acceptable—are made and then adhered to as binding principles of life without ever being questioned or modified, no matter how much our circumstances may change. Dogmatism and rigidity result from these attitudes and are as dangerous in archaeology as they are in life. In archaeology, classification is a research tool, a means for ordering data; since the objectives of classifications may change according to the problems being investigated, archaeologists must be sensitive to the need for revising their classifications when circumstances require it.

Taxonomy and Systematics.   *Taxonomy* is the name given to the system of classifying concepts and terms used by many sciences, including archaeology. The taxonomies of biology, botany, geology, and some other disciplines are highly sophisticated and often very rigid systems that were created in the nineteenth and early twentieth centuries, and in many cases they are now being outgrown. In contrast, archaeology has developed its own taxonomy of specialist terminologies and concepts quite haphazardly. Universal comparisons and classifications have been a virtual impossibility. For example, while the British archaeologists refer to cultures, North American scholars refer to phases, and the French to periods. Each term has basically the same meaning, but there are subtle differences that stem not only from cultural attitudes but also from different field situations (Goggin, 1949; McKern, 1939; Ronse, 1939).

Systematics is essentially a way of creating units that can be used to *categorize* things as a basis for explaining archaeological, or other, phenomena (Dunnell, 1971). It is a means of creating units of classification within a scientific discipline. For example, biologists classify humans within a hierarchy of classification developed by Carl Linnaeus in the eighteenth century. It begins with the *Kingdom* Animalia, the *Phylum* Chordata (animals with notochords and gill slits), the *Subphylum* Vertebrata (animals with backbones), the *Class* Mammalia, the *Subclass* Eutheria, the *Order* Primates, the *Suborder* Hominoidea (apes and hominidae), the *Family* Hominidae, the *Genus Homo,* the *Species Homo sapiens,* and, finally, the *Subspecies Homo sapiens sapien.* This hierarchy is gradually fined down until only *Homo sapien* remains in its own taxonomic niche. The biological classification just described is somewhat arbitrary and is based on each form having common progenitors. It consists of a whole set of empirically defined units arranged in the form of a hierarchy. Each element in the hierarchy is precisely defined and related one to another.

The Objectives of Classification.   Classification in archaeology has three major objectives:

1. *Organization of data into manageable units.* This is part of the preliminary data processing operation, and it commonly involves separating finds on the basis of raw material (stone, bone, and so on) or artifacts from food remains. This preliminary ordering allows much more detailed classifications later on.
2. *Description of types.* By identifying the individual attributes of hundreds of different artifacts, the archaeologist can group them, on the basis of common attributes, into relatively few types. These types are an economical way of describing large numbers of artifacts.
3. *Identification of relationships between different types.* This is done to provide a basis for formulating hypotheses about the meaning of the classification. The hierarchy of types orders the relationships between different artifacts, relationships that stem, in part, from the use of a variety of raw materials, manufacturing techniques, and functions.

Archaeological classifications are artificial formulations that are based on criteria set up by archaeologists. These classificatory systems do not necessarily coincide, however, with those developed by the people who made the original artifacts (Willey and Phillips, 1958).

Typology.   Typology is the process of classification that is based on the comparison of types. The value of typology is that it enables one to *compare* what has been found at two different sites in different levels of a single site. Typology, as James Deetz puts it, has as its main aim "classification which permits comparison. . . . Such comparison allows the archaeologist to align his assemblage with others in time and space" (Deetz, 1967). For example, let's look over a group of archaeologists' shoulders as they sort through a large pile of potsherds, from a single occupation level, on the laboratory table.

First the sherds are separated on the basis of decoration or lack of it, paste, temper, firing methods, and vessel shape. Once the undecorated or shapeless potsherds have been counted and weighed, they are put to one side, unless they have some special significance. Then the remaining sherds are examined individually and divided into different types, according to the features they display. Soon, there are a number of different piles on the table: one consists of sherds painted with black designs; a second, of red-painted fragments, a third, a group of plain sherds that come from shallow platters. Once the preliminary sort is completed, the archaeologists look over each pile in turn. They have already identified three broad types in the pottery collection. But when they examine the first pile more closely, they find that the black-painted sherds can be subdivided into several smaller groupings: one with square, black panels; another with diamond designs; and a third with black-dotted decoration. The other two major piles also yield several subtypes. Eventually, the original three types become nine, as the archaeologists study the collection in minute detail. This is the process of *typology,* classifying artifacts so that you can compare one type with another. Obviously, the nine types from this one site can be compared with other arbitrary types developed during laboratory sorting of collections from nearby sites.

THE PROCESS OF ARCHAEOLOGICAL CLASSIFICATION

As we have emphasized, archaeological classification is the process of ordering data on the basis of shared characteristics. But, how do archaeologists go about this process, and what procedures do they use to do so (Rouse, 1972)?

Attributes. The characteristics used to distinguish one artifact from another are known as *attributes*. As archaeologists work out their typologies, they find themselves examining hundreds of individual fragments, each of which bears several distinctive attributes (Figure 12.2). To return to our hypothetical laboratory, fifty sherds bear black-painted designs, eighty have red panels on the neck, ten are flattened bowls, and so on. A single potsherd, for example, may bear an everted lip, incised decoration applied in a cross-hatched motif, and a red-painted surface. It may have a grit temper, bright red paste, and a slipped interior surface. Each of these many individual features is an attribute, most of them obvious enough. However, only a critically selected few of these attributes will be used in the classification of the artifacts. (If all were used, then no classification would be possible: each artifact would be an individual object identified by several trivial manufacturing or design idiosyncrasies.) The point to remember about attributes is that there is an infinite range of them on any artifact, and

Figure 12.2 Some common attributes of a clay vessel. Specific attributes that could be noted for this pot are concave shoulder, dot and drag decoration, mica temper, round base, and thickness of wall at base.

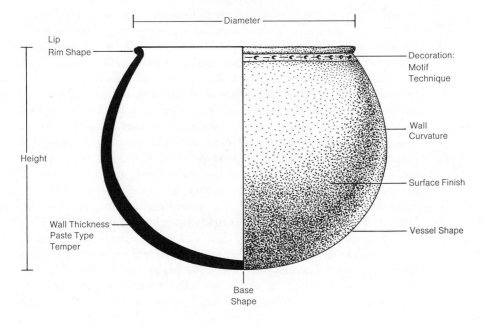

the archaeologist works with those that are considered most appropriate for the classificatory task at hand. All attributes are defined in highly specific terms, often by a measurement. A number of broad groups of attributes are commonly recognized.

Form attributes are features like the shape of the artifact, its measurable dimensions, and its component parts. Normally, they are fairly obvious.
Stylistic attributes include decoration, color, surface finish, and so on.
Technological attributes are those that cover the material used to make an artifact and the way it was made.

The selection of attributes normally proceeds through a close examination of a collection of artifacts. A group of potsherds can be subdivided into different decorative styles based on shapes, surfaces, and colors. The selected attributes are then hand-recorded, and a series of artifact types erected from them. In this case, the definition of the type can depend on the order in which the attributes are examined (see Figure 12.2), and on the researcher's decision as to which are important.

Statistical typologies are derived from attribute clusters which are identified by a computer.

Modes.   Modes are clusters of attributes that define types (Rouse, 1972). They also serve as the means of distinguishing between them. For example, laboratory workers studying the attributes of a group of potsherds realize that such attributes as decorative motifs are the result of human behavior that has been shared and that may recur. Some of these attributes, such as plain, polished surfaces and simple rims on flat platters, are always found together. So archaeologists decide that they represent a deliberate choice by the pot makers to combine these features to produce a certain vessel for a specific purpose, a choice that is cultural. When the archaeologists identify this cluster, they call it a *mode*, a constellation of attributes that have been placed in a cultural context. Modes, then, distinguish characteristics that are cultural at one moment in time from those that are simply part of the natural world. For example, the clay that a pot is made from is a natural attribute; but the choice of a particular type of clay for a specific purpose is cultural.

A mode can also be used to distinguish a widely recognized stage in time and space. For instance, the widespread occurrence of green-tinged clay is characteristic of the 'Ubaid stage of Mesopotamian prehistory, dating from 5300 to 3600 B.C., a mode that has both cultural and technological implications (Redman, 1978). Modes are a useful way of isolating technological and stylistic features for closer study without becoming involved in the complexities of individual types (Rouse, 1972).

Types.   The concept of archaeological type has generated an enormous and often controversial academic literature (Ford, 1954a, b; Kreiger, 1944; Rouse, 1960; Spaulding, 1960). In archaeology, a type is a grouping of artifacts created for purposes of comparison with other groups. This grouping may or may not coincide with the actual tool types designed by the original manufacturers. Everyone agrees that a type is based on modes and on clusters of attributes (Figure 12.3).

But, while the patterns of attributes may be fairly easy to identify, how do archaeologists know what is a type and what is not? Should they try to reproduce the actual categories of pot that the makers themselves conceived? Alternatively, should they just go ahead and

Figure 12.3   A series of Mesolithic arrowhead barbs from Star Carr, England, showing three types based on attributes: oblique bases, triangular shapes, and backed edges. (Actual size.)

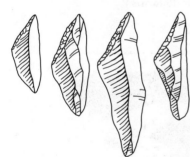

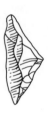

a Obliquely blunted

b Triangular

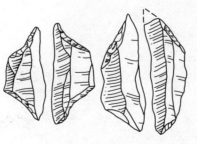

c Elongated trapeze

create quite arbitrary "archaeological" types that are designed purely for analytical purposes? This is the nub of the controversy about types in archaeology.

Natural types. All of us have feelings and reactions about any artifact, whether it is a magnificent wooden helmet from the Pacific Northwest coast (Figure 12.4), or a simple acorn pounder from the southern California interior. Our immediate instinct is to look at and classify these and other prehistoric artifacts from our own cultural standpoint. If laboratory workers were to look at potsherds and identify the flat, plain platters already referred to as "saucers," they would be using their own cultural experience to classify an object that the original prehistoric makers might never have thought of as a saucer. Such *natural typing* is based on the assumption that all artifacts are the results of human behavior, the products of society and culture that placed a series of complex limitations and technological boundaries

Figure 12.4 Tlingit carved wooden helmet from the Northwest Coast, an example of a "natural" type, classified as such when found in an archaeological context. This artifact would obviously be classified as a helmet from the perspective of our cultural experience. (Height, 9 inches; width, 10 inches.)

around the artifacts. The owners of the tools classified them into different groups for themselves, each one having a definite role in the society. This functional, or natural, classification is similar to our own. For example, we assign different roles in the eating process to a knife, fork, and spoon. Knives cut meat; steak knives are used in eating steaks. The prehistoric arrowhead is employed in the chase; one type of missile head is used to hunt deer, another type to shoot birds. Such functional classifications are an intimate part of the culture of the people who made them. The uses of an artifact may be determined not only by convenience and practical considerations, but also by custom or regulation. The light-barbed spearheads used by some Australian hunting bands to catch fish are too fragile for dispatching kangaroo; the special barbs enable the impaled fish to be lifted out of the water. Pots are made by women in most African or American Indian societies, which have division of labor by sex; each has formed complicated customs, regulations, or taboos, that, functional considerations apart, categorize clay pots into different types with varying uses and rules in the culture.

Furthermore, each society has its own conception of what a particular artifact should look like. Americans have generally preferred larger cars, Europeans small ones. These preferences reflect not only pragmatic considerations of road width and longer distances in the New World, but also differing attitudes toward traveling, and on the part of many Americans, a preoccupation with prestige and driveway display, manifested in chromium plate and style changes. We think that a car should have a color-coordinated interior and a long hood to look "right." The steering wheel is on the left, hood ornaments are preferred, and a speedometer is required by law. In other words, we know what we want and expect an automobile to look like, even though minor design details change through time—as do the lengths of women's skirts and the width of men's ties.

Ideally, natural types located by archaeologists would reflect the precise roles and functional classifications made by the members of the society from which they came. Needless to say, such an objective can never be achieved, both because of incomplete preservation and the lack of written records. We have no means of visualizing the complex roles that some artifacts achieved in prehistoric society, nor of establishing the restrictions placed upon their use by the particular society. Although in some cases, obvious functional roles, such as that of an arrowhead for hunting or warfare or of a pot for carrying water, can be correctly established in the laboratory, functional classifications are necessarily restricted and limited. As an example, let us consider the

Figure 12.5   A pressure-flaked Scandinavian flint dagger. (After Oakley; one-half actual size.)

case of a Scandinavian flint dagger (Figure 12.5)—a beautifully made, pressure-flaked tool, a copy of the bronze daggers fashionable at that time in central Europe. This has been classified by generations of archaeologists as a dagger, by implication, a weapon of war and defense, worn by Scandinavian farmers who still had no metals and made a slavish imitation of a more advanced tool. While this instinctive designation may be correct, we really do not know if our functional classification was correct. Was the dagger actually used in warfare and for personal defense? Was it a weapon, or was it purely an object of prestige for the owner, perhaps with some religious function?

The only instances where a classification related to that of the owners themselves can be developed is where the material culture of a modern people shows continuity with the cultural traditions in the archaeological sites excavated. This situation exists in many parts of the world, such as among the Indians of the southwestern United States. But even in these cases, natural types are hard to define, for we often do not know how the actual owners of artifacts viewed or categorized them. How did they define the variations between one artifact type and another? How do people decide upon and maintain their types?

These are questions best considered by taking an example, succinctly described by James Deetz—the case of a basket made by the Chumash Indians of Southern California (Figure 12.6) (Deetz, 1967). The basket has been produced in tangible form by weaving with plant fibers; the design itself has been formed in the maker's mind by several factors, the most important of which is the tremendous reservoir of inherited cultural experience that the Chumash have learned, generation by generation, through the several thousand years they lived in Southern California. The designs of their baskets are almost unconscious; they relate to the feeling that such and such a form and a color are "correct" and traditionally acceptable. But, there are more pragmatic and complex reasons too. This Chumash basket bears a band of decoration around the inside of the rim and rectilinear, stepped patterns and diamond patterns on the body of the basket. The basket is flat and circular, with a simple rim. Each feature mentioned above can be described as a distinctive attribute of the basket and contributes to the characteristic form of the Chumash receptacle.

Figure 12.6   A typical Chumash parching tray.

Each has a good reason for its presence, whether traditional, innovative, functional, or imposed by the technology used to make the basket. As Deetz points out, the band of decoration around the rim of the basket is a feature of the decorative tradition of the Chumash and occurs on most of their baskets. Its rich red-brown color, not mentioned before, is caused by the species of reed used in its manufacture—the best material available. The flat, round shape is determined by its use, for such trays were used for roasting seeds by tossing them with red embers. While the steplike decoration on the body was dictated by the sewing and weaving techniques of all basketry, the diamond motifs between the steps are unique to this particular basket. The woman who made the diamonds was an innovator; her personal stamp on the basket might be a single occurrence, unless it was adopted by others—then, over several generations, it might become an integral part of the basketry trays made by every woman in the group. Most craftspeople can recognize their own work even years later, and other members of the community will as well. The general idea of a basket form or another artifact may well be nowhere but in the heads of its makers, but it is the variation in these artifacts that the archaeologist seeks to study. Our Chumash example serves as a warning that the variations in human artifacts are both complex and subtle. Our task as archaeologists is to measure these variations, to establish the causes for, and directions of, change, and to find out what these variations can be used to measure.

Natural types are thought, by many people, to represent cultural norms, the "right way" in which society produces its artifacts. This is not, however, necessarily true, for numerous ethnographic studies have shown that there can be enormous cultural diversity, even within the confines of a single community. But, while we have shown that many variables can act on the ways people make their artifacts, no one can deny that a reasonable objective of archaeological classifications is to come as close to these "natural" types as possible. But the analytical tools to do so are still in their infancy.

Analytical types.   In contrast to natural types, *analytical types* are purely arbitrary categories set up by archaeologists for their own specific research purposes. Once the laboratory team has studied the attributes in their pottery collection, they sit down and discuss the possible arbitrary analytical types they will use to subdivide their collection for purposes of comparing it to other assemblages. They have a number of choices in front of them. One option is to use a classification of analytical types already set up by someone else; another, to develop their own analytical types employing convenience types, norms, or artifact clusters (Dunnell, 1978).

Convenience types.   A common analytical type is the "convenience type," which is applied to obvious groups of similar objects that stand out relatively clearly and that change throughout time. Flinders Petrie used convenience typing with the pre-Dynastic jars from Diospolis Parva that he used to develop his sequence dating method (see Chapter 6) (Petrie, 1899). His convenience types, based on changing handle designs, were just that—convenient for his purposes.

Convenience typing is commonplace. This approach relies heavily on the archaeologist's intuition and experience, as well as on his other judgmental skills. The classifier assumes that anyone using the report will understand how the types were divided up and will be able to repeat them. Unfortunately, however, under these circumstances, most archaeologists would come up with different results on the same, even quite simple, collection. There are simply too many implicit assumptions made about convenience types for them to be readily duplicated, except under the most favorable conditions or where a group of archaeologists have all received the same training over a long period of time (Sackett, 1977).

Norms and variance.   For accurate and meaningful comparisons to be made, rigorous definitions of analytical types are needed, ones that define not only the "norm" of the artifact type but also its approximate range of variation, at either end of which one type becomes one of two others. Conventional analytical definitions are usually couched in terms of one or more attributes that indicate how the artifact was made, or the shape, decoration, or some other feature that the maker desired the finished product to display. These definitions are set up on the basis of carefully defined technological differences, often bolstered by measurements or statistical clusterings of attributes. In most of these cases, the average artifact, rather than the variation between different individual examples, is the ultimate objective of the definition. Again, we are confronted with a norm. The range of variation between artifacts is less important than the average. A classifier who finds a group, or even an individual artifact, that deviates at all conspicuously from the norm, often erects a new analytical type, for the boundaries between any two types are blurred. Those who are splitters tend to proliferate types, while those who are lumpers do the opposite. The whole operation is more or less intuitive (Dunnell, 1971).

Statistical techniques and clustering of artifacts. The researchers of the past thirty years have produced enormous quantities of new archaeological data, so much so that it is a full-time job to keep track of the myriad records and artifacts from old and new excavations and surveys. Fortunately, the digital computer and a whole battery of statistical techniques have come to our aid. Computers can be used to store information on coded punch cards and to identify patterns of regularity on the artifacts whose attributes are coded on the cards. A computer data bank can be manipulated in such a way as to tell you, for example, what percentage of a collection of projectile points in a Paleo-Indian collection stored in the computer have notched bases and chisel-like tips, or what percentage of painted bowls from an Anasazi assemblage have turned-in rims (Figure 12.7).

Statistical techniques can then be used to determine whether such patterns of regularity, or other distributions, are random or of nonrandom significance. Such determinations may involve highly specialized techniques, most of them beyond the mathematical expertise of most archaeologists. At intervals in these pages, we refer to probability techniques, of which the most widely used is the χ^2 (chi-square) test, and the examples cited speak for themselves (see, especially Chapters

Figure 12.7   Still Life with Hand Axes, 1968. A pleasing group by Derek Roe symbolizing the quantitative approach to artifact classification.

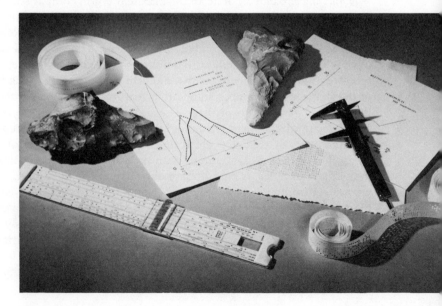

16 and 19). Most people who use such tests have consulted a statistical expert, and the reader is referred to specialist literature for more information on quantitative methods in archaeology (Thomas, 1976; 1978).

As statistical methods have taken a greater hold in archaeology, a new definition of an artifact type laid out by Albert Spaulding (1953) has become popular: "A group of artifacts exhibiting a consistent assemblage of attributes whose combined properties give a characteristic pattern." The key word here is *pattern,* for the Spaulding definition implies that classification into types means discovering the combinations of attributes favored by their makers, not arbitrary combinations set by the classifier. Traditional classificatory methods involved the setting up of types on the basis of inspection and identification of attributes. By using statistical methods, however, one can compare the associations of different attributes one with another on dozens, even hundreds of potsherds. These attributes will cluster in the form of modes. If the distribution of the attributes tests out as an entirely random one, then the distribution is probably not culturally significant. But, if the attributes cluster in a nonrandom fashion, then they are the result of patterned behavior on the part of the makers. By isolating nonrandom clusters, one is assumed to be discovering actual clusters of artifacts recognized by the makers of the artifacts.

The cluster approach is widely used today. The interested reader should read Albert Spaulding's classic and elegant exposition on the subject for further information (Spaulding, 1953; Thomas, 1976).

The chapters that follow describe the various ways in which archaeologists have applied these principles to the classification of common prehistoric technologies.

Guide to Further Reading

The literature on archaeological classification is both complex and enormous. I strongly advise you to obtain expert advice before delving into even key references. Here, however, are some useful starting points.

Dunnell, Robert. *Systematics in Prehistory.* Seattle: University of Washington Press, 1971.
A highly technical introduction to systematic classification in archaeology.

Rouse, Irving. *An Introduction to Prehistory: A Systematic Approach.* New York: McGraw-Hill, 1972.
Describes a basic approach to archaeological classification that has fairly wide application.

Spaulding, Albert C. "Statistical Techniques for the Study of Artifact Types." *American Antiquity* 18,4:305–13.

_____. "Statistical Descriptions and Comparison of Artifact Assemblages." In R. F. Heizer and S. F. Cook, eds. *Quantitative Methods in Archaeology.* New York: Viking Fund, 1960, pp. 60–92.
Two widely read papers on statistical approaches to artifact classification. A reaction to these articles appeared in a series of papers reprinted in American Antiquity *in 1977.*

Thomas, David Hurst. *Figuring Anthropology: First Principles of Probability and Statistics.* New York: Holt, Rinehart and Winston, 1976.
A basic text on quantitative methods that can be strongly recommended to serious students of the past.

Willey, Gordon R., and Phillips, Philip. *Method and Theory in American Archaeology.* Chicago: University of Chicago Press, 1958.
The classic work on culture history construction in New World archaeology. Every advanced student reads this book.

CHAPTER 13 ❧

TECHNOLOGY AND ARTIFACTS

Preview

- One of the main inorganic materials used by prehistoric people was stone, especially siliceous rock, which fractures according to the conchoidal principle.
- We describe the basic techniques of stone tool manufacture, starting with the stone on stone technique, the cylinder hammer method, and the prepared cores used to produce blanks for Middle Paleolithic artifacts. Blade technology came into use about 35,000 years ago, and the first use of pressure flaking was identified among the Solutrean people of some 17,000 years ago.
- Stone technology and artifacts were first studied by means of rigid "type fossil" concepts, which were superseded by functional analyses: artifacts were classified according to shape, dimensions, and assumed use. Attribute analysis has, in turn, replaced functional approaches, and it involves the study not only of finished artifacts but also of the by-products of their manufacture.
- Lithic experimentation and ethnoarchaeology play leading roles in the study of stone technologies; while edge wear and petrological studies throw light on the trade in raw materials and the uses to which tools were put.
- Ceramics (clay objects) are a major preoccupation of archaeologists and date to the past 10,000 years of prehistory. We describe the

process of pottery manufacture, the various methods used, and the surface finishes employed.

- Ceramic analysis proceeds through analogy and experiment, research in which controlled experiments with firing and the properties of clay have played leading parts. The vessels themselves are studied by form and functional analyses, on the assumption that the shape of a vessel is a direct reflection of its function. This assumption can be a dangerous one, however, and many archaeologists prefer to use stylistic analyses. Clusters of attributes are used now, also, in attempts to standardize stylistic classifications.
- Prehistoric metallurgy is a phenomenon of the past 6000 years. We describe the basic properties of copper, bronze, gold, and iron and some of the cultural contexts in which metallurgy developed. Typological and technological analyses are used to study prehistoric metallurgy, with European archaeologists emphasizing typological comparisons based on minute stylistic variations.
- Bone tools are thought to be among the earliest of all artifacts. The so-called osteodontokeratic culture of the Australopithecines has, however, been shown to be of natural origin. They are important in some areas—noticeably, the Arctic—as indicators of typological change. The functional analysis of bone tools is somewhat easier than that of stone tools or ceramics, for the uses of bone objects are often easier to determine. Technological analyses of bone artifacts have concentrated on the ways in which the tools were made. Ethnographic analogy also plays an important role in bone studies.
- Wooden artifacts are a mine of information on prehistoric life. The manufacture of wooden tools involves well-understood mechanical processes, such as cutting and whittling, and these can often be identified even from unfinished artifacts. Stone artifacts and other materials have been found mounted in wooden handles, and this provides insights into the uses of composite artifacts.
- Basketry and textiles are among the least understood of prehistoric technologies, but they offer unique opportunities for studying individual idiosyncrasies in the archaeological record, as well as providing useful chronological markers. We cite an innovative computer mapping project on basketry styles at Ozette, Washington.

"Whatever the ultimate inspiration or the intermediate cause, it was by their hands that the early Europeans dragged themselves out of the primeval mist of savagery, struggled up the long slopes of barbarism and ultimately attained to some kind of civilized existence," wrote Grahame Clark (1952) about prehistoric Europe. His words provide us with ample justification for studying the technology of the ancients.

The tools that people have manufactured throughout their long history have been the means by which they augmented their limbs and extended the use of their environment. The technological achievements of humankind over the past three million years of cultural evolution have been both impressive and terrifying. Today we can land an astronaut on the moon, transplant human hearts, and build sophisticated computers. Yet, in the final analysis, our contemporary armory of lasers, atomic bombs, household appliances, and every conceivable artifact designed for a multitude of specialized needs has evolved in a direct, albeit branching, way from the first simple tools made by the earliest human beings. In this chapter, we examine some of the main technologies used by prehistoric people to adapt to their natural environments and look at some of the ways in which archaeologists study them. We should emphasize, however, that the study of artifacts and technologies is only a small part of the total archaeological process. The data that comes from these studies is designed to verify specific research hypotheses formulated before data collection began.

STONE

Certain categories of rock have, with bone and wood, been the primary raw materials for human technology for most of human existence. The advent of metallurgy is but a recent development, and stone tools have provided the foundation for the classification of many prehistoric cultures since scientific archaeology began. The raw material itself has set severe limits on the extent of people's technological achievements for much of their history, and the evolution of stoneworking over the millions of years during which it has been practiced has been infinitely slow. Nonetheless, people eventually exploited almost every possibility afforded by suitable rocks for making implements.

How People Worked Stone.   The simplest way of producing a stone that will cut or chop, surely the basic tool produced by prehistoric people, is simply to break off a piece and use the resulting sharp edge (Figure 13.1). But to produce a tool that has a more specialized use or that can be employed for several purposes requires a slightly more sophisticated flaking technique. First, an angular fragment or smooth pebble of suitable rock can be brought to the desired shape by systematically

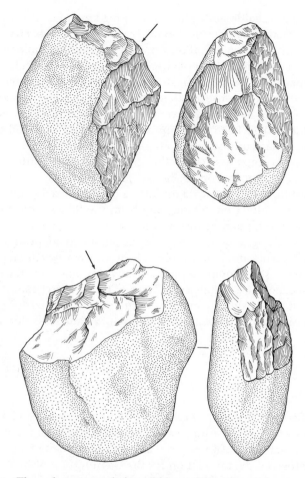

Figure 13.1   These chopping tools from Olduvai Gorge, Tanzania, are some of the earliest human tool forms. Arrows show the working edges. (Three-fifths actual size.)

flaking it with another stone. The flakes removed from this core, or lump, are then primarily waste products, whereas the core becomes the implement that is the intentional end product of the stonemaker. Furthermore, the flakes struck from the core can be used themselves as sharp-edged knives, or they can be further modified to make other artifacts. From this simple beginning, many and complex stone industries have evolved, the earliest tools being simple—many of them virtually indistinguishable from naturally fractured rock.

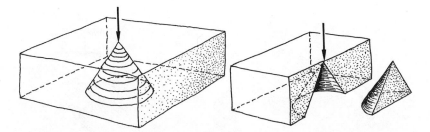

Figure 13.2 How stone fractures: At the left, when a blow is struck on homogeneous types of rock, a cone of percussion is formed by the shock waves rippling through the stone. At the right, a flake is chipped when the block (or core) is hit at the edge and the stone fractures along the edge of the ripple.

Principles of manufacture. Identifying humanly made implements as distinct from naturally broken rocks is something that can be learned only by experience in handling many artifacts. Here is a generalized description of the principles of stone-implement manufacture (Hester and Heizer, 1973; Howell, 1965). Generally, Stone Age people and other makers of stone tools chose flint, obsidian, and other hard homogeneous rocks to fashion their artifacts. All these rocks break in a systematic way, like industrial glass. A sharp blow directed vertically at a point on the surface of a suitable stone dislodges a flake, with its apex at the point where the hammer blow hit the stone. This effects a *conchoidal fracture* (Figure 13.2). When, however, a blow is directed at a stone slab obliquely from the edge and the break occurs conchoidally, a flake is detached. The fractured face of the flake has a characteristic shape, with a bulge extending from the surface of the piece outward down the side. This is known as the *bulb of percussion;* there is a corresponding hollow or flake scar on the core from which the flake has been struck. The bulb of percussion is readily recognized, as the accompanying text figure (Figure 13.3) shows, not only because of the bulge itself but also from the concentric rings that radiate from the center of the impact point, widening gradually away from it. Such deliberate humanly made fractures are quite different from those produced by such natural means as frost, extreme heat or cold, water action, or stones falling from a cliff and fracturing boulders below (Clark, 1958). In these cases the rock may sometimes break in a similar manner, but most of the flake scars are irregular, and instead of concentric rings and a bulb of percussion, there is often a rough depressed area on the surface with concentric rings formed around it.

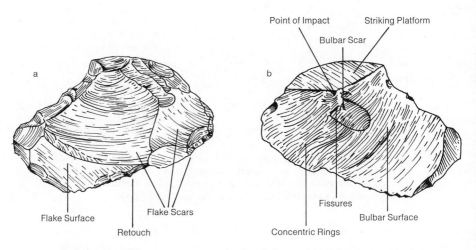

Figure 13.3 The component parts of a flake tool: (a) flake surface; (b) bulbar surface.

Careful examination is needed to distinguish human and naturally fractured stones from one another, a particularly acute problem with tools of the earliest humans. In many cases, their artifacts were made by the simplest of hammerstone techniques, resulting in the removal of two or three flakes from the pebble (Figure 13.1). This produced a jagged edge that was effective, so experiment shows, in dismembering carcasses of game. There have been several famous controversies over alleged "artifacts" found in Lower Pleistocene deposits in Europe and Africa that are contemporary with periods when hominids were already flourishing elsewhere. A celebrated furor arose over a series of alleged tools, named "eoliths," found early in this century in Lower Pleistocene horizons in eastern England (Burkitt, 1955). These were championed for many years as early evidence of human occupation until reexamination of the geological contexts and accurate measurements of the flaking angles on the "eoliths" demonstrated that they were probably of natural origin (Barnes, 1938). Under such circumstances, the only sure identification of humanly fractured stone implements is to find them in association with fossil human remains and broken animal bones, preferably on living sites.

Methods. Figures 13.4–13.7 show some of the major stone flaking methods used by prehistoric peoples. The simplest and earliest used was direct fracturing of the stone with a hammerstone (Figure 13.4).

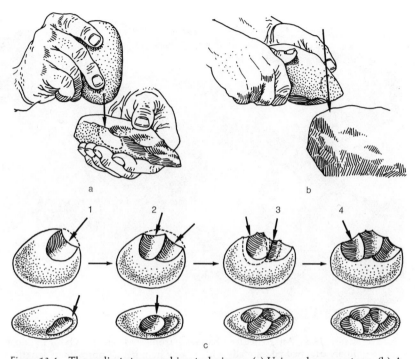

Figure 13.4   The earliest stoneworking techniques: (a) Using a hammerstone. (b) A variant on the hammerstone, striking a core against a stone block, the so-called anvil technique. (c) The earliest stone tools, often crude choppers, were made by a simple process. The top row shows the side view: first, two flakes were struck off (1 and 2); second, the stone was turned over, and two more flakes were removed (3); and third, a fifth flake completed the tool (4), giving it a sharp edge. The bottom row shows the process from above.

After thousands of years, people began to make tools flaked on both surfaces, such as Acheulian handaxes (Figure 13.5). As time went on, the stoneworkers began to use bone hammers to trim the edges of their handaxes. The handaxe of 150,000 years ago had a symmetrical shape, sharp, tough working edges, and a beautiful finish.

As people became more skillful and specialized, such as the hunter-gatherers of about 100,000 years ago, they began to develop stone technologies that resulted in the production of artifacts for highly specific purposes. They shaped special cores that were carefully prepared to provide a single flake or two of a standard size and shape (Figure 13.6). About 35,000 years ago, some stoneworkers developed a new technology based on the preparation of cylindrical cores from which

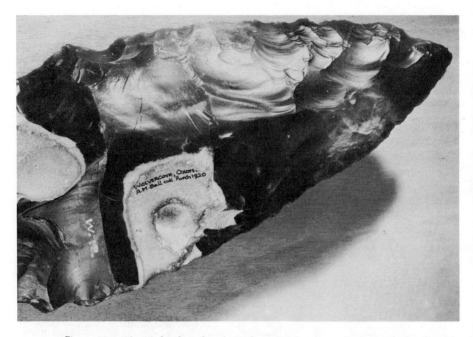

Figure 13.5 An Acheulian handaxe from Wolvercote, Oxford, England, with finely trimmed edges made with a bone hammer. (Approximate length, 5 inches.)

Figure 13.6 The so-called Levallois core, a prepared core carefully shaped in a tortoise-shell profile, with the objective of producing a single, thin flake that was later turned into a knife (the technique is named after a suburb of Paris). The arrow shows where the flake was removed. This specimen comes from the Thames Valley, England. (One-half actual size.)

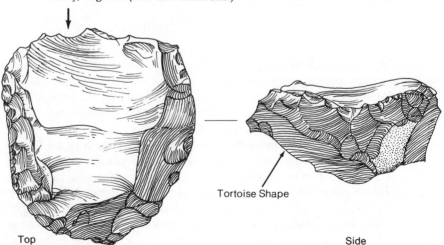

Tortoise Shape

Top   Side

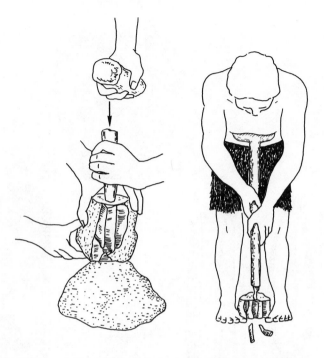

Figure 13.7 Two uses of the blade technique, employing a punch.

long, parallel-sided blades were removed with a punch and hammer-stone (Holmes, 1919) (Figure 13.7). These regular blanks were then trimmed into knives, scraping tools, and other specialized artifacts (Figure 13.8). Blade technology was so successful that it spread all over the world. It was the first stone technology introduced into the Americas (Clark, 1970).

Once blades had been removed from their cores, they were trimmed into shape using a variety of techniques. In some cases, the blade's side was flaked with an antler or piece of wood to sharpen or blunt it. Sometimes the flake would be pressed against another stone, a bone, or a piece of wood to produce a steep, stepped edge or a notch (Figure 13.8a and b). The Australian aborigines and some Plains Indians sometimes nibbled the edges of their tools with their teeth.

The most famous and most common technique used in the later periods of prehistory, especially in the New World, was pressure flaking (Figure 13.8c and d). The stoneworker used a small billet of wood or antler pressed against the working edge in such a way as to exert

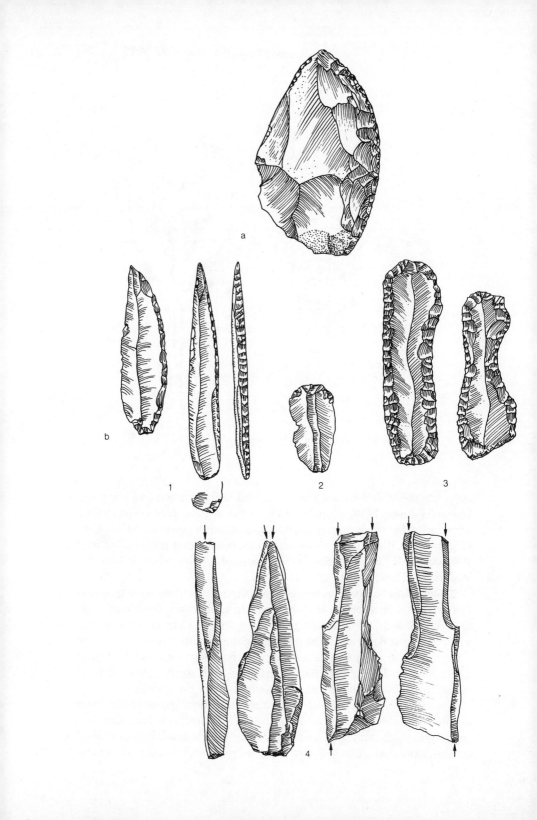

a

b

1

2

3

4

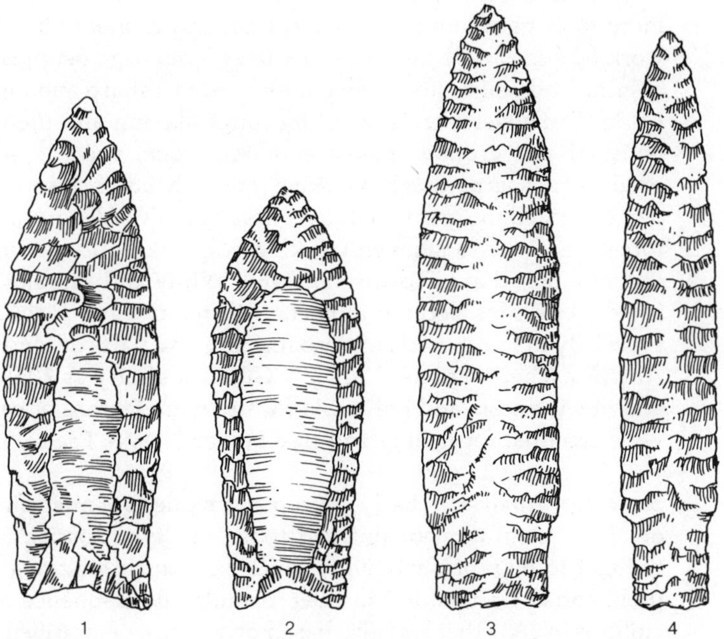

Figure 13.8   Some methods of trimming stone tools: (a) Steep retouch by battering: a Mousterian side scraper. (One-half actual size.) (b) Specialized blade tools made by pressing and sharpening. These artifacts are from southwestern France: (1) backed blades, (2) end scraper, (3) sharpened and notched blades, (4) engraving tools, or burins—their chisel ends were formed by small sharpening flakes removed from the ends. These tools were used for engraving and working antlers and bones. (All actual size.) (c) The pressure-flaking technique. (d) Paleo-Indian pressure-flaked points: (1) Clovis point, (2) Folsom point, (3) Scottsbluff point, (4) Eden point. (All actual size; used with permission of McGraw-Hill Book Company and Thames and Hudson Ltd.)

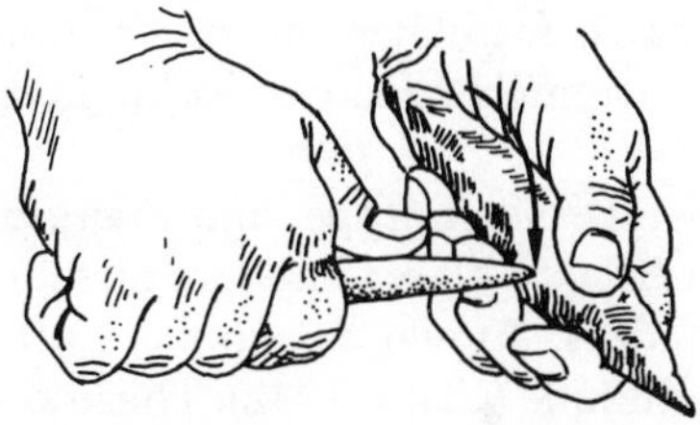

pressure in a limited direction and remove a fine, shallow parallel-sided flake. This formed one of a series of flake scars that eventually covered most of the implement's surfaces. The advantage of pressure flaking is that it facilitates the production of many standardized artifacts with extremely effective working edges in a comparatively short time.

In southwest Asia, Europe, and many parts of Africa and southern and eastern Asia, small blades were fashioned into minute arrowheads, barbs, and adzes, known as *microliths*, often made by a characteristic notching technique (Clark, 1932). These also evolved in Arctic America and Australia.

The blade technologies of later times were capable of producing far more tools per pound of material than earlier methods. Even tougher working edges were developed by later Stone Age peoples, who began to grind and polish stone when they needed a sharp and highly durable blade. The edges were shaped by rough flaking and then laboriously polished and ground against a coarser rock, such as sandstone, to produce a sharp, tough working edge. Modern experiments have demonstrated the greater effectiveness of polished stone axes in felling forest trees, the toughened working edge taking longer to blunt than that of a flaked axe (Townsend, 1969; White and Thomas, 1972). Polished stone axes became important in many early farming societies, especially in Europe, Asia, Mesoamerica, and parts of temperate North America. They were used in New Guinea as early as 20,000 years ago and in Melanesia and Polynesia for the manufacture of canoes, which were essential for fishing and trade (Clark, 1978; Fagan, 1980).

Stone Tool Analysis.   Early attempts at stone tool analysis were based on the classification of finished tools, or "type fossils," which were thought to be representative of different human cultures. The French prehistorian Gabriel de Mortillet formulated a sequence of Paleolithic cultures in 1881 that was also based on a series of stratified type fossils. He and others argued that human progress was inevitable and that, therefore, a slow development of stone tools was inevitable as well. This type of fossil approach was abandoned gradually, as more sophisticated typological methods came into use.

Functional analysis was first developed by nineteenth-century archaeologists. With this approach, well-defined artifact types were named according to their shape, dimensions, and assumed use, such as the Acheulian handaxe (Figure 13.5) and the Mousterian side scraper (see Figure 13.8a). This approach led to the use of type fossils and to a tendency to look for the perfect, typical artifact. Many functional labels still remain in use in modern archaeology, but they are no longer thought of as anything more than a generalized description of the form of an artifact. Functional analysis has reached great refinement in western Europe, where François Bordes, Denise de Sonneville-Bordes, and James Sackett have spent much time trying to refine the functional form classifications of their predecessors (Bordaz, 1970; Bordes, 1968; Bordes and de Sonneville-Bordes, 1970; Sackett, 1966, 1977). Alfred Kidder made great use of functional classifications at Pecos (Kidder, 1924).

Attribute analysis has replaced the functional approach in recent years (Clay, 1976). Attribute analyses are based on the selection of many different artifact features, which can range from technological attributes such as the form of striking platform to a functional attribute such as a steep scraping edge (Figure 13.8a). Stone tools are a revealing source of information on both uses and processes of manufacture. However, any attribute analysis requires the study not only of finished artifacts but also of the waste products, or *debitage* (French: throw-away waste), that were created during stoneworking activity. Sophisticated cluster analyses and probability tests are part of the statistical armory that stone tool experts use to derive classes of artifacts from statistically significant clusterings of attributes. (For details of statistical methods and relevant literature, see Redman, 1978; Spaulding, 1953, 1960; and Thomas, 1976, 1978.)

Archaeologists rely on three other approaches to stone tool analysis:

1. *Lithic experimentation.* Many archaeology laboratories ring to the sound of people trying to make stone tools—and cutting their fingers in the process (Johnson, 1978). Over a century ago, French archaeologists were trying to make copies of handaxes and blade tools. The celebrated Jacques Coutier used to boast that he could make a handaxe in four minutes. Ethnographers described stone toolmaking among the Australians and Tasmanians and compared their techniques to those of Stone Age artisans (Figure 13.9). Modern experimenters, such as François Bordes, Don Crabtree, and L. S. B. Leakey, have drawn on both experimentation and ethnographic observation to work out the techniques used by prehistoric stone-workers (Swanton, 1975). Another fruitful source of analytical data has been professional gunflint makers, such as those at Brandon, in Suffolk, England (R. Clark, 1935; Phillipson, 1969).
2. *Use wear analysis* involves both microscopic examination of artifact working edges and actual experiments with using stone tools (Hayden, 1979). The Soviet archaeologist S. A. Semenov (1964) has

Figure 13.9   Australian aborigines making stone tools.

studied the working edges of hundreds of Upper Paleolithic tools. He found, for example, that the scraping edges of so-called end scrapers bore clear signs not only of scratches but of wear lustre as well. He experimented with such scrapers and found that identical marks could be obtained by using the scraper both as a graver and a scraping tool. Some tools bear wear marks that give a fairly specific clue to their use. An example of this is the flint sickle blade used for harvesting wild or domestic grasses, which often shows a gloss caused by the silica in the grass stems (Garrod and Bate, 1937). It should be pointed out, however, that most functional interpretations of stone artifacts are based on ethnographic analogies (see Chapter 15).

3. *Petrological analyses* have been applied with great success to the rocks from which stone tools are made, especially ground stone axes in Europe. Petrology is the study of rocks (Greek: *petros* = stone). A thin section of the axe is prepared and examined under a microscope. The minerals in the rock can then be identified and compared to samples from quarry sites. British archaeologists have achieved remarkable success with this approach and have identified over twenty different sources of axe blade stone (Clark, 1952; Phillips, 1980). Such researches can lead to vital information on prehistoric trade (see Chapter 17). Spectrographic analysis of distinctive trace

elements in obsidian has yielded remarkable results in the Near East and Mesoamerica, where this distinctive volcanic rock was traded widely from several quarry centers (Cann and Renfrew, 1964; Flannery and Winter, 1976).

CLAY (CERAMICS)

Objects made out of clay are among the most imperishable of all archaeological finds; but pottery is a relatively recent innovation. From the very earliest times, people used animal skins, bark trays, ostrich eggshells, and wild gourds for carrying loads outside the immediate surroundings of their settlements. Such informal vessels were ideal for hunter-gatherers, who were constantly on the move. At one time, it was thought that the advent of pottery coincided with the origins of food production. We now know, however, that both agriculture and domesticated animals existed in the Near East from the eighth millennium B.C., if not earlier. Pottery did not appear until slightly before 6000 B.C. at such early agricultural settlements in the Near East as Jarmo and Jericho (Braidwood and Howe, 1962; Mellaart, 1975). In contrast, in Japan pottery was made by hunter-gatherers as early as 8000 B.C. (Hayashi, 1968; Morlan, 1967). The inhabitants of the Tehuacán Valley in highland Mexico began cultivating crops several thousand years before the first pottery appeared in North America at about 2500 B.C. (MacNeish, 1978).

The invention of pottery seems to coincide with the beginnings of more permanent settlement. Clay receptacles have the advantage of being both durable and long-lived. We can assume that the first clay vessels were used for domestic purposes: for cooking, carrying water, and storing food. They soon assumed more specialized roles in salt making, oil lamps, burial urns, and ceremonial activities. Broken ceramic vessels are among the most common archaeological finds. Their shape, style, and form have provided the foundations for thousands of archaeological analyses.

Pottery Technology.   Modern day industrial potters turn out dinnerware by the millions, using mass production methods and automated technology. Prehistoric artisans created each of their pieces individually, using the simplest of technology but attaining astonishing levels of skill in shaping and adorning their vessels.

The clay used in pot making was invariably selected with the utmost care; often, it was even traded over considerable distances. Of critical importance is the consistency of the clay, which is pounded meticulously and mixed with water to make it entirely even in texture. By careful kneading, the potter removes the air bubbles and makes the clay as plastic as possible, a process that allows it to be moulded into shape as the pot is built up. When the clay is fired it loses its water content and can crack, so the potter adds a *temper* to the clay, a substance that helps reduce shrinkage and cracking. Although some pot clays already contain a suitable temper in their natural state, pot makers commonly add fine sand, powdered shell, or even mica, as artificial temper.

Pot making (ceramics) is a highly skilled art. There are three major methods:

1. *Coil.* The vessel is built up with long coils or wedges of clay that are shaped and joined together with a mixture of clay and water (Figure 13.10). Sometimes the pot is built up from a lump of clay. Hand

Figure 13.10 Making pots using the coil method.

methods were commonplace everywhere that pot making was a part-time activity satisfying local needs.

2. *Mold.* The vessel is made from a lump of clay that is either pressed into a concave mold or placed over the top of a convex shape. Molding techniques were used to make large numbers of vessels of the same size and shape; also figurines, fishing net weights, and spindle whorls. Sometimes several molds were used to make the different parts of a single vessel.

3. *Potter's wheel.* Wheel-made pots came into widespread use after the first invention of potters' wheels in Mesopotamia about 5000 years ago. The vessel is formed by placing a lump of clay on a rotating platform turned by the potter's hands or feet. The wheel method has the advantage of speed and standardization and was used to mass produce thousands of similar vessels, such as the bright red Roman Samian ware (Shepard, 1971). Wheel-made pots can sometimes be identified by the parallel rotation marks on their interior surface.

Surface finishes provided not only a pleasing appearance but also improved the durability of the vessel in day-to-day use. The potter smoothed the exterior surface of the pot with wet hands. Often a wet clay solution, known as a *slip,* was applied to the smooth surface. Brightly colored slips were often used and formed painted decorations on the vessel (Figure 13.11). In later times, *glazes* came into use in some areas. A glaze is a form of slip that turns to a glasslike finish during

Figure 13.11   A painted Zuñi pot of the 1880s. (Height: 9 3/4 inches.)

high temperature firing. When a slip was not applied, the vessel was allowed to dry slowly until the external surface was almost leather-like in texture. It was then burnished with a round stone or similar object to give it a shiny, hard surface. Some pots were decorated with incised or stamped decorations, using shells, combs, stamps, and other tools. Some were even modeled into human effigies or given decorations that imitated the cords used to suspend the pot from the roof (Figure 13.12).

The firing of clay objects requires careful judgment on the part of the potter. Most early pottery was fired over open hearths. The vessels were covered with fast-burning wood, whose ash would fall around the vessels and bake them evenly over a period of a few hours. Far higher temperatures were attained in special ovens, known as *kilns*, which would not only bake the clay and remove its plasticity, but also dis-

Figure 13.12   A spouted Mochica bottle from Peru.

solve carbons and iron compounds. Kilns were used not only to fire vessels at high temperatures, but in the glazing process, when two firings were needed. Once fired, the pots were allowed to cool slowly and small cracks were repaired before they were ready for use.

The making of clay vessels was circumscribed by all manner of social and other variables. Archaeological literature is rich in descriptions of potmaking techniques among people all over the world. Unfortunately, however, few of these studies go beyond technology and processes of manufacture. They may tell us something about the division of labor in making pots, but they reveal little about the potters' status in their own society, their artistic attitudes, or the changing ceramic fashions. In many societies, pottery has a well-defined economic role, and the training of potters is a long, elaborate process. The analysis of ceramics in archaeology must, however, depend on an understanding of the cultural influences that lie behind the variations in pottery in the archaeological record (Fontana, Robinson, Cormack, and Leavitt, 1962; Matson, 1965). Although recent research has focused on the significance of the variations, it is also concerned with the role of the individual potter (Hardin, 1977).

Ceramic Analysis.   Serious potsherd archaeology began in the New World with N. C. Nelson in 1914, and A. V. Kidder a few years later. Within a generation, regional pottery sequences were available for most parts of North America. An enormous expenditure of archaeological energy has gone into ceramic analysis since these pioneer studies, and a sophisticated literature surrounds the common analytical methods (Bennett, 1974; Matson, 1965; Shepard, 1971).

Analogy and experiment.   Controlled experiments to replicate prehistoric ceramic technology have been undertaken to acquire data on firing temperatures, the properties of tempers, and glazing techniques (Coles, 1973; Shepard, 1971). Ethnographic analogy has been a fruitful source of basic information on potters and their techniques, while the direct historical approach traces modern pottery styles back to the prehistoric past.

Form and function analysis.   Two obvious features of prehistoric pottery are immediately obvious upon examination of a collection of vessels—the shape and decoration. Generations of archaeologists have used ethnographic analogy to assign specific functions to different vessel forms. Bowls, for example, are commonly used for cooking and eating, while globular vessels are most suitable for storing liquids.

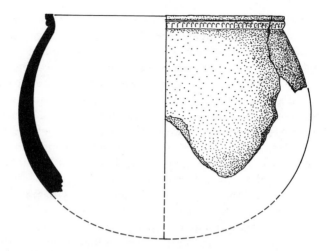

Figure 13.13 A utilitarian clay vessel: an Iron Age pot from the Kalomo culture of Zambia. (One-third actual size.)

Sometimes associations of clay vessels and other artifacts, such as cooking utensils, leave one in no doubt as to the function of the vessels. But such instances are rare, and one usually has to rely on analysis of the vessel form to infer its function.

Form analysis depends on the common assumption that the shape of a vessel is a direct reflection of its function. This assumption, which is based on ethnographic analogies, can be a dangerous one, for there are many intangibles that affect the function of pottery. Intangibles include the properties of the clay used, the technological devices available, and perhaps most important of all, the cultural values that constrain not only the technology but also the uses and fashions of the vessels. Changes in vessel form can sometimes reflect a change in economic activities, but the economic evidence must be complete before such conclusions can be drawn. At the Isamu Pati mound village in Zambia, occupied intermittently for a long period from the seventh to the thirteenth centuries A.D., the uppermost levels contained a much higher proportion of cattle bones than the lower horizons (Fagan, 1967). At the same time, the pottery changed dramatically from a preponderance of simple bag-shaped vessels (Figure 13.13) to an overwhelming dominance of spherical pots with out-turned lips. These could only have contained liquid and were interpreted tentatively as reflecting a change in dietary habits, perhaps an increase in milk consumption. The functional distinction between utilitarian and ceremonial vessels is one of the most evident, but it must be supported not only by vessel form but also by direct association. Ceremonial pots were commonly buried with important people in many parts of the world, especially Mesoamerica.

Form analysis depends on the careful classification of clusters of different vessel shapes. These vessel shapes can be derived from complete vessels, or from potsherds that preserve the rim and shoulder profile of the vessel. It is possible to reconstruct the pot form from these pieces by projecting measurements of diameter and vessel height. Such analyses produce broad categories of vessel form that are capable of considerable refinement. (For an excellent example, see Sabloff, 1975.)

Stylistic analysis.   This is much more commonly used, for it concentrates not on the form and function of the vessel, but on the decorative styles used by the potters. These are assumed to be independent of functional considerations and, as such, are a more accurate reflection of the cultural choices made by the makers. In areas like the American Southwest, pottery styles have been used to trace cultural variations over thousands of years.

Even a cursory glance at pottery reports from different parts of the world will show you that archaeologists have used literally dozens of different stylistic classifications to study their potsherds. It is only in recent years that people have tried to standardize stylistic classifications, using clusters of easily recognized attributes to produce hierarchies of types, varieties, and modes.

With this approach, small numbers of distinctive attributes from different pottery assemblages are recorded. These attributes commonly appear in associated sets of features that provide the basis for erecting types, varieties, and modes of pottery styles. In Chapter 12 we defined these three classifications, which are assumed to represent the social system behind the pots studied. While a *variety* may only represent the activities of a single family of potters, a *type* can represent the work of several villages or an entire community. Thus, goes the argument, standardized pottery types are a reflection of a fairly rigid social system that prescribes what pottery styles are used, while less formalized designs are characteristic of a less restrictive society. James Gifford studied the ceramics from Barton Ramie in the Belize valley and traced the development of Maya pottery from 800 B.C. onward. He argued that the highly localized styles of earlier times reflected a much more flexible social system than in the Late Preclassic period, after 300 B.C., when pottery designs were standardized over large areas and their designs were controlled, perhaps, by rigid cultural values (Gifford, 1976).

Gifford's analysis is based on behavioral assumptions that have yet to be tested. Can one really assume that pottery styles reflect social behavior? The answer must await the day when many more standardized typologies from different areas of the world are available.

Technological analyses.   The manufacturing process used by prehistoric potters is the subject of technological analysis. Anna Shepard of the Smithsonian Institution was a pioneer in this work and spent a lifetime analyzing the constituents of pottery clays and firing techniques (Shepard, 1971). Trace element analyses of mineral elements in clays have provided invaluable evidence for local trading of finished vessels across Lake Malawi in Central Africa (Asaro and Perlman, 1967). Unfortunately, technological analyses of pottery are in their infancy but, nevertheless, they provide an important means of amplifying manufacturing data obtained from archaeological analyses and ethnographic analogy.

METALS AND METALLURGY

The study of metallurgy and metal objects found in archaeological sites is limited by both the state of preservation and our knowledge of primitive metallurgy as a whole (Forbes, 1955–58; Tylecote, 1972). Preservation of metal tools in archaeological horizons is dependent entirely on the soil's acidity. In some circumstances, iron tools are preserved perfectly and can be studied in great detail; in other cases, soil acids have completely reduced the iron to a rusty mass that is almost entirely useless. Copper and gold normally survive somewhat better. Copper was one of the earliest smelted metals, for the ore has a lower melting point than iron has and is readily shaped into artifacts.

Copper.   The earliest metal tools were made by cold-hammering copper into simple artifacts. Such objects were fairly common in Near Eastern villages by 6000 B.C. Copper metallurgy (the process of smelting and working the metal by heating it) came into widespread use about 4000 B.C. (Mallowan, 1965); although European smiths were working copper in the Balkans as early as 3500 B.C. (Cernych, 1978; Coles and Harding, 1979; Tringham, 1971).

In contrast to fine-quality stone and iron, copper ores are rare and

Figure 13.14 Hopewell hammered copper ornaments, found in 1920 in Ross County, Ohio: a raptorial bird and a cut-out breast plate.

concentrated in well-defined regions. The metal was normally, but not invariably, alloyed with tin, which is even rare. In the New World, copperworking was well developed among the Aztec and Inca. The Hopewell Indians of Lake Superior exploited the native copper ore deposits on the southern shores of the lake, and the metal was widely traded and cold-hammered into artifacts from Archaic to Woodland times (Figure 13.14).

Bronze. No one knows quite when prehistoric coppersmiths first learned that alloying copper with small quantities of arsenic, lead, or tin provided a much stronger working edge that could be hammered to make it even tougher. Bronze also has the advantage of a lower melting point than pure copper. Alloying seems to have come into widespread use around 3000 B.C. in several areas, noticeably the Near East, southeastern Europe (Coles and Harding, 1979), and perhaps southeast Asia (Bayard, 1972). The use of tin alloying must have stimulated considerable trading activity, for the metal is relatively rare, especially in the Near East.

Chinese bronze workers, laboring for the rulers of Shang urban centers in the Huangho Valley, were responsible for some of the most sophisticated bronze vessels of prehistoric times. Clay molds were used to cast elaborate legged cauldrons and smaller vessels with distinctive shapes and decoration. Casting was used to produce not only weapons but also elaborate works of art that were valued by early Chinese antiquarians as well as modern collectors (Chang, 1977).

Gold. Gold-decked burials have a curious fascination for many people, but in fact, they are rare finds in archaeological excavations. Gold did, however, play a vital prestigious and ornamental role in many prehistoric societies. It is not without reason that Tutankhamun is sometimes described as the "Golden Pharaoh": his grave was rich in spectacular gold finds. The Chimú peoples of coastal Peru were master goldsmiths of pre-Columbian Latin America (Figure 13.15). The Aztec and Inca also were talented goldsmiths, whose magnificent products were shipped off to Europe and melted down for royal treasuries. The famous artist Albrecht Dürer saw a storeroom full of Aztec gold in Brussels in 1520, in which was included, as he described it: "A Sun all in gold, as much as six feet in diameter . . . there were two chambers full of armor used by these people, and all kinds of weapons, cuirasses, wonderous shields . . . " (Fagan, 1977). Gold was being worked in the Near East almost as early as copper, and it was soon associated with royal prestige. The metal was widely traded in dust, ornament, and bead form in many parts of the Old World (Phillips, 1980; Fagan, 1969).

Figure 13.15   Gold beaker with repoussé decoration and turquoise inlay, attributable to Chimú goldsmiths from Peru. (About two-thirds actual size.)

Iron.   Iron is a more prosaic metal, lacking the lustrous color of fresh copper or bronze, but it yields more effective cutting edges and thus had a far more revolutionary effect on human cultural development than its ornamental relatives. Iron tools were first made on a large scale south of the Black Sea in the second millennium B.C., but objects made of the new metal were uncommon for several centuries. The military advantages of iron may have been appreciated by the Hittite kings, who jealously guarded their monopoly. Even so, the use of iron spread slowly to other areas. Egyptians were working it by the seventh century B.C., whereas iron artifacts are found in Greece and Crete in eleventh-century B.C. contexts. Ironworking was first established on a large scale in continental Europe in the seventh century B.C. by the Hallstatt peoples. In earlier times iron had a comparatively limited economic role, most artifacts being slavish copies of bronze tools before the metal's full potentials were realized. Weapons like swords and spears were the first artifacts to be modified to make use of the new material. Specialized ironworking tools, such as tongs, as well as woodworking artifacts, began to be used as soon as the qualities of iron were recognized.

Iron ore is much more abundant in the natural state than copper. It is readily obtainable from surface outcrops and bog iron deposits. Once its potential had been realized it became much more widespread in use, and stone and bronze were relegated to a subsidiary, often ornamental, role.

The impact of iron was immense, for it made available abundant supplies of tough cutting edges for agriculture. With iron tools, forest clearance became easier, and people achieved even greater mastery over their environment. Ironworking profoundly influenced the development of literate civilizations. Some people, such as the Australian aborigines and the pre-Columbian Americans, did not develop iron metallurgy until they came into contact with European explorers.

Metal Technologies.   Copper technology began with the cold-hammering of the ore into simple artifacts. Copper smelting may have originated in the accidental melting of some copper ore in a domestic hearth or oven. In smelting, the ore is melted at a high temperature in a small kiln and the molten metal allowed to trickle down through the charcoal fuel into a vessel at the base of the furnace. The copper is further reduced at a high temperature and then cooled slowly and hammered into shape. This process of *annealing* (heating, cooling, and hammering) adds strength to the metal. Molten copper was poured into molds and cast into a wide variety of shapes.

Copper ores were obtained from weathered surface outcrops, but the best material came from subsurface ores, which were mined by expert diggers. Copper mines were developed in many parts of the Old World and provide a fruitful field for the student of metallurgy to investigate. The most elaborate European workings were in the Tyrol and Salzburg areas, where there were many oval workings entered by a shaft from above (Clark, 1952). At Mitterburg, Austria, the miners drove shafts into the hillside with bronze picks and extracted the copper by elaborate fire-setting techniques. Many early copper-workings have been found in southern Africa, where the miners followed surface lodes under the ground (Figure 13.16) (Bisson, 1977; Summers, 1969). Fortunately, the traditional Central African processes of copper smelting

Figure 13.16   Excavation in a prehistoric copper mine at Kansanshi, Zambia. The miners followed outcrops of copper ore deep into the ground with narrow shafts, the earth fillings of which yield both radiocarbon samples and artifacts abandoned by the miners.

Figure 13.17   An African ironworker using a goatskin bellows. Similar bellows were also used for copper smelting.

have been recorded. The ore was placed in a small furnace with alternating layers of charcoal and smelted for several hours at high heat maintained with goatskin bellows (Figure 13.17). After each firing, the furnace was destroyed and the molten copper dripped onto the top of a sand-filled pot buried under the fire (Chaplin, 1961).

Bronze technology depended on alloying, the mingling of small quantities of such substances as arsenic and tin with copper. With its lower melting point, bronze soon superseded copper for much metalwork. Some of the most sophisticated bronzeworking was created by

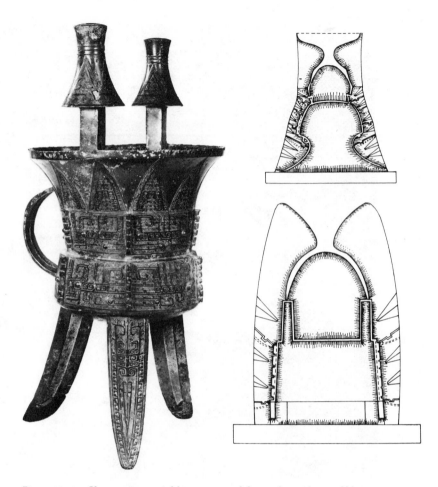

Figure 13.18   Shang ceremonial bronze vessel from about the twelfth century B.C., and diagrams of clay molds for casting such vessels.

Chinese smiths, who cast elaborate vessels in clay molds using the so-called lost-wax method. In this method the mold was assembled with wax in the place of metal, then the wax was replaced with molten bronze, and a cast vessel would emerge from the mold (Figure 13.18).

Ironworking is a much more elaborate technology that requires a melting temperature of at least 1537 degrees centigrade. Prehistoric smiths normally used an elaborate furnace filled with alternate layers of charcoal and iron ore that was maintained at a high temperature for many hours with the aid of bellows. A single firing often yielded only a spongy lump of iron, called a bloom, which then had to be forged and hammered into artifacts. It took some time for the metallurgists to learn that they could strengthen working edges by quenching the tool in cold water. This process gave greater strength, but it also made the tool brittle. The tempering process, reheating the blade to a temperature below 727 degrees centigrade, restored the strength. Iron technology was so slow in developing that it remained basically unchanged from about 600 B.C. to Medieval times (Piggott, 1965).

Analysis of Metal Artifacts.   Typological and technological analyses of metal artifacts are employed.

Typological analyses.   In Europe, metal tools have been analyzed for typology since the early nineteenth century. Stylistic changes in bronze brooches, swords, axes, and iron artifacts were highly sensitive to fashion and to changing trading patterns. As a result, the evolution of bronze pins or iron slashing swords, for example, can be traced across Europe, with small design changes providing both relative dating and occasional insights into the lifeways of the people using them. (Coles and Harding, 1979, summarizes the literature.) In many respects these types of study are similar in intent to those carried out with stone implements or potsherds.

Technological analyses.   In many respects, technological analyses are more important than the study of finished artifacts. Many of the most important questions relating to prehistoric metallurgy involve the manufacturing techniques used. Technological studies start with ethnographic analogies and actual reconstructions of prehistoric metallurgical processes. Chemists study iron and copper slag and residues from excavated furnaces. Microscopic examination of metal structure and ores yields valuable information not only on the metal and its constituents and alloys, but also on the methods used to produce the finished tool. The ultimate objective of the technological analyses is to reconstruct the entire process of metal tool production, from the mining of the ore to the production of the finished artifact.

BONE

Bone as a material for toolmaking probably dates to the very beginnings of human history, but the earliest artifacts apparently consisted of little more than fragments of fractured animal bone used for purposes that could not be fulfilled by wood or stone implements. South

African anatomist Raymond Dart has alleged that *Australopithecus* had a fully fledged bone culture and systematically fractured such bones as jaws and limb bones to form clubs, scrapers, and other artifacts. Dart's "osteodontokeratic"—bone, teeth, horn—culture has been the subject of much controversy, and most scholars reject his hypothesis on the grounds that other, natural factors could have caused such systematic bone fractures (Brain, 1967; Dart, 1957; Wolberg, 1940). Formal bone tools are rare on the Olduvai living floors, but several bone fragments show systematic utilization, as though they were used for scraping skins and similar purposes (M. D. Leakey, 1973).

The earliest standardized bone tools date from later prehistoric times. Splinters of bone were sharpened and used as points in many societies, but bone and antler artifacts were especially favored by the Upper Paleolithic peoples of southwestern France from 30,000 to 12,000 years ago and by postglacial hunter-gatherers in Scandinavia (Bordes, 1968). Bone artifacts as old as 40,000 B.P. may have been located at Old Crow Flats, Alaska (Morlan, 1978). In later times, splinters from long bones were ground and scraped, as well as hardened in

Figure 13.19 Magdalenian harpoons from France, c. 14,000 years B.P. (About two-thirds actual size.)

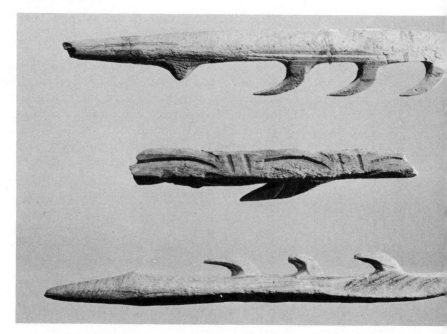

the fire and polished with beeswax, to produce arrowheads, spear-points, needles, and other artifacts. Bone was also carved and engraved, especially during Upper Paleolithic times in western Europe, as was reindeer antler (Grasiozi, 1960).

Deer antler was an even more important material than bone for some later hunter-gatherers. Fully grown deer antler is particularly suitable for making barbed or simple harpoons and spearpoints. One well-known technique involved a beam of reindeer or red deer antler: A series of parallel grooves were made with a suitable stone engraver and the resulting splinters levered from the beam and fashioned into barbed arrowheads or spearheads (Clark, 1954). Bone and antler were much used in prehistoric times for harpoons for fishing and for con-ventional hunting. Numerous harpoons are found in Magdalenian sites in western Europe (Figure 13.19) and also in Eskimo settlements in the Arctic, where they form an invaluable index of cultural development, analogous to that of pottery in the American Southwest.

Bone Tool Analysis.   Bone tools do not throw much light on the mate-rial culture of peoples to whom the by-products of game animals were not particularly important. In woodland areas, where timber is abun-dant, the tendency was to use wood at the expense of bone and antler. But in the Arctic, where bone and ivory are of critical importance, elaborate typological studies have been made of the stylistic and func-tional changes in such diverse items as the harpoons, the winged ivory objects fastened to the butts of harpoons, and other objects (Figure 13.20). Other artifacts include picks made of walrus tusk and snow shovels and wedges of ivory and bone—as well as drills and domestic utensils. Studying such a range of bone artifacts is complicated by the elaborate and variable engraved designs applied to some, but H. B. Collins and others have been able to trace the development of the harpoon of the Northern Maritime Eskimo, from the elaborate types of the Okvik and Old Bering Sea phases to the simpler forms charac-teristic of the Punuk phase and the modern Eskimo weapons (Collins, 1937; Dumond, 1977).

Functional analysis.   Function is easy to analyze, especially in such areas as the Arctic and southern Africa, where contemporary ethno-graphic accounts are available for fruitful analogies. However, there are dangers to this approach. While no one can seriously doubt the func-tional classification of the Old Bering Sea harpoon socket in Figure 13.20, a classification based firmly in analogies, the situation is more complex for the remote past. For example, the Magdalenian peoples

Figure 13.20 Bone and ivory artifacts. Left: Harpoon socket piece, Old Bering Sea style. (9.5 centimeters long.) Right: Turreted ivory object of the Punuk phase. (7 centimeters wide.) From the University of Alaska Museum. Used by permission.

who lived in Southwest France 15,000 years ago made extensive use of bone and antler to produce a wide range of artifacts, ranging from spearthrowers to harpoons and thong straighteners. Are we justified in designating these artifacts by such functional labels as harpoon or thong straightener? The answer is that labels are just that, convenient classificatory terms that may or may not reflect the actual function of the artifact.

Technological analysis. The way in which the tool was made is the subject of technological analysis. The simplest bone technologies involved splitting and flaking bones. Fine points were produced by polishing slivers of bone against grinding surfaces. The Magdalenians used fine lengths of reindeer antler, which they removed from the beam by grooving through the hard outer core of the antler with stone burins or engraving tools. It is no coincidence that their material culture includes a wide range of scraping and graving tools (Clark, 1954).

As with all technological analyses, ethnographic analogy and experimentation with prehistoric bone working methods under controlled modern conditions provide the best insights into early tool making (Coles, 1973).

WOOD

Nonhuman primates sometimes use sticks to obtain grubs, or for other purposes, so it is logical to assume that since the earliest times humans may have used sticks also. Wooden implements form a major part of many modern hunter-gatherer toolkits; occasional, tantalizing glimpses of prehistoric wooden artifacts have come down to us where preservation conditions have been favorable. One of the earliest is a fire-hardened spearpoint found in the Clacton Channel, England, which dates to the Holstein interglacial (*ca.* ?150,000 B.P.) (Clark, 1970). Numerous wooden artifacts, as well as basketry, have come from dry sites in western North America (Jennings, 1978).

The most dramatic discovery of wooden implements in the Americas is undoubtedly that of the Ozette site in the state of Washington, where Richard Daugherty found the remains of several wooden long houses and a wealth of domestic artifacts and fine objects carved from local woods. Preservation conditions at Ozette were so good that the associations of the wooden artifacts with the rest of the site enabled Daugherty to fill in many details of life in this area of the Pacific Coast that otherwise would never have been detected from stone and bone tools alone. He discovered a hitherto unknown art tradition, one ritual whale fin carved in cedar wood and decorated with 700 sea otter teeth (Figure 13.21). The only record of such items was an illustration penned by an artist with Captain Cook during his voyage to the Northwest coast in 1778 (Kirk, 1974).

Wood Technology and Analysis.   The manufacture of wooden tools involves such well-understood mechanical processes as cutting, whittling, scraping, planing, carving, and polishing. Fire was often used to harden sharpened spear points, while oil and paint imparted a fine sheen and appearance to all kinds of wooden artifacts. On the rare occasions when wooden artifacts are preserved, important clues as to their manufacture can be obtained from close examination of the object itself. Unfinished tools are especially useful, especially handles and weapons that have been blocked out but not finished (Coles, Heal, and

Figure 13.21 A whale fin carved from cedar wood and inlaid with more than 700 sea otter teeth, found at Ozette, Washington. The teeth at the base are set in the design of a mythical bird with a whale in its talons.

Orme, 1978). Even more revealing are wooden fragments from abandoned buildings, fortifications, and even track walkways that survive in post holes and other such locations. Microscopic analysis of wooden fragments and charcoals can provide information on the woods used to build houses, canoes, and other such objects. On very rare occasions, stone projectile heads and axes have been recovered in both water-logged and dry conditions where their wooden handles and shafts have survived, together with the thongs used to bind stone to wood. The Ozette excavations yielded complete house planks; even wooden boxes that had been assembled by skillful grooving and bending of planks (Kirk, 1974).

In many instances, the only clues as to the use of wood come from stone artifacts, such as spokeshaves and scrapers used to work it, or from stone axe blades and other tools that were once mounted in wooden handles (Figure 13.22). Only the form of the artifact and occasional ethnographic analogies allow one to reconstruct the nature of the perishable mount that once made the artifact an effective tool.

One often forgets just how important wood was to prehistoric societies. There are thousands upon thousands of ground stone axes in the archaeological record, all of which once had wooden handles. Wood

Figure 13.22 Artifacts as evidence for subsistence: a reconstructed Neolithic stone axe with a handle of ash wood. The handle is a copy of an example found in a Danish bog; only the stone is original, which illustrates how little of an artifact survives under normal conditions. (Approximate length, 30 inches.)

was used for house building, fortifications, fuel, canoes, and containers. Most skilled woodworking societies used the simplest technology to produce both utilitarian and ceremonial objects. They used fire and the ringing of bark to fell trees, stone wedges to split logs, and shells and stones to scrape spear shafts (Drucker, 1968). Wood was probably the most important raw material available to our ancestors. It is a tragedy that it rarely survives in the archaeological record. But, as John Coles points out (Coles, Heal and Orme, 1978), wooden artifacts do occur, with greater frequency than has been believed, and locating them very often is simply a matter of investigating the localities where they are likely to occur.

BASKETRY AND TEXTILES

We do not have the space to discuss basketry in detail, but the production of baskets is estimated to be one of the oldest crafts (Adovasio and Gunn, 1977). Basketry includes such items as containers, matting, bags, and a wide range of fiber objects. Textiles are found in many later, dry sites, and they are especially evident among prehistoric Peruvian artifacts (King, 1978).

Some scholars believe that basketry and textiles are among the most sensitive artifacts for the archaeologist to work with, culturally speaking, on the grounds that people lived in much more intimate association with baskets and textiles than with clay vessels, stone tools, or houses. Furthermore, even small fragments of basketry and textiles display remarkable idiosyncrasies of individual manufacture. Much research has concentrated on methods of manufacture and on raw materials, and it is only in recent years that people have realized their great value as time markers and as potential sources of information on social organization, subsistence activities, and technology.

In a remarkable experiment, Dale Croes and Jonathan Davis (1977) used a computer mapping program to study the baskets made by several families occupying a large house at the waterlogged Ozette site in Washington. They compiled a computer plot of the distribution of basket types, and found that basketry activities were concentrated near the walls of the house. Using the computer, they then plotted and compared different attributes throughout the structure. The clusters that resulted from these analyses were used to show that basketry styles differed from family to family within the group who lived in the house. This is highly experimental research, but it does show the great potential for computer-aided studies of basketry and other artifacts. When preserved, baskets are amenable to the same kind of functional and stylistic analyses as other artifacts.

It is easy for archaeologists to become preoccupied with technology and artifacts, but as the Ozette experiment and other recent studies have emphasized, there is great potential for insights into prehistoric society and subsistence from such research, provided that the ultimate objective is to study people rather than inanimate objects.

Guide to Further Reading

Bordaz, J. *Tools of the Old and New Stone Age.* Garden City, N.Y.: Doubleday Natural History Press, 1970.
A simple manual on stone technology for the beginner.

Clark, J. G. D. *Prehistoric Europe: the Economic Basis.* Palo Alto: Stanford University Press, 1952.
A classic essay on European prehistory that covers the relationship between technology and economic life.

Hill, James, and Gunn, Joel. *The Individual in Prehistory.* New York: Academic Press, 1977.
Essays on ways in which one might identify the work of a single human being in the archaeological record. Especially strong on pottery and basketry. For the more advanced reader.

Matson, F. R. *Ceramics and Man.* New York: Viking Fund, 1965.

A set of conference papers dealing with ceramics. Somewhat outdated, but a thought-provoking beginning for further reading.

Shepard, Anna O. 1971. *Ceramics for the Archaeologist.* Washington, D.C.: Smithsonian Institution, 1971.

The definitive work on ceramics in the New World. Highly technical and informative.

Tylecote, R. F. *Metallurgy in Antiquity.* London: Edward Arnold, 1962.

An introduction to prehistoric metallurgy that is widely respected as a source book.

PART VI 🌿

RECONSTRUCTING PAST LIFEWAYS

And I prophesied as I was commanded; and as I prophesied, there was a noise, and behold, a rattling; and the bones came together, bone to its bone. And as I looked, there were sinews on them, and flesh had come upon them, and skin had covered them . . .

Ezekiel 37:10

A major objective of archaeology is to study the ways in which people have solved the problems of making a living and coping with their environment. Part VI looks more closely at this objective, at research into prehistoric subsistence, settlement archaeology, and the study of religious beliefs and social organization in prehistoric societies. Chapter 14 describes the analysis of food remains, animal bones, vegetable foods, and evidence for prehistoric diet. Archaeologists rely very heavily on ethnographic analogies for the interpretation of prehistoric subsistence and past lifeways. In Chapter 15, we examine some of the latest work in experimental archaeology and ethnoarchaeology, approaches that involve both controlled experiments and observations in the field. Human settlements have changed radically through prehistory. Chapter 16 examines the ways archaeologists study ancient settlement patterns, with special reference to recent research in Mesoamerica. We pay special attention to methods for reconstructing ancient environments. Trade, social organization, and religious beliefs are the special concerns of Chapter 17, which makes the point that much information on these subjects can be obtained with careful research design and meticulous analysis of field data. The study of prehistoric lifeways is an essential preliminary to the interpretation of cultural process, discussed in Part VII.

CHAPTER 14 ❧

SUBSISTENCE AND DIET

Preview

- Archaeologists rely on a wide range of sources to reconstruct prehistoric subsistence methods. These include environmental data, animal bones, vegetable remains, human feces, artifacts, and prehistoric art.
- Zooarchaeology involves the study of animal bones. We describe the process of sorting teeth, horns, and some limb bones. Bone identification is carried out by direct comparison between modern and ancient bones.
- Game animal remains can give insights into prehistoric hunting practices. The proportions of animals present can be affected by cultural taboos, the relative meat yields of different species, and hunting preferences. Overhunting and extinction can also affect the numbers of animals in a site.
- Early domesticated animals are very difficult to identify from their wild ancestors. The process of domestication alters both the characteristics of an animal and its bone structure.
- Slaughtering and butchery practices can be derived from the frequency and distribution of animal bones in the ground. Teeth can be used to establish the age of animals slaughtered, but hunting and slaughter patterns are subject to all manner of subtle variables, including convenience, season of the year, and so on. Understanding

the cultural systems of which the food remains are a part is essential for the interpretation of slaughter and butchery patterns.

- Carbonized and unburnt vegetable remains are recovered from hearths and pits, often using a flotation method that uses water to separate seeds from the matrix around them. Dry sites, such as the rockshelters and camps in the Tehuacán Valley, Mexico, provide abundant evidence for early crop domestication; while grain impressions on European pots are studied to reconstruct prehistoric agriculture in the Old World. Danish archaeologists have used pollen analysis to study forest clearance in temperate zones during early farming times.
- Bird bones have been much neglected, but they provide invaluable information on seasonal occupation; while fish remains reflect specialized coastal adaptations that became common in later prehistoric times. Hooks, nets, and other artifacts, as well as fish remains themselves, provide insights into both coastal and offshore fishing practices.
- Fresh- and saltwater mollusca were both consumed as food and traded over enormous distances as prestigious luxuries or ornaments. We cite the example of the African *Conus* shell, which was an important trade commodity in southern Africa.
- Prehistoric diet and nutrition must be studied together, for they are distinct from subsistence, which is the actual process of obtaining food. It is difficult to estimate the caloric needs of modern peoples, let alone those of prehistoric groups. Despite such recovery methods as flotation, archaeological data can only indicate some of the foods eaten by prehistoric communities and show their importance in general terms. But this is far from ascribing their true caloric importance to prehistoric peoples.
- Human skeletal remains, stomach contents, and feces, are the few direct sources available to us of information on prehistoric diet. The information they yield is limited, at best.

Archaeologists and anthropologists have long been fascinated by the ways in which people have obtained food and essential raw materials. As early as the mid-nineteenth century, Danish scientists were identifying sea shells and animal bones from coastal shell middens to see what their inhabitants lived on (Lubbock, 1865). The study of prehistoric subsistence—subsistence being the means of supporting life through food supplies—has developed in sophisticated ways since the 1860s.

A greater understanding of ecology and its implications for archaeology has led people to view humans and their culture as merely one element in a complex ecosystem. The study of prehistoric subsistence, then, has developed hand-in-hand with attempts to understand the complex interrelationships between the way people make their living and their environment.

THE EVIDENCE FOR SUBSISTENCE

Archaeologists rely on a wide range of data sources to reconstruct prehistoric subsistence. These include the following (Gabel, 1967):

1. *Environmental data.* Background data on the natural environment is an essential prerequisite for studying subsistence. Such data can include information such as animal distributions, ancient and modern flora, and soils.
2. *Faunal remains.* Animal bones are a major source of information on hunting practices and domestic animals. The identification and interpretation of such finds depends on a detailed knowledge of mammalian anatomy, as well as on ethnographic data relating to butchery practices.
3. *Vegetable remains.* These can include both wild and domestic species, obtained by flotation methods or from carbonized contexts. Such materials are less frequently preserved in the archaeological record than animal bones. Sometimes pollen analysis will throw light on prehistoric agriculture and collecting habits.
4. *Human feces.* These yield both tiny fragments of ecofacts and pollen grains and are preserved in dry caves. They are vital evidence for a reconstruction of prehistoric diet (Bryant, 1974).
5. *Artifacts.* The picture of human subsistence yelded by artifacts is necessarily limited. Flint axes, pressure-flaked arrowheads, iron hoes, or digging-stick weights may indicate the outlines of the picture, but they hardly clothe it with substance and intricate detail. Many critical artifacts used in the chase or garden were made from perishable materials, such as basketry, wood, or fiber.
6. *Prehistoric art.* Artists sometimes depicted scenes of the chase and fishing, as well as food-gathering.

ANIMAL BONES (ZOOARCHAEOLOGY)

Zooarchaeology is the study of the animal remains found in the archaeological record. Although some zoologists have specialized in the study of animal bones from archaeological sites, most zooarchaeologists receive training in archaeology and engage in the study of prehistoric faunas as a specialty (Chaplin, 1971; Cornwall, 1956; Olsen, 1972, 1978, 1979).

Sorting and Identification.   Broken food bones are probably the most tangible remains of human subsistence patterns to survive from the past. Bone is one of the more durable raw materials and survives in various environments, either in a fossilized or a fresh form. Most people think skeletal remains occur in a more or less complete state, but rarely does an animal obligingly lie down and die in an archaeological site. Indeed, about the only mammals to do so are small rodents who have died in their burrows or such domestic animals as dogs that normally were not eaten.

Faunal remains are usually fragmentary, coming from dismembered carcasses butchered either at the archaeological site or at the hunting grounds. To some degree, how much of the carcass is carried back to camp depends on the animal's size. Small deer may be taken back whole, slung from the shoulder. Hunter-gatherers sometimes camped at the site of the kill of a large animal, where they both ate and dried parts of the carcass for later use. Almost invariably, however, the bones found in occupation sites literally have been sliced to ribbons. Every piece of usable meat was stripped from the bones; sinews were made into thongs, and the skin into clothing, containers, or sometimes, housing. Even the entrails were eaten. Limb bones were split for their delicious marrow; some bones were made into such tools as harpoon heads, arrow tips, or leather-working tools (Figure 14.1). The fragmentary bones found in an archaeological deposit represent the by-products of many subsistence and cultural activities that can only be inferred from a detailed study of the bones. The archaeologist's job is to attempt to conjure up a picture of the animal that was hunted or kept by the site's inhabitants from the fragmentary bone they dropped into their occupation layer. The archaeologist also has to envisage the role that mammal played in the economy and culture of those who killed it—a difficult problem, for the difference between the "actual animal" slaughtered and the "archaeological animal" found and identified by the archaeologist is considerable (Daly, 1969; Binford, 1978, 1980). The archaeological animal consists of a scatter of broken bones that have been shattered by a butcher, then subjected to thousands of years of gradual deterioration in the soil. It requires careful examination of these fragmentary remains to arrive at an approximation of the once living animal that was felled by a prehistoric hunter.

Bone distributions are carefully plotted on living floor sites to show any significant associations of body parts with artifacts, windbreaks, or

Figure 14.1   A leather-working tool from Star Carr, made of wild ox bone. (Two-thirds actual size.)

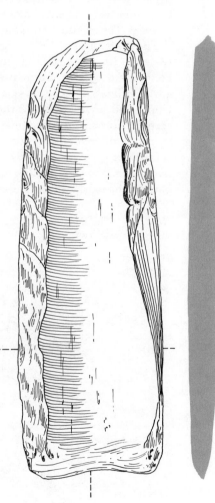

other structures. But unless a living floor is definitely identified, the fragments are normally handled in bulk and bagged carefully for laboratory study.

Most bone identification is done by direct comparison. It is a fairly simple process, easily learned by anyone with sharp eyes (Cornwall, 1956). But only a small proportion of the bones in a collection are sufficiently characteristic for this purpose. As an example, only 2128 fragments of a collection of 195,415 from a Stone Age campsite in Zambia could be identified as to species; another 9207 could be assigned to a particular body part; the remainder of the collection had been smashed into small pieces by hunters in search of marrow, sinew, or meat (Fagan and Van Noten, 1971).

The skeleton of a dog in Figure 14.2 illustrates a typical mammalian skeleton. Small skull fragments, vertebrae, ribs, scapulae, and pelvic bones are normally of little use in identifying a domestic as opposed to a wild animal, or to differentiate one species of antelope from another. Upper and lower jaws and their dentition, individual teeth, the bony cores of horns, and sometimes the articular surfaces of long bones are susceptible to identification (Olsen, 1978). Teeth are identified by comparing the cusp patterns on their surfaces with those on comparative collections carefully taken from the site area (Figure 14.3). In some parts of the world, the articular ends of long bones can be used as well,

Figure 14.2   The skeleton of a dog, showing the most important body parts, from the osteological viewpoint.

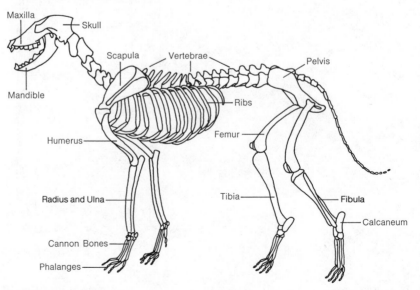

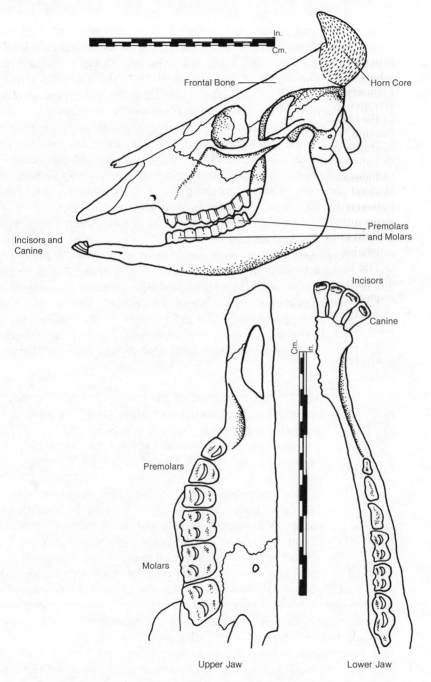

Figure 14.3 The skull and mandible of a domestic ox, showing important osteological features. (One-fourth actual size.)

especially in such regions as the Near East or parts of North America, where the indigenous mammalian fauna is somewhat restricted (Hole, Flannery, Kent, and Neely, 1969). It is even possible to distinguish the fragmentary long bones of domestic stock from those of wild animals of the same size in the Near East, provided that the collections are large enough, and the comparative material sufficiently complete and representative of all ages of individual, and of variations in size from male to female. But in other areas, such as sub-Saharan Africa, for example, the indigenous fauna is so rich and varied, with such small variations in skeletal geography, that only horn cores or teeth can help distinguish between different species of antelope and separate domestic stock from game animals. Even the dentition is confusing, for the cusp patterns of buffalo and domestic cattle are remarkably similar, often only distinguishable by the smaller size of the latter.

The identification stage of a bone analysis is the most important of all, for several fundamental questions need answering: Are domestic and wild species present? If so, what are the proportions of each group? What types of domestic stock were kept by the inhabitants? Did they have any hunting preferences that are reflected in the proportions of game animals found in the occupation levels? Are any wild species characteristic of vegetational associations no longer found in the area today?

Game Animals.   Though the listing of game animals and their habits gives an insight into hunting practices, in many cases, the content of the faunal list gains particular significance when we seek to explain why the hunters concentrated on certain species and apparently ignored others.

Taboos.   The dominance of a particular game species can result from economic necessity or convenience or it can simply be a matter of cultural preference. Many societies restrict the hunting of particular animals or the consumption of certain game meat to one or the other sex. The !Kung San of the Dobe area of Botswana have a complicated series of personal and age- and sex-specific taboos concerning eating mammals (Lee and DeVore, 1976). No one can eat all twenty-nine game animals regularly taken by the San; indeed, no two individuals will have the same set of taboos. Some mammals can be eaten by everyone but with restrictions on what part they may eat. Ritual curers will set personal dietary restrictions on other animals; no one eats primates and some carnivores. Such complicated taboos are repeated with innumerable variations in other hunter-gatherer and agricultural

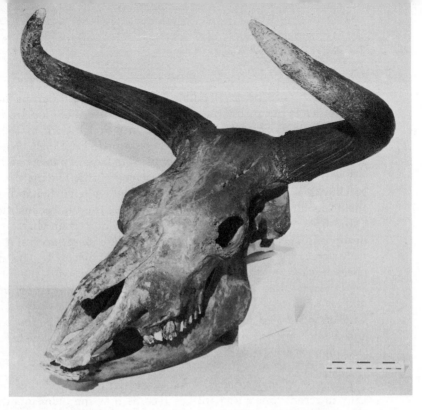

Figure 14.4   A *Bos primigenius* skull from Cambridgeshire, England.

societies and have undoubtedly affected the proportions of game animals found in archaeological sites.

Examples of specialized hunting are common, even if the reasons for the attention given to one or more species are rarely explained. Upper Paleolithic hunters of Solutré in southwestern France concentrated on wild horses, apparently driving them over cliffs in large herds (Smith, 1966). At the eighth millennium B.C. hunting camp of Star Carr in northeast England, Grahame Clark found the remains of a minimum of eighty red deer in the occupation levels, while roe deer—thirty-three individuals—were the next most common game (Clark, 1954). The Archaic Riverton culture peoples of the central Wabash Valley, Illinois, hunted the white-tailed deer as the basic meat staple in their diet to such an extent that the remains of this mammal were more numerous than those of any other species in the sites, except for, in most cases, birds, fish, and turtles (Winters, 1969). The specialized big game hunting economies of the Plains Indians are well known (Frison, 1974).

Overhunting.   Another factor is overhunting, or the gradual extinction of a favorite species (Ewers, 1949). One well-known example is *Bos primigenius* (Figure 14.4), the European aurochs, or wild ox, which was a major quarry of Upper Paleolithic hunters in western Europe and was still hunted in postglacial times and after the advent of food production (Zeuner, 1963). The last aurochs died in a Polish park in 1627. We know from illustrations and contemporary descriptions what these massive animals looked like. The bulls were large, up to six and a half feet at the shoulder, and often had very long horns. The male coat was black with a white stripe along the back and white curly hair between the horns. Professor Lutz Heck of Berlin has tried to reconstitute the aurochs by crossing breeds of cattle that exhibit certain characteristics of the wild ancestor. Heck's experiments were most successful—there were forty "reconstituted aurochsen" living by 1951. The mental characteristics of the aurochs reappeared along with the physical appearance. "Reconstituted aurochsen" are fierce, temperamental, and extremely agile if allowed to run wild. The German experiments have provided a far more convincing reconstruction of a most formidable Pleistocene mammal than could any number of skeletal reconstructions or artists' impressions.

Changes in hunting activities.   Hunting activities have changed drastically in recent times. Richard Lee records how the older members of the San state that in earlier times there were more game animals and a higher hunting population in the central interior of Botswana (Lee and DeVore, 1976). Their forefathers used to hunt in large groups, killing buffalo, giraffe, and elephants. Today, their descendants have a predominantly gathering economy, supplemented by the meat of twenty-nine different mammals, mostly those whose carcasses have a relatively high meat yield. Hunting is a common pursuit, the warthog being the most important source of meat, together with small game. This change in hunting habits directly results from the importation of Victorian rifles and from early hunting safaris, which decimated the wonderful African fauna within three generations.

Domestic Animals.   Nearly all domestic animals originated from a wild species with an inclination to be sociable, facilitating an association with humans (Ucko and Dimbely, 1969). Domestic animals did not all originate in the same part of the world; they were domesticated in their natural area of distribution in the wild. Scholars have assumed that the domestication of wild animals takes place when a certain level of cultural achievement is reached. Domestication everywhere seems to begin when there is a growing population that needs a more regular food supply to feed larger groups of people; domestication is both dependent on such conditions and is a prerequisite for further population growth.

Wild animals lack many characteristics that are valuable in their domestic counterparts. Thus, wild sheep have hairy coats, but their wool is not the type produced by domestic sheep, which is suitable for spinning; aurochs, ancestors of the domestic ox, and wild goats produce sufficient milk for their young, but not in the quantities so important to man. Considerable changes have taken place during the course of domestication, as people develop characteristics in their animals that often render them unfit for survival in the wild (Olsen, 1979).

The history of the domestic species is based on fragmentary animal bones found in the deposits of innumerable caves, rockshelters, and open sites (Reed, 1977). Osteological studies of wild and domesticated animals are inhibited both by the fragmentation of the bones in most sites and by the much greater range of sexual and growth variation in domestic, as opposed to wild, populations. Nevertheless, a number of sites have produced evidence of gradual osteological change toward domesticated animals (Redman, 1978). If the bones of the wild species of prehistoric domesticated animals are compared with those of the domestic animals throughout time, the range of size variations first increases, and eventually, a selection in favor of smaller animals and less variation in size appears. This transition is, however, fluid, and it is difficult to identify wild or domestic individuals from single bones or small collections.

The bones of domestic animals demonstrate that a high degree of adaptability is inherent in wild animals. People have found it necessary to change the size and qualities of animals according to their needs, with corresponding effects on their skeletal remains. Different breeds of cattle, sheep, and other domestic animals have been developed since the beginning of domestication.

Slaughtering and Butchery.   Some insights into peoples' exploitation of wild and domestic animals can be obtained from the study not only of animal bones themselves, but also of their frequency and distribution in the ground. However, as Lewis Binford (1978) points out, the problem is not to record distributions and frequencies alone, but to establish what they mean in terms of human behavior. His recent studies of caribou hunting and exploitation by the Nunamiut Eskimo of Alaska have provided a mass of new data on the ways in which people exploit animals, and have a direct relevance to the interpretation of faunal remains (see Chapter 15).

Slaughtering.   An animal's age is determined by examining the eruption and wear patterns of teeth, as well as the ends (epiphyses) and cross sections of long bones. The epiphyses may be unfused or partially joined in the case of immature animals, and although these make a useful criterion, it is not so significant in areas like Africa or Asia, where the osteology of long bones and other extremities is not well known. Some Near Eastern sites have yielded such large collections that higher proportions of immature epiphyses were used to show the threshold of domestication. Early goat herders such as the inhabitants of Belt Cave in Iran systematically began to kill goats at a younger age than they did when they were hunting the wild species (Reed, 1977). Most aging is determined by studying the dentition, using complete jaws so that the eruption formulae can be compared. Sometimes single teeth are used, the wear on the cusps being measured by a standard scale, but this method is less reliable. The assembled data are then tabulated in graph or table form and are ready for interpretation. Some illustrative slaughter-pattern graphs appear in Figure 14.5. Obviously,

Figure 14.5   Aging graphs derived from skeletal remains for ideal hypothetical cases. (a) Hunting population slaughtered by skilled hunter-gatherers. (b) Typical domestic cattle population. (c) Typical domestic goat population. Note that these graphs are purely hypothetical and take no account of actual systems.

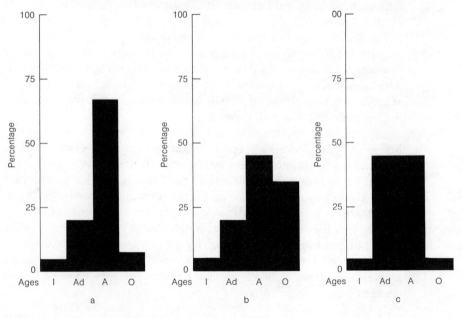

I = Infant   Ad = Adolescent   A = Adult   O = Old age

large samples are essential. The interpretation of such figures is, of course, fraught with difficulty, unless one has an insight into the cultural system within which the hunters or farmers operated.

Hunting and slaughter patterns are subject to all manner of subtle variables; many of which have been described by Lewis Binford (1978). When studying hunting practices among the Nunamiut Eskimo of Alaska, he found that the hunters butchered animals as part of a much broader subsistence strategy. The Nunamiut rely heavily on stored meat for most of the year, and thus, they orient their hunting practices toward storage objectives, as well as many other considerations. In the fall, they may hunt caribou calves to obtain skins for winter clothing, and the heads and tongues of these animals provide the meat for the people who process the skins. Binford stresses that it is difficult to interpret slaughter patterns without a close understanding of the cultural systems of which hunting was a part.

Domestic animals are a controllable meat supply, and subject to quite different selection criteria. In more advanced agricultural societies, cattle or horses might be kept until old age for draught purposes, surplus males being castrated and females being retained until they stopped lactating or were of no further use for breeding or ploughing. Even if riding or work animals were not kept, the problem of surplus males persists. This male surplus represents an abundant source of prime meat, and these animals were often slaughtered at early adulthood. Cattle stood for wealth in many traditional societies, as they do in some today; and they were slaughtered on such special occasions as funerals or weddings. The herd surplus was consumed in this manner, and the owner's obligations were satisfied. Thus, a population of cattle jaws found in a site may reveal a characteristic graph (Figure 14.5b), showing that the animals were slaughtered at different ages. This may reflect distinct slaughtering ages for male and female animals. Or, perhaps the remains of a herd of goats may yield a simple graph (Figure 14.5c), reflecting circumstances in which small stock were slaughtered in their prime for meat purposes. These situations are by no means universal, but they do offer examples of factors that can affect slaughter pattern data.

Butchery.   The fragmentary bones in an occupation level are the end-product of the killing, cutting up, and consumption of domestic or wild animals. To understand the butchery process, the articulation of animal bones must be examined in the levels where they are found, or a close study must be made of fragmentary body parts. For instance, the Olsen-Chubbock kill site in Colorado yielded evidence of a slaughtered bison herd. The hunters camped beside their kill, removing the skin and meat from the carcass of a large mammal, and perhaps drying some surplus meat for later consumption. The butchering tools used by the skinners are found in direct association with the bones, so that the excavations preserve the moment of butchery for posterity (Wheat, 1972).

Interpreting butchery techniques is a complicated matter, for many variables affect the way in which carcasses were dismembered. The Nunamiut relied heavily on stored meat, and the way they dismembered a caribou varied according to storage needs, meat yield of different body parts, and proximity of the base camp. The animal's size may affect the number of bones found at a base site: goats, chickens, or small deer could have been carried to the village as complete carcasses; but often, only small portions of larger beasts were brought in. Sometimes, animals with a high meat yield were consumed where they were killed and every scrap of flesh and entrails utilized. Theodore White (1953) developed a method for studying the distribution of body parts by reducing them to proportions of the most common bone present. He applied the method with success to bison kills in the Great Plains. But his technique although useful, does not solve the problem of interpretation. Once again, the problem is to establish the meaning of archaeological distributions in terms of human behavior. Just how complicated this is in the context of butchery can be appreciated from Binford's comment (1978) that the Nunamiuts' criteria for selecting meat for consumption are the amount of usable meat, the time required to process it, and the quality of the flesh. The only way to interpret archaeological distributions is through a detailed understanding of the cultural systems that generated them (see Chapter 15).

VEGETAL REMAINS

Gathering and agriculture are two major components of prehistoric subsistence that are almost invariably underrepresented in the archaeological record. Seeds, fruits, grasses, and leaves are among the most fragile of organic materials and do not survive long unless they are carbonized or preserved under very wet or arid conditions.

Carbonized and Unburnt Seeds. These are normally found in cooking pots, midden deposits, or among the ashes of hearths, where they were dropped by accident. Though the preservation conditions are not ideal, it is possible to identify both domestic and wild plant species from such discoveries (Ford, 1979; Helbaek, 1969; J. Renfrew, 1973). Much early evidence for cereal cultivation in the Near East comes from carbonized seeds. Many more unburnt vegetable remains occur in waterlogged sites and in dry caves. The Star Carr site in northeastern England yielded a range of fungi and wild seeds, some of which were eaten until recently by European peasants (Clark, 1954). A Stone Age campsite at Gwisho hot springs in central Zambia, situated on the edge of a tract of savannah woodland rich in vegetal foods, contained quantities of seeds and fruit preserved by the high water table in the springs (Fagan and Van Noten, 1971). Ten thousand identifiable vegetal fragments came from the occupation levels at Gwisho, many of them from six species still eaten by southern African hunters: this represents a remarkable continuity of subsistence patterns over more than 4,000 years.

The dry caves of the western United States and Mexico have provided a great quantity of dried vegetable remains. The inhabitants of Tularosa cave in New Mexico were harvesting primitive corn by 2000 B.C., and their successors employed horticulture fully. The lower levels, occupied by hunter-gatherers, yielded the remains of no fewer than thirty-nine species of wild flora that were used for food, tools and raw materials; edible plants included yucca seeds, cacti, walnuts and various grasses (Jennings, 1973).

Tehuacán.   The Tehuacán Valley in the state of Puebla, Mexico, has provided a record of continuous human occupation from the earliest times to the Spanish Conquest (Byers, 1967; MacNeish, 1978). Early inhabitants of the valley lived mainly by hunting rabbits, birds, and turtles. Later, about 6700–5000 B.C., their successors subsisted mostly on wild plants such as beans and amaranth. These people, who lived in caves during the dry season, began to cultivate squashes and avocados; pollens from a plant that some botanists believe is transitional between wild teosinte to corn, through human selection, occur in the cave deposits. Grinding stones, pestles, and mortars were in use for the first time, indicating that seeds were being ground for food.

Richard MacNeish has excavated more than a dozen sites in Tehuacán, five of which contained the remains of ancient corn; 80,000 wild plant remains and 25,000 specimens of corn came from the sites, providing a detailed picture of agriculture's origins in highland Mexico. The transitional pollens and cobs came from the lowest occupation level in San Marcos Cave, and the cobs were no more than twenty millimeters (0.78 inch) long. Coxcatlán Cave contained important botanical evidence, too, for by 5000 B.C., although the inhabitants of this and other sites were still gathering most of their vegetal food, 10 percent of the diet came from domestic cultivation—gourds, squashes, beans, chili peppers, and corn. One-third of Tehuacán subsistence was based on agriculture by 3400 B.C., a period when the domestic dog first appeared; permanent settlement first began soon after that. Pottery was being manufactured by 2300 B.C., and more hybrid types of corn came into use.

So many vegetal remains were found in the settlements of Tehuacán that the history of domestic corn in this area can be written in quite astonishing detail (Figure 14.6). Much controversy surrounds the ultimate ancestry of the maize. One school of thought regards teosinte, a native annual grass, as the ancestor. Another, a long-lived theory, contends that the wild ancestor of maize became extinct some 2000 years ago, as did the early cultivated varieties, which were superseded by more modern forms (Flannery, 1973). Botanical evidence of this completeness is unique in the archaeological record.

Flotation Recovery.   Flotation techniques have been employed systematically to recover seeds in central Illinois, and also at Ali Kosh in Iran. The method uses water or chemicals to free the seeds, which are often of microscopic size, from the fine earth or occupation residue that masks them: the vegetal remains usually float, while the residue sinks. Although this technique enables us to recover seeds from many sites where it was impossible before, by no means can it be applied universally, as its effectiveness depends on soil conditions. Through flotation, Stuart Struever and his colleagues recovered over 36,000 fragments of carbonized hickory nut shell from ovens, hearths, and storage-refuse pits in the Apple Creek site in the Lower Illinois Valley (Struever, 1968). This settlement also yielded 4200 fragments of acorn shell, as well as over 2,000 other seeds from at least three species. Few cultivated seeds were found, which indicated that the inhabitants relied on hickory nuts and acorns for much of their vegetable diet. (Asch, Asch, and Ford, 1972).

Kent Flannery's experiments with flotation at the Ali Kosh site in Iran were also successful—indeed, the results were dramatic (Hole, Flannery and Neely, 1969). After the first season of excavations, Flannery and his colleagues stated confidently that "plant remains were scarce at Ali Kosh." Two years later they used a modified version of Struever's flotation technique and recovered over 40,000 seeds stratified throughout the cultural sequence at the Ali Kosh mound. The data

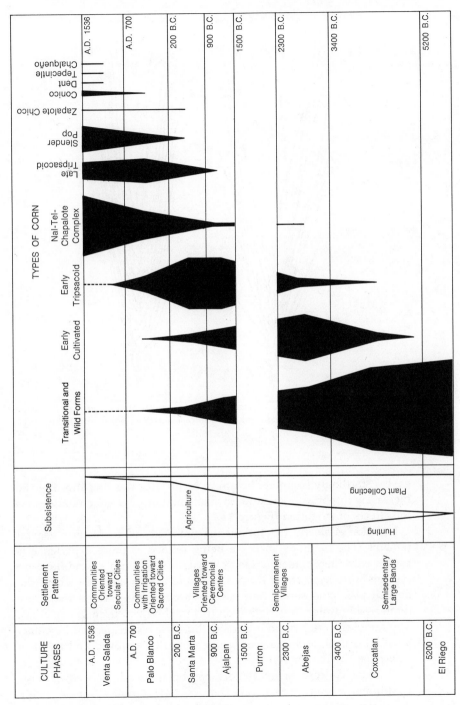

Fig. 14.6 The evolution of maize in the Tehuacán Valley.

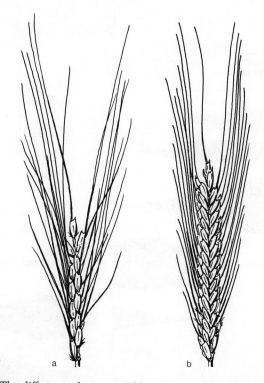

Figure 14.7   The differences between wild and domesticated wheat. (a) The wild ancestor of one-grained wheat (einkorn: *Triticum boeoticum*). (b) Cultivated einkorn (*T. monococum*).

gave a startlingly complete botanical history for the site, showing the increasing importance of emmer wheat and two-row hulled barley and the effects of irrigation (Figure 14.7).

Flotation is slowly revolutionizing the study of prehistoric vegetal remains. The methods used are being refined as more experience is gained with them under varied field conditions. Simple hand flotation systems were used at Ali Kosh and Apple Creek, methods where the deposit was hand sorted and passed through fine meshes that were immersed in water. A variation on this method was used in dry areas. The samples were poured into mesh-lined sieves suspended in water-filled oil drums, and fine seeds were carefully removed and dried in newspaper before study.

A major concern of excavators has been speed, to recover large quantities of seeds in relatively short periods of time (Watson, 1976). A number of ingenious machines have been developed to carry out large-scale flotation: These include a device known as a froth flotation machine, which separates the archaeological material from its matrix in a special flotation chamber, with a mixture of water and chemicals to aid the process (Jarman, Legge, and Charles, 1972). This is an expensive machine to assemble and operate compared with a much simpler device that was assembled for the Mammoth Cave excavations in Kentucky, in which water is forced through a pressure hose and a shower head onto the bottom of a screened container that sits inside the oil drum (Figure 14.8). The sample of earth is poured into the screened container and agitated by the water pouring into the screen. The light plant remains and other fine materials float on the water and are carried out of the container by a sluiceway that leads to fine mesh screens,

Figure 14.8 A simple flotation device used at Mammoth Cave in western Kentucky.

Figure 14.9 A grain impression from a Neolithic pot at Hurst Fen, Cambridgeshire, England.

where the finds are caught, wrapped in fine cloth, and preserved for the botanists to study. The heavy sludge, in the meantime, sinks to the bottom of the container inside the oil drum. This Mammoth Cave system has the advantage of being cheap to make and easy to operate. It is estimated to process about 0.50 cubic meters of deposit a working day. To work most effectively, the system has to be close to a source of running water, whether a river or a faucet.

Flotation, though still in its infancy, promises to rewrite the early history of domestic crops in the New and Old worlds. Recent flotation operations have revealed domestic sunflowers in a site in Tennessee dating to about 900 ± 85 B.C., while finds on Kentucky sites may well push back the origins of horticulture in eastern North America to as early as the late third millennium B.C. (Watson, 1974, 1976). And in the Near East wild einkorn and barley seeds have come from the Mureybit site in Syria, dating to the eighth millennium B.C. (Redman, 1978). These preliminary results have the advantage of being empirical results that can be treated statistically, and—provided that the flotation methods used are carefully defined in each instance—compared one to another.

Grain Impressions.   Apart from the seeds themselves, which reveal what the food plants were, grain impressions in the walls of clay vessels or adobe brick help uncover the history of agriculture or gathering. The microscopic casts of grains that adhered to the wet clay of a pot while it was being made are preserved in the firing process and can be identified with a microscope. Numerous grain impressions have been found on European handmade pottery from the end of the Stone Age (Figure 14.9). Indeed, a remarkably complete crop history of prehistoric Europe has been pieced together from grain impressions. The most abundantly cultivated cereal in prehistoric Europe was emmer wheat (*Triticum dicoccum*); wheat was the most important grain during early farming times, but barley rose into prominence during the Bronze Age (Clark, 1952; J. Renfrew, 1973). Grain impressions have been studied in the Near East and the western Sahara whereas some related work on adobe bricks has been carried out in the western United States (Darrah, 1938).

Palynology has been an invaluable tool for studying European forest clearance (Figure 14.10). Many years ago, Danish botanist Johannes Iversen was studying the pollen diagrams from Scandinavian peat sequences when he noticed that there was a remarkably sudden change in the composition of the forests in the beginning of the sub-Boreal period (Blytt and Sernander, zones VII–VIII) (Iversen, 1941). The ele-

Figure 14.10 Fluctuation in the frequencies of charcoal and fossil pollen brought by Neolithic colonization: Ordrup Mose, Denmark. The amount of grass pollen rises sharply as the forest decreases. (After Iversen.)

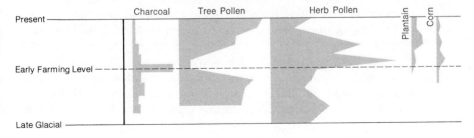

ments of high forest—oak, ash, beech, and elm—simultaneously declined, while at the same time the pollens of grasses increased sharply. At one locality, he found a charcoal layer immediately underlying the zone where forest trees declined. The increase in grass pollens was also associated with the appearance of several cultivation weeds, including *Plantago*, which is characteristically associated with cereal agriculture in Europe and went with European farmers throughout the world, even to North America. Iversen concluded that the tree cover vanished as a direct result of farming activity—humankind's first major imprint on the environment. Similar pollen curves have been plotted from data gathered elsewhere in Europe.

Interpretation of Evidence.   No matter how effective the recovery techniques used for vegetal remains are, the picture of either food gathering or agriculture is bound to be incomplete. A look at modern hunter-gatherers reveals the problem (Lee and DeVore, 1976). The !Kung San of the Kalahari Desert in southern Africa are classic examples of hunter-gathers who appear in every book on ethnography, and yet, until comparatively recently, little was known of their ecology or subsistence patterns, Many early writers on hunter-gatherers assumed the !Kung relied on game alone and lived in a perennial state of starvation that was relieved periodically by meat-eating orgies. Nothing, in fact, could be further from the truth. Much subsistence activity of the San and other hunter-gatherers is conducted by the women, who gather the wild vegetable foods that comprise a substantial part of their diet. Many early observers were naturally preoccupied with hunting techniques and more spectacular subsistence activities, for in former times, many peoples pursued larger game, often cooperating with other bands in the chase.

Today, vegetable foods play a leading part in the San diet and have presumably increased in importance as the large game herds have diminished. The San know of at least eighty-five species of edible fruit, seeds, and plants; of this enormous subsistence base, they eat regularly only some nine species, noticeably the *Bauhinia*. In a famine year or when prime vegetable food sources are exhausted, they turn to other species having an excellent cushion of edible food to fall back on when their conventional diet staple is scarce. Theoretically, therefore, the San can never starve, even if food is scarce at times. Their territory, of course, is delineated in part by available sources of vegetable foods as well as by water supplies; its frontiers in many cases represent a day's walking distance out to the gathering grounds and back to the base camp.

AGRICULTURE AND DOMESTIC AND WILD ANIMALS

Very few subsistence-farming peoples have ever relied on agricultural products or their herds alone to provide them with food the year round. Hunting, fishing, and gathering have always supplemented the diet, and in famine years or times of epidemic the people have fallen back on the natural resources of their environment for survival.

Since, however, food production has led to increased population densities, famine often ensues, because the resource base of wild foods for farmers is smaller than that which may have supported a smaller hunter-gatherer population in comfort (Scudder, 1962). Even in times of plenty, most food producers rely on game for some of their meat, as evidenced by the bones of wild animals in faunal collections where cattle and small stock are also present. The proportions of domestic and wild species in such a collection are considerably important in assessing the roles of hunting and pastoralism in the economy. If such figures are based on how many individuals are represented in the collection, or on some sound formulae, the results can be revealing, especially when a series of collections are available from a cultural sequence extending over several hundred years.

Deh Luran. Just how important an influence domesticated animals had on prehistoric agriculture is well documented on the Deh Luran Plain in Iran (Hole, Neely, and Flannery, 1969). The inhabitants of the Deh Luran Plain first began to cultivate cereal crops and keep goats sometime before 7000 B.C. Their first food production involved plants and animals introduced from the mountains to the rolling steppe of the Plain. As the excavators point out, "What man did, before 7000 B.C., was to domesticate the annuals he could eat, and then domesticate the animals who lived on the perennials." The cultivation system was expanded so that domestic grains increased from 5 percent of the vegetal remains to about 40 percent between 7000 and 6000 B.C. But this early domestic plant and animal complex, based as it was on upland-mountain environmental adaptations, inhibited rapid population growth. Even so, the vegetational pattern of the steppe was altered as field weeds were established and land clearance and grazing removed the natural grass covering.

Between 5500 and 5000 B.C., some simple irrigation techniques were introduced that took advantage of the local drainage pattern. Barley cultivation became of prime importance, and the cultivation areas expanded. Sheep increased in importance, and cattle were introduced, the latter assuming a vital role in the economy only when plows began to be used in around 2000 B.C. Each gradual or rapid change in the subsistence pattern or environment of Deh Luran instituted by humans led to a complicated chain reaction affecting every sector of the inhabitants' culture.

The rate of herd growth is affected by many factors, among them endemic stock disease, the nutrient qualities of grazing grass, the availability of water supplies, and in some areas, the distribution of the dreaded tsetse fly, carrier of *trypanosomiasis*, which is fatal to cattle and harmful to man (Lambrecht, 1964). Similar factors also affect the growth rate of domestic stock, because the size of cattle or smaller stock can vary widely from one environment to another.

BIRDS, FISH, AND MOLLUSCA

Birds.   Bird bones have been sadly neglected in archaeology, although some early investigators did realize their significance. Japetus Steenstrup and other early investigators of Danish shell middens took care to identify bird bones, including those of migrant birds (Lubbock, 1865). In 1902 the famous Peruvianist Max Uhle dug a large Indian mound on the eastern shores of San Francisco Bay. The site was excavated again in 1926, and Dr. Hildegarde Howard studied a large collection of bird remains from the dig. Her report illustrates the potential importance of bird faunas in archaeology (Howard, 1929). She found that water birds were the predominant species, especially ducks, geese, and cormorants, and that land birds distinctive of hill country were absent. All the geese were winter visitors, mostly found in the Bay area between January and April each year. The cormorant bones were nearly all immature, suggesting that the Indians had been robbing cormorant rookeries; most of the cormorant bones equaled an adult bird's in size, but ossification was less complete, equivalent to that in modern birds about five to six weeks old. Dr. Howard examined rookery records and estimated that a date of June 28 each year would be the approximate time when the rookeries could be raided. Thus, from the evidence, she concluded that the Emeryville mound was occupied both during the winter and the early summer, and probably all year.

Bird hunting has often been a sideline in the struggle for subsistence. In many societies, young boys have hunted winged prey with bows and arrows, while training for the hunting of larger game. A specialized bird-hunting kit is found in several cultures, among them the postglacial hunter-gatherer cultures of northern Europe. Though bows and spears were used in the chase, snaring obviously was practiced regularly. The birds found in some African hunting and farming sites are almost invariably species like guinea fowl, which fly comparatively rarely and are easily snared (Dawson, 1969; Fagan, 1967). No traces of the snares have been found in excavations, for normally, they would have been made of perishable materials. Surprisingly little has been written on prehistoric fowling, perhaps because bird bones are fragile and present tricky identification problems.

Fish.   Fishing, like fowling, became increasingly important as people began to specialize in different and distinctive economies and as their environmental adaptations became more sophisticated and their technological abilities improved. Evidence for this activity comes from both artifacts and fish bones.

Freshwater and ocean fish can be caught in various ways. Nets, basket traps, and dams were methods in wide use from postglacial times on, but their remains rarely survive in the archaeological record, except in dry sites or waterlogged deposits. Basket fish traps have been found in Danish peat bogs, dating to the Atlantic vegetational period (Clark, 1975). The ancient Egyptians employed somewhat similar traps, depicted in Old Kingdom tomb paintings (2600–2180 B.C.). Nets remain the most popular fishing device and were used in northern Europe in postglacial times, too. A larger fishweir, constructed of vertical sticks 1.2 to 4.9 meters long (4 to 16 feet), sharpened on one end with a stone axe, enclosed an area of two acres at Boylston Street, Boston (Jennings, 1973). The weir was built about 2500 B.C. and was probably the work of coastal Archaic people. Such traps were evidently widely used along the Atlantic Coast, built in estuary areas where tidal currents were strong. In the Boston weir, brush and flexible withies were placed between the stakes; fish were diverted into the enclosure by "leaders," also made of brush, leading to the trap mouth. Some days' work must have been necessary to build this weir, which provided an almost inexhaustible food supply for its designers.

Fishhooks, harpoons, and barbed spearheads are frequent finds in lake- or riverside encampments. The earliest fishhooks had no barbs, but they did have a U-shaped profile (Figure 14.11). Postglacial hunting peoples, such as the Maglemose folk of Denmark,used such artifacts in the seventh millennium B.C., in all probability to hunt the pike, a prized freshwater fish in prehistoric times (Clark, 1952).

Artifacts alone tell us little about the role of fish in prehistoric economy or about the fishing techniques of prehistoric peoples. Did they fish all year or only when salmon were running? Did they concentrate

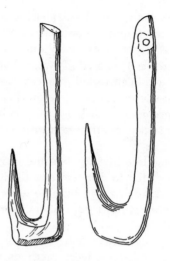

Figure 14.11   Bone fishhooks of the Maglemose culture from northern Europe. (After Clark; two-thirds actual size.)

on bottom fish or rely on stranded whales for protein? Such questions can only be answered by examining the surviving fish bones themselves, or if they survive, which is unusual, actual fish scales. Perhaps the most effective method of collecting fish remains is by taking samples from each level, an approach advocated by Richard Casteel, who found that doing this was nine times less time-consuming than normal collection methods. Furthermore, he succeeded in identifying 30 percent more fish types from his column samples. This type of approach is particularly important on sites like the Glen Cannery site in British Columbia, where fishing was the major economic activity (Casteel, 1976).

The Chumash Indians of Southern California were remarkably skillful fishermen, venturing far offshore in frameless plank canoes and fishing with hook and line, basket, net, and harpoon. Their piscatory skill is reflected in the archaeological sites of Century Ranch, Los Angeles, where the bones of such deep-sea fish as the albacore and oceanic skipjack were found, together with the remains of large deep-water rockfish that live near the sea bottom in water too deep to be fished from the shore (King, Blackburn and Chandonet, 1968). Five other species normally occurring offshore, including the barracuda, were found in the same midden. The bones of shallow-water fish, among them the leopard shark and California halibut, were discovered in the same sites, indicating that both surf fishing and canoe fishing in estuaries with hook and line, basket, or net were also practiced.

The degree to which a community depends on fishing can be impressive. Lake- or seaside fishing encampments tend to be occupied on a more permanent basis than hunting camps, for the food supply, especially when combined with the collection of shellfish, is both reliable and nourishing.

Mollusca. Shellfish from seashore, lake, or river have formed an important part of the prehistoric diet for many thousands of years. Augustin de Beaulieu, who visited the Cape of Good Hope in 1620 with a fleet of ships from Honfleur, France, was a curious and perceptive observer whose wanderings over the Cape Peninsula enabled him to describe the Khoi-Khoi, the indigenous cattle herders and gatherers: "Also they go along the seashore where they find certain shell fish, or some dead whale or other fish, however putrefied it may be, and this they put on the fire for a little and make a good meal of it (Raven-Hart, 1967). The identification of the mollusca in shell middens is a matter for expert conchologists, who possess a mine of information on the edibility and seasons of shellfish. With such data, it was determined that the Khoi-Khoi seem to have depended on shellfish at dry times of the year, when inland pastures were parched and vegetable foods in short supply.

Freshwater mollusca were important to many Archaic bands living in the southeastern United States, but since each mollusk in itself has a limited food value, the amount of mollusca needed to feed even a small band of about twenty-five people must have been enormous. It has been calculated that such a band would need between 1900 and 2250 mussels from the Meramec River each day, and a colossal accumulation of between 57,000 and 67,000 each month (Parmalee and Klippel, 1974). A group of 100 persons would need at least three tons of mussels each month. Confronted with such figures, no one can believe that mollusca were the staple diet of any prehistoric peoples. Rather, they served as an invaluable supplemental food at scarce times of the year or as a source of variety in a staple diet of fish, game, or vegetable foods.

When fresh- or seawater mollusca were collected, the collectors soon accumulated huge piles of shells at strategic places on the coast or on the shores of lakes, near rocky outcrops or tidal pools where mollusca were commonly found. Modern midden analysis involves the systematic sampling of the deposits and the counting and weighing of the various constituents of the soil. The proportions of different shells are readily calculated, and their size, which sometimes changes through time, is easily measured. California shell middens have long been the subject of intensive research, with the changes in frequency of mollusca projected against ecological changes in the site areas.

The La Jolla culture middens of La Batiquitos Lagoon in San Diego are a notable example of such analysis. Claude N. Warren (Crabtree, 1963) took column samples from one shell mound and found that the remains of five species of shellfish were the dominant elements in the molluscan diet of the inhabitants. The changes in the major species of shellfish were then calculated for each excavated level. They found that *Mytilus*, the bay mussel, was the most common in the lower levels, gradually being replaced by *Chione*, the Venus shell, and *Pecten*, the scallop, both of which assumed greater importance in the later phases of the site's occupation, which has been radiocarbon-dated from the fifth to the second millennia B.C. Warren found that *Ostrea*, the oyster, a species characteristic of a rocky coast, was also most common in the lower levels, indicating that the San Diego shore was rocky beach at that time, with extensive colonies of shellfish. By about 6300 years ago La Batiquitos Lagoon was silted to the extent that it was ecologically

Figure 14.12   Ingombe Ilede burial with *Conus* shells, *ca.* fifteenth century A.D. The shells are the circular objects around the neck numbered 1–4.

more suitable for *Pecten* than the rock-loving *Mytilus*. Soon afterward, however, the lagoons became so silted that even *Pecten* and *Chione* could no longer support a large population dependent on shellfish. The inhabitants then had to move elsewhere. Similar investigations elsewhere in California have also shown the enormous potential of mollusca in studying prehistoric ecology.

Both fresh- and seawater shells had ornamental roles, too. Favored species were traded over enormous distances in North America, Europe, and Africa. *Spondylus gaederopus,* a mussel native to the Black Sea, the Sea of Marmora, and the Aegean, was widely distributed as far north and west as Poland and the Rhineland by European farmers in the fifth millennium B.C. The *Conus* shell, common on the East African coast, was widely traded, finding its way into the African interior and becoming a traditional prerequisite of chieftainly prestige. The nineteenth-century missionary and explorer David Livingstone records his visit to Chief Shinte in western Zambia in 1855: the going price for two *Conus* shells at that time was a slave, or five for a tusk of elephant ivory. Archaeological digs have indicated that *Conus* shells were used in the Zambezi Valley 700 years earlier, reflecting a long history of trade in such prestigious ornaments (Figure 14.12) (Fagan, 1969). Indeed, as late as 1910, enterprising merchants were trading china replicas of *Conus* shells to the tribesmen of Central Africa.

Rock Art.   Rock art is a major source of information on economic activities. Some years ago, African archaeologist J. Desmond Clark published an account of late Stone Age hunting and gathering practices in southern Africa, in which he drew heavily on the rock art of Zimbabwe and South Africa. The paintings depict the chase, weapons, collecting, and camp life. Clark remarked, "In the rock art there is preserved an invaluable record of the people's hunting methods, the different kinds of weapons and domestic equipment they used, their customs and ceremonies" (Clark, 1959).

The rock paintings of Natal, South Africa, provide fascinating information on fishing practices and the boats associated with them. Patricia Vinnecombe recorded a fishing scene in the Tsoelike River rockshelter in Lesotho, southern Africa (Figure 14.13) (Vinnecombe, 1960). The fishermen, armed with long spears, are massed in boats, apparently cornering a shoal of fish that are swimming around in confusion. Some boats have lines under their hulls that may represent anchors; the fish cannot be identified with certainty, but they may be freshwater catfish or yellowfish. Vinnecombe's paper generated considerable discussion—some authorities argued that the boats in the paintings were

Figure 14.13   A rock drawing depicting a fishing scene from Lesotho, southern Africa.

probably made of bark (Clark, 1960). Another famous scene from the Cape Province of South Africa depicts a group of ostriches feeding peacefully; among them lurks a hunter wearing an ostrich skin, his legs and bow protruding beneath the belly of an apparently harmless bird. Such vignettes of prehistoric hunting life add enormous insight into data obtained from the food residues recovered from caves and rock-shelters.

PREHISTORIC DIET

So far, the only information on prehistoric subsistence has been gleaned from various archaeological finds. The ultimate objective of economic archaeology is not only to establish how people obtained their food but also to reconstruct their actual diet. Dietary reconstruction is difficult, largely because of incomplete economic information. Yet, the problems involved are fundamental. What proportion of the diet was meat? How diverse were dietary sources? Did the principal sources of diet change from season to season? To what extent did the people rely on food from neighboring areas? Was food stored? What limitations or restrictions did technology or society place on diet? All these questions lie behind any inquiry into prehistoric subsistence.

Diet (what is eaten) and *nutrition* (the measure of the ability of a diet to maintain the body in its environment) have to be studied in close conjunction, for they are quite distinct from subsistence, the actual process of obtaining resources. The baseline for any study of prehistoric diet and nutrition must be surveys of modern hunter-gatherers, subsistence cultivators, and pastoralists. Unfortunately, however, there is such widespread lack of agreement between dietary experts that it is difficult to estimate the caloric needs of prehistoric peoples (Dennell, 1979). So many cultural, medical, and physiological factors have to be weighed—even in modern situations—that research into prehistoric nutrition and food consumption will often be little more than inspired guesswork. Despite such recovery methods as flotation, it is still impossible to assess the intake of vitamins, minerals, and milk products in prehistoric diets. Nor do we have adequate data on the wastage of food in preparation and storage or on the effects of different cooking techniques. Archaeological data can only indicate some of the foods eaten by prehistoric communities, and show, at least qualitatively, how important some of them were in general terms. We are far from being able to ascribe precise food value to animal and plant remains, as would be demanded for precise studies of diet and nutrition.

Sources of Data on Diet and Nutrition.   There are only a few sources of data on prehistoric diet and nutrition, and these are subject to serious limitations (Begler and Keatinge, 1979; Dennell, 1979).

Human skeletal remains can sometimes provide evidence of ancient malnutrition. Some diseases, such as caries, leprosy, and even rickets, leave traces on the human skeleton, which have been identified by physical anthropologists (Brothwell, 1965; Wells, 1964). But signs of malnutrition, although it is frequently disease related, are hard to detect. One promising technique involves the identifications of types of plant foods from the isotopic analysis of prehistoric hair and bone (Brothwell and Burleigh, 1978). Demographic data, obtained from cemetery excavations, if systematically collected, might provide some insights into malnutrition patterns, provided one could establish that a complete cross section of the population was buried in the cemetery.

Stomach contents and feces provide unrivaled momentary insights into meals eaten by individual members of a prehistoric society. However, dietary reconstructions based on these sources suffer from the disadvantage that they are rare, and represent one person's food intake. Furthermore, some foods are more rapidly digested than others. But even these insights are better than no data at all. The stomach of Tollund man, who was executed around the time of Christ, contained the vegetable remains of a finely ground meal made from barley, linseed, and several wild grasses; no meat was found in the stomach contents (Glob, 1969).

Many American scholars have studied *coprolites* (human droppings) from dry caves in the United States and Mexico. Most analyses have consisted of dry sorting and microscopic analysis, but more advanced techniques are being developed. Robert Heizer and his colleagues have analyzed numerous coprolites from the Lovelock Cave in central Nevada (Heizer, 1969). Most of the 101 coprolites analyzed contained bulrush and cattail seeds; they also showed that Lahontan chub from the waters of nearby Humboldt Lake were regularly eaten. Undoubtedly caught with fiber dip nets found in the cave, they were eaten raw or roasted. One coprolite contained the remains of at least fifty-one chub, calculated by a fish expert to represent a total fish weight of 3.65 pounds. Adult and baby birds, the water tiger beetle, and possibly freshwater gastropods were also eaten. Collecting vegetable foods seems to have been done a on casual basis. The remains of large mammals were not found in the feces. Identifying large mammals is particularly difficult, except from hairs or splinters of heavy mammal bones.

Coprolites have been analyzed, also, from stratified cave sequences in the Tehuacán Valley. A diet of grass seeds and a starchy root known as *Ceiba,* eaten as a starvation food, came into vogue at the beginning of the incipient agriculture stage; this diet continued in sporadic use almost up to the time of the Spanish conquest (Bryant and Williams-Dean, 1975). Maize is conspicuously absent from the Tehuacán Valley cave coprolites, as though the crop was grown for tribute purposes and not eaten by the inhabitants—or, alternatively, ground so finely that the meal was digested without a trace. There is always the possibility, too, that the cave dwellers were living in a marginal area where maize cultivation was impossible.

Recent coprolite studies in North America have analyzed pollen grains found in human feces. Fifty-four samples from Glen Canyon in Utah showed that the pollen ingested by their owners could yield valuable information on plants eaten, seasonal occupation, and even on the medicinal use of juniper stem tea (Bryant, 1974). Vaughn Bryant has recently analyzed coprolite pollen from a site near the mouth of the Pecos River in southwest Texas. He found that the inhabitants of the site between 800 B.C. and A.D. 500 spent the spring and summer months at this locality. During their stay they ate many vegetable foods, including several flowers. One danger of using pollen grains is that of contamination from the background pollen "rain" that is always with us. But Bryant was able to show that all but two of the species represented in the pollen were local plants. French archaeologist Henry de Lumley used pollen data from 400,000-year-old coprolites to determine that the Terra Amata Stone Age campsite near Nice was occupied in spring and summer (Lumley, 1969). In all these instances, too, valuable insights were obtained into minor details of prehistoric diet.

Basically, information on prehistoric diets comes from the analysis and the identification procedures described in this chapter. Since the ultimate objective is explaining how people lived in the past, new theoretical frameworks, systematic use of ethnographic analogy, and quantitative methods will, it is hoped, intensify research on the dietary requirements of prehistoric peoples.

This chapter has focused on food remains and subsistence, and not on the manufactured artifacts that also reflect the economic practices of prehistoric peoples. The next chapters deal almost exclusively with artifacts and with the patterning of artifacts. These often reflect specific human activities in the past, including ancient subsistence activities, and we will provide examples of those from time to time in the text that follows.

Guide to Further Reading

Chaplin, R. E. *The Study of Animal Bones from Archaeological Sites.* New York: Seminar Press, 1971.
A summary of faunal analysis. Of wide general use.

Gabel, Creighton. *Analysis of Prehistoric Economic Patterns.* New York: Holt, Rinehart, and Winston, 1967.
A summary of major approaches to reconstruction of prehistoric subsistence. It is somewhat outdated but the only summary available.

Hole, Frank; Flannery, Kent V.; and Neely, J. A. *Prehistoric Human Ecology of the Deh Luran Plain.* Ann Arbor: Memoirs of the Museum of Anthropology, 1969.
An exemplary report on human ecology among early agriculturalists in the Near East.

Olsen, Stanley J. *Osteology for the Archaeologist.* Cambridge: Peabody Museum, 1979.
A primer for archaeologists on bone identification and analysis, oriented toward the New World. Contains numerous references to earlier, invaluable articles by the same author.

Renfrew, Jane. *Paleoethnobotany.* London: Methuen, 1973.
A basic primer on prehistoric vegetal remains, which is oriented toward the Old World but has wide application. A useful introduction to this complex subject.

CHAPTER 15 🌿

LIVING ARCHAEOLOGY

Preview

- The diversity of modern human societies provides us with a unique source of interpretative information about the past. For this reason, archaeologists have been studying living cultures as a means of refining ethnographic analogies.
- Ethnographic analogy has a long history in archaeological research. It is designed to solve the problem of ascribing meaning to the prehistoric past. Analogy itself is a process of reasoning that assumes that if objects have some similar attributes, they will share other similarities as well. It involves using a known, identifiable phenomenon to identify unknown ones of a broadly similar type.
- Early analogies were based on unilinear evolutionary schemes and involved direct comparisons between entire living and prehistoric societies. Such analogies are still employed by Soviet archaeologists.
- Many analogies are based on technology, style, and function of artifacts, as they are defined archaeologically. However, such analogies, based as they are on peoples' beliefs, can be unreliable.
- Direct historical analogies and comparisons made with the aid of texts are commonplace. The use of protohistoric sites provides ways of making analogies with the past based on their proximity to literate peoples. Telehistoric sites are totally prehistoric and are thus subject to much less reliable analogies than later settlements.

- Functionalist analogies stress the notion that cultures are not made up of random traits but are integrated in various ways. Thus, analogies are made between recent and prehistoric societies with closely similar general characteristics.
- Recent analogical research has involved devising test implications, using several different analogies. Each implication is then tested against the archaeological data, as was done at Broken K. Pueblo in the Southwest.
- Experimental archaeology seeks to replicate prehistoric technology and lifeways under carefully controlled conditions. As such, it is a form of archaeological analogy. Experiments have been conducted on every aspect of prehistoric culture, from lithics to housing. Experimental archaeology can rarely produce conclusive answers. It can merely provide some possible insights into the methods and techniques used by prehistoric cultures, for many of the behaviors involved in early lifeways leave no trace in the archaeological record.
- Ethnoarchaeology is ethnographic archaeology, a form of ethnography with a strongly materialistic bias. Archaeologists engage in ethnoarchaeology in attempts to document the relationships between human behavior and the patterns of artifacts and food remains in the archaeological record. We describe examples of ethnoarchaeology among the San of the Kalahari, the Australian aborigines of the western desert, and the Nunamiut Eskimos of northern Alaska. All these studies show that the material remains and food residues recovered in the archaeologial record are reflections of judgments about their current situation, which we try to reconstruct from a perspective thousands of years later in time. This often neglected fact makes the task of archaeological interpretation very difficult.

No archaeologist works in a complete cultural vacuum, for the great diversity of modern humankind provides us with a vital source of information about societies that were until quite recently—or, indeed, still are—living in much the same way as prehistoric peoples. For well over a century, anthropologists have been working among non-Western societies. They have recovered a mass of information of great interpretative value, much of it still buried in museum storerooms and archives. For their part, archaeologists have long recognized the value of comparisons between prehistoric and modern cultures. But it is only in recent years that close attention has been paid to the problems of ethnographic analogy.

This chapter describes some of the problems involved in using ethnographic analogs and some of the fieldwork carried out by archaeologists among living hunter-gatherers. It also focuses on experimental archaeology, the replication of ancient technologies and products under controlled modern conditions. What are the potentials for "living archaeology," as this aspect of archaeology is often called? Are ethnographic analogy and archaeology by experiment viable means of interpreting the prehistoric past?

The general problem has been put forth by Lewis Binford (1978), who undertook a lengthy study of caribou-hunting among the Nunamiut Eskimo in northern Alaska. He points out that his investigations of the archaeological record are an attempt to make systematic observations of the remains of past behavior but that his fieldwork records contemporary phenomena, that is, the archaeological record in its present state: "My interest is in the past but my observations are on the present." In a nutshell, the problem is how to ascribe meaning to contemporary archaeological observations. The patterning of artifacts within a site may reflect changes during prehistoric time, time that can be dated by a variety of methods. But to understand what these changes signify, one has to be able to assign meaning to one's finds. By "meaning," Binford means explaining *why* the patternings are observed today. What ancient behavior led to specific artifact distributions? To answer this question, Binford (1977, 1978) proposed the development of what he called "middle-range theory," which would take into account the processes by which the archaeological record was formed. Living archaeology provides one means for developing such middle-range theory.

ANALOGY IN ARCHAEOLOGY

All living archaeology is undertaken with the ultimate objective of making analogies between living societies or between controlled modern experiments and prehistoric cultures. But what is analogy, and how does it function in archaeological research?

Analogy is a process of reasoning that assumes that if objects have some similar attributes, they will share other similarities as well. It involves using a known, identifiable phenomenon to identify unknown ones of broadly similar type. It implies that a particular relationship exists between two or more phenomena, because the same relationship may be observed in a similar situation. Our abilities to reason by analogy are often tested in aptitude examinations by such questions as: "A fish is to water as a bird is to: (a) a tree (b) a house (c) air (d) grass seed." Obviously, if we grasp the relationship between fish and water, we will not have any trouble completing the question. Analogy in archaeology involves inferring that the relationship between various traces of human activity in the archaeological record is the same as, or similar to, those of similar phenomena found among modern primitive peoples. Thus, on a very simple level, archaeologists infer that small pointed pieces of stone are projectile points, because there are ethnographic records of peoples making small pointed pieces of stone for the tips of lances or arrows. Reasoning by analogy has had a long history in archaeological interpretation.

Early Analogies. In Part I, the discussion about early unilineal evolutionists showed that they considered living tribes to be good examples of successive stages of development in culture history. Each stage of cultural development was correlated with a stage of technology, a form of the family, a kind of religious belief, and a type of political control that could be observed in some living group of people. Because the stages of technology were observed readily in the archaeological record, archaeologists had only to identify the stage of technological development in their sites and then infer, by an analogy to some living group, the kind of social organization and religion appropriate to the stage, as provided by the unilineal scheme. Thus the Australian aborigines, the Eskimos, and the San, who retained a hunting-and-gathering way of life, manufactured stone tools, and had no knowledge of metallurgy, were considered to be living representatives of Paleolithic peoples. The geologist W. J. Sollas made direct analogies between Upper Paleolithic hunters and modern hunting groups (Sollas, 1911). Many early investigators thought that the most primitive Stone Age peoples were matriarchal, had no government, and believed in numerous spirits. The archaeologist who dug a Paleolithic site would interpret his or her findings by analogy to the unilineal scheme. To interpret details not in the scheme, such as the meaning of a particular form of burial, the archaeologist would turn to the literature of the Australian aborigines, the Eskimos, and the San for the "correct" interpretation.

Since the early unilineal schemes have largely been abandoned by Western archaeologists, this kind of simplistic analogy is not often encountered today. In the Soviet Union, however, unilineal schemes of evolution form an important part of Marxist-Leninist doctrine. Even recent Soviet monographs still employ analogy to the "correct stage of development" in order to interpret the social structure of archaeologically known peoples. For example, S. I. Rudenko, writing about the origin of the Eskimo, chides Western scholars for not attempting to describe the development of Eskimo socioeconomic structure. This failure, he writes, "is to be explained by the very simplistic approach of foreign investigators to Eskimo culture, caused by their disregard of the authentic scientific outlook of Marxist-Leninism" (Rudenko, 1961). Rudenko then postulates that the first stage in Eskimo development was characterized by primitive communism and a matriarchal form of the family. Although he admits that all known Eskimo groups are patrilocal, he sees this as a recent development, due to the introduction of trade by American sailors. He then cites the fact that three very important Eskimo spirits are female and leaps to the conclusion that "the Eskimo were matriarchal in the remote past."

Analogy and Technological Generalization.   Outside the Soviet Union, the selection and evaluation of appropriate analogies is a far more complicated problem, and one which has generated a substantial literature. Archaeologists often make use of an ethnographic name, such as *arrowhead*, as a label for an artifact. In doing so, they are assuming that their artifact type, which they recognize by attributes whose presence cannot be explained by natural processes, is identical in form to other, known arrowheads used by the people who made the artifact in question (Figure 15.1). But this simple analogy is a far cry from claiming similarities—or analogies—between the ways in which the prehistoric culture under reference used the arrowhead and the ways a living society uses it. To do the latter is to assume that the relationship between the form and the function of the artifact has remained static through time. If you explain the past simply by analogy with the present, then you are assuming that nothing new has been learned.

Many archaeologists make use of analogies based on the technology, style, and function of cultures as they are defined archaeologically. Enough small pointed pieces of stone have been found imbedded in the bones of animals and people for us to safely acknowledge that such tools were most likely projectile points. Still, we have no way of knowing if the points were a part of ritual activity as well as the hunt. Similarly, the archaeologist will have information about how houses were constructed and what they looked like, what plants were grown and how these were prepared for food, and perhaps some information on grave furniture. But the archaeologist will not know what the people who lived at this site *thought* a proper house should look like, or which

Figure 15.1 Eskimo demonstrating a sinew-backed bow and ivory-tipped arrow at Chicago's Columbian Exposition of 1893. Archaeologists often make use of an ethnographic name, such as *arrowhead*, assuming that their artifact type is identical to arrowheads used by the people who made the artifact. A simple example of analogy.

relatives would be invited to help build a house, or what spirits were responsible for making crops grow, or who in the house customarily prepared the food, or whether or not the people believed in life after death. So, although archaeologists do have direct access to the part of culture that is technological in nature, they have no way of knowing anything about a people's beliefs and ideas; thus, any analogy drawn from the ideas and beliefs of present-day people is probably incorrect.

This cautious approach to analogy is implicit or explicit in many archaeological writings. Raymond Thompson, in a widely read article

on analogy in archaeology, argues that the archaeologist's first inferences *must* be based on technological generalization; but he warns that
anything beyond this is completely subjective and depends on the
archaeologist's abilities and competence (Thompson, 1956). But, how
are we to judge the ability and competence of the archaeologist whose
interpretation we are reading? Thompson does not offer a solution to
this problem.

Direct-Historical Analogy.   Another approach to analogy is that called
folk-culture by European archaeologists and the *direct-historical* by
Americans (see Chapter 8). On both sides of the Atlantic, this approach
uses the simple principle of working from the known to the unknown.
In archaeological problems, the known are the living people with written records of their way of life, and the unknown are their ancestors for
whom no written records exist.

Text-aided analogies involve using written records to interpret archaeological data. For example, archaeologists working at the historic
site of Fort Raleigh in North Carolina found small lead alloy tokens
stamped with the names "Hans Schultes" and "Nuremberg." Normally, without written records, one would not know whether these
tokens were pendants, coins, or IOUs for trade with Herr Schultes
(Harrington, 1956). The historical records tell us, however, that such
lead alloy tokens were used for counting by Elizabethan merchants; the
tokens were moved across a board marked off into rows like an abacus.
Historians also tell us that Hans Schultes of Nuremberg made lead
counters that were very popular on the Continent and in England. The
archaeologists who discovered the tokens at Fort Raleigh confidently
interpreted their finds as counters and inferred that the colonists expected to engage in commerce, not only with the Indians but with their
neighbors and with Europe as well.

Parahistoric sites, which are settlements that belonged to peoples who
had no knowledge of writing themselves but who were contemporary
with literate societies can provide another source for analogy. Their
customs or affiliations may be mentioned in the written accounts of
their literate neighbors. The Iron Age inhabitants of Maiden Castle in
Dorset, although illiterate themselves, were subdued by the legions of
a thoroughly literate Roman Empire; the conquerors left numerous
traces of their campaigns, both in documentary records and in the
archaeological record. Sir Mortimer Wheeler's fine description of the
investment of Maiden Castle in the first century A.D. owes much to the
Roman records of the conquest (Figure 15.2) (Wheeler, 1943).

Telehistoric sites are those that are far removed from any area having written records. Star Carr, the Olsen-Chubbuck bison-kill site in Colorado, and Olduvai Gorge are all "telehistoric," and as such, they are remote from documentary evidence of the human past.

According to proponents of the direct historical approach, confidence in the interpretation of past lifeways diminishes as we move from historic to parahistoric to telehistoric sites; analogies to living peoples become less and less secure the more remote we become from written records. Furthermore, the earlier the site, the more likely it is that there have been major environmental changes in the area. Although it would seem that text-aided archaeology is certainly useful, confidence in particular interpretations of past lifeways seems to depend on more than the presence or absence of written documents. And, the difficulties of analogy are compounded as one moves from purely technological comparisons to economic, religious, or social analogies.

Figure 15.2 Aerial photograph of Maiden Castle, Dorset, England, stormed by the Romans in A.D. 43, an event described through excavation by Mortimer Wheeler.

Functionalist Analogies.   The emphasis on functionalism in enthnology has also influenced archaeological thinking about the use of analogy and behavioral interpretation. Functionalist ethnographies integrate various aspects of culture with each other and with the adaptation of the culture as a whole to its environment. Functionalism stresses the notion that cultures are not made up of a random selection of traits but that cultural traits are integrated in various ways and influence each other in fairly predictable ways. Functionalist thinking is evident in the way that many archaeologists select analogies from the ethnographic data to help them interpret their archaeological finds. Given that several ethnologically known cultures might provide reasonable analogies, functionally oriented scholars suggest selecting those that most closely resemble the archaeological culture in subsistence, technology, and environment—and those that are the least removed from the archaeological culture in time and in space. As an example, let us say we wish to find ethnographic analogies for the Desert Culture sites—the term *Desert Culture* refers to the very old (10,000 B.C. to *ca.* 500 B.C.) occupations of the arid western United States (Aikens, 1978). The archaeological remains in these sites—grinding stones, basketry, sandals, cores, choppers, and some stemmed projectile points—indicate a reliance on food gathering and small game hunting; signs of pottery and agriculture are lacking. The desertic environment was harsh but not devoid of food resources. The functionalists would argue that appropriate analogies might be drawn from the literature on the San of the Kalahari Desert in southern Africa or on the desert Australians, both of whom rely on gathering and small game hunting in desiccated regions. But the San and the Australian aborigines are far removed from the Desert Culture in both time and space when compared with the modern Pueblo Indians of the southwestern United States, who inhabit some of the same territory once occupied by Desert Culture peoples. The Pueblo are, in fact, probably descendants of Desert Culture peoples and might, for this reason, provide appropriate analogies. But they have adopted pottery, agriculture, and a settled, village way of life, and their entire adaptation to desert conditions differs from that of their desertic, hunter-gatherer ancestors.

We might go so far as to assume that we could use the San and the Australian aborigines for analogies regarding subsistence and technology, but that for a Desert Culture trait not obviously dependent upon subsistence or technology, the Pueblo Indians might provide the more appropriate analogy. The problem is that we often do not know which aspects of culture are most closely integrated in a functional manner.

For example, perhaps we want to know about the role of sandal-making among the Desert Culture people—whether sandals were produced by men, women, individuals on their own initiative, or by formal groups working together. If we consider sandal-making an aspect of technology, we might turn to the literature on San or Australian material culture, in which sandals are sometimes featured. Among both the San and the Australian aborigines, domestic tasks are generally done by women working alone or with one or two helpers. The analogy might lead us to argue that sandal-making was regarded as a domestic task by Desert Culture people and carried out by women who usually worked alone. On the other hand, weaving is men's work among the Pueblo Indians and is carried out in special ceremonial rooms; since much ritual performed there today reflects very ancient Pueblo Indian practices, we might be led to infer by analogy that in Desert Culture times the weaving of sandals was not regarded as a domestic task and was carried out by men. No matter which alternative we chose, we would probably not have much confidence in our choice.

Testing of Implications Derived from Analogy.   The most recent literature in archaeology reflects a shift in attitude toward the use of analogy in archaeological interpretation. The selection of possibly appropriate analogies from the ethnological literature is increasingly being seen as only the first step toward interpretation. Once several different analogies are chosen, the implications of each one are explicitly stated and then are tested against the archaeological data. In our example of sandal-making among Desert Culture peoples, the ethnographic literature provided conflicting analogies. If we want to gain confidence in selecting one or the other analogy, we must state explicitly the implications each would have for the archaeological data and then examine the latter again in the light of each implication. If sandal-making were a domestic task done by women working alone, we might expect to find the raw materials for sandal manufacture associated with tools that more surely represent women's work, such as grinding stones for food preparation. We might also expect to find tools for sandal-making (such as awls and scrapers for preparing fiber) among the debris of most domestic sites. We could anticipate that women working alone might introduce more variation into the finished product than might be the case in products made by group effort or by individuals working in the company of other specialists. A contrasting list of implications for the possibility that men produced sandals could also be made, and both sets could be tested against the archaeological data.

Devising test implications is not an easy task. For example, to find a measure for the amount of variation in a finished product that one would expect under certain production conditions requires sophisticated measurements, various statistical tests, and often, experimentation among groups of living people. Archaeologists willing to make the effort entailed in this approach, however, have found that they are able to discover more about ancient societies than was previously thought possible. Reasoning by analogy is, of course, an important part of this process, but it is only one step in the archaeologist's task. Analogies provide the material from which test implications are drawn; they are no longer ends in themselves.

Broken K. Pueblo.   The use of analogy as only one phase of the interpretative process in archaeology is demonstrated by James N. Hill's analysis of room variability at the Broken K. Pueblo in Hay Hollow Valley, Arizona (Hill, 1970). The ninety-five rooms of the Pueblo were occupied from about A.D. 1150 to 1280. Hill analyzed their functional categories using sampling techniques and artifact patterning for the purpose. He divided the Broken K. rooms into three groups: large rooms containing ventilators, firepits, and mealing bins; small rooms with none of the preceding features; and a third type that was similar to the large rooms in all respects, but that had such additional special features as wall niches, benches, and slab-lined floors. Hill turned to the ethnography of living Pueblo peoples and found that there were three kinds of rooms in modern pueblos, each of which was used for specific purposes. Large rooms without special features serve as living areas where most domestic activities are conducted; small rooms are primarily for storage; some large chambers served as special ceremonial rooms. Hill then hypothesized that the differences among the room types at Broken K. reflected the differences in room functions as observed in the modern pueblos. To test this, Hill turned to the ethnographic data for test implications of the functional differences in rooms and listed sixteen different implications that could be tested against the archaeological data. For example, if the small rooms were used as storage areas, they would be expected to contain large quantities of food remains, such as corncobs, seeds, and pollen; on the other hand, small rooms should not contain evidence of food preparation or eating, such as small grinding stones, animal bones, and charred food remains. If the large rooms were used for living space, they should contain a greater variety of cultural debris than the small rooms. If the large rooms with special features were ceremonial in function, they should have no evidence of food preparation, although they might contain serving bowls and certainly some traces of ritual paraphernalia. Hill tested each implication of functional difference against the archaeological data and found that most of his implications were confirmed.

Analogy, then, can suggest possible interpretations of the past. These interpretations are restated as hypotheses and tested with an appropriate technique. The goal is to develop specific procedures for testing or evaluating archaeological statements objectively, so that confirmation does not depend on the competence, skill, or imagination of any particular archaeologists.

EXPERIMENTAL ARCHAEOLOGY

Another form of analogy is that derived from experiments with prehistoric subsistence and technology. Experimental archaeology began in the eighteenth century, when people tried to blow the spectacular bronze horns recovered from peat bogs in Scandinavia and Britain. The exaggerated claims for the qualities of the horns fascinated the gullible public. One ardent experimenter, a Dr. Robert Ball of Dublin, Ireland, blew an Irish horn so hard that he was able to produce "a deep bass note, resembling the bellowing of a bull." Sadly, a subsequent experiment with a trumpet caused him to burst a blood vessel, and he died several days later. Dr. Ball is the only recorded casualty of experimental archaeology, for most modern experiments have been conducted with greater precision and perhaps less gusto (Coles, 1973).

Scientific archaeologists have been interested in experimenting with prehistoric technologies and lifeways ever since the early days of anthropology. As we showed earlier, much experimental effort went into stone toolmaking and the study of prehistoric stone technology by replication. One French archaeologist even went so far as to make stone tools by casting pebbles into a cement mixer! In a sense, the early stoneworking experiments were the product of academic curiosity, and it was not until the early years of this century that experimental archaeology involving stone tools took on a more immediate relevance. One reason that it did was because of the capture and observation of Ishi, one of the last California Indians to follow a traditional lifeway.

Ishi. Ishi, the last "wild" Yahi Indian, was captured near Oroville, California, in 1913 (Kroeber, 1965). Fortunately, the story of his capture came to the notice of University of California anthropologists

Alfred Kroeber and Thomas Waterman. They managed to assume responsibility for Ishi, who resided at the University Museum at Berkeley for four-and-a-half years before he died of tuberculosis. Ishi became a local attraction, a living museum exhibit that brought hundreds of visitors to the campus. But he was far more than an exhibit; he proved to be a mine of information about the hunter-gatherer lifeway and about the simple technology that the Yahi had enjoyed. Kroeber, Waterman, and a doctor named Saxon Pope from the University of California Medical School accompanied Ishi to his homeland, and observed him as he stalked game and used his bow and snares. They acquired a mass of vital anthropological and linguistic information that would otherwise have been lost for ever. Pope, an archery expert, not only apprenticed himself to Ishi, but also spent years studying bows and arrows in the museum collections. He subsequently published a monograph on the subject, which did much to make archery the popular sport it is today.

Stone Technology. Ishi left a wonderful legacy to archaeologists, a mass of data that made people realize just how ignorant we were about prehistoric technologies. Only the sketchiest historical accounts of stoneworking and other craft activities survived in the records of early explorers. Some of the Spanish friars, noticeably Juan de Torquemada, saw Indian stoneworkers flaking obsidian knives. In 1615, he described how the Indians would take a stick and press it against a stone core with their "brest." "With the force of the knife there flies off a knife," he wrote. But, until recently, no one knew just how pressure flaking, as it is called, was done.

Since the 1920s, Idaho rancher Don Crabtree has spent a lifetime trying to learn lithic technology. He began making Folsom projectile points, and for over forty years, has tried to replicate the beautiful fluted points (Figure 13.8d), arguing that they required a great deal of time and a special technique to manufacture. His reports on the experiments (1966; 1972) describe no less than eleven methods that he tried in order to reproduce the flute at the base of the artifact. Eventually, he came across Torquemada's account of pressure flaking and used a chest punch to remove flakes from the base of unfinished points gripped in a vise on the ground. The result was points that were almost indistinguishable from the prehistoric artifacts. Crabtree's long-term experiments raise the basic question: Does the production of an exact replica mean, in fact, that modern experimentation has recovered the original technique? The answer, of course, is that we can never be certain. However, our hypotheses about prehistoric technology are now on a firmer footing than ever before.

Criteria For Experimental Archaeology.   Experimental archaeology can rarely provide conclusive answers. It can merely provide some possible insights into the methods and techniques used in prehistory; for many of the behaviors involved in, say, prehistoric agriculture have left no tangible traces in the archaeological record. But some general rules must be applied to all experimental archaeology. First, the materials used in the experiment must be those available locally to the prehistoric society one is studying. Second, the methods must conform with the society's technological abilities. Obviously, modern technology must not be allowed to interfere with the experiment. Experiments with a prehistoric plough must be conducted with a ploughshare made correctly, with careful reference to the direction of wood grain, the shape and method of manufacture of working edges, and all other specifications. If the plough is drawn by a tractor, the experiment's efficiency will be radically affected; thus, for accuracy, you will need a pair of trained, paired oxen. The results of the experiment must be replicable and consist of a series of tests that lead to suggested conclusions.

Some Examples of Experimental Archaeology.   One of the most famous instances of experimental archaeology is that of the *Kon-Tiki* expedition, on which Thor Heyerdahl attempted to prove that Polynesia had been settled by adventurous Peruvians who sailed balsa log rafts across thousands of miles of ocean (Heyerdahl, 1950). He did succeed in reaching Polynesia, but his expedition merely showed that long ocean voyages in *Kon-Tiki* rafts were possible; he did not prove that the Peruvians settled Polynesia.

Much experimental archaeology is far more limited in scope. Many experiments have been done on the clearance of forests in Europe and elsewhere. Stone axes have been surprisingly effective at clearing woodland, one Danish experiment yielding estimates that a man could clear 0.2 hectare of forest in a week. Tree-ringing and fire have been shown to be effective tree-felling techniques in West Africa and Mesoamerica (Shaw, 1969). Experiments with agriculture over eight or more years have been conducted in the southern Maya lowlands and the Mesa Verde National Park. The latter experiment lasted seventeen years. A hectare of heavy red clay soil was cultivated and planted with maize, beans, and other small crops. Good crop yields were obtained in all but two of the seventeen years, when drought killed the young crop. The test revealed how important careful crop rotation is to preserve the land's carrying capacity.

Housing experiments.   Houses of poles and thatch, logs, or hut clay normally survive in the form of postholes, foundation trenches, or collapsed rubble. Traces of the roof and information on wall and roof heights, unfortunately, are normally lacking. But this has not deterred experimenters from building replicas of Mississippian houses in Tennessee, using excavated floor plans associated with charred poles, thatching grass, and wall-clay fragments (Nash, 1968) (Figure 15.3). Two types of house, dating to A.D. 1000–1600, were rebuilt. One of these was a "small pole" type with slender poles bent over to form an "inverted" basketlike rectangular structure with clay plaster on the exterior. Later houses were given log walls, which supported a steep, peaked roof. In this, as in many other instances, many details of the rafter and roof design are probably lost. A logical next stage in housing experiments is to observe how the structure decays. The Danes have carried out valuable observations on the decay of reconstructed "Neolithic" houses at Allerslev, where they found that rising dampness was a major cause of decay. Eventually, a house burned down by accident, and they excavated the pile of poles and rubble that resulted. The success of this experiment prompted the Danish Television Service to finance the reconstruction and destruction by fire of an Iron Age long house near Roskilde (Hansen, 1962). The foundation plan of a house excavated in 1937 was chosen as a model, and the complete structure was reconstructed. Thermocouples were placed at key locations to

Figure 15.3   Reconstruction of a Mississippian house.

record fire temperatures, the timbers were marked with metal numbers, and domestic objects were placed inside the house. It was then burned on a windy day, with spectacular results. After thirty-five minutes nothing was left of the hut, which disintegrated completely except for the large upright posts. Six months later the archaeologists returned and excavated the remains. They recovered a floor plan that coincided remarkably closely with that of the original Iron Age house, as well as valuable information on the types of features, such as door frames, which could be identified from careful excavation and analogy with the Roskilde experiment.

Overton Down.   One of the longest experiments in archaeological interpretation is that of the Overton Down earthwork in England, which will last as long as 128 years. In 1960 the British Association for the Advancement of Science built an experimental earthwork at Overton Down, Wiltshire (Jewell and Dimbleby, 1966). The earthwork and its associated ditch were built on chalk subsoil, with profiles approximating those of prehistoric monuments. Archaeological materials including textiles, leather, wood, animal, and human bones as well as pottery were buried within and on the earthwork. The Overton Down earthwork was partly built with modern picks, shovels, and hatchets and partly with red deer antlers, ox shoulder blades, wicker baskets, and other prehistoric digging tools, in an attempt to establish relative work rates for different technologies. The difference was about 1.3:1.0 in favor of modern tools, mostly because modern shovels were more efficient. Overton Down was then abandoned, but small and very precise excavations of the ditch and bank were to take place at intervals of 2, 4, 8, 16, 32, 64, and 128 years. The digs were to be used to check the decay and attrition of the earthwork and the silting of the ditch over a lengthening period of time. The project will yield invaluable information of great use for interpreting archaeological sites of a similar type on chalk soils.

ETHNOARCHAEOLOGY

Ethnoarchaeology, or ethnographic archaeology, is a form of ethnography that has a strongly materialist bias. Archaeologists engage in ethnoarchaeology because they are trying to document the relationships between human behavior and the patterns of artifacts and food remains that are found in the archaeological record. One effective way to do this is to examine such relationships in living societies as a basis for interpreting the past. Ethnoarchaeology is a logical development of analogy, a way of gathering data for testing hypotheses about the relationship between cultural process and the surviving archaeological data that document it. (For an interesting set of essays on this subject, see Gould, 1978.)

Archaeologists use ethnographic evidence all the time, either consciously or unconsciously. If a projectile point is classified as an arrowhead, the assumption used to make this classification derives ultimately from ethnographic observations. Many archaeologists regard ethnography as being simply a mass of observed data on human behavior from which they can draw up suitable hypotheses to compare to the finds from their excavations and laboratory analyses. Often, however, the ethnographic data have been too meager to allow specific and valid comparisons, because ethnographers studying hunters and gatherers have dealt more with social and ritual organization, as well as other less tangible aspects of culture.

Ethnoarchaeology Among the San.   One interesting example of ethnoarchaeology comes from the Kalahari desert of southern Africa, where Richard Lee has spent many years studying the human ecology of the !Kung San hunter-gatherers (Lee and DeVore, 1976). Lee spent a great deal of time observing the food-collecting and hunting habits of the San and accumulated a mass of information of great use to archaeologists. In one of his later expeditions, an archaeologist accompanied the research team and made detailed studies of butchery techniques and fractured animal bones and also drew plans of abandoned settlements of known age. John Yellen's research has yielded a wealth of facts on house and camp arrangements, hearth locations, census information, and bone refuse, all of which is of fundamental importance to archaeologists in southern Africa (Yellen, 1977). He points out that a !Kung camp develops through conscious acts, such as the construction of windbreaks and hearths, as well as through such incidental deeds as the discarding of refuse and manufacturing debris (Figure 15.4). He recognized communal areas in the campsites, often in the middle of the settlement, that belonged to no one in particular, and family areas centered around hearths that belonged to individual families. The communal activities of the camp members, such as dancing and the first distribution of meat, take place in the open spaces that belong to no one family. Such activities leave few traces in the archaeological record. Cooking and food processing as well as manufacturing of artifacts normally take place around family hearths. Yellen points out some interesting variations on this pattern: manufacturing activities

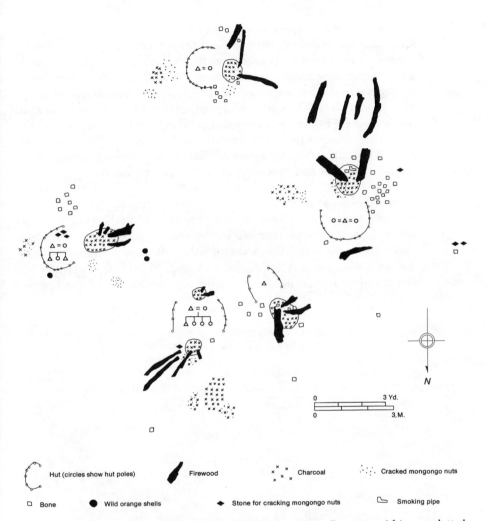

Figure 15.4   A San camp in the ≠ Tum = /toa grove, Botswana, Africa, as plotted by John Yellen to show the layout of activity areas and artifacts. (After Lee and DeVore.)

taking place at one hearth will sometimes involve people from other families; large skins will normally be pegged out for treatment away from main living areas because of vermin and carnivores. And activity areas are sometimes shifted around on hot days to take advantage of patches of heavy shade. Such activity areas can be identified on recently abandoned sites where a scatter of discarded mugongo nuts and charcoal fragments lies outside the encampment. The !Kung study showed that it is dangerous to assume that activities with the greatest archaeological visibility, such as meat preparation or cracking of nuts, take place in special places. In most !Kung instances, except for some small, temporary encampments where some specific, and temporary, food-gathering activities took place, manufacturing, food preparation, and other such activities took place within the family residence area of the campsite. The activity patterning at !Kung campsites relates, for the most part, directly to family groups. And, argues Yellen, hypothetically, it should be possible to use artifact clusters through time to study the development and evolution of such social structures.

Ethnoarchaeology in Australia. A pioneer study of systematic ethnoarchaeology was carried out by Richard Gould in the Western Desert of Australia. He pointed out (1978) that what most ethnographers study first is the nature and transformation of whole cultures, but that the archaeologist as ethnographer considers sites as particular instances of patterned behavior. Gould observed some of the few re-

Figure 15.5 Comparison of a prehistoric campsite at Pututjarpa Rockshelter, Australia, at the right, with a modern aborigine campsite.

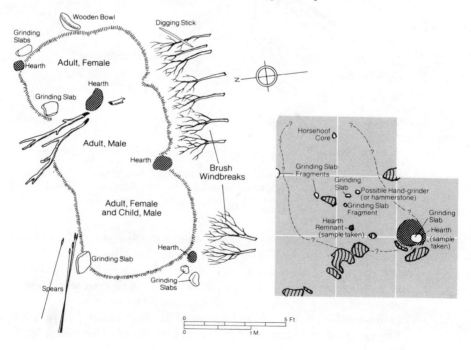

maining bands of nomadic, foraging aborigines in an area where he was searching for archaeological sites. Most of the sites were found with the help of aboriginal informants, who supplied valuable information on the people who had lived at the sites, their activities, and the sacred traditions associated with the settlements.

One such locality was Puntutjarpa Rockshelter, where excavations revealed a record of human occupation extending from modern times back to about 6,800 years ago (Gould, 1977). Indeed, the site is still visited by aborigines, although they no longer live there. The stone implements at the site consisted of cores, flake tools, and smaller artifacts, which in their later forms, were indistinguishable from modern Ngatatjara implements still in use today. Gould made detailed comparisons between the tools found in the rockshelter and modern examples. The local people use a simple technology of hafted and unhafted tools used for cutting meat and skin and for woodworking. By examining traces of edge wear on modern stone tools and artifacts found at Puntutjarpa, Gould was able to demonstrate a remarkable continuity between prehistoric and modern tools, and he was able to say that some of the implements that were more than 5,000 years old had been hafted, when no traces of the wooden handle survived. He also compared modern living surfaces with equivalent features found in the rockshelter (Figure 15.5). He attempted some tentative population estimates and came up with a figure of 3.55 persons per camp in the area. In the Western Desert, living archaeology could be brought to bear on at least three levels of archaeological research. The first was the practical level, where the local people were able to direct Gould to sites and give him information on them. The second was the specific, functional interpretation of artifacts and living surfaces. The final level was that of general interpretation, where broad interpretations of culture history were attempted, taking form as general hypotheses about an Australian desert culture. Gould's work was successful because he combined archaeology and ethnography into a holistic, site-oriented approach, working with a site at which direct connections with modern peoples were still possible.

Ethnoarchaeology Among the Nunamiut Eskimo. Perhaps the most carefully designed living archaeology project yet undertaken is Lewis Binford's study of the Nunamiut Eskimo (Binford, 1978). Binford undertook this research as a result of long months spent examining Upper Paleolithic tools and faunal remains from rockshelters in Southwestern France. He found that he had no reliable way of giving meaning to his observations on the frequencies of artifact types and animals in the occupation levels he examined, so he decided to study the Nunamiut Eskimo, 80 percent of whose subsistence comes from hunting caribou. His aims were to find out as much as he could about "all aspects of the procurement, processing, and consumption strategies of the Nunamiut Eskimo and relate these behaviors directly to their faunal consequences." He chose to concentrate on animal bones rather than artifacts, because although the bones were not humanly manufactured, the patterns of their use were the result of cultural activity.

The Nunamiut depend more heavily on meat than any other known hunter-gatherers. Indeed, Binford estimates that each adult eats around a cup-and-a-half of vegetable foods a year, supplemented by the partially digested stomach contents of caribou. In an environment that has a growing season of only twenty-two days, the Eskimo relies on stored food entirely for eight-and-a-half months a year, and partially on it for an additional month and a half. Fresh meat is freely available for only two months a year. Binford soon realized that the strategies they used to feed themselves were based not only on game distributions but on other considerations as well. For example, given such a heavy reliance on stored food, the problem of bulk was always important. Was it easier to move people to where fresh meat was available, or to carry the meat back to a base camp where precious stored food was kept? It is no coincidence that the Nunamiut move around the most in late summer and early fall, when stored foods are at their lowest levels. The Nunamiut's lifeway involved a whole set of complicated and interacting decisions that were related to the distribution of food resources at different seasons, the storage potential of different animals and of different parts of an animal, and also the logistics of procuring, carrying, and storing meat. All these, and many other variables, make up the cultural system of the Nunamiut. Binford points out that the linkage between the facts of animal anatomy and the realities of lifeway strategies among the people are the keys to any meaningful analysis of animal bones.

By close study, not only of the Nunamiuts' annual round of activities, but also of their butchery and storage strategies, Binford was able to develop a series of indices that measured, in exhaustive detail, the utility of different body parts of caribou and described the butchering techniques, distribution of body parts, and food preparation methods used. He showed that the people have an intimate knowledge of caribou anatomy, a knowledge that is related to meat yield, storage potential, and consumption needs relative to the logistical, storage, and social needs of the moment. The field study also included an analysis of forty-two archaeologically known locations that dated to earlier times.

The Nunamiut adaptation depended on long-term storage strategies that were keyed to two aggressive periods of caribou hunting in spring and fall. That they were able to hunt the caribou twice a year was a factor of the topography of their homeland, which lies close to the borders of both summer and winter caribou feeding ranges. The movement of the people was keyed to seasonal game movements and to storage and other needs. For example, fall hunting was directed toward calves, whose skins were used to make winter clothing. Small, mobile parties of Nunamiut would pursue them, knowing that their prey would yield not only skins but the added bonus of heads and tongues to feed the people who processed the skins. Without taking account of this fact, the Nunamiut were unable to maintain a viable cultural system.

What is the importance of the Nunamiut research? In the first place, it provides a mass of empirical data on human exploitation of animals that is applicable not only to the Nunamiut and other caribou hunters, but also to the interpretation of different types of archaeological sites in many parts of the world. Binford showed how local any cultural adaptation is, that of the Nunamiut depending on a whole set of interacting topographic, climatic, logistical, and other realities. These adaptations are so local that he was able to draw a number of important conclusions:

1. The ongoing dynamics of a local adaptation can result in considerable variation in archaeological sites.
2. There may be considerable interregional variations within a culture, which are reflected in different archaeological remains. Yet the inhabitants of one site were well aware of the general cultural variations displayed at other sites nearby.
3. The adaptive strategies and the factors affecting the peoples' decision making may remain constant, even if the archaeological remains show great variability.
4. Perhaps most important of all, changes in, for example, stone tool frequencies or pottery forms, may not reflect any significant change in adaptation at all. It is impossible to tell without an understanding of the strategies behind the local adaptation through time. And such understanding can only be obtained from sites where food remains and other such data are available.

"There is an unrelenting demonstration that the Nunamiut behave rationally in their treatment of animal foods," says Binford. "This rationality is facilitated by a truly remarkable knowledge of animal anatomy. It is facilitated by an outlook that is future-oriented. . . . The

Eskimo are pragmatic, they are empiricists, and they are very skeptical of statements as to the 'right' way to do something." At the center of the Nunamiut's and, we may suspect, most other prehistoric peoples' lives, are judgments about their present situation relative to some desired end in the future. The archaeologist can no longer assume that all variability in the archaeological record is directly related to cultural similarity and difference. Before one can give meaning to archaeological patterns in time and space, one must understand the systems that lie behind the finds. Empirical studies, such as the Nunamiut research, offer a possible avenue for such understanding. The objective of all living archaeology is greater understanding of the complicated, interacting strategies that determined the ways in which people looked at their world, made their livelihood, and behaved toward their environment and toward other groups.

Guide to Further Reading

Binford, Lewis R. *Nunamiut Ethnoarchaeology.* New York: Academic Press, 1978.
A descriptive monograph about ethnoarchaeology among caribou hunters. A must for the serious student.

Coles, John *Archaeology by Experiment.* London: Heinemann, 1973.
An introduction to experimental archaeology with numerous examples, mainly from the Old World.

Gould, Richard A., ed. *Explorations in Ethnoarchaeology.* Albuquerque: University of New Mexico Press, 1978.
A volume containing many useful articles on ethnoarchaeology in many parts of the world.

Yellen, John E. *Archaeological Approaches to the Present.* New York: Academic Press, 1977.
Ethnoarchaeology among the San of the Kalahari Desert. A technical work with broad implications.

CHAPTER 16 ~

SETTLEMENT ARCHAEOLOGY AND SPATIAL ANALYSIS

Preview

- Settlement archaeology, the study of changing human settlement patterns, is part of the analysis of adaptive interactions between people and their environment.
- Settlement patterns are determined by many factors, among them, the environment, economic practices, and technological skills. Learned cultural skills and established networks of human behavior also affect settlement, as do practical political considerations, population growth, and social organization. Settlement archaeology involves examining the complex relationships between different parts of a cultural system and the natural environment.
- Bruce Trigger defines three levels of settlement: the single building, the arrangement of structures within individual communities, and the distribution of communities across the landscape.
- Single structures can be studied from the perspective of form and material or from a functional viewpoint. Social and political institutions also affect the design of individual houses.
- Archaeologists working in Mesoamerica have studied households and household clusters in Early Formative villages. They did so by studying artifact patternings, using each house, and the occupation debris around it, as separate analytic units. Activity sets in the same sites provided evidence of specialist activity in the villages.

- A community is a maximal group of people that normally resides in face-to-face associations. The layout of communities is much affected by political and social considerations. The archaeologist looks for clusters of settlement attributes that may indicate a grouping of social units. Teotihuacán in the Valley of Mexico is an example of settlement archaeology. Early Formative villages in the Valley of Oaxaca were studied using similar approaches, and some of these were found to be divided into residential zones. However, estimates of population are very difficult, indeed, to obtain from even comprehensive archaeological data—there simply are too many intangible variables that affect the archaeological record.

- Prehistoric environmental data is obtained from both Pleistocene geology and from animal bones, especially small mammals. Pollen analysis is one of the most effective methods of reconstructing ancient environments. We cite examples from Star Carr and Kalambo Falls to show how people adapted to environments that were very different from those of today.

- Site catchment analysis is a method used to inventory resources within range of prehistoric sites. It is a study of the relationships between technology and available natural resources. We use examples from Israel and Oaxaca to demonstrate its applications.

- Site distribution maps are used to study prehistoric settlement patterns; these are analyzed using rigorous, objective criteria, which take into account sampling errors and other variables. The objective of such analyses is to establish the factors that governed human settlement in prehistoric times.

- Spatial analyses in archaeology make use of a variety of techniques that were developed by geographers. They include Central Place Theory, cluster analysis, and other concepts.

- Population estimates for prehistoric sites have been made by subjective guesswork, mathematical formulae, and by using sophisticated estimates of carrying capacity of the land. Such estimates rarely are precise.

- Population growth has been a major factor in later prehistory. Most archaeologists agree with Thomas Henry Malthus that humankind's reproductive capacity far exceeds available food supplies. But, Ester Boserup and her colleagues disagree with this, arguing that people intensify their food gathering or production efforts in the face of rising population. This controversy highlights the necessity for archaeologists to examine the many intangible variables that affect cultural change over long periods of prehistoric time.

In the preceding chapters we examined the ways in which archaeologists study artifacts and prehistoric subsistence and the various technologies that people developed to adapt to their environments. We also glanced briefly at some methods used to reconstruct the prehistoric environment itself. But, what about the relationships between different prehistoric settlements and the environment? This chapter examines some of the ways in which archaeologists have studied changing settlement patterns in prehistoric times.

One of the pervasive theoretical frameworks for archaeology is that of cultural ecology, the study of the interrelationships between people and their environment. But the term "environment" covers not only the natural environment, but the social environment as well (Jochim, 1979). Technology and subsistence play central roles in the study of prehistoric settlement patterns, and the research methods used rely heavily on both systems models and cultural ecology, as well as on large bodies of information manipulated by computers and quantitative methods.

SETTLEMENT ARCHAEOLOGY AND SETTLEMENT PATTERNS

Settlement archaeology, the study of changing human settlement patterns, is part of the analysis of adaptive interactions between people and their external environment, both natural and cultural (Chang, 1968).

Settlement patterns, the layout of human settlements on the landscape, are the result of relationships between people who decided, on the basis of practical, political, economic, and social considerations to place their houses, settlements, and religious structures where they did. Thus, settlement archaeology offers the archaeologist a chance to examine not only relationships between different communities, but trading networks, the ways in which people exploited the resources in their environment, and social organization as well. The study of settlement patterns involves examining the degree to which human settlement reflects a society and its technology's adaptation to a specific environment.

The Determinants of Settlement Patterns. Settlement patterns are determined by many factors: the environment, economic practices, and technological skills. Inherited cultural patterns and established networks of human behavior have an impelling influence on settlement patterns in some societies. For examples, the distribution of San camps in the Kalahari desert is dependent on the availability of water supplies and vegetable foods; and ancient Maya settlements in Mexico were laid out in segments dictated by political and religious considerations.

Village layout may be determined by the need to protect one's herds against animal predators or war parties. Other settlements may be strung out at regular intervals along an important trade artery, such as a river. Even the positioning of individual houses is dictated by a complex variety of social, economic, and even personal factors that can defy explanation.

The determinants of settlement patterns operate on at least three different levels, each formed by factors that differ in quality or degree from those that shape other levels (Trigger, 1968).

1. *The single building, or structure.* Houses, household clusters, and activity areas are minimal units of archaeological analysis.
2. *Communities.* The arrangement of single structures within a single group constitutes a community. The term community is defined as a "maximal group of persons who normally reside in face to face association" (Murdock, 1949).
3. *Distribution of communities.* The density and distribution of communities, whatever their size, is determined, to a considerable extent, by the natural resources of their environment and by the economy, nutritional requirements, and technological level of the population, as well as by social and religious constraints.

A critical part of settlement archaeology is understanding the factors that interact to determine a settlement pattern at any of these three levels. These factors can best be understood with reference to anthropological analogy with modern societies (see Chapter 15). And, the ultimate objective of the exercise is to study prehistoric settlement systems as an aspect of the total picture of a prehistoric society.

STRUCTURES AND COMMUNITIES

Structures. Human dwelling places occur in infinite size and variety, from the crude windbreak of the Tasmanian aborigine to the magnificent palaces of King Henry VIII. Temples, fortifications, and even cattle pens are all forms of standardized structures. Domestic architecture may be standardized, or it may differ according to strict modes of variation dictated by a number of factors. The study of individual structures can be approached from several standpoints.

Form and material are among the major determinants of house design. For example, 20,000 years ago the mammoth hunters of the western Russian plains lived in semisubterranean dwellings with roofs made of skins and mammoth bones and with interior hearths (Klein, 1969). Theirs was a treeless, arctic environment, where protection from icy cold winds was vital. The people made use of the only abundant raw materials available to them—the bones and skins of the huge mammoths they hunted. In contrast, the Tonga peoples of the Middle Zambezi Valley in Central Africa, where the midday temperature is often over 100° Fahrenheit, and the nights are hot throughout most of the year, spend more of their lives in the shade of their pole-and-mud huts than they do inside them. So, their dwellings have thatched roofs that project far from the walls to form large and shady verandas (Reynolds, 1967) (Figure 16.1).

The nature of the raw materials used to build a structure affected not only its form but also its preservation in the archaeological record. For example, unfired mud brick was used throughout the Near East for house building, and it is still employed today. Once a house is abandoned, the unmaintained brick literally melts and reverts to clay. It took archaeologists generations to learn how to recover traces of mud brick houses from their matrix (Lloyd, 1963). As we saw in Chapter 11,

Figure 16.1   Tonga hut from the Middle Zambezi valley, Central Africa.

wooden structures often leave no trace in the soil except, perhaps, postholes or foundation trenches.

Function radically affects house design, too. The earliest humans lived in temporary brush shelters that reflected their mobile life style and the fact that the nights were rarely cold. More sedentary communities, such as subsistence farmers in the Near East, built houses that combined a need for shelter with a need for storage and cooking facilities for each family.

Social and political organization can affect the design of structures also, for the size and layout of a dwelling can reflect the family organization of the occupants, as well as their social standing. For instance, a polygamous family may live in a house with several kitchen areas, each owned by a different wife. Sometimes, with controlled use of anthropological data, particular house types in the archaeological record can be related to specific forms of family organization. Within a single

Figure 16.2 Temple I at Tikal, Guatemala, which dates to about A.D. 700, an example of a ceremonial structure.

house, a family unit can only be distinguished by interpreting the use of the artifacts found in it, in order to identify different rooms, especially cooking areas.

Many societies developed special architectural styles and structures that were associated with political or religious activities or with leadership. Classic Maya temples, exemplified by the pyramids at Tikal (Figure 16.2), provide an excellent instance of such structures. The plazas and pyramids were designed to create a sense of awe. Artisan's houses can be identified by distinctive artifact clusters, such as the potters' workshops found by James Mellaart at the early town of Hacilar in Turkey, dating to about 5300 B.C. (Mellaart, 1975).

Recovering Houses and Households.   Evidence for individual houses and households is obtained by careful excavation of features, household clusters, and activity sets in the archaeological record. In many societies, limited economic opportunities and an even distribution of wealth resulted in standardized floor plans. Such houses, which served as shelters for their occupants, provide the archaeologist, centuries afterwards, with convenient analytic units, provided the house remains isolated from surrounding occupation debris. The variations between houses may reflect a variation between families in subsistence activities, social status, manufacturing activity, wealth, and so on.

Early Mesoamerican houses.   Between 1350 and 850 B.C. the one-room, thatched wattle and daub house became the most common dwelling type in Early Formative Mesoamerican villages. In the Valley of Oaxaca, Early Formative houses were generally rectangular. The floors were sand covered and dug out from the subsoil, and the thatched roof was supported by pine posts. The puddled clay walls were smoothed and sometimes whitewashed (Flannery, 1976).

House contents.   In studying such houses, Kent Flannery and his colleagues distinguished carefully between the households themselves, the household cluster of associated features, such as storage pits and graves, and the various activity areas sometimes associated with them (Winter, 1976) (Figure 16.3). Many of the houses were swept clean before abandonment, but several of them contained accumulations of debris that included not only potsherds and bone tools but food remains as well. Marcus Winter broke down the house contents into at least five possible activities, including sewing and basketry (needles), cooking and food consumption (pots and food remains), and cutting

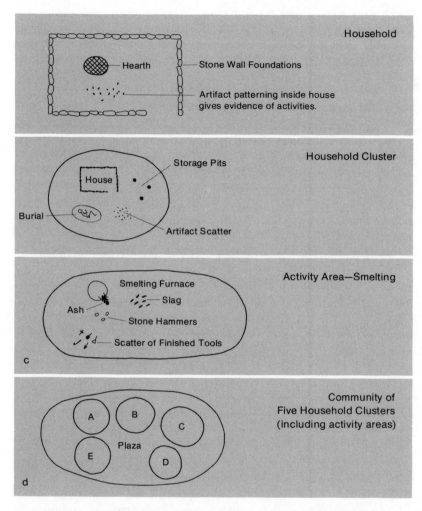

Figure 16.3   Various spatial units used by archaeologists in studying human settlement: (a) household; (b) household cluster; (c) activity area; (d) community.

and scraping (stone tools). He plotted the house contents (Figure 16.3c) in an attempt to distinguish the craft activities of the family who occupied each dwelling.

Household cluster.   It was possible for the archaeologists to isolate the household clusters in Oaxaca. These included bell-shaped storage pits large enough to contain a metric ton of maize; and some of them contained maize pollen and grinders. Human burials were associated with some houses, perhaps those of the family, but archaeologists were unable to prove this. The Oaxaca household clusters also included various types of ovens, refuse middens, and drainage ditches (Figures 16.4 and 16.5).

Figure 16.4   Plan of a house at Tierras Largas, Oaxaca, *ca.* 900 B.C., with selected artifacts plotted on the floor.

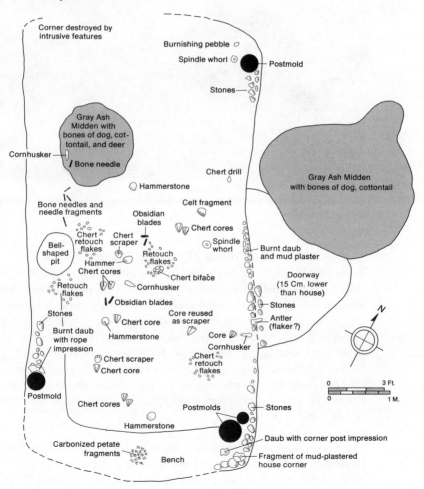

Figure 16.5 Features near houses at San José Mogote: storage pits, drainage canals, and a large cistern.

Activity sets (a set of artifacts associated with specific activities, ie a bow and arrow with hunting). Twenty-two household clusters were analyzed for traces of specialist activities. Food procurement, preparation, and food storage activities were common to all households; these were identified by grindstone fragments, storage pits, and jars, as well as by food remains. Every household chipped local stone and made baskets; but there were also signs of specialist activities. One large pit at Tierras Largas contained large quantities of pressure-flaking debris, while other household clusters yielded no such fine debitage. Perhaps this household boasted of a part-time specialist who made fine stone artifacts for others.

The Oaxacan study offered some potentials for identifying division of labor within a household and artifacts used by children rather than adults. Unfortunately, the excavated samples were too small for definitive study, but Figure 16.6, from Evon Vogt's classic study of the Maya of Zinacantan in Chiapas, shows some of the long-term possibilities (Vogt, 1967).

Communities.   Many variables act to determine the layout of communities, both large and small (Figure 16.7).

Environment and economy limit the size and permanence of a settlement, because the ability to gather and store food is as important as the technology necessary to transport and process it into edible form.

Figure 16.6 Modern highland Maya house from Zinacantan, Chiapas, Mexico, conceptually divided into male and female work spaces.

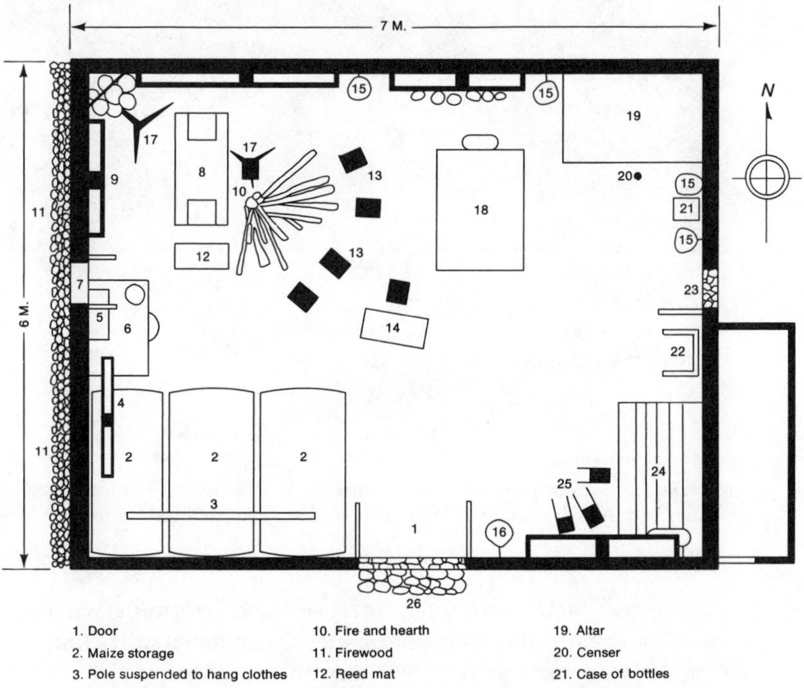

1. Door	10. Fire and hearth	19. Altar
2. Maize storage	11. Firewood	20. Censer
3. Pole suspended to hang clothes	12. Reed mat	21. Case of bottles
4. Shelf suspended by rope	13. Movable chair	22, 25. Table and chair stored
5. Shelf supported by a pole	14. Movable table	23. Door
6. Table and chair	15. Wooden stake in adobe wall	24. Plank bed
7. Window	16. Metal hanger	26. Stoop
8. Grinding table	17. Forked stake	
9. Metate	18. Reed mat for sleeping	

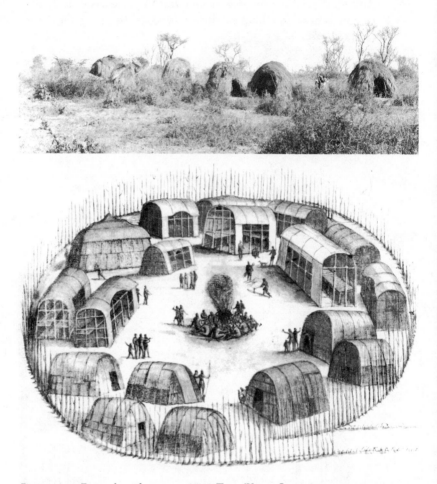

Figure 16.7   Examples of communities. Top: !Kung San winter camp at a water hole; Bottom: Algonquin village in North Carolina, painted by John White in 1585.

These two factors are vital, because they determine whether a community lives in one place permanently or must shift camp at regular intervals during the year. For example, preliterate 'Ubaid farmers in Mesopotamia (*ca.* 4500 B.C.) relied on simple irrigation agriculture. They had no need to move in order to achieve a stable subsistence cycle, so they lived at the same location for centuries, forming large *tells* (Redman, 1978).

Social and political factors are also strong determinants, even in simple societies. Family and kinship considerations are important in camps and small villages. State-organized societies reserved special precincts for ceremonial centers, palaces, and official buildings where the business of the state was conducted (see Figure 16.2). Whole sectors of towns were sometimes reserved for minority religious groups or foreign traders living under the protection of the local ruler. These quarters may be reflected in the archaeological record by exotic objects, unusual architecture, or religious objects. At the trading port of Kilwa on the Tanzanian coast, the Sultan lived in a magnificent palace, a special precinct with its own mosque. The fine artifacts in the palace are not duplicated in any numbers elsewhere in the site, where a cosmopolitan population of Arabs and Africans lived and traded (Chittick, 1974).

Studying a Community: Teotihuacán.   The behavior of a complete community, insofar as it can be discerned as having a pattern is reflected in its artifact grouping and in the characteristic settlement pattern of the location as a whole—house design and layout, and the distribution of household clusters and activity areas. The archaeologist uses site survey and selective excavation, as well as sampling techniques, to look for systematic and statistical associations of settlement attributes—in the same way as for artifact attributes—that may reflect a grouping of social units.

The most ambitious settlement pattern study of a community ever undertaken was really a study of many communities—George Cowgill and René Millon's survey of the Classic city of Teotihuacán in the Valley of Mexico, which flourished from *ca.* A.D. 100 to 700 (Millon, 1973). Their objective was to examine the changing settlement pattern of the urban complex during the vital period when the city was growing rapidly. How large was the population? How did it come into being? What was the social composition of the city, and how was it organized?

Cowgill and Millon spent years mapping and sampling the city (see Chapter 10). They found that it was built in four quadrants, following a master plan that was adhered to for centuries. The basic cruciform layout was established very early, when the great Street of the Dead (Figure 16.8) was laid out. The oldest part of the city lies in the northern quadrant, where most of the city's craftspeople lived. It contains many more structures than the southern quadrants, where exceptionally fertile soils, ideal for irrigation agriculture, are located. The archaeologists found that the city spread southwards from the northern quadrant and that it was organized into neighborhoods, or *barrios*, groups of apartment compounds separated from one another. Teotihuacán's population may have reached a peak of over 125,000 people in A.D. 600. There were more than 2,000 compounds that contained thousands of standardized, one-story apartments that shared courtyards and temples with their neighbors. Some of these compounds contained large concentrations of obsidian flakes or potters' artifacts, and were identified as specialist precincts or groups of workshops.

There were foreign traders' quarters, too. One Oaxacan *barrio* seems to have flourished in the western part of the city, a compound where Oaxacan pottery and artifacts were common. The percentages of Oaxacan wares was very high in this area compared with other precincts, and Millon has hypothesized that there may have been a Oaxacan quarter in Teotihuacán for centuries.

A major objective of the Teotihuacán research is to understand the diverse internal workings of this remarkable city as a going concern throughout its long history. This can only be done by comprehensive

Figure 16.8   Teotihuacán, Mexico, Pyramid of the Sun.

surveys that rely heavily on samples of artifact patternings and analyses of house contents and entire neighborhoods conducted all over this enormous site.

Analysis of Smaller Communities. Communities much smaller than Teotihuacán can be investigated somewhat more easily, but a large amount of archaeological data is still involved. For example, Early Formative villages in the Valley of Oaxaca were investigated to test a number of hypotheses about the relationships between different parts of the settlement. Were the villages subdivided into a number of *barrios*, which are still an organizational unit in modern Indian communities that have well-defined communal and ceremonial responsibilities (Flannery, 1976)? By studying artifact patterns and inventories, the archaeologists found traces of at least four residential wards at San José Mogote, each separated from its neighbors by an erosion gully where the trash was dumped. This larger village displayed some different craft specializations between the wards.

In many smaller communities, the distinctions between different zones of the settlement may be inconspicuous. At Santo Domingo Tomaltepec in Oaxaca, Michael Whallon (1976) managed to isolate three distinct zones in the village of four or five households, occupied between 1150–1000 B.C. He found a cemetery, a zone with two houses containing more trade goods, perhaps a "higher status residential area," and another zone with almost no imports. However, there was little separation between the zones. Unlike Teotihuacán, there was no formal layout for the village, nor were any public buildings discernable.

Population Estimates for Communities. How does one estimate community populations? Obviously, as in the case of the Algonquin historical villages (see Figure 16.6), written records can sometimes provide a fairly accurate estimate. Modern censuses of villages and towns, however, are only of marginal use, for many different variables affect even nineteenth-century population densities relative to those of prehistoric times. Some investigators have attempted to estimate population sizes using mathematical formulae that allocate a certain amount of living space to each individual and each family. But again, one is dealing with so many intangible variables, such as social restrictions, that it is difficult to be accurate. Estimates of the rates at which people accumulate refuse middens over long periods of time have also been used to calculate population size (Cook, 1972; Zubrow, 1976), but this method has the same serious disadvantages as the others mentioned.

About the only reliable estimates of population are based on the number of households at any one specific moment in a community's history. Millon's guesses about Teotihuacán's population are based on such house counts. Using samples of early Mesoamerican village households, Joyce Marcus (1976) showed that perhaps ninety percent were small hamlets that contained from one to ten or twelve households and up to sixty people. But, some villages were much larger than this average. The contemporary Olmec site of San Lorenzo in Vera Cruz may have housed as many as 1,200 people. Thus, it can be seen that this method, too, is far from accurate.

Community population estimates are important, because they can give insights into the maximum size that a settlement can achieve. What, for example, was the maximum size that early Mesoamerican hamlets and villages could reach before further growth was impossible? Characteristically, societies that are not organized in large states tended to live in small villages, which frequently split off from one another as further growth at the mother settlement was cut off. This process is straightforward enough, and in Formative Mesoamerica many villages split off in just this manner. But others, such as the Olmec settlement at San Lorenzo, were able to grow larger and still remain viable settlements. Why was this possible? The search for explanations of evolving settlement patterns takes us onto a broader area of research, that of the layout of communities against the background of their natural environment.

RECONSTRUCTING THE NATURAL ENVIRONMENT

The density and distribution of communities, whatever their size, are determined, to a considerable extent, by the natural resources of the region in which they flourish and by cultural factors. The requirements of hunter-gatherers, for example, differ from those of agriculturalists, and those of cattle herders are different from them both. In Africa, for example, the distribution of cattle is determined by zones of tsetse-fly infested country, for the insect's bite is fatal to stock and dangerous to humans. Pastoral populations tend to concentrate their settlements in grassland areas that are free from these flies and where good fodder and abundant standing water is available (Clark, 1967).

By the same token, the settlement patterns of agricultural populations are determined by equally critical factors. Such shifting cultivators as the Bemba farmers of northern Zambia, have an understanding of their environment that is astonishingly detailed. They can rate a garden's fertility and its suitability for different crops by examining the vegetational cover and the soil's physical characteristics. Critical factors are the land's staying power, the number of seasons during which it can be cropped with satisfactory results, and the fallow period required before it can be reused. As land is exhausted, the Bemba use new or regenerated plots and move their settlements accordingly (Allan, 1965). Like the Bemba, the archaeologist has to achieve a detailed understanding of the environmental variables that affected prehistoric settlement patterns.

The dynamics of human behavior are closely tied to those of the natural environment, the dynamics of such resources as soils, plants, and animals. The changes and patterns of behavior in these resources are just as variable as those of human populations, and they condition the way in which people plan their hunting-and-gathering activities and plant their crops. Increasingly, archaeologists are becoming involved not only with cultural ecology but also with modern ecological research on feeding activities, energy inputs and outputs, and data on the ways in which modern populations utilize natural resources (Hardesty, 1977; Jochim, 1979).

By way of illustration, the hunter-gatherers of the Tehuacán valley in Mexico are known to have concentrated in larger camps during the wet season and to have dispersed over a much wider area in smaller settlements during the scarce months of the dry season. Their food procurement activities were scheduled carefully from season to season (MacNeish, 1978). These activities, in terms of energy maximization and specialization and clustering of population, are much better understood now that archaeologists are beginning to use the concepts of modern ecology. We lack the space for a detailed consideration of these concepts here, and the reader is referred to Hardesty's recent synthesis (1977) for further information.

Reconstruction of the natural environment can be achieved by the use of archaeological, biological, or geological evidence, or by the inventorying of natural resources within reach of a given settlement.

Archaeological, Biological, and Geological Evidence.   A diverse spectrum of sources provides at least generalized information on prehistoric environments. However, in most instances, this data is incomplete at best.

Pleistocene geology is one source. The broad fluctuations of Pleistocene climate are known from geological deposits, such as glaciations, lake beds, raised sea levels, and so on (see Chapter 6). However, these broad fluctuations are too general for study of individual site ecology.

Animal bones can provide broad-based information on climate change, such as that which comes from the study of Pleistocene elephants (see Chapter 6). Unfortunately, many animals taken by Pleistocene hunters were tolerant of temperature changes and rainfall fluctuations, making them less useful as sources for environmental reconstruction. Small rodents and birds are more useful, and they have been used with success in studying British caves (Campbell, 1977). Snails and mollusca are a source of valuable ecological information, too.

Tree rings have been used with success in the Southwestern United States to trace changes in rainfall throughout the past 3000 years. Unfortunately, tree-ring data comes from only some areas of the world (see Chapter 7).

Vegetable remains preserved in archaeological sites can provide insights into the local environment, as long as one remembers that people's exploitation of the local flora can determine the plants brought home to the site (see Chapter 14).

Pollen analysis (palynology) is by far the most useful method for environmental reconstruction and has been applied with success not only to Pleistocene sites but to recent settlements as well (Faegri and Iverson, 1966) (see Chapter 6). Palynology can provide a vivid impression of the surroundings of a prehistoric site, especially if combined with evidence from other sources. Pollen samples can be used, also, to measure the effect of human activities on vegetational cover, and they provide a means of dating the first appearance of agriculture and forest clearance (Iversen, 1941).

The study of pollen remains enabled a detailed ecological reconstruction to be made of the Stone Age hunting camp at Star Carr, England—a tiny birch platform sited in some reeds at the edge of a small lake (Clark, 1954, 1972)—which was occupied in the eighth millennium B.C. The waterlogged deposits yielded both pollens and wood fragments. They showed that the camp was surrounded by birch trees that came down to the water's edge, some pine and willow trees grew nearby, and water plants and fungi were common. The occupation levels extended out through the reeds into deeper water (Figure 16.9).

Unfortunately, not all archaeological sites contain pollen remains, so such reconstructions as the Star Carr example are not as common as one would like.

Inventorying Environmental Resources: Site Catchment Analysis. Cultural adaptation to any environment can only be understood in the context of two categories of data: the ancient environment and resources available therein, and the technology of the culture being studied. Once this data is on hand, the archaeologist can proceed to

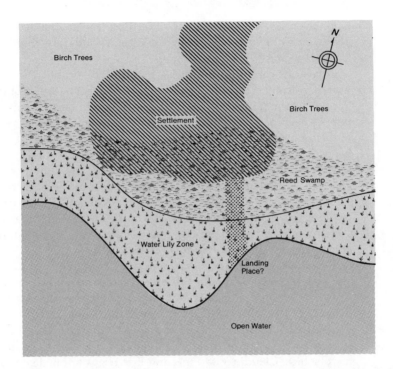

Figure 16.9 A reconstruction of the vegetational surroundings of the Star Carr site in England.

establish which subsistence and economic options the people chose, given the available resources and their technological ability to exploit them.

It is easy enough to make an inventory of the natural resources available in an area, but it is not sufficient merely to list them, for it is the ways in which they can be exploited—the seasons of availability of vegetable foods, the migration patterns of game, and the months when salmon runs take place—and not just the resources themselves that are significant. These many variables, to say nothing of soil distributions, rainfall patterns, and distributions of valuable raw materials, determine the critical element of a settlement pattern—the carrying capacity of the land.

Carrying capacity is the number and density of people that any tract of land can support. It is a flexible statistic that can be affected by factors other than those of the available resources in an area. People can alter the carrying capacity of their land by taking up agriculture, or by cultivating a new crop that needs deeper plowing and thus exhausts the land faster. Or, the introduction of fertilizer can enable people to settle permanently in one village because their lands are kept fertile by artificial means.

Prehistoric carrying capacities are difficult to establish, except by the use of carefully controlled experimental data, such as that obtained for Southwestern agriculture and Maya cultivation (see Chapter 15). Attempts have been made to measure the amount of meat available to prehistoric hunters in the Mississippi valley (Smith, 1974), and it has been clear for some time that Classic Maya populations were much larger than those that could be supported from the felling and burning of forest gardens (Adams, 1977). One problem has been that earlier settlement models were far too simple to accommodate the complexity of the data. Recent research has concentrated on resource inventories, systems models, and even computer simulation of the variables that affect carrying capacity (Hodder, 1978).

Site catchment analysis is a technique of resource inventorying that assumes that every human settlement has a *catchment area* around it. This is a zone of domestic and wild resources within easy walking distance of the settlement. For instance, the !Kung San of the Kalahari Desert in Southern Africa are unlikely to forage much farther away from their base camps than ten kilometers, a comfortable day's walking distance. Claudio Vita-Finzi and Eric Higgs applied site catchment analysis to prehistoric sites near Mount Carmel, Israel, and studied the relationships between technology and the natural resources lying within economic range of individual sites (Hodder and Orton, 1976; Roper, 1979; Vita-Finzi and Higgs, 1970). The fundamental assumption is a simple one: the further the resources in an area are from a site, the less likely they are to be exploited.

Mount Carmel.   Vita-Finzi and Higgs started by drawing a series of five-kilometer concentric rings around their late hunter-gatherer and farming sites. Then they calculated the number of hectares of arable land, rough grazing land, marsh, sand dunes, and other acreage in each circle (Figure 16.10). Each of these land categories formed a percentage of the total catchment area and was exploited more-or-less intensively according to its distance from the site. The catchment areas were plotted on a map and then sampled on foot, using transects to check walking times to allow for different terrains. The investigators based their environmental data on modern sources, but they applied it to show what resources were available to the earlier inhabitants of the Mount Carmel area.

Site catchment analysis is a reasonably objective way of comparing sites lying in the same area or in different regions. The Mount Carmel

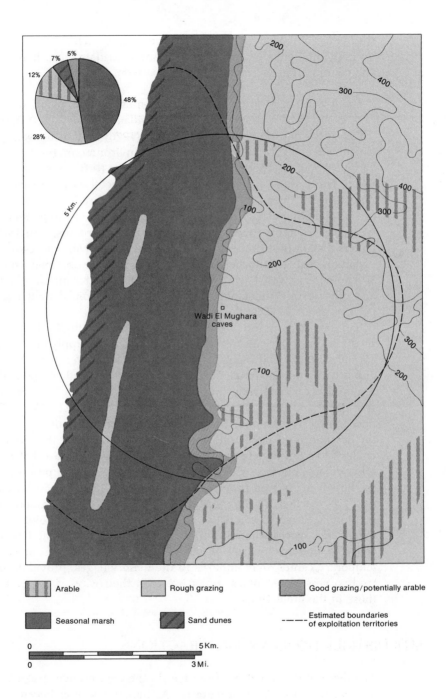

Figure 16.10 Classification of land use at Mount Carmel.

study was somewhat generalized, and recent research has concentrated on individual sites where rigorously analyzed data from households and communities is available for comparison.

San José Mogote.   From how far away must animal, plant, and mineral resources have come to this Oaxaca village between 1150–850 B.C.? This was the question that Kent Flannery (1976) tried to answer by site catchment analysis of the surrounding environment. He tested the various resources: those from within the village (turkeys, stored maize, edible fruit); those from the river, one kilometer away (reeds, sand, mud turtles); those on the high alluvium, within 2 to 5 kilometers (maize and other crops); those on the piedmont, 0 to 5 kilometers away (seasonal vegetable foods); and those in the mountains, 5 to 15 kilometers distant (hut timbers, game, and firewood). Mineral resources— essentials such as salt, chert, and pottery clay—were obtained from 3 to 50 kilometers away. Pacific marine shells, freshwater mussels, jadeite, and other exotic substances and objects came from distant regions, perhaps as far as 200 kilometers away.

San José Mogote thus needed a circle of under 2 to 5 kilometers to satisfy its basic agricultural needs, 5 kilometers to supply basic minerals and seasonal wild vegetable foods, and 15 kilometers for game meat and construction materials. Exotic trade materials and ceremonial life required occasional collecting trips of up to 50 kilometers from the settlement and some contacts with even greater distances. When Flannery plotted the San José Mogote catchment areas relative to those of the neighboring Early Formative villages, he found that the innermost circles (2 to 5 kilometers) of one village did not overlap that of any other village, but that wider circles did, as the exclusive possession of catchment areas was progressively reduced. Once the 50-kilometer ring was reached, all the villages of Oaxaca shared a common catchment area. Seasonal campsites were placed at strategic points on the outer rings, places where hut timbers, game, and trade materials were collected, perhaps by three or four villages sharing the same area. Such temporary camps were annexes to the main villages, providing more ready access to resources, which were, in their way, as important as those in the inner rings.

SITE DISTRIBUTIONS AND INTERACTIONS

The distribution of natural resources in the environment was but one determinant of settlement patterns. As human societies became more complex, so did the interactions between them; and these interactions were reflected in evolving settlement patterns. The study of entire settlement patterns brings into play a number of basic research methods that require large quantities of archaeological data.

Distribution Maps. The distribution map, which plots site distributions against the environmental background, has been used by archaeologists for a long time. One of the early pioneers in this field was the Englishman Sir Cyril Fox, whose classic monograph, *The Personality of Britain* (1932), plotted archaeological sites against base maps of the reconstructed prehistoric vegetation and modern topography. Other studies soon followed, as people found that prehistoric settlement patterns did tend to coincide with many environmental zones.

Distribution maps, and the settlement patterns plotted on them, are normally derived from aerial photographs and ground reconnaissance. As such, they are subject to several obvious sources of error, among them, the location of archaeologists in the field, site destruction by modern construction, and the difficulties of dating sites without excavation. Most early interpretations of distribution maps were based on "eyeballing" distributions to show, using radiocarbon dates, the direction of spread of a culture trait, such as a sword type, or to explain how a scatter of site clusters came to take shape on the landscape. Obviously, however, such impressionistic interpretations are far too superficial.

Ultimately, the objective is not only to describe the distribution or settlement pattern itself, but to look at the factors that generated the settlement pattern in the first place. These factors cannot be deduced from archaeological evidence alone, but they can be deduced by use of computer simulations or statistical techniques of probability.

SPATIAL ANALYSIS

Any attempt to analyze a settlement pattern must begin with the development of a site typology. Such a classification should provide objective criteria for separating different sites on the basis of size, function, and other features. Archaeologists in the Valley of Mexico, for example, use a local classification that distinguishes between primary and secondary regional centers, nucleated and dispersed villages, hamlets, camps, and residences, on the basis of population size, architecture, and other specific criteria. Each of these site types has a relationship to the others; the sites form a constellation that makes up a settlement pattern on a local, regional, and even a continental level. And the precise definitions of site types—ceremonial centers, villages,

and so on—supply us with an explicit administrative hierarchy, a series
of successive levels of settlement that organizes our patterns of dots on
the map hierarchically (Figure 16.11). This hierarchy raises the fundamental question: What were the rules that shaped it on the landscape?

Site Distribution Analyses.   Our thinking about site hierarchies, settlement spacing, and hypothetical rules of settlement patterning depends on accurate distribution information, and even more important,
on one's evaluation of the significance of the various "clusters" of sites
that can be discerned on the map. Are these clusterings accidental, the
result of deliberate human planning, or due to modern factors?

A number of statistical techniques can be used to analyze site distributions, most of them borrowed from geographers. For example,
David Thomas used a method called *cluster analysis* to study socioeco-

Figure 16.11   (a) A hypothetical population pyramid of archaeological site types.
(b) A simplified diagram showing possible and hypothetical interactions between
different Early Formative settlement types in the Valley of Oaxaca.

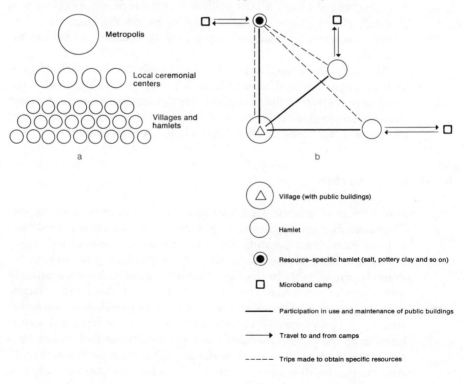

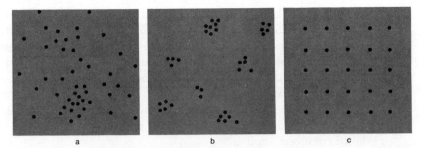

Figure 16.12   Three possible models for archaeological distributions: (a) A random distribution, with the points scattered at random. All points have an equal probability of being located at any given place on what is assumed to be a featureless landscape. (b) Clusters of points, representing artifacts or sites grouped in clumps. Distributions in clumps can occur when people are attracted toward a valuable resource or when a village, for example, generates new settlements that are located nearby. An extreme example is, of course, a distribution in which everyone is located at the same point. (c) A spaced distribution, which has the sites or artifacts at more-or-less regular intervals. Here, people are spaced at regular intervals because they are competing with each other for resources or in some other way.

nomic patterns in the Great Basin, where he found striking differences in site distributions. He discovered that "harvesting village and rabbit-driving implements are in a clumped distribution, while hunting artifacts tend to be distributed over pinon-juniper and upper sagebrush-grass zones." He was able to compare the theoretical distributions of the artifacts with his observed patterns (Thomas, 1969, 1976).

Other approaches include *point pattern analysis,* in which site distributions are plotted on a grid and tested for nonrandom patterning (Figure 16.12). The *nearest neighbor statistic* of the geographers is another. It has been used experimentally on Olmec sites as a test for measuring the intensity of a settlement pattern (Earle, 1976; Earle and Ericson, 1977). Timothy Earle found that Olmec ceremonial centers were spaced at regular intervals in territories that were 44 kilometers in diameter, with lesser centers within each territory. He tried to use that statistic to examine the intensity of interaction between major and minor centers. All these techniques are still in an experimental stage; and all require sophisticated statistical manipulations and data of meticulous quality to be effective.

One essential ingredient for an understanding of settlement patterns—one that Earle attempted to find in studying the Olmec—is a knowledge of how site hierarchies came into being and of the intensity of interaction between the inhabitants of each site type. One useful concept for this end is that of *central place theory.*

Central Place Theory.   Central place theory, which was first developed by the German geographer Walter Christaller (1933) in a study of southern German communities, is a series of statements about the relationship between settlement systems. Christaller stated that "if the population distribution and its purchasing power, as well as the to-pography, its resources, and transport facilities, are all uniform, then all central places providing similar services, performing similar functions, and serving areas of equal size, will be spaced at an equal distance from one another."

After this general definition, Christaller went on to develop a hierarchy of central places, one that divided groups of centers of decreasing size and facilities into various hierarchical groups. In these hierarchies it was assumed that there were fewer large places than small ones, which provided the widest range of services possible. The largest places performed not only the services of the smaller ones, but they also performed central functions that distinguish them from their lesser neighbors.

The simple Christaller model has been modified by later research to allow the size of a service area to vary with the size of the central place that services it. Under this rubric, the central place function of Teotihuacán, for example, affects a much larger area than that serviced by smaller service centers lying within, say, twenty miles of the city. These latter merely duplicate services available at Teotihuacán and are less likely to develop close to the city as they are to develop close to one another. Behind these modifications is the assumption that the location of any form of center will be determined, at least in part, by convenience to its clients. It will be located where it can be reached with the minimum effort.

Ideally, a single service center that provides multiple services to a surrounding population situated on a flat plain will service a circular area, with the center being located in the middle. But, when there are several types of central place, each fulfilling different functions within a single region, then the most logical shape of service territory would be a hexagon.

The hexagon is a theoretical configuration, to be sure, but it is one that reflects the essential regularity of service areas. This shape of territory minimizes the distance to the centers from the boundaries of the area and keeps population movement to a minimum (Figure 16.13). This model has been tested using southern English market towns, which were spaced 6 to 10 kilometers (4 to 6 miles) apart in medieval times, a convenient day's journey by cart from the surrounding rural

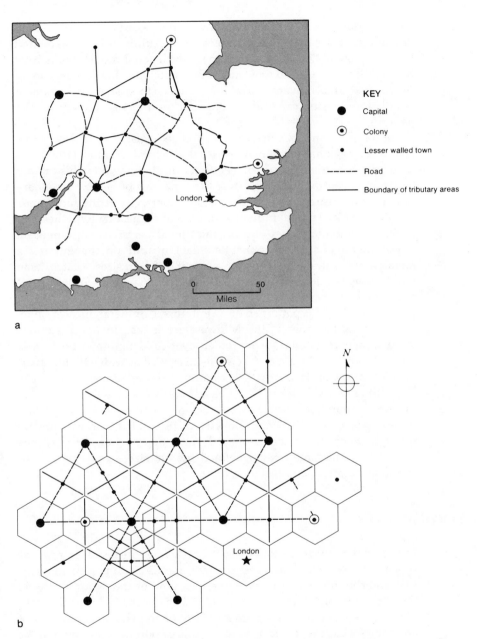

Figure 16.13 Hodder and Hassall's map of Romano-British settlement in southern Britain during the third century A.D. (a) The site hierarchy plotted on a conventional map. (b) The hexagonal lattice that they erected over the hierarchy.

villages. Indeed, a twelfth-century law expressly forbade the placement of markets closer than 10 kilometers apart. Although Ian Hodder and Mark Hassall (1972) have shown that a hexagonal model works relatively well when applied to Romano-British towns, this spacing cannot be claimed as a universal law, for many factors, such as terrain or population density, can still act on even the most seemingly regular patterns.

Central place theory's main use to archaeologists is as a descriptive device for regional settlement patterns. Richard Blanton (1978) has used it to document the rise of Teotihuacán, showing how this rapidly burgeoning central place took over the functions of nearby secondary centers and affected the entire settlement hierarchy at the same time. The central place model provides a means of suggesting hypotheses as to what economic moves and organizational decisions were needed. These can then be tested against field data. In addition, the notion of a hierarchy of central places serving areas of different sizes—that is, in an interlocking relationship in space—is vital to archaeology. A number of attempts have been made to show that the distribution of specific prehistoric sites was patterned on a centralized, or hierarchical, system. The Hopewell people of the Midwest are a case in point. Famous traders, their cult objects were traded over the length and breadth of Ohio, Illinois, Michigan, and Wisconsin, as well as wider afield. Stuart Struever and Gail Houart (1972) examined the relationships between different Hopewell sites in the Midwest and were able to suggest that the large mound sites found were regional centers, where important trading was focused. They developed a picture of the hierarchy of sites through which the various Hopewell trade objects were handled, the levels of the hierarchy being defined by site size, similarity of construction, location, and distance apart.

POPULATION

In the final analysis, settlement patterns evolve in response to three broad variables: environmental change, alterations in population density, and the interaction between people. One of the major factors in the later cultural evolution of humankind has been, undoubtedly, rapidly growing population densities. Many of the classic arguments of archaeology have revolved around the role of population growth in the origins of agriculture, urban life, and civilization. Unfortunately, however, as mentioned previously, the estimation of population densities is a task fraught with serious difficulties.

Estimating Populations.   As yet, no one has developed a fool-proof method of estimating prehistoric population densities: there are simply too many variables to contend with, many of them impossible to reconstruct from archaeological data.

Methods based on settlement data rely on information from excavated household clusters and ethnographic information to provide an estimate of the amount of floor space, or living area, needed by an individual. The average family size is first calculated and then multiplied by the available living space. Efforts have been made to estimate the amount of living space required by individuals in many different societies. R. Naroll (1962), conducted one such experiment that produced a figure of ten square meters per person. Clearly, however, such estimates could not possibly apply to all societies, let alone to both hunter-gatherers and city dwellers. Others, such as Millon at Teotihuacán, have used the amount of sleeping area required as the formula. Although there may be instances where a relatively reliable population estimate can be obtained, much depends on precise ethnographic analogy, very careful control of the archaeological data, and the excavation of considerable areas of the site.

Methods based on *food consumption* have been used to calculate populations of hunter-gatherer camps in Europe and of shell middens in the western United States. A clever, but mainly theoretical, calculation—but one that may give a reasonable estimate of general population size—was made by a group of California archaeologists, who estimated that about 30 people occupied the Scripps Estate in Southern California between about 5500 and 3500 B.C. (Cook, 1972). They based their estimates on the amount of shell refuse and the number of grindstones found there.

Cemeteries and burial grounds have been used to estimate population also, but this evidence has the disadvantage that it is seldom representative of the population as a whole. Most cemeteries are used over long periods of time, and as such, they represent a cumulative population rather than the number of people living at a given moment in time.

Most demographic figures from large geographic areas are clearly little more than feasible guesses. For example, one estimate has placed the average population of the early Sumerian states in Mesopotamia at about 17,000 souls (Sanders and Price, 1968); and the Late Glacial population of Britain, at about 10,000 people (Clark, 1952).

Population Growth.   While accurate population estimates on a settlement-by-settlement basis are obviously of great interest, especially if one assumes that the growing size of a village represents a growing population, the consequences of population growth and decline are even more important. Population is a key element in cultural process, for there is a clear cause-and-effect relationship between population and the potential carrying capacity and productivity of agricultural land. Competition and cooperation between different communities may result from a shortage of resources engendered by population growth, and these interactions may, in turn, affect both settlement pattern and population density.

The classic hypothesis on world population was formulated by Thomas Henry Malthus in the late eighteenth century. Malthus believed that humankind's reproductive capacity far exceeds available food supplies; in other words, people must compete for the necessities of life. Competition causes famine, war, and misery. The Malthusian thesis has dominated archaeological thinking for generations, to the extent that many scholars believed that population carrying capacity of land and other resources, as well as that of technology, places limits on population growth.

The Malthusian viewpoint has been challenged by economist Ester Boserup, who developed the thesis that population growth should be treated as a quite independent variable when studying technological and cultural change. "As population grows," she argued, "more people per unit of land are faced with the necessity of providing more food per unit of land, and they are able to do this by intensifying their relationship with the land—technology—moving from hunting and gathering through stages of cultivation with ever shorter fallow periods up to the final stage of intensification, which is multicropping with no fallowing." She went on to argue that people only intensify their agricultural efforts when forced by population pressure to do so. The implication is that more intensive land use is accompanied by parallel processes of intensification of other aspects of culture and society (Spooner, 1972).

Boserup's theoretical viewpoint serves to highlight population as another variable in settlement archaeology. Unfortunately, few regions have been surveyed in sufficient archaeological detail to enable population estimates or data on intensity of agriculture to be made with any statistical confidence. Elizabeth Brumfiel (1976) used site catchment analysis and modern agricultural data to study population growth in Formative villages in the Valley of Mexico. She recorded a slight increase in the settlement area at the end of the Formative, but the ratio of productive potential of the agricultural land to site size remained almost the same as before, and climatic conditions also had remained the same. But, three of the larger sites had a much higher population to productivity ratio than the smaller settlements. From this, she concluded that there were political and social reasons why this situation developed. Conceivably, she argued, the smaller villages had to pay taxes for services to larger settlements. So, the smaller settlements boosted their agricultural production, while the larger centers enjoyed greater population densities but did not have to raise their own agricultural production.

The Brumfiel research, and that of other investigators, such as Jeffrey Parsons, in the same region (Sanders, Parsons, and Santley, 1979), and Robert Adams (1974), on irrigation in Mesopotamia, clearly demonstrate the complex economic and social variables that can affect population growth in prehistory. Much of the time, settlement archaeology involves hypothesizing about intangibles, those aspects of human society that are never preserved in the archaeological record. But, as Chapter 17 shows, much of our understanding of cultural evolution and changing settlement patterns comes from the insights we can obtain into the interactions between different communities reflected in their trading, social, and religious practices.

Guide to Further Reading

Chang, K. C., ed. *Settlement Archaeology.* Palo Alto: National Press, 1968.
   A fundamental set of essays on settlement archaeology that covers both general theory and specific examples.

Flannery, Kent V., ed. *The Early Mesoamerican Village.* New York: Academic Press, 1976.
   A modern classic, a study by a team of Michigan archaeologists of settlement patterns in the Valley of Oaxaca. Enlivened by some hypothetical, but highly entertaining, debates between fictitious archaeologists of different theoretical viewpoints.

Hodder, Ian, and Orton, Clive. *Spatial Analysis in Archaeology.* Cambridge: Cambridge University Press, 1976.
   A study of this new field, of a rather technical nature but full of useful concepts and ideas.

Sanders, William T.; Parsons, Jeffrey R.; and Santley, Robert S. *The Basin of Mexico: Ecological Processes in the Evolution of a Civilization.* 2 vols. New York: Academic Press, 1979.
   A settlement-ecological study just completed, which gives an admirable impression of the state of the art research in this field.

Willey, Gordon R. *Prehistoric Settlement Patterns in the Virú Valley, Peru.* Washington, D.C.: Bureau of American Ethnology, Bulletin 155, 1953.
   The pioneer settlement study that uses aerial surveys and distribution maps. Still a definitive study.

CHAPTER 17 ❧

SOCIAL ORGANIZATION, TRADE, AND RELIGIOUS LIFE

Preview

- Human subsistence is based on natural resources and on the exploitation of the environment, whether or not people produce food. Trade may have had its beginnings when people moved to a new territory where a previously available raw material was no longer abundant. Much early trade probably took the form of gift exchanges and the bartering of food and other commodities between neighboring settlements. The pattern of the trade was established by the distance between settlements and available raw material sources.

- Trade is normally recognized in the archaeological record by the discovery of objects exotic to the material culture of the economy of the host society. Prehistoric trade networks are studied by examining the distributions of such objects and of tool patterns in individual households and household clusters.

- Trading activity is closely tied to growing complexity in social and political organization among prehistoric peoples. It is not enough simply to identify trading activity in the archaeological record, one also has to understand the exchange processes that lay behind the trading.

- We cite two examples of prehistoric trading to show how trade cannot be studied except with reference to the cultural systems of which it was a part. Our first example is Maya trade in the lowlands, an area where trade in *metates*, jadeite, and other raw materials was essential for survival. Long-distance trading served as an integrative factor for the emergence of lowland Maya civilization. At Tepe Yahya in Iran, steatite trading assumed great importance, but it was controlled by middlemen and depended on a demand for luxury objects in Mesopotamia, hundreds of miles away.

- The redistribution of trade objects through a society is often controlled politically by chiefs and other leaders. We use an example of obsidian trading in Mesoamerica to show how such redistribution mechanisms can be studied in the archaeological record.
- Social organization is difficult to study from archaeological evidence, although a systematic view of human culture makes it possible to examine it as one variable among the many that affect cultural change. The Tucson Garbage Project suggests that the use of artifacts and food remains for the study of ancient social organization has great potential.
- Leslie White and other anthropologists have developed an evolutionary model of social organization that envisages four broad levels: bands, tribes, chiefdoms, and state-organized societies.
- Social organization can be studied in the archaeological record by using burials and associated grave furniture, as was done at Ur-of-the-Chaldees, and by using structures or artifact patternings.
- The use of artifact patternings to study prehistoric social organization is still at an experimental stage. We cite William Longacre's study of Carter Ranch, Arizona, to exemplify some of the difficulties involved.
- Religion has been studied traditionally through burials, burial rites, and sacred buildings. Organized religions were a feature of many of the more complex prehistoric societies, and they were often centered on elaborate ceremonial areas that were a focus for state-organized societies. The rituals that ensured the continuity of religious belief are reflected in architecture and art, and the presence or absence of sacred artifacts in the archaeological record may reveal valuable information on prehistoric religion, provided careful research designs are developed.

So far, we have discussed human cultures as more-or-less self-sufficient entities, each with their own territory and constellation of natural resources. Very few human societies have lived in complete isolation from their neighbors, however. One major theme of world prehistory is the increasing interdependence and competition between different communities, the culmination of which is the highly interdependent, industrialized world we live in today. In this chapter we examine the ways in which archaeologists study these evolving interactions, interactions reflected not only in the exchange of resources and trading but also in kinship, marriage, and more complex social structures, as well as in shared religious beliefs.

TRADE AND EXCHANGE SYSTEMS

Trade has been defined as the "mutually appropriative movement of goods between hands" (Renfrew, 1975). People develop trade connections and the exchange systems that handle trade goods when they need to acquire goods and services that are not available to them within their own site catchment area. The movement of goods need not be over any great distance, and it can operate internally, within a society, or externally, across cultural boundaries. In all cases, trade involves two elements: the goods and commodities being exchanged, and the people doing the exchanging. Thus, any form of trading activity implies both the procurement and handling of tools and raw materials and some form of social system that provides the people-to-people relationships within which the trade flourishes.

Trade is recognized in the archaeological record by the discovery of objects exotic to the material culture or economy of the host society. Glass, for example, was never manufactured in sub-Saharan Africa during prehistoric times, yet imported glass beads are widespread finds in archaeological sites of the first millennium A.D. (Beck and Schofield, 1958). Prehistoric exchange networks can be studied through the distribution of exotic artifacts and materials, using not only the artifacts but also trace elements and other characteristic features of such raw materials as obsidian, the volcanic glass so highly prized for ceremonial and utilitarian artifacts in Mesoamerica, North America, and the Near East (Figure 17.1).

Pioneer studies of obsidian were made by Colin Renfrew and others in the Near East, where spectroscopic analysis was used to identify no fewer than twelve early farming villages that had obtained obsidian from the Ciftlik area of central Turkey (Renfrew, Dixon, and Cann, 1966). The study showed that eighty percent of the chipped stone in villages within 300 kilometers of Ciftlik was obsidian. Outside this "supply zone," the percentages of obsidian dropped away sharply with

Figure 17.1   An obsidian mirror from Mesoamerica, showing the reflection of a figurine.

distance, to five percent in a Syrian village, and 0.1 percent in the Jordan Valley. Renfrew and his colleagues argued that regularly spaced villages were passing about half the obsidian they received to their more distant neighbors (Figure 17.2).

The study of prehistoric trade through artifacts and raw materials is of critical importance to archaeology, for it provides a unique opportunity to examine not only the mechanics of trading networks but also the changing social institutions that regulated them.

Social Interaction and Organization.   *Gift giving* is a common medium of exchange and trade in societies that are relatively self-supporting. The exchange of gifts is primarily designed to reinforce a social relationship, both of an individual and of a group as a whole. This form of trade is commonplace in New Guinea and the Pacific, widespread in Africa during the past 2000 years, and in the Americas as well. Much depends on the types of commodity being exchanged. The exchange of sea shells, for example, may have involved individuals of higher status, while that of foodstuffs and hut poles was a more commonplace form of transaction involving many individuals and families. And, of course, not only objects but also information can be exchanged, information that may lead to technological innovation or social change. Gift-giving and bartering formed a basic trading mechanism for millennia, a simple means of exchanging basic commodities. But this sporadic interaction between individuals and communities reduced people's self-sufficiency, and eventually, it made them part of a larger, functioning society whose members were no longer so self-sufficient and who depended on one another not only for basic commodities but also for social purposes.

The decision to engage in trading—to acquire commodities from afar—depends on both how urgent the need for the goods is and the

Figure 17.2   Obsidian trade routes in the Neolithic Near East. The nuclear zone was the center of obsidian mining.

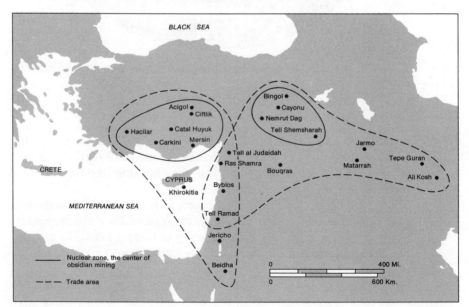

difficulties in acquiring and transporting them. Clearly, such items as cattle or slaves are more easily transported than tons of iron ore or salt cakes. The former move on their own, but metals require human or animal carriers or wheeled carts. To ignore these differences is to oversimplify the study of prehistoric trade.

Reciprocity, the exchange of goods between two individuals or groups, is at the heart of much gift giving and barter trade. It can happen at the same place year after year and be focused on a central place, one that can be as humble as someone's house. Such central places become the focus of gift giving and trade. When a village becomes involved in both the production of trade goods and their exchange with other communities, it will probably become an even more important center, a place to which people will travel to trade.

Redistribution of trade goods from a central place throughout a culture requires some form of organization to ensure that the redistribution is equitable. A redistributive mechanism may be controlled by a chief, a religious leader, or some form of management organization. Such an organization might control production of copper ornaments, or it might simply control distribution and delivery of trade objects. Redistribution of any commodity requires someone to both collect and redistribute it, something that requires considerable social organization for collection, storage, and redistribution in the case of grain and other commodities. The chief, whose position is perhaps reinforced by religious power, has a serious responsibility to his community, one that can extend over several villages, as his lines of redistribution stretch out through people of lesser rank to the individual villager. A chief will negotiate exchanges with other chiefs, substituting the regulatory elements of reciprocal trading for a redistributive economy in which less trading in exotic materials is carried out by individual households.

Prehistoric trade was an important variable that developed in conjunction with sociopolitical organization. It has been assumed that trade proceeded from simple reciprocal exchange to the more complex redistribution of goods under a redistributor. In other words, trading is closely tied to growing complexity in social and political organization.

Markets are both places and particular styles of trading administration and organization that encourage people to develop one place for trading and relatively stable, almost fixed, prices for staple commodities. This does not mean regulated prices; but some regulation is needed in a network of markets in which commodities from an area of abundant supplies are sold to one with strong demand for the same materials. The mechanisms of the exchange relationship, in particular, require some regulation. Markets are normally associated with more

Figure 17.3   A ceremonial Maya *metate,* a carved stone slab used for grinding corn and other materials.

complex societies. No literate civilization ever developed without strong central places, where trading activities were regulated and monopolies developed over both sources of materials and trade routes themselves.

Successful market trading required predictable supplies of basic commodities and adequate policing of trade routes. It is not without significance that most early Mesopotamian and Egyptian trade was riverine, where policing was easier. With the great caravan routes opened, the political and military issues—tribute, control of trade routes, and tolls—became paramount. The caravan, predating the great empires, was a form of organized trading that kept to carefully defined routes set up and maintained by state authorities. The travelers moved along set routes, looking neither left nor right, bent only on delivering and exchanging imports and exports. These caravans were a far cry from the huge economic complex that accompanied Alexander the Great's army across Asia, or the Grand Mogul's annual summer progress from the heat in Delhi in India to the mountains, which moved a half million people, including the entire Delhi bazaar.

Studying Market Networks.   Emphasis on these mechanisms has led Johnson, Lamberg-Karlovsky, Rathje, and others to study market networks and the mechanisms by which suppliers are channeled down well-defined routes and by which profits are regulated and fed back to the source, providing further incentive for more supplies (Sabloff and Lamberg-Karlovsky, 1975). There may or may not be a physical marketplace; it is the state of affairs surrounding the trade that forms the focus of the trading system and the mechanisms by means of which trade interacts with other parts of the culture. Taking a systems approach to trading activity means emphasizing the role of archaeological finds as the material expressions of interdependent factors. These factors include the need for goods—which prompts a search for supplies. The supplies themselves represent production above local needs and are created to satisfy external demands. Other factors are the logistics of transportation and the extent of the trading network, as well as the social and political environment. With all these variables, no one aspect of trade can be reasonably viewed as an overriding cause of cultural change or of evolution in trading practices. Hitherto, archaeologists have concentrated on the objects of trade or on trade as an abstraction—trade as a cause of civilization; but they have had no profound knowledge about the workings of even one trading network from which to build more theoretical abstractions.

EXAMPLES OF TRADE IN PREHISTORY

Mayan Trade. What were the remarkable forces that brought the Maya of Mesoamerica together in one state organization? Most people now agree that a series of complicated variables connected with cosmo-magical symbolism, trade, and resource conservation were involved. William Rathje believes that trade was one critical variable for people like the Maya who were living in uniform environments (Rathje, 1971; Parsons and Price, 1971). He suggests that the Maya's lowland rainforest environment was very deficient in many vital resources, including stone for grinding maize, salt (always vital for agriculturalists), obsidian for knives and weapons, and many luxury materials (Figure 17.3). All these could be obtained from the highlands in the north, from the Valley of Mexico, and from Guatemala and other regions, if the necessary long-distance trading networks and mechanisms could be set up. Such connections, and the trading expeditions to maintain them, could not be organized by individual villages alone. The Maya lived in a uniform environment, where the rainforest provided similarly deficient resources for every settlement. Cooperation was therefore advantageous to all. Trade networks could thus be developed through the authority of the ceremonial centers and their leaders. The integrative organization needed must have been considerable, for communications in the rainforest, especially in areas remote from the highlands, were extremely difficult to maintain.

Rathje carried his argument one stage further. Obviously, peoples living on the border between the lowlands and the highlands had the best opportunities for trade. Those who lived farther away, like the Maya, were at a disadvantage in this respect. But they offered the same agricultural commodities and craft exports as their more fortunate neighbors, and they had one competitive advantage—a complex and properly functioning state organization and the knowledge to keep it going. This knowledge itself was very exportable. Along with pottery, feathers, specialized stone materials, and lime plaster, they exported their political and social organization and their religious beliefs. Beyond establishing the idea that trade was a major factor in the emergence of the Mayan state, Rathje has shown that objects can bring about the evolution of social organization.

Regulated Trade: Tepe Yahya.   Trading was an integral part of early Sumerian civilization in the Near East, too, a many-faceted operation that absorbed the energies of thousands of people. Sumerian trade was much more tightly organized and controlled than, say, Hopewell trading. The redistribution systems of the cities combined many activities, all controlled by the centralized authority that ruled the settlements. Food surpluses were redistributed, and raw materials were obtained from far away for the manufacture of ornaments, weapons, and prestigious luxuries. Demands for raw materials appear to have risen steadily, spreading market networks into territories remote from the home state. For these long-distance routes to succeed, political stability at both ends of the route was essential. An intricate system of political, financial, and logistical checks and balances had to be kept in place, requiring an efficient and alert administrative organization.

The raw materials traded by the Sumerians included metals, timber, skins, ivory, and such precious stones as malachite. Many could be found only in the remote highlands to the north and east of Mesopotamia. The trade in steatite (soapstone—an easy-to-work material) shows how far-flung Mesopotamian trade became (Lamberg-Karlovsky, 1973; 1975). Steatite was used to make stone bowls as early as 10,000 B.C., but it suddenly became a highly fashionable material around 2750 B.C. Steatite bowls are found in Early Dynastic Mesopotamian tells and also occur at Moenjo-daro in the Indus Valley, one of the great cities of the Indus civilization, and at contemporaneous sites on islands in the Persian Gulf. Objects of the same materials are also common in settlements near today's Iran-Pakistan border, the hinterland between Indus and Mesopotamian civilizations. Most of the steatite objects are stone bowls bearing intricate designs, the same designs being found all over the area where steatite is found.

Experiments with physiochemical analysis have identified at least a

Figure 17.4   The tell at Tepe Yahya, Iran, an important center of steatite trade.

dozen sources for the stone, but so far only Tepe Yahya in Iran is
known to have been a center of steatite bowl production (Figure 17.4).
Abundant steatite deposits occur near the site. The bowls produced at
Tepe Yahya and elsewhere were definitely items of luxury; they were
so prized in Mesopotamia that they may have caused keen competition
among those rich enough to afford them. The competition for luxury
goods generally may have been intense enough to affect production
rates in the source areas, with political vicissitudes in the Mesopotamian city-states constantly shifting production rates of steatite centers
and making profits from the trade fluctuate. Interestingly, the demand
for steatite around Tepe Yahya was minimal, and the occurrence of few
finds in the Indus Valley contrasts sharply with the very large quantities found in Mesopotamia. Most of the trade was with the west,
depending on the demand for luxuries among the increasingly wealthy
elites of the Mesopotamian cities. Local artisans seem to have produced
the steatite near Tepe Yahya, perhaps working part-time or at selected
seasons. But the trade itself was not in the artisans' hands; it was run by
middlemen and ultimately by the exploitative elite of Mesopotamia.
C. C. Lamberg-Karlovsky calls this trade a form of economic imperial-
ism: "Economic exploitation of foreign areas without political control."

The study of prehistoric trade is a vital source of information on social organization and the ways in which societies became more complex. Trade itself developed a great complexity, in terms of both goods traded and the interactions of people involved. Colin Renfrew (1975) has identified no less than ten different types of interaction between people that can result from trading, ranging from simple contact between individuals to trading by professional traders, such as the *pochteca* of the Maya and the Aztec, who were not above acting as spies (Figure 17.5).

SOCIAL ORGANIZATION

"Data relevant to most, if not all, components of past sociocultural systems *are* preserved in the archaeological record," argued Lewis Binford some years ago (Binford, 1968). Traditionally, archaeologists had regarded the more intangible aspects of human society, such as religious and social organization, as particularly difficult to infer from archaeological data. Many minor differences between prehistoric peoples—speech, religion, and social organization among them—are, it is true, seldom obvious in the archaeological record, and traditional definitions of culture only help us to recognize differences when they are detectable in the data obtained by excavation, analysis, and induction. But, Binford's approach sees human cultures in archaeology as sociocultural systems that enable one to think of social and religious factors as vital subsystems in regulating cultural change. These intangibles can be reconstructed, he believes, at least partially, through a study of artifact patterning and stylistic changes in national culture. Other archaeologists have pointed out that material culture is extremely sensitive to changes in ideology, a sensitivity reflected in stylistic changes in such items as tombstones in New England churchyards (Deetz, 1967).

The Tucson Refuse Project.   University of Arizona archaeologist William Rathje has demonstrated this same theory with his study of garbage from the city of Tucson. In this remarkable project the latest archaeological methods and research designs were applied to investigate the relationships between resource management, urban demography, and social and economic stratification in a modern context where some control data from interviews and other perspectives are available to amplify an archaeological study of the type that is conducted at an ancient urban center. The project has yielded remarkable results, showing how resource management varies from one segment of the city's population to another. Patterns of waste and consumption can be studied for different households, and the various trends show up clearly in the discarded food residues and artifacts.

Rathje and his colleagues found, for example, that the average middle-class Tucson household wasted $100 of edible beef a year.

Figure 17.5 The ten different ways in which prehistoric trade can operate, as determined by Colin Renfrew. The diagram illustrates the wide variety of means by which trade goods are exchanged, each of which has specific implications for settlement patterns.

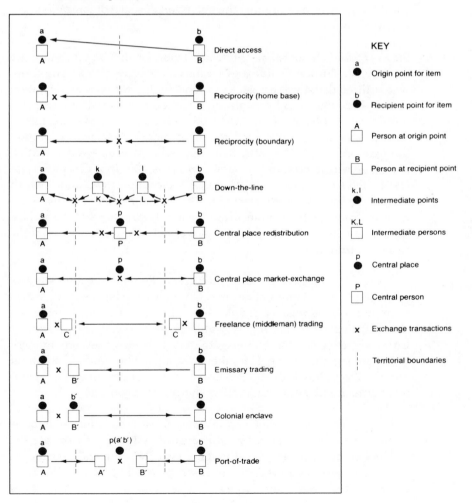

White middle-class families ate proportionately more ham, lamb, pork, and chicken than Black, American Indian, and Asian families. In contrast, lower-income groups consumed many more vitamins, liquor, and bread. The recently discarded refuse in Tucson revealed the surprising fact that high-income residences were associated with relatively little waste of food or artifacts and that it was the middle-income families that were the most wasteful.

Most of the Tucson garbage research is based on modern artifact patterning, and its conclusions may have bearing on the study of prehistoric social organization. Rathje's work, however, does throw light on social organization within a single society, whereas much other effort has gone into examining the evolution of social organization on a much larger scale.

Stages of Social Organization.   Edward Tylor, Lewis Morgan, and more recently, V. Gordon Childe and Leslie White were also among those who realized that it was a mistake to consider human cultural evolution as divorced from social organization. Childe recognized this with his formulations of Neolithic and Urban Revolutions; Leslie White, Elman Service, and others developed a simple model of societal evolution through prehistory that attracted, and still attracts, wide attention among archaeologists. In his classic *Profiles in Ethnology,* Elman Service (1971) defined several broad levels of sociocultural evolution, which provided a framework for tracing the evolution of human social organization from the first simple, primitive family structures of the earliest hunter-gatherers to the highly complex state-organized societies of the early civilizations.

Bands.   For most of its long prehistory, humankind flourished in small bands, associations of families that may have been no larger than some twenty-five to sixty people. These bands were knit together by close kinship ties. This highly viable form of social organization is extremely effective for hunter-gatherers and survives into modern times among the !Kung San, the Australian aborigines, and other groups. The tightly knit organization of the band encourages cooperative hunting and gathering and the sharing of resources.

Tribes.   The social level of the band proved effective as long as humans were hunter-gatherers. But once they began to cultivate the soil and domesticate animals, the more sedentary life and demanding requirements of food production caused people to associate in aggregates of bands that were linked by class into tribes. A clan unites families within an organization where all its members claim descent from a common ancestor. Tribal societies are essentially democratic, for the leadership of this much larger social unit is normally conducted through a tribal council of some type whose membership consists of band and clan representatives. A tribe may also possess nonkinship social units that transcend kinship ties, often units that foster a particular activity, such as canoe navigation or potmaking. These sodalities are but one of several new forms of social organization that tribes employ to manipulate their growing populations. At the core of tribal life is the notion that all resources are owned by the tribe as a whole and are to be controlled in a basically egalitarian manner.

Chiefdoms.   Tribal societies develop chiefdoms in situations where the egalitarian principles of the society are replaced by a new order, where different kin groups assume a form of ranking within society as a whole. One kin group may achieve prominence because its members, all descended from a common ancestor, are associated with extraordinary deeds or are believed to have unusual religious or other abilities. This particular lineage may soon enjoy a special status within society, one that gives its leaders organizational powers to cater to the needs of society as a whole. The lineage chieftains do not actually control or own the products or services of the society that they manipulate or redistribute. Rather, they act as the social instrument for the redistribution of goods and services for their society as a whole. These chiefdoms are headed by lineage leaders who coordinate the management of food surpluses and the products of the diverse part-time specialist craftspeople that even a tribal society possesses.

Once food supplies are regularly produced and the division of labor within a society has diversified far beyond that of simple male-female roles, then the leaders of the principal lineage or lineages assume an important role in redistributing specialist products throughout the tribe on a fair basis, keeping a proportion of the supplies for their own use and for storage in communal food reserves. The authority of such leaders is commonly backed by their spiritual powers, their intermediary role with the society's deities, and their abilities at regulating the cycles of planting, harvesting, and even rainmaking. The leaders of chiefdoms may even be specialists themselves, priests with extraordinary spiritual powers, who were the only people permitted access to certain types of exotic cult objects, certain clothing, and even certain types of food. Chiefdoms, such as those of the Hopewell people of the Midwest, are really a transitional stage between tribal society and the much more organized state societies of the early civilizations.

Figure 17.6 Ramesses II, seated upon a cushioned chair, receives a foreign dignitary. Ramesses II and Queen in Audience, stela from eighteenth dynasty (09.287). Gift of Mrs. Frank E. Peabody. Courtesy of the Museum of Fine Arts, Boston.

The state-organized society.   This stage developed out of the chiefdom. Lineage chieftains enjoyed a social and economic status that relieved them of many of the day-to-day burdens of agriculture or stock breeding. Their authority was based on spiritual and managerial roles bolstered by the wealth of their possessions, visible signs of their immense prestige. A state-organized society, on the other hand, is governed by a full-fledged ruling class, one whose privileges and powers are bolstered by a hierarchical secular and religious bureaucracy; some, at least rudimentary, system of justice; and a system of ranked classes of nobility, warriors, traders, priests, bureaucrats, peasants, and perhaps slaves. The ruler enjoys great wealth and is often regarded as semidivine. Ancient Egyptian pharaohs, for example, were divine monarchs with absolute powers. The ownership of land and the administration of state religion were vested in their hands (Figure 17.6). The pharaohs ruled by centuries of legal precedent, through an elaborate hierarchy of bureaucrats, whose principal officials represented practically hereditary dynasties (Aldred, 1961). Many state societies, such as those of the Maya and the Inca, were organized along rigid lines, with strict classes of nobles, craftsmen, and others. Only the most extraordinary act of military skill or religious devotion would allow a few lucky people entry into the highest classes of society.

When French explorers visited the Natchez people of the Mississippi Valley in the early eighteenth century, they found a state society so rigid that the Great Sun and his noblemen at the pinnacle of Natchez society referred to the commoners as "stinkards" (Swanton, 1911). Yet, all noblemen, even the Great Sun, were required to marry stinkards. Everyone knew exactly where they stood in society, even slaves. State-organized societies were the foundation of the early civilizations of the Near East, China, and the Americas, indeed, they were the precursors of the Classical civilization of Greece and Rome.

SOCIAL ORGANIZATION IN THE ARCHAEOLOGICAL RECORD

The archaeological evidence that bears directly on prehistoric social organization comes from several sources, each of which can give us insights into the general level of social organization of a prehistoric society and into much more specific social details as well.

Burials. Human burials are one important source of information about prehistoric social organization (Brown, 1971). The actual disposal of the corpse is really a minimal part of the entire sequence of mortuary practice within a society. Funerary rites are a ritual of passage, and they are usually reflected not only in the position of the body in the grave but also by the ornaments and grave furniture that accompany it. The contents of a grave, whether spectacular or extremely simple, are useful barometers of social ranking. In some cases, the differing status of burials may indicate that a society was rigidly ranked.

When Leonard Woolley excavated the Early Dynastic royal burials of Ur-of-the-Chaldees in Mesopotamia (Figure 17.7), he found a great cemetery containing 1850 graves (Woolley, 1943). Sixteen of them stood out by virtue of their remarkable grave furniture. The royal tombs were sunk into the earlier levels of the mound, and a sepulchre consisting of several rooms was erected in the middle of a huge pit. The royal corpses were decked out in a cascade of gold and semiprecious stone ornaments; gold and silver ornaments were placed next to the biers; and several attendants were slaughtered to accompany the dead. Once the royal sepulchre was closed, the entire court filed into the grave pit, drank poison, and lay down to die in correct order of protocol. Woolley was able to identify the different rankings of the courtiers from their ornaments. In contrast to all this luxury, the average person was buried in a matting roll or a humble coffin.

Physical anthropologists have just begun to look at groups of skeletons as another means of identifying the family relationships between groups of burials. The minute study of skeletal geography is an approach that is still in its infancy.

Structures.   Evidence of social organization can sometimes be inferred from buildings. Teotihuacán, for example, shows every sign of having been an elaborately planned city, with special precincts for markets and craftspeople, while the houses of the leading priests and nobles were located near the Street of the Dead, a street that bisected the city. In instances like this, it is easy enough to locate the houses belonging to each of the different classes of the society, both by their architecture and the distinctive artifacts found in them.

Some civilizations seem to have regulated the houses occupied by the various classes of society with almost stultifying monotony. A

Figure 17.7   The Royal Cemetery at Ur-of-the-Chaldees, excavated by Leonard Woolley.

classic example is the Harappan civilization of the Indus Valley. Both Harappa and Moenjo-daro were dominated by great citadels, with rectangular grids of monotonous workers' houses surrounding them. Special quarters of the city were reserved for craftspeople and for storage purposes. In these, and many other cases, one can study the relationships between different segments of society by examining the spacing between the different structures within the site.

Artifact Patterning: Houses and Settlement Patterns. Theoretically, at any rate, distinctive artifact patternings within houses, household clusters, and communities should provide data on prehistoric social organization. Few archaeologists have ventured into this difficult research field, partly because no one has yet developed a battery of tested methods for studying and manipulating the many pottery design elements that form the basis of most studies of prehistoric organization.

At issue, too, is the role of the individual potter and artifact user. Can one use artifact styles to identify individual fashions and social groupings in the archaeological record? Some stylistic attributes of basketry or pottery could be the result of individual effort, while others could be the work of a group of craftspeople or a social unit. The study of social organization from artifacts depends on making such distinctions (Hill and Gunn, 1977). It is only recently, however, that archaeologists have confronted the problem in rigorous methodological terms.

James Hill has argued that it should be possible to identify the work of individual craftspeople in some instances, and he has carried out experiments with assemblages of painted pottery from the Southwest. He suggests that there are five areas in which progress can be made:

1. By studying artifact classes closely to see if one can identify the number of people making the objects and calculating the degree of craft specialization. Do we find, for example, a reduction in the number of people making such artifacts throughout time? Does this reflect increased craft specialization? And, by studying the tools, can we identify the individual tasks assigned to specialists within the group?
2. By studying trade and identifying specific artifact classes that were exchanged outside the community. Can we identify objects made by an individual and establish their distribution in space and their maximum concentration at, presumably, the place of manufacture?
3. By examining residence units and pottery styles associated with them in minute detail, as has been done with Southwestern pueblos (Longacre, 1970). If one could identify individual craftspeople, then, perhaps, one could say something about social organization.

4. By examining burials, which are a potential source of information about relationships between individuals and groups of individuals. Graves may be clustered in different places, and can be associated with artifacts found in nearby communities.
5. By finding artifacts made by the same individual in more than one community, we may be able to identify population movements.

This type of research is highly complex, and it involves methodologies that may not even exist yet. The problem is not only the identification of the work of individuals, but also the controlling of the many variables affecting, say, pottery making. As Margaret Ann Hardin has pointed out, variables, such as the choice of paint brush and paint composition, have to be controlled before individual variations can be identified (Hill and Gunn, 1977).

Example: Carter Ranch Pueblo.   The Carter Ranch Pueblo in the Hay Hollow Valley, Arizona, was occupied for a period of 150 years from around A.D. 1050 or 1100. William Longacre was confronted with the problem of untangling five periods of occupation and the contents of 39 rooms and several subterranean ceremonial structures, known as *kivas.* But he wanted to go even further than that; he sought to isolate and explain the social systems of the occupants as a means of achieving a better understanding of their adaptive changes to environmental stress (Longacre, 1970).

Longacre began by setting up a series of testable hypotheses based on the assumption that the occupants of the pueblo had lived according to residence rules that led to related families living in the same place for generations. Thus, he argued, pottery styles would be passed down from mother to daughter within the household. He also assumed that the potsherds found in the rooms were the result of the "patterned behavior" of the occupants. Using 175 design elements identified on more than 6,000 potsherds, he used computer-calculated statistical studies to not only identify groups of elements but also to correlate these groups with occupation floors in the pueblo rooms.

The Carter Ranch rooms fell into two distinct clusters, one at the south end of the Pueblo, and the second associated with a *kiva* at the north end. When a burial area on the east side of the site was subjected to similar analysis, Longacre found that the northern graves contained pottery designs from the northern group, and those at the south end contained designs from the southern rooms. The archaeological evidence, in the form of *kivas,* associated burial practices, and jointly owned storage areas, favored a corporate residential area maintained by a social unit larger than a family.

Longacre found it far harder to identify households, the basic economic and landholding unit in a pueblo. They probably consisted of groups of adjoining rooms that formed residence areas. After lengthy analyses of room contents, Longacre concluded that they had many different functions, ranging from cooking to sleeping and storage, even though different structures had varying purposes—a pattern found in modern pueblo architecture today. As a result, the household unit is hard to delimit at this site, in contrast to settlements where the rooms' activities tend to be more specialized.

The Longacre study has been criticized on the grounds that the research fails to demonstrate the "assymetry between presumed products of the two sexes" (Dumond, 1977). Dumond also feels that Longacre's data patterns reflect variations in occupation during the 150-year life of the site rather than a coincidence of pottery design elements and residence units. (For another example of this type of research, see Hill, 1970.)

The average archaeologist will probably be daunted at the sophisticated statistical methods needed to test archaeological data for its possible social implications. Several of the pioneer studies in this field, regarded as modern classics by many people, have been shown to be inadequate measures of social phenomena (Dumond, 1977). However, relatively simple statistical tests can be used to correlate artifact patternings with sites on the basis of objects whose exact provenance is accurately established.

RELIGION AND RITUAL

An anonymous archaeologist once wrote cynically that "religion is the last resort of troubled excavators." At one time archaeologists tended to ascribe any artifact or structure with even vaguely religious associations to a category broadly named "ritual." There are many famous instances in which the religious associations of an artifact or a structure can be determined readily enough. The Pyramid of the Sun at Teotihuacán is clearly a structure of religious significance; so are the Temple of Amun at Karnak in Egypt and the famous stone circles at Stonehenge in England (Atkinson, 1969; Hawkins, 1965; Thom, 1974). The "Venus" figurines of the European Upper Paleolithic have been widely interpreted as fertility symbols, and later human figures have received similar interpretation; but the ritual associations of such objects are still in doubt (Grasiozi, 1960) (Figure 17.8). The cave art of Altamira and Lascaux has been called a manifestation of "sympathetic hunting

Figure 17.8   A Venus figurine from Dolní Věstonice, Czechoslovakia.

magic" by many observers, and new investigative methods are dealing with this interpretation. (Leroi-Gourhan, 1967; Marshack, 1972). Burial mutilations, oral tradition, and even astronomy have been used to infer religious activities from archaeological data. Mother Goddess cults, Baal-Astarte rituals, and earth worship are only a few of the fascinating manifestations of ritual found in archaeological literature—a delight to the eccentric and entertainment to the serious student of prehistory (Ucko, 1962).

Religion and Burials.   The traditional archaeological evidence for religious rituals has come from burials. The first humans to deliberately bury their dead were the Neanderthal peoples of 70,000 years ago. The bodies of Neanderthal families have been found in French caves, such as La Ferrassie, buried in shallow pits, the skeletons covered with the red ochre powder that was scattered over their corpses. Ralph Solecki found Neanderthal burials in the Shanidar Cave in Iraq. One deformed individual had been killed in a rockfall from the cave roof and was buried with some choice cuts of game meat. Another skeleton was found in association with many pollens of some brightly colored wild flowers and a piney shrub. Perhaps, Solecki felt, this individual was covered with wild flowers before his grave was filled in. "No longer," he wrote, "can we deny the early men the full range of human feelings" (Solecki, 1972).

There are clear signs that highly organized religions were a feature of many of the more complex prehistoric societies. We have only to mention the Chavín and Olmec art styles and religious beliefs that spread so widely in Peru and Mesoamerica just before the emergence of state-organized societies to verify this. Such organized religions can be detected by the patterning of characteristic art objects or other artifacts clearly associated with religious rituals or by the emergence of public temples or ceremonial centers in small villages and towns. The ceremonial centers of the Mesopotamians were towering *ziggurats* that gave rise to the legend of the Tower of Babel, while Maya centers consisted of pyramids and other large structures grouped around huge, open plazas. The ceremonial center became a focus for a group of independent settlements, "the sanctified terrain where were manifested those hierophanies that guaranteed the seasonal renewal of cyclic time, and where the splendor, potency, and wealth of their rulers symbolized the well being of the whole community (Wheatley, 1971). According to Mircea Eliade, the ceremonial center ensured the continuity of cultural traditions; the religious and moral models of society were laid down in sacred canons recited in temples in reassuring chants passed from generation to generation (Eliade, 1954).

The distinctive religious art and architecture of Teotihuacán reflects such a concern with cultural continuity and ritual; so do the cult objects of the Hopewell and the endless religious friezes and inscriptions of the ancient Egyptians. Maya calendars, too, are convincing evidence that the priests of one generation considered it their responsibility to ensure the continuity of religion for future generations.

Religious Systems.   Religious beliefs have often linked large areas of the world into gigantic spheres of common cosmology and ritual practices, even if the many peoples unified under a common religious banner enjoy widely disparate governmental, societal, and economic institutions. One has only to look at the distribution of Christianity and Islam to realize the importance of religion as an integrative force. Yet the many peoples who follow either religion are linked merely by a very generalized common belief, by some religious practices, and perhaps by some shared artistic or architectural traditions. Thousands of prehistoric societies, too, were linked by common beliefs and cosmologies, which are reflected in the archaeological record by common artistic traditions, temple and ceremonial center architecture, wall paintings, and even trade in cult objects. The Adena and Hopewell preoccupation with burial and death spread far beyond the confines of their Illinois and Ohio heartlands. The megalithic (large-stone) monuments of western Europe (Daniel, 1973), Mapungubwe and Zimbabwe in southern Africa, ceremonial centers connected with the Shona peoples—all are archaeological manifestations of widely distributed religious cults and beliefs (Garlake, 1973).

Until recently, religion and ritual have been thought of in isolation, not as an integral part of social organization, economic life, and political systems; but the ideas and beliefs, the core of all religions, are reflected in many aspects of human life, especially in art and architecture. Over the past decade, ethnologist Roy Rappaport has examined this problem of integration (Rappaport, 1968, 1971). His conceptual framework ties religion to other aspects of human life (Figure 17.9). Every society has its own model of how the world is put together, its own ultimate beliefs. An origin myth and other sacred propositions can shape the entire world of a society.

Rappaport argues that these sacred propositions are interpreted for the faithful through a body of theology and rituals associated with it. The rituals are more or less standardized, religious acts often repeated at regular times of the year—harvests, plantings, and other key times. Others are performed when needed: marriages, funerals, and the like. Some societies, such as those of the ancient Egyptians and the Maya, developed regular calendars to time religious events and astronomical cycles. These regular ceremonies performed important functions not only in the integration of society but also in such activities as redistribution of food, population control through infanticide, and dispersing of surplus male cattle in the form of ritually accumulated wealth. Any ritual is, according to Rappaport, designed to produce in the believer a religious experience that reinforces beliefs and ensures the maintenance of belief. Religious experiences are predominantly emotional, often supernatural and awe-inspiring. Each aspect of religion— sacred propositions, ritual, experience—supports the other. A religion will operate through sanctified attitudes, values, and messages, an ethic, as it were, that adds a sacred blessing, derived from the ultimate sacred propositions of the society, to elicit responses that ensure predictable responses from the people. Such predictability, sparked off by directives from some central religious authority, ensures the orderly operation of society. In time, as in Mesopotamia, that authority can become secular as well. The institutions and individuals associated with these messages can become sanctified, for they are associated with the very sacred propositions that lie at the heart of the society's beliefs. As societies became more complex, so did the need for a stable framework to administer the needs of the many increasingly specialized subgroups that made up society as a whole.

By 3000 B.C. in Egypt and Mesopotamia, and between 1150 and 850 B.C. in Mesoamerica, there are signs that administrative authority became more institutionalized, dealing with all manner of social and economic problems, such as new rankings in society (reflected in burials), specialist communities and households of specialists in each village, and an increased need for predictable social behavior and mutual interdependence. It is during these periods that the first of the more elaborate public buildings appear in the Near East and Mexico, temples and monumental works that reflect not only the involvement of individual communities but also that of other villages without ceremonial structures of their own. The emergence of such ceremonial buildings, and presumably, administrative centers had, as we showed earlier, a major effect on the hierarchies and spacing of settlements. So, in a sense, a circular relationship links the ultimate sacred beliefs and rituals of a society with the processes of social and environmental change that act upon them. And the link between administrative policy and belief is in ritual and the sanctified message.

To attempt to detect religion and ritual in the archaeological record without a careful research design is to invite disaster. As has frequently been pointed out, religious beliefs are intangible and survive only in the form of temples, ritual paraphernalia, and art. Viewed in isolation, the study of ancient religion seems a hopeless task, if archaeological finds are the only available source of information. But, if one views

Figure 17.9   The circular relationship between Rappaport's ultimate sacred propositions, ritual, and religious experience. Ritual is also an articulation point between religion and socioenvironmental processes.

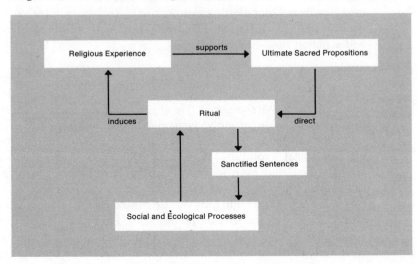

religion and ritual as an integral part of a society closely tied to all other aspects of its activities, then there is some hope that, armed with a theoretical framework, such as that of Rappaport, we may be able to look at ritual and religious artifacts in the context of a society as a whole.

Formative Oaxaca.   The presence or absence of distinctive ritual artifacts or buildings in a site or society may be significant. In Formative Oaxaca, for example, public buildings appear between 1400 and 1150 B.C., many of them oriented eight degrees west of north and built on adobe and earth platforms (Flannery, 1976). Rare conch-shell trumpets and turtle-shell drums traded from the coastal lowlands were apparently used in public ceremonies in such buildings. Clay figurines of dancers wearing costumes and masks that make them look like fantastic creatures and animals, as well as pottery masks are also signs of communal ritual (Figure 17.10). The personal ritual of self-mutilation by bloodletting was widespread in early Mesoamerica. The Spanish described how the Aztec nobles would gash themselves with knives or fish and stingray spines in acts of mutilation that were penances before the gods imposed by religion (Valliant, 1941). A few stingray spines have come from Middle Formative villages, probably traded into the far interior for the specific use of community leaders. Marine fish spines have been found in public buildings, houses, and even in refuse heaps of the Early Formative. Kent Flannery suggests that bloodletting fish spines were kept and used at home and that they were also used in public buildings. The ritual artifacts in the Oaxacan villages enabled Flannery and his colleagues to identify three levels of religious ceremony: personal bloodletting; dances run by sodalities, which cut across household lines; and public rituals in ceremonial buildings, involving a wider region than one village.

The Olmec Religion.   Robert Drennan, in studying the Olmec religion, used Rappaport's scheme to look closely at the role of religion in social change in early Mesoamerica. He argued that the sudden diffusion of the Olmec art style through Mesoamerica resulted from "the increased need for mechanisms of sanctification in various regions owing to internal social evolution" (Drennan, 1976). This diffusion occurred after the exchange networks for handling ritual objects, such as stingray spines, had been in operation for centuries. This interaction between lowlands and highlands was disrupted by the sudden collapse of Olmec society in the first millennium B.C. Drennan looked at the accumulated evidence on settlement patterns, population, and prehistoric agriculture in Olmec country. At the height of their prosperity,

Figure 17.10 Four clay figurines grouped deliberately to form a scene, found buried beneath an Early Formative house at San José Mogote in Oaxaca, Mexico. (No scale given.)

the two great Olmec centers of San Lorenzo and La Venta would have been strong magnets for increased human settlement, for drawing goods and services into the immediate vicinity of the ceremonial center. On the other hand, the outlying villages were dependent on tropical rainforest agriculture, a shifting form of cultivation that tends to make people spread outwards from their home base as their fields become exhausted and new forest is cleared. The land around San Lorenzo may have supported a peak population of some 2500 people living in those villages within 2 to 8 kilometers of each other. This would have left little margin of land to cover fluctuations in productivity caused by flooding and other environmental phenomena. And, if the continued concentration of population and overuse of land continued, the resistance of society as a whole to environmental fluctuations would be drastically reduced. The result could be a process of desanctification, the populace at large being unable to support the burden of a ritual system that regulated the checks and balances of their entire society. A social calamity ensued, one that resulted not only in the collapse of San Lorenzo and La Venta but also of the socioeconomic system and beliefs behind them. Perhaps the reason many of the large Olmec statues at both sites were mutilated is that such disfigurement was the final defiant act of desanctification of the entire belief system upon which the Olmec once thought their very existence depended.

It should be stressed that Drennan's desanctification hypothesis is highly tentative. It does, however, demonstrate the importance of considering religious beliefs and the rituals that go with them as a part of the many complex regulatory mechanisms affecting not only prehistoric societies but our own as well.

The study of prehistoric religion depends heavily on not only the study of sacred artifacts and temples but also on careful research design. The most effective way to study such intangibles as social organization or religious beliefs and rituals is to consider them as integral parts of a society, closely tied to all other aspects of its activities.

Guide to Further Reading

Earle, T. K., and Ericson, J. E., eds. *Exchange Systems in Prehistory.* New York: Academic Press, 1977.
Articles dealing with method and theory in the study of prehistoric trade. For the more advanced reader.

Rappoport, Roy A. *Pigs for the Ancestors.* New Haven: Yale University Press, 1968.
A fascinating study of the role of ritual in the cultural ecology of a New Guinea tribe. Essential reading for anyone interested in ritual as an integral part of a cultural system.

Sabloff, Jeremy A., and Lamberg-Karlovsky, C. C. *Ancient Civilizations and Trade.* Albuquerque: University of New Mexico Press, 1975.
A set of conference papers that covers a wide range of problems in the studying of prehistoric trade. Strong on theory and actual case studies.

Woolley, C. L. *Ur Excavations, vol. 2: The Royal Cemetery.* London and Philadelphia: British Museum and University of Pennsylvania Museum, 1943.
This detailed description of the pre-Dynastic royal cemetery is one of the classics of archaeology and provides fascinating insight into the study of prehistoric social organization.

PART VII

INTERPRETING CULTURE CHANGE IN THE PAST

Is it too late for salvation? If not, please let me have the analytical expertise of the New Archaeology—and the humility and common sense of the Old.

KENT V. FLANNERY
The Early Mesoamerican Village, 1976

It is only in recent years that archaeologists have become preoccupied with not only describing the past but also explaining it. Part VII looks at the explanation of the past from two perspectives: the culture historical perspective, which is an inductive form of archaeological research; and the processual perspective, which is based on deductive research. Neither of these two approaches to archaeological explanation is mutually exclusive. Much processual archaeology, for example, is based on data derived from inductive research.

Part VII shows what an amazing battery of powerful analytical tools are being brought to bear on archaeological interpretation. Archaeology is on the threshold of a quantum jump in analytical sophistication, one in which the work of mathematicians, statisticians, and scientists will play a leading part. As Colin Renfrew (1979) has recently observed, archaeologists are "replacing anecdote by analysis."

CHAPTER 18 ❦

CONSTRUCTING CULTURE HISTORY

Preview

- The study of culture history is based on inductive research methods and on a normative view of culture, which assumes that there are a set of abstract rules that govern what a given culture considers normal behavior.

- The process of constructing culture history begins with the identification of a research area, with reconnaissance and surface survey. These efforts yield at least a tentative chronological sequence for the area, which is based on attributes and artifact types that have been seriated in their correct order. Then, carefully selected excavations are made to test, refine, and expand the sequence. The data are then analyzed and classified. Artifacts and structures are used as sensitive barometers of cultural change; they are divided into complexes, each of which is used to chronicle a particular aspect of technological and cultural change.

- The process of synthesis in culture history is based on the construction of precise chronological sequences. Expanding these chronologies beyond a single site or occupation layer is a cumulative process, in which seriation and cross-dating play key roles.

- A series of arbitrary archaeological units are used to aid in this synthesis. Local chronological sequences lie at the core of all culture historical research. These are based on phases, which are cultural units in a local sequence that possess culture traits sufficient to distinguish them from all other phases. Normally, the boundaries of a phase are set arbitrarily. The term *component* is used to describe a single manifestation of a phase at a single site.

- Archaeological regions are normally defined by natural geographical boundaries, while culture areas are much larger and coincide with major ethnographic culture areas—for example, the Southwest.
- Horizons link together a number of phases in neighboring areas, phases that contain certain rather general cultural patterns, which are often distinguished by characteristic art styles, as, for example, the Chavín of Peru. The term *tradition* is used to describe a long-lasting artifact type—assemblages of tools, architectural styles, and so on—which last for a much longer time than a phase, or even a horizon.
- The interpretation of culture history depends on analogy and descriptive cultural models that are used to identify variables that operate when culture change takes place.
- The commonly accepted models of culture change are: inevitable variation, cultural selection, diffusion, and migration.

In Part II, we discussed how the reconstruction of culture history was a major preoccupation of archaeologists from the early years of this century. Culture history itself is the description of human cultures in the past, and it is based on the chronological and spatial ordering of archaeological data. This approach is an excellent way of describing the past, but it is of much less use for explaining cultural process or the causes of major developments in prehistory. This chapter describes the culture historical approach and some of its limitations.

THE CULTURE HISTORICAL METHOD

The study of culture history is based on two fundamental principles that were enumerated as long ago as the early years of this century by Franz Boas, N. C. Nelson, and A. V. Kidder (Willey and Sabloff, 1975). These principles are: *inductive research methods,* the development of generalizations about a research problem that are based on numerous specific observations (see Chapter 9); and *a normative view of culture,* which is based on the notion that there are a set of abstract rules that govern what the culture considers normal behavior. The normative view is a descriptive approach to culture, one that can be used to describe culture during a single time period or throughout time. Archaeologists base it on the assumption that surviving artifacts, such as potsherds, display stylistic and other changes that represent the changing norms of human behavior throughout time.

Most archaeological interpretation in the New and Old Worlds has been based on normative models. The culture historical approach has resulted in a descriptive outline of prehistory in time and space for much of the world. The interpretation of culture historical data is based on analogies from historical and ethnographic data, using techniques described in Chapter 15. Within its limitations, culture historical reconstruction is a wonderful organizational tool, one that has added some degree of descriptive order to human prehistory.

The Process of Constructing Culture History.   All culture history research is based on inductive methods, which acquire specific data from one or many archaeological sites that are not only accumulated but also subjected to gradual synthesis, a process that leads to generalizations based on the data.

The sequence of research begins with the identification of a research area, with reconnaissance and surface survey. These surveys yield a mass of surface collections, which allow the researcher to develop at least a tentative chronological sequence for the area, one based on attributes and artifact types that are seriated according to the principles outlined in Chapter 12. The research continues with carefully selected excavations that are designed not only to test the validity of the sequence, but to refine and expand it as well. Although the excavations may be concerned, ultimately, with the recovery of structures and village layouts, their primary goals are always stratigraphic—the observation and recording of occupation layers and the development of relative and absolute chronologies. The data from the excavations are then analyzed and classified and used to refine the preliminary classifications and chronologies developed before digging began.

This data base consists not only of artifacts and structures but also of food remains and other information. The process of classification involves the analysis of all these categories of data. Artifacts and structures are the primary concern of culture historians, for they provide a sensitive barometer for studying technological and cultural change throughout time and space. Often, artifacts and structures are divided into a series of *complexes,* chronological subdivisions of different artifact forms, such as stone tools, pottery, bone objects, and so on, each of which can be used to chronicle an aspect of technological and cultural change. Some artifact complexes, such as pottery, are more sensitive than others, and these are the ones that are used for correlating cultural sequences with one another. Archaeologists have developed a series of arbitrary time-space units to aid them in this process.

SYNTHESIS: ARCHAEOLOGICAL UNITS

The basis of all culture historical reconstruction is the precise and carefully described site chronology. The synthesis of these chronologies beyond the confines of a single site or local area involves not only repeating the same descriptive processes at other sites, but also the constant refining of the original cultural sequence from the original excavations. The synthesis is cumulative, for some new excavations may yield cultural materials that are not represented in the early digs. It is here that the techniques of seriation and cross-dating come into play.

The archaeological units used to aid the synthesis form an arbitrary, hierarchical classification for this purpose. They represent the combining of the formal content of a site or sites with its distribution in time and space. For example, three different occupation levels in a Utah cave each have distinctive artifact assemblages that have been sorted into types. Occupation levels at a dozen nearby sites contain examples of these three assemblages. What arbitrary units can we use to help us compare these various sites and occupation levels with their different contents? What arbitrary units will assist us to study cultural change as well? The archaeological units used most widely in the Americas are those developed by Gordon Willey and Philip Phillips (1958), and we describe some of these below.

Phases and Components. The local chronological sequence is what Willey and Phillips call "the very stuff of archaeology," the basis of all culture historical synthesis. Local sequences are based on sites and localities occupied by one or more prehistoric societies. These local sequences may be broken down into two units.

Phases are cultural units in a local sequence that possess culture traits sufficient to distinguish them from all other phases. They are made up of several artifact complexes, each of which may be evolving at a different rate. The boundaries of phases are set arbitrarily; normally, they cover a relatively brief period of time. But, artifacts from the same phase may be found at many sites, not just at one settlement. Wherever they occur, they can be isolated in time; and their spatial distribution, also, can be established within the locality or region where they occur.

Components are single manifestations of a phase at a single site. A single occupation site will consist of a single component, but a settlement occupied at three different times will contain three distinct components. Each may belong to a separate cultural phase. The Koster site in Illinois could be described as an excellent example of a multicomponent site, with its various living surfaces representing different components separated by sterile layers of soil (Struever and Holton, 1979).

Regions and Culture Areas. Culture historical synthesis involves working with much larger areas in time and space than those covered by phases or local sequences. The two major divisions are archaeological regions and culture areas.

Archaeological regions are normally defined by natural geographic boundaries. They may also be defined, however, by a heavy concentration of archaeological sites. Normally, a region will display some cultural homogeneity. Examples are the Santa Barbara channel region and the valley of Oaxaca in Mexico.

Culture areas define much larger tracts of land, and they often coincide with the broad ethnographic culture areas identified by early anthropologists. Many areas tend to coincide with the various physiographic divisions of the world. The southwestern United States is one such area, as it is defined, in part, by its history of research, and in part, by cultural and environmental associations that lasted over 2000 years. Such large areas can be divided into subareas, where differences within the culture of an area are sufficiently distinctive to separate one subarea from another. The Southwest, for example, was divided by Gordon Willey (1966) into the Anasazi, Hohokam, and Mogollon subareas, among others (Figure 18.1). But the term *area* does not imply anything more than a very general and widespread cultural homogeneity. Within any large area, societies will adapt to new circumstances—some evolving more quickly than others—and enjoy quite different economies.

Stages, Periods, Horizons, and Traditions. In Chapter 6 we described the three-age system, an evolutionary framework of cultural stages that still provides a broad framework for Old World prehistory. This evolutionary scheme has no exact counterpart in the Americas, where the

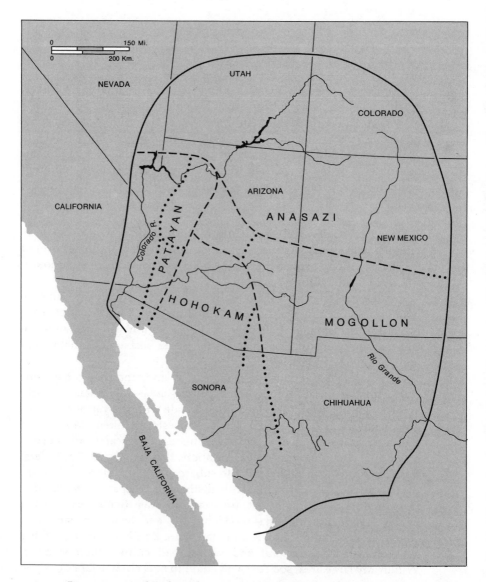

Figure 18.1 Archaeological regions and subareas in the North American Southwest. (After Gordon Willey.)

early archaeologists deliberately avoided evolutionary models. For generations, Old World archaeologists have been filling in details of the three-age framework. The Stone Age, the Bronze Age, and the Iron Age are the broadest of technological stages. All of them are purely arbitrary technological labels, that in no way coincide exactly with any levels of social evolution. Periods, on the other hand, are units of time, during which specific cultural phenomena are observed. For example, the Stone Age is a technological stage that, although it ended in Mesopotamia about 6000 years ago, is still in progress in parts of the Amazon Basin. In contrast, the Inca period in Peru lasted from about A.D. 1200 to 1534.

New World archaeologists have developed two units that synthesize archaeological data over wide areas: horizons and traditions.

Horizons link together a number of phases in neighboring areas, phases that contain certain rather general cultural patterns in common, even if there are major local differences. Horizons are usually distinguished by some specific art style or highly characteristic artifact or set of artifacts widely distributed over a large area at a well-defined period of time. The Chavín art style of coastal Peru, for example, was associated with distinctive religious beliefs and rituals shared by many Peruvian societies between 900 B.C. and 200 B.C. (Willey, 1971). This commonality of belief is manifested in the archaeological record by Chavín art; hence the common use of the term *Chavín horizon* (Figure 18.2).

The term *tradition* has widespread application in archaeology. It is used to describe a long-lasting artifact type, assemblages of tools, architectural styles, economic practices, or art styles that last for a much longer period of time than one phase or even the duration of a horizon. The tool-making tradition, for example, may continue in use while the many cultures that share it develop in entirely different ways. Tradition implies a degree of cultural continuity, even if shifts in cultural adaptation have taken place in the meantime. A good example of such a tradition is the so-called Arctic small-tool tradition of Alaska, which originated at least as early as 4000 B.C. (Dumond, 1977). The small tools made by these hunter-gatherers were so effective that they continued in use until recent times and led to the modern Eskimo cultures of the far north.

INTERPRETATION

The interpretation of culture history depends on analogy and descriptive cultural models, which are used to identify the variables that are in operation when culture change takes place. These models are used to account for changes in the archaeological record. However, this record does not show invariably a smooth and orderly chronicle of culture change. For example, a seriated pottery sequence from six sites may display the sudden arrival of a new ware that is radically different from others in the sequence. An entire new artifact inventory may suddenly appear in components at eight sites, while the toolkits of earlier centuries rapidly vanish. The economy of sites in a local sequence may change completely within fifty years as the plow comes into use in the locality. Such changes are readily observed in the thousands of local sequences found in the archaeological record. But how did these

Figure 18.2   Chavín carving on a pillar in the temple interior at Chavín de Huantar, Peru. The Chavín art style formed one of the bases for identifying the Chavín horizon in Peruvian prehistory.

changes come about? What processes of cultural change were at work to cause major and minor alterations in the archaeological record? A number of models have been formulated to characterize culture change: some of these are cultural models, others noncultural; several involve internal change, others external influence.

Cultural Models.   The commonly accepted models of culture change in archaeology are inevitable variation, cultural selection, and the three classic processes—invention, diffusion, and migration (Trigger, 1968).

Inevitable variation.   This is somewhat similar to the well-known biological phenomenon of genetic drift. As people learn the behavior patterns of their society, inevitably, some minor differences in learned behavior will appear from generation to generation; although minor in themselves, these differences accumulate over a long period of time, especially if the populations are isolated. Today we live in a far more complex society than people did even thirty years ago. The "snow-balling" effect of inevitable variation and slow-moving cultural evolution can be detected in dozens of prehistoric societies, not least among them the Adena and Hopewell cultures of the American Midwest, whose burial customs and religious beliefs gradually assumed a great complexity between 1000 B.C. and the early centuries of the Christian era (Snow, 1976). The story of culture change in prehistory has been one of gradual acceleration in cultural evolution, with an attendant increase in the rate of technological invention, population movements, and the spread of new ideas.

Cultural selection.   This concept is somewhat analogous to that of natural selection in biological evolution. It is the notion that human cultures accept or reject new traits—whether technological, economic, or intangible—on the basis of whether or not they are advantageous to society as a whole. Cultural selection results in cumulative cultural change, and it operates within the prevailing values of the society. This tends to make it harder for a society to accept social change as opposed to technological advance, which is less circumscribed by restrictive values. For example, the emergence of state-organized societies in Mesopotamia and Mexico resulted from centuries of gradual social evolution, where centralized political and religious authority was perceived to be advantageous.

Invention.   The first of the three classic processes that contribute to culture change involves creating a new idea and transforming it—in archaeological contexts—into an artifact or other tangible innovation. Unfortunately, many inventions, such as new religions or ideas, leave little tangible trace in the archaeological record. An invention implies either the modifying of an old idea or series of ideas, or the creation of a completely new concept; it may come about by accident or by intentional research. The atom was split by long and patient investigation, with the ultimate objective of fragmentation; fire was probably the result of an accident. Inventions spread, and if they are sufficiently important, they spread widely and rapidly. The transistor is in almost universal use because it is an effective advance in electronic technology; plows had an equally dramatic effect on agriculture in prehistoric Europe. How inventions spread has been studied extensively by archaeologists and anthropologists, for the quality of inventiveness is an essential part of the human genius, as our society defines it.

Invention can appear in the archaeological record as a radically new product or subsistence strategy. The earliest occurrence of, say, iron-working can be dated to the Mitanni area of Anatolia about 1500 B.C. (Tylecote, 1972). Iron tools appear in the archaeological record of Egypt (Figure 18.3) and temperate Europe much later. We can say that Anatolia was the place where iron was invented, for the earliest dates for iron artifacts occur there.

In the early study of prehistory, people assumed that metallurgy and other major innovations were invented in only one place, a notion that led to the great diffusionist theories of fifty years ago. But as people have come to understand the importance of environment and adaptation in prehistory, they have realized that many inventions have been

Figure 18.3 Iron-bladed dagger of the Egyptian pharaoh Tutankhamun, *ca.* 1340 B.C. This weapon was probably made of native hammered iron. The Egyptians tried, without success, to obtain iron tools from the Hittites after hearing of the revolutionary new metal.

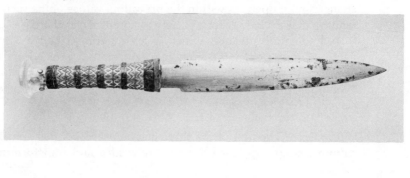

made in several parts of the world, where identical adaptive processes occurred. Agriculture, for example, is known to have developed quite independently in the Near East, Southeast Asia, Mesoamerica, and Peru, quite apart from its supposed origins in Northern China.

Diffusion.   This is defined as the processes by which new ideas or cultural traits spread from one person to another or from one group to another—often, over long distances. Diffusion can proceed through such diverse mechanisms as trade, warfare, frequent visits between neighboring communities, and migrations of entire populations. A key issue here is the formal or informal mechanisms of contact between the members of separate groups that account for the spread and acceptance of a new idea. Rates of diffusion may vary considerably, and the reasons for these variations in speed of transmittal must be understood clearly as part of the interpretation. Traditional interpretations of diffusion have been rather simplistic, as we saw in the work of Grafton Elliot Smith (see Chapter 3), for little attempt was made to understand the mechanisms of diffusion. A clear distinction must be made between the transmittal of abstract ideas, such as religious beliefs, and the diffusion of material goods and their methods of manufacture. A classic example is that of the Hopi Indians, who received American trade goods but retained their own culture, social institutions, and religious beliefs.

Figure 18.4 is a diagram of the spread of a culture trait in space and time. Let us say that a new type of painted clay pot is invented in a single village in A.D. 1400. The advantages of this new pot are such that villagers ten miles away learn about the vessel at a beer party five years later. Within ten years, their potters are making similar receptacles. Within a short time the pot form is found not only in one village but in three within a circle of ten miles. By A.D. 1450, the pot form is so widely used that dozens of villages within a fifty-mile circle of the original settlement are making the same vessels. Plotting this development on paper yields the *cone effect* shown in Figure 18.4; and it is this cone effect that is the principle we apply when we study diffusion.

Several criteria must be satisfied before we can decide whether a series of artifacts in archaeological sites distant from one another are related to each other in a historically meaningful way. First, the traits or objects must be sufficiently similar in design and typological attributes to indicate that they probably have a common origin. Second, it must be shown that the traits did not result from convergent evolution. To do this, the earlier development of the trait, perhaps as general as a

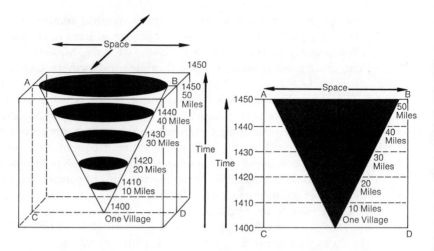

Figure 18.4 The spread of a culture trait in time and space: the *cone effect.*

form of architecture or a domestic animal, must be carefully traced in both cultures. Third, the distributions of the surviving traits must be carefully studied, as well as those of their antecedents. The only acceptable evidence for the diffusion of a trait is a series of sites that show, when plotted on a map, a continuous distribution for the trait or, perhaps, a route along which it spread. Accurate chronological control is essential, with either a time-gradient from either end of the distribution, or one from the middle. In many cases, the archaeological criteria may be difficult to establish; indeed, they are rarely satisfied, but the importance of reliable evidence is obvious. Theoretical speculations are all very well, but they may result in completely false conclusions, sometimes supported by uncritical use of scanty archaeological evidence (Thompson, 1956).

Instances of diffusion in prehistory are legion. There are innumerable cases where ideas or new technologies have spread widely from their place of origin, although none of them are as grandiose as Elliot Smith's schemes or Thor Heyerdahl's attempts to prove that the Egyptians colonized Mesoamerica. A well-documented instance is the religious beliefs of the Adena and Hopewell peoples of the Midwest, who enjoyed a set of beliefs associated with death that spread far beyond the relatively narrow confines of the Midwest. Religious beliefs are expressed in the form of distinctive rituals, which in the case of Adena and Hopewell, involved extensive earthwork and mound building.

Such monuments are found far outside the Adena and Hopewell heartlands, as are the cult objects associated with Hopewell ritual. In the case of the Hopewell, we know that widespread exchange networks carried raw materials and fine cult objects all over the Midwest, as well as further afield (Struever and Houart, 1972) These networks were the means by which religions and rituals and the material culture associated with them were transmitted to other groups. The exchange transactions were probably handled through kin connections that involved individual bonds of friendship between people in different communities. These friendships involved the regular exchange of luxury goods, in situations where the gift could not be refused. These ties not only cemented friendships but aided the process of diffusion as well (Figure 18.5).

The effectiveness of diffusion depends, of course, on the willingness of the receiving society to adopt the new idea or technological artifice. It is here that cultural selection comes into play, as new ideas are assimilated or rejected. (For more examples of diffusion models, see Clarke, 1968.)

Migration. The third classic process involves the movement of populations, both large and small. Migration can be peaceful, or it can be the result of deliberate aggression, resulting in invasion and con-

Figure 18.5 A Hopewell craftsman cut this human hand from a sheet of mica. It was found in an Ohio burial mound with the body of its owner, who lived 370 miles from the nearest mica source. An example of the consequence of diffusion of religious beliefs, this hand probably had powerful shamanistic associations in Hopewell society.

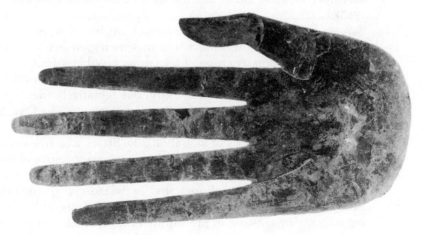

quest. In every case, people make a deliberate decision to expand their sphere of influence into new areas. English settlers moved to the North American continent, taking their own culture and society with them; the Spanish occupied Mexico. Such population movements result not only in a diffusion of ideas but also in a mass shift of people, with wide-ranging social and cultural changes accompanying it.

For migration to be recognized in the archaeological record, one would need to find series of local sequences where the phases show a complete disruption of earlier cultural patterns by an intrusive new phase—not just of one tool type, or even several. Of course, some elements in earlier cultural traditions might survive and become an acculturated part of the peoples' new culture. Perhaps the classic instance of migration in world prehistory is that of the Polynesians, who settled the remote islands of the Pacific by deliberate voyaging from archipelago to archipelago (Bellwood, 1979). In each case, the islands were discovered by an act of deliberate exploration, by voyagers who set out with every intention of returning. Hawaii, Easter Island, and Tahiti were first settled by deliberate colonization, a colonization that was, perforce, a migration of a small number of people to a new, uninhabited land mass. The kind of total population movement, or in some cases, population replacement, that occurs with mass migrations of this type is rare in human prehistory. It will be reflected in the archaeological record either by totally new components and phases of artifacts or by skeletal evidence. When a total replacement is violent, a result of widespread warfare, for instance, the occurrence of such an event must be proved by excavation. It is not sufficient just to find a few skeletons lying in confusion and then to claim that a city was sacked, as Mortimer Wheeler did at Moenjo-daro in the Indus Valley (Wheeler, 1963).

A second type of migration, on a much smaller scale, occurs when a small group of foreigners move into another region and settle there as an organized group. A group of Oaxacans may have done just that at Teotihuacán in the Valley of Mexico (Millon, 1973). They settled in their own special precinct of the city, one tentatively identified by a concentration of Oaxacan potsherds and ornaments. The Oaxacan enclave lasted for centuries.

There are other forms of migration, too. Slaves and artisans wander as unorganized migrants. Artisans are an important source of diffusion of techniques and ideas. This type of unorganized migration is difficult to discern in the form of culture traits, for the individual migrant leaves little behind except, perhaps, some specialist artifacts, as bronzeworking migrant artisans did in prehistoric Europe. Finally, there are great warrior migrations, such as those of the Eastern nomads in temperate Europe and the warlike Nguni tribes of southern Africa (Omer-Cooper, 1966). In both cases, warrior bands swept over an indigenous, sedentary r opulation, causing widespread disruption and population shifts. But, within a few generations the warrior newcomers had adopted the sedentary way of life of their neighbors and were virtually indistinguishable from them. Such migrations leave few traces in archaeological sites.

Noncultural Models.   Cultural change triggered by alterations in the natural environment is an integral part of culture history. The model for this type of change is a simple one. For example, earlier models for the origins of agriculture in the Near East were based on the notion that the climate became progressively drier. Animal and human populations were forced into oases, where people started to domesticate animals and grow wild cereal grasses so that they could survive (Redman, 1978). In other words, climatic changes caused cultural modifications. However, more recent research has shown that, actually, a large number of highly complex variables were involved in the development of food production in this area, environmental change being only one of them.

Of course, human cultures can modify their environments, either accidentally or deliberately. For example, enormous areas of the Sahel regions of the southern Sahara have been stripped of vegetation by the overgrazing of goats and other domestic animals. These areas are now deserts, and the local people are starving, as a result of their long term cultural practices. One should emphasize the words "long term," for such modifications are not simply a phenomenon of recent times.

The most recent research in archaeology has focused heavily on specific details of the relationship between the environment and prehistoric cultures. The complex models that are emerging from this research show that earlier models were far too generalized to explain what are complex and ever-changing environment-culture relationships.

In the final analysis, the reconstruction of culture history is a descriptive process, one that is very difficult and complex and that depends on the availability of large amounts of basic data to be effective. In itself, inductive research of the type involved in culture history takes little account of the role of artifacts in the total cultural system. Thus, the explanation of cultural process requires far more complex models based on a quite different approach to archaeology. These are described in Chapter 20.

Guide to Further Reading

Childe, V. G. *Piecing Together the Past.* London: Routledge and Kegan Paul, 1956.
Although outdated, this is still an eloquent and easy to understand exposition of the basic principles of constructing culture history—European style.

Rouse, Irving. *Introduction to Prehistory: A Systematic Approach.* New York: McGraw-Hill, 1972.
A basic account, which is widely quoted, of archaeological units at the synthetic level.

Willey, Gordon R., and Phillips, Philip. *Method and Theory in American Archaeology.* Chicago: University of Chicago Press, 1958.
I have heard this work described as the culture historian's bible. Certainly, it is a fundamental source on the methods of culture history, which forms part of the training of every professional archaeologist.

CHAPTER 19 ❧

THE STUDY OF CULTURAL PROCESS
PROCESSUAL ARCHAEOLOGY

Preview

- Processual archaeology is based on deductive research methodology that employs formal research design, explicit research hypotheses, and the testing of these against basic data. Its methods are cumulative; that is, synthesized archaeological data is interpreted on the basis of successive generations of working hypotheses that are tested again and again.
- The processual approach is based firmly on culture history and on data obtained from inductive research. The differences between it and the inductive approach lie in the orientation of the research, which is deductive rather than inductive.
- Processual archaeologists who use the deductive nomological approach are committed to a highly formal, scientific methodology that is based on the study of general laws and the work of philosophers of science. They consider the world to be composed of observable phenomena that act in an orderly way. In other words, according to them, the world can be explained by predicting when a set of phenomena that indicate a particular law is in operation occur.
- General laws governing human behavior are derived from anthropology and other social sciences. But many archaeologists reject the assumption that such general laws exist and believe that the highly specific, deductive scientific methods of physics and other sciences

are inappropriate to archaeological data. They do, however, recognize the value of deductive research.

- Most processual archaeology embraces a systems-ecological approach that is concerned with the ways in which cultural systems function, both internally and in relation to external factors, such as the environment. This approach is based on General Systems Theory, cultural ecology, and multilinear cultural evolution.

- The systems approach provides a way of looking at relationships between different traits within a cultural system. In contrast to closed systems, such as a heating thermostat, which is self-regulating, archaeologists deal with open systems that are regulated, at least in part, by external stimuli. In the case of cultural systems, these stimuli are the elements in the environment. The regulatory mechanisms that govern the system maintain it in equilibrium and sometimes trigger further cultural change through positive feedback.

- Cultural ecologists see human cultures as subsystems interacting with other subsystems, all of which are part of a total ecosystem. Under this rubric, human culture is, ecologically speaking, a way in which humans compete successfully with other plants, animals, and human beings.

- Multilinear cultural evolution recognizes that cultural adaptations are complex processes, fine-tuned to local conditions, with long-term cumulative effects. For instance, the four stages of the evolution of social organization described in Chapter 17 are defined in terms of social complexity, subsistence strategy, and population size, among other factors.

- Processual archaeology has proved effective in studying the origins of literate civilization, for explanations for cultural change are now couched in terms of multiple causes rather than single prime movers. The new multicausal models resulting from the systems ecological approach will require the development of new, rigorous methodologies for data collection, comparative studies of cultural variables in the archaeological record, and the tracing of the development of these variables in the millennia immediately preceding the origins of civilization.

- Future research in processual archaeology undoubtedly will make a great deal of use of mathematical models, for biologists and archaeologists are facing the same problem: How do forms, whether living or cultural, emerge and stabilize? The research problems being faced are very complex, and the sciences provide archaeologists with new and sophisticated tools with which to solve them.

Processual archaeology, defined in Chapter 5, is a phenomenon of the 1960s and 1970s that stemmed from the research of W. W. Taylor, Albert Spaulding, and Lewis Binford, among many others (Binford, 1972). It provides a vehicle for a close examination of cultural process and a viable means of searching for explanations of culture change in prehistory (Plog, 1974). This chapter describes some of the applications of processual archaeology.

THE PROCESSUAL APPROACH

Processual archaeology is based on deductive research methodology that employs research design, the formulation of explicit research hypotheses, and the testing of these against basic data. Its methods are cumulative; that is, initial hypotheses are designed that propose a working model to explain culture change. These hypotheses are tested against basic data, and some are discarded, while others are retested again and again, until the factors that affect cultural change are isolated in highly specific terms. The synthesized archaeological data is interpreted on the basis of successive generations of working hypotheses that are tested many times.

The processual approach is firmly based on culture history and data obtained from inductive research. It has to be, for the chronological and spatial frameworks for prehistory come from descriptive methods developed over many years of arduous fieldwork and analysis. The difference between the two approaches lies in the *orientation* of the research. Processual archaeologists rely on deductive strategies that begin with the formulation of testable hypotheses and then proceed to the gathering of data to test them. Very often, however, the initial hypotheses are based on data derived from inductive culture history.

The early days of processual archaeology were marked by furious academic controversy between not only culture historians and those espousing processual methodology but also between proponents of different approaches to the study of cultural process (Flannery, 1973). Two methods are commonly espoused: the deductive nomological approach and the systems-ecological approach.

The Deductive-Nomological Approach.   Archaeologists who use this approach are firmly committed to a highly formal, scientific methodology, which is based on the work of Carl Hempel and other philosophers of science (Watson, Redman, and Le Blanc, 1971). Nomology is the study of general laws; a deductive-nomological approach is based on the philosophy of logical positivism. This philosophy considers the world to be composed of observable phenomena that act in an orderly way. It views the world as being governed by general laws that can be identified through the use of rigorous research methods. In other words, the world can be explained by predicting when a set of phenomena occur that indicate that a particular law is in operation.

In archaeology, these general laws are derived from anthropology and other social sciences. Laws have been formulated about the relationships between human cultures and the environment, about ecological adaptation, and about cultural evolution (Sahlins and Service, 1960). Most of them are so generalized, however, that it is difficult to test them with specific data. Nevertheless, some archaeologists believe that archaeological data can be used to formulate and test hypotheses that serve to identify the general and universal laws that govern cultural process.

At the heart of this approach to processual archaeology is the notion that there actually are general laws that govern human behavior. Proponents of the deductive-nomological approach also assume that formal scientific experiments, which can be repeated and can produce predictable results, can be used to identify instances when a particular law is in operation. Their explanations of cultural change are based on the predictability of these results. In other words, the hypothesis that allows accurate prediction of similar phenomena in one area under the same circumstances elsewhere is the one that can be justified as the best explanation.

Most archaeologists reject the assumption that there are general laws governing human behavior and feel that the highly specific deductive methods applied to physics and other hard sciences are far less applicable to archaeological data, much of which is governed by intangible variables, such as values and beliefs. They believe that deductive research is extremely valuable for study of the past, provided that realistic account is taken of the unique nature of archaeological data.

The Systems-Ecological Approach. The second, and more common, processual approach is concerned with the ways in which cultural systems function, both internally and in relation to external factors, such as the natural environment. It involves three basic models of cultural change: *systems models*, which are based on General Systems Theory; *cultural ecology*, which provides complicated models of the interactions between human cultures and their environments; and *multilinear cultural evolution*, which combines both systems approaches and cultural ecology in a theory of the cumulative evolution of culture over long periods of time through complex adaptations to the environment.

As Kent Flannery pointed out some years ago (1973), archaeologists using these models are intent on "the search for the ways human populations (in their own way) do the things that other systems do." Human cultural behavior displays properties unknown in other living systems. We, as archaeologists, study these peculiarities, using systems, ecological, and evolutionary models to look at how and why cultural systems flourished and survived throughout time. The only way to do this is to examine the many components and dynamic interrelationships that make up human cultural systems.

THE SYSTEMS APPROACH

General systems theory was first developed in the 1950s. It is a body of theoretical concepts that provides a way of searching for "general relationships in the empirical world." By the same token, a system is defined as "a whole which functions as a whole by virtue of the interdependence of its parts" (Rapoport, 1968). Systems theory has been widely applied in physics and other hard sciences, where relationships between different parts of a system can be defined with great precision. It has obvious appeal to archaeologists, for it assumes that any organization, however simple or complex, can be studied as a system of interrelated components (Salmon, 1978). A change in one of these components will trigger reactions in many of the other parts. The notion of cultural systems, which was described in Chapter 5, is derived, in part, from systems theory.

Systems experts distinguish between two general types of system: the closed system and the open system.

Closed systems are self-regulating and operate without any information or instructions from outside. The classic example of this is a household heating and cooling system, which is regulated by the air temperature within the dwelling. A change in temperature triggers the thermostat, which operates the heater or air conditioner. This particular type of system is designed to keep the air temperature at a precise level, and it operates to maintain this steady state. Feedback between the air temperature and the thermostat ensures that equilibrium is maintained.

Open systems are ones that are regulated, at least in part, by external stimuli. This concept is most applicable to human cultures that interact intimately with the natural environment. Human organizations are adaptive systems that can react to their environment in ways that can be favorable to the continued operation of the system; these systems are far from being preprogrammed machines like closed systems are. They achieve their direction not only from preprogrammed instructions, but also from decisions made by their members. When the behavior resulting from these decisions is more adaptive to new conditions, then changes in organization will occur.

The classic, and often quoted, example of an application of an open systems model to an archaeological problem comes from Mesoamerica, where Kent Flannery (1968) studied the ecology of early food production in highland Mexico. He was trying to understand why the population of the southern highlands gave up food gathering and took up agriculture. He began by assuming that the southern highlands and their inhabitants were part of a single, complex open system consisting of many subsystems—economic, botanical, social, and so on—which interacted with one another. Between 8000 and 2000 B.C. the highland peoples used no less than five different food collecting systems, each with its own distinctive artifact technology. These five systems were carefully scheduled to take maximum advantage of the seasonal abundance of different resources in each season. By a combination of scheduling and judicious use of seasonal foods, the people were able to interact with their environment without overexploiting any of their available food sources. Thus, the system as a whole was in equilibrium.

The highland system was maintained in equilibrium by this same careful scheduling and seasonal collecting. These regulatory mechanisms—they were nothing less—are sometimes called *deviation-counteracting processes*, just like the thermostat in the closed system. After 5000 B.C., wild maize cobs found in dry caves ripened with larger cobs, and these were crossed with related wild corn to produce a hybrid species, which was the ancestor of modern domesticated maize. Thus, the people began to experiment with the deliberate planting of foods, and they intentionally expanded the range of their food procurement areas. This triggered a series of *deviation-amplifying processes*, which not only caused a minor alteration in one aspect of the food procurement system, but also eventually led to a whole series of cumulative changes throughout the society, which occurred because of *positive feedback*.

The planting of maize crops upset the annual round, for the new farmers had to spend more time near their gardens during the seasons of planting and harvesting. Their scheduling patterns gradually changed as the more sedentary populations spent more and more time improving their agricultural techniques and crop yields. The positive

feedback resulting from these experiments caused the Indians to develop a self-perpetuating food procurement system with entirely different scheduling demands—those of planting and harvesting. This
system competed with the traditional gathering systems and proved to
be far more effective. By 2000 B.C., then, cumulative deviation-amplifying processes had changed Indian society beyond recognition.

The advantage of the systems approach is that it frees one from
having to look at only one agent of cultural change, such as irrigation or
diffusion; and it allows one to focus attention, instead, on regulatory
mechanisms and on the relationships between different components of
a cultural system and the system as a whole and its environment. But it
must be kept in mind that the data used to test the hypotheses derived
to validate this model is acquired by the same methods used to acquire
culture historical information.

CULTURAL ECOLOGY

As we saw in Chapter 4, processual archaeology relies not only on the
concepts of systems theory but also on the study of cultural ecology
(Nelting, 1977). Cultural ecology is a way of obtaining a total picture of
how human populations adapt to and transform their environments.
These environments include not only the natural landscape but also
vegetational and animal populations as well as other cultures.

This method is being hailed widely as a possible explanation for
many major cultural changes in prehistory. Cultural ecologists see
human cultures as subsystems interacting with other subsystems, all
forming part of a total ecosystem with three major subsystems: human
culture, the biotic community, and the physical environment. Thus the
key to cultural process lies in understanding the interactive relationships between the various subsystems. William Sanders has pointed
out that every biological and physical environment offers problems for
human utilization (Sanders and Price, 1968). Furthermore, the human
response to diverse environments will be different and distinctive.
Although the possibilities for human adaptation to an environment are
almost unlimited, the number of probable adaptations to a specific
environment is limited. Thus, communities with highly differing cultures may occupy the same or similar environments and the level of
technological achievement and effectiveness of the hunting and gathering or food-producing economy involved naturally affects the varied
response in other aspects of culture. Some environments are inherently

less productive than others, a factor that can limit population growth as well as other cultural responses.

The adaptation of any population is achieved primarily by effective subsistence strategies and technological artifices, but social organization and religious beliefs are important in assuring cooperative exploitation of the environment as well as technological cooperation. Religious life provided an integrating force in many societies, not least among them the Maya and Sumerians. Human cultures are as dynamic as all other components of an ecological system, and any human culture can be thought of as what William Sanders and Barbara Price call "a complex of techniques adaptive to the problems of survival in a particular geographical region." Human culture is, ecologically speaking, a way in which humans compete successfully with animals, plants, and other humans. Sanders and Price point out that: "The product of plant and animal evolution is more effective utilization of the landscape in competition with individuals of the same and other species. This effectiveness is usually expressed in population growth, and this growth can therefore be taken as a measure of success in a given area at a given point."

There are obvious difficulties in studying the interactions between people and their environment, especially when preservation conditions limit the artifacts and other data available for study. Fortunately, however, artifacts and other elements of the technological subsystem often survive. Since technology is a primary way in which different cultures adapt to their environment, detailed models of technological subsystems allow archaeologists to obtain a relatively comprehensive picture of the cultural system as a whole. It is in research of this type where the storage capacity of the digital computer has come into play. Cultural ecological studies depend for their effectiveness on enormous quantities of basic data. Once this data is stored on the computer, one can use simulation techniques to model possible cultural outcomes, by inserting hypothetical variables into the surviving cultural system. The techniques used are somewhat like those used for business forecasting, but they are still in a highly experimental stage.

MULTILINEAR CULTURAL EVOLUTION

Anthropologist Julian Steward argued many years ago (1955) that people living in similar environments tend to solve the problem of adaptation in similar ways. This argument led him and others to develop the concept of *multilinear cultural evolution*. This is not the single-line evolutionary theory of the early evolutionists, but rather, a branching, cumulative process, which results from cultural adaptations over long periods of time.

There was a stultifying inevitability about the earlier unilinear theories that put twentieth-century civilization at the pinnacle of human achievement. Multilinear evolutionary theory is far more flexible; it recognizes that there are many different evolutionary tracks, from simple to complex, the differences resulting from individual adaptative solutions (Mill, 1977). Despite these variations, there are some broad evolutionary developmental stages that can be recognized in the world's societies. The four-stage evolutionary classification of bands, tribes, chiefdoms, and state-organized societies was described in Chapter 17 (Service, 1971). These highly flexible stages are defined with reference to social complexity, subsistence strategy, and population size. None of them ar rigidly defined, for multilinear evolutionary theory recognizes that cultural adaptations are complex processes that are fine-tuned to local conditions, with long term, cumulative effects.

Multilinear cultural evolution, then, is the vital integrative force that brings systems theory and cultural ecology together into a closely knit, highly flexible way of studying and explaining cultural process (Sanders and Webster, 1978).

PROCESSUAL ARCHAEOLOGY APPLIED: THE ORIGINS OF LITERATE CIVILIZATION

Theoretical approaches are meaningless unless they are tested against actual field data. The models of processual archaeology have been applied successfully to many small-scale problems, and they have provided new means of studying major developments in world prehistory. The origins of literate civilization in the Near East some 5,000 years ago illustrate the effectiveness of the processual approach very clearly.

Prime Movers.   Early theories on the origins of cities and civilization in the Near East assumed that Sumerian civilization developed as a result of a major invention or technological advance, often called a *prime mover*, which was the ultimate cause of dramatic cultural change. Many people believed, for example, that the development of irrigation, with all its complex administrative problems, caused the growth of early civilization; others believed that population growth was the cause of the major changes in settlement patterns and agriculture that resulted in civilization. Warfare, trade, religious beliefs—all have been claimed as prime movers of early civilization. In truth, however, none of these prime mover hypotheses is adequate to explain the complex cultural changes that preceded the emergence of the first civilizations. As Kent Flannery pointed out, "complex societies are simply not amenable to the simple types of structural, functional, or 'culturological' analyses that anthropologists have traditionally carried out." (Flannery, 1972).

Multicausal Explanations. To replace the prime mover hypotheses, Flannery proposed a many-sided approach to the origins of literate civilization. Instead of prime movers, he argued that there was a "whole series of important variables with complex interrelationships and variations between them." He said that, for example, the behavior of the people living in Mesopotamia at the time when the first city-states were formed was "a point of overlap (or articulation) between a vast number of systems, each of which encompasses both cultural and non-cultural phenomena—often much more of the latter."

Under this rubric, the rise of civilization should be thought of as a series of interacting and cumulative processes, which were triggered by favorable cultural and ecological conditions and which continued to develop cumulatively, as result of continual positive feedback. Just how complex the interactions may have been is shown in Figure 19.1 (Redman, 1978b). The process began with the establishment of agricultural communities in the Mesopotamian delta about 7300 years ago. These settlements triggered three processes that set up critical positive feedback relationships:

1. slow but steady population growth within the delta region
2. increased specialization in food production by different groups within the society
3. a demand for, and acquisition of, raw materials from outside the delta

Each of these processes set off feedback reactions that became more and more complex as time went on. For example, an increase in population led to either more extensive fields or more intensive cultivation of existing acreage. The need for increased agricultural production leads to more centralized planning and administration of irrigation works and other communal food-producing activities. The inhabitants of the delta lived within a restricted area, and as populations rose, were

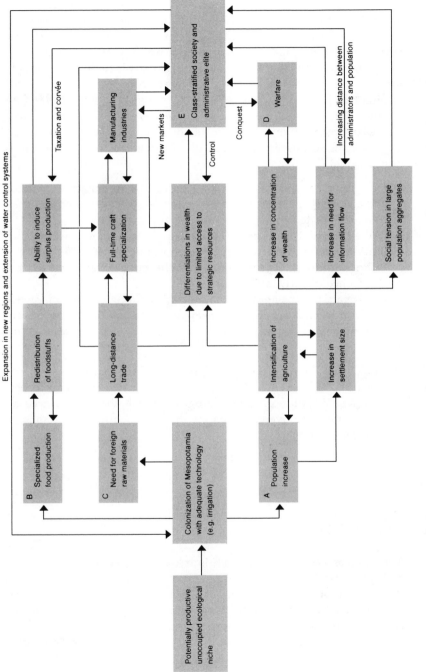

Figure 19.1 A tentative system model that attempts to document the interrelationships between cultural and environmental variables leading to the increasing stratification of class structure in Mesopotamian society between 5000 and 2000 B.C.

forced to live in larger, more densely populated settlements that took up the minimum agricultural land and required extremely intensive exploitation of the closest fields. And finally, an administrative elite that controlled peoples' access to strategic agricultural resources eventually emerged. As Figure 19.1 shows, it is possible to develop a highly complex, multicausal model for the emergence of Mesopotamian civilization that is based on a set of logical, interlocking hypotheses. The problem is to test this model and its many hypotheses in the field.

In a lengthy essay on the origins of civilization, Charles Redman has suggested three possible avenues of research for testing the multicausal model (Redman, 1978b):

1. Develop a rigorous methodology based on quantitative methods and historical analogies for identifying the variables, whether social, economic, or technological, in the archaeological record.
2. Make comparative studies of these variables in regions where civilization emerged and in areas where it did not. This could lead one to an understanding of what were the crucial variables for the emergence of early civilization.
3. Investigate the societies that immediately preceded the emergence of civilization to see if the critical variables identified above were present before civilization, or whether they emerged afterwards.

The acquisition of the data to test even a small proportion of these research topics will require large-scale multidisciplinary research, extensive use of statistical testing and computer simulations, and continued refinement of the systems-ecological models that have served already to show the complex reality that lay behind the origins of civilization.

THE FUTURE: MATHEMATICAL MODELS AND CULTURAL PROCESS

The systems-ecological approach is but the beginning of a new and highly complex period of experimentation with new approaches to the study of cultural process. Some of the most promising and sophisticated models are being derived from cooperation between mathematicians and archaeologists (Renfrew and Cooke, 1979).

Processual archaeologists have long understood that individual human actions and decisions are an important part of human history. But these actions and decisions were made within a framework of checks and balances that were not only cultural and biological but also environmental. They regard the understanding of these frameworks to establish the circumstances under which cultural process takes place as one of their primary tasks. In recent years, mathematicians have developed some approaches and techniques that are very suitable to the study of the evolution and change of structures and frameworks. In many ways, the biologist and the archaeologist are facing the same problem: How do forms, whether living or cultural, emerge and stabilize?

At first glance, the problems of applying mathematical models to archaeology seem daunting (Doran and Hodson, 1975). Few archaeologists have a sophisticated understanding of mathematics, and there is the inevitable feeling that the use of such models will dehumanize archaeology (Renfrew, 1979). There can only be one reply to such suggestions: the problems we are trying to solve are very complex and difficult, and so are the concepts needed to solve them.

Our knowledge of world prehistory grows more complex every day. We can discern some regularities, yet the more general relationships and processes that have led to these regularities are still little understood. "We may glimpse," writes Colin Renfrew, "that there are relationships which may one day find formal expression, just like those of chemistry have done . . . we may aspire to express them by means of the precision and generality of mathematics."

The few general experiments in this fascinating area that have appeared are tantalizing and highly technical contributions that lie beyond the scope of this book, and indeed, the technical competence of many professional archaeologists. But one can predict that future processual archaeologists will rely heavily on mathematical studies of relationships, forms, and processes that enable us to explain how and why human societies have taken the forms and followed the courses they have. (For technical information, read Renfrew and Cooke, 1979.)

Archaeology is becoming an increasingly complex and sophisticated discipline that relies heavily on the sciences. But its reliance on systems models and on highly technical concepts from mathematics and other fields, in no way threatens the magic of human experience or downplays the importance of our beliefs and passions in shaping our destiny. The sciences provide archaeologists interested in explaining our past with new and sophisticated tools of awesome authority and power to do so.

Guide to Further Reading

Binford, Lewis R. *An Archaeological Perspective*. New York: Seminar Press, 1972.
*Binford's autobiographical account of how he developed his ideas on processual ar-
chaeology. Polemical, but essential reading; the volume contains Binford's early papers.*

Clarke, David L. *Analytical Archaeology*. London: Methuen, 1968.
*A massive discussion of processual archaeology written by an archaeologist who many
scholars regarded as as a genius. European orientation, but worth close attention by
the serious student.*

Flannery, Kent V., ed. *The Early Mesoamerican Village*. New York: Academic
Press, 1976.
*The "dialogues" that introduce each paper in this volume on settlement archaeology
are a mine of entertaining, and frank, information on the uses and limitations of
processual archaeology.*

Redman, Charles L., ed. *Research and Theory in Current Archaeology*. New York:
John Wiley Interscience, 1973.
*Useful articles on processual archaeology, especially those by Kent Flannery and Albert
Spaulding, which offer a perceptive critique.*

Watson, Patti Jo; LeBlanc, Steven; and Redman, Charles L. *Explanation in
Archaeology*. New York: Columbia University Press, 1971.
*A basic primer on processual archaeology. Good on the deductive-nomological ap-
proach.*

PART VIII

CULTURAL
RESOURCE
MANAGEMENT

We have now completed our journey through the complexities of contemporary archaeology, a journey that should have given you some insights into the processes of archaeological research.

Our discussion of contemporary archaeology would be incomplete, however, without a discussion of cultural resource management, one of the most pressing and complex aspects of the discipline. A major crisis confronts archaeologists, a crisis of destruction of finite resources. In the two chapters that follow we survey the problems of managing the world's archaeological resources and look at the various ways in which one can become involved in archaeology, both as a pastime and as a professional career.

CHAPTER 20 ✤

MANAGEMENT OF THE PAST

Preview

- This chapter surveys the destruction of archaeological sites in the United States and outlines the history of federal legislation designed to protect antiquities and archaeological sites. One of the key pieces of legislation was the Historic Preservation Act of 1966, which called for a National Register of Historic Places and appropriated funds for state-level planning for inventorying of sites. Another, the Reservoir Salvage Act of 1960, authorized salvage archaeology and led to some valuable large-scale surveys, such as the Navajo Reservoir project.
- The 1960s saw the development of the concept of cultural resource management, overall strategies for conservation priorities and management of a finite resource—the archaeological record. The National Environmental Policy Act of 1969 laid down comprehensive government land-use and resource policies that require environmental impact reports on all federally owned land that was to be developed or modified. Executive Order 11593 brought historians and archaeologists together with the common goal of managing cultural resources and developing long-term goals. These new laws had an immediate effect on archaeology and led to a dramatic expansion of cultural resource management activity on thousands of acres.
- The Archaeological Resources Protection Act of 1979 defines an archaeological resource as any artifact over one century old, but it still

offers very limited protection to antiquities on privately owned land. Despite this, and other laws, archaeology still faces a serious crisis.

• There are important sources of conflict between cultural resource management archaeologists and academic scholars, the former often considering archaeology to be an inductive, rather than a deductive, science. The tendency was to assume that each site threatened with destruction should be investigated and described, on the assumption that it would one day become part of a wider synthesis. Relatively few cultural resource management projects were based on specific research designs, until federal agencies began to take a stronger interest in land-use management, and state historic preservation plans began to take effect.

• As a result of these conflicts, and of the crisis in general, the Society of Professional Archaeologists has developed a set of ethics for people engaged in field research. These guidelines have drawn criticism, especially from people who have failed to realize that archaeology, as an academic discipline, is adapting to completely new conditions; under these conditions, most research in North America is funded as part of a cultural resource management project.

• Archaeologists have an obligation to police unethical operators, to keep charges for contract work within reasonable bounds, and to develop strategies for making the public aware of the importance of cultural resource management and of the results and benefits obtained from it. The Alexandria, Virginia, project is cited as an excellent example of public involvement in archaeology.

• Chapter 20 ends with a detailed examination of the Cache River project in Arkansas, an exemplary cultural resource management project that gives an excellent insight into the processes involved in this important type of archaeological research.

All archaeological excavation is destruction, the destruction of a finite resource. But, while archaeologists themselves have destroyed thousands of sites in the course of their research, far more damage has resulted from looting, treasure hunting, and modern agricultural and industrial activity (Gumerman and Schiffer, 1977; King, Hickman, and Berg, 1977). This chapter looks at ways in which archaeologists have sought to halt the destruction of sites by legislative means and at the practical problems of management of cultural resources.

The inexorable destruction of archaeological sites has accelerated rapidly in the past twenty years. Deep plowing, freeway construction, water control schemes, and unprecedented urban development have all played havoc with the archaeological record. In many areas, the situation has reached crisis proportions. It is estimated, for example, that less than five percent of all archaeological sites in Los Angeles County are still undisturbed. Charles McGimsey (1972) estimated that at least twenty-five percent of the archaeological sites in Arkansas have been destroyed by agricultural and other land use, to say nothing of looters, in the previous ten years. Archaeologists in Britain, worried about the wanton destruction of archaeological sites by industrial development and by treasure hunters using metal detectors, have formed an organization named RESCUE that helps fight to save key sites and to prevent looting (Rahtz, 1974) (Figure 20.1). Perhaps the most famous example of "rescue" archaeology was the international effort, sponsored by UNESCO, that resulted in the moving of the Abu Simbel temples in Egypt from the banks of the Nile behind the Aswan High Dam to a

Figure 20.1   Rescue speaks for itself: "Tomorrow may be too late."

Tomorrow maybe too late.
Rescue

new site clear of the rising waters of Lake Nasser. The Aswan project also resulted in the discovery of hundreds of additional sites in the area to be flooded (Macquilty, 1965).

EARLY ANTIQUITIES LEGISLATION

People have been concerned about the destruction of archaeological sites for a long time. There were loud outcries in 1801 when Lord Elgin removed the stunning marbles that now bear his name from the Parthenon and bore them away to chilly London (Bracken, 1975). When the British built a dam across the Nile at the First Cataract in 1898, they flooded the temples on the island of Philae, one of the most glorious legacies of ancient Egypt (Fagan, 1975). The furious protests of the archaeologists were ignored in the interests of industrial progress. Only now, three-quarters of a century later, are the temples being rescued from the waters of the Nile, with the help of UNESCO. Apart from their enormous historical value, the temples are simply too lucrative a tourist attraction to remain partially submerged.

Archaeological preservation has a long and respectable history in the Americas, too. The earliest proponents of historic preservation included late-nineteenth-century architects, archaeologists, anthropologists, and historians, who realized that a valuable part of America's heritage was slipping away in the face of colonization and vigorous industrial development (Lee, 1970). John Wesley Powell, the famed explorer of the Colorado, and later, director of the newly formed Bureau of American Ethnology attached to the Smithsonian, was one eminent American who spent years organizing the preservation of American Indian artifacts, customs, and languages. An early triumph of archaeological conservation occurred in 1886, when Frederick Putnam of Harvard's Peabody Museum managed to save the Serpent Mound in Ohio, by the simple expedient of buying it with subscriptions contributed by wealthy ladies of Boston and Cambridge (Fagan, 1977). This unique effigy monument (Figure 20.2) was then restored and fenced for posterity.

But even by the 1880s the damage done to America's prehistoric past was incalculable. Thousands of Adena and Hopewell mounds in the Midwest had been quarried away for topsoil or razed to make way for the streets of Cincinnati or other cities. In the Southwest, pioneer farmers, who settled near the same streams as their prehistoric predecessors, soon found that the painted pots and other artifacts from

Figure 20.2   The Great Serpent Mound, Ohio.

abandoned pueblos fetched a ready price in Chicago and other cities. Within a few years the farmers had dug into the Aztec site, Pueblo Bonito, the Mesa Verde region, and other famous sites with abandon, destroying many of the Southwest's most precious cultural resources. So many collectors and pot hunters, many of them actively encouraged by large museums, descended on the Southwest that many sites soon resembled a battleground. The few professional archaeologists working in the region, men such as Edgar Hewitt and Nels Nelson, pooled their efforts and formed an archaeological field school; they lobbied in Washington for the passage of an Antiquities Law to protect at least well-known sites.

The early preservation movement, if one can call it that, although somewhat involved with archaeology, was concerned primarily with historic landmarks, the acquisition of the homes and birthplaces of founding fathers and famous pioneers, and with architectural preservation. The efforts of this loosely knit group of influential citizens and scholars resulted in the passage of the Antiquities Act of 1906, the so-called Lacey Law. This was an important first step, as it extended some measure of protection to America's embattled archaeological sites—though only those on land owned or controlled by the United States government.

By the 1930s, the preservation of America's past had become a far more complex business, one whose thrust was accelerated by the "make-work" programs of the Depression. Hundreds of architects and historians were employed documenting, interpreting, and restoring old buildings, occasionally with the collaboration of archaeologists. The La Purisima mission near Lompoc, California, is an example. Founded in 1813, it remained in active use until 1844, when it gradually went into disuse. During the Depression a team of experts aided by large numbers of Works Progress Administration (WPA) and Civilian Conservation Corps (CCC) laborers descended on the ruined buildings and slowly restored them to a state approaching that of the original mission. La Purisima is now a state park, one that gives the visitor a perception of life at the early Spanish missions. The experts who restored La Purisima spent a great deal of time researching a wide range of topics, from Spanish tile-making methods, adobe brick construction, and ecclesiastical furniture, to archival information on the missionaries themselves. Much of this data has formed the basis for historical preservation in California ever since.

Although some archaeologists were employed in historic preservation, many more became involved in archaeological salvage, excavating sites with WPA labor in river basins and other areas where federal dams were being constructed. The Tennessee Valley Authority (TVA) employed many archaeologists, whose published reports recorded vast quantities of data on site distributions and key cultural sequences before they vanished forever. Some of these publications are now classics of North American archaeology (Thomas and Lewis, 1961; Webb, 1939).

LEGISLATION AND SALVAGE ARCHAEOLOGY

The lobbying efforts of the historic preservationists gave rise to the Historic Sites Act of 1935. This gave the National Park Service a broad mandate to identify, protect, and preserve cultural properties of fundamental importance to Americans *in situ*, such as Gettysburg. The

Historic Sites Act stressed permanent, physical preservation of actual "living" properties. It meant that the federal government acknowledged a broad responsibility for the nation's historic properties (including archaeological sites) both on and off federally owned land. Archaeologists, meanwhile, continued their increasingly deep involvement in salvage, both in reservoir areas and elsewhere. Two Federal Aid to Highway acts (1956 and 1958) authorized use of highway funds for archaeological salvage. In 1960 the Reservoir Salvage Act was passed, directing the Secretary of the Interior to oversee salvage operations in the river basins that were still being flooded with considerable abandon. The funds provided the Secretary never really matched the need, however, and great losses continued to occur.

The Historic Preservation Act of 1966.   Theoretically, the ultimate goal and philosophic assumption of historic preservation is that everything of historical value should be preserved. This is obviously impracticable, so one has to develop strategies that maximize preservation. This is what historical preservationists have done, especially through the Historic Preservation Act of 1966, a complex but carefully assembled piece of legislation that required the federal government to establish a nationwide system for the identification, protection, and rehabilitation of what are commonly called "historic places" (Gumerman and Schiffer, 1977). The Act called for a National Register of Historic Places (a "historic place" could include archaeological sites), and it appropriated funds for historic preservation organizations to carry out surveys and planning in each state. It required federal agencies to protect Register properties when development projects were planned, and it established a National Advisory Council to oversee compliance with this requirement. This was an act that set up a national framework for historic preservation.

The Reservoir Salvage Act of 1960.   In contrast, the Reservoir Salvage Act merely authorized archaeologists to dig and salvage sites that were in immediate danger of destruction. While the Historic Preservation Act was a first attempt at cultural resource management, the Reservoir Salvage Act was merely a "last-ditch" measure. Its enactment did, however, make possible some fairly substantial surveys that were not only valuable salvage operations but useful pieces of archaeological research as well. Salvage archaeology rapidly became a watchcry among archaeologists in the 1960s, as thousands of sites were excavated hastily and then lost in the face of bulldozers and deep plowing. Rough-and-ready methods often had to suffice, for there was little time for sophisticated research designs or leisurely excavation. Such archaeology was—and still is—practiced all over North America, as well as in Britain and Europe. Larger-scale salvage operations have often consisted of wide-ranging surveys yielding considerable information on site distributions, despite the rudimentary character of the research designs. But only a small, arbitrarily selected sample of sites could be excavated—sites chosen in the hope that they were representative of many others (Figure 20.3).

The Navajo Reservoir. One early large-scale salvage operation in North America, in the late fifties, resulted from the construction of the Navajo Reservoir in New Mexico (Dittert, Hester, and Eddy, 1961). The dam was to form a lake thirty-four miles long, which would flood many prehistoric sites. The National Park Service drew up a series of contracts with the School of American Research attached to the University of New Mexico for a salvage survey of the area to be lost. The report on this survey has become a minor classic of salvage archaeology, for many of the survey techniques used by the investigators have been employed since by others. The survey area was divided into nine sections, each of which was investigated on foot and by jeep. A standard site recording form was used, upon which not only details of the sites but also evaluations for salvage purposes were entered; these forms constituted a form of evaluation of the total inventory of sites from the flooded area. A summary report described the various stages of prehistoric culture in the inundated area, inventoried sites and finds, and attempted to relate the area to surrounding regions. But the investigators did not, nor were they asked to, recommend mitigation factors that might lead to the saving of some sites for the future. Neither had they been involved in the planning and siting of this water project when archaeological considerations could have been taken into account. Everyone assumed that the archaeological resources were to be destroyed forever. Interested persons were gratified simply to recover at least some of the archaeological material and information from the endangered area.

Glen Canyon. The archaeologists who surveyed Glen Canyon on the Upper Colorado River in Utah and Arizona before Lake Powell came into being were lucky enough to have considerable time to carry out a salvage survey. Jesse Jennings, who ran the Glen Canyon project in the late 1950s with W. Adams, described the project as a "very special kind of archaeological work," one defined by limitations beyond the archaeologist's control (Jennings, 1966). The entire project was a compromise with time, one in which "total sampling of all cultures, and all

Figure 20.3 Salvage archaeology. Top: In Arkansas, four land-leveling machines work while archaeologists try to salvage the bottoms of trash pits and crushed burials exposed by the machines. Bottom: In California, emergency salvage in the wake of huge machinery recovers only scattered remnants of occupation.

the periods to be found in the area" was essential. Jennings and his colleagues insisted on working on the highlands outside the canyon in order to place their finds in a wider context. They also placed great emphasis on accurate records and publication of results—since no one would be able to check their results in the field later. The Glen Canyon project stands out as a prime example of an early, and relatively effective, form of salvage archaeology on a large scale. But the emphasis was on *recovery* of data, not on *management* of resources.

MANAGING ARCHAEOLOGICAL SITES

The rate of destruction of archaeological sites still accelerated, and it still does, far faster than the expansion of even the most superficial salvage archaeology efforts. By the mid to late 1960s, important historic places were being destroyed faster than they could be placed on the National Register of Historic Places, and the philosophical and practical concept of salvage archaeology was becoming outmoded. The idea of salvage archaeology appealed to archaeologists of what one authority has called the "have trowel, will travel" mentality, people who lived from contract to contract job, working in advance of bulldozers and contractors. The reports from much of this work were so sketchy as to be almost useless. All too frequently, there was no report at all. Clearly, the problem of site destruction had many more dimensions than merely that of salvage. Like the historic preservationists, archaeologists had to think in terms of overall strategies, conservation priorities, and field research designs that ensured a close marriage between the latest methodological and theoretical approaches and practical salvage excavation in the field.

The National Environmental Policy Act of 1969.   The changing attitudes toward historical preservation in the widest sense during the 1960s led to new federal legislation that, again, affected the course of American archaeology radically. The National Environmental Policy Act (NEPA) of 1969 laid down a comprehensive policy for government land use planning and resource management. This act, and accompanying regulations, required federal agencies to consider the environmental, historical, and cultural values to be weighed whenever federally owned land is modified or private land modified with federal funds. The regulations required documented environmental impact statements and reports that considered the impact of any project on the environment, an environment that included archaeological sites. The idea was that information on the nature, extent, and significance of archaeological resources should be inventoried, on the assumption that this information would affect planning of land use in the future. But, while impact reports were required, there was no guarantee that either preservation of a site or measures to mitigate the impact of new land-use projects on the area would be taken.

Executive Order 11593. In 1971, President Nixon issued Executive Order 11593, which helped tie NEPA, the National Historic Preservation Act, and other legislation together into a sensible federal policy on archaeological and historic preservation. The executive order directed all federal agencies to take the lead in historic preservation; they were to study lands under their jurisdiction to locate properties that might qualify for the National Register and nominate them; they were to exercise caution to make sure that such properties were not inadvertently damaged; and they were to develop programs to contribute to the protection of important historic properties on nonfederal lands. By this time, the Advisory Council on Historic Preservation, authorized by the Historic Preservation Act, had become fully operational. At the same time, those programs of the National Park Service that were concerned with historic preservation outside the parks were consolidated, together with the Interagency Archaeological Salvage program, into the Office of Archaeology and Historic Preservation. In addition, each state had begun to develop historic preservation programs of their own, each headed by a state historic preservation officer designated by the governor and partly funded by the National Park Service. Each state's historic preservation office was required to have a professional archaeologist (as well as an architectural historian and an historian) on its staff. Thus, archaeologists and historic preservationists were brought back together after years of division to begin to work toward a common goal—preservation of the nation's historical environment.

The Effects of Legislation. The new laws and programs had an immediate and profound effect on not only salvage archaeology but also on North American archaeology as a whole. NEPA and Executive Order 11593 made it essential for archaeologists to prepare and maintain extremely comprehensive information on archaeological resources on federal, state, and privately owned land that would enable them to assess, often at short notice, the effect of many different projects on these resources. Research strategies to meet the requirements of NEPA alone are still being worked out. Federal agencies are now contracting for archaeological surveys on a scale that has never been undertaken before. Indeed, the major sources of support for North American archaeology in the 1970s were such federal agencies as the Forest Service, the National Park Service, and the Army Corps of Engineers, as well as some private companies that were funding research on a contract basis (Wendorf, 1979).

This dramatic expansion of archaeological effort was hailed by some as the greatest opportunity for scientific advance in archaeology in this century, provided that archaeologists could adjust to the new situation. But others feared that a rapid expansion of survey and contract research would result in catastrophic declines in the quality of field research and research designs. One thing was certain: any archaeological work conducted under the general rubric of cultural resource management must have more sophisticated objectives than merely the production of site distribution maps. Key issues, such as the significance of sites and priorities of preservation and excavation are obviously critical to any research designs for cultural resource management.

Black Mesa.   When the Black Mesa Pipeline Company and the Peabody Coal Company contracted with the archaeologists working on the Black Mesa archaeological project, designed to recover archaeological information on the right-of-way for a coal-slurry pipeline in the area, the immediate concern was the management of resources in the way (Gumerman and Euler, 1976). The 274-mile right-of-way from Black Mesa to Nevada was 50-feet wide, and the survey was coordinated with the two-phase construction schedule. It also covered the proposed construction of truck routes. The affected areas were surveyed by helicopter, and obvious sites were easily spotted. The helicopter landed at each one, and archaeologists George Gumerman and Robert Euler investigated them at once. The company had the option to pay for excavations or to divert the pipeline. In most cases, it was easier to realign the pipeline to avoid the sites. Once the surface survey was complete and the pipeline route settled, the excavation of the trench began. The archaeologists watched the sides of the excavation, which varied in depth from about 6 to 15 feet. A number of sites came to light during digging operations, ones that could not be detected on the surface. By the end of construction, 58 new prehistoric and historic sites, 5 of them burial places, had been located. They ranged from a sheep-herding camp occupied in 1968 to Basketmaker II locations dating from about A.D. 1.

The pipeline survey was only a small part of a much longer-term Black Mesa archaeological project, but it was a salvage project designed with the goals of the multidisciplinary, long-term research being carried out in Black Mesa as a whole very much in mind. Every effort was made to minimize the impact of the pipeline on archaeological resources and to make the survey a significant piece of academic work. In both these goals, the investigators were more than partially successful.

The Archaeological and Historical Preservation Act of 1974.   NEPA and Executive Order 11593 are but a small part of an elaborate framework of laws, regulations, and statutes that the archaeologist concerned with cultural resource management now works with. There are state, county, city, and Indian tribal laws to amplify federal legislation and adapt it to local conditions. Keeping abreast of changes in the laws is itself practically a full-time job.

One final piece of federal legislation in 1974 added a new dimension to NEPA and EO 11593, neither of which provided special funds for preservation or recovery of archaeological and historical resources when these are endangered by federal projects. An amendment to the Reservoir Salvage Act in 1974 (the Archaeological and Historical Preservation Act) authorized federal agencies to provide such funds, either by contract, by allocating up to one percent of the cost of a project to the National Park Service, or by trying to persuade the Service to do the work from its own funds. Most important of all, the 1974 amendment provided funds not only for digging but also for the analysis of finds and the publication of results.

The Archaeological Resources Protection Act of 1979.   The latest piece of federal legislation gives somewhat more stringent protection to archaeological sites on federal lands. Archaeological resources under this act are defined as being at least 100 years old, a serious loophole that affects many historic sites. People removing archaeological materials from federal lands without a valid permit are subject to fines of up to $10,000 and one year in prison, unless the objects removed have a commercial value of more than $5,000, in which case the penalties rise sharply. Fines can reach a level of $100,000 for repeated offenses. The Act bans the assessment of civil penalties on individuals removing arrowheads "located on the surface of the ground," and tightens up much of the earlier legislation. This legislation is aimed at commercial vandals, and as such tightens earlier laws. Unfortunately it offers no protection to archaeological resources on privately owned land.

A CRISIS OF QUALITY

Although a morass of laws and regulations at all levels and a growing body of legal opinions and court decisions provide an elaborate framework for long-term cultural resource management in American archaeology, archaeologists themselves are facing a serious crisis within their discipline (King, 1971; Lipe and Lindsay, 1974). Everyone suddenly wants archaeological surveys completed, often at short notice, and on a scale unthinkable a few years ago. Apart from the fact that pressures for more and more surveys are causing some temporary shortages of archaeologists, the sudden upsurge in contract-supported archaeological research generated by NEPA and other legislation has produced an avalanche of contract reports that are of very poor quality.

The poorly documented salvage archaeology of the 1950s and 1960s has now assumed the dimensions of a small industry, whose products are often worse than useless. In 1975, Michael Schiffer wrote—provocatively—that contract archaeology's record was a dismal one. Moreover, he added, "A glance at the bibliography of any compendium of method and theory will attest to the negligible impact of contract 'research' on modern archaeological thought" (Schiffer and House, 1976). Not all archaeologists agree with him; some claim that the reservoir surveys of the 1950s and 1960s brought many archaeologists to look more closely at prehistoric settlement patterns than before. Much modern interest in research design, too, stems from Lewis Binford's experiences with the Carlyle Reservoir salvage project in Illinois, experiences that led him to formulate explicit statements about research design (Binford, 1964).

But among the worst outcomes of contract archaeology of this period is the fact that some agencies and contractors were quietly accepting second-rate reports and claiming that even minimal surveys were fulfilling both the requirements and the spirit of existing legislation. The situation became so bad that by 1972 federal agencies and such organizations as the Arizona Archaeological Center began to compile official and unofficial guidelines for contract research to ensure that surveys complied with the law.

In 1974, the Society of American Archaeology began to develop proposals for a registry of professional archaeologists and a code of ethics. The Society for Professional Archaeologists was founded in 1976 specifically to handle the registration process, draw up minimal standards, and to enforce, insofar as this is possible, a code of ethics for contract research (McGimsey and Davis, 1977). These developments should mitigate, at least to some extent, the problem of quality. But, in the final analysis, the problem is so large and the amount of activity so intense that the only long-term solution to the crisis of quality lies in a close interrelationship between the goals and research techniques of a sophisticated scientific archaeology, on the one hand, and the realities and demands of cultural resource management and what can loosely be called "contract archaeology," on the other.

Sources of Conflict.   Specifically, the source of conflict between academic, scientific archaeology and the requirements of cultural resource management has been that the latter assumes archaeology to be an inductive science, whereas, in the 1970s, archaeology itself has been increasingly concerned with deductive thinking and hypothesis-testing (Gumerman and Schiffer, 1977).

Certainly, the traditional methods of archaeological research have been inductive ones. That is, they assume that sufficient facts can be collected to eventually provide enough data for synthesis and inference from the data. Thus, as much information as possible should be gathered, subject only to the limitations of time, money, and other constraints. Of course, inductive research is useful, especially in the sort of general exploratory work that is carried out in many large survey areas.

But until recently, the agencies that distributed salvage archaeology funds thought of archaeology purely as an inductive discipline, one quite prepared to undertake piecemeal projects that would dig or survey a particular site or area. The assumption was that each site, excavation, or area survey would eventually—somehow—become part of a grand, final synthesis. In the meantime, all that was needed was an isolated investigation to solve an immediate problem. This type of archaeology was, in fact, attractive to those with some command of excavation techniques, whose final objective was to produce a descriptive site report. The sites, or areas, were preselected by such criteria as imminence of destruction or availability of salvage funds.

The changing direction of archaeology in the 1960s, however, with its emphasis on deductive strategies, took many archaeologists in a new direction, to a viewpoint that excavation and field work were to be carried out only when a specific research hypothesis required testing. In some cases, indeed, such research might not even yield a descriptive report (Binford, 1964). To these archaeologists, salvage archaeology for its own sake was an entirely inconsistent activity, one that simply did not mesh with the specific problem orientation of deductive research. There was a real danger that archaeologists would divide into two camps: those deductive researchers concerned with specific problems, and the majority of technicians, who dug the soil, found artifacts, and wrote the descriptive reports that contracting agencies expected.

Land-Use Management. Fortunately, some contract agencies began to take a broader view of land-use management in the early 1970s. They turned away from piecemeal land use planning to broader regional schemes that regarded all types of natural resources as a total entity, with archaeological sites being but one element in the total resource base. This shift should mean several changes in how contract archaeology is carried out. First, and most important, it should give prospective sites more time. Heretofore, cultural resource management practices have required archaeologists not only to gather data in considerable haste but also to make quick, on-the-spot evaluations of the significance of the sites studied as a basis for justifying their preservation. Needless to say, such evaluations *should* be made on a broad rather than a narrow base: individual sites should be assessed largely by how they relate to regional research problems and also to theoretical issues in archaeology as a whole. Second, this broader management outlook allows archaeological work to be carried out in several stages, as part of an overall research design. In addition, it allows—indeed requires—archaeologists reporting on sites to consider, and include in their recommendations on preservation, elements in the resource base, such as wildlife and wetlands, elements that affect the future of a site area.

Although longer-term thinking and planning is spotty at best in federal agency circles, there is at least a slow movement toward integration of long-term contract archaeology objectives with formal historic preservation plans. But these moves, in turn, create new problems for archaeologists. They, too, must come to agree that the goals and methods of contracted cultural resource management archaeology may be compatible with those of scientific archaeology. They have to develop new, cooperative organizations that work together on long-term planning and that include archaeologists who work on all time periods and come from all manner of theoretical and methodological viewpoints.

State Historic Preservation Plans. One such vehicle for cooperation is the state historic preservation plans called for under the Historic Preservation Act of 1966. Under this act, a state historical preservation officer is responsible for developing a plan to guide the preservation and use of the state's cultural resources. The Secretary of the Interior, in 1976, developed regulations for the formulation of these plans, regulations that call for professional supervision. States are now required to undertake statewide surveys of all kinds of cultural resources (United States Department of the Interior, 1976). The surveys are to include not only nominations for the Register of Historic Places, but also inventories and *predictions* of where cultural properties may exist. The intent is to integrate all types of cultural resource management programs in each state and to assist federal agencies and others in complying with existing and future legislation. Federal agencies have very broad responsibilities for cultural resource management under a new constellation of acts dealing with housing and community development (1974), water pollution (1973), and coastal zone management (1973), among others.

All these new laws, as well as the state historic preservation plans, offer archaeologists unique opportunities to become involved with government in developing and implementing preservation plans, assisting with statewide surveys, and establishing research priorities. Above all, the program as a whole provides an opportunity for most major contract research to be coordinated on much more than a piecemeal basis, something that is long overdue. Whether this theoretical ideal will be achieved depends not only on the Department of the Interior but also on archaeologists themselves.

Problems of Cultural Resource Management.   The problems facing cultural resource management in archaeology revolve around a number of key issues: proper training of archaeologists; an end to haphazard salvage methods; and proper regional planning of both preservation and investigative excavation, when required, against a background of careful assessment of the priorities involved in preservation and destruction. The beginnings of a new era are in sight. But reaction to archaeological preservation on the grounds of both intrinsic value and expense is beginning to surface.

Training and ethics.   Anyone involved professionally in cultural resource management has to receive a thorough training in not only basic archaeological skills but also in methods of legislation, conservation, and administration. Anyone running even a medium-sized project will need management expertise, as well as considerable experience in the morass of regulations that now surround the average CRM contract. A few institutions, noticeably the universities of Arizona and Arkansas, have fully fledged M.A. training programs for this, which are duplicated at other schools across the nation. But, it remains an uncomfortable fact that many of the archaeologists involved in cultural resource management projects have received little or no formal training in anything more than basic archaeological method and theory—and that is simply not enough.

The Society of Professional Archaeologists (SOPA) has drawn up some basic ethical guidelines that focus on the training and qualifications for carrying out cultural resource management. But these ethical guidelines have drawn fire, partly on the grounds that they do not reflect the reality of carrying out archaeology under commercial contract conditions (Fitting and Goodyear 1979). The fact of the matter is that the academic discipline of archaeology is busy adjusting to a completely new environment, one in which most financial support comes from federal and state agencies and private companies involved with projects on federal land (Wendorf, 1979). One authority has estimated that no less than $200,000,000 was spent on archaeology by federal agencies alone in 1978 (King, 1979). What have we to show for the expenditure of this enormous sum?

Results and reactions.   The expenditure of $200 million would be fine, if we had results to show for it. While one can argue that knowledge is intangible, and as such is worth spending money on, one has to show at least something for the money, other than an abundance of technical reports and preserved sites. To begin with, one has to convince people that the sites are worth preserving in the first place. There is a growing concern—and the beginnings of a backlash—over the prohibitive cost of archaeological research. In at least one area of the United States, archaeologists charge a flat $1500 per cubic meter for an excavation. It pays them to excavate sites rather than work out other ways of preserving them. A recent series in the *Kansas City Times* went as far as to charge that archaeology had fallen into the hands of profiteers (King, 1979). Government officials are beginning to talk about an "archaeology problem." The problem has been compounded by the recent formation of the Energy Mobilization Board, which will have the power to waive environmental restrictions altogether if they are perceived to delay an important project. The question of questions that is beginning to be asked can be easily stated: Is the public benefiting in practical ways from the expenditure of such huge sums on archaeology?

The only people who can answer that question are the archaeologists themselves, who have several immediate obligations. The first is to police unethical archaeologists and keep charges for contract work within controlled limits that are realistic and not exorbitant. The second is to develop strategies for making the public aware of the importance of their work (Lipe and Lindsay, 1974). And the third is to see to it that much greater attention is paid to research planning and to the development of carefully formulated research designs before excavation begins.

Public involvement.   The Alexandria Urban Archaeology Project was founded within the city of Alexandria, Virginia, in 1977, with the specific objective of integrating academic and archaeological needs under the auspices of a single organization. The center conceives of itself as having four major activities: research, conservation, interpretation, and education. It has developed a research design for survey and excavation within the city that includes investigation of nineteenth-century ethnic neighborhoods. Sample excavations have been conducted, which are used as a basis for drawing up a data base of archaeologically sensitive areas and to establish conservation priorities. In addition to all this technical activity, the center maintains a museum area, where interested people are trained to assist in archaeological work and the public can learn about Alexandria's past. This closely integrated project is one of the few urban archaeology centers in the United States, and it provides a possible blueprint for great public participation in, and appreciation of, archaeological research (Cressey, 1980).

Research design.   There is no longer any excuse for contract archaeology to fail to use problem-oriented research designs, *provided* the archaeologist is given sufficient lead time to design research. Unfortunately, many agencies still have unrealistic goals and ask the contract archaeologist to locate every site traversed by a power line passage or situated in an area to be flooded by a dam scheme with an unrealistic time deadline. And every day archaeologists sign contracts agreeing to find them in that time frame, apparently without demur. Most such contract requirements are never met—they are impossible in the first place. But, as archaeological studies are increasingly incorporated into long-range planning, archaeologists are given more opportunities to break up contract projects into manageable stages, so that earlier survey stages can feed later ones. This makes larger-scale projects much easier to handle. An initial survey can establish the correct survey methods to be used, find out where the densest concentrations of archaeological sites lie, and work out accurate costs, as well as formulate much more specific research designs for later, more detailed surveys and excavations (Plog, 1978).

Such types of resource management confront any archaeologist with a very difficult set of practical, logistic problems. So many and diverse skills are required of an archaeologist these days that no one scholar can do everything—excavation, bone identification, studying pottery, programming a computer, writing the final report. The days of the Renaissance archaeologist are over. Any large-scale contract archaeology project has to rely on archaeologists with many different skills— theoreticians to put research designs together, with the aid of methodologists and field workers; experts on bone and plant analysis; pottery and computer specialists; and others. Lest this seem like a pipe dream, let us remember that the issue is the survival of a finite cultural resource, not a leisurely research project dealing with one site or some long-term academic problem. Contract projects of any size have to involve several investigators, perhaps even by subcontract; and the collective objective must be to design, execute, and publish a comprehensive research project on a site or area being threatened by immediate or future land modification.

All of this may seem a radical departure from the needs of what used to be called salvage archaeology. But, while the archaeologist's approach to the problem of site destruction may have changed, the fundamental issue has not: archaeological resources are finite ones that can never be replaced. The archaeological record, however much endangered, can be exploited only within the context of properly planned and executed research designs.

CASE STUDY: THE CACHE RIVER PROJECT

It is difficult to choose between examples of sound contract archaeology to illustrate the ways in which large-scale projects of this nature can be executed. But we make no apologies for dwelling at length on the Cache River Basin archaeological project, for it represents an excellent example of a long-term project with sound research strategies (Schiffer and House, 1977).

The Cache River Basin lies in northeast Arkansas and covers an area some 2,018 square miles in extent, most of it in the Mississippi alluvial valley. Its alluvial soils are used for growing soybeans and other cereal crops. In recent years, increased agricultural activity has resulted in the clearance of hundreds of acres of woodland from marginal soils. These, like the rest of the basin, are liable to periodic flooding. For over thirty years the Army Corps of Engineers studied these inundation problems. Then, in 1972, they submitted a seventeen-page environmental impact statement for the basin, as grounds for implementing a twenty-year channelization project on the river (Figure 20.4). One long-term consequence of this project would have been the clearance of several thousands of acres of woodland for conversion to agricultural use. Not only would wildlife and wetlands have been affected, but many archaeological sites as well. Hundreds of sites were in imminent danger of destruction by the canal project, the proposed land clearance, and the intensification of agriculture on already cleared land.

After prolonged hearings and a successful suit by the Environmental Defense Fund, the Corps of Engineers was ordered to stop construction work and to submit a new environmental impact statement that would meet NEPA requirements.

Archaeology was completely neglected in the original 1972 statement, but the new report had to contain comprehensive archaeological coverage. The corps signed a contract with the Arkansas Archaeological Survey in 1973 for an archaeological inventory and reconnaissance of the Cache River Basin. This contract, highly specific in its requirements, was funded to the tune of $48,000. A precise and specific report was required in just over a year. The contract called for an inventory of archaeological resources, an assessment of their relative significance, and an estimate of probable future changes affecting these resources if the project did go ahead. The archaeologists were asked to determine the effects of alternative, specified improvement plans and to provide a basis for planning conservation measures.

The Contract and Preliminary Survey.   The contract was even more specific about the stages of archaeological research to be conducted. First, the archaeologists were to use existing records as much as possible to cover the whole drainage basin; then, reconnaissance was to be made to supplement existing data. The third stage was to be a comprehensive inventory of a direct impact zone along the routes of the proposed Army Corps channel, extending for an average of 1000 feet on either side of the proposed channel routes. The contract even specified the actual lower reaches of the alluvial plain, where construction was to resume, which were to receive the most attention. This was a far cry from a generalized directive to "find all the sites in the area" of many equivalent projects.

A preliminary survey of the lower reaches of the basin, designed as a basis for an interim report requested by the corps for September 1973, was completed by archaeologist John House in June and July. At the outset, no fewer than 546 archaeological sites had been known in the Cache River Basin. This prior information was now combined with the preliminary survey results to design a multistage program of further archaeological survey and testing. The preliminary survey showed that a comprehensive inventory of sites in the direct impact zone on either side of the proposed channel was neither feasible nor, indeed, necessary to provide the corps with information for assessing the archaeological resources at this planning level. Instead, Michael Schiffer, John House, and other colleagues designed a two-part sampling survey. The first element in the survey was a 12.5 percent stratified random sample of the direct impact zone; the second was a stratified random transect survey of the Cache River Basin as a whole (see Figure 20.4). This research strategy enabled completion of a relatively reliable survey of the direct impact zone. Because of time constraints, only two transects of the rest of the basin were completed. But they both yielded valuable information for supplementing the data from prior survey records and from the direct impact zone survey.

Research Designs, Sampling, and Excavation.   The June–July survey and the carefully controlled surface collections that came from the sites located during fieldwork were used to write a preliminary report for the corps. Three months were then spent reviewing previous archaeological surveys and contract research elsewhere, in attempts to define the research designs more specifically. Then, in December 1973, a two-week survey in the northern part of the basin was used to test the range of site density in the basin, to try out record forms developed for the survey, and to check other classification systems before beginning the intensive survey work of the remaining six months of the project. The two-week survey yielded thirty-four sites, all within the direct impact zone along a four-mile stretch of the river channel. This was a density several times greater than that of the lower end of the basin. Furthermore, much more of the survey area was accessible than that further downstream.

The logistics were now obvious. A comprehensive survey of the entire direct impact zone of 65–67 square miles was impossible. Indeed, Schiffer and House estimated that it would take about five years and $150,000 to carry out such a survey, more than three times the budget available. Since there was good reason to believe that the Corps of Engineers would permit further work in the future, the best approach was to use random sampling techniques. These would allow reliable sampling of 12.5 percent of the direct impact zone and permit at least some prediction of the impact of the corps project on site densities. The sample figure of 12.5 percent was reached by randomly selecting one three-mile-long unit from each 24-mile-long "stratum"

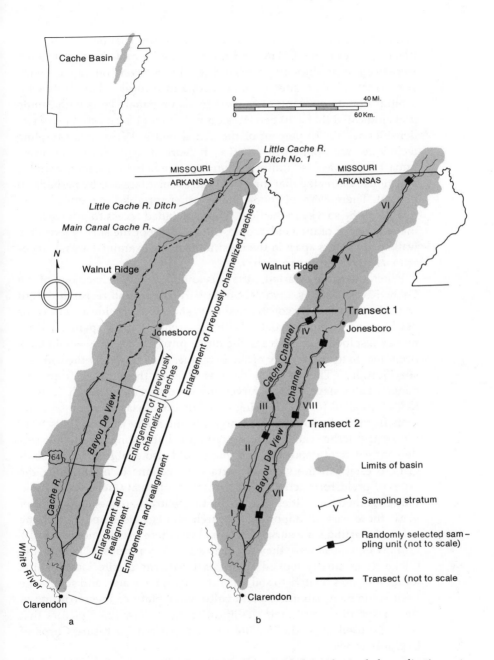

Figure 20.4   The Cache River Basin Project: (a) the authorized channelization outline; (b) the sampling design.

of the direct impact zones on either side of the channels. Nine such units were examined. The preliminary results and existing records were used to produce an artificial direct impact zone on paper, which was "stocked" with sites from surveys and records. Then, tests with arbitrary random sample sites were made on paper. Tests with 3-mile units indicated that a 10 percent sample would give an estimate of site densities within 10 percent of the actual figure. When this sampling technique was applied in practice, it worked well. Since the direct impact zone was less uniform than that predicted on paper, Schiffer and House estimated that their final site estimate was off by perhaps 20 percent. There were, of course, many other variables that affected the quality of the survey in the field. These included access to private land, the experience of the field people, the intensity of the survey (workers walked 60 meters apart in the most intensively examined areas), vegetational cover, and map accuracy.

When the survey started, little was known of the archaeology of the Cache River Basin as a whole. So, in part, the overall research design was set up in a loosely constructed way, simply to provide a context for newly acquired survey data. Had the archaeologists spent all their money just looking for sites in the direct impact zone, they would have been unable to answer any of the data questions posed by the contract specifications. The research designs steered them away from this danger. Later stages of the survey involved specific research designs, too. One called for the devising of a functional classification of stone tools from the basin, mainly to organize the many isolated finds from the area. Another called for a design aimed at testing an Archaic settlement pattern hypothesis, one that would also enable the archaeologists to establish the value of surface collections in establishing the types of prehistoric activity that had taken place at Cache River Basin hunter-gatherer localities. And, from the contract archaeology point of view, there was an important research strategy designed to test the value of existing state survey records. Was there bias in older records? Of how much use were they for contract survey purposes? Finally, the Cache River survey looked at the past patterns of site location—the location of sites relative to soil types, topography, water, and so on—the basic settlement patterns behind cultural adaptation. The recording of such associations and their classification might provide a picture that could be used in predicting site location patterns in future Corps of Engineer projects.

During March 1974, six Cache Basin sites were excavated, with specific objectives in mind. These were: to assess the amount of information potentially recoverable from shallow sites under cultivation, to test the "principles by which inferences about the extent and contents of a site were made from surface observations during the archaeological survey," and to test the feasibility of future pollen analysis research in the basin. It should be noted that these excavations were conducted as part of the overall research designs and to answer specific questions—not just to see at random what was there.

Final Report and Mitigation Recommendations.   The final report on the Cache River survey used the results of the archaeological work to show that the dragline and bulldozer operations needed to channelize the river would damage many sites and render many others inaccessible. And the numerous ancillary construction operations—road making, bridge building, and so on—would destroy many sites as well. Then, the archaeologists made recommendations regarding "mitigation" efforts to minimize the impact of Cache River channel operations on the archaeological record. They recommended close and highly specific cooperation between archaeologists and the Corps during the final two years of planning, when the channel routes were being finalized immediately before construction. They also recommended a future, two-phase program of intensive archaeological survey to minimize the destruction. This was to consist of a surface reconnaissance in advance of construction to act as a basis for decisions about location of construction activities and actual monitoring of the direct impact zone during construction, so that unexpected finds could be recorded and preserved. This called for close vigilance over construction to recover sites buried in alluvial silt, whose existence could not be detected on the surface. Since this salvage excavation might be needed, the archaeologists recommended building flexibility into the construction schedule to enable such digs to take place.

The archaeologists were concerned, too, about longer-term destruction, that resulting from the intensified agricultural activities that would flow from the completed channel project. They recommended the purchase of representative sites to be saved, sites of all time periods and functional types. These sites should be drawn from the data bank of known locations and from new ones found during future land clearance. This recommendation called for consultation with archaeologists over said purchases, for education of the public by the Corps as to the significance of the preserved sites, and for close coordination with wildlife and recreation needs when purchase was considered. This particular recommendation called for a remarkable change in the ways in which archaeologists look at their data. It called for precisely drawn decisions on an active "bank" of sites, where certain localities could be preserved intact for posterity, others destroyed. A classic confrontation with a finite resource was involved.

A final mitigation measure called for a long-term, multidisciplinary research project to be coordinated closely with every planning and construction phase of the Cache River Basin project. The recommendation noted there was sufficient time for a large-scale, long-term investigation of human occupation in the Cache River Basin from *ca.* 12,000 B.C. to the present. The proposed project should be conducted on a broadly based format that drew heavily on experts in many fields. Both survey and excavation would be undertaken, some of it outside the geographic confines of the Cache River Basin. It is in this way, argued the archaeologists, that the significance of the archaeological resources of the Cache River could be placed in their true, meaningful, historical context. And this is part of what cultural resource management is all about.

Conservation of a Finite Resource.   Does the Cache River survey, for all its admirable archaeology, comply with existing law? It is probably too early to say, given both the fast-moving legislative picture and the relative inexperience of both federal agencies and archaeologists in dealing with cultural resource management. But Cache River certainly serves as an admirable example of a thoughtful and well-executed contract survey for future archaeologists to build on.

In addition, the Cache River project is an example of the distinction that can be made between emergency excavation and more leisurely salvage, when longer-term construction work is threatened. But the issue goes deeper than the notion that a site should be dug if it is threatened. Archaeology now involves conservation of a finite resource, where every planned excavation or construction project causes us to draw on a "bank account" of precious sites, an account that is not ours alone to deplete but the property of future generations of archaeologists as well. It must be archaeologists who recommend which *managed* archaeological resources are preserved intact, and which excavated.

All archaeologists are managers of a finite resource, which is banked in various ways—in the ground, within the pages of a report, or by finds and records in a museum storeroom. The problem of cultural resource management can be described as *the* central issue in contemporary archaeology and one that will never disappear—unless, of course, we succeed in leading archaeology down the easy pathway to extinction.

Guide to Further Reading

Cultural resource management has yet to generate an extensive methodological and theoretical literature, and many of the best field projects are still not yet widely available. The following are some of the key volumes to start with.

Gumerman, George J., and Schiffer, Michael, eds. *Conservation Archaeology.* New York: Academic Press, 1977.
Basic essays of variable quality on the beginning of the art. Some very useful case studies and theoretical arguments are included.

King, T. F.; Hickman, Patricia P.; and Berg, Gary, eds. *Anthropology in Historic Preservation: Caring for Culture's Clutter.* New York: Academic Press, 1977.
More articles on the state of the art, with both case study and theoretical orientation.

McGimsey, Charles. *Public Archaeology.* New York: Seminar Press, 1972.
An eloquent essay drawing attention to the destruction of sites, with hard data from Arkansas. A landmark book.

McGimsey, Charles, and Davis, Hester, eds. *The Management of Archaeological Resources.* Washington, D.C.: National Park Service, 1977.
Proceedings of a conference on various aspects of cultural resource management and public archaeology. Useful essays to read as a starting point.

CHAPTER 21 ❦

ARCHAEOLOGY
AND YOU

Preview

- Career opportunities for professional archaeologists can be found in universities, colleges, museums, and government service, both in the United States and overseas. Most archaeological jobs require a minimum of an M.A., and very often, a Ph.D.
- Do not consider becoming a professional archaeologist unless you have an above-average academic record, some field experience, strong support from your professors, and a moral commitment not to collect artifacts for profit.
- Even people who have no intention of becoming professional archaeologists can gain digging experience by attending a field school or by digging overseas.
- Archaeology can give you insight into the past and the potential for involvement as an informed layperson. It will also enable you to enjoy the major archaeological sites of the world in a unique way and to aid in archaeologists' attempts to preserve the past.
- All of us have ethical responsibilities to the past: *not to collect artifacts;* to report new finds; and to obey federal, state, and tribal laws that protect archaeological sites. Unless all of us take our responsibility to the past seriously, the past has no future.

W̲e have two final questions to answer: How can I become an archaeologist? Even if I do not become one, what are my responsibilities as an informed citizen?

ARCHAEOLOGY AS A PROFESSION

Professional archaeologists are much more commonplace than they were even a generation ago. This is mostly because there are many more different career tracks within the discipline. Most American archaeologists teach in universities and colleges and some teach in high schools. Others head archaeology departments of national, city, state, or local museums all over the country, or direct state archaeological surveys. Still other archaeologists work for the National Park Service and other federal agencies; support themselves by part-time teaching; undertake contract work on federal projects; or work for companies seeking cultural resource management services. The research interests of these archaeologists range from early Indian Plains settlements to historical sites in New England, from theoretical models of early agriculture to computer simulation. A considerable number of America's archaeologists work overseas—in Africa, Europe, Mesoamerica, Peru, and even farther afield.

But, a word of warning! Jobs in archaeology, except those involved in cultural resource management, are often hard to come by, even with a doctoral degree.

Qualifications.   Most archaeological jobs, whether in a college, museum, or university require a minimum of an M.A. degree, but most often, a Ph.D. is needed. The doctorate is a research degree that requires comprehensive seminar, course, and field training in graduate school followed by a period of intensive field work that, in written form, constitutes the Ph.D. thesis. The average doctoral program takes between four and seven years to complete. The M.A. degree is normally completed in one or two years and gives you broad, general training in the basic methods and theory of archaeology and world prehistory. In addition to this general knowledge, you will specialize in a local area or in cultural resource management. You may have to write a library thesis and obtain some digging experience as well. The M.A. qualifies you to teach at two-year colleges and some state universities. Although it does not give you as much access to research funds and opportunities as a Ph.D., you can do invaluable work in cultural resource management or local archaeology.

Do *not* consider becoming a professional archaeologist unless you have the following qualifications:

1. A well above-average academic record with in-depth coverage of anthropology and archaeology. An A— grade point average is a minimal requirement for good graduate schools.
2. Some field experience on a dig or survey.

3. Strong and *meaningful* support from at least two qualified archaeologists, who are able to write letters for you.
4. A strong motivation to become an archaeologist, and for the Ph.D., a specific research interest.
5. The type of personality that thrives on hard work and some discomfort, a mass of detail, and long hours of routine laboratory work.
6. The ability to face up to a very tight employment situation.
7. An interest in teaching.
8. A moral commitment not to collect artifacts for profit or personal gratification.

Gaining Digging Experience.   Many people want to gain some digging experience, whether or not they intend to go to graduate school. The best way to learn is to take a course in field methods and then volunteer to dig for a period of time on a summer excavation. Details of these excavations are normally posted on anthropology department bulletin boards or at local museums. Some people elect to go on a university-sponsored field school and to obtain academic credit for their work. Many such schools are designed mainly for graduate students, but again, you should consult your own department. General field schools, like the Koster dig in Illinois, are worthwhile because they combine excavation, laboratory analysis, and academic instruction into one intensive experience. And, the camaraderie among the participants of such digs can be a memorable experience.

Some people venture farther afield and join an excavation overseas for several weeks. By contacting such organizations as the Council for British Archaeology in London, it is possible to obtain details of excavations in progress where volunteers are needed. (Very few digs, either in this country or overseas, pay you to be an excavator.) At the other end of the spectrum, there are package travel tours that take students to such places as Israel to dig and learn archaeology under close supervision. These tend to be expensive experiences, often of variable academic quality. Whatever type of dig you choose, an excavation experience is a good way of testing out your commitment to archaeology.

What an Undergraduate Degree Gives You.   It is possible to get a low-level job in archaeology with a B.A., a job, either as a fieldworker or a laboratory assistant. However, you will probably need further qualifications at some point, and it is best to acquire these as soon as possible.

Most people who take a B.A. with a major in or emphasis on archaeology never become professionals. But nevertheless, they can enjoy the achievements and perspectives derived from archaeology for the rest of their lives. There are many ways to enjoy archaeology as a lay person. You can join a local archaeological society, participate in excavations and volunteer museum programs, and keep an eye on endangered sites in your neighborhood. Your background in archaeology will enable you to visit famous sites all over the world as an informed observer and to enjoy the achievements of prehistoric peoples to the fullest extent. Only last week, I received a postcard mailed from Stonehenge from a former student. "Thank you for introducing me to archaeology," it read. "I enjoyed Stonehenge so much more after having taken your course." His postcard made my day, for in the final analysis, archaeology cannot survive without the involvement and interest of many more people than just professional archaeologists. And, as an interested lay person, you have responsibilities.

WHAT ARE OUR RESPONSIBILITIES TO THE PAST?

Professional archaeologists have ethical responsibilities as members of a demanding profession. But everyone interested in and concerned about archaeology has responsibilities, too. The world's archaeological sites are under attack from many sources: from industrial development, mining, and agriculture, as well as from treasure hunters, collectors, and professional tomb robbers. In these inflated times, even modest antiquities fetch high prices on the antiquarian market. No government on earth can hope to free the necessary funds to protect its antiquities adequately. And countries like Egypt, Guatemala, and Mexico, with rich archaeological heritages, have almost overwhelming problems protecting even their well-known sites. As long as there is a demand for antiquities among collectors and we maintain our materialist values about personal possessions, the destruction of archaeological sites will continue unabated. Even the necessary legal controls to prevent the destruction of archaeological sites are just barely in place in most parts of the world.

Yet, there is still hope, hope that stems from the enormous numbers of informed people who have gained an interest in archaeology from university and college courses or from chance encounters with archaeologists or the prehistoric past. If sufficient numbers of lay people can influence public behavior and attitudes toward archaeological sites and the morality of collecting, then there is still hope that our descendants will have archaeological sites to study and enjoy.

Is there a future for the past? Yes, but only if *we all* help, not only by influencing other people's attitudes toward archaeology, but also by obeying the following simple code of ethics:

1. To treat all archaeological sites and artifacts as a finite resource.
2. Never to dig an archaeological site.
3. Never to collect artifacts for ourselves or to buy and sell them for personal gain.
4. To adhere to all federal, state, local, or tribal laws that affect the archaeological record.
5. To report all accidental archaeological discoveries.
6. To avoid disturbing any archaeological site, and to respect the sanctity of Indian burial sites.

Some Useful Addresses

Here are three addresses from which you can obtain information about archaeological activities and excavations that need volunteers:

> Archaeological Institute of America
> 53 Park Place
> New York, New York 10007

Members receive the journal *Archaeology*.

> Society for American Archaeology
> 1703 New Hampshire Avenue NW
> Washington, D.C. 20009

Members receive *American Antiquity*, a more technical journal.

For excavation opportunities overseas, contact:

> The Council for British Archaeology
> 112 Kennington Road
> London SE11 6RE
> England

This admirable organization publishes a monthly *Calendar of Excavations*, which you can obtain by airmail subscription. It contains complete details of volunteer excavations in Britain, and sometimes, in other parts of the world.

Information on Archaeological Field Schools can be obtained from fliers that are posted on university department bulletin boards.

SUGGESTED READINGS ✻
IN WORLD ARCHAEOLOGY

The bibliography of world prehistory is enormous and highly confusing. The list of books that follows is designed as the most superficial of guides.

World Prehistories

Grahame Clark's *World Prehistory* (Cambridge University Press: New York, 3rd ed., 1978), is the pioneer work that emphasizes Europe and the Near East. Brian M. Fagan, *People of the Earth* (Little, Brown: Boston, 1980), is widely used in introductory courses. Try also: Robert Wenke, *Patterns in Prehistory* (Oxford University Press, New York, 1980)

Popular Archaeologies

There are surprisingly few popular accounts of archaeological discoveries, but the most famous of all must be C. W. Ceram, *Gods, Graves and Scholars* (Alfred A. Knopf: New York, 1953). The same author's *The First American* (Harcourt Brace: New York, 1971), is widely read. For the earliest humans, John Pfeiffer, *The Emergence of Man* (Harper and Row: New York, 1978), is articulate and fascinating. See, also, Brian M. Fagan, *The Quest for the Past* (Addison-Wesley: Reading, Mass.; 1978). The Time/Life series of books on archaeology are justly famous and are especially suitable for beginners.

Africa

The ancient Egyptians are well described by Paul Johnson, *The Civilization of Ancient Egypt* (Weidenfeld and Nicholson: London 1978). J. Desmond Clark's *Prehistory of Africa* (Praeger: New York, 1970), is a summary account of the whole span of African prehistory. Roland Oliver and Brian M. Fagan, *Africa During the Iron Age* (Cambridge University Press: New York, 1975), covers the later centuries of African prehistory, while the history of Africa is well synthesized by Roland Oliver and John Fage, *A Short History of Africa* (Pelican Books: Baltimore, 1963).

Australia

Derek J. Mulvaney, *The Prehistory of Australia* (Pelican Books: Baltimore, 1977), is recognized as the fundamental source.

China

Kwang-Chih Chang, *The Archaeology of Ancient China* (Yale University Press: New Haven, 3rd ed., 1977), is a mine of detailed information, while W. Watson, *China* (Praeger: New York, 1959), deals mainly with the later periods.

Europe

It is a bold archaeologist who attempts to summarize European prehistory. As a result there are few syntheses to choose from. Try: J. M. Coles and A. F. Harding, *The Bronze Age in Europe* (Methuen: London, 1979); Sarunas Milisanskas, *European Prehistory* (Academic Press: New York, 1979); Patricia Phillips, *The Prehistory of Europe* (Allen Lane: London, 1980); D. H. Trump, *The Prehistory of the Mediterranean* (Allen Lane: London, 1980). Colin Renfrew's *Before Civilization* (Alfred A. Knopf: New York, 1973), describes the impact of new dating techniques on the study of later European prehistory. It should be read in conjunction with Stuart Piggott, *Ancient Europe* (Edinburgh University Press: Edinburgh, 1965). François Bordes, *The Old Stone Age* (McGraw-Hill: New York, 1968), offers some coverage of earlier millennia and stone tool types.

India and Pakistan

Walter Fairservis, *The Roots of Ancient India: The Archaeology of Early Indian Culture* (Macmillan: New York, 1971), is one commonly used source. See, also, Mortimer Wheeler, *Early India and Pakistan* (Praeger: New York, 2nd ed., 1963), and the same archaeologist's *The Indus Civilization* (Cambridge University Press: New York, 1968). B. and R. Allchin, *The Birth of Indian Civilization* (Pelican Books: Baltimore, 1968), is another source.

Japan

J. E. Kidder's *Japan* (Praeger: New York, 1959), is now outdated. Chester Chard's *Northeast Asia in Prehistory* (University of Wisconsin Press: Madison, 1974), is a useful synthesis, but those interested in reading about this area are advised to consult a specialist.

Near East

Jacquetta Hawkes's *The First Great Civilizations* (Alfred A. Knopf: New York, 1973), is an attractive synthetic description of the early civilizations. Samuel N. Kramer's *The Sumerians* (University of Chicago Press: Chicago, 1973), is a widely available account of this remarkable society. Earlier cultures: James Mellaart, *Neolithic Cultures of the Near East* (Thames and Hudson: London, 1975).

North America and Mesoamerica

Gordon R. Willey's *Introduction to American Archaeology* (Prentice-Hall: Englewood Cliffs, N.J.; 1967), vol. 1, *North and Middle America*, is a massive and authoritative account that is heavy going for the beginner. Try instead, perhaps, Jesse D. Jennings, *The Prehistory of North America* (McGraw-Hill: New York, 2nd ed., 1973). The same author has recently edited *Ancient Native Americans* (W. H. Freeman: San Francisco, 1978), a collection of essays on American culture history. Dean Snow, *The American Indians* (Viking Press: New York, 1976), is easily the most attractive book for lay people and is lavishly illustrated. Mesoamerica is well served by Richard Adams, *Prehistoric Mesoamerica* (Little, Brown: Boston, 1977) and by Muriel Porter Weaver, *The Aztecs, Maya, and Their Predecessors* (Academic Press: New York, 1972). Kent V. Flannery, ed., *The Early Mesoamerican Village* (Academic Press: New York, 1976), is a description of cultural process in early Mesoamerica that deserves wide circulation.

Pacific Ocean Area, New Zealand, and Southeast Asia

Peter Bellwood's two books, *Man's Conquest of the Pacific* (Oxford University Press: Oxford, 1979) and *The Polynesians* (Thames and Hudson: London, 1978) cover most of the ground. New Zealand archaeology is described by Jack Golson and Peter Gathercole, "New Zealand Archaeology," *Antiquity*, 1962 (36), 168–174. Wilhelm Solheim, "An Earlier Agricultural Revolution," *Scientific American*, 1972, 218, 1: 34–41 describes the potential of Southeast Asia for our understanding of world prehistory.

South America

Gordon R. Willey's *Introduction to American Archaeology* (Prentice-Hall: Englewood Cliffs, N.J.; 1971), vol. 2, *South America*, does for South America what his first volume did for North America. Geoffrey Bushnell, *Peru* (Praeger: New York, 1963), and Betty J. Meggers, *Equador* (Praeger: New York, 1965), are widely read regional syntheses. D. W. Lathrap, *The Upper Amazon* (Praeger: New York, 1970), is informative on rainforest settlement and agriculture. Another widely read book is Eric Lanning, *Peru before the Incas* (Prentice-Hall: Englewood Cliffs, N.J.; 1967). The South American chapters in Jesse K. Jennings, ed., *Ancient Native Americans* (W. H. Freeman: San Francisco, 1978) are useful sources.

Union of Soviet Socialist Republics

Richard Klein, *Man and Culture in the Late Pleistocene* (Chandler: San Francisco, 1969), is one of the few accounts of Russian Stone Age sites in English. It deals with West Russia. His *Ice Age Hunters of the Ukraine* (University of Chicago Press: Chicago, 1973), is a companion volume. A. Mongait, *Archaeology in the USSR* (Pelican Books: Baltimore, 1959), and Tadeusz Sulimirski, *Prehistoric Russia: An Outline* (Methuen: London, 1970), are two basic syntheses. *The Scythians* by T. T. Rice deals with these important nomadic peoples (Praeger: New York, 1957), while M. W. Thompson's translation of Sergei Rudenko, *Frozen Tombs of Siberia: The Pazyryk Burials of Iron Age Horsemen,* is a wonderful insight into the remarkable culture of steppe nomads (Berkeley: University of California Press, 1970). For extreme northeast USSR, consult Chester Chard's *Northeast Asia in Prehistory* (University of Wisconsin Press: Madison, 1974).

BIBLIOGRAPHY ✣

This Bibliography is not intended as a comprehensive reference guide to method and theory in archaeology. Rather, it is a compilation of both the majority of the sources used to compile this book and a cross-section of the most important methodological and theoretical research. Readers interested in probing even more deeply into the literature should consult the references given in the text.

Adams, R. E. W. 1975. "Stratigraphy." In Thomas R. Hester, Robert F. Heizer, and John A. Graham, eds., *Field Methods in Archaeology*. 6th ed. Palo Alto: Mayfield Publishing Company, pp. 147–62.

———. 1977. *Prehistoric Mesoamerica*. Boston: Little, Brown.

Adams, Robert M. 1974. *The Uruk Landscape*. Chicago: University of Chicago Press.

Adovasio, J. M. 1979. *Basketry Technology: A Guide to Identification and Analysis*. Chicago: Aldine.

Adovasio, J. M.; Gunn, J. D.; Donahue, J.; and Stuckenrath, R. 1975. "Excavations at Meadowcroft Rockshelter, 1973–74," *Pennsylvania Archaeologist* 45:1–30.

Adovasio, J. M., and Gunn, Joel. 1977. "Style, Basketry, and Basketmakers." In James Hill and Joel Gunn, eds., *The Individual in Prehistory*. New York: Academic Press, pp. 137–54.

Aikens, C. Melville. 1970. *Hogup Cave*. University of Utah Anthropological Papers, no. 93.

———. 1978. "The Far West." In Jesse D. Jennings, ed., *Ancient Native Americans*. San Francisco: W. H. Freeman, pp. 131–82.

Aitken, Mark. 1977. "Thermoluminescence and the Archaeologist," *Antiquity* 51:11–19.

Aldred, Cyril. 1961. *The Egyptians*. New York: Praeger.

Alexander, John. 1970. *The Directing of Archaeological Excavations*. London: John Baker.

Allan, William. 1965. *The African Husbandman*. Edinburgh: Oliver and Boyd.

Anderson, J. E. 1969. *The Human Skeleton: A Manual for Archaeologists*. Ottawa: National Museum of Canada.

Arnold, J. R., and Libby, W. F. 1949. "Age Determinations by Radiocarbon Content." *Science* 110:678–80.

Asaro, Fred, and Perlman, I. 1967. *Determination of Provenience of Pottery from Trace Element Analysis*. Berkeley: Lawrence Radiation Laboratory.

Asch, David L. 1975. "On Sample Size Problems and the Uses of Non-Probabilistic Sampling." In James W. Mueller, ed., *Sampling in Archaeology*. New York: Academic Press, pp. 170–91.

Asch, Nancy B.; Ford, Richard I.; and Asch, David L. 1972. *The Paleoethnobotany of the Koster Site: The Archaic Horizon*. Springfield: Illinois State Museum.

Atkinson, R. J. C. 1953. *Field Archaeology*. London: Methuen.

———. 1957. "Worms and Weathering." *Antiquity* 31:46–52.

———. 1969. "Moonshine on Stonehenge." *Antiquity* 43:212–16.

Avebury, Lord (Sir John Lubbock). 1865. *Prehistoric Times*. London: Williams and Norgate.

Bada, Jeffrey L., and Hoffman, Patricia M. 1975. "Amino Acid Racemization Dating of Fossil Bones." *World Archaeology* 7,2:160–73.

Baker, C. M. 1978. "The Size Effect: An Explanation of Variability in Surface Artifact and Assemblage Content." *American Antiquity* 43:288–93.

Bannister, Bryant, and Robinson, William J. 1975. "Tree Dating in Archaeology." *World Archaeology* 7,2:210–25.

Bannister, R. 1969. "Dendrochronology." In D. R. Brothwell and Eric Higgs, eds., *Science in Archaeology.* London: Thames and Hudson, pp. 191–205.

Barker, Philip. 1977. *Techniques of Archaeological Excavation.* London: Batsford.

Barnes, A. S. 1938. "Les Outils de l'Homme Tertiaire en Angleterre: étude critique." *L'Anthropologie* 47:1–31.

Bass, G. F. 1966. *Archaeology Under Water.* New York: Praeger.

———. 1970. *A History of Seafaring from Underwater Archaeology.* London: Thames and Hudson.

Bass, W. M. 1971. *Human Osteology: A Laboratory and Field Manual of the Human Skeleton.* Columbia, Mo.: Missouri Archaeological Society.

Bayard, D. T. 1972. "Early Thai Bronze: Analysis and New Dates." *Science* 196:1411–12.

Beck, Horace, and Schofield, J. F. 1958. "Beads." In Roger Summers, ed., *Inyanga.* Cambridge: Cambridge University Press.

Begler, Elsie B., and Keatinge, Richard W. 1979. "Theoretical Goals and Methodological Realities: Problems in the Reconstruction of Prehistoric Subsistence Economies." *World Archaeology* 11,2:208–26.

Bellwood, Peter. 1979. *Man's Conquest of the Pacific.* New York: Oxford University Press.

Bennett, W. J. 1974. *Basic Ceramic Analysis.* Eastern New Mexico University Contributions in Anthropology, vol. 6, no. 1.

Biddle, Martin. 1961. "Nonsuch Palace, 1959–60: An Interim Report." *Surrey Archaeological Collections* 58:1–20.

Biddle, M., and Kjølbye-Biddle, B. 1969. "Metres, Areas, and Robbing." *World Archaeology* 2:208–19.

Binford, Lewis R. 1962. "Archaeology as Anthropology." *American Antiquity* 28:217–25.

———. 1964. "A Consideration of Archaeological Research Design." *American Antiquity* 29:425–41.

———. 1980. "Willow Smoke and Dog's Tails: Hunter-Gatherer Settlement Systems and Archaeological Site Formation." *American Antiquity* 45, 1:4–20.

———. 1968. "Archaeological Perspectives." In Sally R. Binford and Lewis R. Binford, eds., *New Perspectives in Archaeology.* Chicago: Aldine, pp. 5–32.

———. 1972. *An Archaeological Perspective.* New York: Seminar Press.

———, ed. 1977. *For Theory Building in Archaeology.* New York: Academic Press.

———. 1978. *Nunamiut Ethnoarchaeology.* New York: Academic Press.

Bisson, Michael S. 1977. "Prehistoric Copper Mining in North West Zambia." *Archaeology* 29:242–47.

Blanton, Richard E. 1978. *Monte Alban: Settlement Patterns at the Ancient Zatopec Capital.* New York: Academic Press.

Boardman, J., and Palmer, L. R. 1963. *On the Knossos Tablets.* Oxford: Clarendon Press.

Bordaz, J. 1970. *Tools of the Old and New Stone Age.* Garden City, N.Y.: Natural History Press.

Bordes, F. 1968. *The Old Stone Age.* New York: McGraw-Hill.

Bordes, F., and de Sonneville-Bordes, D. 1970. "The Significance of Variability in Palaeolithic Assemblages." *World Archaeology* 2:61–73.

Boserup, Ester. 1965. *Conditions of Agricultural Growth: The Economics of Agrarian Change under Population Pressure.* Chicago: Aldine.

Bracken, C. P. 1975. *Antiquities Acquired.* Newton Abbott: David and Charles.

Bradford, John. 1957. *Ancient Landscapes: Studies in Field Archaeology.* London: G. Bell.

Braidwood, Robert J., and Howe, Bruce. 1962. "Southwestern Asia Beyond the Lands of the Mediterranean Littoral." In Robert J. Braidwood and Gordon R. Willey, eds., *Courses Toward Urban Life.* New York: Viking fund, pp. 132–46.

Brain, C. K. 1967. "Hottentot Food Remains and Their Bearing on the Interpretation of Fossil Bone Assemblages." *Scientific Papers of the Namib Desert Research Station* 32,6:1–7.

Brill, R. H. 1964. "Applications of Fission-Track Dating to Historic and Prehistoric Glasses." *Archaeometry* 7:51–57.

Brothwell, D. R. 1965. *Digging Up Bones.* London: British Museum (Natural History).

Brothwell, D. R., and Higgs, Eric., eds. 1969. *Science in Archaeology.* London: Thames and Hudson.

Brown, James A., ed. 1971. *Approaches to the Social Dimensions of Mortuary Practices.* Memoirs of the Society for American Archaeology, vol. 25.

Brown, James A., and Struever, Stuart. 1973. "The Organization of Archaeological Research: An Illinois Example," In Charles L. Redman, ed., *Method and Theory in Current Archaeology.* New York: John Wiley Interscience, pp. 261–80.

Brumfiel, Elizabeth O. 1976. "Regional Growth in the Eastern Valley of Mexico." In Kent V. Flannery, ed., *The Early Mesoamerican Village.* New York: Academic Press, pp. 234–47.

Bryant, Vaughn. 1974. "Prehistoric Diet in Southwest Texas: The Coprolite Evidence." *American Antiquity* 39:407–20.

Bryant, Vaughn, and Williams-Dean, Glenna. 1975. "The Coprolites of Man." *Scientific American* 232:100–109.

Buchanon, R. A. 1972. *Industrial Archaeology in Britain.* Baltimore: Pelican Books.

Burghardt, Andrew F. 1959. "The Location of Towns in the Central Lowland of the United States." *Annals of the Association of American Geographers* 49:305–23.

Burkitt, Miles C. 1955. *The Old Stone Age.* Cambridge: Cambridge University Press.

Burleigh, R., and Brothwell, D. R. 1978. "Studies on Amerindian Dogs," *Journal of Archaeological Science* 5:355–62.

Butzer, Karl. 1974. *Environment and Archaeology.* 3d ed. Chicago: Aldine.

Byers, Douglas S., ed. 1967. *The Prehistory of the Tehuacán Valley.* Austin: University of Texas Press.

Campbell, John B. 1977. *The Upper Palaeolithic of Britain.* Oxford: Oxford University Press.

Cann, J. R. and Renfrew, Colin. 1964. "The Characterization of Obsidian and Its Application to the Mediterranean Region." *Proceedings of the Prehistoric Society* 30:111–33.

Cartailhac, Emil. 1901. "Les Cavernes Ornées de Dessins: La Grotte d'Altamira. Mea Culpa d'un Sceptique." *L'Anthropologie* 12:671.

Carter, Howard, and others. 1923–33. *The Tomb of Tutankhamun.* London: Cassell.

Casteel, Richard W., ed. 1976. *Fish Remains in Archaeology and Paleo-Environmental Studies.* New York: Academic Press.

Ceram, C. W. 1953. *Gods, Graves, and Scholars.* New York: Alfred A. Knopf.

Cernych, E. N. 1978. "Aibunar—A Balkan Copper Mine of the Fourth Millennium B.C." *Proceedings of the Prehistoric Society* 44:203–18.

Chang, K. C., ed. 1968. *Settlement Archaeology.* Palo Alto: National Press.

———. 1977. *The Archaeology of Ancient China.* 3d ed. New Haven: Yale University Press.

Chaplin, J. H. 1961. "Notes on Traditional Smelting in Northern Rhodesia." *South African Archaeological Bulletin* 16, 63:53–60.

Chaplin, R. E. 1971. *The Study of Animal Bones from Archaeological Sites.* New York: Seminar Press.

Chartkoff, J. L. 1978. "Transect Interval Sampling in Forests." *American Antiquity* 43:46–53.

Childe, V. G. 1925. *The Dawn of European Civilization.* London: Routledge and Kegan Paul.

———. 1942. *What Happened in History.* Baltimore: Pelican Books.

———. 1956. *Piecing Together the Past.* London: Routledge and Kegan Paul.

———. 1958. "Retrospect." *Antiquity* 32:69–74.

Chisholm, Michael. 1968. *Rural Settlement and Land Use.* London: Hutchinson.

Chittick, H. N. 1974. *Kilwa.* Nairobi: British Institute in Eastern Africa.

Christaller, Walter. 1933. *Die Zentralen Orte in Suddeutschland.* Jena: Karl Zeiss.

Clark, J. Desmond. 1958. "The Natural Fracturing of Pebbles from the Batoka Gorge, Northern Rhodesia, and Its Bearing on the Kafuan Industries of Africa." *Proceedings of the Prehistoric Society* 24:64–77.

———. 1959. *The Prehistory of Southern Africa.* Baltimore: Pelican Books.

_____. 1960. "A Note on Early Fishing-Craft and Fishing Practices in Southeast Africa." *South African Archaeological Bulletin* 15:77-79.

_____, ed. 1967. *Atlas of African Prehistory.* Chicago: University of Chicago Press.

Clark, J. G. D. 1932. *The Mesolithic Age in Britain.* Cambridge: Cambridge University Press.

_____. 1939. *Archaeology and Society.* New York: Barnes and Noble.

_____. 1952. *Prehistoric Europe: The Economic Basis.* Palo Alto: Stanford University Press.

_____. 1954. *Star Carr.* Cambridge: Cambridge University Press.

_____. 1970. *Aspects of Prehistory.* Berkeley: University of California Press.

_____. 1972. *Star Carr: A Case Study in Bioarchaeology.* Reading: Addison-Wesley Modules in Anthropology, no. 10.

_____. 1975. *The Early Stone Age Settlement of Scandinavia.* Cambridge: Cambridge University Press.

_____. 1978. *World Prehistory in New Perspective.* 3d ed. Cambridge: Cambridge University Press.

Clark, Rainbird. 1935. "The Flint Knapping Industry at Brandon." *Antiquity* 9:38-56.

Clark, R. M. 1975. "A Calibration Curve for Radiocarbon Dates." *Antiquity* 49:251-66.

Clarke, David L. 1968. *Analytical Archaeology.* London: Methuen.

_____, ed. 1977. *Spatial Archaeology.* New York: Academic Press.

Clay, R. B. 1976. "Typological Classification, Attribute Analysis, and Lithic Variability." *Journal of Field Archaeology* 3:303-11.

Coe, Michael D. 1962. *Mexico.* New York: Praeger.

_____. 1967. *Tikal: A Handbook of the Ancient Maya Ruins.* Philadelphia: University Museum.

_____. 1976. *The Maya.* 2d ed. New York: Praeger.

Coles, John M. 1972. *Field Archaeology in Britain.* London: Heinemann.

_____. 1973. *Archaeology by Experiment.* London: Heinemann.

Coles, J. M. and Harding, A. F. 1979. *The Bronze Age in Europe.* London: Methuen.

Coles, J. M.; Heal, S. V. E.; and Orme, B. J. 1978. "The Use and Character of Wood in Prehistoric Britain and Ireland." *Proceedings of the Prehistoric Society* 44:1-45.

Collins, H. B. 1937. *The Archaeology of St. Lawrence Island.* Smithsonian Miscellaneous Collections, no. 96.

Cook, S. F. 1972. *Prehistoric Demography.* Reading: Addison-Wesley Modules in Anthropology.

Cornwall, I. W. 1956. *Bones for the Archaeologist.* London: Phoenix.

Crabtree, Don E. 1966. "An Introduction to Flintworking. Part I: An Introduction to the Technology of Stone Tools." *Occasional Papers of the Idaho State University,* vol. 28.

_____. 1972. "A Stoneworker's Approach to Analysing and Replicating the Lindenmeier Folsom." *Tebiwa* 9:3-39.

Crabtree, Robert M. 1963. "Archaeological Investigations at Batiquitos Lagoon, San Diego County." *California Archaeological Survey Annual Report,* pp. 319-462.

Crawford, O. G. S. 1953. *Archaeology in the Field.* New York: Praeger.

Crawford, O. G. S., and Keiller, Alexander. 1928. *Wessex from the Air.* Oxford: Clarendon Press.

Cressey, Pamela J. 1980. "Studying the American City: The Alexandria Urban Archaeology Project," Unpublished paper read at the Society for American Archaeology meetings, Philadelphia, 1980.

Croes, Dale R., and Davis, Jonathan O. 1977. "Computer Mapping of Idiosyncratic Basketry Manufacturing Techniques in the Prehistoric Ozette House, Cape Alava, Washington." In James Hill and Joel Gunn, eds. *The Individual in Prehistory.* New York: Academic Press, pp. 155-66.

Curtis, Garniss H. 1975. "Improvements in Potassium-Argon Dating, 1962-1975." *World Archaeology* 7, 2:198-209.

Dalrymple, G. Brett, and Lamphere, Mason A. 1970. *Potassium Argon Dating.* San Francisco: W. H. Freeman.

Daly, Patricia. 1969. "Approaches to Faunal Analysis in Archaeology." *American Antiquity* 34:146-53.

Daniel, Glyn. 1962. *The Idea of Prehistory.* London: Watts.

———. ed. 1967. *The Origins and Growth of Archaeology.* Baltimore: Pelican Books.

———. 1973. *Megaliths in History.* London: Thames and Hudson.

———. 1975. *One Hundred and Fifty Years of Archaeology.* London: Duckworth.

———. 1976. "Stone, Bronze, and Iron." In J. V. S. Megaw, ed., *To Illustrate the Monuments.* London: Thames and Hudson, pp. 35–42.

Daniels, S. G. H. 1972. "Research Design Models." In David L. Clarke, ed., *Models in Archaeology.* London: Methuen, pp. 201–29.

Däniken, Erich von. 1970. *Chariots of the Gods?* New York: Bantam Books.

———. 1971. *Gods from Outer Space.* New York: Bantam Books.

Darrah, W. C. 1938. "Technical Contributions to the Study of Archaeological Materials." *American Antiquity* 3:269–70.

Dart, R. A. 1957. *The Osteodontokeratic Culture of Australopithecus Prometheus.* Pretoria: Transvaal Museum.

Darwin, Charles. 1859. *On the Origin of Species.* London: John Murray.

———. 1881. *The Formation of Vegetable Mould Through the Actions of Worms with Observations on Their Habits.* London: Faber and Faber. (Republished in 1945.)

David, N. C. 1971. "The Fulani Compound and the Archaeologist." *World Archaeology* 3,2:111–31.

Dawson, Elliot W. 1969. "Bird Remains in Archaeology." In D. R. Brothwell and Eric Higgs, eds., *Science in Archaeology.* London: Thames and Hudson, pp. 359–75.

Dean, Jeffrey S. 1970. "Aspects of Tsegi Phase Soil Organization." In W. A. Longacre, ed., *Reconstructing Prehistoric Pueblo Societies.* Albuquerque: University of New Mexico Press.

Deetz, James. 1967. *Invitation to Archaeology.* Garden City, N.Y.: Natural History Press.

De Laet, S. J. 1956. *Archaeology and Its Problems.* London: Phoenix.

De Mortillet, Gabriel. 1867. *Promenades Préhistoriques à L'Exposition Universelle.* Paris.

De Perthes, Boucher. 1841. *De La Création: Essai Sur L'Origine et la Progression des Etres.* Abbeville.

Dennell, R. W. 1979. "Prehistoric Diet and Nutrition: Some Food for Thought." *World Archaeology* 11,2:121–35.

Dent, John. 1962. *The Quest for Nonsuch.* London: Pall Mall Press.

Dethlefsen, Edwin, and Deetz, James. 1966. "Death's Heads, Cherubs, and Willow Trees: Experimental Archaeology in Colonial Cemeteries." *American Antiquity* 31:502–10.

Deuel, Leo. 1969. *Flights into Yesterday.* London: Macdonald.

Digby, Bernard. 1926. *The Mammoth and Mammoth-Hunting in North-East Siberia.* London: Macmillan.

Dittert, Alfred E., Jr.; Hester, Jim J.; and Eddy, Frank W. 1961. *An Archaeological Survey of the Navajo Reservoir District of Northwestern New Mexico.* Monographs of the School of American Research and Museum of New Mexico, no. 23.

Doran, James. 1970. "Systems Theory, Computer Simulations, and Archaeology." *World Archaeology* 1,3:289–98.

Doran, J. E., and Hodson, F. R. 1975. *Mathematics and Computers in Archaeology.* Cambridge: Harvard University Press.

Dowman, Elizabeth A. 1970. *Conservation in Field Archaeology.* London: Methuen.

Drennan, Robert D. 1976. "Religion and Social Evolution in Formative Mesoamerica." In Kent V. Flannery, ed., *The Early Mesoamerican Village.* New York: Academic Press, pp. 345–63.

Drucker, Philip. 1966. *Cultures of the North Pacific Coast.* San Francisco: Chandler.

———. 1972. *Stratigraphy in Archaeology: An Introduction.* Reading: Addison-Wesley Modules in Anthropology, no. 30.

Dumond, Don E. 1977. *The Eskimos and Aleuts.* London: Thames and Hudson.

Dunnell, Robert C. 1970. "The Seriation Method and Its Evaluation." *American Antiquity* 35, 3:305–19.

————. 1971. *Systematics in Prehistory.* New York: Free Press.

————. 1977. "Science and Archaeology: When the Saints Go Marching In." *American Antiquity* 42:33–49.

————. 1978. "Style and Function: A Fundamental Dichotomy." *American Antiquity* 43:192–202.

Dymond, D. P. 1974. *Archaeology and History.* London: Thames and Hudson.

Earle, Timothy. 1976. "A Nearest Neighbor Analysis of Two Formative Settlement Systems." In Kent V. Flannery, ed., *The Early Mesoamerican Village.* New York: Academic Press, pp. 196–224.

Earle, Timothy, and Ericson, J. E., eds. 1977. *Exchange Systems in Prehistory.* New York: Academic Press.

Eliade, Mercea. 1954. *The Myth of the Eternal Return.* New York: Pantheon.

Evans, John. 1849–50. "On the Date of British Coins." *Numismatic Chronicle* 12:127.

————. 1860. "On the Occurrence of Flint Implements in Undisturbed Beds of Gravel, Sand, and Clay." *Archaeologia* 38:280–308.

Ewers, John C. 1949. "The Last Bison Drives of the Blackfoot Indians." *Journal of the Washington Academy of Sciences* 39, 11:355–60.

Faegri, K., and Iverson, J. 1966. *Textbook of Pollen Analysis.* New York: Hafner.

Fagan, Brian M. 1967. *Iron Age Cultures in Zambia,* vol. 1. New York: Humanities Press.

————. 1969. "Early Trade and Raw Materials in South Central Africa," *Journal of African History* 10: 1–26.

————. 1975. *The Rape of the Nile.* New York: Charles Scribner's.

————. 1977. *Elusive Treasure.* New York: Charles Scribner's.

————. 1978a. *Quest for the Past.* Reading: Addison-Wesley.

————. 1978b. *Archaeology: A Brief Introduction.* Boston: Little, Brown.

————. 1979. *Return to Babylon.* Boston: Little, Brown.

————. 1980. *People of the Earth.* 3d ed. Boston: Little, Brown.

Fagan, Brian M., and Van Noten, F. 1971. *The Hunter-Gatherers of Gwisho.* Tervuren: Musée Royal de l'Afrique Centrale.

Fell, Barry. 1977. *America B.C.* New York: Viking.

Finley, M. I. 1971. "Archaeology and History." *Daedalus* 100:168–86.

Fitting, James F., and Goodyear, Albert C. 1979. "Client Oriented Archaeology: An Exchange of Views." *Journal of Field Archaeology* 6:352–60.

Flannery, Kent V. 1968. "Archaeological Systems Theory and Early Mesoamerica." In Betty J. Meggers, ed., *Anthropological Archaeology in the Americas.* Washington: Anthropological Society of Washington, pp. 67–87.

————. 1972. "The Cultural Evolution of Civilizations." *Biennial Review of Ecology and Systematics,* pp. 399–426.

————. 1973a. "Archaeology with a Capital S." In Charles L. Redman, ed., *Research and Theory in Current Archaeology.* New York: John Wiley Interscience, pp. 337–54.

————. 1973b. "The Origins of Agriculture." *Biennial Review of Anthropology* 12:271–310.

————, ed. 1976. *The Early Mesoamerican Village.* New York: Academic Press.

Flannery, Kent V. and Winter, Marcus C. 1976. "Analyzing Village Activities." In Kent V. Flannery, ed., *The Early Mesoamerican Village.* New York: Academic Press, pp. 34–44.

Fleischer, Robert L. 1975. "Advances in Fission Track Dating." *World Archaeology* 7, 2:136–50.

Fontana, Bernard L. 1968. "Bottles, Buckets, and Horseshoes: The Unrespectable in American Archaeology." *Keystone Folklore Quarterly* 13, 3:171–84.

Fontana, Bernard; Robinson, W. J.; Cormack, C. W.; and Leavitt, E. E. 1962. *Papago Indian Pottery.* Seattle: University of Washington Press.

Forbes, R. J. 1955–58. *Studies in Ancient Technology.* The Hague: Brill.

Ford, J. A. 1954a. "A Comment on A. C. Spaulding 'Statistical Techniques.' " *American Antiquity* 19:390–91.

———. 1954b. "On the Concept of Types." *American Antiquity* 56:42–54.

———. 1962. *A Quantitative Method for Deriving Cultural Chronology.* Washington: Pan American Union.

Ford, J. A., and Willey, Gordon R. 1941. "An Interpretation of the Prehistory of the Eastern United States." *American Anthropologist* 43, 3:325–63.

Ford, Richard I. 1979. "Paleoethnobotany in American Archaeology." *Advances in Archaeological Method and Theory* 2:286–336.

Fox, Sir Cyril. 1932. *The Personality of Britain.* Cambridge: Cambridge University Press.

Frankfort, Henri. 1951. *The Birth of Civilization in the Near East.* New York: Doubleday.

Frazer, James. 1890. *The Golden Bough.* London: Macmillan.

Friedman, I.; Clark, D.; and Smith, R. L. 1969. "Obsidian Dating." In D. R. Brothwell and Eric Higgs, eds., *Science in Archaeology.* London: Thames and Hudson.

Frison, George. 1974. *The Casper Site: A Hell Gap Bison Kill on the High Plains.* New York: Academic Press.

Fritts, H. C. 1976. *Tree Rings and Climate.* New York: Academic Press.

Gabel, Creighton. 1967. *Analysis of Prehistoric Economic Patterns.* New York: Holt, Rinehart and Winston.

Garlake, Peter. 1973. *Great Zimbabwe.* London: Thames and Hudson.

Garrod, D. A. E. and Bate, Dorothea. 1937. *The Stone Age of Mount Carmel,* vol. 1. Cambridge: Cambridge University Press.

Gifford, E. W. 1916. "Composition of California Shell Middens." *University of California Publications in Archaeology and Anthropology* 12:1–29.

Gifford, J. C. 1976. *Prehistoric Pottery Analysis and the Ceramics of Barton Ramie in the Belize Valley.* Memoirs of the Peabody Museum, no. 18. Harvard University, Cambridge, Mass.

Glob, P. V. 1969. *The Bog People.* London: Faber and Faber.

Goggin, J. W., ed. 1949. *The Florida Indian and His Neighbors.* Winter Park, Florida: Rollins College.

Goodyear, A. C.; Raab, L. A.; and Klinger, T. C. 1978. "The Status of Archaeological Research Design in Cultural Resource Management." *American Antiquity* 43:159–73.

Gould, Richard. 1977. *Puntutjarpa Rockshelter.* New York: American Museum of Natural History.

———, ed. 1978. *Explorations in Ethnoarchaeology.* Albuquerque: University of New Mexico Press.

Grange, Roger T. 1972. "Pawnee Potsherds Revisited: Formula Dating of a Non-European Ceramic Tradition." *The Conference on Historic Site Archaeology Papers* 7:318–36.

Grasiozi, Paolo. 1960. *Palaeolithic Art.* New York: McGraw-Hill.

Graybill, Don. 1978. "The Destruction of Archaeological Sites," *Journal of Field Archaeology* 3:25–38.

Grootes, P. M. 1978. "Carbon–14 Time Scale Extended: Comparison of Chronologies," *Science* 200, 4337:11–15.

Griffin, J. B. 1946. "Culture Change and Continuity in the Eastern United States." In F. Johnson, ed., *Man in Northeastern North America.* Andover: Peabody Foundation.

Grinsell, L. V.; Rahtz, P.; and Williams, D. P. 1970. *The Preparation of Archaeological Reports.* London: John Baker.

Gumerman, George J., and Euler, Robert C. 1976. *Papers on the Archaeology of Black Mesa, Arizona.* Carbondale: Southern Illinois University Press.

Gumerman, George J., and Lyons, T. R. 1971. "Archaeological Methodology and Remote Sensing." *Science* 210:11–15.

Gumerman, George J., and Schiffer, M., eds. 1977. *Conservation Archaeology.* New York: Academic Press.

Hamblin, Dora Jane. 1970. *Pots and Robbers.* New York: Simon and Schuster.

Hanson, H. O. 1962. *I Built a Stone Age House.* London: Phoenix.

Hardesty, Donald. 1977. *Ecological Anthropology.* New York: John Wiley.

Hardin, Margaret Ann. 1977. "Individual Style in San José Pottery Painting: The Role of Deliberate Choice." In James Hill and Joel Gunn, eds., *The Individual in Prehistory.* New York: Academic Press, pp. 109–36.

Harp, Elmer. 1978. *Photography for Archaeologists.* New York: Academic Press.

Harp, E., Jr., ed. 1975. *Photography in Archaeological Research.* Albuquerque: University of New Mexico Press.

Harrington, J. C. 1948. "Evidence of Manual Reckoning in the Cittie of Raleigh." *North Carolina Historical Review* 33, 1:1–8.

Harris, Edward C. 1979. *Principles of Archaeological Stratigraphy.* New York: Academic Press.

Harris, Marvin, 1968. *The Rise of Anthropological Theory.* New York: Thomas Crowell.

Hatch, Elvin. 1973. *Theories of Man and Culture.* New York: Columbia University Press.

Hatt, C. 1957. "Norre Fjord, and Early Iron Age Village in West Jutland." *Archaeologiske Kunthistorische* 2, 2:1–25.

Hawkins, Gerald. 1965. *Stonehenge Decoded.* New York: Doubleday.

Hayashi, Kensaku. 1968. "The Fukui Microblade Technology and Its Relationships in Northeast Asia and North America." *Arctic Anthropology* 5:128–90.

Hayden, Brian, ed. 1979. *Lithic Wear Analysis.* New York: Academic Press.

Heizer, Robert F. 1969. "The Archaeology of Great Basin Coprolites." In D. R. Brothwell and Eric Higgs, eds., *Science in Archaeology.* London: Thames and Hudson, pp. 244–50.

Helbaek, Hans. 1969. "Plant Collecting, Dry-Farming, and Irrigation Agriculture." In Frank Hole, Kent V. Flannery, and James Neely, eds., *The Prehistoric Human Ecology of the Deh Luran Plain.* Ann Arbor: Memoirs of the Museum of Anthropology, no. 1.

Hess, John L. 1974. *The Grand Acquisitors.* Boston: Houghton Mifflin.

Hester, Thomas; Heizer, Robert F.; and Graham, John. 1975. *Field Methods in Archaeology.* 6th ed. Palo Alto: Mayfield.

Hester, Thomas, and Heizer, Robert F. 1973. *Bibliography of Archaeology—I: Lithic Technology and Petrography.* Reading: Addison-Wesley Modules in Anthropology, no. 29.

Heyerdahl, Thor. 1950. *The Kon Tiki Expedition.* London: George Unwin.

Hill, James N. 1970. *Broken K Pueblo: Prehistoric Social Organization in the American Southwest.* Tucson: University of Arizona Press.

————, ed. 1977. *Explanation of Prehistoric Change.* Albuquerque: University of New Mexico Press.

Hill, James, and Gunn, Joel, eds. 1977. *The Individual in Prehistory.* New York: Academic Press.

Hill, James N., and Hevly, Richard H. 1968. "Pollen at Broken K: Some New Interpretations." *American Antiquity* 33:200–10.

Hodder, Ian, ed. 1978. *Simulation Studies in Archaeology.* Cambridge: Cambridge University Press.

Hodder, Ian, and Hassall, M. 1972. "The Non-random Spacing of Romano-British Walled Towns." *Man* 6:391–407.

Hodder, Ian, and Orton, Clive. 1976. *Spatial Analysis in Archaeology.* Cambridge: Cambridge University Press.

Hole, Frank; Flannery, Kent V.; and Neely, J. A. 1969. *The Prehistory and Human Ecology of the Deh Luran Plain.* Ann Arbor: Memoirs of the Museum of Anthropology, no. 1.

Hole, Frank, and Heizer, R. F. 1973. *An Introduction to Prehistoric Archaeology.* 3d ed. New York: Holt, Rinehart and Winston.

Hole, Frank, and Shaw, M. 1967. "Computer Analysis of Chronological Seriation." *Rice University Studies* vol. 53, no. 3.

Holmes, W. H. 1919. *Handbook of Aboriginal American Antiquities, Part I: Introductory: The Lithic Industry.* Bureau of American Ethnology, Bulletin no. 60.

Howard, Hildegaard. 1929. "The Avifauna of Emeryville Shellmound." *University of California Publications in Zoology* 23:378–83.

Howell, F. Clark. 1965. *Early Man.* New York: Time-Life Books.

Hudson, Kenneth. 1976. *Industrial Archaeology: A New Introduction.* 3d ed. London: Thames & Hudson.

Huxley, Thomas. 1863. *Man's Place in Nature.* London: Macmillan.

Ingersoll, Daniel; Yellen, John E.; and Macdonald, William, eds. 1977. *Experimental Archaeology.* New York: Columbia University Press.

Isaac, Glynn L., and McKown, Elizabeth, eds. 1977. *Human Origins: Louis Leakey and the East African Evidence.* Menlo Park: W. A. Benjamin.

Iversen, Johannes. 1941. "Land Occupation in Denmark's Stone Age." *Danmarks Geologiske Undersøgelse,* II Raekke 66:70–76.

Jarman, H. N.; Legge, A. J.; and Charles, J. A. 1972. "Retrieval of Plant Remains from Archaeological Sites by Froth Flotation." In E. S. Higgs, ed., *Essays in Economic Prehistory.* Cambridge: Cambridge University Press, pp. 39–48.

Jennings, Jesse D. 1966. *Glen Canyon: A Summary.* Salt Lake City: University of Utah Anthropological Papers.

———. 1973. *The Prehistory of North America.* 2d ed. New York: McGraw-Hill.

———, ed. 1978. *Ancient Native Americans.* San Francisco: W. H. Freeman.

Jewell, P. A., and Dimbleby, G. W. 1966. "The Experimental Earthwork at Overton Down, Wiltshire, England." *Proceedings of the Prehistoric Society* 32:313–42.

Jochim, Michael A. 1979. "Breaking Down the System: Recent Ecological Approaches in Archaeology." *Advances in Archaeological Method and Theory* 2:77–119.

Johnson, L. 1968. *Item Seriation as an Aid for Elementary Scale and Cluster Analysis.* Bulletin of the Museum of Natural History, no. 15. University of Oregon, Eugene.

Johnson, L. L. 1978. "A History of Flint Knapping Experimentation, 1838–1976," *Current Anthropology* 19:337–72.

Johnson, Paul. 1968. *The Civilization of Ancient Egypt.* London: Weidenfeld and Nicholson.

Judge, James W., and Dawson, J. 1972. "Paleo-Indian Settlement Technology in New Mexico." *Science* 176:1210–16.

Keesing, R. M. 1974. "Theories of Culture." *Annual Review of Anthropology* 3:71–97.

Kidder, A. V. 1924. *An Introduction to the Study of Southwestern Archaeology.* New Haven: Yale University Press.

King, Chester; Blackburn, Thomas; and Chandonet, Ernest. 1968. "The Archaeological Inventory of Three Sites on the Century Ranch, Western Los Angeles County, California." *California Archaeological Survey Annual Report* 10:12–161.

King, M. E. 1978. "Analytical Methods and Prehistoric Textiles." *American Antiquity* 43:89–96.

King, T. F. 1971. "Resolving a Conflict of Values in American Archaeology." *American Antiquity* 36:255–62.

———. 1979. "Preservation and Rescue: Challenges and Controversies in the Protection of Archaeological Resources." *Journal of Field Archaeology* 6:351–52.

King, T. F.; Hickman, Patricia; and Berg, Gary, eds. 1977. *Anthropology in Historic Preservation: Caring for Culture's Clutter.* New York: Academic Press.

Kirk, Ruth. 1974. *Hunters of the Whale.* New York: Morrow.

Klein, Richard. 1969. *Man and Culture in the Late Pleistocene.* San Francisco: Chandler.

———. 1977. "Environment and Subsistence of Prehistoric Man in the Southern Cape Province, South Africa." *World Archaeology* 5:249–84.

Kluckhohn, Clyde. 1940. "The Conceptual Structure in Middle American Studies." In A. M. Tozzer, ed., *The Maya and Their Neighbors.* New York: Appleton-Century-Crofts.

_____. 1943. "Bronislaw Malinowski, 1884–1942." *Journal of American Folklore* 56:208–19.

Kreiger, A. D. 1944. "The Typological Concept." *American Antiquity* 9:271–88.

Kroeber, Alfred L., and Kluckhohn, Clyde. 1952. *Culture: A Critical Review of Concepts and Definitions.* Papers of the Peabody Museum of American Archaeology and Ethnology. Harvard University, Cambridge, Mass.

Kroeber, Theodora. 1965. *Ishi in Two Worlds.* Berkeley: University of California Press.

Kuhn, T. S. 1970. *The Structure of Scientific Revolutions.* 2d ed. Chicago: University of Chicago Press.

Lamberg-Karlovsky, C. C. 1970. *Excavations at Tepe Yahya, Iran, 1967–1969.* Cambridge: Bulletin of the American School of Prehistoric Research.

_____. 1975. "Third Millennium Modes of Exchange and Modes of Production." In Jeremy A. Sabloff, and C. C. Lamberg-Karlovsky, eds., *Early Civilization and Trade.* Albuquerque: University of New Mexico Press, pp. 341–68.

Lambrecht, Frank L. 1964. "Aspects of the Evolution and Ecology of Tsetse Flies and Trypanosomiasis in the Prehistoric African Environment." *Journal of African History* 5:1–24.

Layard, A. H. 1849. *Nineveh and Its Remains.* London: John Murray.

Leakey, L. S. B. 1951. *Olduvai Gorge, 1931–1951.* Cambridge: Cambridge University Press.

_____. 1971. *Olduvai Gorge,* vol. 1. Cambridge: Cambridge University Press.

Leakey, M. D. 1973. *Olduvai Gorge,* vol. 3. Cambridge: Cambridge University Press.

LeBlanc, Steven A. 1975. "Microseriation: A Method for Fine Chronologic Differentiation." *American Antiquity* 40:22–30.

Lee, Richard B., and DeVore, Irven, eds. 1976. *Kalahari Hunter-Gatherers.* Cambridge: Harvard University Press.

Lee, Ronald F. 1970. *The Antiquities Act of 1906.* Washington, D.C.: National Park Service.

Leone, Mark P. 1978. "Time in American Archaeology." In Charles L. Redman and others, eds., *Social Archaeology.* New York: Academic Press, pp. 25–36.

Leroi-Gourhan, André. 1967. *Treasures of Prehistoric Art.* New York: Abrams.

Libby, W. F. 1955. *Radiocarbon Dating.* Chicago: University of Chicago Press.

Limbrey, Susan. 1972. *Soil Science in Archaeology.* New York: Seminar Press.

Lipe, William D. 1970. "A Conservation Model for American Archaeology." *The Kiva* 3,4:213–43.

Lipe, William D., and Lindsay, Alexander J., Jr. 1974. *Proceedings of the 1974 Cultural Resource Management Conference.* Flagstaff: Museum of Northern Arizona.

Lloyd, Seton. 1963. *Mounds of the Near East.* Chicago: Aldine.

Longacre, W. 1970. *Archaeology as Anthropology.* Tucson: University of Arizona Press.

Lubbock, Sir John (Lord Avebury). 1865. *Prehistoric Times.* London: Williams and Norgate.

Lumley, Henry de. 1969. "A Palaeolithic Camp at Nice." *Scientific American* 220:42–50.

Lyons, Thomas R., and Avery, Thomas. 1977. *Remote Sensing: A Handbook for Archaeologists and Cultural Resource Managers.* Washington, D.C.: National Park Service.

McBurney, C. B. M. 1959. "First Season's Fieldwork on British Upper Palaeolithic Cave Deposits." *Proceedings of the Prehistoric Society* 25:260–69.

McGimsey, Charles. 1972. *Public Archaeology.* New York: Seminar Press.

McGimsey, Charles, and Davis, Hester. 1977. *The Management of Archaeological Resources.* Washington, D.C.: National Park Service.

McHargue, George, and Roberts, Michael. 1977. *A Field Guide to Conservation Archaeology in North America.* Philadelphia: Lippincott.

McKern, W. C. 1939. "The Midwestern Taxonomic System as an Aid to Archaeological Culture Study." *American Antiquity* 4,4:301–13.

MacNeish, Richard S., ed. 1970. *The Prehistory of the Tehuacán Valley,* vol. 3. Austin: University of Texas Press.

_____. 1978. *The Science of Archaeology?* North Scituate, Mass: Duxbury Press.

Macquilty, William. 1965. *Abu Simbel.* London: Macmillan.

Mallowan, Max L. 1965. *Early Mesopotamia and Iran.* New York: McGraw-Hill.

Marcus, Joyce. 1976. "The Size of the Early Mesoamerican Village." In Kent V. Flannery, ed., *The Early Mesoamerican Village.* New York: Academic Press, pp. 79–88.

Marshack, Alexander. 1972. *The Roots of Civilization.* New York: McGraw-Hill.

Martin, Paul S., and Plog, Fred. 1973. *The Archaeology of Arizona.* Garden City, N.Y.: Doubleday Natural History Press.

Marquardt, William H. 1978. "Advances in Archaeological Seriation." *Advances in Archaeological Method and Theory,* vol. 1.

Matson, F. R. 1965. *Ceramics and Man.* New York: Viking Fund.

Mehringer, Peter J., and Haynes, Vance. 1965. "The Pollen Evidence for the Environment of Early Man and Extinct Animals at the Lehner Mammoth Site, Southeastern Arizona." *American Antiquity* 31:11–23.

Mellaart, James. 1975. *The Neolithic of the Near East.* London: Thames and Hudson.

Mercati, Michael. 1717. *Metallotheca Vaticana.* Rome.

Mewhinney, H. 1957. *A Manual for Neanderthalers.* Austin: University of Texas Press.

Meyer, Karl. 1977. *The Plundered Past.* 2d ed. Baltimore: Pelican Books.

Michael, H. N., and Ralph, E. K., eds. 1971. *Dating Techniques for the Archaeologist.* Cambridge: MIT Press.

Michels, J. W. 1973. *Dating Methods in Archaeology.* New York: Seminar Press.

Millon, René. 1973. *The Teotihuacán Map. Urbanization at Teotihuacán, Mexico,* vol. 1. Austin: University of Texas Press.

Moorehead, Alan. 1961. *Darwin and the Beagle.* London: Hamish Hamilton.

_____. 1966. *The Fatal Impact.* London: Hamish Hamilton.

Morgan, J. W. W. 1975. "The Preservation of Timber." *Timber Grower* 8:55.

Morgan, Lewis. 1877. *Ancient Society.* New York: Holt, Rinehart and Winston.

Morlan, Richard E. 1967. "The Preceramic Period of Hokkaido: An Outline." *Arctic Anthropology* 4:164–220.

_____. 1978. "Early Man in Northern Yukon Territory: Perspectives as of 1977." In Alan L. Bryan, ed., *Early Man in America.* Edmonton: Archaeological Research International, pp. 78–95.

Movius, H. L. 1974. "The Abri Pataud Program of the French Upper Palaeolithic in Retrospect." In Gordon R. Willey, ed., *Archaeological Researches in Retrospect.* Cambridge: Winthrop.

_____. 1977. *Excavation of the Abri Pataud, Les Eyzies (Dordogne).* Cambridge: Peabody Museum.

Mueller, James A. 1974. *The Use of Sampling in Archaeological Survey.* Memoirs of the Society for American Archaeology, no. 28, Washington, D.C.: U.S. Government Printing Office.

_____, ed. 1975. *Sampling in Archaeology.* Tucson: University of Arizona Press.

Murdock, George P. 1949. *Social Structure.* New York: Macmillan.

Naroll, R. 1962. "Floor Size and Settlement Population." *American Antiquity* 27:587–88.

Nash, C. H. 1968. *Residence Mounds. An Intermediate Middle Mississippian Settlement Pattern.* Memphis: Memphis State University Anthropological Research Center, Occasional Paper no. 2.

Nelson, N. C. 1914. *Pueblo Ruins of the Galisteo Basin, New Mexico.* New York: Macmillan.

Netting, R. McC. 1977. *Cultural Ecology.* Menlo Park: Cummings.

Noël Hume, Ivor. 1969. *Historical Archaeology.* New York: Alfred A. Knopf.

Oakley, K. P. 1969. *Frameworks for Dating Fossil Man.* 2d ed. Chicago: Aldine.

Olsen, S. J. 1972. *Zooarchaeology: Animal Bones in Archaeology and Their Interpretation.* Reading: Addison-Wesley Modules in Anthropology, no. 12.

_____. 1978. *Fish, Amphibians, and Reptile Remains from Archaeological Sites.* Cambridge: Peabody Museum.

_____. 1979a. *Osteology for the Archaeologist*. rev. ed. Cambridge: Peabody Museum.

_____. 1979b. "Osteologically, What Constitutes an Early Domesticated Animal?" *Advances in Archaeological Method and Theory* 2:175–97.

Omer-Cooper, John. 1966. *The Zulu Aftermath*. London: Heinemann.

Organ, R. M. 1968. *Design for Scientific Conservation of Antiquities*. Washington, D.C.: Smithsonian Institution Press.

Pallottino, Massimo. 1968. *The Meaning of Archaeology*. New York: Abrams.

Parmalee, Paul, and Klippel, Walter E. 1974. "Freshwater Mollusca as a Prehistoric Food Resource." *American Antiquity* 39:421–34.

Parsons, J. A., and Price, B. J. 1971. *Mesoamerican Trade and Its Role in the Emergence of Civilization*. University of California Archaeological Research Facility Contribution, no. 11, Berkeley.

Pavlish, L. A. and Banning, E. B. 1980. "Revolutionary Developments in Carbon 14 Dating." *American Antiquity* 45, 2:290–296.

Petrie, Flinders. 1889. "Sequences in Prehistoric Remains." *Journal of the Royal Anthropological Institute* 29:295–301.

Phillips, Patricia. 1980. *The Prehistory of Europe*. London: Alan Lane Books.

Phillips, P.; Ford, J. A., and Griffin, J. A. 1951. *Archaeological Survey in the Lower Mississippi. 1940–1947.* Papers of the Peabody Museum of American Archaeology and Ethnology, no. 25. Harvard University, Cambridge, Mass.

Phillipson, D. W. 1969. "Gunflint Manufacture in North-Western Zambia." *Antiquity* 43:301–04.

Piggott, Stuart. 1965. *Ancient Europe*. Chicago: Aldine.

_____. 1968. *The Druids*. London: Thames and Hudson.

Pires-Ferreira, Jane. 1976. "Obsidian Exchange in Formative Mesoamerica." In Kent V. Flannery, ed., *The Early Mesoamerican Village*. New York: Academic Press, pp. 293–305.

Pitt-Rivers, General Lane Fox. 1887. *Excavations in Cranborne Chase*. Farnham, England: privately published.

Plenderleith, H. J., and Werner, A. E. A. 1973. *The Conservation of Antiquities and Works of Art*. 2d ed. London: Oxford University Press.

Plog, F. T., ed. 1974. *The Study of Prehistoric Change*. New York: Academic Press.

_____. 1978. "Cultural Resource Management and the 'New Archaeology.' " In Charles L. Redman and others, eds., *Social Archaeology*. New York: Academic Press, pp. 421–29.

Plog, S. 1976a. "Relative Efficiencies of Sampling Techniques for Archaeological Surveys." In Kent V. Flannery, ed., *The Early Mesoamerican Village*. New York: Academic Press, pp. 136–58.

_____. 1976b. "Measurement of Prehistoric Interaction between Communities." In Kent V. Flannery, ed., *The Early Mesoamerican Village*. New York: Academic Press, pp. 255–72.

Plumb, J. H. 1969. *The Death of the Past*. London: Macmillan.

Polyani, Karl. 1975. "Traders and Trade." In Jeremy A. Sabloff and C. C. Lamberg-Karlovsky, eds., *Early Civilization and Trade*. Albuquerque: University of New Mexico Press, pp. 133–54.

Rahtz, P. A. 1974. *RESCUE Archaeology*. Baltimore: Pelican Books.

Rapoport, Anatol. 1968. "Foreword." In W. Buckley, ed., *Modern Systems Research for the Behavioral Sciences*. Chicago: Aldine.

Rappoport, Roy A. 1968. *Pigs for the Ancestors*. New Haven: Yale University Press.

_____. 1971. "Ritual, Sanctity, and Cybernetics." *Current Anthropology* 73:59–76.

Rathje, William. 1970. "Socio-Political Implications of Maya Lowland Burials." *World Archaeology* 1:359–74.

_____. 1971. "The Origin and Development of Lowland Classic Mayan Civilization." *American Antiquity* 36, 3:275–85.

_____. 1974. "The Garbage Project: A New Way of Looking at the Problems of Archaeology." *Archaeology* 27, 4:236–41.

_____. 1979. "Modern Material Culture Studies." *Advances in Archaeological Method and Theory* 2:1–38.

Rathje, W. H., and McCarthy, W. 1977. "Regularity and Variability in Contemporary Garbage." In Stanley A. South, ed., *Method and Theory in Historical Archaeology*. New York: Academic Press.

Raven-Hart, R. 1967. *Before Van Riebeeck*. Capetown: Struik.

Read, D. W. and LeBlanc, Steven A. 1978. "Descriptive Statistics, Covering Laws, and Theories in Archaeology." *Current Anthropology* 19:307–35.

Redman, Charles L., ed. 1973. *Research and Theory in Current Archaeology*. New York: John Wiley Interscience.

_____. 1974. *Archaeological Sampling Strategies*. Reading: Addison-Wesley Modules in Anthropology, no. 55.

_____. 1975. "Productive Sampling Strategies for Archaeological Sites." In James Mueller, ed., *Sampling in Archaeology*. Tucson: University of Arizona Press, pp. 147–54.

_____. 1978a. *The Rise of Civilization*. San Francisco: W. H. Freeman.

_____. 1978b. "Multivariate Artifact Analysis: A Basis for Multidimensional Interpretations." In Charles L. Redman and others, eds., *Social Archaeology*. New York: Academic Press, pp. 159–92.

_____. 1978c. "Mesopotamian Urban Ecology: The Systemic Context of the Emergence of Urbanism." In Charles L. Redman and others, eds., *Social Archaeology*. New York: Academic Press, pp. 329–48.

Redman, C. L., and Watson, P. J. 1970. "Systematic, Intensive Surface Collection." *American Antiquity* 35:279–91.

Reed, Charles A., ed. 1977. *The Origins of Agriculture*. The Hague: Mouton.

Renfrew, A. C.; Dixon, J. E.; and Cann, J. R. 1966. "Obsidian and Early Cultural Contact in the Near East." *Proceedings of the Prehistoric Society* 32:1–29.

Renfrew, Colin. 1971. *Before Civilization*. New York: Alfred A. Knopf.

_____. 1979. "Transformations." In Colin Renfrew and Keith L. Cooke, eds., *Transformations: Mathematical Applications to Cultural Change*. New York: Academic Press, pp. 3–44.

Renfrew, Colin, and Cooke, Keith L., eds. 1979. *Transformations: Mathematical Applications to Cultural Change*. New York: Academic Press.

Renfrew, Colin. 1975. *The Emergence of Civilization*. London: Methuen.

Renfrew, Jane. 1973. *Paleoethnobotany*. London: Methuen.

Reynolds, Barrie. 1967. *The Material Culture of the Gwembe Tonga*. Manchester: Manchester University Press.

Roper, D. C. 1979. "The Method and Theory of Site Catchment Analysis: A Review." *Advances in Archaeological Method and Theory* 2:120–42.

Rouse, Irving. 1939. *Prehistory in Haiti: A Study in Method*. New Haven: Yale University Press.

_____. 1960. "The Classification of Artifacts in Archaeology." *American Antiquity* 25:313–23.

_____. 1972. *Introduction to Prehistory: A Systematic Approach*. New York: McGraw-Hill.

Rudenko, S. I. 1961. "The Ancient Cultures of the Bering Sea and the Eskimo Problem." *Arctic Institute of North America: Anthropology of the North, Translations from Russian Sources*, no. 1. Toronto: University of Toronto Press, pp. 163–64.

_____. 1970. *Frozen Tombs of Siberia: The Pazyryk Burials of Iron Age Horsemen*. Translated by M. W. Thompson. Berkeley: University of California Press.

Sabloff, Jeremy A. 1975. *Excavations at Seibal: Ceramics. Memoirs of the Peabody Museum of American Archaeology and Ethnology*, vol. 13, no. 2, Harvard University, Cambridge, Mass.

Sabloff, Jeremy A., and Lamberg-Karlovsky, C. C., eds. 1975. *Early Civilization and Trade*. Albuquerque: University of New Mexico Press.

Sabloff, Jeremy A., and Rathje, W. L., eds. 1975. *A Study of Pre-Columbian Commercial Systems: The*

1972–1973 Seasons at Cozumel, Mexico. Memoirs of the Peabody Museum, no. 3, Harvard University, Cambridge, Mass.

Sackett, James. 1966. "Quantitative Analysis of Upper Paleolithic Stone Tools." *American Anthropologist* 68, 2:356–94.

———. 1977. "The Meaning of Style in Archaeology." *American Antiquity* 43:369–82.

Sahlins, Marshall, and Service, Elman, eds., 1960. *Evolution and Culture.* Ann Arbor, Mich.: University of Michigan Press.

Salmon, M. 1978. "What Can Systems Theory Do for Archaeology?" *American Antiquity* 43:174–83.

Sanders, W. T., and Price, Barbara J. 1968. *Mesoamerica: Evolution of a Civilization.* New York: Random House.

Sanders, W. T.; Parsons, Jeffrey R.; and Santley, Robert S. 1979. *The Basin of Mexico: Ecological Processes in the Evolution of a Civilization.* New York: Academic Press.

Sanders, W. T., and Webster, David. 1978. "Unilinealism, Multilinealism, and the Evolution of Complex Societies." In Charles L. Redman and others, eds., *Social Archaeology.* New York: Academic Press, pp. 249–302.

Schiffer, Michael. 1976. *Behavioral Archaeology.* New York: Academic Press.

Schiffer, Michael, and House, John H. 1976. *The Cache River Archaeological Project.* Fayetteville: Arkansas Archaeological Survey.

———. 1977. "Cultural Resource Management and Archaeological Research: The Cache Project." *Current Anthropology* 18:43–68.

Schiffer, M. B.; Sullivan, A. P.; and Klinger, T. C. 1978. "The Design of Archaeological Surveys." *World Archaeology* 10:1–28.

Schliemann, Heinrich. 1881. *Ilios.* New York: Benjamin Blom. (Reissued in 1968.)

Schuyler, Robert L., ed. 1978. *Historical Archaeology: A Guide to Substantive and Theoretical Contributions.* Farmingdale, N.Y.: Baywood Publishing Company.

Scudder, Thayer. 1962. *The Ecology of the Gwembe Tonga.* Manchester: Manchester University Press.

Selkirk, Andrew, and Selkirk, Wendy. 1970. "Winchester: The Brooks." *Current Archaeology* 2:250–55.

Semenov, S. A. 1964. *Prehistoric Technology.* Translated by M. W. Thompson. London: Cory, Adams, and MacKay.

Service, Elman. 1971. *Primitive Social Organization.* New York: Random House.

Shackley, M. L. 1975. *Archaeological Sediments.* New York: John Wiley.

Sharer, Robert J., and Ashmore, Wendy. 1979. *Fundamentals of Archaeology.* Menlo Park: Cummings.

Shaw, Thurstan. 1960. "Early Smoking Pipes in Africa, Europe, and America." *Journal of the Royal Anthropological Institute* 90:272–305.

———. 1969. "Tree Felling by Fire." *Antiquity* 43:52.

Shawcross, F. C. 1967. "Prehistoric Diet and Economy on a Coastal Site at Galatea Bay, New Zealand." *Proceedings of the Prehistoric Society* 33, 7:125–30.

Shepard, Anna O. 1971. *Ceramics for the Archaeologist.* 2d ed. Washington, D.C.: Smithsonian Institution.

Slotkin, J. S., ed. 1965. *Readings in Early Anthropology.* New York: Viking Fund.

Smith, B. D. 1974. "Middle Mississippian Exploitation of Animal Populations: A predictive model." *American Antiquity* 39:274–91.

Smith, Eliot Grafton. 1911. *The Ancient Egyptians.* London: Macmillan.

Smith, Philip E. L. 1966. *Le Solutréen en France.* Paris: Payot.

Snow, Dean. 1976. *The North American Indians.* New York: Viking.

Solecki, Ralph. 1972. *Shanidar: the Humanity of Neanderthal Man.* New York: Penguin Press.

Sollas, W. J. *Ancient Hunters.* London: Macmillan, 1911.

South, Stanley. 1972. "Evolution and Horizon as Revealed in Ceramic Analysis in Historical Archaeology." *The Conference on Historic Sites Archaeology Papers* 6, 2:71–106.

———, ed. 1977. *Method and Theory in Historical Archaeology.* New York: Academic Press.

South, Stanley, and Widmer, Randolph. 1977. "A Subsurface Strategy for Archaeological Reconnaissance." In Stanley South, ed., *Method and Theory in Historical Archaeology.* New York: Academic Press.

Spaulding, A. C. 1953. "Statistical Techniques for the Study of Artifact Types." *American Antiquity* 18, 4:305–13.

_____. 1960a. "The Dimensions of Archaeology." In G. E. Dole and R. L. Carneiro, eds., *Essays in the Science of Culture in Honor of Leslie A. White.* New York: Crowell, pp. 437–56.

_____. 1960b. "Statistical Description and Comparison of Artifact Assemblages." In Robert F. Heizer and S. F. Cook, eds., *Quantitative Methods in Archaeology.* New York: Viking Fund, pp. 60–92.

_____. 1973. "Archaeology in the Active Voice: The New Anthropology." In Charles L. Redman, ed., *Research and Theory in Current Archaeology.* New York: John Wiley Interscience, pp. 337–54.

Spencer, Herbert. 1855. *Social Statistics.* London: Macmillan.

Spooner, Brian, ed. 1972. *Population Growth: Anthropological Implications.* Cambridge: MIT Press.

Stephens, John Lloyd. 1841. *Incidents of Travel in Central America, Chiapas, and Yucatan.* New York: Harper and Brothers.

Steponaitis, V. P., and Brain, J. P. 1976. "A Portable Differential Proton Magnetometer." *Journal of Field Archaeology* 3:455–63.

Steward, Julian. 1938. *Basin-Plateau Aboriginal Sociopolitical Groups.* Bureau of American Ethnology, Bulletin no. 120. Washington, D.C.: The Smithsonian Institution.

_____. 1955. *A Theory of Culture Change.* Urbana: University of Illinois Press.

Steward, Julian, and Setzler, F. M., eds. 1977. *Evolution and Ecology.* Urbana: University of Illinois Press.

Stone, Irving. 1975. *The Greek Treasure.* New York: Doubleday.

Story, Ron. 1976. *The Space Gods Revisited.* New York: Harper and Row.

Strong, W. D. 1935. *An Introduction to Nebraska Archaeology.* Washington, D.C.: Smithsonian Institution Miscellaneous Collections, vol. 93, no. 10.

Struever, Stuart. 1968. "Woodland Subsistence-Settlement Systems in the Lower Illinois Valley." In Sally R. Binford and Lewis R. Binford, eds., *New Perspectives in Archaeology.* Chicago: Aldine: pp. 285–312.

_____. 1971. "Comments on Archaeological Data Requirements and Research Strategy." *American Antiquity* 36:10.

Struever, Stuart, and Holton, F. A. 1979. *Koster.* New York: Anchor Press/Doubleday.

Struever, Stuart, and Houart, Gail L. 1972. "An Analysis of the Hopewell Interaction Sphere." *Anthropological Papers of the University of Michigan* 46:47–79.

Suess, Hans E. 1965. "Secular Variations of the Cosmic-Ray-Produced Carbon 14 in the Atmosphere and Their Interpretations." *Journal of Geophysical Research* 70:23–31.

Summers, Roger. 1969. *Ancient Mining in Rhodesia.* Salisbury: National Museums of Rhodesia.

Swanton, E., ed. 1975. *Lithic Technology: Making and Using Stone Tools.* Aldine: Chicago.

Swanton, John R. 1911. "Le Page de Pratz's *Histoire de Louisiane.*" *Bureau of American Ethnology Bulletin* 41:144–49.

Taylor, R. E., and Meighan, C. W., eds. 1978. *Chronologies in New World Archaeology.* New York: Academic Press.

Taylor, W. W. 1948. *A Study of Archaeology.* Menasha, Wisconsin: American Anthropological Association.

Terrell, J. 1967. "Galatea Bay: The Excavation of a Beach-Stream Midden Site on Poniu Island in the Hauraki Gulf, New Zealand." *Transactions of the Royal Society of New Zealand* 2, 3:31–70.

Thom, Alexander, and others. 1974. "Stonehenge." *Journal for a Study of Astronomy* 5:71–90.

Thomas, David Hurst. 1969. "Regional Sampling in Archaeology: A Pilot Great Basin Research Design." *UCLA Archaeological Survey Annual Report* 11:87–100.

_____. 1973. "An Empirical Test for Steward's Model of Great Basin Settlement Patterns. *American Antiquity* 38:155–76.

_____. 1974. *Predicting the Past.* New York: Holt, Rinehart and Winston.

_____. 1976. *Figuring Anthropology: First Principles of Probability and Statistics.* New York: Holt, Rinehart and Winston.

_____. 1978. "The Awful Truth about Statistics in Archaeology." *American Antiquity* 43:231–44.

_____. 1979. *Archaeology.* New York: Holt, Rinehart and Winston.

Thomas, M. N. and Lewis, Madeleine K. 1961. *Eva: an Archaic Site.* Knoxville: University of Tennessee Press.

Thompson, J. E. S. 1972. *Maya Hieroglyphs without Tears.* London: British Museum.

Thompson, M. W. 1977. *General Pitt Rivers.* London: Moonraker Press.

Thompson, R. H. 1956. "The Subjective Element in Archaeological Inference." *Southwestern Journal of Anthropology* 12, 3:327–32.

Thomsen, C. J. 1836. *Ledestraad til Nordisk Oldkyndighed.* Translated by Lord Ellesmere in 1848 as *A Guide to the Northern Antiquities.* Copenhagen.

Tite, M. S. 1972. *Methods of Physical Examination in Archaeology.* New York: Academic Press.

Townsend, William H. 1969. "Stone and Steel Tool Use in a New Guinea Society." *Ethnology* 8, 2:199–205.

Traling, D. H. 1971. *Principles and Applications of Paleomagnetism.* London: Chapman and Hall.

_____. 1975. "Archaeomagnetism: The Dating of Archaeological Materials by Their Magnetic Properties." *World Archaeology* 7, 2:198–209.

Trigger, Bruce. 1968a. *Beyond History: the Methods of Prehistory.* New York: Holt, Rinehart and Winston.

_____. 1968b. "The Determinants of Settlement Patterns." In K. C. Chang, ed., *Settlement Archaeology.* Palo Alto: National Press, pp. 53–78.

_____. 1971. "Archaeology and Ecology." *World Archaeology* 2, 3:321–36.

_____. 1978. *Time and Tradition.* Edinburgh: Edinburgh University Press.

Tringham, Ruth. 1971. *Hunting, Fishers, and Farmers of Southeastern Europe, 6000 to 3000 B.C.* London: Hutchinson.

Tylecote, R. F. 1972. *Metallurgy in Antiquity.* London: Edward Arnold.

Tylor, Edward. 1871. *Primitive Culture.* London: John Murray.

Ucko, Peter J. 1962. "The Interpretation of Prehistoric Anthropomorphic Figurines." *Journal of the Royal Anthropological Institute* 92:38–54.

Ucko, Peter J., and Dimbleby, G. W., eds. 1969. *The Domestication and Exploitation of Plants and Animals.* London: Duckworth.

United States Department of the Interior. 1976. "National Register of Historic Places: Criteria for Statewide Surveys and Plans." *Code of Federal Regulations, Title 36.* Chapter 1, Part 60.

Valliant, C. G. 1941. *The Aztecs of Mexico.* New York: Doubleday.

Vinnecombe, Patricia. 1960. "A Fishing Scene from the Tsoelike River, Southwestern Basutoland." *South African Archaeological Bulletin* 15:15–19.

Vita-Finzi, Claudio. 1978. *Archaeological Sites in Their Setting.* London: Thames and Hudson.

Vita-Finzi, Claudio, and Higgs, E. S. 1970. "Prehistoric Ecology in the Mount Carmel Area of Palestine: Site Catchment Analysis." *Proceedings of the Prehistoric Society* 36:1–37.

Vogt, Evon Z. 1967. *A Maya Community in the Highlands of Chiapas.* Cambridge, England: Belknap Press.

————, ed. 1974. *Aerial Photography in Anthropological Field Research*. Cambridge: Harvard University Press.

Watson, Patti Jo. 1974. *Archaeology of the Mammoth Cave Area*. New York: Academic Press.

————. 1976. "In Pursuit of Prehistoric Subsistence: A Comparative Account of Some Contemporary Flotation Techniques." *Mid-Continental Journal of Archaeology* 1, 1:77–100.

Watson, Patti Jo; LeBlanc, Steven A.; and Redman, Charles A. 1971. *Explanation in Archaeology*. Columbia: Columbia University Press.

Watson, R. A. 1976. "Inference in Archaeology." *American Antiquity* 41:58–66.

Wauchope, Robert. 1972. *Lost Tribes and Sunken Continents*. Chicago: University of Chicago Press.

Webb, William S. 1939. *An Archaeological Survey of Wheeler Basin on the Tennessee River in Northern Alabama*. Bureau of American Ethnology, no. 122. Washington, D.C.: The Smithsonian Institution.

Wells, Calvin. 1964. *Bones, Bodies, and Disease*. London: Thames and Hudson.

Wendorf, Fred. 1979. "Changing Values in Archaeology." *American Antiquity* 44, 4:641–43.

Wendorf, Fred, and others. 1968. *The Prehistory of Nubia*. Dallas: Southern Methodist University Press.

Whalen, Michael A. 1976. "Zoning within an Early Formative Community in the Valley of Oaxaca." In Kent V. Flannery, ed., *The Early Mesoamerican Village*. New York: Academic Press, pp. 75–78.

Wheat, Joe Ben. 1972. *The Olsen-Chubbock Site: A Paleo-Indian Bison Kill*. Society for American Archaeology, Memoir 26. Washington, D.C.: The Smithsonian Institution.

Wheatley, Paul. 1971. *The Pivot of the Four Quarters*. Chicago: Aldine.

Wheeler, R. E. M. 1943. *Maiden Castle*. London: Society of Antiquaries.

————. 1954. *Archaeology from the Earth*. Oxford: Clarendon Press.

————. 1967. *The Indus Civilization*. Cambridge: Cambridge University Press.

White, J. Peter. 1974. *The Past Is Human*. New York: Taplinger.

White, J. Peter, and Thomas, David Hurst. 1972. "What Mean These Stones?" In D. L. Clarke, ed., *Models in Archaeology*. London: Methuen, pp. 275–308.

White, Leslie. 1949. *The Evolution of Culture*. New York: McGraw-Hill.

White, Theodore. 1953. "Observations on the Butchery Techniques of Some Aboriginal Peoples." *American Antiquity* 19, 2:160–64.

Willey, Gordon R. 1953. *Prehistoric Settlement Patterns in the Virú Valley, Peru*. Bureau of American Ethnology, Bulletin 155. Washington, D.C.: The Smithsonian Institution.

————. 1962. "The Early Great Styles and the Rise of the Pre-Columbian Civilizations." *American Anthropologist* 64:1–14.

————. 1966. *An Introduction to American Archaeology, Volume I: North America*. Englewood Cliffs, N.J.: Prentice-Hall.

————. 1971. *An Introduction to American Archaeology, Volume 2: Middle and South America*. Englewood Cliffs, N.J.: Prentice-Hall.

————, ed. 1974. *Archaeological Researches in Retrospect*. Cambridge: Winthrop.

Willey, Gordon R., and Phillips, Philip. 1958. *Method and Theory in American Archaeology*. Chicago: University of Chicago Press.

Willey, Gordon R., and Sabloff, Jeremy A. 1980. *A History of American Archaeology*. 2d ed. San Francisco: W. H. Freeman.

Winter, Marcus C. 1976. "The Archaeological Household Cluster in the Valley of Oaxaca." In Kent V. Flannery, ed., *The Early Mesoamerican Village*. New York: Academic Press, pp. 25–30.

Winters, Howard D. 1969. *The Riverton Culture*. Urbana: Illinois Archaeological Survey.

Wolberg, Donald L. 1940. "The Hypothesized Osteodontokeratic Culture of the Australopithecines: A Look at the Evidence and the Opinions." *Current Anthropology* 11, 1:23–38.

Wood, W. Raymond, and Johnson, Donald Lee. 1978. "A Survey of the Disturbance Processes in Archaeological Site Formation." *Advances in Archaeological Method and Theory,* vol. 1.

Woolley, C. L. 1943. *Ur Excavations Volume II: The Royal Cemetery.* London and Philadelphia: British Museum and University Museum.

_____. 1954. *Excavations at Ur.* New York: Barnes and Noble.

Worsaae, J. J. A. 1843. *Danmarks Oldtid.* Copenhagen.

Wright, Thomas. 1852. "Wanderings of an Antiquary: Part VII." *Gentleman's Magazine,* p. 569.

Yellen, John E. 1977. *Archaeological Approaches to the Present: Models for Predicting the Past.* New York: Academic Press.

Zeuner, F. E. 1958. *Dating the Past.* 3d ed. London: Methuen.

_____. 1963. *A History of the Domesticated Animals.* London: Hutchinson.

Zubrow, Ezra. 1976. *Demographic Anthropology: Quantitative Approaches.* Albuquerque: University of New Mexico.

GLOSSARY ❧

This glossary is *not* designed as a comprehensive dictionary of archaeological terms. Rather, it seeks to give informal definitions of technical words, terms, and concepts used in the text, particularly ones that are theoretical. While we have tried to keep jargon to a minimum, inevitably some technical words enter a book like this. Terms in common use in many contexts as well as in archaeology, like, for example, "adaptation," "mutation," and so on, are not listed here. A good dictionary will give clarification in such cases.

Absolute dating: dating in calendar years before the present; chronometric dating.
Activity area: a patterning of artifacts in a site that indicates that a specific activity, such as stone toolmaking, took place.
Activity set: a set of artifacts that reveals the activities of an individual.
Alluvium: geological deposit laid down by the action of a river or stream.
Analogy: a process of reasoning whereby two entities that share some similarities are assumed to share many others.
Analysis: a stage of archaeological research that involves the description and classification of artifactual and non-artifactual data.
Analytical type: arbitrary groupings that an archaeologist defines for classifying humanly manufactured artifacts. Analytical types consist of groups of attributes that define convenient types of artifacts for use in site comparisons in space and time. They do not necessarily coincide with actual tool types used by prehistoric people.
Anthropology: the study of humankind in the widest possible sense. Anthropology studies humanity from the earliest times up to the present, and it includes cultural and physical anthropology and archaeology.
Antiquarian: someone interested in the past who collects and digs up antiquities in an unscientific manner, in contrast to the scientific archaeologist.
Arbitrary sample unit: a carefully defined unit of a total population of artifacts, or whatever is being sampled, selected by absolutely artificial criteria, without reference to cultural yardsticks. A typical example is a grid of squares laid out over a site.
Amino acid racemization: a chronometric dating method that uses the cumulative changes in amino acids in bone tissue to date human skeletons and other fossils.
Archaeological context: see Context.
Archaeological culture: a group of assemblages representing the surviving remains of an extinct culture.
Archaeological data: material recognized as significant as evidence by the archaeologist and collected and recorded as part of the research. There are four main classes of archaeological data: artifacts, features, structures, and food remains.
Archaeological reconnaissance: systematic attempts to locate, identify, and record the distribution of archaeological sites on the ground and against the natural geographical and environmental background.
Archaeological theory: a body of theoretical concepts which provide both a framework and a means for archaeologists to look beyond the facts and material objects for explanations of events that took place in prehistory.
Archaeological unit: arbitrary unit of classification set up by archaeologists to separate conveniently one grouping of artifacts in time and space from another.

Archaeologist: someone who studies the past using scientific methods, with the motive of recording and interpreting ancient cultures rather than collecting artifacts for profit or display.

Archaeology: a special form of anthropology that studies extinct human societies using the material remains of their behavior. The objectives of archaeology are to construct culture history, reconstruct past lifeways, and study cultural process.

Archaeomagnetic dating: chronometric dating using magnetic alignments from buried features, such as pottery kilns, that can be compared to known fluctuations in the earth's magnetic field to produce a date in years.

Archaic: in the New World, a period when hunter-gatherers were exploiting a broad spectrum of resources and may have been experimenting with agriculture.

Area excavation: excavation of a large, horizontal area, normally used to uncover houses and prehistoric settlement patterns.

Artifact: any object manufactured or modified by humans.

Assemblage: all the artifacts found at a site, including the sum of all subassemblages at the site.

Association: the relationship between an artifact and other archaeological finds and a site level, or other artifact, structure, or feature in the site.

Assyriologist: a student of the Assyrian civilization of Mesopotamia.

Attribute: a well defined feature of an artifact that cannot be further subdivided. Archaeologists identify various types of attributes, including form, style, and technology, in order to classify and interpret artifacts.

Attribute analysis: analysis of artifacts using many different artifact features. These attributes are normally studied statistically to produce clusters of attributes that can be used to identify statistical artifact classes.

Auger: a drill, either hand or power driven, used to probe subsurface deposits.

Australopithecus: primates whose fossil remains have been found mainly in East and southern Africa. They are thought to be closely related to the first humans, who may, indeed, have evolved among them.

Band: the simple form of human social organization that flourished for most of prehistory. Bands consist of a family or a series of families and normally range between twenty and fifty people.

Battleship curve: a term used to describe the rise in popularity of an artifact, its period of maximum popularity, and its eventual decline, as seen in a seriation graph.

Blades: parallel-sided stone flakes, normally removed from a carefully prepared core, often by means of a punch.

Bowsing: a technique of subsurface detection that involves thumping the ground to detect buried features through differing earth compaction.

Bulb of percussion: the conelike effect caused by conchoidal fracture on siliceous rocks.

Bulbar surface: the surface upon which the bulb of percussion occurs.

Burin: blade tool, flaked on either or both ends to form a small chisel or grooving tool.

Cambium: a viscid substance lying under the bark of trees, in which the annual growth of wood and bark takes place.

Carrying capacity: the number and density of people per square mile that a given area of land can support, given a particular subsistence level.

Causes: in archaeology, events which force people to make decisions about how to deal with new situations.

Central place theory: a geographical theory applied to archaeology, which states that human settlements will space themselves evenly across a landscape depending on the availability of natural resources and other factors. Eventually, these will evolve into a hierarchy of settlements of different size that are dependent on one another.

Ceramics: objects of fired clay.

Chiefdom: a more complex form of social organization than a tribal society, one that has evolved some form of leadership structure and some mechanisms that distribute goods and services throughout society. The chief who heads such a society, and the specialists who work for the chief, are supported by the voluntary contributions of the people.

Chronometric dating: dating in years before the present, absolute dating.

Clan: group of people from many lineages who live in one place and have a common line of descent—a kin grouping.

Class: a general group of artifacts, like "handaxes," which will be broken down into specific types, like "ovates," and so on.

Classic: in Mesoamerica and Peru, the period of vigorous civilization in both areas, characterized by numerous ceremonial centers and small states.

Classical archaeologist: a student of the Classical civilizations of Greece and Rome.

Classification: the ordering of archaeological data into groups and classes, using various ordering systems.

Closed system: a system that is internally self-regulating and receives no feedback from external sources (a good example is a household heating and cooling system).

Cluster analysis: the process of analyzing clusters of sites in space.

Community: in archaeology, the tangible remains of the activities of the maximum number of people who together occupy a particular settlement at any one period in time.

Complex: in archaeology, a chronological subdivision of different artifact types like stone tools, pottery, etc.

Component: an association of all the artifacts from a single occupation level at a site.

Conchoidal fracture: characteristic fracture pattern that occurs in siliceous rocks, such as obsidian and flint.

Conchologist: one who studies shells.

Conservation archaeology: another term for cultural resource management.

Context: the position of an archaeological find in time and space, established by measurement and assessment of its associations, matrix, and provenience. The process of assessment includes study of what has happened to the find since it was buried in the ground.

Coprolite: excrement preserved by desiccation or fossilization.

Core: in archaeology, a lump of stone from which humanly struck flakes have been removed.

Core borer: a hollow, tubelike instrument used to collect samples of soils, pollens, and other materials from below the surface.

Cranial: of, or pertaining to, the skull (cranium).

Crop marks: differential growth in crops and vegetational cover that reveals the outlines of archaeological sites from the air.

Cross dating: dating of sites by use of objects of known age, or artifact associations of known age.

Cultural anthropology: those aspects of anthropology focusing on cultural facets of human societies (a term widely used in the United States).

Cultural ecology: the study of the dynamic interactions between human societies and their environments. Under this approach, culture is the primary adaptive mechanism used by human societies.

Cultural evolution: a theory similar to that of biological evolution, which argues that human cultures change gradually throughout time, as a result of a number of cultural processes.

Cultural process: a deductive approach to archaeological research that is designed to study the changes and interactions in cultural systems and the processes by which human cultures change throughout time. Processual archaeologists use both descriptive and explanatory models.

Cultural resource management: the conservation and management of archaeological sites and artifacts as a means of protecting the past.

Cultural selection: the process that leads to the acceptance of some cultural traits and innovations that make a culture more adaptive to its environment. This is somewhat akin to natural selection in biological evolution.

Cultural system: a perspective on culture that thinks of culture and its environment as a number of interlinked systems in which change occurs through a series of minor, linked variations in one or more of these systems.

Cultural tradition: in archaeology, a distinctive tool kit or technology that lasts for a considerable period of time, longer than the duration of a single culture, at a single locality or several localities.

Cultural transformations: changes in the archaeological record resulting from later human behavior, like, for example, the digging of a rubbish pit into earlier levels.

Culture: human culture is a set of designs for living that help mold our responses to different situations. It is our primary means of adapting to our environment. A "culture" in archaeology is an arbitrary unit meaning similar assemblages of artifacts found at several sites, defined in a precise context of time and space.

Culture area: an arbitrary geographical, or research, area in which general cultural homogeneity is to be found.

Culture history: an approach to archaeology that assumes that artifacts can be used to build up a generalized picture of human culture and descriptive models in time and space and interpret them.

Cumulative recording: a process of stratigraphic recording in excavation that involves excavating and recording a trench in three dimensions, using both horizontal and vertical observations to reconstruct events at the site.

Cuneiform: from the Greek word *cuneus,* meaning a wedge. The earliest known, wedgelike script from Mesopotamia.

Curation: deliberate attempts by prehistoric peoples to preserve key artifacts and structures for posterity.

Cybernetics: general systems theory.

Cylinder hammer technique: stone flaking technique using a bone hammer that removes small, flat flakes from a core.

Data universe: a defined area of archaeological investigation, bounded in time and space, often a geographical region or an archaeological site.

Datum point: a location from which all measurements on a site are made. The datum point is tied into local survey maps.

Debitage: waste byproducts resulting from the manufacture of stone tools.

Deductive: a process of reasoning that involves the testing of generalizations by generating hypotheses and testing them with data. Deductive research is cumulative and involves constant refining of hypotheses. This contrasts with inductive approaches where one proceeds from a set of specific observations to a set of general conclusions.

Deductive-nomological reasoning: a way of explaining observable phenomena by means of formal scientific methods, testing hypotheses generated from general laws governing human behavior. Some archaeologists believe this is the appropriate way to explain cultural process.

Demography: the study of population.

Dendrochronology: tree-ring chronology.

Detritus: debris or droppings.

Diffusion: the spread of a culture trait from one area to another by means of contact between people.

Direct historical approach: archaeological technique of working backwards in time from historic sites of known age into earlier times.

Drift: a glacial deposit laid down by ice or water in glacial streams, lakes, or arctic oceans.

Ecofact: archaeological finds that are of cultural significance but that were not manufactured by humans, for example, bones, vegetal remains, and so on. This is not a very commonly used term.

Egyptologist: a student of the cultures of Ancient Egypt.

Epigrapher: one who studies inscriptions.

Epiphysis: the articular end of a long bone, a process that fuses at adulthood.

Escarpment: a hill range or cliff (a geological term).

Eolith: a controversial artifact, identified by European archaeologists in the early twentieth century and claimed to be the earliest human tools. Eoliths are now considered to be of natural origin.

Ethnoarchaeology: living archaeology, a form of ethnography that is mainly concerned with material remains. Archaeologists carry out living archaeology to document the relationships between human behavior and the patterns of artifacts and food remains in the archaeological record.

Ethnography: a descriptive study, normally an in-depth examination of a particular culture.

Ethnology: a cross-cultural study of particular aspects of various cultures, usually theoretically based.

Excavation: the process of digging archaeological sites, removing the matrix and observing the provenience and context of the finds contained therein, and recording them in a three-dimensional way.

Exchange system: a system developed to exchange goods and services between individuals and different communities.

Exogamy: a rule requiring marriage outside a social or cultural unit (*endogamy* means the opposite).

Experimental archaeology: the use of carefully controlled modern experiments to provide data to aid in the interpretation of the archaeological record.

Extrasomatic: outside the body.

Faience: glazed terracotta.

Feature: an artifact that, being too large to remove from a site, normally is recorded only; for example, houses, storage pits, and so on.

Feces: excrement.

Feedback: a concept in archaeological applications of systems theory that reflects the continually changing relationship between a set of cultural variables and their environment.

Fire setting: a technique for quarrying stone by using fire to shatter the outcrops of rock.

Fission track dating: observation of accumulations of radioactivity in glass and volcanic rocks to produce absolute dates.

Flake tools: stone tools made of flakes removed from cores.

Flotation: in archaeology, a technique for recovering plant remains by using water to separate seeds from their surrounding deposit.

Focus: approximately equivalent to a phase.

Form: the physical characteristics—size and shape or composition—of any archaeological find. Form is an essential part of attribute analysis.

Form analysis: analysis of artifacts based on the assumption that the shape of a pot or other tool is a direct reflection of its function.

Formative: in Mesoamerica, the period when more complex societies and settlement patterns were emerging, ones that led to the complex states of later times (contemporary with the rise of argriculture).

Form attributes: attributes relating to the shape of an artifact.

Form types: artifact types based on the shape of an artifact.

Formulation: in archaeology, the process of making decisions about a research project as a preliminary to formal research design.

Foot survey: archaeological reconnaissance on foot, often with a set interval between members of the survey team.

Fuller: a clothmaker.

Functional type: an archaeological classification based on the supposed function of the artifact.

General systems theory: the notion that any organism or organization can be studied as a system broken down into many interacting subsystems, or parts. This is sometimes called cybernetics.

Geochronology: geological dating.

Glacial eustasy: the adjustments made in sea levels and the earth's crust as a result of the expansion and contraction of Pleistocene ice sheets.

Half-life: the period of time required for the decay of one half of a radioactive isotope into a stable element. Used as a basis for radiocarbon dating and other dating methods.

Heuristic: serving to find out; a means of discovery.

Hieroglyphs: ancient writing form using pictographic or ideographic symbols; used in Egypt, Mesoamerica, and elsewhere.

Historical archaeology: the study of archaeological sites in conjunction with historical records. It is sometimes called historic sites archaeology.

Historiography: the process of studying history.

History: the study of the past through written records.

Hominid: a member of the family *Hominidae,* represented today by a single species, *Homo sapiens.*

Homo erectus: humans who evolved from Lower Pleistocene hominids. They possessed larger brains and made more elaborate stone tools than their predecessors and settled in far more extreme environments, as far apart as western Europe, Asia, and tropical Africa.

Homotaxial: strata or cultures that have the same relationship to one another but are not necessarily contemporaneous.

Horizon: a widely distributed set of culture traits and artifact assemblages whose distribution and chronology allow one to assume that they spread rapidly. Often, horizons are formed of artifacts that were associated with widespread, distinctive religious beliefs.

Horizontal (area) excavation: archaeological excavation designed to uncover large areas of a site, especially settlement layouts.

Household cluster: an arbitrary archaeological unit used to define artifact patterns reflecting the activities that take place around a house and are presumed to belong to a single household.

Hydrology: the scientific study of water—its properties and laws.

Ideology: the knowledge or beliefs developed by human societies as part of their cultural adaptation.

Induction: a reasoning process by which one proceeds from a set of specific observations to a set of general conclusions.

Industry: the industry at a site is all of the particular artifacts (bone, stone, wood) found at one site and made at the same time by the same population.

Industrial archaeology: the study of sites of the Industrial Revolution and later.

Inevitable variation: the notion that cultures change and vary throughout time, in a cumulative manner. The reasons for these changes are little understood.

Inorganic materials: material objects which are not part of the animal or vegetable kingdoms.

Interpretation: the stage in the research process in which the results of archaeological analyses are synthesized and attempts to explain their meaning are made.

Interstadial: a period of slightly warmer climate between two cold periods of a major glaciation.

Kinship: in anthropology, relationships between people that are based on real or imagined descent, or sometimes, on marriage. Kinship ties impose mutual obligations on all members of a kin group, ties that were at the core of most prehistoric societies.

Knapper: someone who manufactures stone artifacts.

Leaching: water sweeping through the soil and removing the soluble materials in it.

Levallois technique: stoneworking technique that involves preparation of a bun-shaped core from which a single, preshaped flake is removed.

Limited area reconnaissance: door-to-door inquiries on a comprehensive level, supported by actual substantiation of claims that sites exist by checking on the ground. This method fails to give information of proportions of different sites in an area.

Lineage: a kinship that traces descent through either the male or female members.

Lithic: of, or pertaining to, stone, as in *lithic technology*.

Lithic experimentation: the process of experimenting with the manufacture of stone tools. A useful analytical approach to the interpretation of prehistoric artifacts.

Loess: windblown glacial soil.

Lost-wax technique: a method of bronzeworking in which a mold of the object is made. The mold is assembled with wax in place of the artifact. The wax is then melted and replaced with molten bronze. This technique was much used by the Shang bronzeworkers of China.

Magnetometer: a subsurface detection device that measures minor variations in the earth's magnetic field and locates archaeological features before excavation.

Material culture: normally refers to technology and artifacts.

Matriarchal: family authority rests with the woman's family.

Matrilineal: descent reckoned through the female line only.

Matrilocal: married couples live with or near the wife's mother.

Matrix: the surrounding deposit in which archaeological finds are situated.

Mesolithic: rather outdated term, sometimes used by Old World archaeologists to refer to the period of transition between the Paleolithic and Neolithic eras. No precise economic or technological definition has ever been formulated.

Mica: a mineral, occurring in a glittering scaly form, widely prized for ornamental purposes.

Midden: a deposit of occupation debris, rubbish, or other by-products of human activity.

Midwestern Taxonomic System: system of archaeological units developed before World War II to organize artifacts and sites in North America, which is still in widespread use in a modified form.

Mitigation: in archaeology, measures taken to minimize the impact of destructive forces on archaeological sites.

Mode: a cluster of attributes that has cultural meaning and can be interpreted as such.

Model: a theoretical reconstruction of a set of phenomena, devised to understand them better. Archaeological models can be descriptive or explanatory.

Modified diffusionism: form of diffusionist theory, espoused by Gordon Childe and others, which allowed for some local cultural evolution.

Monotheistic: religion recognizing one god.

Moraine: deposit of debris left by an advancing or retreating glacier.

Multilinear cultural evolution: a theory of cultural evolution that sees each human culture evolving in its own way as a result of adaptations to diverse environments. It is sometimes defined in terms of four broad stages of evolution of social organization (band, tribe, chiefdoms, and state-organized societies).

Natural transformations: changes in the archaeological record resulting from natural phenomena that occur after the deposition of artifacts in the ground.

Natural type: an archaeological type that coincides with an actual category recognized by the original toolmaker.

Negative feedback: a response to a stimulus given a system that tends to dampen change.

Neolithic: an outdated Old World term, used to refer to that period of the Stone Age when people were cultivating without the use of metals.

Nonarbitrary sample unit: a sample unit chosen with reference to cultural and other factors, such as geographical proximity or layout of rooms in a pueblo. These types of sample unit are often clustered.

Nonprobabilistic sampling: sampling using instinctual criteria, such as the archaeologist's experience, or factors that affect access to a research area.

Normative view: a view of human culture that argues that one can identify the abstract rules that regulate them: a commonly used basis for studying archaeological cultures throughout time.

Nuclear family: mother, father, and children.

Obsidian: black volcanic glass.

Obsidian hydration: a dating method that measures the thickness of the hydration layer in obsidian artifacts. The hydration layer is caused by the absorption of water on exposed surfaces of the rock.

Open system: in archaeology, cultural systems that interchange both energy and information with their environment.

Oral tradition: historical traditions, often genealogies, passed down from generation to generation by word of mouth.

Ordering: in archaeology, the process of arranging artifacts in logical classes, and in chronological order.

Organic materials: materials like bone, wood, horn, or hide, which were once living organisms.

Ossification: the fusion of a limb bone with its articular end. The term is also used to imply the stagnation, or calcification, of soft tissue into bonelike material.

Osteologist: one who studies bones.

Paleoanthropologist: an archaeologist who studies the archaeology of the earliest humans.

Paleobotanist: one who studies prehistoric botany.

Paleoecology: the study of ecology in ancient times.

Paleolithic: the Old Stone Age.

Paleontology: the study of fossil (or ancient) bones.

Palynology: pollen analysis.

Parahistoric sites: archaeological sites of preliterate peoples who were contemporary with cultures with writing.

Patination: the natural weathering on the surface of rocks and artifacts.

Patrilineal: descent reckoned through the male line only.

Patrilocal: married couples live with or near the husband's father.

Patterns of discard: Remains left for investigation after natural destruction processes have affected artifacts and food remains abandoned by their original users.

Pedology: the scientific study of soil.

Periglacial: surrounding a glacial area.

Period: an archaeological unit defining a major unit of prehistoric time; it will contain several phases and pertain to a wide area.

Permafrost: permanently frozen subsoil.

Petrological analysis: examination of thin sections of stone artifacts to determine the provenience of the rock used to make them.

Petrology: the study of rocks, in archaeology, the term normally refers to the analysis of trace elements and other characteristics of rocks used to make such artifacts as axe blades, which were traded over long distances.

Phase: an archaeological unit defined by characteristic groupings of culture traits that can be identified precisely in time and space. It lasts for a relatively short period of time and is found at one or more sites within a locality or region. Its culture traits are sufficiently distinctive for it to be distinguished from other phases.

Physical anthropology: basically, biological anthropology, which includes the study of fossil humans, genetics, primates, and blood groups.

Planimetric maps: maps used to record details of archaeological sites: they contain no topographic information.

Pleistocene: the last major geological epoch, which extended from about two million years ago until about 11,500 B.P. It is sometimes called the Quaternary, or the Great Ice Age.

Population: in sampling methods, the total sum of sampling units selected within a data universe.

Positive feedback: a system's response to external stimuli that leads to further change and reinforces it.

Postclassic: a period of Mesoamerican and Andean prehistory, which saw the rise of militaristic stages, such as those of the Aztec and the Inca.

Potassium argon (K/A) dating: an absolute dating technique based on the decay rate of potassium ^{40}K, which becomes Argon ^{40}Ar.

Potsherd: a fragment of a clay vessel.

Preclassic: see *Formative*.

Prehistory: the millennia of human history that preceded the development of written records. Prehistorians study prehistoric archaeology.

Pressure flaking: a stoneworking technique in which thin flakes are removed from a core or artifact by applying hand or chest pressure.

Primary context: an undisturbed association, matrix, and provenience.

Prime movers: an early concept in the study of the origins of civilization, meaning a single, and primary, cause of the emergence of urban societies. For example, many people considered irrigation a prime mover of Egyptian civilization.

Probabilistic sampling: archaeological sampling based on formal statistical criteria. This method enables one to use probability statistics in the analysis of data.

Process: in archaeology, the process of cultural change that takes place as a result of interactions between a cultural system's elements and the system and its environment. The study of this process is the ultimate goal of archaeology.

Provenience: the recorded position of an archaeological find in time and space, recorded three-dimensionally.

Proximal: opposite to distal: the end of a bone nearest to the skeleton's center line.

Pulse radar: use of a pulse induction meter that applies pulses of magnetic field to the soil. This method can be used to find graves, metals, and pottery.

Quadrat; a unit of spatial analysis used to divide up an area into cells for purposes of analysis.

Quaternary: geological time since the beginning of the Pleistocene up to recent times. The exact date of its commencement is still uncertain, but it is over two million years old.

Radiocarbon dating: an absolute dating method that is based on measuring the decay rate of the carbon isotope, Carbon 14, to stable nitrogen (E12). The resulting dates are calibrated using tree-ring chronologies, from radiocarbon ages into dates in calendar years.

Random sampling: sampling techniques that are based on the totally random selection of sample units to be investigated.

Reciprocity: in archaeology, the exchange of goods between two parties.

Redistribution: the process of dispersing of trade goods from a central place throughout a society, a complex process that was a critical part of the evolution of civilization.

Region: a geographically defined area in which ecological adaptations are basically similar.

Relative chronology: time scale developed by the law of superposition or artifact ordering.

Remote sensing: reconnaissance and site survey methods that use such devices as aerial photography to detect subsurface features and sites.

Research design: a carefully formulated and systematic plan for executing archaeological research.

Resistivity survey: the measurement of differences in electrical conductivity in soils, used to detect buried features, such as walls and ditches.

Sampling frame: lists of chosen sampling units that form the sample of the total population to be tested. It is compiled as a means to proceed to the selection of units for investigation.

Sample unit: an arbitrary or non-arbitrary unit of the data universe, used for sampling archaeological data.

Scanner imagery: a method of recording sites from the air using infrared radiation that is beyond the practical spectral response of photographic film. Useful for tracing prehistoric agricultural systems which have disturbed the topsoil over wide areas.

Science: a way of acquiring knowledge and understanding about those parts of the natural world that can be observed. A disciplined and highly ordered search for knowledge carried out in a systematic manner.

Scientific method: the operational methodology of science, used for observing and testing natural phenomena.

Secondary context: a context of an archaeological find that has been disturbed by subsequent human activity or natural phenomena.

Selective excavation: archaeological excavation of parts of a site using sampling methods or carefully placed trenches that do not uncover the entire site.

Seriation: methods used to place artifacts in chronological order, under which artifacts with close similarities in form or style are placed in close proximity to one another.

Settlement pattern: distribution of human settlement on the landscape, and within archaeological communities.

Shadow sites: archaeological sites identified from the air, where oblique light can show up reduced topography of sites invisible on the ground.

Site: any place where humanly manufactured or modified objects, features, or ecofacts are found. A site can range from a living site to a quarry site, and it can be defined in functional and other ways.

Site catchment analysis: the inventorying of natural resources within a given distance of a site.

Site plans: specially prepared maps for recording the horizontal provenience of artifacts, food remains, and features. They are keyed to topographic maps.

Site survey: the collection of surface data and the evaluation of the archaeological significance of each site.

Slip: fine, wet clay finish applied to the surface of a clay vessel prior to firing and decoration of same.

Social anthropology: the British equivalent of cultural anthropology, but with an emphasis on socio-logical factors.

Sociocultural: combining social and cultural factors.

Sodality: a nonkinship organization within a society that cuts across kinship groups and lineages for specific purposes that add to the cohesiveness of that society.

Sondage: see *Test pit.*

Spectrographic analysis: chemical analysis that involves passing the light from a number of trace elements through a prism or diffraction grating that spreads out the wavelengths in a spectrum. This enables one to separate the emissions and identify different trace elements. A useful approach for studying metal objects and obsidian artifacts.

Stage: a technological subdivision of prehistoric time that has little chronological meaning but denotes the level of technological achievement of societies living within it, for example, the Stone Age.

Stela (or stele): a column or stone slab, often with an inscribed or sculptured surface.

Stratified sampling: a probabilistic sampling technique used to cluster and isolate sample units, when regular spacing is inappropriate for cultural reasons.

Stratigraphy: the process of observing the superimposed layers of an archaeological site.

Stratum: a single-deposited or cultural level.

Stylistic attributes and types: such phenomena based on stylistic features.

Stylistic analysis: artifact analysis that concentrates not only on form and function, but on the decorative styles used by the makers—a much used approach to ceramic analysis.

Subarea: subdivision of an archaeological area, normally defined by geographic or cultural consid-erations.

Subassemblage: association of artifacts that denotes a particular form of prehistoric activity practiced by a group of people.

Surface survey: the process of collecting archaeological finds from sites, with the objectives of gathering representative samples of artifacts from the surface. Surface survey also establishes the types of activity on the site, locates major structures, and gathers information on the most densely occupied areas of the site that could be most productive for total or sample excavation.

Synthesis: the process of assembling and analyzing data preparatory to interpretation.

Systematics: in archaeology, procedures for creating sets of archaeological units derived from a logical system for a particular purpose.

Systematic sampling: a refinement of random sampling in which a single unit is chosen, then others chosen at regular intervals from the first. Useful for studying artifact patterning.

Taxonomy: an ordered set of operations that results in the subdivision of objects into ordered classifications.

Technological analysis: study of technological methods used to make an artifact.

Technological attributes (technological types): attributes based on technological features of an object.

Tectonic: a term referring to the earth's crust; an example of a tectonic movement is an earthquake.

Telehistoric sites: sites far removed from written records: prehistoric sites.

Tell: a mound; a term used to refer to archaeological sites of this type in the Near East.

Temper: coarse material such as sand or shell added to fine potclay to make it bond during firing.

Tempering: a process for hardening iron blades, involving heating and rapid cooling. Also, material added to potters' clay.

Test pit: an excavation unit used to sample or probe a site before large-scale excavation or to check surface surveys.

Thermoluminescence: a chronometric dating method that measures the amount of light energy released by a baked clay object when heated rapidly. This gives an indication of the time that has elapsed since the object was last heated.

Three-age system: a technological subdivision of the prehistoric past developed for Old World prehistory in 1806.

Topographic maps: maps that can be used to relate archaeological sites to basic features of the natural landscape.

Total excavation: complete excavation of an entire archaeological site. Normally confined to smaller sites, such as burial mounds or camp sites.

Trace elements: minute elements found in rocks that emit characteristic wavelengths of light when heated to incandescence. Trace element analysis is used to study the sources of obsidian and other materials that were traded over long distances.

Tradition: persistent technological or cultural patterns that are identified by characteristic artifact forms. These persistent forms outlast the duration of a single phase and can occur over a wide area.

Transformational processes: processes that transform an abandoned prehistoric settlement into an archaeological site through the passage of time. These processes can be initiated by natural phenomena or human activity.

Tribe: a larger group of bands unified by sodalities and governed by a council of representatives from the bands, kin groups, or sodalities within it.

Trypanosomiasis: sleeping sickness.

Tsetse: a fly that carries trypanosomiasis. Because of belts of tsetse fly country in Africa, inhabitants are prevented from raising cattle.

Tuff: solidified volcanic ash.

Type: in archaeology, a grouping of artifacts created for purposes of comparison with other groups. This grouping may or may not coincide with the actual tool types designed by the original manufacturers.

Type fossil: a tool type characteristic of a particular "archaeological era," an outdated concept borrowed from geology.

Typology: the process of classification of types.

Unaerated: not exposed to the open air.

Underwater archaeology: the study of archaeological sites and shipwrecks beneath the surface of the water.

Uniformitarianism: the doctrine that states the earth was formed by the same natural geological processes that are operating today.

Unilinear cultural evolution: a late-nineteenth-century evolutionary theory that envisaged all human societies as evolving along a single track of cultural evolution, from simple hunting and gathering to literate civilization.

Unit: in archaeological terms, an artificial grouping used for description of artifacts.

Use wear analysis: microscopic analysis of artifacts to detect signs of wear through their use on their working edges.

Varves: annual clay deposits made by retreating and melting glaciers. Used to measure recent Pleistocene geological events.

Vertical excavation: excavation undertaken to establish a chronological sequence, normally covering a limited area.

Votive: intended as an offering as a result of a vow.

Zooarchaeology: the study of animal remains in archaeology.

Brown, "The Organization of Archaeological Research: An Illinois example," Fig. 1, p. 278 in Charles L. Redman, *Research and Theory in Current Archaeology*; New York: John Wiley and Sons, 1973.

11.3   The University Museum, University of Pennsylvania.

11.4   Courtesy of Sir Mortimer Wheeler and the Society of Antiquaries of London.

11.5   J. A. Tuck, Memorial University of Newfoundland.

11.6   Redrawn from Ivor Noël Hume, *Historical Archaeology*, Fig. 10; New York: Alfred Knopf, Inc., 1968. By permission of the publisher and Curtis Brown, Ltd. Copyright © 1968 by Ivor Noël Hume.

11.7   From *Techniques of Archaeological Excavation* by Philip Barker, Fig. 72, p. 236. London: B. T. Batsford Ltd., 1977.

11.9   a. & b. Peabody Museum, Harvard University, Cambridge, Massachusetts.

11.10   Peabody Museum, Harvard University. Photograph by A. L. Smith.

11.11   Carl W. Blegen and Marion Rawson, *The Palace of Nestor at Pylos in Western Messenia*, Vol. I, Part 2, Plates copyright © 1966 by Princeton University Press, Fig. 9. Reprinted by permission of Princeton University Press and The University of Cincinnati.

11.12   Redrawn from Ivor Noël Hume, *Historical Archaeology*, Fig. 15; New York: Alfred A. Knopf, Inc., 1968. Redrawn by permission of the author, the publisher, and Curtis Brown, Ltd. Copyright © 1968 by Ivor Noël Hume.

11.13   Mesa Verde National Park.

11.14   By courtesy of the Society of Antiquaries of London.

11.15   M. D. Leaky, *Olduvai Gorge*, Vol. 3, Fig. 13; London: Cambridge University Press, 1971.

11.16   R. S. Peabody Foundation for Archaeology, Andover, Massachusetts.

11.17   Wilfred Shawcross.

11.19   By courtesy of the Society of Antiquaries of London.

11.21   Patricia M. Christie.

11.22   Winchester Excavations Committee, Winchester, England.

Chapter 12

12.1   By courtesy of the Society of Antiquaries of London.

12.3   After J. G. D. Clark, *Star Carr*, Fig. 35; London: Cambridge University Press, 1954.

12.4   Lowie Museum of Anthropology, University of California, Berkley.

12.5   By permission of the Trustees of the British Museum (Natural History).

12.6   Figures from *Invitation to Archaeology* by James Deetz, illustrated by Eric G. Engstrom. Copyright © 1967 by James Deetz. Reproduced by permission of Doubleday & Company, Inc.

12.7   Pitt Rivers Museum, Oxford.

Chapter 13

13.1   Redrawn from M. D. Leakey, *Olduvai Gorge*, Vol. III; London: Cambridge University Press, 1971.

13.2   *Life Nature Library/Early Man* © 1965, 1973 Time, Inc.

13.4   *Life Nature Library/Early Man* © 1965, 1973 Time, Inc.

13.5   Pitt Rivers Museum, Oxford.

13.6   Reprinted by permission of Faber and Faber Ltd. From *The Archaeology of Early Man* by J. M. Coles and E. S. Higgs.

13.7   Adapted from: F. Bordes, *The Old Stone Age*, London: Weidenfeld & Nicholson, 1968. Fig. 34.

13.8   a. Adapted from F. Bordes, *The Old Stone Age*, London: Weidenfeld & Nicholson, 1968. Fig. 55. b. *Ibid*. Fig. 54. d. After G. H. S. Bushnell, *The First Americans*, Fig. 2, copyright © 1968. Thames and Hudson Ltd., London; McGraw-Hill, New York.

13.9   Courtesy of Robert Edwards, Aboriginal Arts Board.

13.10   Maria Martinez photographer; Courtesy of Museum of New Mexico.

13.11   Photo by Carmelo Guadagno, Courtesy of Museum of the American Indian/Heye Foundation, New York.

13.12   Courtesy of the Art Institute of Chicago.

13.14   The Ohio Historical Society, Columbus, Ohio.

13.15   From the Miguel Majico Gallo Collection.

13.16   Michael S. Bisson.

13.18   From K. C. Chang, *The Archaeology of Ancient China* © 1971, Yale University Press, and Courtesy of the Smithsonian.

13.19   Photo by Jean Vertut, taken at the British Museum.

13.20   University of Alaska Museum.

13.21   Ruth Kirk with Richard D. Daugherty, *Hunters of the Wale*, New York: Wm. Morrow & Co., 1974. Photo by Harvey Rice.

13.22   By permission of the Trustees of the British Museum (Natural History)

Chapter 14

14.1   After J. G. D. Clark, *Star Carr*, Fig. 73; London: Cambridge University Press, 1954.

14.3 Reproduced by permission of Blackwell Scientific Publications.

14.4 Copyright reserved: University Museum of Archaeology and Ethnology, Cambridge, England.

14.6 Copyright © 1970 by the Regents of the University of California. Reprinted by permission of the University of California Press.

14.7 By permission of the Trustees of the British Museum (Natural History).

14.8 Cave Research Foundation Archaeological Project, Photo by Roger W. Brucker.

14.9 Copyright reserved: University Museum of Archaeology and Ethnology, Cambridge, England.

14.10 Redrawn from *Prehistoric Europe: The Economic Basis* by J. G. D. Clark, Fig. 44, with permission of the publishers, Stanford University Press. Copyright © 1952 by J. G. D. Clark; London: Methuen and Company Ltd.

14.11 Redrawn from *Prehistoric Europe: The Economic Basis* by J. G. D. Clark, Fig. 17, with permission of the publishers, Stanford University Press. Copyright © 1952 by J. G. D. Clark; London: Methuen and Company Ltd.

14.13 Patricia Vinnecombe, "A Fishing scene from the Tsoelike River, South-Eastern Basutoland," *South African Archaeological Bulletin,* Vol. 15, No. 57, March 1960, p. 15, Fig. 1.

Chapter 15
15.1 Smithsonian Institution Photo No. T13301.

15.2 By courtesy of the Society of Antiquaries of London.

15.3 Reconstructions by Nelson Reed. Courtesy of Illinois State Museum.

15.4 Redrawn from Richard Lee and Irven DeVore, *Kalahari Hunter Gatherers,* Cambridge: Harvard University Press. Used by permission.

15.5 Redrawn from Richard A. Gould, "The Archaeologist as Ethnographer," *World Archaeology,* 1971, 3, 2, pp. 143–177, Fig. 18.

Chapter 16
16.2 Carl Frank/Photo Researchers, Inc.

16.4 Redrawn from Marcus C. Winter and Kent V. Flannery, "Analyzing Household Activities," Fig. 2.17 in *The Early Mesoamerican Village,* Kent V. Flannery (ed.); New York: Academic Press, 1976.

16.5 Marcus C. Winter, "The Archaeological Household Cluster in the Valley of Oaxaca," Fig. 2.10 in *The Early Mesoamerican Village,* Kent V. Flannery (ed.); New York: Academic Press, 1976.

16.6 Redrawn from E. Z. Vogt, *Zinacantan,* Cam-

bridge: The Belknap Press of Harvard University Press. Used by permission.

16.7 Top: Melvin Konner/Anthro Photo File. Bottom: Reproduced by Courtesy of the Trustees of the British Museum.

16.8 Lee Boltin.

16.9 After J. G. D. Clark, *Star Carr,* Fig. 8; London: Cambridge University Press, 1954.

16.10 Redrawn from Ian Hodder and Clive Orton, *Spatial Analysis in Archaeology;* Oxford: Cambridge University Press, 1976, and with permission of the proceedings of The Prehistoric Society.

16.11 Redrawn from Kent V. Flannery, "Empirical Determination of Site Catchments in Oaxaca and Tuhuacan" Fig. 4.6 in *The Early Mesoamerican Village,* Kent V. Flannery (ed); New York: Academic Press, 1976.

16.13 Redrawn from Hodder and Orton, *Spatial Analysis in Archaeology,* New York: Cambridge University Press, 1976, p. 461. Courtesy of Cambridge University Press and the Royal Anthropological Institute of Great Britain and Ireland.

Chapter 17
17.1 Courtesy of the American Museum of Natural History.

17.3 Museum of the American Indian/Heye Foundation, New York.

17.4 Peabody Museum, Harvard University, Cambridge, Massachusetts.

17.5 After Renfrew, 1976, as redrawn in Sharer-Ashmore, *Fundamentals of Archaeology,* The Benjamin Cummings Publishing Co., Inc., 1979, from *Ancient Civilization and Trade,* ed. J. A. Sabloff and C. C. Lamberg-Karlovsky, University of New Mexico Press, 1975.

17.6 *Ramesses II and Queen in Audience.* Stela from 18th Dynasty, 09.287, Gift of Mrs. Frank E. Peabody; Courtesy, Museum of Fine Arts, Boston.

17.7 The University Museum, University of Pennsylvania.

17.8 Used with permission of Museé de L'Homme.

17.9 Redrawn from Robert D. Drennan, "Religion and Social Evolution in Formative Mesoamerica," Fig. 11.8 in *The Early Mesoamerican Village,* Kent V. Flannery (ed); New York: Academic Press, 1976.

17.10 Kent V. Flannery, "Contextual Analysis of Ritual Paraphernalia from Formative Oaxaca," Fig. 11.9 in *The Early Mesoamerican Village,* Kent V. Flannery (ed); New York: Academic Press, 1976.

INDEX ⚜

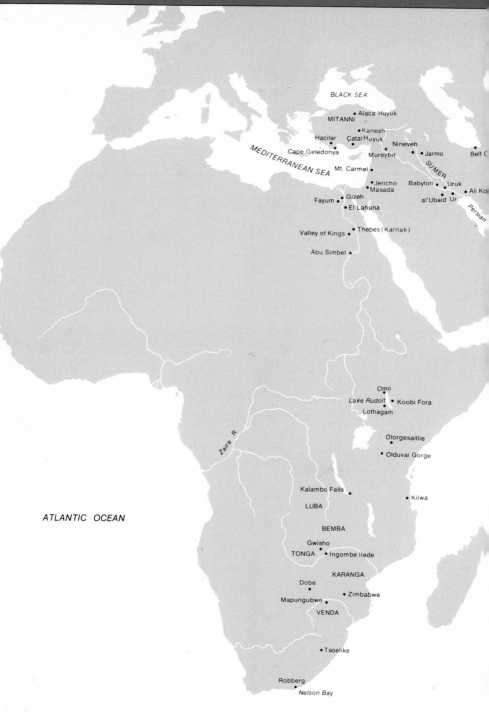

BLACK SEA

MITANNI
• Alaca Huyuk
• Kanesh
Hacilar • Çatal Huyuk
Cape Geledonya Nineveh
Mureybit • Jarmo Belt C
Mt. Carmel • SUMER
• Jericho Babylon • Uruk
Masada • Ali Kol
Fayum • • Gizeh al'Ubaid • Ur
• El Lahuna Persian

Valley of Kings • • Thebes (Karnak)

Abu Simbel •

Omo
Lake Rudolf • Koobi Fora
Lothagam

Olorgesaillie •
• Olduvai Gorge

ATLANTIC OCEAN

Kalambo Falls •
• Kilwa
LUBA

BEMBA

Gwisho
TONGA • Ingombe Ilede

KARANGA
Dobe •
• Zimbabwe
Mapungubwe •
VENDA

Zaire R.

• Tsoelike

Robberg •
• Nelson Bay

MEDITERRANEAN SEA

Archaeological Sites in Africa and the Near East